MAP OF THE

UNITED STATES
of
AMERICA.

The British Provinces, Mexico, the West Indies and
Central America, with part of New Granada and Venezuela

NEW YORK

ECSTATIC NATION

ECSTATIC NATION

CONFIDENCE, CRISIS, AND
COMPROMISE, 1848–1877

BRENDA WINEAPPLE

HARPER
www.harpercollins.com

Endpapers: Courtesy of the Lionel Pincus and Princess Firyal Map Division, the New York Public Library, Astor, Lenox and Tilden Foundations.

Emily Dickinson, "The Heart is the Capital of the Mind," J1354/F1384, reprinted by permission of the publishers and the Trustees of Amherst College from *The Poems of Emily Dickinson: Variorum Edition*, edited by Ralph W. Franklin, Cambridge, Mass.: The Belknap Press of Harvard University Press. Copyright © 1998 by the President and Fellows of Harvard College. Copyright © 1951, 1955, 1979, 1983 by the President and Fellows of Harvard College.

Part I: *Sleighing in New York*, Thomas Benecke. Courtesy of the Library of Congress, LC-pga-03406.

Part II: *Bodies of Confederate Artillerymen near Dunker Church*, Alexander Gardner. Courtesy of the Library of Congress, LC-ppmsca-32887.

Part III: *Massacre of the Innocents*, Thomas Nast (March 30, 1867), pp. 200–201. Courtesy of HarpWeek.
Let Us Clasp Our Hands Over the Bloody Chasm, Thomas Nast (September 21, 1872), p. 732. Courtesy of HarpWeek.

FIRST EDITION

Designed by Renato Stanisic

Library of Congress Cataloging-in-Publication Data

Wineapple, Brenda.
Ecstatic nation : confidence, crisis, and compromise, 1848–1877 / Brenda Wineapple.—First edition.
p. cm.
Includes bibliographical references and index.
ISBN 978-0-06-123457-6
1. United States—History—1849–1877. 2. Slavery—United States—History—19th century. 3. Antislavery movements—United States—History—19th century. 4. United States—Territorial expansion—History—19th century. 5. United States—History—Civil War, 1861–1865—Causes. 6. United States—History—Civil War, 1861–1865. 7. Reconstruction (U.S. history, 1865–1877) I. Title.
E415.7.W75 2013
973.6—dc23   2012051538

13 14 15 16 17   OV/RRD   10 9 8 7 6 5 4 3 2

To Michael Dellaira

The Heart is the Capital of the Mind
The Mind is a single State—
The Heart and Mind together make
A single Continent—

One—is the Population—
Numerous enough—
This ecstatic Nation
Seek—it is Yourself.
— EMILY DICKINSON, CIRCA 1875

Fellow citizens, we cannot escape history.
The fiery trial, through which we pass, will light
us down, to the latest generation.
— ABRAHAM LINCOLN, 1862

CONTENTS

ECSTATIC
NATION

PROLOGUE: THE END OF EARTH

They called him Old Man Eloquent, but he was more than that, more than eloquent; he was resolute, canny, cantankerous. And though he liked to quote the Bible and Shakespeare and to frame an irrefutable argument, he could also be eloquently brusque. In fact, he had just uttered one unwavering word that day in the House. *No*, he had said, and "no" summarized how John Quincy Adams had spent his long life—and where, in a sense, his country was heading: to a series of negatives, for good and for ill, that brooked no compromise or conversation.

No: "No is the wildest word we consign to the language," as Emily Dickinson would say. The sixth president of the United States, eighty-one years old and a crusty member of the House of Representatives, had spoken loud and clear. It was the early afternoon on Monday, February 21, 1848. With his bald head fringed with a crown of white hair and a permanent scowl carved deep into his broad face, Adams struck his colleagues as the same as ever—hale, hearty, forthright—despite of course the minor stroke he had suffered not too long ago. Yet he still could pursue an objective with unrelenting, single-minded focus. His grandson Henry Adams long remembered the summer day when he had been about six or seven and had rebelled against going to school until his grandfather, having emerged from his study, appeared at the top of the steps, descended the stairs, put on his hat, took the boy's hand, and silently walked Henry the mile or so to the schoolhouse, whereupon Henry took his seat and his grandfather let go his hand and returned home, never having said a word.

A New England Puritan who loved scribbling in his colossal diary and arguing on behalf of his country, John Quincy Adams was never eclipsed by his own brass or mahogany, as another outspoken man, the radical Reverend Theodore Parker, would say. Known as wild or, at best, contentious in his views, according to Parker, he had encountered more political opposition than any other man in the nation. Persistently, he had battled for public education, improved transportation, civil rights, freedom of expression—and against the extension of slavery. Morally austere, without humor, glacially scrupulous, the bleak Old Man frequently reread his Cicero, and just the day before, he had twice attended church. In the evening he had read a sermon by the Reverend William Wilberforce, the British antislavery evangelical, for pleasure. It was about the passing of time.

The Old Man's habits had been unchanged for years. On Monday morning Adams woke early and rode by carriage from his home on F Street to the House of Representatives, where he represented Massachusetts, his cherished state. He adored Washington too, that rough and ready town—the city of magnificent intentions, Charles Dickens had called it—and a work in progress to which Adams was devoted. Mud might clog the streets, if that's what you could call those unpaved passageways and lanes, pigs rooted for garbage, and summers were unbearable, what with the brackish swamps breeding disease and the city reeking with the bittersweet smell of horse manure. Neither the Washington Monument nor the Capitol was finished; they stood undressed, symbolic of the city and country that were to come. "Public buildings that need but a public to complete," Dickens observed.

It was winter now, crisp and clear and not at all malarial or murky. At the House, Adams chatted with a few colleagues, nothing more. In the early afternoon, Speaker of the House Robert C. Winthrop (a friend) called the question of whether or not to suspend the rules in order to vote to award gold medals to various generals for their gallant action in what Adams, unequivocally, considered an "unrighteous" war—the war with Mexico. So Adams said no.

His face reddened. He had evidently muttered something else, too. "Look to Mr. Adams! Look to Mr. Adams!" several representatives cried. Adams grabbed for the corner of his desk and then slumped to the left of his chair. David Fisher of Ohio, seated next to him, caught Adams in his arms, and another quick-acting colleague ran for ice water and a compress.

"Mr. Adams is dying!" House members rushed forward to lift the elderly statesman to the space in front of the clerk's table before several others brought in a sofa. Carefully lifted onto it, Adams was carried into the Rotunda. Winthrop adjourned the session.

As the members of the House dashed here and there, several senators, on hearing that Adams was stricken, thronged around the old man. So too did anxious visitors to the House, who had come to witness the day's roll calls. They had not expected this. The thickening crowd prompted one of the House members to recommend that the sofa be removed to the East Portico, which might be better for the ex-president because a fresh east wind was blowing there. The physicians who were members of the House thought the place too damp. Winthrop suggested they go to the speaker's room, where they would have more privacy. They bled Adams and applied mustard plasters, which seemed to give the poor man some relief even though his entire right side was paralyzed.

Adams asked for Henry Clay, who had been his secretary of state. Old Harry had also helped engineer what was known as the Missouri Compromise of 1820 (admitting Maine to the Union as a free state and Missouri as a slave state while pledging that the territory north of 36 degrees, 30 minutes latitude, would be forever free). Like Adams, Clay had run for president more than once and as recently as four years ago. He dashed out of the Senate chamber, tears streaming down his face.

"This is the end of earth," Adams was heard to say. "But I am composed."

Louisa Adams hurried in to see her husband, who by that time could not recognize her. Distraught, she left the room. Joshua Giddings, the passionate antislavery representative from Ohio, felt Adams's pulse and wiped the sweat from his brow.

All business in the hushed Capitol was suspended through the next day and the next day and the next. The celebration of Washington's birthday was canceled. On the evening of February 23, 1848, after sixty years of public service, John Quincy died as he lay, fittingly, in the Capitol building. The electric telegraph madly tapped out the news.

NEWSPAPERS THROUGHOUT THE country chronicled the funeral's every detail. The Stars and Stripes flew at half-mast while statesmen from the South as well as the North paid homage to the tough old contrarian as he lay in his glass-covered coffin in the House of Representatives. Thousands of people filed by, even those who had hated him during his long years as their public servant.

Had he died much earlier, Old Man Eloquent would not have been remembered with the outpourings of love and praise that accompanied his funeral train all the way to his ancestral home in Quincy, Massachusetts. For whatever his failures as president, whatever his want of judgment, whatever his intransigence, this was the man who had subsequently fought with all his might for the right of free speech when the House of Representatives passed a series of "gag rules" tabling all petitions or propositions related to slavery and its abolition. This was the man who had tried to establish relations with the independent state of Haiti and who, in 1841, when he was seventy-three, had successfully argued the *Amistad* case before the Supreme Court on behalf of freedom for a boatload of black men kidnapped from their African homes to be sold into slavery in Cuba. This was the man once called the Madman of Massachusetts whom irate representatives from the South had unsuccessfully tried to censure; this was the man who had hunkered down and won, over sectional dissensions, the right of slaves to petition Congress. This was the son of a president and a president himself, who, after he left the executive office, had broadened. He had possessed a capacity for growth, and he had loved a good fight, and his constituents loved him for that, all the more so after he was gone. When a motion was proposed in the House that a committee escort his body back to Massachusetts, a Southern representative objected. "What's the use of sending him home?" he asked a fellow member. "His people think more of his corpse than they do of any man living and will reelect it, and send it back." He put sulfuric acid, Ralph Waldo Emerson said, in his tea. And he bequeathed to his son Charles Francis Adams the words that he believed he and the country should live by: "a stout heart and a clear conscience, and never despair."

In the Senate, the brawny Democrat of Missouri Thomas Hart Benton, an adversary, summed up what many congressmen felt when they thought of old Adams: "Where could death have found him but at the post of duty?"

"We cannot find it in our hearts to regret he has died as he has died," said Speaker Winthrop. "He himself could not have desired any other end." The tributes were warm, for he was the greatest man in the House, admitted even those who liked him least. "There have been, I confess, moments in my life—perhaps not a few," Speaker Winthrop noted in his diary, "when John Quincy Adams has seemed to me the most credulous, prejudiced, and opinioned of mortal men. As a rule, however," he continued, "he either endeared himself to me by his attractive conversation, or electrified me by his energy and eloquence."

South Carolina Representative Isaac Holmes praised his former enemy as a diplomat, statesman, peacemaker, sage, and patriot who had "crushed no heart beneath the rude grasp of proscription." Holmes, who had wanted to eject Adams from the House, reminded the mourners that the two men, representing North and South, had "battled for a common cause, and rejoiced in common triumph"—and that in grief, they were united. Governor James McDowell of Virginia, another former foe, eulogized his colleague as "unapproachable by all others in the unity of his character and in the thousand-fold anxieties which centered upon him." North and South could join hands. Death was their bond as it would later prove—alas—to be.

A POIGNANT HARBINGER of the national funerals to come, the rites were undertaken with laborious and protracted solemnity. Adams lay in state for two days in a gloomy Capitol, where the portraits of Lafayette and Washington, behind the coffin, were covered with black cloth. Black cloth had also been draped over Adams's chair, and dark funeral wreaths were placed in the windows. The coffin was decorated with evergreens.

At dawn on Saturday, February 25, thirteen cannon ceremoniously boomed to indicate that this would be no ordinary day. Afterward, every thirty minutes, a single gun was fired. At nine, the crowd began to mill around the Capitol, and by noon, when the procession started, and the bells on Capitol Hill began to toll, the Rotunda was jammed with people. James K. Polk, the slaveholding president of the United States, trailed by his cabinet, solemnly entered the Hall in the House of Representatives. The president took his seat beside the Speaker. The Supreme Court justices, all black-robed, came next, just ahead of the foreign diplomatic corps, smartly clothed in their formal costumes, and then the officers of the army and navy, whose sparkling regalia contrasted with the dimness of the setting.

The senators walked into the Hall followed by the self-effacing vice president, George M. Dallas, who would sit on the left of the Speaker. The members of the Adams family minus his widow, who was too grief-stricken to attend, walked ahead of the silver-mounted coffin, which came to rest in front of the speaker. There was silence.

The Massachusetts senators, John Davis and the black-eyed orator Daniel Webster, walked into the Hall.

The Reverend R. R. Gurley offered up a prayer and a hymn.

The choir sang. The Reverend Gurley read from Job: "And thine age shall be clearer than the noon-day; thou shalt be as the morning; and thou shalt be secure, because there is hope."

After a closing hymn, a huge procession formed at the Portico and moved from the east front to the north gate and then around to the west. Thomas Hart Benton was one of the pallbearers, as was the brilliant Senator John Calhoun of South Carolina. They had been preceded by the funeral band, the chaplains, the attending physicians, and the Committee of Arrangements, which included a young Whig representative from Illinois named Abraham Lincoln.

The family followed the hearse in their carriage, and behind it came carriages packed with representatives from Massachusetts and from Congress and with President Polk. Toward the end of the procession stood officers and students from the institutions of higher learning, such as Georgetown, which Adams had long championed. Citizens and strangers came last. The military band played a dirge, their drums muffled. They passed houses and the public buildings shrouded in black cloth until they arrived at the Congressional Burying Ground, where the venerable Old Man waited patiently for his last train ride to Quincy, Massachusetts. There he would rest, near his famous mother and his famous father.

At sunset a salute of twenty-nine guns brought the day to its end.

WHEN THE FUNERAL cortege slowly rumbled over five hundred miles of railroad track, all along the way businesses were closed, flags were lowered, and men and women silently bowed their heads or doffed their hats. Newspapers printed eulogies, tributes, and whatever scraps of verse or wise sayings they thought might please and console the public that reverently visited the casket in city after city. In Baltimore, Adams's coffin lay in the rotunda at the Mercantile Exchange, and in Philadelphia, it rested in Independence Hall, where Adams's father had helped birth the country. In New York City, ten thousand citizens paid their respects at City Hall before the funeral train chugged to Springfield, Massachusetts, and then on to Boston, where thousands of local citizens, many of them holding placards, had come to bid Adams good-bye as the city's bells tolled. At the Boston Theater, there was a special performance followed by the singing of the national anthem. For days, sorrowful citizens bought mourning badges from the more enterprising of the grievers, but a blizzard ripped through the city, canceling all outdoor events.

A hearse drawn by six black and plumed horses delivered the mortal remains of the ex-president to storied Faneuil Hall, another symbol of American independence, where patriots, among them two Adamses, had debated liberty and freedom and unfair taxation without representation in the rooms above the marketplace. Built in 1742 and redesigned and enlarged at the turn of the nineteenth century by Charles Bulfinch, Faneuil Hall had been made into a crypt, said one reporter. The tall arched windows were now wrapped in black gauze, the American flag wrapped in black crepe, and the panels in the galleries told of Adams's long career: private secretary to the minister to Russia; minister to the United Netherlands and then Prussia; senator in the Massachusetts legislature; senator in Congress; minister to Russia; peace negotiator and minister to Great Britain; secretary of state; president; member of the House of Representatives.

After the eulogies and orations, many of the speechmakers trotted off to a banquet. Boston Yankees and Northern Whigs were feeling good about themselves even as they admitted that with the death of Adams they were irrevocably cut off from the past. "The last relic of our Revolutionary age has departed," wrote the editor of the *New-York Tribune*. "He has been a public servant for more years than any one who survives him; and his career is of inestimable value for the striking proof it affords that a Politician need not be tricky, nor hollow, nor time-serving."

On March 11, from Penn's Hill, where as a boy John Quincy Adams had watched the Battle of Bunker Hill, the sound of guns could be heard ricocheting through the countryside. Adams was being celebrated as the president and son of a president who had stood firm and unmoved during a storm. The storm was over freedom, and these days he had been thundering about slavery. That didn't matter, not right now anyway. One Southern member of Congress who was escorting the coffin on the day of Adams's interment walked up to the vault and, with the gentleness and gallantry of a cavalier, trembled with respect as he said, "Good-bye, Old Man!"

This unnamed mourner must have known that in 1839 Adams had offered a doomed amendment to the Constitution declaring that from July 4, 1842, onward, there should be no hereditary slavery in the United States; that on that day and afterward, every child born in the United States should be free; and that no state should be admitted into the United States that tolerated slavery.

Speaking before the New York State legislature, William Henry Seward, one of the younger eulogists to whom Adams had entrusted the future, would remember Adams as someone who "knew that the only danger incident to political reform, was the danger of delaying it too long."

On that point, Adams had been tragically and presciently correct: reform had been delayed far too long.

THE COUNTRY HAD been founded in compromise, and to compromise it was dedicated. The Constitution had been composed by men hammering together a new government, bargaining and conceding and settling their differences to do so, or thinking that they had, especially when it came to the thorny issue of slavery: they did not call for its abolition; they just omitted the word "slave" from the document.

Compromise was therefore a strategy and not necessarily a capitulation. The discovery of a common ground, or the creation of one, on which men and women could meet and maneuver, compromise was art; it was statesmanship. But this conception of compromise was in trouble, and the word would, in the next years, become an epithet.

It would be said that compromise was acceptance, cowardice, a series of piecemeal concessions. Compromise was wholesale surrender, inch by shameful inch, to expedience, a surrender that sacrificed the very ideal on which the country rested: a more perfect union in which the blessings of freedom were secured. And yet, as the historian David Brion Davis noted, "all idealism is compromised by tactical expediency, and all opportunism, no matter how ruthless, is compromised by idealism."

The year of Adams's death was a year of exuberance, exultation, and promise: a women's rights convention in New York, revolutions across Europe, the acquisition of 525,000 square miles of land from Mexico, a new political party (Free Soil), the discovery of gold in California. It was a time of optimism and energy, revivalism and great hope—even frenzied belief—a time to turn at last against tyranny in all forms, especially slavery, so that the great sin of the country could be eradicated and the nation could fulfill its promise of liberty: for the immigrants flooding to America; for the enslaved, brought unwillingly; for women and men committed to equality. "America is the country of the Future," Ralph Waldo Emerson had already said. "It is a country of beginnings, of projects, of designs, and expectations."

But the present was and the future would also be a time of delirium, failure, greed, violence, and refusal: refusal to listen and to find—or create—that hard common ground of compromise; refusal to bend, so great was the fear of breaking; refusal to change and refusal to imagine what it might be like to be someone else. John Quincy Adams knew how to say "no," but that negative could be inflexible, ideological, fanatical, particularly when some considered refusal a better tool than compromise or when compromise itself was so flaccid and unjust as to be meaningless, particularly if it evaded matters of human rights and dignity. In short, America was an ecstatic nation: smitten with itself and prosperity and invention and in love with the land from which it drew its riches—a land, grand and fertile, extending from one sea to another and to which its citizens felt entitled. Yet there was a problem—a hitch, a blot, a stain. The stain was slavery. That John Quincy Adams knew, and because of it, he forecast with doom the price the country would have to pay.

SOME OF THE people and many of the events in this book are so familiar they seem ready-made: Lincoln and his grief-stricken face, the Confederate general George Pickett's charge at Gettysburg, the elegant and battle-weary Robert E. Lee meeting the scruffy, cigar-smoking, and oddly gentle Ulysses S. Grant at Appomattox. But the richness and variety of American life during this time of confidence and crisis and putative consolidation bring into focus other events, other characters: the impounding of the schooner *Pearl* as it tried to flee Washington, D.C., with a group of fugitive slaves; a shoot-out in Christiana, Pennsylvania; the day hungry women ran through the streets of Richmond begging for bread; Susan B. Anthony and Elizabeth Cady Stanton riding on wagons without springs through Kansas to secure the ballot for women; exuberant men such as Walt Whitman—and P. T. Barnum—embracing multitudes; the anguished honesty of Herman Melville; the powerful editor Horace Greeley changing his political stripes; the execution of the Lincoln conspirators and the head of the Andersonville prison, and then the impeachment of a president; Anna (not Emily) Dickinson on the stump; Chief Red Cloud at New York's Cooper Union; the saga of the antislavery general Rufus Saxton, fired from the Freedmen's Bureau by a soon-to-be-disgraced chief executive; and the grandeur and allure and promise of freedom, whether to the Mormons, or to men such as Clarence King, who possessed nature in the wild, or so he thought. And there was the war, that terrible war, and all the while, before, during, and after it, the idea of compromise, which was being bandied about, debated, and often held responsible for the country's failure to face its fatal flaws, for its selfishness and short-sightedness, and for the reconciliation, at the end of Reconstruction, that opened a new era (beyond the scope of this book) of Jim Crow.

I don't presume to say what people should or should not have done, which is not to suggest I am without judgment, sorrow, or at certain times astonishment. Still, by placing persons, events, contradictions, principles, and, yes, compromises next to one another, perhaps we can empathize with the choices people may or may not have felt they had, given the exigencies within which they lived and the very mixed motives we come to understand, if we do, but through a glass darkly. For in the roiling middle of the nineteenth century, when Americans looked within, not without, there was an unassailable intensity and imagination and exuberance, inspirited and nutty and frequently cruel or brutal. There was also a seemingly insatiable and almost frenetic quest for freedom, expressed in several competing ways, for the possession of things, of land, and—alas—of persons. And in many instances there was a passion, sometimes self-righteous, sometimes self-abnegating, for doing good, even if that good included, for its sake and in its name, acts of murder.

PART ONE

{ 1848—1861 }

(1)

HIGHER LAWS

New Orleans, 1851

I t is the third of August. Just before daybreak, bands of men and women, hats and handkerchiefs waving, gather at the dock at the end of St. Mary's Street in a New Orleans suburb. Before them looms the *Pampero*, the 500-ton ship soon to head to Cuba. "Cuba, Cuba, Cuba," the men and women chant from the wharf. They've been chanting for days, milling around street corners and meeting halls and talking endlessly of Cuba, Cuba, Cuba, and emblazoning the newly drawn Cuban flag on posters and handbills and banners. Now, finally, at any minute, the *Pampero* will pull out of the slip, General Narciso López at the helm. There in fact he stands—he boarded around 1 A.M.—the stocky fifty-four-year-old Venezuelan eager to export American freedom to Cuba and annex the island to the United States, as if it were a jeweled brooch destined for the lapel of Uncle Sam. The crowd (some estimated it was ten thousand strong) cheers. López bows.

The expedition is a matter of some urgency. Less than two decades ago, when the British abolished slavery in 1833 in the West Indies, many Southern slaveholders feared the Spanish might free the slaves of Cuba, which would mean that Cuba could become, according to John A. Quitman, the brash governor of Mississippi, a "strong negro or mongrel empire." Even old John Quincy Adams had warned before he died that if the United States seized Texas—which it just had—and permitted slavery there, England might retaliate by invading Cuba and emancipating Cuban slaves. (An Anglophobe, Adams calculated that Cuba was better left to the Spanish than to the British.) Besides, any talk of abolition in the Caribbean from any quarter could spark a series of slave insurrections: after all, that was what had happened in Haiti, setting the slaves free; the fire next time might sweep across the South, razing everything and everyone in its path.

Unless, that is, the United States annexed Cuba. The South could then carve out of the island at least two more slave states for itself. That would preserve the peace and be good for the Creole planters and sugar producers who craved direct access to the U.S. market; it would be good for the American speculators invested in Cuban sugar plantations and very good for those American citizens—Southerners—who were riled by the recent admission of California to the Union as a free state, which had cost the South its parity in the Senate.

Sighing in relief when the *Pampero* departed, Laurent J. Sigur lit his cigar. A wealthy slave owner in the greatest slave-trading center of the South, Sigur had recently purchased the *Pampero* solely for the purpose of López's expedition. Committed to the country's expansion southward, he also assumed that after López and his men landed on the Cuban coast, they would be joined by enough disgruntled Cubans to overthrow the Spanish once and for all. Open arms and loving crowds would then greet the liberators: that was Sigur's dream and that was López's dream, as it seems to be the dream of all besotted redeemers.

Besides, who could resist the call to freedom? Hadn't all of Europe convulsed in 1848? Wasn't the United States founded in liberty for—almost—all? In his newspaper, the New Orleans *Daily Delta*, Sigur had been running engravings of López on the front page and publishing letters from Cuba that told of ongoing revolution there. He had also issued and sold Cuban bonds signed by López himself to finance the invasion. Still, as one skeptical correspondent noted, "every fool declared his determination to go over to Cuba, to exterminate the odious Spaniards, and to give freedom to the Cubans; whilst, not a single fool or knave, expressed this determination, without calculating how much he could make by the speculation." Sigur was a smart businessman.

And López was the perfect figurehead and foil. Silver-haired, dark-eyed, and spoiling for a crusade, the mustachioed López looked the part of the liberating hero, although now, from this distance, it's difficult to piece together who he was, where he was, when or what exactly he wanted from his quixotic mission. Formerly a general in the Spanish army but the son of a former Venezuelan landowner, López seems less a revolutionary than a gold-plated opportunist, part idealist, part fanatic, and part capitalist with a penchant for grandiosity. Yet dogged of purpose, he was perfectly suited to do the dirty work for those Americans who supported a self-serving Cuban revolution.

He was also a shrewd survivor, or so it seemed. As a boy of fifteen he had fought on the side of the Spanish against Simón Bolívar, but after the Spanish defeat in Caracas in 1813, he retired from the Spanish army and headed to Cuba to avoid execution. By 1824, he was a Cuban citizen; he had married into the Creole aristocracy, taken up cockfighting and philandering, dabbled in iron and coal and copper mines, and squandered his wife's inheritance, although some say he amassed a small fortune that he deposited in New York banks.

He left Cuba in 1827, at age thirty, and sailed to Spain in search of further advancement. As aide-de-camp to General Jerónimo Valdés, he fought on the side of Queen Maria Cristina during the war between the liberals and the Carlists. The Spanish queen draped him in medals, but after she was deposed, "we find him in hostile array against Christina [sic]," drily noted one of his chroniclers, "and in command still, under her enemies." López had the ability, remarked a historian without irony, to make friends.

López remained in Spain until Valdés was transferred to Cuba in 1841, where he served as lieutenant governor of Matanzas and head of the Military Commission. Two years later, after Valdés was replaced as captain-general of Cuba, López joined or founded a group called the "Conspiracy of the Cuban Rose Mines." The organization was a cover, for López was plotting against the Spanish. But, a boastful, self-deceived man unable to keep a secret, in 1848 he confided his revolutionary plans to Robert Campbell, the U.S. consul in Havana. Campbell promptly leaked the information to Secretary of State James Buchanan. Though an expansionist, Buchanan didn't want trouble, so he in his turn tipped off the Spanish minister in Washington about López.

López's men were arrested, but the slippery López had already hopped aboard the *Neptune*, a brig bound for Bristol, Rhode Island, and then made his way to New York, where he immediately met the members of the Club de la Habana, a group of wealthy sugar planters, bankers, merchants, and intellectuals. "The annexation of Cuba holds out temptations to the commercial, navigating and manufacturing interests of New York and New England that no anti-slavery feeling can withstand," the *Charleston Courier* tartly observed.

To most of these annexationists—López included—a liberated Cuba meant freedom to conduct business unencumbered by Spanish governmental regulations and taxation but not, obviously, freedom for the slaves. "López was not particularly interested in the emancipation of the slaves," one of his followers blithely explained. "He thought that they were necessary for the successful cultivation of the island, and he could not successfully visualize a free black population. He felt that a Cuba unbound by any ties to any other nation meant free blacks. He therefore favored annexation to the United States."

The Cuban junta had selected López as its leader, but since he didn't speak a word of English, he needed an interpreter, and in this he was ably, if not craftily, assisted by the Cuban-born Ambrosio José Gonzales, an expert marksman and fine linguist who happened to be a boyhood friend of the future Confederate general Pierre Beauregard, at whose dashing side Gonzales would stand when Beauregard fired on Fort Sumter. Educated in the United States and steeped in the ideology of expansionism, Gonzales had good contacts, so in 1849 he had been able to secure a meeting for López with four senators, including John Calhoun. Calhoun had already crossed swords over Cuba with John Quincy Adams years earlier, during the administration of James Monroe.

Though he might have liked to annex Cuba sooner rather than later, Calhoun was evasive. States' rights and the matter of regional sovereignty had been keeping the tubercular senator awake at night, and he didn't want Cuba to distract him or his fellow Southerners from these issues. Yet according to Gonzales, Calhoun had not discouraged López. "You have my best wishes," the senator had allegedly said, "but whatever the result, as the pear, when ripe, falls by the law of gravitation into the lap of the husbandman, so will Cuba eventually drop into the lap of the Union."

Calhoun shrewdly introduced López to senators Henry S. Foote of Mississippi, Stephen A. Douglas of Illinois, and Daniel S. Dickinson of New York—each man from a different region, each of whom had his eye on the prosperous island. López also met with the newly elected senator from Mississippi, Jefferson Davis, who cordially turned down his offer to command the expedition and receive $100,000 up front for his trouble. In his stead, Davis suggested a West Pointer from Virginia, Robert E. Lee. Lee too turned López down.

So López and Gonzales took up sewing. They designed a new Cuban flag with a five-pointed white star—similar to the one on the flag of Texas—set against a red background and, on the right, four blue and white stripes. In New Orleans, Laurent Sigur immediately hoisted it over his office at the *Delta*, and before the *Pampero* expedition, a representative of the Mexican Gulf Railroad Company presented López with a finely wrought rendition in silk.

Today it may seem that only a fool would have believed that a mere handful of men, without the sanction of their own or any other government, could land in Cuba and bring the Spanish government to its knees. Still, the cockamamie plan to incite a revolution was not all that different from John Brown's ill-conceived raid on Harpers Ferry, Virginia, a few years later, even if their goals were decidedly dissimilar: Brown and his tiny band of revolutionaries were perfervid abolitionists, intent on freeing slaves. Yet like Brown—at least initially—Narciso López was able to entice young men to join him, men who might be adventurers or freedom lovers or land grabbers. His company eventually included a former state senator, the attorney general's nephew, and a large number of Mexican War veterans lured by the promise of $4,000 on signing up and a parcel of land after one year. "We should remember that we are sons of Washington and had come to free a people," López said, wrapping his cash offer in the flag of liberation.

But unlike Brown, López could raise lots of money. Speculators in the North as well as the South were backing him: speculators in Boston, New York, and Philadelphia recognized the commercial significance of Cuban sugar and turned a blind eye to the increased numbers of slaves brought to Cuba from Africa—as many as 8,700 in 1849, with the number growing each year. The slaves worked about eighteen hours a day under a blazing sun; they were stuffed into small quarters at night and fed salt fish and a few vegetables if lucky; they were beaten, humiliated, and on occasion murdered. But López handily won the approval of such Democratic Party organs as John O'Sullivan's *United States Magazine and Democratic Review*, which published a sixteen-page biography of the general, no doubt written by O'Sullivan himself. As the man who presumably coined the phrase "manifest destiny" in reference to the American West, O'Sullivan considered the destiny of Cuba just as manifest: annexation via an armed expedition, known as a filibuster.

In the middle of the nineteenth century, the term "filibuster" referred not to long-winded speeches in Congress aimed at delaying or railroading the passage of legislation but rather the invasion of a country by force. (The term derives from the Dutch *vrijbuiter*, or "freebooter," and Spanish *filibustero*, which referred to the pirates of the seventeenth century who sacked colonies in the West Indies and Yucatán.) President Polk and, in particular, Secretary of State Buchanan had looked kindly on the annexation of Cuba, but they were cautious and politically prudent men. They had hoped to purchase the island from Spain, not to invade it. Buchanan had offered the Spanish $100 million. The Spanish replied that they'd sooner see Cuba sunk in the ocean than sold to the Americans. Buchanan had dropped the matter but snappishly promised that the United States would seize that damned Caribbean island in a coup d'état someday. "I feel it in my finger ends," he said.

General Zachary Taylor, the Whig who had succeeded Polk to the presidency, condemned the Cuban filibusters. He did not want a war with Spain, and he did not want to violate the 1818 Neutrality Act. In the fall of 1849, working hard to thwart López and his network, the federal government had impounded their ships, weaponry, and ammunition. But stopping them completely was not easy, what with several newspapers in New Orleans and New York clamoring for Cuban annexation to the point where the New York *Sun* jumped the gun with the headline "Cuba Is Free!"

Having relocated his base of operations from New York and Washington to New Orleans, López canvassed the South. Soon he stood in the governor's mansion of John Quitman, the recently elected straight-in-the-saddle slavery zealot of Mississippi who during his military stint in Mexico had been briefly appointed governor of Mexico City. "I possess absolute power," Quitman had bragged to his wife at the time. Quitman suited López to a T. He was a rich slave owner with a plantation that boasted over 450 slaves, and, as an unshakable advocate of slavery, he hoped to see the institution spread into as many new territories as possible. Cuba was just the place for the extension of his and the country's commerce.

With a map of Cuba spread on the table, he and López discussed the invasion. López offered Quitman a million dollars and promised an army of four thousand for him to lead. After the revolution, Quitman could then command the entire Cuban army (before the island's annexation to the United States, that is). Tempted, the silver-haired Quitman nonetheless turned López down but provided him with contacts. And with the help of O'Sullivan, by May 1850, López had secured three ships. Volunteers for the expedition had been rounded up in New Orleans, and it's likely that John Henderson, a former U.S. senator from Mississippi, helped underwrite the expedition along with the Cuban émigrés and New Orleans merchants still involved.

López left New Orleans on May 7, 1850, and by May 18 he was bound for Cárdenas on Cuba's northwest coast on one of his ships, which were disguised as emigrant vessels. Planning to capture the railroad, he was quickly routed by the Spanish infantry (Gonzales was wounded soon after they landed), and though he and his men managed to burn the governor's mansion, they were forced to retreat to Key West, where the people in the street did hail them as liberating heroes. Not so the U.S. government, which called them outlaws and pirates. Secretary of State John M. Clayton said that "the honor of the Government requires that no just effort be spared to bring him [López] to trial and punishment."

Now under federal investigation, Quitman resigned the Mississippi governorship and surrendered himself to federal officials. López was arrested in New Orleans on the charge of violating the Neutrality Act: leading a hostile expedition against a country with which the United States was at peace. López was unflappable. "If it be a crime to solicit the aid of freemen to achieve the liberation of oppressed and enslaved Cubans—men like themselves—and to place the Queen of the Antilles in the path of her magnificent destiny," López said, "I am determined to be a criminal now and to the very last moment of my life—a pertinacious, unrepenting and open criminal—for I shall implore that assistance from noble and sympathizing men wherever I shall meet them—from my judges, from President Taylor, from his cabinet and from Congress—as I shall ever beseech it from God, with every pulsation of my heart." López saw himself as battling for a just and transcendent cause.

Two trials ended in a hung jury, and when the jury deadlocked again, a third mistrial was declared and the charges were dropped. "If the evidence against López were a thousand-fold stronger," a New Orleans paper editorialized in June 1850, "no jury could be impaneled against him because public opinion makes law."

True to his vow, López would try again. In August 1851, financed with at least $50,000 from avid supporters—women were urged to contribute their jewels—and officially condemned by the federal government, López was ready to depart at dawn from New Orleans on the *Pampero*.

The expedition was doomed from the start. López was jittery: he had heard that U.S. marshals were going to seize the *Pampero*. And he was impatient: he had also heard that the rebellion in Cuba had already begun in Puerto Príncipe (what he hadn't heard was that the Spanish had planted the rumor). Why wait for Gonzales, his lieutenant, who had not yet arrived in New Orleans, López wondered, or for more volunteers (hundreds would assemble in the Crescent City during the next week); why wait for more ships; and why sail to Jacksonville, Florida, as initially intended, where more than five hundred men were ready to join him? He didn't want the revolution to begin without him. Ripeness was all.

López started up the *Pampero*'s engines. But with one engine dead, the ship had to be towed to the mouth of the Mississippi and then stop for repairs in Key West. And though Sigur had bought and outfitted the *Pampero*, his coal dealer had delivered only about half of the 160 tons needed to reach Puerto Príncipe, so when the *Pampero* finally left Key West, it chugged toward Bahía Honda, about fifty miles west of Havana. Because the current had pushed it off course, it passed within easy sight of the lighthouse at Havana harbor. Not until eight on the evening of August 11 did it approach Bahía Honda.

The Spanish had of course been watching. Unaware of this, López, on landing, divided his troops and left about a hundred men under the command of Colonel William Logan Crittenden, a nephew of the U.S. attorney general (and last in his class at West Point). He was instructed to guard the supplies and ammunition until López, marching inland with the rest of his men, could round up wagons and oxen. But left to themselves, Crittenden and his men were vulnerable. When, in a matter of hours, the Spanish attacked, the frantic Crittenden sent half of his troops to find López while he and the rest headed to the coast; but with their backs to the sea, they were captured, taken to Havana, and summarily shot in groups of ten the next morning in the public square—like dogs, growled one observer.

Writing to friends and family before his execution, young Crittenden denounced López. "When I was attacked, López was only three miles off," he cried. "If he had not been deceiving us as to the state of things, he would have fallen back with his forces and made fight. Instead of which he marched immediately to the interior."

It may be that López was unaware of what had happened; Crittenden might well have been a victim of López's poor planning and boundless arrogance. In either case, a driving rain had destroyed what was left of López's ammunition, most of his men were shoeless, the roads were thick with sucking mud, and López had lost his saddle and his sense of direction. Desperate, he killed his own horse to feed his troops before they trudged over the mountains, their feet bloody. On August 28, López was surrounded by seventeen Creoles. He was seated upon a rock, his pistols in his girdle. "He had not courage to put one to his head, and blow his brains out," a former supporter remarked, "preferring to live a few hours longer, and die in the manner a traitor should." In the early-morning hours of September 1, 1851, Narciso López stood atop a wooden tower in Havana and, clad in a white gown and white cap, was ignominiously garroted with an iron collar. The bulk of López's men were sentenced to hard labor in a Spanish prison on the African coast.

The handkerchief-waving women and men of New Orleans erupted in anger. "Fifty-one Americans Captured and Butchered in Cold Blood," raged the New Orleans *Picayune*. Rioters snatched the

Spanish flag from the consulate, sliced it to ribbons, and set it afire in Lafayette Square. Another crowd wrecked the offices of the printing press of the Spanish newspaper, *La Unión*, and flung the presses into the street. In Philadelphia, in Independence Square, almost fifteen thousand outraged citizens stood in a drizzling rain to hear speeches demanding that the United States order the Spanish to withdraw from Cuba. It was reported that in Pittsburgh a rally to protest the "massacre" in Cuba was the largest such gathering ever held there. There were mass meetings in Memphis, Montgomery, and in Raymond, Mississippi. In Cincinnati, citizens once opposed to the Cuban expedition condemned the brutality of the Spanish. In Baltimore, the U.S. consul in Havana was burned in effigy.

Since such a diplomatic scuffle could have led to a war that no one wanted, the U.S. government decided to pay Spain a sum of $25,000 for the damages inflicted by the New Orleans mobs, and it publicly condemned López as a blackguard who had led gullible if idealistic American boys astray. In return the Spanish released the imprisoned Americans. The situation cooled.

But behind the fracas, the hubris, the loss of life, the lust for riches and power and property, behind the tangled motives that tied the extension of slavery to the name of freedom and knit them sentimentally together, poorly concealing the violence at its core—behind all that lay the tragic fragility and the folly of the Compromise of 1850.

THE COMPROMISE OF 1850 had been the brainchild of Henry Clay, the venerable, aging, and charismatic senator from the slave state of Kentucky who was widely admired for his ability to forge alliances— and for his unwavering loyalty to the Union. Born in 1777—"the infant nation and the infant child began the race of life together" said his faithful admirer, Abraham Lincoln—Clay had long served the Union. Now in this, his last grand senatorial stand, with the fluency for which he was known, he proposed a solution to the legislative impasse bitterly, even violently, racking the country.

That impasse (and the accompanying rancor) had been largely caused by the vast expanse of new territory the United States had acquired after the Mexican War. For by 1850 there were three million slaves in America, and North and South were at bitter odds over whether to exclude slavery from those more than 525,000 acres, which included land that would become part of the states of Texas, California, Nevada, Utah, most of New Mexico and Arizona, and parts of Colorado and Wyoming. Making matters worse, California was pressing for statehood. Flush with gold prospectors and gold seekers and immigrants, it had ratified a constitution that prohibited slavery, but its entrance into the Union would throw off the ticklish economic balance between South and North.

Soon to be known as the Compromise of 1850, Henry Clay's solution would, he hoped, mollify both slaveholding and non-slaveholding states by dividing that territory, Solomon-like, into slave and free. California could be admitted to the Union as a free state. The territories of New Mexico and Utah would be organized without mention of slavery until, at a later time, the territorial legislatures could decide whether or not to permit it. (Who could argue with self-rule?) The huge slave trade, not slavery itself, would be abolished in Washington, D.C., yet Congress should not interfere with interstate slave trade. Plus, Clay proposed settling the Texas and New Mexico boundary dispute by stipulating that the federal government pay Texas $10 million if that state abandoned its claim to New Mexico east of the Rio Grande. Finally, he proposed a more stringent Fugitive Slave Act.

Of course, friction over territorial expansion and the extension of slavery had preceded the war with Mexico, and though dispelled temporarily by the Missouri Compromise of 1820, it stretched all the way back to the founding of the country—and the framing of its Constitution. Drafted during the muggy summer of 1787, the Constitution had annulled Thomas Jefferson's charming notion that "all men are created equal." "I tremble for my country when I reflect that God is just: that his justice cannot sleep for ever," Jefferson admitted in his *Notes on the State of Virginia*, also published in 1787. It did not. In 1842, the abolitionist William Lloyd Garrison denounced the Jeffersonian equivocation. The Constitution was a covenant with death, he said, cruelly struck to create a country.

Garrison knew—and didn't much care—that without guarantees for their institution of slavery, the Southern states would have walked out of the Constitutional Convention. Moderate Southerners knew that too. Hugh Williamson of North Carolina said he was against slavery but, taking all circumstances into account, he thought it better in the long run to grant South Carolina and Georgia their way rather than exclude them from the Union. Hence the deal: the Constitution would protect the African slave trade until 1808, when, presumably, Congress would regulate it. (James Madison, a slaveholder, gloomily predicted, "twenty years will produce all the mischief that can be apprehended from the liberty to import slaves." He was right.) Free states were prohibited from emancipating runaway slaves, who were to be returned to their owners. Those conditions more or less satisfied the South. But denied citizenship and the vote along with their freedom, would the slaves be represented in government at all? Northern delegates did not want to count slaves as persons since doing so would produce a huge imbalance in congressional representation—and the North wanted to maintain its edge. So North and South compromised again with the "three-fifths compromise": for every five slaves, three would be added to the count determining representation in the House of Representatives.

Those uneasy about all this vaguely hoped that someday slavery would wither away. It did not. Who could foresee, for instance, the invention of the cotton gin, for one thing, which would make cotton easier to clean—and slavery wildly profitable.

And morally untenable, or so John Quincy Adams thought, although he believed that, to prevent a horrific war, practical politics had to override moral principle. "Great prudence and caution become indispensably necessary to me," Adams had told the antislavery Quaker poet John Greenleaf Whittier in 1837. Before his death, though, he proposed gradual emancipation as well as financial recompense to slave owners. "I have abstained, perhaps too pertinaciously abstained from all participation in measures *leading* to that conflict for Life and Death between *Freedom* and *Slavery*," he had earlier admitted, "through which I have yet not been able to see how this Union could ultimately be preserved from passing." The forecast was very gloomy.

Adams and the so-called Conscience Whigs (the antislavery wing of the party) also opposed the extension of slavery into new territory; so would several Democrats and Free Soilers, the coalition of antislavery Democrats and former Whigs who very much wanted to keep western lands open and free. But in 1846, it was a Democratic congressman from Pennsylvania, David Wilmot, who added a controversial amendment to an appropriations bill that prohibited slavery in the new territories. Of course, Wilmot insisted that his purpose was only to "preserve free white labor, a fair country, a rich inheritance, where the sons of toil, of my own race and own color, can live without the disgrace which association with Negro slavery brings upon free labor."

Familiarly known as the Wilmot Proviso, the amendment infuriated Southerners, especially the formidably articulate Senator John Calhoun, who predicted, "The day that balance between the two sections of the country—the slaveholding States and the non-slaveholding States—is destroyed, is a day that will not be far removed from political revolution, anarchy, civil war, and widespread disaster." The Wilmot Proviso threatened that balance, and Calhoun did not take threats lightly. So he linked his position to the Constitution, which protected the South, he said. "I see my way in the Constitution," he declared. "I cannot in a compromise. A compromise is but an act of Congress. It may be overruled at any time. It gives us no security. But the Constitution is stable. It is a rock. On it we can stand. It is a firm and stable ground, on which we can better stand in opposition to fanaticism, than on the shifting sands of compromise. Let us be done with compromises." The proviso passed the House in a sectional vote and failed in the Senate.

Now, with the war over and Clay's compromise being debated, Southern extremists were again angry. Robert Toombs of Georgia, who had made his fortune as a slave-holding planter, cried, "If you seek to drive us from the territories of California and New Mexico, purchased by the common blood and treasure of the whole people, and to abolish slavery in this district, thereby attempting to fix a national degradation upon half the States of this Confederacy, *I am for disunion*." But disunion meant war, Clay warned, a war "so furious, so bloody, so implacable, so exterminating [that]—none—none, none of them raged with such violence, or was ever conducted with such bloodshed and enormities, as will that war which shall follow that disastrous event—if that event ever happens—of dissolution."

To many Americans, Whig and Democrat alike, including the Whig from Illinois Abraham Lincoln, Henry Clay epitomized civic wisdom, so when Clay proposed the eight resolutions that became known as the Compromise of 1850, the spectators crowding the gallery seemed to sigh with relief. Yet Clay's notion of compromise offended many Northerners, who interpreted it as craven weakness and dire submission. The Conscience Whig Charles Francis Adams—certainly no radical—said that Clay's compromise doomed the Wilmot Proviso, and, as far as he was concerned, "years of piecemeal concessions . . . had brought the country to its present plight." Philip Hone, a former mayor of New York, complained, "The fever of party spirit is beyond reach of palliatives. The fanatics of North and the disunionists of the South have made a gulf so deep that no friendly foot can pass it. Compromise is at an end." Thaddeus Stevens, a representative from Pennsylvania, said the nefarious compromise, with its fugitive slave rider, bartered away a black person's freedom. "If it will save the Union," Stevens sharply noted, "let these gentlemen introduce a 'compromise,' by which these races may change conditions."

In the Deep South, the radicals commonly known as "fire-eaters" scorned the compromise's braying assumption of the moral high ground, for they were irritated over and over again by the self-righteousness of the increasingly rich and populous industrial

North. Slaves mistreated? Mississippi senator Jefferson Davis scoffed at the idea. "The slave trade, so far as the African was concerned, was a blessing," he said. "It brought him from abject slavery and a barbarian master, and sold him into a Christian land."

And John Calhoun was implacable. "The most majestic champion of error since Milton's Satan," as the historian David Potter called him, Calhoun was too ill to deliver his own denunciation of Clay's compromise. His flesh loose, his long skeleton practically poking out of it, this shrunken, haggard man was swaddled in warm flannel to ward off the chill in the Senate chamber. But his ominous and obdurate message, read by his colleague James Mason of Virginia, was clear: the South, he said, "has no compromise to offer but the Constitution, and no concession or surrender to make."

It was therefore a measure of Clay's success, said one historian, that extremists in both the North and the South condemned his compromise.

On March 7, 1850, the famed Daniel Webster rose from his Senate seat. A leading statesman for thirty years, a consummate attorney, and a man committed to perpetual Union, this towering (if short) congressman from Massachusetts was already legendary for the erudite and theatrical speeches he delivered in a carefully modulated and often booming voice. Remembered and hailed for patriotic rhetoric about the "sentiment, dear to every true American heart,—Liberty and Union, now and forever, one and inseparable!," Webster had spoken out against slavery and the slave trade, which he called "odious and abominable"—shameful for New Englanders and for the country. "I hear the sound of the hammer," he had said, "I see the smoke of the furnaces where the manacles and fetters are still forged for human limbs."

That day, March 7, the sixty-eight-year-old Webster wore a blue coat with gleaming brass buttons, but the shine had come off his great career. He drank too much, he was not well, he was in debt, and he had no use for antislavery agitators, as he called them. Still, in the overheated chamber, men and women were tense with excitement; what might the country's grandest orator say?

"I wish to speak today, not as a Massachusetts man nor as a Northerner," Webster began, "but as an American." That meant he spoke as a Unionist. And as a backer of Clay. He talked for almost four hours, wooing both Southerners and Northerners even as he chastised them, censuring the South for yelping about secession, declaring that runaway slaves should of course be returned to bondage, and excoriating the abolitionists of the North as silly women and sillier men.

Someone from the crowded gallery shouted, "Traitor!" Though Webster succeeded in appeasing the Senate chamber temporarily and placating conservatives in both the North and the South, his speech wrecked what remained of his reputation in the North, at least among the antislavery groups he had mocked. The South must have offered Webster the presidency; what else could explain such perfidy? Webster had crossed the line, said Ralph Waldo Emerson, who noted with aspersion that the North was protecting its factories and capital. "The south does not like the north, slavery or no slavery, and never did," he said. "The north likes the south well enough, for it knows its own advantages." Theodore Parker called Webster a Benedict Arnold.

Four days later, William Henry Seward, a former governor of New York and now its freshman senator, took the floor. Slight and slim, hook-nosed and homely, he was described by Henry Adams as having a "head like a wise macaw; a beaked nose; shaggy eyebrows; unorderly hair and clothes; hoarse voice; offhand manner; free talk; and perpetual cigar." Often people could not hear his low and husky voice; he wasn't by nature a gifted orator. But he was a gifted and intelligent politician. Born in upstate New York and previously a state senator, Seward had served as governor under the tutelage of the wily political boss Thurlow Weed, the editor of the influential *Albany Evening Journal*. He had entered the Senate in 1849 as a steady antislavery Whig who as governor had refused to return fugitive slaves, arguing that New York did not recognize slavery. He had also backed Zachary Taylor for president and, it seemed, had influenced him in the awarding of patronage positions.

On March 11, though he began his speech in a shuffling undertone, he soon warmed to his purpose. You could almost hear a pin drop,' reported a journalist, and next to what Seward had to say, Webster's speech was humbug. For on that day, in his three-hour speech, Seward denounced not only Clay's compromise but also the provision that fugitive slaves be recaptured, and he denounced compromise in general when it came to slavery. "There is a higher law than the Constitution," he declared—that of inalienable human freedom—and it should supersede the Constitution's protection of slavery.

The notion was not new: after all, the Declaration of Independence had implied a higher law—the self-evident truths derived from the Creator. John Quincy Adams had invoked the idea of a higher law, and the transcendentalists of New England had been citing it for years. Ralph Waldo Emerson had claimed in his 1836 bible of transcendentalism, *Nature*, "We make fables to hide the baldness of the fact and conform it, as we say, to the higher law of the mind. But when the fact is seen under the light of an idea, the gaudy fable fades and shrivels. We behold the real higher law." And as the writer Orestes Brownson explained it, "The law of God is supreme, and overrides all human enactments, and every human enactment incompatible with it is null and void from the beginning, and cannot be obeyed with a good conscience."

But after Seward spoke, Brownson took exception. "Mr. Seward had no right, while holding his seat in the Senate under the Constitution, to appeal to this higher law against the Constitution, because that was to deny the very authority by which he held his seat." What about the law of the land? In New Hampshire, the Democratic press called the speech infamous, revolting, impious, and anti-Christian and went on to say that if Seward's "doctrines were to be endorsed by the people at large, there would be an end not only of the Union but of every rational form of government for either section." Even Thurlow Weed told Seward that the speech had "sent me to bed with a heavy heart." In Georgia, a newspaper said Seward should be carted away in a straitjacket as a lunatic. In Tennessee, the Whig press called him hateful. Henry Clay oozed contempt: "Who are they who venture to tell us what is divine and what is natural law?"

"A Kentuckian kneels only to God," Crittenden had reportedly said when the Spanish executioner had ordered him to turn around and fall to his knees. Flying under the flag of liberty and hoping to sustain slavery, López had invoked the same authority as Seward had: a higher law.

The Washington *Republic*, an organ of the administration, accused Seward of superseding the Constitution even though Seward's speech actually mirrored part of President Taylor's position. Taylor had warned Congress before a special session that he would quickly recommend California for statehood as soon as it applied; ditto New Mexico, even if the latter move alienated Texas, which was threatening to invade and absorb the territory. An absentee slave owner, Taylor was nonetheless a Unionist. The new states should decide for themselves about slavery—and Taylor was willing to go to war if Texas took Santa Fe.

So rife with acrimony and suspicion were both Northerners and Southerners that when Taylor died suddenly on July 9, 1850, after an attack of gastroenteritis, it was rumored that he had been poisoned. Suspicion erupting into aggression erupting into assault: this was not new in the Senate chamber. But Zachary Taylor's sudden death, the new presidency of Millard Fillmore, the appointment of Daniel Webster as secretary of state, and above all the inspirited and aggressive young Democratic senator from Illinois, Stephen A. Douglas—known as the Little Giant because he stood only five feet four inches tall—combined forces to pass Clay's compromise that September.

An enactment of Hell, abolitionists called it. And the Fugitive Slave Act was galling. ("I hate to see the poor creatures hunted down, and caught, and carried back to their stripes," Abraham Lincoln would say, "but I bite my lip and keep quiet.") The black activist author and doctor Martin Delany noted with bitterness, "A people capable of originating and sustaining such a law as this, are not the people to whom we are willing to entrust our liberty at discretion." When Clay died just two years later, the abolitionist Frederick Douglass, a former slave, remarked that the man had done more than any other to ensure the perpetuation of slavery: the Compromise maintained the balance between slave and free states and thus preserved the status quo, which was slavery itself. Conciliation bled into concession.

Although Kentucky, Virginia, Tennessee, Arkansas, Maryland, Missouri, and Delaware accepted the measures adopted by Congress, the fire-eaters of the Deep South were incensed, it seems, because the Compromise had stolen their thunder. By the time of their June convention in Nashville, there was but little enthusiasm for disunion, although John Quitman warned, "There is no effectual remedy for the evils before us but secession."

In Washington, D.C., the Compromise rang the city's bells, and approving bonfires glowed in the night. The Marine Band played "The Star Spangled Banner," and cannon were loaded and fired. Looking northward toward those cannon, the editor of the *Charleston Mercury* cheerlessly forecast the future: "The burning of powder may not stop with Washington."

THE COMPROMISED CENTER, if that's what it was, could not hold. The era of the strong executive had passed. Taylor was dead, and the short presidency of Millard Fillmore was followed by the fumbling presidency of Franklin Pierce. What remained were a fragile coalition of states' rights advocates in the South and nationalists in the North and a delicate truce between proslavery and antislavery forces. Continued compromise—real compromise, demanding concessions from both sides and not just a shabby makeshift of placating laws that sold out an entire people—would depend on imaginative statesmanship and far-reaching vision, qualities that the pliable Pierce and James Buchanan, the mealy-mouthed president following him, sorely lacked.

Northerners who considered the eventual elimination of slavery to be a moral absolute could not compromise. Many Southerners were absolutists too, for they considered states' rights and hence slavery their constitutional prerogative; to them what lay beneath it was the integral right of the white male to steer his own boat. That meant that to them the legal claim was a moral one too, writ large on the cope of heaven. As a consequence, they could secede. But they waited, for party bonds were still strong.

There was more. The inclusion of the Fugitive Slave Act radicalized many a placid Northerner, for it permitted slave catchers to pursue escaped slaves into the free states—all the way to Maine, for instance—where federal marshals could require citizens to assist in their capture. And once captured, the alleged fugitives, denied trial by jury and the right to testify on their own behalf, did not stand a chance. All over New England vigilance committees were established to aid the fugitives. In Massachusetts, the radical minister Theodore Parker said he kept a brace of pistols in his desk, and the clergyman Thomas Wentworth Higginson counseled citizens to disobey the so-called Kidnap Act "and show our good citizenship by taking the legal consequences!"

For black men and women, the question was not one of good citizenship; they had none. Nor was the question an academic one; it was real. They stood up when they could. As Samuel Ringgold Ward, himself a fugitive slave and the editor of *The Impartial Citizen*, wrote, "Let the men who would execute this bill beware." In New York, the Reverend Jermain W. Loguen, another fugitive slave, cried out, "I don't respect this law—I don't fear it—I won't obey it! It outlaws me, and I outlaw it."

The next year, 1851, López undertook his last and fatal journey.

"THE NEVER CEASING song of the negroes as they raise the sugar and coffee into the ships is enough to create a slow fever," Sophia Peabody had confided to her Cuba journal. To Peabody, the future wife of Nathaniel Hawthorne, Cuba was a realm of enchantment, of avocado and lime, rich in sugar and coffee plantations as well as a balmy paradise for invalid Americans who might recover there from cold winters, chronic illnesses, and industrialization. There the ailing Miss Peabody, afflicted with headaches, was soon flushed with health. Her cheeks pink, she closed her eyes to the institution of slavery that lay at the heart of the island's wealth.

To Lucy Holcombe Pickens, one of the Southern belles waving her handkerchief at the wharf as the *Pampero* was towed to sea, the López filibuster was "glorious, a holy mission," a mission promising liberation, though not for the slave of course. (A decade later, Pickens's pretty face would be put on the hundred-dollar Confederate bill.) And a few years after the López debacle, in 1855, she published a novel, *The Free Flag of Cuba; or, The Martyrdom of López: A Tale of the Liberating Expedition of 1851*, which was glowingly dedicated to John Quitman.

Under the pseudonym H. M. Hardimann, Pickens intended to vindicate the brave mission of such self-sacrificing patriots as López and Crittenden (who was rumored to have been her fiancé). "Don't say Filibusters! Call them by their proper names—Patriots! Liberators!" she cried, anticipating what would be known, ten years or so later, as the Lost Cause. "Young America, like a true knight, he stands ready at any moment to resume arms in a cause so worthy his chivalrous devotion."

That was how John O'Sullivan saw himself: as a true knight. Also a Democrat, he bristled at privileges vested in class or rank, and, as if sprung from the novel by Lucy Holcombe Pickens, he was a nationalist, a pacifist, a spiritualist, an expansionist, and a racist who cared not a fig for the slaves. During the war, as a Confederate sympathizer, he went to England to drum up support for the Southern side.

Years earlier, in 1837, he'd founded *The United States Magazine and Democratic Review*, a party organ devoted not just to politics but to good literature, which attracted a band of writers of various political stripes: William Ellery Channing, John Greenleaf Whittier, Edgar Allan Poe, Henry Wadsworth Longfellow, Hawthorne, Catharine Maria Sedgwick, Walter (later Walt) Whitman, William Gilmore Simms, Orestes Brownson, William Cullen Bryant, James Russell

Lowell, and Jane McManus Storm Cazneau, who wrote under the pen name Cora Montgomery and was an outspoken backer of López. O'Sullivan was also the brother-in-law of the wealthy Cuban planter who presided over the Cuban Council in New York. Joining the campaign to buy Cuba and, if that failed, to grab it, O'Sullivan worked closely with Moses Yale Beach, whose newspaper, the New York *Sun*, whipped up enthusiasm for the taking of Cuba and helped print the bilingual newspaper *La Verdad*, bankrolled by wealthy Cuban planters. So the movement to seize Cuba had contacts in the Northeast as well as the South, and in Washington.

To the abolitionist author Lydia Maria Child, though, the discussion of the need for a Cuban democracy was a smoke screen. The filibusterers and their allies, she felt, simply wanted to steal the island and extend the slave empire. Horace Greeley, the antislavery editor of the *New-York Tribune*, agreed. "'The revolution in Cuba' proposes to leave the cultivators of *her* soil in the position of beasts or chattels," he wrote, "subject to be flogged, starved, sold, or tortured as the caprice or fancied interest of the landlord caste shall dictate." Martin Delany too told a far different story from Pickens, O'Sullivan, or the mobs of people protesting the summary execution of López and his hapless men. In his novel *Blake, or The Huts of America* (serialized from 1859 to 1862 in *The Anglo African Magazine* and the *Weekly Anglo African Magazine*) half-naked Cuban slaves were chased at night by bloodhounds and by day surrounded by secret guards "to keep in check the disposition to rebellion." As for the filibusters: "As soon as they got to the island, they would deny the Negros the rights they now have."

What should the Cuban slave or, for that matter, the American slave do? Rebel? Indeed, it was the specter of such a rebellion that scared many a Southerner most of all.

(2)

WHO AIN'T A SLAVE?

Hydesville is a sleepy rural town in upstate New York, just twenty miles east of Rochester, where two young girls, ages twelve and fifteen, claim to hear odd tapping sounds in the night. Their mother decides the noise must be what Maggie and Kate say it is—the sound of the dead, come knocking. She hears it herself on March 31, 1848, after shooing her daughters upstairs to an early bedtime (the dead have been keeping her daughters awake). But Maggie and Kate did not intend to go to sleep. Instead, they tied an apple to a string and thumped it on the floor and, having learned to crack the knuckles on their toes, they also staged a whole new series of rappings.

Ghosts rattled about the little farmhouse for a week.

These garrulous ghosts were friendly, and when asked, they obligingly tapped out answers to all Mrs. Fox's questions. Excited, she called over the neighbors so they too could hear the dead communicate from the world beyond. Soon a whole lot of other folks were dropping by. They came from all over, in wagons and buckboards, and a lawyer from Canandaigua decided he simply had to tell about these weird events in a pamphlet.

News of the strange noises at the Fox house was traveling fast, and Maggie and Kate Fox were growing famous. Their elder sister, Leah, who lived in Rochester, brought Maggie and Kate to her house to conduct what had by now become known as seances. Crowds were flocking into Rochester; people who were desperate, scared, beguiled, and hopeful, all of them had questions for the Fox sisters, who would translate the taps into letters of the alphabet—and into answers.

Amy and Isaac Post had asked the Fox sisters to contact their deceased daughter Matilda, and if Amy and Isaac Post actually believed the sisters were legitimate, then they should be taken seriously. For the Posts were serious people, uncompromising abolitionists, in fact, who had parted ways with many of their fellow Quakers to organize a dissident group of Congregational Friends (later called "Progressivists") over the issue of slavery. The Posts knew Frederick Douglass, the eloquent man who had written the best-selling narrative about his escape from slavery and was now editing his abolitionist newspaper, *The North Star*, in Rochester, and they'd protected the runaway slave Harriet Jacobs at their home on Sophia Street, which served as a stop on the Underground Railroad. In just one night, they might help as many as fifteen runaway slaves on their journey north to Canada and freedom, and now they'd help the spirits. Isaac Post's late mother told the Posts that the spirits were on their side. There was no slavery in the netherworld.

Thomas Higginson, also an abolitionist, would explain why the idea of spirits lit up the country. "In the midst of a world full of despondency, of doubt, of sadness, with a sad and weary life, in many cases bounded by a sadder and more weary view of eternity, comes a new hope," he said, "a new excitement, a new aspiration." Higginson was not the only hopeful abolitionist partial to spiritualism. William Lloyd Garrison, Joshua Giddings, Senator Benjamin Wade, and William Cullen Bryant were some of the other better-known antislavery activists with at least one foot in the spiritualist movement, and the editor Horace Greeley and his wife, after the death of a son, started attending seances. Meanwhile, Maggie and Kate Fox were performing at Rochester's huge Corinthian Hall. Admission cost a quarter, and people began queuing for tickets at daybreak. Among the four hundred in attendance were skeptics, of course, who assumed the girls were ventriloquists, but these doubters were also won over. The Fox sisters were genuine; they had to be.

The Fox sisters were tapping out higher laws, much as that new-fangled telegraph tapped out more pedestrian messages, for this was an age of technological miracle and, one hoped, of miracles of even greater, more transcendent and liberating magnitude. The railroad had spiritualized travel, as the writer Nathaniel Hawthorne had said (even though he was being sardonic); but hadn't it? Hadn't it diminished the distance between place and place? And hadn't the telegraph made distance almost irrelevant with messages sent through immaterial ether? Couldn't one then contact the spirit world with some human invention? Consider the miracle of the daguerreotype. When Louis-Jacques-Mandé Daguerre brought to the public a machine that rendered the visible world in two-dimensional images on polished plates, the daguerreotype effectively replaced the transitory with the permanent and allowed the past to live in the present. Photographs keep "the form of the dead among the living," said the main character, a daguerreotypist, in Hawthorne's 1851 novel, *The House of the Seven Gables*. The dead *were* among the living; and if you could see them, you might hear them too.

The world was changing fast, to be sure, while managing to preserve, liberate, and extend itself. The telegraph and railroad could connect the country, the New Englander could talk to the Californian, or they might meet one another without having to travel around Cape Horn, if only that transcontinental railroad managed to get built. As for the daguerreotype, you didn't have to be wealthy or well born to have your likeness taken. For two and a half dollars, your image could appear in a small, portable, often leather-lined packet. And you could own images of the rich and famous. An ambitious daguerreotypist with poor eyesight named Mathew Brady had realized that early on, and he'd realized that there was a market in images. Formerly a jewel case manufacturer, Brady published a daguerreotype of President Andrew Jackson that he'd taken just before

Jackson died and in 1850 released twelve daguerreotyped portraits, called *The Gallery of Illustrious Americans*, that included Zachary Taylor, John Calhoun, Daniel Webster, and Henry Clay: Democrats and Whigs, Northerners and Southerners: it was a pictorial translation of the Compromise of 1850.

People wanted to see the politicians they'd read about. John O'Sullivan also used the daguerreotype in his magazine, *The United States Magazine and Democratic Review*, where he included a segment called "Political Portraits with Pen and Pencil." Steel engravings made from daguerreotypes were strategically placed at the front of any issue with a profile of a government official. And when O'Sullivan was about to publish an essay about Hawthorne, he suggested that the reticent author sit for a daguerreotype to accompany the piece. "By manufacturing you thus into a Personage," O'Sullivan explained, "I want to raise your mark higher." Manufacture, yes; the Fox sisters were marketing a spectacle too.

For if the dead are never dead, then one can hear as well as see them—for a fee. That's what the Fox sisters demonstrated, and soon men of probity such as Isaac Post were communicating with Benjamin Franklin, George Washington, the founder of the Quakers, George Fox, Voltaire, and William Penn. Most seances, however, were conducted by women; women were presumed to be the perfect, passive instrument for channeling the dearly departed. Yet there was power too in their presumed passivity, and mediumship converted what seemed to be compliance into coin—and sometimes into social action. The early women's rights activists Elizabeth Cady Stanton, Mary Ann McClintock, Lucretia Mott, Jane Hunt, and Martha Coffin Wright sat around a spirit table hoping the dead would talk, and on the same table, Stanton composed the Declaration of Rights and Sentiments read at the women's rights convention in Seneca Falls, twenty miles from Hydesville. That was on July 19 and 29, 1848, not four months after the Fox sisters began tapping.

After attending the World's Anti-Slavery Convention in London, where women were cordoned off in their own separate section of the hall, Mott and Stanton had decided to call for a women's rights meeting in America to demand suffrage, equal pay, and a woman's right to divorce or own property. It was a success. In the boiling heat of July 1848, three hundred men and women arrived in Seneca Falls. (The largest contingent was the antislavery Quakers from the Rochester and Waterloo area.) A second convention was held a few weeks later in Rochester, to which Amy Post went directly after a Fox seance, for she felt strong enough—inspired enough—to argue that a woman should chair the meeting, which a woman did. She knew that the spirits were backing women's rights as well as abolition.

But the apostles of such liberation and equal rights—and abolition—struck many people as fanatics, not reformers; they were monsters of sentiment and vanity who believed that they alone could read by the light of a divine or higher law. "They have no heart, no sympathy, no reason, no conscience," complained Hawthorne in *The Blithedale Romance*, a coruscating satire of such reformers published just after *The House of the Seven Gables*. "They will keep no friend, unless he make himself the mirror of their purpose; they will smite and slay you, and trample your dead corpse under foot, all the more readily, if you take the first step with them, and cannot take the second, and their third, and every other step of their terribly straight path."

Composed shortly after the Rochester rappings and the Seneca Falls convention, *The Blithedale Romance* is one of the strangest novels to come from the strange pen of the New Englander who, stranger still, had passed one spring among the utopian socialists of Brook Farm, where he'd hoed manure in the presence of such living spirits as Charles Anderson Dana, later the managing editor of Greeley's *New-York Tribune*. (During the war, Dana was sent by Secretary of War Edwin Stanton to report on General Grant's susceptibility to drink; later still, he published the New York *Sun*, which he had purchased in a fire sale from the filibusters' backer Moses Y. Beach.)

Blithedale, then, takes place in an eponymous pastoral community modeled on the short-lived Brook Farm. Founded in 1841 by George and Sophia Ripley and located on about 170 acres in West Roxbury,

Massachusetts, Brook Farm was an experiment in cooperative living that intended to spiritualize manual labor by sharing it: "Thought would preside over the operations of labor," Ripley said in trying to entice Ralph Waldo Emerson, who did not join. "We should have industry without drudgery, and true equality." The Brook Farm Institute of Agriculture and Education, as the community was formally called, eschewed rank, status, privilege, enforced labor (slavery) as well as wage slavery and formal attire. It welcomed everyone: farmers, mechanics, writers, and preachers. Children were educated in the community school, and the place was funded as a joint-stock company that paid a fixed 5 percent interest to its subscribers.

To Hawthorne, though, the experiment merely spawned the same old society with the same old problems that the benighted reformers had hoped to leave behind. ("No sagacious man will long retain his sagacity," Hawthorne wrote, "if he lives exclusively among reformers and progressive people, without periodically returning into the settled system of things, to correct himself by a new observation from that old stand-point.") Among those benighted reformers is the beautiful Zenobia, a character based on the women's rights journalist Margaret Fuller. Magnificent but doomed, Zenobia is also the half sister of the far more passive and moony Priscilla, a veiled young woman who onstage mumbles hocus-pocus divinations dispatched, it's widely assumed, directly from the spirit world. The other side of freedom and strength, Hawthorne was suggesting, is mumbo-jumbo, and as if to prove that women are never really tough or free, the once powerful Zenobia eventually kills herself.

Yet Hawthorne's quarry in *Blithedale* was not just the counterfeit arcadia of the 1840s, the women's movement, or the recent vogue in spiritualism; it was a fractious America in which all three were interwoven as so many threads in a national carpet, where women and men insisted that they spoke of higher laws with "authority from above." The radical minister Theodore Parker thought *Blithedale* had been written just for him; perhaps William Seward, if he read the novel, thought the same.

Hawthorne was no reformer and certainly no abolitionist, and though his opposition to that movement embarrassed some of his acquaintances and later his admirers, the novelist did sign a Free Soil petition protesting the Fugitive Slave Act. Hawthorne regarded any law that ceded control to the federal government as absurd. "This Fugitive Law is the only thing that could have blown me into any respectable warmth on this great subject of the day," he said, "—if it really be the great subject."

The great subject, though, was America, particularly to Hawthorne's onetime and uncategorizable neighbor, Herman Melville, a seafarer turned novelist, who lived near Hawthorne in western Massachusetts and loudly banged the drum for America: "We are rapidly preparing for that political supremacy among the nations," he said, "which prophetically awaits us at the close of the present century."

Melville wrote this in an erotic review of Hawthorne's story collection *Mosses from an Old Manse* in the summer of 1850. Pretending to be a Virginian on summer holiday in Vermont, the ersatz Southerner says he feels Hawthorne "expands and deepens down, the more I contemplate him; and further and further, shoots his strong New-England roots into the hot soil of my Southern soul." Undeniably ardent, the passage also suggests Melville is laying claim to a national literature with its roots in New England. But the soil that nurtures those roots is hot and Southern and presumably more fertile than New England's. A true national literature, then, is a product of North and South.

The Compromise of 1850 had not yet passed. It was as if Melville were calling for it.

Still, Melville's politics cannot be ascertained with any more certitude than his sex life. Even the colossal novel he was presently writing combined American history and politics with the lore of whaling, current events, philosophy, Shakespeare, Milton, Virgil, the Bible, Andrew Jackson, John Bunyan, and George Washington. Sounding much like O'Sullivan or even Emerson—"the world is as young today, as when it was created"—Melville asks his reader to "contemn all imitation . . . and foster all originality," to take risks, to speak without bounds, to support American authors. That is, declaiming that the American must seize the moment, not sound like anyone else, and scrap all "leaven of literary flunkeyism towards England," Melville brooked no compromise. And so he intended to blast open the conventions of the novel. Its rhythms bursting forward and upward, *Moby-Dick* contains multitudes: natural history and drama, cetology and science, philosophy and crude humor.

Sprawling and gargantuan as the great white whale that the protagonist, Captain Ahab, pursues round the globe, *Moby-Dick* is a riotous examination of human knowledge, its limits and circumference, as well as a meditation about morality and the ethical actions that make sense, if any do, in an indifferent universe. "Who ain't a slave?" wonders the novel's narrator, Ishmael, in a statement that, out of context, places the bitter debate over American slavery on an altogether nongeographic plane: "Let America add Mexico to Texas, and pile Cuba upon Canada; let the English overswarm all India, and hang out their blazing banner from the sun; two thirds of this terraqueous globe are the Nantucketer's. For the sea is his; he owns it, as Emperors own empires."

On that sea glides Ahab's ship, the *Pequod*, and on that ship hides the black cabin boy Pip, who hails from Connecticut or Alabama or both (it's not quite clear—which is to say he may also be a fugitive). When Pip one day leaps from the side of a whaleboat as the men go in for the kill, he flounders in the ocean, nothing in sight, until Stubb, the second mate, rescues him. Stubb tells Pip not to jump again. "We can't afford to lose whales by the likes of you," he says; "a whale would sell for thirty times what you would, Pip, in Alabama." Of course Pip gets frightened again, and he jumps again, and this time Stubb is in no hurry to rescue him. So Pip bobs in the ocean, his soul drowned in its immense heartlessness, and by the time Stubb finally fetches him, Pip has gone mad. But it's Ahab, of all people, who recognizes Pip and his suffering. "I feel prouder leading thee by thy black hand," says the monomaniacal captain, "than though I grasped an Emperor's!"

If the brooding, angry, fire-defying Ahab would chase the white whale round the Horn into perdition's flames—and he could—who might stop him? The person best suited to the task seems to be Starbuck, Ahab's chief mate, a moral man, a brave man, an honest and steadfast and prudent man who will not persist "in fighting a fish that too much persisted in fighting him." Starbuck would not have a man in his boat who is not afraid of a whale. "By this, he seemed to mean," Melville explained, "not only that the most reliable and useful courage was that which arises from the fair estimation of the encountered peril, but that an utterly fearless man is a far more dangerous comrade than a coward." Starbuck is looking for compromises; he's a Henry Clay man.

Starbuck tries to influence Ahab by appealing to reason. " 'Vengeance on a dumb brute!' cried Starbuck, 'that simply smote thee from blindest instinct! Madness! To be enraged with a dumb thing, Captain Ahab, seems blasphemous.' " Ahab's zeal is no match for Starbuck's logic. But if Ahab's obsession will destroy the ship, Starbuck must consider slaying his captain. "Is there no other way? no lawful way?" he wonders, much as the men of moderation wondered when assaulted by fanatics, or fire-eaters, or even by the Fugitive Slave Act. But Starbuck would have to be Ahab to kill Ahab, and this far he cannot go. Insurgents sow insurgency, lawlessness, immorality.

Yet to Melville, moderation—"the incompetence of mere unaided virtue"—can itself be a crime. With no one stopping him, Ahab takes down the *Pequod* and its whole multiracial crew, all except Ishmael.

Moby-Dick is not a political parable. Melville was composing a novel unlike any other America had ever seen; he was not a political practitioner like his older brother Gansevoort, a Democratic booster. Rather, Melville is an Ishmael, the outsider and outcast who perceives that an ineffable, unutterable phantom swims before all human hearts, luring and evading, luring as it evades. Perhaps that phantom is freedom; it's hard to know. But Melville is also Ahab, of course, and as Ahab, radically breaks through the mask—which is the novel: "If man will strike, strike through the mask! How can the prisoner reach outside except by thrusting through the wall?" Called crazy when the book appeared, Melville reached far and then burrowed deep into the human heart, where there is freedom but no law—and no moderation.

"SO YOU'RE THE little woman who wrote the book that started this great war," Abraham Lincoln reportedly quipped to the diminutive Harriet Beecher Stowe—she stood under five feet tall—when they met in 1862. Though likely apocryphal, the remark encapsulates what was and remains Stowe's ability to place the antislavery movement squarely on the American table. Mrs. Stowe's *Uncle Tom's Cabin*, Henry James would drily remark, was the "irresistible cause." George Orwell would call it "a good bad book" that was also "deeply moving and essentially true."

Published around the same time as *Moby-Dick* and *Blithedale*, Stowe's *Uncle Tom's Cabin: or, Life Among the Lowly* was a whopping best seller: 10,000 copies flew off the shelves in the United States during the first week of publication, 300,000 in the first year. "Let us hope there are no more Blithedales," groaned Hawthorne's publisher. "The writer of *Uncle Tom's Cabin* is getting to be a millionaire." *Blithedale* had not been a commercial success, and *Moby-Dick* would fail utterly, its author vilified as vain or vulgar or a little crazy.

Initially serialized in *The National Era*, Gamaliel Bailey's Washington-based antislavery magazine, *Uncle Tom's Cabin* had been written by a woman who later said she wrote it with her "*heart's blood*." Harriet Beecher Stowe was no stranger to people whose blood was up. The daughter of the noted preacher Lyman Beecher, the sister of the pioneering female educator Catharine, the sister of the women's rights activist and spiritualist Isabella, she was also the wife of Bowdoin College instructor Reverend Calvin Stowe and the mother of six living children. Her famous and histrionic brother was the antislavery clergyman Henry Ward Beecher. It was as if Mrs. Stowe's family were a microcosm of the culture, politics, and evangelical religion of the Northeast, which included her own evangelical condemnation of slavery.

Because of its propaganda, the novel and its aesthetic merits have long been a question of some dispute and were even contested at the time of its publication. Hawthorne's wife, who disparaged most abolitionists, haughtily remarked, "I have felt all along that Mrs. Stowe's book was overrated—that it was not profound but exciting—too much addressed to the movable passions—not to the deeper soul. Also that it would do no good to the slave." Yet despite its pieties, its glorification of submission and martyrdom and despite its racism, *Uncle Tom's Cabin* is a story of female liberation. With slave catchers in pursuit, the slave Eliza, clutching her baby, crosses the Ohio River into freedom as ice floes heave beneath her; the slave woman Cassy foils the cruel slave owner Simon Legree with a cunning plan that plays on the man's superstitions. Woman's wit triumphs, even if slavery persists. Though the putative hero of the book, even the Christian slave Uncle Tom is something of a lady, albeit the most docile sort, and his miserable fate ironically suggests the wages of female passivity.

"When I thought of slavery, with its democratic whips—its republican chains—its evangelical blood-hounds, and its religious slave-holders—when I thought of all this paraphernalia of American democracy and religion behind me, and the prospect of liberty before me," wrote William Wells Brown, an escaped slave, "I was encouraged to press forward." A white woman, Stowe excoriates North and South alike, and at story's end, didactically and without apology, predicts that the wrath of "Almighty God" will be visited on the country if it does not eradicate slavery.

Thus a small, overburdened female writer rocking the baby's cradle in freezing Maine was more a monomaniacal Ahab than a compromising Starbuck—at least in terms of the very act of writing—for Stowe broke the unstated, domestic law of the Victorian novel simply by producing one of anger, outrage, and of contempt for a system that allowed the slave trader to consider himself ill-used, the politician to consider himself humane, the abolitionist to consider herself without racism, and the man of moderation to shrug his shoulders and hope for better days. The author was flinty and unflinching, as a reviewer in the prominent Southern magazine *DeBow's Review* noted with contempt. "It is a melancholy exemplification of the facility with which a philanthropist, who devotes himself exclusively to the eradication of one form of evil, can deceive himself, and come to regard any means justifiable, in the pursuance of a supposed good end," the reviewer said. "That subtle analyst of character, Nathaniel Hawthorne, has ably dissected this species of delusion in the Blithedale romance." He recommended that Stowe reread Hawthorne.

Yet Stowe's book is not just a jeremiad. Tackling a controversial subject, she argued it with characters—audacious character, stereotyped character, three-dimensional character, and flat predictable character. Taken together, they present a range of real and harrowing views on slavery. And if Stowe could not reach beyond the platitudes of colonization or Christian charity, or if she trapped herself in a mire of racial pigeonholes, the very fact of her writing at all and writing and selling as she did and questioning the religious precepts she herself lived by—could her character George Harris, a former slave, ever again believe in God after what he'd seen of slavery?—made *Uncle Tom's Cabin* a cultural event. So, this is the little woman who started the war.

When initially offered the book, the publisher Phillips, Sampson, & Co. declined. A novel about a touchy topic—by a woman, no less? If women were to appear in public unshawled and unbonneted, as the New York *Christian Inquirer* fussed, "what becomes of her modesty, her virtue?" "It does seem to me to deprive women of all delicacy," Hawthorne groused. "It has pretty much such an effect on them as it would to walk abroad through the streets, physically stark naked." A proper lady keeps her clothes on, which is why she shouldn't write. A western editor objected to the women's rights groundswell by warning, "If it should prevail, we may yet see some Mrs. Stowe in the Presidential chair." But as the abolitionist Thomas Higginson said,

"The anti-slavery movement had hardly made its way to the masses till a woman undertook to explain it."

Stowe explained it in a book that ultimately gave no crisp solutions. "Of course, in a novel," Stowe wrote in *Uncle Tom's Cabin*, "people's hearts break, and they die, and that is the end of it; and in a story this is very convenient. But in real life we do not die when all that makes life bright dies to us. There is a most busy and important round of eating, drinking, dressing, walking, visiting, buying, calling, talking, reading, and all that makes up what is commonly called living, yet to be gone through."

Everyday life composed of obligation, grief, and slavery: who ain't a slave to something? That was what technology, spiritualism, the women's convention, and the antislavery movement, all of them, were hoping against hope to circumvent.

BECAUSE HE SEEMED so safe, so moderate, and so principled, Horace Mann had been elected in April 1848 to fill John Quincy Adams's empty seat in the House of Representatives. Congressional tempers were hot that spring. Representative John Gayle of Alabama was grilling the abolitionist Joshua Giddings of Ohio about his alleged involvement in the *Pearl* affair, which involved the attempted escape by schooner of fugitive slaves in the District of Columbia. In the Senate, the slave owner Henry Foote of Mississippi was haranguing the antislavery John Hale of New Hampshire, inviting him to come down to Mississippi, where Hale "would grace one of the tallest trees of the forest, with a rope around his neck." So the hand of Old Man Eloquent might have been on Mann's otherwise temperate shoulders, for when asked, he felt he couldn't really refuse to oversee the defense of Captain Daniel Drayton, who had sailed the *Pearl*, and of Captain Edward Sayres, who owned it, even though he hadn't practiced law in twelve years.

Yet Mann wasn't feeling altogether well that spring. Prematurely white-haired, he suffered from bouts of insomnia and periods of depressions as powerful as his passion for reform. Imagining a better and more democratically educated world than the one he inherited, he had been born in 1796 to moderately well off farmers without connections to Harvard and Yale. But he was industrious and determined and worked successfully toward implementing a vibrant public school system and establishing so-called normal schools devoted solely to teacher training. An antislavery (or Conscience) Whig, he'd also been the head of the Massachusetts Board of Education, which he had in fact helped to create, and as a Massachusetts state senator, he worked to pass legislation to build the state's first insane asylum; to him, insanity was not a disgrace.

Devastated by the death of his first wife, when Mann finally remarried, the sleepless reformer whisked his bride away to Europe for a honeymoon—along with his best friend, Samuel Gridley Howe, and Howe's bride, Julia Ward. Together, they would all study the Prussian school system and visit a few prisons, workhouses, and lunatic asylums. For the Howes, it was their first excursion into an unhappy marriage, but Mann had married a woman as devoted to him as he was to public life even though, as his sister-in-law once observed, Horace Mann had "the spirit of a Martyr."

His new brother-in-law happened to be Nathaniel Hawthorne, and some members of the family thought Mann resembled the egomaniacal philanthropist in *Blithedale*. In fact, Hawthorne had completed the book while he was subletting Mann's house. Yet Mann was less an obsessive idealist than a person who adhered closely to the rule of law. Admitted to the Massachusetts bar in 1823, he was prudent and cautious, said his own wife, and he preferred nonpartisanship to popularity. "A partisan cannot be an honest man," he claimed. The abolitionists of Massachusetts therefore distrusted him.

Yet in 1848 they turned to him. Staunch antislavery men such as Salmon P. Chase of Ohio and William Henry Seward of New York were too busy to defend the captain and owner of the *Pearl*, and Daniel Webster (still considered antislavery in 1848) charged too much money. The case went to the safe, judicious, and principled

Horace Mann. "No man in the country will make more out of a bad case than you can," his best friend encouraged him.

The schooner *Pearl* had been impounded in the lower Chesapeake with seventy-six slaves aboard; Drayton had been indicted for stealing and transporting them to freedom. On Sunday, April 16, 1848, the *Pearl* had departed without a hitch from White-house Wharf, a fairly out-of-the-way dock. But since the Potomac is a tidal river, and the *Pearl* was sailing against the tide, it had moved very slowly. Then a northerly squall stopped it cold before it had reached the mouth of the river. Anchored temporarily for shelter at Cornfield Harbor, located just above Point Lookout, Maryland, and about 140 miles from the District of Columbia, the vessel was waiting for the winds to calm, when, at two in the morning, a posse of thirty musketed men, tipped off about the *Pearl*'s mission, had sneaked onto the ship from their steamer, the *Salem*.

Wakened by the clack of footsteps above their heads, the slaves scrambled to the deck, ready to fight. Drayton told them not to do that; they hadn't a chance. They were unarmed.

Drayton and Sayres and the crewman, Chester English, were hustled aboard the *Salem* while the black men, women, and children were kept on the *Pearl*, which was towed back to the District. By the time they disembarked, a mob had gathered at the steamboat wharf. "Lynch them!" the crowd yelled at the white men. "Shoot him! Shoot the hell hound!," they screamed at Drayton. One man jumped forward and with a knife sliced off part of Drayton's ear.

For three days, the angry mob threw stones and shattered the windows of a two-story brick building across from the Patent Office building, which happened to house the antislavery paper *The National Era*. Gamaliel Bailey, its editor, denied having any connection with the *Pearl*. "Believing that the extinction of slavery can be effected in accordance with Constitution and Law, and that this is the better way," Bailey insisted, "no system of unconstitutional or illegal measures will find in us a supporter." The rational Starbuck had spoken, or so fervid abolitionists felt. But Bailey firmly believed that helping slaves escape from Washington was too risky for the fugitives. If they were caught, as was likely, they'd be hauled back into slavery and sold farther south, where conditions were even worse.

At the trial of Dayton and Sayres, the courtroom was hot and stuffy and, as Horace Mann dourly noted, as packed as a slave ship. Men in the gallery carried pistols. Drayton was indicted on 115 counts, his bail set at the astronomical amount of $76,000. Mann argued that the number of indictments and the cost of bail were excessive, for the slaves had not been "stolen" but had run away. Mann's defense moved the question at hand from the rights of property owners to the moral meaning of so-called human property. Moreover, he asked, was the color of one's skin sufficient proof of enslavement; and how could the court prove that these men and women and children were actually slaves? And, in any case, wasn't slavery unconstitutional? Or wrong? "I feel in this case as if I were not working for Drayton," Mann wrote his wife, "but for the whole colored race."

After twenty-one hours of deliberation, the jury found Drayton guilty. He was sentenced to twenty years in prison. (Sayres was subsequently acquitted for stealing slaves though he pled guilty to the charge of transporting them.) Mann tried to have the verdict set aside and, failing that, appealed it in a higher court. Not only did he wish to free Drayton and Sayres but, as he said, "get the principles on record."

There were three more trials. The convictions of Drayton and Sayres were reduced to a misdemeanor but not until 1852 and after being censured by abolitionists—William Lloyd Garrison ran a piece in The Liberator called "Inquiry after a 'Back-Bone' "—did Charles Sumner, the tall, regal senator from Massachusetts, manage to get Drayton and Sayres an executive pardon. (Sumner then rushed Drayton and Sayres out of the city because he feared they'd be rearrested.) As Mann drily pointed out, Millard Fillmore had just lost his party's nomination for president, which made it easier for him to issue a pardon—although the conservative Fillmore was fretting over what would now happen to his reputation. "I shall be abused and misrepresented for pardoning them," he cried.

And what had happened to the fugitives? As Mann explained in his opening remarks, they'd been inspired partly by the speeches they heard in Washington, especially on the night of April 15, when bonfires blazed in celebration of the revolutions of 1848 and congressman after congressman proclaimed a new reign of free men. Representative Staunton of Tennessee likened the Tree of Liberty to Mississippi's huge cottonwood (the same tree, likely, on which Henry Foote wanted to hang John Hale). Mann read from Staunton's speech, and he read another one by Foote, extolling liberty. Perhaps these were the men who should be charged with inciting slaves to escape, snapped the Boston papers.

Yet they had tried to escape, and the court would not free them. Instead, the fugitives were marched through the streets of Washington and held in a pen until a gray slave trader from Baltimore named Slatter came to town to purchase a number of them, saying they would fetch good money down South. A pretty young woman would bring even more money, Horace Mann noted with disgust: a slave trader "knew how he could transmute her charms into gold through the fires of sin." One such young woman, Elizabeth Russell, killed herself en route to escape her fate.

The men and women whom Slatter left behind were taken by the slave-traffickers, Bruin and Hill, of nearby Alexandria. This group included six of the children of Amelia and Paul Edmondson, four boys and two girls (Mary and Emily), who sold for $4,500. Held in the slave pens in Alexandria, right across the Potomac from the nation's capital, they were eventually packed up and shipped off to New Orleans. In her *Key to Uncle Tom's Cabin* (Stowe was trying to stem Southern criticism of her book by authenticating its sources), Harriet Beecher Stowe told what had happened to the Edmondsons: how they were clothed in blue pants and shirts, how the brothers' mustaches had been shaved, how their mouths were pried open to check their teeth, how they had been staged, paraded, manhandled. One of the brothers was never seen again; another, luckier one was freed with funds from the grandson of the fur trader John Jacob Astor.

After yellow fever decimated much of New Orleans, the two remaining Edmondson brothers, Ephraim and John, and their two sisters, Mary and Emily, were hauled back to Virginia, where their father desperately tried to save the girls. Advised by the New York branch of the Anti-Slavery Society to consult the Reverend Henry Ward Beecher, Edmondson went to Beecher's home in Brooklyn, New York, but could not bring himself to pull the Beecher bell.

The reverend found Edmondson crying on the stoop and invited him inside, and soon the Edmondson sisters were Beecher's cause. He preached at the large Broadway Tabernacle on behalf of the girls, thundering and cajoling—and appalling—the audience, when he sounded as though he were an auctioneer bidding for the girls' freedom from flesh peddlers. "A thousand—fifteen hundred—two thousand—twenty-five hundred! Going, going! Last call! *Gone!*"

Beecher's church raised the money, and Mary and Emily were freed before being shipped back to New Orleans. Harriet Beecher Stowe and her brother, afterward, supported them through their years at Oberlin College. Horace Mann walked out of the House of Representatives to become the first president of the newly founded Antioch College, which admitted men and women, black and white. He died of fever and overwork in 1859, two years before the firing on Fort Sumter. He was sixty-three. His brother-in-law Hawthorne died in 1864, disgusted by the carnage of what he believed to be an ill-conceived war.

IN THE EARLY morning of September 11, 1851, in Lancaster County, Pennsylvania, a white man from Maryland, Edward Gorsuch, rode up to a stone house located in the small community of Christiana. The house was being rented by William Parker, a tall, strong, light-skinned man, himself once a slave in Maryland, whose rights as a freeman, he said, "were, under God, secured by my own right arm." In his teenage years, Parker had escaped to Pennsylvania, where he had found work but was always looking over his shoulder for someone who might throw him back into slavery. As a result, he decided that he'd assist "in liberating every one within my reach at the risk of my life," slavery was so terrible, freedom so good.

That September day in 1851 in Pennsylvania, Edward Gorsuch went to the Parker place with a six-man posse, which included his son Dickinson, his two nephews, and the well-known slave-catching constable Henry H. Kline, deputy U.S. marshal. Carrying arrest warrants in his satchel, Gorsuch was searching for slaves who had run away from him and were reportedly hiding at the Parker place.

When the posse attempted to enter the house, Parker met them at the landing and asked who they were. "I am the United States marshal," Kline replied and read his warrants aloud. Parker answered that he cared little for him or the United States and that if Kline took another step, he'd break Kline's neck. Kline turned around, or so he later claimed, to leave. Other testimony claimed that Kline hadn't turned around but that he and his men had attempted to force their way upstairs while Parker tried to bide his time. Still other testimony claims that Gorsuch and his men said that if the slaves inside the house didn't surrender, they'd burn the place down and shoot the occupants. "Go in the room down there, and see if there is anything there belonging to you," Parker allegedly told Gorsuch. "There are beds and a bureau, chairs, and other things. Then go out to the barn; there you will find a cow and some hogs. See if any of them are yours." The message was clear; men were not property.

The people in the house began to sing a popular spiritual: "Leader, what do you say / About the judgment day? / I will die on the field of battle, / Die on the field of battle, / With glory in my soul."

Eliza Ann Parker, Parker's wife, went up to the garret and blew a horn to signal to her husband's friends that there was trouble. Those friends were a group of armed black men dedicated, like Parker, to resisting slave catchers and the Fugitive Slave Act "at the risk of our own lives." Hearing the horn, Kline ordered his men to shoot whoever was blowing it. Two of his men climbed up the peach tree near the house and started to fire but the thick stone of the house protected Eliza Parker from the flying bullets.

By now black men and women from the neighborhood had gathered, as many as two hundred, some reckoned, although Parker said that there weren't that many blacks within eight miles. Parker's friends had guns, axes, staves, and corn cutters. Two white men, Castner Hanway and Elijah Lewis, both of them Quakers, also appeared. They warned Gorsuch and Kline not to mess with Parker. Gorsuch and Kline, in reply, ordered the Quakers to help the posse. The Quakers refused. Gorsuch then strode back up to the Parker house, around which more men were collecting. He argued with Parker while his son Dickinson asked him if he'd "take all this from a nigger?"

Young Gorsuch opened fire, but the balls passed through Parker's hat, just grazing his scalp. "How many times each party fired," it was later said, "it is impossible to tell." Edward Gorsuch fell to the ground with a bullet in his chest. He lay in a pool of blood. He was the boldest of the lot, said Parker, for he'd stood firm while Kline turned tail, leaped over a fence, and disappeared. Dickinson Gorsuch died a few days later from his wounds.

The telegraph wired news of the fracas across the country. "Awful Loss of Life in an Attempt to Capture Fugitive Slaves," ran the headline of the Baltimore *Sun* two days later; it was afterward changed to "The Christiana Outrage." Parker's black neighbors were indicted for levying war against the government, even though they were not themselves considered citizens of that government or allowed to vote in it. Parker and several others took off for Canada.

En route, while riding the rails, Parker met a white man who, not recognizing the fugitive, said that he thought this man Parker a brave man. "All you colored people should look at it as we people look at our brave men, and do as we do. You see Parker was not fighting for a country, nor for praise. He was fighting for freedom: he only wanted liberty, as other men do."

(3)

ONE AGGRESSES

James Buchanan had not forgotten Cuba.

Once something caught his fancy, James Buchanan could not let go, and Cuba had undoubtedly caught his fancy. It was time to purchase from Spain that pesky and rich Caribbean island, he surmised from his perch in London, where he was serving as consul under President Franklin Pierce.

In the fall of 1852, Pierce, a friend of Hawthorne and a New Hampshire Democrat, had been elected to the presidency in a landslide by winning over 80 percent of the electoral vote. As the straight Jacksonian he was, Pierce had campaigned foursquare for states' rights and unfettered territorial expansion, helped purge the Democratic Party in New Hampshire of Free Soilers, and he backed the Compromise of 1850. As a good politician, however, he fell prudently silent—he had a "talent for silence," said the New York diarist George Templeton Strong—on the incendiary Fugitive Slave Act once the Democrats had nominated him at their national convention in Baltimore in June. (Disgusted, Horace Mann concluded that the convention had been a sham in which the slavery faction of the party had succeeded in picking and embracing a Southern-sympathizing candidate as party unifier.) Pierce won the nomination with 282 votes on the forty-ninth ballot. When he received the news by telegram, his wife fainted.

A genial person short on specific talent, the handsome Pierce was to the Whigs of New England something of a joke: "just an average man—such as are found in every considerable town in the U.S.—of popular manners & convivial habits, but as a statesman, an orator, or even a lawyer, of no account at all." Disliked by antislavery activists, even moderate ones such as Mann, who called Pierce "a thorough, unmitigated, irredeemable pro-slavery man," he'd been a brigadier general under Winfield Scott during the Mexican War but had been mocked there too as the hero of many a hard-fought bottle, Whigs joked, referring to Pierce's taste for strong drink. But Pierce pleased the Young America Democrats such as John O'Sullivan, and he pleased Southerners, and even that once mighty Whig Daniel Webster had voted for him.

Pierce's inauguration took place just ten weeks after an awful train accident in which his youngest surviving child, eleven-year-old Benjamin, was killed right before Pierce's eyes. His other two children, both boys, had already died, one at four years old of typhus and the other in infancy. It was not an auspicious or happy beginning for the president. Yet he took the oath of office in his own way, "affirming" rather than "swearing," his allegiance, presumably on religious grounds. A strict Congregationalist, he was also a strict constructionist in all things, beginning with the Bible and ending with the Constitution. "If the Federal Government will confine itself to the exercise of powers clearly granted by the Constitution," he declared in his inaugural address, "it can hardly happen that its action upon any question should endanger the institutions of the States or interfere with their right to manage matters strictly domestic according to the will of their own people."

That meant the Northern abolitionists and antislavery activists ought not to bother the South—or slavery—and that Pierce as president believed that enforcing the Constitution also meant enforcing the Fugitive Slave Act.

Reciting his inaugural address without notes before fifteen thousand people, Pierce also spoke of America's manifest destiny—its need and its right to acquire territory. "It is not to be disguised that our attitude as a nation and our position on the globe render the acquisition of certain possessions not within our jurisdiction eminently important for our protection, if not in the future essential for the preservation of the rights of commerce and the peace of the world."

Pierce was evidently thinking of Cuba.

GOOD-NATUREDLY CONSCIOUS OF his good looks, Pierce liked to be liked. In his early White House days, he often appeared clad in a cherry-colored silk dressing gown, as if a host at a salon. But his vanity left him pliable and weak. Even his most reliable supporters sometimes balked. "General Pierce is not the equal of Calhoun in intellect and learning, or of Jackson in intuitive comprehension," said *The United States Magazine and Democratic Review.*

Yet he was a solid Democrat and an expansionist, and he'd made Cuba a campaign subject. In Washington, General Gideon Johnson Pillow, a Tennessee soldier put on trial for insubordination during the Mexican War by Winfield Scott, whom Pierce had just defeated for the presidency, was pushing for a military takeover of Cuba. (Later, during the Civil War, while commanding a Tennessee brigade, Pillow hid behind a tree during the battle at Stones River.) The rationale for seizing the island had stayed the same as it had been: if Spain were to emancipate Cuban slaves (the new Spanish governor in Cuba had announced he might just do that), then the United States would be justified in taking over the island to protect the South from the slave insurrections it feared emancipation in Cuba might set off in America. Pierce also worried that France and England might join together to prevent the United States from legally purchasing Cuba in order to curb American development. Even moderate newspapers such as *The New York Times* had been suspicious: "What possible interest has Great Britain in preventing the United States from acquiring Cuba," it asked, "—except that of checking their growth and putting limits upon their territorial expansion?"

Pierce turned to his foreign ministers, those men, as the *New-York Evening Post* quipped, who could be out of the country for four years without being missed. First of all, there was James Buchanan himself, sent to Great Britain probably because Pierce wanted him out of the way; Buchanan had for a very long time been eyeing the presidency. But Buchanan abroad was a problem. Never comfortable around people, Buchanan had immediately touched off a diplomatic ruckus by not wearing full court dress at a royal dinner. Instead, he'd rather ostentatiously clad himself as a statesman of the people, in the people's dress: black coat, white waistcoat, black pantaloons, cravat, dress boots, a three-cornered hat, all dignified, of course, but not the regalia of monarchs.

Pierce's minister to France was John Y. Mason, who owned a plantation and slaves in Virginia and was known to be something of a hedonist. He "only required having his stomach full of oysters and his hands full of cards to be perfectly happy," joked Thomas Hart Benton. Formerly a member of the U.S. House of Representatives and a secretary of the navy under John Tyler and James Polk, Mason could be tractable. Though fond of finery, unlike Buchanan—he preferred to wear a blue coat trimmed with gold lace topping his white breeches—he stood before a bedecked Louis Napoleon in the plain black of the American republican, just as Pierce's secretary of state, William L. Marcy, had in this case ordered him to do.

Pierre Soulé, the minister to Spain, was the most controversial and complex of the three appointees. Born in the French Pyrenees in 1801, he had studied for four years in a Jesuit seminary, then trained as a lawyer in Paris—after, that is, spending a year as a shepherd in Navarre, where he hid from the Bourbons. They had rightly suspected him of conspiring to depose Charles X, and in 1823, he was arrested, tried, and convicted. He left France, escaped to England, and eventually landed by way of Haiti in New Orleans, where much of the population spoke his native language. By working as a gardener at the Dominican monastery in Bardstown, Kentucky, he perfected his English so well that after a subsequent—and lucrative—career as a criminal attorney in New Orleans, Soulé was elected to the U.S. Senate, where he was considered one of the best orators in the country. Like Mason, he was one of the most extreme, vituperative, and proslavery expansionists in Congress. To Pierre Soulé, a Cuban filibustering mission was an expression of freedom.

His detractors and admirers considered Soulé superficial, arrogant, brilliant, melancholic, impetuous, proud, and relentlessly vain—a character sprung from the pages of Alexandre Dumas, who was his friend for a while. Not surprisingly, then, as soon as Soulé landed in Madrid in his velvet embroidered coat, he was associated with scandal: two duels, one with the French minister to Spain; an alleged flirtation with the queen; and the claim that he intended to bring down the monarchy. He had also supported López and the annexation of Cuba—positions that did not endear him to the Spanish.

The Spanish continued to be wary not just of Soulé—whose diplomacy was far from diplomatic—but also of Pierce and his entire administration. Remembering the expeditions of Narciso López and on the lookout for arms smuggled into Havana harbor, they boarded a U.S. steamer, the *Black Warrior*, to search for weapons, claiming it had violated port regulations. This was just the pretext Pierce needed. The seizure of the *Black Warrior* was a "wanton injury," Pierce declared, and he demanded an indemnity of $300,000. He also warned Congress that he would not "hesitate to use the authority and means which Congress may grant to insure the observance of our just rights." John Slidell, also of Louisiana, proposed a suspension of all neutrality laws, and the ever ready John Quitman began arming for another invasion.

Then the Pierce administration changed course. Likely, the profilibusters in Pierce's cabinet, such as Secretary of War Jefferson Davis, realized that the free blacks of Cuba would fight—and there were more and more of them. Buchanan, meanwhile, still wanted to purchase Cuba and hoped to pressure Spain by getting the support of European bondholders, who could urge Spain to sell the island in order to pay its creditors. Ready to listen, Pierce restrained the fili-busters by publicly reaffirming the neutrality laws but opted to send a special commission to Madrid to carry out instructions earlier sent to Soulé by Secretary of State William L. Marcy, who had authorized the purchase of Cuba for as much as $130 million and, failing that, "to detach that island from the Spanish dominion and from all de-pendence on any European power."

What did "detach" mean?

Britain and France were more concerned about the Crimea than about Cuba. That did not reassure U.S. expansionists, who feared that Spain might liberate the slaves or that Britain might somehow force Spain to emancipate them and turn Cuba into another Haiti, right on America's doorstep. Cuba was an obsession, a mystery, a menace, a prize. Pierce too was fixated on Cuba, and Marcy suggested that the three ministers, Buchanan, Mason, and Soulé, meet in early October in Ostend (in present-day Belgium), the place chosen as one where there would be little publicity and few spies.

Mason represented the hope of a Southern Confederacy, Soulé represented Manifest Destiny, and Buchanan wanted to be president. Together, they would try to map out foreign policy. But if Soulé was involved, there could be trouble. With his gift for back-stabbing, he had been suspected of helping foment the (failed) republican insur-rection in Madrid that August. Several newspapers demanded that Pierce recall him, which he refused to do, and by fall, the public-ity, all of it bad, convinced the three ministers to leave Ostend for the quieter Aix-la-Chapelle in Prussia. It was there, in October, that Soulé and Buchanan and, to a degree, Mason composed the bellig-erent document. "Judge Mason can scarcely be held accountable," wrote the antislavery Democrat Donn Piatt. "It depended very much whether it was before or after dinner that he signed the paper."

The so-called Ostend Manifesto, later considered by historians as calamitous, sanctioned the use of force. It recommended that the United States purchase Cuba and, if unable to accomplish that, to consider whether Cuba then threatened national security. "Should this question be answered in the affirmative," the ministers blustered, "then by every law human and divine, we shall be justified in wresting it from Spain, if we possess the power." The implication was clear: there might be war. "Self-preservation is the first law of nature, with states as well as individuals." Somehow Soulé had pushed Buchanan, which was not hard to do, in the direction of a martial solution, for Buchanan was a Southern sympathizer, his eye still firmly fixed on the White House.

When news of the Ostend Manifesto leaked—it was apparently intended as an internal memorandum—Horace Greeley in the *Tribune* called it "The Manifesto of the Brigands." He was not alone. "It is said that the collision of wits produces wisdom," sniggered *The Boston Daily Atlas*, "but this collision of Buchanan, Mason, and Soulé has proved nothing but blank stupidity and hopeless nonsense, and irreconcilable inconsistency, and dreary columns of mere commonplace." If nothing except annexation, by any means, could save the United States from disunion, death, revolution, and so-called Africanization, as the manifesto suggested, then what was Pierce doing? Even the sympathetic *United States Magazine and Democratic Review* found the manifesto hasty, rambling, abrupt, and inconclusive. Marcy coolly renounced it and snubbed Soulé, whom he never much liked anyway. He was now able to settle the *Black Warrior* affair with Spain without much fuss; Soulé was recalled in early 1855, and in relief, Spain offered to compensate the owners of the ship. Pierce distanced himself from Ostend; no military takeover for him—he knew the North would not tolerate it. Already the general feeling was that the three ministers at Ostend had gone too far: they were called buccaneers, highwaymen—and filibusterers who, in the words of the *New York Herald*, said to Spain, "Your money or your life." Their aggression too had been a form of "higher law."

Unfazed, Soulé predicted that no Democrat would win the 1856 nomination for president without backing the outrageous Ostend doctrine.

. . . .

John O'Sullivan liked controversy. And grateful that Pierce had appointed him minister to Portugal, he began shilling for the Kansas-Nebraska bill, another Pierce administration fiasco with far-reaching and bloody results.

Introduced in January 1854 by Illinois senator Stephen A. Douglas (partly because he, as chairman of the Committee on Territories, maneuvered the building of the transcontinental railroad through his state and partly because he could promise land to white settlers), the Kansas-Nebraska bill was intended to organize territorial governments in the regions acquired by the Louisiana Purchase, which included the huge Nebraska territory and Kansas. The bill also allowed the inhabitants of the territory to hold a referendum on slavery.

To Douglas, this referendum was a compromise measure that would squelch any fight over slavery—which he considered a nuisance anyway—by simply letting people in the territory vote slavery up or down. And a compromise it was, to a degree. By permitting slavery in the territories previously considered untouchable, the Kansas-Nebraska bill triggered a deadly controversy, for the Missouri Compromise of 1820 had prohibited all slavery in the Louisiana Territory above 36 degrees, 30 minutes latitude. But in exchange for the support of Jefferson Davis and Missouri's foulmouthed proslavery senator David Rice Atchison, along with Robert M. T. Hunter of Virginia, a defender of Southern rights, Douglas had agreed to include that territory in his referendum. Where slavery had once been forbidden, it could now be sanctioned by vote. But Douglas said he was appealing to a "higher and a more solemn obligation"—that of the "great fundamental principle of Democracy and free institutions which lie at the basis of our creed, and gives every political community the right to govern itself in obedience to the Constitution of the country."

And so the Pierce administration acquiesced to the naked repeal of the Missouri Compromise, but no one is quite sure why or whether, for instance, anyone bullied the president on the Sunday that several senators, including Douglas, gained entrance to the White House—no small thing, for Pierce typically refused meetings on the Sabbath. Whatever happened, the bill infuriated the North, which well understood that it threatened to make Kansas a slave state. And Secretary of State Marcy knew that the bill meant, at the very least, no more Cuban sprees; the addition of Cuba to the roster of Southern slave states would be unthinkable if Kansas was a slave state. Meanwhile, antislavery Democrats were angry enough to leave the party. "The Nebraska question," Marcy concluded, "has sadly shattered our party in all the free states and deprived it of that strength which was needed and could have been much more profitably used for the acquisition of Cuba." It didn't matter, for the Pierce administration had launched the Ostend fiasco and destroyed whatever opportunity there may have been for that acquisition.

In the North, the Nebraska bill rang the fire bell that Jefferson had ominously heard so many years before, after the Missouri Compromise, when he contemplated slavery and its extension: "this momentous question, like a fire bell in the night, awakened and filled me with terror. I considered it at once as the knell of the Union." The *National Era* said the Nebraska bill would yoke the nation to a "slaveholding despotism." And so when Charles Sumner condemned the bill as a slaveholders' plot, Douglas retorted that Senator Sumner represented "the pure unadulterated representatives of Abolitionism, Free Soilism, and Niggerism."

William Seward, the passionate and savvy antislavery senator from New York, tried to outmaneuver Douglas by urging Southern Whigs to demand total repeal of the Compromise. But since the Conscience Whigs of the North deplored the bill, Southern Whigs, whose interests were now regional, felt forced to back it in opposition. Not all Southerners were happy about that, for they felt the bill would reignite the slavery issue and not to their advantage. Certainly Northerners would allege that the Southern slavocracy still wielded power, and westerners would grow more and more suspicious of Southern designs on western land. Plus, the party was in tatters anyway, and the nativist element within its ranks was growing stronger.

As for the Democrats, they too were splitting, with many Northerners preferring to leave the slavery issue alone since they believed white migrants would populate the West and (they hoped) render the issue of slavery moot. Free labor for free men. Keep the Free Soil status quo. Believing as he did in the manifest perpetuation and extension of the Union, O'Sullivan argued that "the old policy of congressional intervention in this matter of slavery in new Territories ought to and must be abandoned, no sane and candid man who is not a *disunionist for the sake of abolitionism can now deny*. Establish that principle, and there is clearly and at once an end of the Union. The non-intervention principle is the only alternative." Let Kansans decide their future for themselves. O'Sullivan reasoned that the cold, raw, dry climate of Kansas and Nebraska wouldn't support slavery anyway. Better to focus instead on an annexed Cuba, where slavery would be profitable. So the extension of slavery didn't really bother O'Sullivan; nor did, evidently, the fact of slavery itself.

In this he was not alone. To him and to Douglas, it was the "abolition party" stirring up another "political tornado of fanaticism" that made for all the trouble.

Other Democrats violently disagreed. Missouri's Thomas Hart Benton, no abolitionist but a longtime opponent of the extension of slavery, condemned the bill, and the lifelong Democrat and influential editor William Cullen Bryant called it disgraceful. The prescient George Bancroft, also a Democrat, told Secretary of State Marcy that "this cruel attempt to conquer Kansas into slavery is the worst thing ever projected in our history. Pierce will be handed over to contempt; for posterity will find for him no apology but in the feebleness of his intellect." And two antislavery men from Ohio, Salmon Chase and the evangelical Joshua Giddings, composed an "Appeal of the Independent Democrats in Congress to the People of the United States," which ran in the *National Era*. It called the Kansas–Nebraska bill a "gross violation of a sacred pledge [the Missouri Compromise]."

The bill passed in May 1854 with Pierce's blessing. He signed it into law on the thirtieth of that month.

EXPECTING A FIGHT, the energetic Stephen Douglas went home to Illinois to defend the bill to his constituents. In Chicago in the fall of 1854, the Little Giant was shouted down by a furious crowd at North Market Hall. Never a retiring man, Douglas lost his temper, and after midnight finally burst out, before stalking off the stage, "It is now Sunday morning; I'll go to church and you may go to hell!"

What the intemperate Douglas had not yet grasped was that the Kansas-Nebraska Act had pushed settlers—indeed, the entire country—into polarized and aggressive positions, each side insulted, stigmatized, and experiencing the kind of paranoia that leads, almost inevitably, to the rifle and the bowie knife. And what gave form and then meaning to their outbursts was the irrepressible issue of slavery. Abraham Lincoln understood this. And he understood the stakes.

In Illinois, most people knew or would soon know about Lincoln's background, which wholly personified the twice-told American tale of the self-made man. This story, in fact, lay at the moral heart of Lincoln's political philosophy. For to him, "self-made" meant the "right to rise" in this world, to achieve or make something from nothing, and to keep and enjoy the fruits of one's labor. Born in 1809 into poverty, his mother dead of the "milk sickness" when he was nine, and the son of a restless father, young Abe Lincoln, six foot four in stocking feet, had read at night by the fire, etched out his thoughts on the back of a shovel, and in his early years worked as a farmer, rail-splitter, surveyor, ferryman, postmaster, and storekeeper, whatever he could, to better himself. By the age of twenty-eight he was an avid student of Blackstone's *Commentaries* and Aesop's *Fables* as well as a skillful lawyer and a formidable Whig leader in the Illinois House of Representatives.

Now forty-four years of age, Lincoln had been out of politics for five years, working diligently and successfully at his law practice. But the Kansas-Nebraska Act seemed to galvanize him—he was thunderstruck and stunned, he said—and with Senator Stephen Douglas back on the Illinois stump defending his unpopular position, Lincoln took to the road. In fact, the famous Lincoln-Douglas debates of 1858 actually began in the fall of 1854, with the issues of slavery, compromise, racism, and the Declaration of Independence passed back and forth by each orator in a kind of relay race of rhetoric. Douglas's speeches had been articulate, persuasive, and fluent even if he often boiled with indignation and hurled the occasional sarcastic epithet, particularly about abolitionists, for which he became known. Lincoln too was articulate, persuasive, and down-home. His pants were often too short, his humor often of the barnyard and the field; yet he was logical, well prepared, often mesmerizing. With perfectly pitched self-confidence and an eye to the ballot box, he ratcheted up the argument. Standing very tall in his broadcloth coat, he was an eloquent Ichabod Crane on a backwoods stump, wielding a moral cudgel.

On September 26 and then again on October 4, at an Illinois State Fair brimming with pigs and pies, the former one-term congressman delivered by candlelight a three-hour address that's rightly considered his first major speech. In a high, reedy voice, Lincoln spoke from a written text and immediately claimed that he had no intention of questioning the existing state of slavery, just its extension, and he did so by adverting to the basic right of slavery, which he said he considered a monstrous injustice, albeit constitutional. "When the white man governs himself that is self-government," Lincoln explained; "but when he governs himself, and also governs *another* man, that is *more* than self-government—that is despotism. If the negro is a *man*, why then my ancient faith teaches me that 'all men are created equal;' and that there can be no moral right in connection with one man's making a slave of another." Yet Lincoln judiciously distinguished himself from the abolitionists. He adhered to the laws that allowed slavery and, moreover, he would not know how to rid the country of the institution anyway. But, as he insisted, the political will of the nation, "a universal feeling, whether well- or ill-founded," could and should not be disregarded. Laws are made by people. Whether well or ill founded, they are the laws. Lincoln was walking a fine line, of course, between moral truths and the law. And he knew it.

For the general sentiment in antebellum America did not list toward abolition, nor in fact did Lincoln. He did not advocate immediate emancipation (a constitutional impossibility anyway) or political or social equality with blacks. As Frederick Douglass later declared, "viewed from the genuine abolition ground, Mr. Lincoln seemed tardy, cold, dull, and indifferent." But from his own ground—moral indignation at the defeat of Clay's compromise—he was plain-spoken, direct, pragmatic, and careful. Arguing against the extension of slavery, he agreed that the Nebraska territory should be available for free white people. "Slave States are places for poor white people to remove FROM; not to remove TO. New free states are the places for poor people to go to and better their condition." This brand of freedom— the freedom to better one's (white) condition—lay at the heart of his argument. It was also freedom, he averred, as defined in the Declaration of Independence. Thus Lincoln defined freedom for white people as a basic right. Yet he also declared that freedom should exist for black people too as a moral right. Regarding humans as property is a flat contradiction, impossible, unjust, absurd. This he could not say quite as directly, but he did parse the notion of compromise on which, as he explained, the nation was founded. That compromise had to do with slavery—slavery was necessary, he quickly reasoned, because it already existed, but *not* as a right and *certainly* not a moral right. "Necessity drove them [the fathers of the republic] so far, and farther, they would not go." A compromise, then, occurs when both sides yield something because they have to; that was true of the Constitution, the Missouri Compromise, the Compromise of 1850. And underlying these compromises was a faith in moral progress—that is, his conviction that slavery would eventually perish from the globe.

Until then, there must be compromise. "Ask us not to repeal, for nothing, what you paid for in the first instance." It was Lincoln the rational lawyer now speaking. "If you wish for a thing again, pay again. That is the principle of the compromises of '50, if indeed they had any principles beyond their specific terms—It was the system of equivalents." But this was only half the story. To repeal the Missouri Compromise would imperil the country. "Is it not probable that the contest will come to blows, and bloodshed?" Lincoln prophetically asked. "And if this fight would begin, is it likely to take a very peaceful, Union-saving turn? Will not the first drop of blood so shed, be the real knell of the Union?" The lawyer turned apocalyptic soothsayer seemed to know the answer.

"For who after this will ever trust in a national compromise?" he wanted to know.

"The spirit of mutual concession—that spirit which first gave us the constitution, and which has thrice saved the Union—we shall have strangled and cast from us forever. And what shall we have in lieu of it? The South flushed with triumph and tempted to excesses; the North, betrayed, as they believe, brooding on wrong and burning for revenge. One side will provoke; the other resent. This one will taunt, the other defy; one aggresses, the other retaliates."

Only a middle ground would save the nation, but the center would not hold.

SOOTHSAYERS WITH RATIONAL gifts were few in number. More prevalent were the hotheads who dreamed of freedom, who equated filibustering expeditions with freedom, or for whom freedom came, as it did in California, in the form of golden nuggets; often they saw themselves as freedom fighters in the mold of Europe's revolutionary heroes, men such as Italy's Giuseppe Mazzini and Hungary's Louis Kossuth. Discounting his own absolutist tendencies, Melville's Captain Ahab had dreamed of a world without evil, and Hawthorne's Hester Prynne, wearing her scarlet letter, had dreamed of freedom for women. Margaret Fuller told women they could be sea captains, if they would—even before Seneca Falls, when women declared and demanded and petitioned for their civil rights. As slaves, William

Parker and Frederick Douglass knew the meaning of freedom, and they knew it could not be won without a fight.

In Boston, on the evening of May 26, 1854, a cadre of black and white men tried to spring the jailed fugitive slave, Anthony Burns, and whisk him to freedom. The police resisted with swords and billy clubs, and the rescuers, also armed, fired at least two shots. The men guarding Burns may have fired as well. A twenty-four-year-old teamster, come to help the police, was killed that night, and the U.S. marshal in Boston called for federal troops.

The next day, vacillating antislavery people waffled no more. "We went to bed one night old fashioned, conservative, Compromise Union Whigs," said Amos Lawrence, a wealthy textile manufacturer, "& waked up stark mad Abolitionists." Yet less than a week later, with thousands of troops on horseback patrolling the city's cobblestones and someone hanging a small coffin, the word "Liberty" painted on it, from State Street, Anthony Burns, escorted by a martial entourage—the soldiers' bayonets fixed, their swords drawn—was taken to the Boston wharf, where the U.S. cutter *Morris* blankly waited to take him back south.

In Concord, Massachusetts, Ralph Waldo Emerson's wife covered the front gate of the Emerson home with black bunting, and the otherwise reclusive Henry David Thoreau, who was anxiously awaiting the publication of *Walden*, went to the Massachusetts Anti-Slavery Society meeting on July 4 in Framingham to protest. The picnic area was crowded with over six hundred people despite the scorching heat. The platform was decorated with two white flags labeled "Kansas" and "Nebraska." The renowned editor of *The Liberator*, William Lloyd Garrison, burned a copy of the Fugitive Slave Act, but when the bespectacled and bald-headed newspaperman torched the Constitution, some members of the audience jeered while others, still louder, cheered. Famously, Garrison denounced the founding document as a "covenant with death and an agreement with hell." As his copy wrinkled in flames, he added, "So perish all compromises with tyranny! And let all the people say, Amen!"

Lank, lean, and formidably eloquent, the former slave Sojourner Truth took to the platform to remind her audience, "The white people owed the colored race a big debt, and if they paid it all back, they wouldn't have anything left for seed. All they could do was to repent, and have the debt forgiven them." Then Thoreau delivered what Horace Greeley called a "higher-law speech." The violation of the moral law, said Thoreau, makes for defiance: "Who can be serene in a country where both the rulers and the ruled are without principle?" the author asked. " . . . My thoughts are murder to the State, and involuntarily go plotting against her."

IN 1854, AT the age of twenty-two, the Scottish-born blowhard James Redpath traveled to the South, partly on foot and partly by railroad and steamer. Redpath had already left Michigan, where his immigrant family had settled, and gone to New York, where he had found work with Greeley's *Tribune*, but peripatetic and exuberant, he needed to see slavery with his own eyes. In particular he wished to hear what the slaves said about their own condition.

From Virginia and Georgia and North Carolina, Redpath dispatched a series of graphic antislavery letters to abolitionist newspapers. And during his travels, convinced that rational arguments could never appeal to the Southerner, who was obliged to believe his or her system was right—that wrong was actually right, as their churches told them—Redpath decided that the abolitionist's duty was to appeal to the slaveholder's fear. "Let us teach, urge, encourage insurrections," he wrote, "and the South will soon abandon her haughty attitude of aggression. Then it will be time to advocate schemes of compensation; then it will be time to ascertain whether or not the Constitution gives us the power to abolish slavery everywhere."

Though readying himself for the insurrection soon to be promised by John Brown, Redpath knew that no slave insurrection was imminent, not in the South anyway, and he wanted to go where the action was. A romantic individualist, young and idealistic, itching for a fight and buoyed by the spirit of reform in the air, he headed to Missouri, which, as one scholar noted, was a place for young men determined to make history, not watch it from afar. In St. Louis, he joined the staff of the *Daily Missouri Democrat* in the midst of what amounted to a civil war, which he later admitted he'd wanted to foment all along.

In March 1855, just after the Ostend Manifesto was bruited in the press as a ridiculous attempt to extend slavery, heavily armed Missourians, or "border ruffians" as they were called, crossed from Missouri into Kansas to fight the antislavery homesteaders being sent to the territory by the New England emigrant aid societies. Do-good settlers with a Bible in one hand and a rifle in the other, sneered Stephen Douglas. Douglas wasn't entirely wrong. Through organizations such as the well-financed Massachusetts Emigrant Aid Society, initially chartered to colonize the West in order to make money, it wasn't long before these Yankee land-speculating companies were labeled Free Soil usurpers come to rob Missouri folk. Besides, what were Yankees anyway, if not abolitionists? Countered the Yankees, with equal hyperbole, what were Missourians but backwoods slave owners?

Cold, hungry, and beleaguered, many of the emigrants from the East crossing into Kansas soon turned their wagons around to go back. But with men such as David Atchison inciting Missourians "to kill every God-damned abolitionist in the district," gritty settlers continued to flood the territory. Hostile and wary, they nonetheless aimed to make the place their home. And many of them were abolitionists who knew how much hostility they faced. For to Missourians, if Kansas became a free state, Missouri would be bound by free states to its west as well as to its north and its east. "I say let the Indians have it [Nebraska] *forever*," fumed Missouri state senator Claiborne Fox Jackson. "They are better neighbors than the abolitionists, by a damned sight."

After hundreds of Missourians—"full of whiskey and resentment," said one eminent historian, succumbing to the name-calling of both sides—poured into Kansas for the day in order to vote, a pro-slavery majority swiftly elected a proslavery legislature. (The Kansas-Nebraska Act had not stipulated residency requirements for voters.) In turn, the new legislature passed the so-called Bogus Laws forbidding antislavery talk of any kind. They also mandated ten years' hard labor, if not the death penalty, to anyone caught helping fugitive slaves. When free-staters countered by setting up their own legislature in Topeka, the violence escalated. "The territory was covered with guerillas, gangs of highwaymen, horse-thieves, and housebreakers from Missouri, Georgia, Alabama, and South Carolina," Redpath reported.

In May 1856, a gang of riled-up proslavery men mobbed the Free Soil town of Lawrence, Kansas, burned the hotel, sacked the governor's house, and demolished two antislavery newspaper offices. In retaliation, the abolitionist crusader John Brown rounded up two of his sons—he had sired twenty children—along with his son-in-law and two other men and rode out to Pottawatomie County where they dragged five settlers from their cabins at midnight and hacked them with cavalry broadswords. Brown evidently did not participate in the attack, except to shoot an unconscious man to make sure he was dead.

In the Senate chamber that same May, Massachusetts senator Charles Sumner inveighed for two days against the sacking of Lawrence, verbally drubbing colleagues such as South Carolina's Andrew Butler, a man with chalk white hair and genteel manners. (Sumner said Butler had chosen a mistress, that harlot slavery, to cherish and adore, and belittled Butler as Stephen Douglas's Sancho Panza.) Two days later, on May 22, Senator Butler's less dignified protégé, Congressman Preston Brooks, avenged the honor of his slandered cousin and their state when he entered the Senate chamber, sauntered over to the wooden desk where Sumner sat writing, and whacked him senseless with a gutta-percha cane while some of his colleagues egged him on. It took Sumner more than three years to recover and return to the Senate, and emotionally he never recovered at all.

A few days after Sumner's caning, in Syracuse, New York, radical abolitionists held a convention during which they harked back to old John Quincy Adams. In 1842, Adams had declared that during war, slaves could be freed by martial law: "that the military authority takes for the time the place of all municipal institutions, slavery among the rest. Under that state of things, so far from its being true that the states where slavery exists have the exclusive management of the subject, not only the President of the United States, but the commander of the army, has power to order the universal emancipation of slaves." To those radical abolitionists, the country was in a state of war. Frederick Douglass recalled what the bold Adams had said and what the bold Adams had meant: that "liberty and slavery are eternally forbidden to be at peace. There is no middle ground; the choice it leaves to liberty, is kill or be killed."

IF THE OSTEND MANIFESTO and its implications for Cuba—and slavery—had to most Americans seemed far away or forgettable; if the Kansas-Nebraska Act seemed too cerebral or not worth fighting for; if the Anthony Burns case in Boston represented the furor of dozing fanatics, now awakened; if Abraham Lincoln moralizing about the repeal of the Missouri Compromise among prize cattle seemed quaint and far-fetched; if the sacking of Lawrence seemed an instance of frontier justice; if the radical abolitionists symbolized the frenzied "ultraism," not to be taken seriously, of a handful of white people and of ("insolent") blacks, then the brutal caning of Charles Sumner "silently epitomized," as one historian put it, "the white men's right to speak, whether in the U.S. Senate or in Kansas."

With its classical allusions tightly coiled around insults to Southern manhood and gentility, Sumner's mean-spirited speech had been sophomoric, admitted George Templeton Strong, who regarded antislavery agitation as mistaken in principle and mischievous in policy. "But the reckless, insolent brutality of our Southern aristocrats," he concluded, "may drive me into abolitionism yet."

(4)

DEMOCRACY

After his death it was said that Phineas Taylor Barnum was more alive than anyone still living. Gray-eyed, affable, and six foot two, his jowls a little flabby, he had been funny, extroverted, and aphoristic. And as a producer and prolific writer (though he himself was his best and truest subject), Barnum had represented America to Americans, or so he had hoped. In that way, he was oddly like his contemporary, the controversial poet Walt Whitman; in fact he was the Whitman of the stage: cocky, optimistic, self-centered, a purveyor of the American scene and in a way its singer. He celebrated the variety, the innocence, the agitations that Whitman declared quintessentially American.

Born in rural Connecticut in 1810, as a boy Barnum peddled molasses candy but by 1855, the year of his first autobiography, the budding impresario had edited a newspaper, been sued for libel, worked for a dry goods store, opened a museum, and as a loyal Democrat paid a call on Andrew Jackson when his circus troupe performed in Tennessee. He had also successfully promoted Joice Heth, a former slave said to be the 161-year-old blind, toothless, wrinkled ex-nurse of the infant George Washington. Slavery had dressed the founding father, Barnum symbolically suggested, his eye on the box office. (Barnum had bought Heth, which of course made him a slave owner.)

Barnum declared that people got their money's worth in the untruths they happily paid for. And besides, the greater the fiction, Barnum said, the greater the truth.

In 1841 he bought Scudder's Museum at the corner of Broadway and Ann Street in lower Manhattan and opened his famed American Museum, a medley of crowded rooms that over time displayed bearded ladies, four-legged chickens, whale carcasses, educated dogs, wax figures, American Indian artifacts, and the ugly, popular "Feejee Mermaid" (a fishtail grafted onto a monkey's torso). He included scientific exhibits, paintings, and a few marvels of the mechanical world, such as the "knitting machine." All were jumbled together: the dubious, the peculiar, the inventive, the technological, the grotesque, and the made-up. Millions of people—from Bowery boys to Henry David Thoreau, from farmers to the Prince of Wales and the young Henry James—paid the twenty-five-cent price of admission.

Entrepreneur, national historian, and peerless promoter, Barnum was a manipulator of images who understood advertising, publicity, and the American propensity for self-making. He did not aspire to literary greatness or to poetry. Instead, he worked with the country's scramble of opportunity, squalor, idealism, and mistrust to create a weird hall of mirrors in which people unwittingly saw themselves. But Barnum loved his audience. In fact, he didn't say there was a sucker born every minute, though the phrase has been attributed to him. Rather, his hodgepodge of curiosities was a kind of democracy in action, embracing everybody and everything.

Walt Whitman learned a great deal from Barnum. Interviewing him in 1846 after Barnum returned from Europe (where he had exhibited the midget General Tom Thumb to the young Queen Victoria), Whitman asked the showman if there was anything he'd seen abroad that made him "love Yankeedom less." Barnum answered immediately, "No! Not a bit of it! Why, sir, you can't imagine the difference.— There everything is frozen—kings and *things*—formal, but absolutely frozen: here it is life." Whitman presciently commented, "a whole book might be written on that little speech of Barnum's."

In 1850 Barnum shrewdly orchestrated the American tour of the coloratura soprano Jenny Lind, the so-called Swedish Nightingale, and turned it into a series of hugely lucrative publicity events aimed at all classes. The programs included ballads, arias, folk tunes, and bel canto—and attracted raving, screaming crowds that tossed bouquets at her white-shod feet. In New York City, twenty thousand people gathered on Broadway in front of the entrance to the Irving House just for a peek, and a sellout crowd of five thousand elbowed into Castle Garden in Battery Park on opening night. Among the ranks of those who heard her sing during her fabulous American tour through Pittsburgh and Baltimore and Richmond and Charleston and Natchez was Emily Dickinson's father, Edward, who went to a performance in Northampton, Massachusetts. Daniel Webster saw her in Washington, and a disappointed Walt Whitman in New York thought the Nightingale's performance glitzy. She was scheduled to give 150 concerts in the United States and Cuba. She sat for Mathew Brady, the newly minted photographer of celebrity. Soon there were Jenny Lind shawls, riding hats, bonnets, gloves, sofas, pianos, and poems. George Templeton Strong summed up the commotion, and the reasons behind it, when he noted that the Nightingale reminded him "of the good little girl in the fairy story who spat pearls and diamonds out of her mouth whenever she opened it to speak." Jenny Lind, however, produced five-dollar bills, "a variation that suits the more prosaic imagery of the nineteenth century." The Gilded Age was arriving early.

Barnum's bubbling energy, his beguiling falsehoods, his seeming ease, and his canny affectation of civic duty (his exhibits were supposed to educate) delighted or, more to the point, distracted Americans frustrated by bloody Kansas and bloodied senators and weary of talk of wage slavery, never mind chattel slavery, railroads, and tariffs. In 1853 Barnum staged an expurgated version of *Uncle Tom's Cabin*. Familiarly known as the "Compromise" *Uncle Tom's Cabin*, Barnum let Little Eva and Uncle Tom survive. Slavery wasn't so bad, William Lloyd Garrison scoffed, as long as most of it was omitted. But Barnum couldn't have cared less what a nut such as Garrison might say. True, the story had been toned down, but the play was the only "sensible Dramatic version of Stowe's book," he insisted, because it didn't give fanaticism a platform. Besides, there was no use in being glum, as one of the advertisements declared; this is America.

And remember that for the same ticket of admission, you could see the Bearded Lady.

In 1855, Barnum published his first autobiography, a book he'd write and rewrite over the course of his lifetime, as if he was saying that behind every story lay another version of the same story and that behind every person another side of that person. By the time he published his autobiography's final rewrite, it was the second most widely read book in the country, after the Bible. Barnum's revisions were not exactly falsehoods; in fact they reflected Ralph Waldo Emerson's idea that the self (even the idea of the self) was always growing, always evolving: "Our life is an apprenticeship to the truth, that around every circle another can be drawn; that there is no end in nature, but every end is a beginning."

Emerson's so-called theory of expansion was the spiritual counterpart of O'Sullivan's manifest destiny, except that O'Sullivan and the Young America movement defined expansion in territorial, not spiritual, terms. Democracy, for them, was an America of growth and change and progressive, outward movement. And that's what Whitman celebrated in his first, 1855, edition of *Leaves of Grass*, which he, like Barnum, would revise over the course of his life:

My sun has his sun, and round him obediently wheels,
He joins with his partners a group of superior circuit,
And greater sets follow, making specks of the greatest inside
    them.
There is no stoppage, and never can be stoppage.

"WE HAD CEASED, we imagined, to be surprised at anything America could produce," remarked a British journalist. "We had become stoically indifferent to her Wooly Horses, her Mermaids, her Sea Serpents, her Barnums." Then came Walt Whitman.

The first edition of *Leaves of Grass* was a Barnumesque celebration of democracy, of an America "growing among black folks as among white, / Kanuck, Tuckahoe, Congressman, Cuff." And if Barnum eschewed higher laws by bridging the gap between the real and the fake and acknowledging that people liked their deceptions—self-deceptions best of all—Whitman in his way also reconciled the divisions between high and low, male and female, young and old, urban and rural. Right inside all of them were higher laws. These laws, then, were not higher at all; they were inherent, immanent, innate. And the poet embodied these laws; the poet contained all things, "the enormous diversity of temperature and agriculture and mines— the tribes of red aborigines—the weather-beaten vessels entering new ports or making landings on rocky coasts—the first settlements north or south—the rapid stature and muscle—the haughty defiance of '76, and the war and peace and formation of the constitution . . . the union always surrounded by blatherers and always calm and impregnable."

A Union calm and impregnable: this was what Lincoln offered in his speeches in Illinois in 1854 on the Kansas-Nebraska Act. This was the fluid world that entrepreneur Barnum managed, exhibited, relished, and exploited. This was the diverse audience Whitman addressed (or imagined) when he declared America the greatest poem and he, its poet:

Walt Whitman, an American, one of the roughs, a kosmos,
Disorderly fleshy and sensual . . . eating drinking and
   breeding,
No sentimentalist . . . no stander above men and women or
   apart from them . . . no more modest than immodest.

Whoever degrades another degrades me . . . and whatever is
   done or said returns at last to me,
And whatever I do or say I also return.

Through me the afflatus surging and surging . . . through me
the current and index.
I speak the password primeval . . . I give the sign of
democracy;
By God! I will accept nothing which all cannot have their
counterpart of on the same terms.

Like Barnum, Whitman had gray eyes, said Bronson Alcott, the
Orphic oracle from Concord whom very few people read; he was also
a friend of Emerson's and the father of Louisa May, and he'd arranged
to meet Whitman, "the very God Pan," in New York. Alcott, who
was not at all buttoned up, noticed right away that Whitman wore
a concoction of clothes—including trousers tucked into his cowhide
boots and an open shirt—and seemed out of place in parlors. There
was certainly nothing "New Englandy" about him, to use Emily
Dickinson's phrase. Dickinson claimed never to have read Whitman,
who she'd heard was scandalous.

Visiting Whitman at his home on Classon Avenue in Brooklyn,
Alcott was accompanied by Henry David Thoreau and the abolitionist Sarah Tyndale. Though Whitman liked Mrs. Tyndale, he was ambivalent about the prickly Thoreau, who, before Whitman arrived,
had helped himself to the biscuits Mrs. Whitman was baking. Still,
Whitman pressed on Thoreau a copy of the new (1856) second edition of *Leaves of Grass*.

Thoreau later told a friend that with the poet's "heartiness &
broad generalities he puts me into a liberal frame of mind prepared
to see wonders—as it were sets me upon a hill or in the midst of a
plain." That was high praise coming from Thoreau, particularly since
Whitman later remembered strolling with the woodsy writer over
Brooklyn streets when Thoreau suddenly turned and asked, "What is
there in the people? Pshaw! What do you (a man who sees as well as
anybody) see in all this cheating political corruption?"

"Thoreau's great fault was disdain—disdain for men (for Tom,
Dick and Harry)," Whitman would say.

In *Walden*, Thoreau's recently published spiritual autobiography, Thoreau had included a chapter aptly called, with sly reference to William Seward, "Higher Laws." In it, Thoreau had insisted he loved the wild in nature not less than the good—though, in fact, he staked his life on the higher, more evolved side of being. Whitman placed his bets on the lower, which to him was also the higher.

The cool recluse of Concord thus met the democratic humanitarian of the kosmos who loved high and low, the good and the wild, which were just two sides of a seemingly different coin: union, without compromise or confrontation.

THE FIRST (1855) EDITION of *Leaves of Grass*, twelve poems and a preface, all untitled, had been published on the Fourth of July. Whitman had not included his name on the title page though on the frontispiece was a portrait of a bearded man, without cravat, his shirt open, one hand on his hip, the other in his pocket, his hat rakishly tipped back. Here he was, a poet of the people for the people, without pretension or pomp. "The best writing," he would say, "has no lace on its sleeves."

Whitman mailed a copy of his book to Ralph Waldo Emerson, who responded kindly and with true admiration. "I greet you at the beginning of a great career," he promptly wrote.

Then, for publicity, Whitman published Emerson's letter in the *Tribune* without Emerson's consent. He also quoted a section of it on the cover of the next edition of *Leaves of Grass*, which included the new and sensual poems that would predictably annoy Emerson, who later called Whitman "priapic."

That was not all: in Barnumesque style, Whitman continued to breach etiquette by publishing three anonymous reviews of *Leaves of Grass* in which he hailed his own arrival as the American bard whom Emerson had been awaiting: "I look in vain for the poet whom I describe," Emerson had written in 1844. Look no more, Whitman effectively said. *The New York Times* caustically replied, "Mr. Walt Whitman . . . was not content with writing a book, but was also determined to review it." Yet in this second edition of *Leaves of Grass*, no matter how jauntily he had pushed himself or America, Whitman more somberly surveyed the territory before him—the rascal and thief (his words) who was president (Franklin Pierce), the Anthony Burns case, the beating of Charles Sumner, the federal government's backing of the proslavery Kansas government, and the nomination for president of the weak, toadying James Buchanan on the Democratic ticket.

Whitman's optimism frayed at the edges, and in the open letter to Emerson that he placed at the end of the second edition he warned, "In every department of These States, he who travels with a coterie, or with selected persons, or with imitators, or with infidels, or with the owners of slaves, or with that which is ashamed of the body of a man, or with that which is ashamed of the body of a woman, or with any thing less than the bravest and the openest, travels straight for the slopes of dissolution."

The slopes of dissolution: even for the ebullient Walt Whitman, talk of disunion was in the wind.

"YES, THE WORLD'S a ship on its passage out, and not a voyage complete," Melville had written in *Moby-Dick*. Barnum had included a mobile panorama of the Mississippi River in his production of *Uncle Tom's Cabin*; the Mississippi River spelled adventure, which is how Samuel Clemens would come to use it; and panoramas of the great wilderness were very popular forms of entertainment. And there was the sea, as Melville knew, and foreign ports. Commodore Matthew C. Perry's four "black ships" (as the Japanese called them) stubbornly anchored themselves in the Bay of Yedo, prying open Japanese ports to U.S. trade. Elisha Kent Kane, infatuated with the spirit rapper Maggie Fox, would soon publish his best-selling *Arctic Explorations*, about his quest to find the lost explorer Sir John Franklin—and about the harrowing, seductive pursuit of the Northwest Passage and an open polar sea: manifest destiny in different dress.

Americans loved a journey. They loved the ocean, the forests, the fauna, the vastness, the Barnumesque variety, even the sublimity of it all and, Thoreau notwithstanding, they loved to consider its rich land ripe for the taking. Unable to distinguish between spectatorship and ownership, they loved to plant their flags, which the surveyor John Frémont had done in the Rocky Mountains. And they loved the explorer and adventurer, especially if he was a daring and handsome man, part patriot, part expansionist, part rogue filibusterer. That too was John Frémont.

By 1856 Frémont was a national celebrity who had undertaken five exploring expeditions and rather enjoyed the notoriety he earned from them. Known as the Pathfinder, he'd mapped out a route from Missouri to Oregon (the Oregon Trail) as well as routes through Utah, Nevada, New Mexico, and of course California, where in 1849, as the fledgling state's very first senator, he voted for abolition of the slave trade in the District of Columbia. "The West," one historian wrote, "was also the chessboard in the Great Game between North and South."

John C. Frémont was very much a player in this expansionist game. Born in 1813 in Savannah, Georgia, Frémont was the son of a French émigré, Jean-Charles Fremon, and Anne Beverley Whiting Pryor, a Virginia belle. But his parents had never married, and distressed by his illegitimate birth, after his father's death, Frémont added the accent and the "t" to his name, as if to give himself the pedigree he likely felt he lacked. An indifferent student expelled from the College of Charleston, he knew how to position himself, securing a post on the USS *Natchez* on a two-year expeditionary voyage to South America and then one with the team mapping out a railroad route through Cherokee land. The goal was to remove the Indians from land where gold had been discovered.

Commissioned as a second lieutenant in the U.S. Army Corps of Topographical Engineers, Frémont met the famous senator Thomas Hart Benton, a man with his own dream of empire, and eloped with Benton's brilliant seventeen-year-old daughter, Jessie. But that didn't leave him—or Jessie, for that matter—homebound. In 1842, he headed a twenty-five-man, four-month expedition to survey the region between the Missouri River and the Continental Divide, and then John and Jessie together wrote about the expedition; or he told of it, and she turned what he told into such vividly melodramatic prose that it thrilled the public almost as much as Barnum did. (Years later, the western writer Wallace Stegner would call Frémont more of a Path-publicizer than Path-finder.) They romanticized the buffalo herds and prairie dogs, the exhausted horses and the antelope they ate for supper, and the pine nuts supplied by Indians—but not the Indians who left blood on the bushes after a raiding party.

Frémont the Pathfinder was articulate, charismatic, and slightly reserved, a shabby aristocrat but self-made—albeit with the help of political patronage—and a man who, like Whitman, wore no lace on his buckskin sleeves. He also liked the limelight, and as an aggressive trailblazer he was perfect for the smudgy pages of the penny press. In 1846, believing his hour had come, he headed what might be considered a filibustering mission in Alta California, when he declared California independent of Mexico on the Fourth of July in Sonoma. Early the next year, Commodore Robert Stockton appointed Frémont governor, but when General Stephen Watts Kearney challenged Stockton's authority, Frémont was caught in the middle. Refusing to follow Kearney's orders, Frémont was soon court-martialed; this was the first in a series of disputes and disagreements that would characterize the erratic Pathfinder's spotty career.

Shrewdly, Frémont had invested in the Las Mariposas gold mines in California, where gold had been famously discovered, and there, above the San Francisco Bay, Jessie Frémont held court to an array of optimists, go-getters, and transplanted easterners, including the Unitarian minister and naturalist Thomas Starr King and the writer Bret Harte. By then a well-known figure, rich and prominent, Frémont was a successful candidate for Senate from California should California enter the Union, which it did in September 1850. That year, the Frémonts returned to Washington—briefly, for he was not reelected.

In 1855, though, the Pathfinder's name was seriously being tossed around by the fledgling Republican Party as its candidate for president of the United States.

THE REPUBLICAN PARTY was an amalgam of Conscience (antislavery) Whigs, disgruntled Democrats, and former members of the Liberty Party (abolitionists, unlike Garrison, committed to political action as well as moral suasion). All of them had been galvanized by the failed Kansas policy and opposed the further extension of slavery into the territories. The small cadre of men who first formed the Republican Association in Washington included men such as Francis Blair, a Democrat of note who had for many years published the renowned Democratic Party newspaper, *The Globe*. Soon Republican clubs were springing up nationwide, and a convention was held in Pittsburgh in early 1856 to form an Executive Committee. In June, then, the Republicans met in Philadelphia and nominated John Frémont as their presidential hopeful. He was just what they needed: a man with name recognition and not much else. Men such as William Seward had a record that could be used against them, and anyway Republicans didn't really think they'd win this time out. They needed just a placeholder. So with his ties to the powerful Benton family and also to Missouri's influential Blair family, Frémont was their man.

"The merest baby in politics," sniggered Horace Greeley. But that was what the new party wanted; at forty-three years old, the explorer became the Republican poster boy who, during the campaign, rarely opened his mouth.

"FREE SPEECH, FREE PRESS, Free Soil, Free Men, Frémont, and Victory," the Republicans cried during torchlight parades, their platform one of excluding slavery from the territories. "Whether or not Frémont won," observed the editor Evert Duyckinck, "the moral victory at any rate will be for Free Soil—for Slavery must in the end be a losing game."

That was in part true: the antislavery Republicans won eleven of the sixteen free states and voter turnout was very high. But James Buchanan, their Democratic rival, received the prize he had long sought. Because the Kansas-Nebraska Act had destroyed the reputation of Franklin Pierce and fatally tarnished the reputation of Buchanan's chief Democratic rival, Stephen Douglas, the way had at last been cleared for his nomination on the Democratic ticket—and his victory. For Buchanan was running against a splintered Whig Party: some few Whigs had rallied around Millard Fillmore on an anti-Catholic, anti-immigrant American (Know-Nothing) party ticket; the rest of them voted for Frémont and the newly organized Republicans.

The campaign against the Republicans and Frémont had been ugly and was fueled by paranoia. Democrats said slaves and free blacks would use Frémont's victory as an excuse to revolt; absurd rumors reached the Hawthornes in England, for instance, where the novelist was working for the Pierce administration as the U.S. consul to Liverpool: "the negroes received an idea or instruction that he [Frémont] would aid them with an army—& they began to rise." Even Frémont's father-in-law, Thomas Hart Benton, who had lost his seat in the Senate and then in the House when he had opposed the extension of slavery, predicted disunion if Frémont won. He'd campaigned for Buchanan. And the corpulent Howell Cobb of Georgia, a genial man and Unionist, warned that if Frémont was elected, the South would secede.

Cobb was not the only one talking about secession, nor was such talk confined to the South. In Massachusetts, William Lloyd Garrison and the skilled Boston abolitionist Wendell Phillips were accusing the Republicans of not standing strongly enough against slavery. Thomas Higginson began planning a disunion convention in Worcester "to consider the practicality, probability and expediency of a separation between the free and slave states."

Millard Fillmore tried to position himself as the compromise candidate, which he definitely was not. "We are treading upon the brink of a volcano," Fillmore warned, "that is liable at any moment to break forth and overwhelm the nation." To his mind, both of the other candidates represented sectional interests, while *he* spoke for compromise, the Union, and the Union's salvation. Buchanan presented himself the same way, but Frémont supporters retaliated by dressing "Old Buck," as Buchanan was called, in women's clothes and arguing he was a Southern servant bent on preserving slavery, even in Kansas. Though formerly sympathetic to the South, James Gordon Bennett, the Democratic editor of the powerful *New York Herald*, backed Frémont.

Such were the divisions, prejudices, aspersions, and fears. And when the pro-Southern Buchanan won, he had to know that Republicans had achieved their own kind of victory. They were stronger than he dared admit. They had done well; they had proved themselves a competitive, viable party, not a will-o'-the-wisp. And henceforward Whigs and Know-Nothings would eventually vanish from the national scene.

Yet Buchanan may have felt protected by the Supreme Court as early as inauguration day. On March 4, right before being sworn in as chief executive, Buchanan was seen in a tête-à-tête with Chief Justice Roger Taney of Maryland, who would administer the oath of office. Then, in his inaugural address, Buchanan referred to the Court's impending and crucial decision about the slave Dred Scott. Suing for his and his family's freedom in Missouri, where they lived, Scott had argued all the way to the Supreme Court that his family's earlier residence in free states or territories had made them free. (After a delay of three years, the Missouri court had declared them unequivocally free, but shortly afterward, in a partisan decision, the Missouri Supreme Court reversed the decision of the lower court and sent Dred Scott back to slavery.)

"To their decision, in common with all good citizens," promised Buchanan, referring to the U.S. Supreme Court, "I shall cheerfully submit, whatever this may be."

Did Buchanan already know the decision? Republicans suspiciously took note of his little chat with Taney. But whether or not a confidence had been breached, it was true, and more heinous, that just a month earlier President-elect Buchanan had written Supreme Court Justice John Catron of Tennessee, a Southern rights man, that he would like to refer to the Dred Scott case in his inaugural. Catron responded by telling Buchanan that he might "safely say" the Supreme Court would "settle a controversy" that had rocked the nation, though he also informed Buchanan that the judges were split. So Catron recommended that Buchanan lobby his fellow Pennsylvanian, Supreme Court Justice Robert Grier, to make sure that the court arrived at a comprehensive solution, once and for all, to the problem of slavery. Thus Catron not only violated confidentiality, he suggested that Buchanan intervene in Court affairs, and Buchanan complied. According to the historian Kenneth Stampp, Buchanan along with several of the justices thereby "secretly made a pawn of Dred Scott in a game of judicial politics."

In the stunning 7–2 decision delivered on March 6, the Court ruled that blacks were, in fact, property and as such had no rights of citizenship, meaning they could not petition the courts and, in addition, had never been citizens. Moreover, the Court declared unconstitutional and void all congressional acts excluding slavery from the territories, meaning that slavery might exist anywhere it wanted. In other words, it declared the Missouri Compromise unconstitutional. A staggering blow to Free Soil and antislavery activists, the decision deepened the rift in the Democratic Party and strengthened the Republicans, who looked forward to the next round of elections.

The decision did nothing for Dred Scott and his family. Fortunately, they were all soon emancipated. By a quirk of inheritance, they were now "owned" by Dr. Calvin Clifford Chaffee, a Massachusetts abolitionist, but because he did not live in Missouri and therefore could do nothing legally to free them, he transferred ownership to a Missouri family living close to the Scotts (and their previous owners). They signed the freedom papers, but Scott died of tuberculosis the following year.

Proslavery Southerners hailed the Dred Scott ruling as a vindication of slavery, and Northern Democrats such as Stephen Douglas twisted the interpretation of the ruling so it wouldn't vitiate popular sovereignty (the freedom to vote up or down for slavery). But the decision did, in fact, impair it: if Congress couldn't restrict slavery in the territories, did Congress then have any power over the territorial legislatures at all? Republicans deplored the decision, claiming it perverted the Constitution. At the anniversary of the American Anti-Slavery Society in New York, Frederick Douglass called the ruling the infamous product of the Supreme Court's slaveholding wing—and he went on to invoke the higher law of the British abolitionist Henry Lord Brougham: "Man cannot hold property in man."

"The sun in the sky is not more palpable to the sight than man's right to liberty is to the moral vision," Douglass continued. "To decide against this right in the person of Dred Scott, or the humblest and most whip-scarred bondman in the land, is to decide against God."

Yet Douglass did not, as Garrison had, call for dissolution of the Union. That would, as he shrewdly noted, "withdraw the emancipating power from the field."

Abraham Lincoln, who also said man cannot hold property in man, deplored the Dred Scott decision, but to many it seemed as though he tiptoed around the question of how to counter it—if, that is, one does not bear in mind what he said at the Springfield, Illinois, statehouse on the evening of June 26, 1857. After studying a recent speech in which Stephen Douglas had defended the Dred Scott ruling, Lincoln forcefully argued, in reply, that the decision had been "erroneous." The decision, he said, was based on a misinterpretation of historical facts and was by no means a settled doctrine. And by answering Stephen Douglas's suggestion—if the framers of the Declaration of Independence had wished to include African Americans, they would have made them equal to white men—Lincoln responded by noting that the framers "did not mean to say all were equal in all respects. They did not mean to say all were equal in color, size, intellect, moral developments, or social capacity," but they did say "with tolerable distinctiveness, in what respect they did consider all men created equal—equal in 'certain inalienable rights, among which are life, liberty, and the pursuit of happiness.'"

Lincoln's speech was as dramatic, in its way, as the Dred Scott decision, for he understood that Dred Scott threatened to make slavery the law of the land. That is, the issue was no longer the protection of slavery where it already existed but the legitimization, even the tacit encouragement, of its extension. The nation was being redefined. Compromise was more impossible than ever. Again, the Dred Scott decision not only failed to accomplish what it was intended to do—put a lid on the explosive subject of slavery—it annulled the Compromise of 1850 and, further, deprived the slaves of liberty in places where there were actually no slaveholders. The moral, political, and symbolic consequences would be huge.

Lincoln declared that though a slave "in some respects . . . is not my equal; but in her natural right to eat the bread she earns with her own hands without asking leave of any one else, she is my equal, and the equal of others." Decidedly not an abolitionist, Lincoln believed in the humanity—the inalienable right—of all people to freedom, and he was, as well, an adroit politician, disgusted by slavery though cautious about how far he would go denouncing it, especially since the Springfield speech was his opening bid in a run for the U.S. Senate seat against Stephen Douglas himself.

Lincoln was a moderate and willing to compromise, and the abolitionists thus regarded him as conservative. Southern fire-eaters considered him a toxic radical.

Whitman likely read Lincoln's Springfield speech—the poet was a Brooklyn journalist at the time—but whether or not he did, years later he wondered if "you noticed that the time to look for the best things in best people is the moment of their greatest need? Look at Lincoln: he is our proudest example: he proved to be big as, bigger than, any emergency—his grasp was a giant's grasp—made dark things light, made hard things easy."

. . . .

"LAND! LAND! IS the cry."

On mules, in wagons, buggies, stagecoaches, on horses, on foot, aboard riverboats, settlers poured into Kansas, where land sold for about ninety cents an acre; there were timber lands and town lots and amber waves of grain. To Thomas Higginson, who went there, everyone seemed full of hope.

But that depended on which Kansas you were in. There were two governments in Kansas: one, with a proslavery legislature, sat in Lecompton, a small town on the Kaw River, which consisted of a large wooden shack and a muddy street as well as several taverns. The other government, the free-state government, was located fifteen miles west in Topeka. There was a post office in the log cabin that served as a blacksmith shop, a new sawmill, two boardinghouses, and two stores in Topeka, and more and more were coming. The town was booming, and its free-state government represented three times as many Kansans as Lecompton. But since its constitution barred slavery from the territory, President Pierce had not recognized the Topeka constitution or government, which he called treasonable, and when its legislature tried to meet in 1856, it was dispersed at the point of a gun.

In March 1857, shortly after taking office, Buchanan appointed Robert J. Walker of Mississippi as territorial governor of Kansas to replace the failed governors from the Pierce administration, and he expected Walker to do his bidding. Though a lifelong Democrat descended from a staunch Jacksonian father, Walker was no lackey. He fully expected Buchanan to fulfill the pledge he had made to him: that Walker was to have a free hand in Kansas and that, moreover, any Kansas constitution had to be ratified by a vote of the people.

The Lecompton government, however, planned to elect (proslavery) delegates to a constitutional convention by allowing day-trippers from Missouri to vote; these delegates could then draft a proslavery constitution. Free-staters boycotted the election, and out of the 9,000 or so males eligible to vote in Kansas, only 2,000 actually voted, and many of them were not even Kansas residents; they'd merely crossed the border. The election was a sham. Then too, abolitionists and free-staters were wary of Governor Walker; the journalist James Redpath reported with concern that "Walker is all things to all men." But when he spoke in Topeka, Walker gained their confidence and, encouraging them to vote in the upcoming elections of a new legislature, he assured them that their votes would be counted.

A second election was held in October, and when a huge number of votes were again cast by day-trippers from Missouri, Walker was outspoken in denouncing the fraud and throwing out the illegal ballots. Southerners savagely reviled Walker as a heartless free-stater and Buchanan as a traitor for having appointed him. Buchanan was livid. Southern politicians were beside themselves.

To them, Kansans had rightly elected a proslavery body, pure and simple, and Walker should be removed. But the citizens of Kansas clearly preferred a free state; that much was clear to Stephen Douglas, who vehemently reminded Democrats that any attempt to jam a proslavery legislature down the throat of Kansans would push their party directly into the arms of the Republicans. And it would gut the entire notion of popular sovereignty. He too was livid. "By God, sir, I made Mr. James Buchanan," he reportedly said, "and by God, sir, I will unmake him."

Regardless, by November 1857 the proslavery delegates had indeed drafted a constitution guaranteeing the right of private property (meaning slaves). Though scorned by one Kansas newspaper as "broken-down political hacks, demagogues, fire-eaters, perjurers, ruffians, ballot-box stuffers, and loafers," the delegates were savvy enough to try to send the constitution, known as the Lecompton constitution, to Congress as quickly as possible—without a popular vote ratifying it—so that Kansas could be promptly admitted to the Union as a slave state.

When moderate delegates to the convention were offended, a compromise was reached. Voters would not be allowed to vote on the constitution with or without slavery; rather they could vote on whether new slaves might be imported. That is, voters could approve the constitution with the provision for importing slaves or vote for the constitution without the provision. It was, of course, a false choice. Voters could not vote to accept or reject the proslavery constitution, which Buchanan had promised Walker they would be able to do and which cut to the heart of popular sovereignty. Moreover, there was no option for voting against slavery per se; as one Kansan noted, he could choose to take his arsenic with bread and butter or without bread and butter.

Convinced that popular sovereignty, never mind the future of the Democratic Party, was at stake, a feisty Walker argued that Lecompton had been a swindle and that any attempt of the administration to support it would lead to more violence. ("Cuba! Cuba! (and Porto Rico, if possible) should be the countersign of your administration, and it will close in a blaze of glory," he advised Buchanan.) Buchanan wasn't budging, particularly since members of his cabinet, such as Secretary of the Treasury Howell Cobb and Attorney General Jeremiah Black, were in favor of Lecompton. The eminent Democrat George Bancroft begged Buchanan to avert disaster and walk away from Lecompton. Honor your pledge to Walker for free and fair elections by the people. Buchanan refused.

Walker tendered his resignation, which Buchanan readily accepted in December, and Buchanan announced that he endorsed Lecompton. In so doing, he split the Democrats along virulent Northern and Southern lines. Unfazed, Buchanan denounced the free-staters, sent the Lecompton constitution to Congress to push it through "naked," as he said, which meant without amendments, and he defined Kansas as much of a slave state as Georgia or South Carolina.

"The fractious cabal of fire-eaters, which has so much more power than it deserves, has made up its mind to disunion or the Lecompton Constitution," noted George Templeton Strong in his diary. "I doubt if the North can submit to the latter."

Strong was right; the North could not. Though Buchanan lobbied, promising jobs, cash, building contracts, and, it was later alleged, even prostitutes to recalcitrant congressmen, with Douglas and Northern Democrats now working against him, Buchanan lost the vote in the House.

Democrats, such as Walker, believed that popular sovereignty returned to the people a right, inalienable, to choose how they wanted to live, a choice not administered by banks or factory owners or operatives in Washington (though it may have been) but a choice founded on the very principle of democracy. This too was the position of Stephen Douglas, who irreparably broke with Buchanan, whom he never much liked. In Congress, the Republicans challenging Buchanan believed more in the elimination of slavery than in popular sovereignty, for theirs was moral passion based on their sense of human dignity, and this was to them the higher law. But here popular sovereignty would have worked; had all eligible Kansans been able to choose, they would have voted against slavery.

Harder to understand are the Southern intransigents such as the prominent publisher James Dunwoody Brownson DeBow, a literary and idealistic man devoted to all things Southern who deplored what he considered the South's economic backwardness. He believed slavery to be good for the economy—and good for the slave. The DeBows of the time were aggrieved and outraged and proud, all the more so because they regarded themselves as occupying a minority position—and, perhaps, they knew that slavery and its perpetuation was a morally untenable one. Popular sovereignty portended the elimination of slavery, and they could not give it up even if that meant abandoning their democratic principles. The former filibusterer from Mississippi, Congressman John Quitman, threatened secession if Kansas were to become a free state. "I am sick to death of compromises," he'd said, "and will not bend an inch."

Then there were men such as the wizened Georgian Alexander Hamilton Stephens, a former Whig and firm believer in what he considered the higher law of slavery; he'd backed the Lecompton constitution even though he knew it to be a fraud. This son of a

Georgia schoolteacher was a scholarly, often dyspeptic, and moralistic man who as a frail youth, born in 1812, was initially headed for the ministry. Studying law instead, he joined the Whigs in 1834, and by 1843, was elected to the U.S. House of Representatives. He greatly admired Clay, Webster, and Edmund Burke, and though he was a powerful leader and deft parliamentarian, he was rebuffed by fellow Southerners when he coauthored a resolution insisting the war with Mexico not be waged over slavery. Called a traitor to the South, Stephens was subsequently in a brawl with a fellow Georgian, who slashed him with a knife.

In 1854, as floor manager in the House, Stephens helped push through the Kansas-Nebraska bill but, breaking with Douglas, he fought hard for Lecompton, almost as if he had to prove his loyalty to the South. Caught between Southern extremists and antislavery Republicans, or so he felt, at the height of his career, in 1859, Stephens retired from Congress in disgust, gloomily telling a friend, "When I am on one of two trains coming in opposite directions on a single track, both engines at high speed, and both engineers drunk, I get off at the first station."

Whigs turned Republican such as William Seward and even Horace Greeley temporarily allied themselves with Stephen Douglas; these were Free Soil, antislavery Northern men who had reviled the Little Giant for his role in passing the Kansas-Nebraska Act. At present their goals were the same even if their purposes differed. Douglas argued for popular sovereignty, the rest against slavery. The fire-eaters and the Buchanan administration remained stubbornly unmovable, and Congress was deadlocked.

William English, Democrat of Indiana, proposed another referendum: Kansans could vote on whether or not they would accept or reject the Lecompton constitution. If they approved Lecompton and slavery, they would be granted statehood immediately as well as a federal land grant (reduced from the initial request of twenty-three million acres to four million). This was a shabby bribe of no real consequence, for Congress would also give the same amount of land to Minnesota when it joined the Union. But the bribe satisfied the Democrats.

However, if Kansans voted against Lecompton and slavery, they could not apply for statehood again until the population reached 93,000.

All parties accepted the expedient proposal except Stephen Douglas, who denounced the compromise as unfair. He stood his ground for democracy.

The Senate and House passed the English bill. In August the people of Kansas overwhelmingly voted to reject Lecompton.

Kansas remained a territory until 1861, when it entered the Union with an antislavery constitution.

(5)

SOVEREIGNTY

The date had been set: September 1, 1858. The city braced itself. When the day finally came, it was clear and crisp, technically still summer, and in the morning there was a prayer of thanks offered within the lovely neo-Gothic Trinity Church in lower Manhattan, where worshippers entered through the large bronze doors and squeezed into the pews. The bells rang over and over, and a procession of more than fifteen thousand men and women marched the four miles from the Battery to Fifth Avenue and the Crystal Palace at 42nd Street to listen to the lawyer David Dudley Field praise his brother Cyrus—although anyone standing in the back of the giant hall could barely hear him. Still, many of them knew by heart what he was saying: how a series of steps and missteps, of snapped wires and of reconfigurations, of financing and finagling and the shouldering of ridicule finally led to this grand moment, this wonderful celebration of the laying of the transatlantic cable.

For barely a month before, on the twenty-ninth of July, two large ships, one American and one British, each carrying half the amount of cable needed to cross the Atlantic, had met at the ocean's midpoint. Field explained to those who could hear him what had happened next. "The end of the cable which the U.S.S. *Niagara* bore was carried to the *Agamemnon* and there spliced to the end of hers," he told his happy audience. "It was then lowered into the sea, and the ships moved, each towards its own country, at first creeping slowly till the cable had sunk far down, and then faster, to a speed of five or six miles an hour."

This moment was a dream come true for Cyrus Field, who had made so much money in the paper business that he was able to realize his ambition, that of laying a cable across the Atlantic and connecting the United States to Great Britain. And now, after several failed attempts, it had actually happened, and his name was written in bold letters on huge signs and placed next to those of Benjamin Franklin and Robert Fulton, Samuel Morse and Eli Whitney: American geniuses, all of them. In upstate New York, Senator William Henry Seward attended a rally in his hometown of Auburn, where he said that from now on the country would cry, "American Mind, American Opinions, American Systems, shall rule throughout the earth," and that he could see "despotic systems of oppression and slavery, of infidelity and paganism, in the progress of thick coming centuries, disappearing, and mankind in all nations, becoming all free." The "Age of Progress," proclaimed the signs on the lampposts in New York City. The papers were jubilant, reporting that "two continents have been penetrated to their remotest extremities by an electric thrill . . . 'THE ATLANTIC TELEGRAPH CABLE HAS BEEN LAID!' " Messages between Ireland and Newfoundland pulsed back and forth. "Glory to God in the highest, and on earth, peace, good will to men," Queen Victoria congratulated President Buchanan, who replied with sangfroid that this feat was more glorious—and far more useful—than any success on the field of battle.

Extra ferryboats were shuttling the crowds to Manhattan from Brooklyn, and the trains from New Jersey and Long Island were crammed. Ships and scows in the harbor raised colorful flags, and the Stars and Stripes flapped from windows of the telegraph offices on Wall Street. After the sun set, a torchlight parade lit up Broadway as far as the eye could see, and candles and colored lanterns cast a saffron glow along the crooked streets downtown. A wagon drawn by several horses carried a section of the magical cable; in fact, sections of the surplus cable had been selling for as much as $360 a mile—that is, before Charles Tiffany purchased the entire leftover stock to cut into four-inch pieces. Every American could have a bit of it, for a price. Capped with a brass ferrule, the cable came with a certificate of authenticity signed by Field himself; soon you could buy watch fobs and earrings made from the cable or a brass snuff-box with a segment of the cable inserted into the lid, which was engraved with the Stars and Stripes and the Union Jack.

A candle glowed from every window of Barnum's Museum, and you could hear the kettle drums beating from inside, where a band played long into the night. The city had been celebrating since the middle of August, when cannon were booming every day, it seemed, and extra editions of newspapers sold on every corner. There were extra broadsides, extra policemen, and more Roman candles than ever. The fireworks set the cupola of City Hall ablaze and nearly burned the place to the ground, the statue of Justice fell to the flames, and George Templeton Strong noted the furor in his sidelong way: "Yesterday's *Herald* said that the cable (or perhaps Cyrus W. Field, uncertain which) is undoubtedly the Angel in the Book of Revelation with one foot on sea and one foot on land, proclaiming Time is no longer."

New York wasn't the only city wrapping itself in flags and fire. In San Francisco, 120 little girls, representing each state, each territory, and the many European nations, wore white dresses trimmed with blue ribbons and rode through the streets in vans. They were followed by the Knickerbocker Fire Company and then the fire companies from Stockton, Sacramento, and Solana. A wagon outfitted to resemble a small boat hauled a coiled rope of cable on its ersatz deck, and a team of ten oxen hauled another wagon made to look like one of the prairie schooners that conveyed emigrants to Kansas. On its side was a banner. "Give us a Pacific Railroad," it said. "Don't wait for the Wagon."

"There is no such thing as impossible now," declared the *Savannah Morning News*.

Yet the cruel fact was that the telegraphic signal had been in the last few days growing fainter and fainter. The cable's insulation was giving way under the pressure of voltages far too high. Soon it was almost impossible to hear any messages, and not three weeks later, on September 18, there was no sound at all.

Charles Tiffany decided to sell his leftover cable souvenirs to a Vermont farmer.

THE THIRTY-TWO STATES in the Union certainly weren't united, at least not about matters of tariffs or internal improvements or immigration or Pacific railroads or religion. And in addition to Kansas and Nebraska and slavery, there was the territory of Utah to contend with.

This was the territory increasingly settled by members of the Church of Jesus Christ of Latter-day Saints, also known as Mormons, which had been founded by a charismatic young man from upstate New York. Joseph Smith claimed to have discovered golden plates on a hillside near Palmyra, New York, to which he'd been directed by an angel calling himself Moroni. In 1830 he translated and published a religious text, the Book of Mormon, which purportedly the prophet Mormon had transcribed in the fourth century from the recoded tales of the prophets themselves.

Smith had been for a very long time subject to visions of brightness and glory so common in upstate New York that the area was dubbed "burned-over." The term referred to the religious revivals in the Hudson and Mohawk valleys. In camp meetings William Miller had preached that the Second Coming (the Advent) would occur in the spring of 1843 and that those who followed him, the Millerites, who soon numbered one million people, would ascend to heaven a year later. In Adams, New York, Charles Grandison Finney, after seeing a brilliant light in his office, had undergone a conversion to what was called New School Presbyterianism. As a revivalist Finney spoke emotionally about the individual's moral responsibility and one's ability to distinguish between good and evil. In Oneida, John Humphrey Noyes founded a utopian community, based on free love, in 1848. Of course there were also the cities Hydesville and Rochester, where the Fox sisters had first heard those spirit rappings, and Seneca Falls, where dedication to a different kind of conviction was yielding controversial results: Amelia Jenks Bloomer had published the temperance and women's rights paper *The Lily* from Seneca Falls in 1849, and the next year she was showing a new outfit for women, a short skirt worn over trousers and called "bloomers," which would revolutionize women's clothing.

Joseph Smith too sprang from burned-over soil and the revivals that promised direct revelation and a new Kingdom of God on earth. The prophet Mormon was telling Smith and his followers that Christ would come to America, that Christ was God, and that the prophet Nephi had migrated to the Americas in 600 B.C. with his light-skinned Nephites and the darker Lamanites. Since Native Americans were also descended from the original prophets, the Mormons were to bring the Book to them too.

Having organized the Church of Christ of Latter-day Saints and having named himself its main prophet and leader, Smith said he'd been instructed to build a New Jerusalem in the beckoning West and among the Indian tribes who dwelled there. After another revelation, Smith rounded up his worshippers—he'd inspired a number of disciples—and left New York for Ohio. In Kirtland, now a suburb of Cleveland, Smith and his Latter-day Saints built a church, trained apostles, and dispatched missionaries abroad. He also organized a central bank, the Kirtland Safety Society, which intended to issue its own currency.

Such religious and economic apostasy, to say nothing of their reputed abolitionism, their tolerance of Native Americans, and their growing population—they numbered about ten thousand, a large voting bloc—infuriated the local citizenry, who wanted to be rid of this strange group of people in their midst, people who in addition did not drink or smoke. There were skirmishes, there was violence, Mormons were killed, Smith was tarred and feathered and nearly castrated.

Mormons had also settled in Jackson County, Missouri, and near Independence, where Smith, taking no chances, had organized a secret militia, the Sons of Dan, or Danites, or, as they were popularly called, the "Destroying Angels." Although Mormons later denied their existence, it seems that these guerrilla bands stole from and even murdered non-Mormons. Or perhaps they were simply defending the faithful. There were accusations and assassinations on both sides. One group of irate Missourians, for instance, rode into a Mormon farming community and killed at least seventeen Mormon men and young boys. By 1838, Lilburn W. Boggs, the governor of Missouri, was fed up, and he ordered the Mormons out of Missouri. If they stayed, they faced execution because, as Boggs declared, "They instituted among themselves a government of their own, independent of and in opposition to the government of this state."

Arrested and detained, Smith managed to bribe his way out of jail and catch up with his peripatetic followers, led by a man named Brigham Young. The group built a new church in Commerce, Illinois, which Smith renamed Nauvoo the Beautiful, and in 1840, the more lenient Illinois state legislature granted the Mormons a liberal charter for the new city.

The number of converts grew, for Mormonism offered not just security, comfort, and hierarchy, it provided ritual: washing, anointing, even the wearing of underwear were all prescribed. And as a self-sustaining collective, it endowed each person with the purpose of a saint. "In temporal things you shall be equal," Smith had said. Mormons believed their long pilgrimages from one place to another to be a westward exodus, divinely ordained. Their hardships were a test; their successes, a blessing. Persecution united them in their faith and toughened it.

As a political force, the Mormons were greatly resented and, they believed, further persecuted since their numbers had grown too large for non-Mormons to tolerate. Joseph Smith was accused of being an accessory before the fact in an attempted assassination of Governor Boggs. When he was extradited to Missouri, though, the judge declared the writ of extradition invalid. More ominous, though, was the schism within the community, which played to the general non-Mormon mistrust of their religion and growing political clout. Many Latter-day Saints—Christians for whom bigamy was taboo—were balking at the idea of plural or celestial marriage, which Smith evidently preached, having been divinely instructed to do so. One of Smith's counselors, John Cook Bennett, himself excommunicated for adultery, then wrote an exposé of Smith (whom he called the Holy Joe), which included salacious information about the Mormon system of secret wives.

By 1844 there was more trouble, especially after Smith declared himself a presidential candidate and sent Mormon elders to campaign for him. When he selected a secret Council of Fifty to help with his presidential bid—and which crowned him king of the Kingdom of God—a group of dissenting Mormons, tired of Smith's grandiosity and what they considered hypocrisy, published a newspaper, the *Nauvoo Expositor*, that threatened to expose polygamy in the community. (Until then, though it had been rumored, polygamy had been a secret shared only by the church hierarchy.) Smith swiftly ordered the newspaper office closed, and after one of his henchmen kicked down its door and torched the place, the governor of Illinois interceded. Smith and his brother surrendered to the authorities. Charged with inciting a riot, they were jailed in Carthage, Illinois. They were awaiting trial when on June 27, 1844, a mob of men, their faces blackened with gunpowder, entered the jail and murdered the two of them.

Brigham Young, Smith's special assistant, assumed the leadership of the Mormons. Born in 1801 in Vermont, Young had worked as a carpenter for a while in the burned-over area of New York after his mother's death, when he was fourteen. (He had helped construct the house in Auburn that William Seward later occupied.) Married in 1824, he was a religious seeker and Methodist who first read the

Book of Mormon at the age of twenty-nine. Baptized two years later, the year his first wife died, the young convert set out to meet Joseph Smith. Smith liked him, and he sent Young to preach in the northeast though Young also worked on the erection of the Mormon temple in Kirtland. Subsequently dispatched to England, Young published an edition of the Book of Mormon there and converted so many of the British that he set up a shipping agency to transport thousands of them to America.

With his talent for missionary work and empire-building, Young soon emerged as the apostle best suited to lead the Mormons out of Illinois after the death of Joseph Smith. He resettled 16,000 Mormons in Iowa and Nebraska, and once the Illinois legislature revoked the Nauvoo charter in 1845, Young led the Mormon migration to the new state of Deseret in the Great Salt Lake Valley. By then the international ministry had almost 35,000 members.

At Salt Lake City, or the City of Zion in the Promised Valley, Young oversaw the seeding and planting of crops, the building of homes, the enlargement of farms, the manufacture of plows and wagons, the local processing of timber and hides, the establishment of regional banks and education centers, and the creation of probate courts vested with powers not authorized by Congress. Each family received land, and most settlements possessed livestock herds. Each settlement had a general store. Families paid tithes to the church. Young converts mined iron, lead, and coal for the church. Their settlements flourishing and expanding westward (especially after gold was discovered in California), their businesses and enterprises lucrative, and their church membership still increasing, the Mormons had created a theocratic state within a territory. The Southern journal *DeBow's Review* carped that "they desire a kingly government in order to make their patriarchal institutions more harmonious."

After the creation of the Utah Territory, which extended from the Colorado Rockies to the Sierra Nevada, via the Compromise of 1850, President Millard Fillmore named Brigham Young the superintendent of Indian affairs and governor. But the federal government grew suspicious of what amounted to a shadow country aping America's dominant values: westward expansion, religious freedom, moneymaking. Plus, Mormons also believed in obedience to the group; individualism was vanity, except in the case of the prophets, who included Smith and, now, Brigham Young. Mormons were a closed society, disciplined, organized, cohesive, colonizing. And there was that matter of polygamy, which was anathema to proper American culture. The Church of Latter-day Saints was a "Religion of Sensuality," George Templeton Strong scoffed.

Democrats had always treated the Mormons with benign neglect—though sometimes with a degree of support (presumably Stephen Douglas had helped the Mormons win the liberal Illinois charter). And Mormons were likewise hospitable to Democrats such as Douglas. With his doctrine of popular sovereignty, Douglas in the White House would likely let them alone or even go so far as to let the Mormons enter the Union; Young had been lobbying the federal government in vain to admit Deseret as a state. (Much larger than the Utah Territory, Deseret, which meant "honeybee" to the Mormons, would include the Great Basin and stretch out to the Pacific coast.) But this was an opportunity for Republicans, who could charge that popular sovereignty effectively sanctioned moral malfeasance. The Republican presidential candidate, John Frémont, had pledged in 1856 to wipe out "those twin relics of barbarism—Polygamy and Slavery."

The press had obliged the Republican campaign by unleashing a series of anti-Mormon reports from disgruntled federal officials who had fled the territory; these were sensational stories about bloody baptisms, about murder, prostitution, and persecution, about the shooting of elders and the selling of young girls. What shall we do with the Mormons?, nervously asked *The New York Times* in the spring of 1857. "At whatever cost, the United States must declare and vindicate its supremacy," declared *Harper's Weekly*. Even Stephen Douglas had to turn against the Mormons, who, he said, were forming alliances with Indian tribes to rob and murder U.S. citizens. Plus, the Church of Latter-day Saints was a "loathsome, disgusting ulcer," Douglas said, invoking a higher law—that of monogamy.

Ironically, the Mormons had forced Douglas's hand, for their claim to popular sovereignty and self-government placed the Little Giant in an untenable position. How could he support a group that voted for polygamy even if, by his reasoning, the group could vote as it wished? His solution was to rescind the Utah territorial charter "upon the ground," he said, "that it is run by outlaws perpetrating treason." Of course, before he would place Utah under the jurisdiction of the federal government, Douglas wanted the allegations against the Mormons to be proved, even though, as *The New York Times* noted, he "seemed to believe all of them to be true."

An Illinois Republican, Abraham Lincoln, was happy to take this opportunity to refute Douglas. "Why deprive the Mormons of the sacred right of 'squatter sovereignty'?" he jeered. "This thing of squatter sovereignty was never anything but a humbug, generated in the marshes and pools of South Carolina, and used as a pretext to run and pour slaves out of the land as hot lava is belched out from the crater of the fire mountain. It stinks of fraud."

The issue, then, was not Mormonism. It was still slavery.

Slavery: to President James Buchanan the Mormons of Utah could serve as a convenient distraction from the mess in Kansas. "Supersede the Negro-Mania with the almost universal excitements of an Anti-Mormon Crusade," Robert Tyler, a son of former president Tyler, advised. In the spring of 1857, Buchanan fired Young as governor of Utah without the courtesy of informing him and, assuming Young wouldn't step aside quietly, dispatched 2,500 troops to impose order. In retaliation, Young declared martial law, closed the territory, and demanded that overland immigrants crossing through Utah Territory show a permit. The governor of California protested; closing those trails cut off immigration to the West. Young's response was that Buchanan had violated the Constitution's protection of religious freedom when he interfered with the Mormon settlements, and Buchanan had also abrogated the right of a territorial government to

self-rule. On September 11, 1857, more than a hundred settlers traveling on the Baker-Fancher wagon train from Arkansas en route to
California were besieged, supposedly by a coalition of Paiute Indians
and Mormons. The emigrants fought for five days and then surrendered to the attackers, who murdered everyone save seventeen children, none over six years old. The incident would become known as
the Mountain Meadows Massacre.

GRAIN PRICES HAD fallen, inventories of merchandise languished in
peeling warehouses, stocks had plummeted, railroads had defaulted,
and the land boom had collapsed. Iron mills shut down; publishers
closed their doors; ships lay idle. The lines of the unemployed at soup
kitchens had grown long. And as the country suffered in what was
known as the Panic of 1857, easterners previously unconcerned about
or opposed to westward expansion now looked for new markets near
the Pacific. The Mormons were thriving.

Buchanan asked Congress for authorization to send four additional regiments to Utah. "At the present moment of depression in
the revenues of the country," he smoothly apologized, "I am sorry
to recommend such a measure." Only an "imposing force," he said,
could convince "these deluded people" of the error of their separatist
and barbaric ways. According to Buchanan, the autocratic Young had
authorized "acts of hostility" against the soldiers already dispatched
to Utah to remove him, and since Young considered himself "governor of the Territory by divine appointment," and since his people
therefore "obey his commands as if these were divine revelations
from Heaven," Buchanan declared that these zealots would fight to
the death to keep Young in power—and, not coincidentally, to exclude all other settlers from the territory who didn't bow to Young's
allegedly divine will. Land had to be available to all white settlers,
Mormon and non-Mormon alike. Mormon settlements, as Buchanan's secretary of war had noted, "lie in the grand pathway which leads
from our Atlantic States to the new and flourishing communities

growing up upon our Pacific seaboard." And as Buchanan told Congress, Young had already "tampered" with Indian tribes, turning them "against the United States."

Persecution again toughened the Mormons. And Young was a very capable leader. During the subsequent Utah War, as it was called, he outsmarted Buchanan. Instead of confronting the army directly, he ordered that its supply lines be cut, its horses stampeded, its trains torched. Livestock was to be driven off. When winter came early, in November, Colonel Albert Sidney Johnston and his troops found themselves trapped with scant supplies in the charred remains of Fort Bridger, which the Mormons had also burned. Young, meanwhile, urged the residents of Salt Lake City and northern Utah to evacuate temporarily to central and southern Utah, where they had stored a part of their harvest.

Buchanan apparently awoke to the fact that this was a war he was going to lose, at least on the publicity front, since the skillful Young and the well-organized Saints were ready to martyr themselves rather than confront the U.S. Army. The press had already turned against Buchanan, and Congress was dubious about the whole affair. Or Buchanan may have realized he could not put down an open and potentially armed rebellion against the Constitution in the West if he would refuse, should the need arise, to do so in the rebellious South. So instead he recurred to the cardinal principle of local government over which the federal government had no constitutional authority.

Young's replacement, the governor-elect of the Utah Territory, Alfred E. Cumming, was encamped with the troops and planned to meet with Young. Buchanan also sent the Mormon-friendly Thomas L. Kane to join them. The men came to an agreement—a compromise—to end the war. Young retained ecclesiastical power and a great deal of local authority but yielded the governorship to Cumming and allowed the army to occupy the territory as long as it left Salt Lake alone. Although Colonel Johnston and his men remained in Camp Floyd, about forty miles to the southwest of Salt Lake City, they would not attack. Instead, Johnston stayed in Utah until early

1861. When he left, the Saints bought Camp Floyd for ten cents on the dollar. Not long after that, Albert Sidney Johnston, serving as a general in the Confederate army, would be killed at the Battle of Shiloh.

"THE EYES OF the whole Union are fixed on the contest now going on in Illinois between Stephen A. Douglas and Lincoln," exclaimed the *Dallas Herald*.

As the Atlantic cable became more and more silent, the country's internal divisions played out on the Illinois prairie, where the hard-fighting, hard-drinking, pragmatic, and recently principled Stephen Douglas was running for reelection to the Senate against Abraham Lincoln, who had been, until now, unknown except locally. "You are like Byron," a friend told Lincoln, "who woke up one day and found himself famous."

The *Chicago Press & Tribune* had thrown down the gauntlet—"Let Mr. Douglas and Mr. Lincoln agree to canvass the state together, in the old western style," it had taunted. Knowing Lincoln had nothing to lose and everything to gain from Douglas's celebrity, the senator would have preferred to ignore the press. Yet he had no choice but to accept the challenge; otherwise he'd be labeled a coward.

And so the contest between the pugnacious, ambitious, famous Little Giant and the gangling, ambitious Honest Abe took shape. It was a test of endurance, not just in terms of the arduous debate schedule between August 21 and October 15 but also in terms of the intensity with which both men argued their positions on the slavery question. Because they knew they were performing on a national stage, Douglas and Lincoln did not discuss tariffs or sugar or land grants and railroads, subjects of local interest in Illinois. Instead, their impassioned subject was slavery, only slavery, pure and simple—though it was neither pure nor simple, since neither debater knew what to do with a whole population of freed slaves, should that come to pass. But the subject was cloaked under the guise of popular sovereignty;

that is, the matter of whether citizens had the right to decide for themselves if their government would or would not sustain slavery. Lincoln had been arguing against it since the Kansas-Nebraska Act had been passed, believing that popular sovereignty could be used as a means for perpetuating slavery and denying an entire people their human rights.

Douglas knew he had his hands full. "He is the strong man of the party," he said of Lincoln, "—full of wit, facts, dates, and the best-stump-speaker, with his droll ways and dry jokes, in the West."

The debates took place in seven of the nine congressional districts, where the debaters were typically encircled by picnic tables and drums, by hecklers and horses and peddlers, by plates of ice cream and banners and torchlight processions, by scribbling newspapermen and children not particularly interested in either Douglas or Lincoln, one short, one tall, who had come to town amid a great deal of hoopla.

Neither man was a zealot. In their different ways, both Douglas and Lincoln wished to occupy a middle ground between the abolitionists and the Southern fire-eaters in a country that could and should be committed to its own democratic principles. Both men were what we'd certainly call racists today: as typical nineteenth-century Americans, both considered blacks an inferior people and shared the white supremacist beliefs of most Democrats and Republicans. Yet the racism of each man demonstrated that American racism in general was not monolithic: Lincoln differentiated between what he considered the inferior cast of black people and the right—their natural right—to freedom and the fruits of their labor. Douglas did not differentiate. To him, freedom meant white people deciding for themselves whether or not to own slaves or to extend slavery. Yet he had stood up—and would continue to do so—to the Southern intransigents. "If slavery be a blessing," he'd told his Southern colleague Henry Foote, "it is your blessing." He wanted no part of it.

Lincoln had already stated his point of view on a humid June night in Springfield after he had been nominated by Republicans for the Senate seat. "'A house divided against itself cannot stand,'" the forty-nine-year-old had declared. "I believe this government cannot endure, permanently half slave and half free. I do not expect the Union to be dissolved—I do not expect the house to fall—but I do expect it will cease to be divided. It will become all one thing or all the other. Either the opponents of slavery will arrest the further spread of it, and place it where the public mind shall rest in the belief that it is in the course of ultimate extinction; or its advocates will push it forward, till it shall become alike lawful in all the States, old as well as new—North as well as South."

Douglas too had staked out his position. Alienating Buchanan and the pro-Southern Democrats, Douglas said the proslavery Lecompton constitution in Kansas had been a fraud. That is, he held fast to the notion of popular sovereignty which had become, to him and to others, the fundamental right of a democratic nation, and he earned Republican points for it. "The general recognition of the principle of popular sovereignty is all that is needed to restore peace to the country, and to allay the agitation of the Slavery question," said the moderate *New York Times*, praising Douglas. "He has shown constancy to this principle [of popular sovereignty] at a cost which proves his sincerity," claimed a Portsmouth, New Hampshire, newspaper. Other Republican papers applauded Douglas's courage; he had not flinched when the Buchanan Democrats drubbed him. For that, prominent Republicans such as Horace Greeley supported Douglas for the Illinois Senate seat; he seemed to be one of them, and his *Tribune*, much read in Illinois, said so. (A well-known Democrat who could stand up to Buchanan and Southern Democrats would serve the Republican cause better than an unknown hick.)

Douglas needed to squash the idea that he might be a Republican in disguise. Quickly he distanced himself from Lincoln's notion of a house divided by shifting the discussion to war. For the phrase suggested a country divided permanently over slavery until that division brought on a civil war, "a war of sections, a war of the North against the South, of the free states against the slave states—a war of extermination to be continued relentlessly until the one or the other shall be subdued and all the states shall either become free or become slave." Who wanted a divided country, a broken country, a country warring over such a benighted issue as slavery, especially when the matter could be so easily resolved by popular sovereignty? Massachusetts could vote itself a free state, which it had; South Carolina was a slave state; and the territories could decide for themselves: easy.

Douglas, in July 1858, had initially opened his campaign before thirty thousand people. Lincoln sat near him on the podium. "In my opinion," Douglas shouted, "this government of ours is founded on the white basis. It was made by the white man, for the benefit of the white man, to be administered by the white man, in such a manner as they should determine. It is also true that a negro, an Indian, or any other man of inferior race to a white man, should be permitted to enjoy, and humanity requires that he should have all the rights, privileges and immunities which he is capable of exercising consistent with the safety of society. I would give him every right and every privilege which his capacity would enable him to enjoy, consistent with the good of the society in which he lived. But you may ask me, what are these rights and these privileges? My answer is, that each State must decide for itself the nature and extent of these rights."

The moral apathy of Douglas is staggering—but from the point of view of his argument, he made sense: popular sovereignty, he contended, guaranteed democracy, and people could vote for or against slavery, and such freedom to vote safeguarded a republic of "diversity, dissimilarity, variety in all our local and domestic institutions."

The rules of engagement were such that one man would speak for an hour, the other would reply for an hour and a half, and then the first man would rebut for another thirty minutes. It was a grueling schedule. Covering about ten thousand miles in a hundred days, Douglas and Lincoln stood for hours in riverboats or sat for hours on uncomfortable seats in hot steamy trains. They ate at odd times, they did not sleep, they were trailed by the press and greeted by cheering or hooting mobs. They shook hands and each man listened carefully, very carefully, to his opponent in the summer heat. Douglas often wore a ruffled shirt, dark blue coat, light trousers, and a white felt hat. His shoes were shined. Exhausting himself, he traveled relentlessly from fairground to blistering fairground, bringing an entourage that included private cannon. He occasionally lost his temper—some said he drank too much—and he sputtered the withering invective for which he was famous, accusing Lincoln, for instance, of an alliance with the abolitionists.

Lincoln, in turn, wore trousers too short for his long thin legs and a stovepipe hat that accentuated his height, giving him a physical advantage over Douglas. He also wore plain, rough boots, sturdy as a Conestoga wagon, but his sentences could incorporate biblical itera-tion, and he had schooled himself in politics and oratory, studying the law alongside the Bible, Milton, and Shakespeare. He peppered his speech with a laconic, self-deprecating humor that little disguised his tough, forensic reasoning. His task was formidable: he had to dis-sociate himself from the epithet of "ultra" or (radical) abolitionist that the Democrats hung around his neck like an advertising placard. At the same time he had to show how he differed from Douglas, who had recently joined forces with Lincoln's fellow Republicans to help defeat Lecompton.

When the debates began in the dusty city of Ottawa, Illinois, about eighty miles southwest of Chicago, in the heat of a late August day, Lincoln reread part of the speech he had given in Peoria in order to swat away Douglas's charge against him that he sought either im-mediate emancipation or equality for black men and women. "If all earthly power were given me, I should not know what to do, as to the existing institution," Lincoln declared. "I think I would not hold one in slavery, at any rate," he said. "Yet the point is not clear enough to me to denounce people upon. What next? Free them, and make them, and make them politically and socially our equals? My own feelings would not admit of this; and if mine would, we well know that the mass of white people will not. Whether this feeling accords with justice and sound judgment, is not the question, if indeed, it is any part of it. A universal feeling, whether well or ill founded, cannot be safely disregarded. We cannot then make them equals."

He then added that he had "no purpose to introduce political and social equality between the white and black races. . . . But I hold that notwithstanding all this, there is no reason in the world why the negro is not entitled to all the rights enumerated in the Declaration of Independence,—the right of life, liberty and the pursuit of happiness. I hold that he is as much entitled to these as the white man. I agree with Judge Douglas that he is not my equal in many respects, certainly not in color, perhaps not in intellectual and moral endowments," and here he again hammered his point, "but in the right to eat the bread, without the leave of anybody else, which his own hand earns, he is my equal, and the equal of Judge Douglas, and the equal of every living man."

As for clarifying the matter of the "house divided," Lincoln said that the country was really a house united after all; "the great variety of the local institutions in the States, springing from differences in the soil, differences in the face of the country, and in the climate, are bonds of Union." That is, "if they produce in one section of the country what is called for by the wants of another section, and this other section can supply the wants of the first, they are not matters of discord, but bonds of union, true bonds of union." The bonds of union had to be built on common ground, not just economic interdependency but on the ground of compromise, though he did not say so.

These were cagey, sophistical answers, measured and direct and evasive at the same time. Lincoln was careful to separate the matter of racism from the institution of slavery; the one—the institution of slavery—he wanted to contain. Lincoln continued to believe vociferously that slavery violated the principle of human equality on which the Declaration had been founded, but he read the Constitution as an instrument whose necessary concession to slave owners had made the nation possible—no small thing. And though the Constitution compelled the protection of slavery where it existed, the document said nothing about restricting its expansion, which Lincoln assumed would (and should) hasten its eventual demise. Lincoln thus initially intended not to end slavery per se but to implement what he thought was a consensus about its fundamental wrongness so that, in its due time, slavery would disappear.

Lincoln did cling to the curious idea, bandied about for years, of colonizing free blacks in Liberia or Central America. Yet the moral heart of Lincoln's political philosophy remained the "right to rise" in this world, which meant to achieve or make something from nothing, and, significantly, to keep and enjoy, as he had said, bread earned from one's labor. Slavery denied basic human rights.

It was on the matter of race—race, not the institution of slavery—where, to certain later observers, Lincoln stumbled. "I am not nor ever have been," he had said more than once, "in favor of bringing about in any way the social and political equality of the white and black races—that I am not, nor ever have been, in favor of making voters or jurors of negroes, nor of qualifying them to hold office, nor to intermarry with white people; and I will say in addition to this that there is a physical difference between the white and black races which I believe will forever forbid the two races living together on terms of social and political equality. And inasmuch as they cannot so live, while they do remain together there must be the position of superior and inferior, and I as much as any other man am in favor of having the superior position assigned to the white race."

But he emphatically added that while "I do not perceive that because the white man is to have the superior position the negro should be denied everything. I do not understand that because I do not want a negro woman for a slave I must necessarily want her for a wife. My understanding is that I can just let her alone. I am now in my fiftieth year, and I certainly never have had a black woman for either a slave or a wife. So it seems to me quite possible for us to get along without making either slaves or wives of negroes."

Again his reasoning was clear.

And he outwitted Douglas on the matter of popular sovereignty.

At Freeport, in northwest Illinois and the site of the second debate, Lincoln argued that the Supreme Court's Dred Scott decision countermanded Douglas's beloved notion of popular sovereignty since the decision specifically allowed slaveholders to bring their slaves into whatever territory they saw fit to take them. He therefore asked Douglas whether he actually believed residents could exclude slavery from their territory before it entered the Union. The question was a trap. Douglas supported, as Lincoln did not, the Dred Scott decision. Yet he had to reply that, notwithstanding Dred Scott, people had the lawful means (the vote) to introduce or exclude slavery as they pleased. Though Douglas's reply, which came to be known as the Freeport Doctrine, was nothing more than a reiteration of his popular sovereignty plank, it cost him his already dwindling Southern support. Southerners considered the Freeport Doctrine an abomination that implicitly challenged Dred Scott and potentially prohibited slavery in the territories.

Douglas's reply also became good copy because a backwoodsy prairie lawyer had caught the seasoned politician in a contradiction. "Does he [Douglas] mean to say that he has been devoting his life to securing to the people of the Territories the right to exclude slavery from the Territories?" Lincoln asked. "If he means so to say, he means to deceive; because he and every one knows that the decision of the Supreme Court, which he approves and makes especial ground of attack upon me for disapproving, forbids the people of a Territory to exclude slavery. This covers the whole ground from the settlement of a Territory till it reaches the degree of maturity entitling it to form a State constitution. So far as all that ground is concerned, the Judge is not sustaining popular sovereignty, but absolutely opposing it."

On September 15, at the fairgrounds in Jonesboro, Illinois, in the rural and Democratic area of Illinois known as Egypt (because of its proximity to Cairo), Douglas tried to restore his credibility. He brought up Cuba. "When we get Cuba we must take it as we find it," Douglas declaimed, "and leave the people of Cuba to decide the question of slavery for themselves without the interference of the federal government or any other State in the Union." Of course, he was assuming that Cuba would vote to uphold slavery and thus be a slave state. The ruse didn't work.

Standing tall on a platform made out of rough planks, Lincoln again posed the Freeport question. "If the slaveholding citizens of a United States Territory should need and demand congressional legislation for the protection of their slave property in such territory, would you, as a member of Congress, vote for or against such legislation?" he wanted to know. Which was more important: the Dred Scott decision or popular sovereignty? Again Douglas was cornered.

John Hay and John George Nicolay, the two promising young men who had become Lincoln's private secretaries, later said that when Douglas hesitated, he lost whatever chance he had of reunifying the Democrats. "Compared with this," they noted, "his Lecompton revolt had been a venial offense."

Gone too was his hope of unsplintering a country splintered among West, East, South, and North; there was no transcontinental railroad linking East and West, and communication between opposing parties had grown as muffled as those electric pulses in the failed transatlantic cable.

Though Lincoln won the popular vote, Douglas won the Illinois Senate seat. Senate seats were determined not by popular vote but by the state legislature, and the Democratic majority in the Illinois legislature voted for Douglas 54–46. Douglas was momentarily elated, and as he traveled from Chicago to Washington, he continued to stump for popular sovereignty and the need for cooperation between the free and slave states while America grew and grew and inevitably fulfilled its "glorious destiny."

"We live in a rapid age," he said, "and things will come along, naturally enough." But Douglas had lost what trust the Democrats in the South had vested in him. Several Southern senators—along with President Buchanan—moved to strip Douglas of his chairmanship of the Committee on Territories. Judah Benjamin, a senator from Louisiana, noted that on the matter of Dred Scott, popular sovereignty, and the Freeport Doctrine, "the Senator from Illinois faltered." To be sure, "he got the prize for which he faltered," Benjamin said, but he forfeited "the grand prize of his ambition."

Stephen Douglas would never be president of the United States. The South would see to that.

"I TAKE SPACE to be the central fact to man born in America," the poet Charles Olson would say years later, in 1947. He was writing about Melville and the sea, but he was also referring to freedom and liberty and land, always land. It was to overcoming or to owning land that Americans were committed: western land, southern land, Caribbean land, Central American land.

William Walker is a case in point. This slender, small man had the tacit, if not explicit, support of men in government and was touted as an American hero, brave and restless and colorful enough to be the subject of theatrical reviews and song. Born in Nashville, Tennessee, in 1824, Walker was a doctor, a lawyer, and the editor of the San Francisco *Herald*. Walker was also a man who fought four pistol duels and a swashbuckler who enjoyed the unspoken support of men in government. Called "King of the Filibusters," he wanted to make Baja, California, and Mexico's Sonora region his private empire, and when he and his tiny army of recruits failed in 1853, and he was arrested, he popped up again in 1855 and aimed for Nicaragua. Like the megalomaniacal Narciso López and with the same bullheadedness, Walker was consumed by his own imperial calling.

And he would settle for nothing less than a nation. Nicaragua, with its transit route to the West, beckoned. Fortunately for Walker, Nicaragua had been in the midst of a civil war for several years.

With the backing of several wealthy entrepreneurs and a group of armed Americans, Walker actually managed to seize control of the government by arriving at just the right time, having commandeered a steamboat on Lake Nicaragua, and having captured the city of Granada from the rear. After ordering that the Nicaraguan minister of war be shot, Walker set up a provisional government, named himself president, reinstituted slavery, pillaged the country, and in 1856 stupidly seized the property and revoked the railroad charter of Cornelius Vanderbilt, whose company conveyed Americans overland across Nicaragua and then on to California by steamship.

Officially, Washington had done nothing about Walker. Franklin Pierce, then still president, naively hoped to be nominated on the Democratic ticket for president in the spring, and he did not want to offend the South or Jefferson Davis, who supported Walker. To Davis, a Nicaragua under Walker held open the same promise as Cuba: territory for slavery. But Vanderbilt was not a man to be trifled with. He embarked on what his biographer called "an independent foreign policy," closed the Nicaragua line, and, negotiating with countries such as Costa Rica that were hostile to Walker, he declared unofficial war on Walker. And Walker was no help to himself, especially when it was discovered he had no plans to let the United States annex Nicaragua.

So the American who had conquered Nicaragua had to leave the country in 1857, foiled by a coalition of forces from El Salvador, Honduras, and Guatemala—and by Cornelius Vanderbilt, who had financed the military operation against him.

Walker again bounced back. Bankrolled by men in several Southern states, he launched another invasion of Nicaragua that fall. Again he was defeated, more quickly this time by the howitzers at the command of Commodore Hiram Paulding of the U.S. Navy operating with the authority of the new president, James Buchanan. Walker was arrested and taken off to America, where Buchanan's condemnation of him inflamed Southern fire-eaters. But Walker still wasn't finished, or so he thought. He raised money in the South and mounted yet another—an astounding third—invasion of Nicaragua, this time traveling through Honduras to avoid U.S. patrols. The British navy captured him and turned him over to the Hondurans, who finally executed him by firing squad.

Citing neutrality laws, Buchanan had condemned Walker, yet in his annual address to Congress in late 1858, he tried to unite Democrats by whetting their appetite for land, which was to say expansion of its slave territory. Again, this meant Cuba.

The wealthy John Slidell of Louisiana introduced to the Senate a bill authorizing $30 million to purchase the island. But the call for appropriations ran smack into the Republican bid for homestead legislation that would open western territories to all settlers—and not coincidentally help those ravaged by the economic downturn in 1857, promising them a fresh start. Republicans insisted that the homestead bill be passed before they broached the subject of Cuba, and this set off another debate. "As soon as the Cuba question is disposed of," promised Andrew Johnson, a Democrat from Tennessee, "we shall make one common and united effort to bring up the homestead bill and procure the action of the Senate upon it." Cuba first, then homestead legislation, which Johnson supported. So did Stephen Douglas, though he expediently decided to put Cuba ahead of homestead legislation in order, he hoped, to unite his party and to boost his standing with Southerners, some of whom were now calling him Black Douglas. But Republicans such as Lyman Trumbull distrusted any Democratic promise to pass homestead legislation, and so did William Seward, who believed the Southern Democrats would postpone and postpone because they feared homestead legislation would do nothing more than lead to another Kansas, which was to say restrict the expansion of slavery.

Mindful of his political future, Seward directed the debate about Cuba away from the issue of slavery. Wouldn't the government incur a huge fiscal debt if the Cuban appropriations bill was passed, he wanted to know? He also attempted to undermine Buchanan by playing to the Senate's sense of its autonomy. Did the question of Cuba and its possible statehood even fall under executive jurisdiction? Wasn't the executive wading into congressional waters?

Yet to Seward the most important issue was, in fact, slavery: "The Senate is the propagandist of slave labor," he cried in frustration. Benjamin Wade, Republican senator from Ohio, was even more outspoken. Rising to his feet, Wade summarized the discussion in the ugly invective of the day. "Shall we give niggers to the niggerless," he asked, "or land to the landless?"

Audacious, aggressive, and often eloquent, Robert Toombs of Georgia stood up, his long black hair streaked with gray. In his youth, he had studied for a brief time at Franklin College in Athens (now the University of Georgia), but at heart he was a gambler who preferred cards to books. And though he never earned a degree, he'd also been enrolled at Union College in Schenectady, New York, where Seward had studied. An intelligent and often short-tempered man who had been teased as a runt when a boy, Toombs had been elected to the House of Representatives four times. Now a senator, he joined fellow Georgians Howell Cobb and Alexander Stephens to form part of a formidable Southern triumvirate. Loyal to Georgia and to the South, he also loved the Union and tried to prevent factionalism. He had even lectured at the Tremont Temple in Boston, where he wooed a crowd that had come to hiss him for his proslavery views. He'd pointed out that the Declaration of Independence, drafted while slavery was a fact of American life, did not emancipate anyone. Besides, as Toombs smoothly explained, African peoples were inferior to whites—and in the South, they were better treated than many whites in the North and elsewhere. "The injustice and despotism of England toward Ireland has produced more separation of Irish families and sundered more domestic ties within the last ten years than African slavery has effected since its introduction into the United States," Toombs reminded a Boston audience, which likely included a large number of Irish immigrants.

He had spoken in Boston, yes, but he had no use for the likes of Sumner, whose brutal caning he had approved of. And Toombs hated William Seward. "He may go tell foolish old men and spinsters and old maids in New York that he has done a thriving business in freeing negroes," Toombs jeered, "but he has never freed one. He has never sacrificed one acre of land to liberty—not one inch—and he never will. These are not the people to do it."

Personal insults notwithstanding, Democratic politicians knew that the issue of Cuba might unify the Democratic Party in the upcoming presidential election of 1860 by bringing together North and South on a single, popular issue; it could revive disheartened Democrats in the wake of the acrimonious Lecompton debates; it might even mollify Southern fire-eaters, who were already speaking, yet again, of secession. Surely a foreign war, if it came to that, would prevent the Union from breaking apart. But Toombs was right that the Republicans wanted to replace the Cuba bill with a homestead bill as a delaying tactic, and as a result, both came to naught. "The social intercourse between North and South, or rather between Dems. and Reps.," Toombs told Alexander Stephens, "seems almost to have ceased and all sides seem sullen and ill-natured."

Toombs was not finished. He did not denounce Douglas, and he very much wanted to unite the Democrats, who were falling asunder. "If you will stand with me," Toombs beseeched the Democrats of Georgia, "we shall conquer faction in North and South, and shall save the country from the curse of being ruled by the combination now calling itself the opposition. We shall leave the country to our children as we found it—united, strong, prosperous and happy."

And enslaved.

(6)

REVOLUTIONS NEVER
GO BACKWARD

Have we been listening to a thing, a piece of property, or a man?" shouted William Lloyd Garrison.

"A man! a man!" five hundred voices yelled back.

The mostly white audience that had gathered at the large building covered in salt-weathered shingles wasn't referring to Abraham Lincoln or Stephen Douglas but to that other Douglass, the one who spelled his name differently from the Illinois senator's, the handsome black man with the large head who had just finished speaking. The throng of antislavery enthusiasts had come to Nantucket Island for the annual convention of the Massachusetts Anti-Slavery Society.

That was in the summer of 1841, when Frederick Douglass was still in his twenties and lived in the whaling port of New Bedford with his wife and family. Virtually unknown and shaking with nervousness, he spoke with such feeling of his life as a slave that he held the audience and the bespectacled William Lloyd Garrison spellbound. Afterward, John A. Collins, the executive director of the Anti-Slavery Society, asked Douglass to work for the group as a lecturer. Douglass consented and was such an enormous stump success that Yankee naysayers doubted whether the man could have really been a slave. "Better have a *little* of the plantation manner of speech than not," one man advised Douglass, " 'tis not best that you seem too learned."

Four years later, in the spring of 1845, Douglass published a stirring account of how he, Frederick Augustus Washington Bailey, born a slave in Talbot County, Maryland, to a black mother and a white man whom he had never known, had escaped from bondage to remake himself as Frederick Douglass, man of freedom and conviction. Told with a verbal dexterity unparalleled except, perhaps, by the speeches of Abraham Lincoln, *The Narrative of the Life of Frederick Douglass, an American Slave*, was an international sensation. Ironically, however, it exposed Douglass to the threat of recapture. He took off for England, where his lectures helped him earn enough money to purchase his freedom on his return.

Settling in the abolition-minded Rochester, New York, in 1847, within the year Douglass was speaking at the women's rights convention in Seneca Falls. He also started his own newspaper, *The North Star* (later renamed *Frederick Douglass' Paper*), with its masthead announcing "Right is of no sex—Truth is of no color—God is the Father of us all, and we are all Brethren." But he broke with Garrison when in 1854 Garrison burned a copy of the Constitution, calling it a pact made with the devil. For Garrison shunned violence. Not Douglass. He neither spurned the Constitution nor rejected violence as a means of securing liberty, though he preferred a politics of intervention.

Disillusioned with the Republican Party, which, as he said, "refuses to oppose slavery where it is, and opposes it only where it is not," Douglass joined with the philanthropist Gerrit Smith and the rump of the Liberty Party (which later merged with the Radical Abolition Party). With its headquarters near Rochester, the Liberty Party had originally been formed in 1840 and looked to U.S. history for its precedents and found in men such as John Quincy Adams (with whom Smith had corresponded) an argument for abolition. Adams had said, for instance, that if the Constitution granted Congress and the president the right to exercise war powers as they saw fit, they could then abolish slavery if they defined slavery as a state of war. And Gerrit Smith believed it was a state of war.

With the success of his book, his newspaper, and with his sure command of himself, Douglass was soon the most famous ex-slave in America. And an amazing orator, fearless and proud. "What, to the Slave, is the Fourth of July?" Douglass trenchantly asked in 1852. "To him, your celebration is a sham; your boasted liberty, an unholy license; your national greatness, swelling vanity; your sounds of rejoicing are empty and heartless; your denunciation of tyrants brass fronted impudence; your shout of liberty and equality, hollow mockery; your prayers and hymns, your sermons and thanks-givings, with all your religious parade and solemnity, are to him, mere bombast, fraud, deception, impiety, and hypocrisy—a thin veil to cover up crimes which would disgrace a nation of savages."

The other Douglas, the senator from Illinois, had invoked Frederick Douglass's name to manipulate his audience during his debates with Lincoln. "Why, they brought Fred Douglass to Freeport when I was addressing a meeting there in a carriage driven by a white owner, the negro sitting inside with the white lady and her daughter," the Little Giant sniped. "Shame," replied the Jonesboro audience. They knew what Douglas meant: do you really think your wife and child ought to ride in a carriage with a black man, while you are reduced to driving the carriage? If so, vote for Lincoln.

OPPRESSION MAKES A wise man mad, Frederick Douglass explained—mad enough to dispense with reason, with argument, and believe that only violence would end the oppression. "We need the storm, the whirlwind, and the earthquake," he said. A storm, a whirlwind, an earthquake: one of Douglass's most devoted subscribers, a white man, some say mad, wanted more than anything to rain an apocalypse down on slavery. The abolitionist and freedom fighter who hadn't yet begun to fight with swords and guns—though he would before long—was named John Brown.

Possessed like Melville's Ahab with one besetting idea, the elimination of slavery, John Brown glowed with "that religious elevation," an acquaintance recalled, "which is itself a kind of refinement,—the quality one may see expressed in many a venerable Quaker face at yearly meeting." When speaking of Brown, the Yankee abolitionist Wendell Phillips called him "a strange, resolute, repulsive, iron-willed, inexorable old man. He stands like a solitary rock in a more mobile society, a fiery nature, and a cold temper, and a cool head,—a volcano beneath a covering of snow."

Eloquent and shrewd, he had already been lionized far in excess of his dubious accomplishments, which included a so-called battle at Osawatomie, Kansas, in 1856 against proslavery men from Missouri that resulted in the town's being burned to the ground and the death of one of his sons. Brown was undaunted; he was a Puritan of the old school. Just under six feet tall, with the lines etched on his face making him look hard and sculptural, he would be compared to Oliver Cromwell and Jesus Christ. To Henry David Thoreau, Brown was "a transcendentalist above all."

Perhaps so. He certainly adhered to higher laws. A longtime abolitionist who had presumably vowed to fight slavery after the murder of the abolitionist Elijah Lovejoy eighteen years earlier, in 1855 Brown joined five of his sons in what became known as Bleeding Kansas. It was he who stood up at a public meeting, early on, and declared the Negro the equal of any white person there. But according to one observer, he didn't much like discussion. "Talk is a national institution," Brown reportedly said, "but it does no good for the slave." Instead, border ruffians in Kansas would learn to fear him. As one supporter noted, Old Brown "swallows a Missourian whole, and says grace after the meal"; that was the kind of accolade abolitionists accorded "Weird John Brown" (as Melville would call him). His hatred of slavery was hard, deep, bloody, and unmerciful.

When Abraham Lincoln's secretaries, John Nicolay and John Hay, in later years belittled Brown's speech as coarse, Brown's admirers complained. There were by then many champions of Brown's prose, his mission, his dedication to a righteous cause. These same enthusiasts had turned a blind eye to Brown's role in the 1857 massacre near Pottawatomie Creek, when five proslavery settlers were dragged out of their homes around midnight and butchered with broadswords. "Lynch-law is terrible always," rationalized a supporter; "but Kansas was the seat of guerilla warfare, and this was its sternest phase." Other people, less enamored of Brown, called him a madman, a fanatic, a rabble-rouser, and an idiot.

Born in Torrington, Connecticut, in 1800, John Brown was a self-taught antislavery evangelist who had been a tanner, a postmaster, a farmer, a shepherd, a successful wool merchant, an unsuccessful wool merchant, and after Lovejoy's death an abolitionist who talked easily and with passion of the cause, which even at this early date included an armed force acting in the heart of the South. Henry Highland Garnet, the black Presbyterian clergyman who supported black emigration, and Jermain Wesley Loguen, the black clergyman in Syracuse who claimed to have helped usher 1,500 slaves to freedom, both lowered their voice when they mentioned Brown, afraid they would be overheard. They suggested Douglass meet him. Brown was living with his family in an unostentatious wooden house on a back street in Springfield, Massachusetts. When Douglass arrived in 1848, he noticed that the inside of the house was as plain as its outside: nothing pretentious or fancy. As Douglass later recalled, there was nothing pretentious or fancy about Brown either. He was "lean, strong, and sinewy, of the best New England mould, built for times of trouble, fitted to grapple with the flintiest hardships." Douglass ate with the Browns: beef soup, cabbage, and potatoes, all served on an unvarnished pine table.

"Slavery was a state of war, and the slave had a right to anything necessary to his freedom," Douglass remembered Brown as saying. "Even if the worst came, he could but be killed; and he had no better use for his life than to lay it down in the cause of the slave." The next year, 1849, Brown relocated his family to North Elba, near Lake Placid in the Adirondack Mountains of New York on the land (known as Timbucto) that Gerrit Smith had given to the black community. Brown hoped to help make Timbucto a self-sustaining black settlement. But the deteriorating situation in Kansas was a magnet for Brown, who followed his sons there in 1855, supposedly to homestead. The call to action, to right the country's wrongs, and to eradicate slavery all beckoned. After the Pottawatomie massacre in 1856—likely Douglass knew of it—Brown confided to Douglass that he intended to open a corridor through Virginia, Pennsylvania, and New York to enable slaves to flee to Canada. It would be a corridor not unlike that of the Underground Railroad but more militant; squadrons of armed men, posted five miles apart, would guard the route. The guards would subsist on the land, avoid violence except in self-defense, and raid the slaveholders' so-called property, thus freeing the slaves.

Brown also dreamed of a separate black state in the Allegheny Mountains, a country within a country (not unlike Brigham Young's). As recalled by Douglass, however, the plan was shapeless. During his stay at the Douglass home in Rochester in 1858, Brown composed the constitution for the new state using a piece of board for a desk. He gave Douglass a copy of the "Provisional Constitution and Ordinances for the People of the United States," which Douglass held on to for the rest of his life.

Though Brown insisted that he pay Douglass rent, he couldn't afford it. For months he'd been reaching out to prominent individuals in the black community such as James N. Gloucester in New York and John Jones in Chicago—and the famed Harriet Tubman. (W. E. B. DuBois said about Tubman that she was the woman who, "like some dark ghost," guided more than three hundred fugitive slaves to freedom.) He didn't raise as much cash as he had hoped, but several prominent men did volunteer to back him, for his effect was mesmeric: "Napoleon himself had no more blind and trusting confidence in his own destiny and resources," said one of the men who heard Brown speak. And when Brown lectured in Concord, Massachusetts, he convinced Bronson Alcott of his courage and conviction: "I think him equal to anything he dares," said Alcott, "the man to do the deed if it must be done, and with the martyr's temper and purpose." The Reverend Henry Ward Beecher said that Brown spoke bullets.

"The Beechers of our age are only useful in proportion as they prepare the way for the John Browns," James Redpath said. Among Brown's converts and recruits was the radical Concord schoolteacher Franklin Sanborn, whose students included two of Alcott's daughters and two of Henry James's brothers. There were the abolitionist Thomas Higginson, who had recently given up his pulpit for abolition and Kansas, and the self-made financier George Luther Stearns, who had made a fortune in lead pipes. And there was the mercurial, large-hearted Gerrit Smith, on whose land the Brown family lived. The Reverend Theodore Parker, ailing from congenital tuberculosis, joined the group, as did the Byronic Samuel Gridley Howe, the founder of the Perkins Institute for the Blind, who, in younger days, had fought the Turks in Greece. These men—Sanborn, Higginson, Stearns, Smith, Parker, and Howe—formed a clandestine group soon widely known as the "Secret Six." They were to help finance Brown and to ignite, so they initially hoped, an insurrection that would eradicate slavery once and for all.

Since Congress had passed the Lecompton compromise and Kansas seemed no longer the battle's frontier, Brown decided to take his war elsewhere—to Virginia, to attack the federal arsenal in Harpers Ferry. The raid would set off a rebellion of huge proportions, fugitives and free slaves rushing to his side, all of them armed with revolvers purchased by Stearns and the pikes forged by New England smithies. The Secret Six were privy to Brown's plans, which were nearly foiled when another recruit, the Englishman Hugh Forbes, turned against Brown. A volatile idealist who had fought alongside Giuseppe Garibaldi, Forbes parted with Brown when Brown did not pay him, he said, for writing an important tactical handbook on guerrilla warfare. Anyway, Forbes had also wanted to replace Brown as head of the undertaking, which would never have happened.

Hurt and angry, Forbes leaked news of Brown's plan to Senator

William Seward, who later said the whole thing was too wild to believe. Forbes also spilled information to Massachusetts senator Henry Wilson, who would disingenuously deny that he knew anything of the plans. Pretending to abandon his scheme to attack in Virginia, Brown headed to Kansas, alienated many of the Free Soil Kansans, and was said to be insane. Meanwhile, the Six decided that the raid should be delayed, and many of the handpicked black abolitionists whose support Brown had enlisted were hesitating. Kansas voters had defeated the Lecompton constitution once and for all in August 1858 and seemed to defeat Brown's cause along with it.

So Brown shook off his timid advisers and raised more money.

James Redpath admired the older man and when Redpath published *The Roving Editor*, his book about slavery, he dedicated it to Brown. "You, Old Hero! believe that the slave should be aided and urged to insurrection, and hence do I lay this tribute at your feet. . . . You went to Kansas, when the troubles broke out there—not to 'settle' or 'speculate'—or from idle curiosity: but for one stern, solitary purpose—*to have a shot at the South*."

UPSTATE NEW YORK shimmers in October. The oaks and maples are bright with color on crisp, clear days, although on October 25, 1858, it had been raining all afternoon. The lights in Rochester's Corinthian Hall weren't working, and the gas lamps were sputtering. By evening, though, the rain was just an annoying drizzle, not enough to keep the thousand or so people from lining the street outside the building, the same one where the Fox sisters had communed with the dead just a decade earlier. Corinthian Hall had hosted Jenny Lind, the Nightingale who had sung her Swedish folk tunes there, P. T. Barnum, and Frederick Douglass, who had asked his now-famous question, "What, to the Slave, is the Fourth of July?"

It was a perfect setting for Senator William Seward, come to rally support for the Republican Party—especially since he intended to run for president in 1860. That was no secret.

The gas lamps continued to flicker, and at first, it was hard to see Seward. But the people in the hall knew just who he was—the most famous man in America, the newspapers had claimed, even if that may not have been quite true. Doubtless he hoped it was. And bad press was still press. An antislavery man (no matter what his critics alleged about his commitment to the cause), Seward had spoken so fervently against the Dred Scott decision that Chief Justice Taney vowed that if Seward were ever elected president, Taney wouldn't administer the oath of office.

Yet Seward needed to bolster his credentials among antislavery activists, for if he wished to defeat the Democrats, he would need to lure Gerrit Smith's Liberty people into the Republican ranks. He did not want to split the antislavery vote. So here he was in Rochester stumping for Edwin D. Morgan as governor. Morgan had to run a tough fight against a running Democrat as well as against Smith himself. Of course, Smith's nomination for governor was largely symbolic; he didn't expect to win. But he might be a spoiler, and if he was, and continued to be, and if he attracted more Republicans to his more radical point of view, then Seward might not be hanging his hat in the White House after all.

That damp night at Corinthian Hall, Seward spoke for almost ninety minutes. "Our country is a theatre which exhibits, in full operation, two radically different political systems; the one resting on the basis of servile or slave labor, the other on the basis of voluntary labor of freemen," he told his audience. Pacing back and forth, and poking the air with his unlit cigar, Seward explained that "hitherto, the two systems have existed in different States, but side by side within the American Union. This has happened because the Union is a confederation of States. But in another aspect the United States constitute only one nation," he continued. "Increase of population, which is filling the States out to their very borders, together with a new and extended net-work of railroads and other avenues, and an internal commerce which daily becomes more intimate, is rapidly bringing the States into a higher and more perfect social unity or consolidation."

One nation: that was Seward's theme. By combining the idea of "higher laws" with the idea of a "more perfect social unity," he provided a definition of the Republican Party. It was "a party of one idea; but that is a noble one—an idea that fills and expands all generous souls; the idea of equality—the equality of all men before human tribunals and human laws, as they all are equal before the Divine tribunal and Divine laws."

Yet because the Republicans represented a national party founded on the principle of equality, they could not help but come into conflict with those who did not believe in nationhood or equality. The time had come, moreover, for a collision, the inevitable collision between antagonistic systems. "Shall I tell you what this collision means?" Seward asked, his cigar still unlit. "They who think that it is accidental, unnecessary, the work of interested or fanatical agitators, and therefore ephemeral, mistake the case altogether. It is an irrepressible conflict between opposing and enduring forces, and it means that the United States must and will, sooner or later, become either entirely a slave-holding nation, or entirely a free-labor nation."

"Irrepressible conflict": that was the phrase, the prophecy, the slogan that would catch fire. Perhaps Seward guessed how volatile those two words would be though he later said he hadn't anticipated the backlash. He continued to speak. The failure to "apprehend this great truth, induces many unsuccessful attempts at final compromise between the slave and free States," he declared, "and it is the existence of this great fact that renders all such pretended compromises, when made, vain and ephemeral."

Compromise did not exist, for it could not; or, if it could exist, it would have to be a real one. As it stood, there were no grounds for real compromise, not between "opposing and enduring forces." Make no mistake, Seward continued, the Democrats *were* the slave party, and they would extend slavery west, south, and, most terrifyingly, north. He grimly outlined a future of bondage: "By the action of the President and the Senate, using their treaty-making power, they will annex foreign slave-holding states. Thus relatively increasing the number of slave states, they will allow no amendment to the Constitution prejudicial to their interest; and so, having permanently established their power, they expect the Federal judiciary to nullify all state laws which shall interfere with internal or foreign commerce in slaves. When the free states shall be sufficiently demoralized to tolerate these designs, they reasonably conclude that slavery will be accepted by those states themselves."

The country must become free—or, as Seward warned, "Boston and New York [would] become once more markets for trade in the bodies and souls of men." The danger was clear and imminent. Only the Republican Party could save New York and Boston and Vermont and Maine from bondage by defeating Democrats once and for all.

The fearmongering, articulate, well-wrought speech concluded portentously, "I know, and you know, that a revolution has begun. I know, and all the world knows, that revolutions never go backward."

SEWARD'S AUDIENCE MAY have stomped its feet and clapped loudly when he finished speaking, and Morgan may have won the race for governor, but nationwide, there was little applause when Seward's speech hit the papers. In New York, the Democratic *Herald* said Seward was as delirious as the Reverend Henry Ward Beecher or the radical Reverend Theodore Parker. The Albany *Atlas & Argus* complained that the hypocritical Seward had held out a flag of truce while declaring war. *The Washington Union* shuddered at Seward's vision of the "plantations of our Southern states . . . cultivated by free labor—meaning free negro labor—such as that is in vogue in Jamaica," which would invariably lead to "decay, waste, and desolation." In the South, the headline of a Richmond paper blasted Seward, declaring, "Roguery Overreaches Itself." It went on to say that both Seward in the North and "his co-workers in the South" were spewing venom at each other and damaging themselves far more than their enemy, whoever that was.

What offended and frightened most was the notion of an irrepressible conflict, which actually was not a new idea. Abraham Lincoln had suggested something similar in his "house divided" speech, and before that, Horace Greeley had been editorializing in the *Tribune* that "We are two peoples. We are a people for Freedom and a people for Slavery. Between the two," he concluded, "conflict is inevitable." But Seward's phrase "irrepressible conflict" struck a chord. Oddly, though, Seward seemed to have learned little from the well-publicized debates of Abraham Lincoln, who, having been taken to task for the "house divided" speech, had explicitly vowed to protect slavery where it already existed. Lincoln knew he had to appeal to southern as well as northern Illinois—to Little Egypt and to Chicago. Rather, when speaking in upstate New York at a main stop on the Underground Railroad, Seward was trying to prove to Gerrit Smith's radicals that his antislavery position was real, even more real than they may have thought. He therefore vilified the Democrats in much the same way that the fire-eaters and certain Southern Democrats vilified Republicans: each party, to the other, was a band of extremists bent on perverting the entire way of life of a region. Southerners believed that the North would emancipate the slaves and, in the bargain, replace Southern governments with an autocratic, centralized, and bourgeois Yankee monster.

The wonder is not the predictable responses to Seward's speech. The wonder is that while many people in the North and the South could analyze with clarity the sectional division rocking the country and could even forecast what might happen as a result of the deepening rift, they seemed not to be listening to themselves. Both sides understood the differences dividing them, but by calling them "enduring," they consequently had rightly to regard compromise as appeasement—that is, submission to a hated enemy. To the South, the flouting of the Fugitive Slave Act showed Southerners that the North would disregard laws—even the Constitution—when it so chose and in support of a nebulous and discretionary idea called a higher law; and besides, hadn't Garrison called the Constitution a covenant with death and then ground it under his heel? How could Northerners be trusted to be Americans? For their part, Northerners disdained those "doughfaces" (their term for Southern sympathizers) in the White House, Pierce and Buchanan, who made no secret of their partiality to Southern demands for extending slavery, no matter if that meant now and then turning a blind eye to guerrillas or filibusterers or even the very popular sovereignty that Buchanan, for one, had said he endorsed. Who, then, could be trusted?

And both sides took refuge in the vernacular of the Revolutionary War: America was special, its founding was special, its mission was special, its democracy was special, its Declaration of Independence had declared the importance of life and liberty. Both sides saw their side as representing self-government and freedom; both sides saw themselves incarnating that same desire that animated the revolutions, abroad, of 1848. Both sides indulged in apocalyptic rhetoric, perhaps without realizing they would help bring about a very bloody future.

The Republican aim was surer than that of the failed Whigs or of the Democrats, and they commanded more authority than the anti-immigrant Know-Nothings. Republicans targeted slavery. That was their abiding issue, and that issue changed everything. It provided moral force. And in any event the Democrats were reeling from their own irrepressible conflict, the rift between Stephen Douglas, whose denunciation of Buchanan and Lecompton had alienated Southerners such as Jefferson Davis. Machiavellian though he may have been, a shrewd political operator though he was, and despite his unreflective racism, Douglas did believe in pure popular sovereignty as a matter of democratic principle. For him, it harked back to Thomas Jefferson, and he placed it at Jefferson's feet. The people should decide. It was that simple. What Douglas failed to see—and this was his personal flaw as well as the moral pitfall of nineteenth-century America—was that popular sovereignty would eventually mean nothing if voters could cast a ballot about whether or not to buy and sell other people. And the moral issue aside, if one can essentially vote on who is allowed to vote, there also can be a legitimate vote to eliminate popular sovereignty: popular sovereignty is therefore moot if it declares its own undoing—it declares that the population is not sovereign. Lincoln understood this self-contradiction. It foreshadows his argument against secession: there would be no end to secession if secession were "legal": that is, any dissatisfied group could secede from the larger group, ad infinitum and to a logical absurdity, and hence secession too would declare the end of itself.

Then there was William Seward, poking the air with his unlit cigar. Addressing the staunch antislavery men and women of Rochester and beyond, he made himself a target even for somewhat moderate Southerners, such as Toombs, for whom irreparable conflicts foretold disunion. So while some Seward enthusiasts claimed that in Rochester he clinched the Republican nomination for president, just the opposite seems true. *The New York Times* speculated that after Rochester, Seward's name struck terror into the heart of the South.

Yet one might reasonably ask whose name would spark more fear, more dread, more dismay, more hysteria: that of William Seward or of Old John Brown?

In August 1859, almost a year after Seward's speech, John Brown invited Frederick Douglass to meet with him at an abandoned quarry in Chambersburg, Pennsylvania, about fifty miles north of the quiet village of Harpers Ferry and not far from where, under the alias of John Smith, Brown was hiding out in a rented farmhouse. On the day he met Douglass, Brown carried fishing tackle, though he had no intention of fishing, and he wore a scruffy old hat. Douglass thought Brown looked as raggedy as that hat but was impressed at Brown's plans, eagerly outlined in full, for a raid on Harpers Ferry. Another man, named Shields Green (sometimes called "Emperor"), a fugitive slave who had come with Douglass, stood by and listened too: Brown was planning to strike the federal arsenal and then distribute its weapons to the nearby slaves and free blacks who would rush to his side—he assumed they would—and then all of them together would launch guerrilla raids against slaveholders in Tennessee and the Deep South, sowing terror and freeing slaves along the way.

To succeed, Brown very much needed Douglass or at least his approval, which would go a long way in the black community. Douglass would not sign on. "I told him, and these were my words," Douglass would recall, "that all his arguments, and all his descriptions of the place, convinced me that he was going into a perfect steel-trap, and that once in he would never get out alive." Yet the two men talked for two days. Brown didn't give up and neither did Douglass, who warned Brown that Virginia would "blow him and his hostages sky-high rather than he hold Harper's Ferry an hour." And, of course, Brown's plan endangered the entire black community, which, after the raid, would surely suffer horrific reprisals in the South. Years later, though, Douglass wondered whether it was cowardice or prudence that had protected him from Brown's fierce courage and his folly, his addiction to violence and his self-destructive but in many ways good political sense.

Shields Green said he would join Old Brown.

Sunday, October 16, 1859, was the day scheduled for Brown's Armageddon. By that Sunday, though, Brown had recruited only twenty-one men, including three of his sons and five blacks, but they managed to seize ten slaves, their owner, and several horses. Armed with their pikes as well as rifles and wearing long gray shawls, they then stormed the federal armory building. But rather than strike quickly and escape to the Virginia hills, Brown and his gang hovered nearby for thirty-six hours. He didn't have an exit strategy.

That was a tremendous blunder. Alerted of the attack, a local militia quickly cut off any escape routes, forcing Brown and his men, including two of his sons, to barricade themselves within a small firehouse in the armory yard. Lieutenant Colonel Robert E. Lee and Lieutenant J. E. B. "Jeb" Stuart rode into town with a company of one hundred marines, under a flag of truce, and Stuart delivered a note from Lee, which offered Brown a chance to surrender unconditionally. Two thousand onlookers—news of the raid had traveled fast—waited for the reply. The parley took a long time, according to Stuart, because Brown wanted free passage out of Harpers Ferry for himself and his men and without that—which he was not going to get—Brown refused to give up.

Waving his cap, Lieutenant Stuart ordered his squadron forward. They slammed the door of the firehouse with sledgehammers, and when the door didn't budge, the soldiers took a battering ram to it. One of Brown's raiders, having fled the armory, was shot, his dead body used for target practice by snipers encircling the area. Spectators cheered. Inside, Brown, who had been stabbed with a decorative dress sword, lay wounded on the ground. Stuart snatched Brown's bowie knife. Governor Henry Wise, who had arrived on the scene, leaned over the bloody man, who introduced himself with resonant dignity. "My name is John Brown," he said.

In all, seventeen people had died, including two of Brown's sons, two slaves, the slave owner, a marine, and three residents of Harpers Ferry. Brown and seven of his men were taken prisoner, though Jeb Stuart told his mother had he been in charge, his saber would have saved Virginia the cost of Brown's trial.

News of the raid shocked the country. "Some sort of insurrection, an armed gang getting possession of the United States Armory; railroad trains stopped, x + y hundred fugitive slaves under arms, government troops, marines, and other forces sent on," George Templeton Strong chronicled the rumors. "Seems to have been a fight this morning (and the rebellion quashed, of course), but the whole transaction is as yet most obscure, and our reports probably much exaggerated."

Prosecuted almost immediately in a Virginia court even though Brown had assaulted federal property, Brown was given a speedy trial. Governor Wise told the Virginia legislature that Brown had confessed that he had intended to arm slaves, who would then turn on the slaveholders—and that once word got out, he would be joined by whites and free blacks from every state in the union. He might have been deluded, but he was bold and he was sincere, and, like many Southerners, Governor Wise ungrudgingly pronounced Brown the gamest man he had ever met. Brown thanked Wise for the compliment. Perhaps had everything been different, Ralph Waldo Emerson wondered, men such as Governor Wise and Captain Brown would have been friends.

Of the conspirators, John Brown was tried first. The trial began on Wednesday, October 26, a year after Seward's speech. More than six hundred spectators jammed into the courthouse to watch the proceedings while they nibbled peanuts and tossed the shells on the floor. The prosecutor showed up drunk. He was replaced. Because of his injuries, Brown lay on his back on a cot. Yet the trial wasn't a farce. Brown refused to plead insanity, and the defense argued against the charge of treason on the grounds that "no man is guilty of treason unless he be a citizen of the state against which the treason so alleged has been committed," and Brown was a citizen of New York. The defense also argued that Brown had intended only to liberate slaves, not kill slave owners.

In forty-five minutes, the jury returned a guilty verdict. No one spoke after the verdict was read.

At his sentencing on November 2, Brown rose from his cot in the courtroom, and what he had to say transfixed the nation. "I am yet too young to understand that God is any respecter of persons. I believe that to have interfered as I have done, as I have always freely admitted I have done, in behalf of His despised poor, I did no wrong but right," he said. "Now, if it is deemed necessary that I should forfeit my life for the furtherance of the ends of justice, and mingle my blood further with the blood of millions in this slave country whose rights are disregarded by wicked, cruel and unjust enactments, I say, let it be done." Gritty to the end, he reminded the country that while it might readily dispose of him, "this question is still to be settled." He had not given up; the slaves were not free.

In New York, George Templeton Strong observed, "The supporters of any institution are apt to be staggered and startled when they find that any one man, wise or foolish, is so convicted of its wrong and injustices as to acquiesce in being hanged by way of protest against it."

Brown also refused to name the names of his coconspirators. Papers found in his possession pointed in the direction of the Secret Six, and the U.S. Senate was issuing warrants for several of them and their colleagues, including Frederick Douglass, who hadn't been involved in the least. Aware that he, as a black man, could be summarily hanged, Douglass left the country once again. His white compeers did the same, more or less. Franklin Sanborn took off for Canada, and Gerrit Smith committed himself to an insane asylum in Utica, New York, after methodically destroying all incriminating documents. Stearns and Howe also ran, and Howe went so far as to publish a public letter distancing himself from Brown. "Gerrit Smith's insanity—& your letter," Higginson chided Howe, "—are to me the all too sad results of the whole affair."

Yet Howe, along with Ralph Waldo Emerson and Higginson, had signed a circular soliciting funds for Brown's defense. Higginson, for his part, was proud of his involvement with Brown's raid, and his pride turned into sympathy. He traveled to the Adirondacks to escort Brown's wife to Boston, in case she wanted to go there, and he planned to accompany her all the way to Virginia, where he hoped she would urge her jailed husband to escape; sympathy had its calculated side, of course. The latter scheme was part of Higginson's dubious plot to rescue Brown and his raiders. Brown was unwilling to participate. He knew he was far more effective as a martyr than as a fugitive.

As a passionate Northern sympathizer and a woman, the writer Lydia Maria Child could not bear what had happened. By 1859, Child was well known not just in the world of letters but in the world of politics—and though she was beloved as a writer for children, she was also despised as an abolitionist, the one who had the audacity to write, as early as 1833, *An Appeal in Favor of That Class of Americans Called Africans*, which called for immediate, uncompensated emancipation of the slaves. *An Appeal* influenced a number of abolitionists, including Charles Sumner, Wendell Phillips, and Higginson himself. No doubt Brown had read it too. On its publication, the Boston Athenaeum, which had supplied the popular author with a free library card, rescinded her privileges.

Born in 1802, Child was prolific and daring and conventional, all at the same time, in her quiet but devastating way. She had written a novel about racial intermarriage (*Hobomok*) and about homemaking (*The Frugal Housewife*), both published in the 1820s. In the 1830s, she had compiled a *History of the Condition of Women*, having already edited a magazine for children, and in the 1840s, she had produced a weekly column about life in New York for the *National Anti-Slavery*, which she also edited for two years. That made perfect sense: the well-known phrenologist Lorenzo Fowler, after rubbing her skull, declared that the woman could not be satisfied with the world as it is.

Unhappily married to a man who had served in the Massachusetts legislature (and had supported John Quincy Adams), this contradictory and childless woman wrote often for or about children; she represented domestic virtues but left her husband to move to New York where she apparently fell in love with another man. While in New York, she visited Barnum's American Museum—and, not at all amused, she protested his use of Native Americans for cheap display, along with monkeys and flamingos. In the 1850s, she wrote a didactic novella, "The Kansas Emigrants," which Greeley serialized in the November 1856 *Tribune*—interrupting Charles Dickens's serial *Little Dorrit* to do so.

Having reconciled with David Child, she tucked them both into her elderly father's house, which she had inherited, in Wayland, Massachusetts, west of Boston and out of the fray, for the Childs had little money, little ability to travel, and they were aging. But one thing had never changed: Lydia Maria Child hated slavery. "If the monster had one head," she said, "assuredly I should be a Charlotte Corday." Perhaps for that reason, in the twentieth century and later, she would be remembered, if remembered at all, only for the Thanksgiving Day jingle "Over the river, and through the wood, / To Grandfather's house we go."

In 1859, with John Brown lying on his blood-soaked pallet in a Virginia jail, the fifty-seven-year-old Lydia Maria Child decided to contact Governor Wise and request permission to travel to Virginia to nurse him. It was an odd request by any standards—and it was of course a political one, which Wise immediately understood. Child did not mince words. Introducing herself as an "uncompromising abolitionist" who admired Brown, though she preferred peace to violence, she said she wanted simply to comfort him.

Governor Wise answered with pointed civility. "Virginia and Massachusetts are involved in no civil war," he said, "and the Constitution which unites them in confederacy guarantees to you the privileges and immunities of a citizen of the United Sates in the State of Virginia." But he knew who Mrs. Child was; the country knew who Mrs. Child was, and he held her responsible, in part, for what Brown had done: it was a "natural consequence," he said, "of your sympathy." Mrs. Child took umbrage. "Your constitutional obligation, for which you profess so much respect," she replied, "has never proved any protection to citizens of the Free States, who happened to have a black, brown, or yellow complexion; nor to any white citizen whom you even suspected of entertaining opinions opposite to your own."

This was a children's versifier who would not be trifled with. Because slaveholders had "recklessly sowed the wind in Kansas," Child continued her argument, "they reaped a whirlwind at Harper's Ferry." Child did not go to Virginia—Brown had replied that he'd rather she raise money for his family than tend to him—but instead entered a heated and public exchange of letters with Governor Wise and then with Senator James M. Mason's wife, Margaretta. Sparring with Governor Wise, she outlined the events of the past decade—the filibustering and fraud, as she called it, the pretense of "squatter sovereignty," which allowed slavery in the territories, the near murder of Charles Sumner. Then Mrs. Mason, enraged, sent her own letter to Child, lambasting her. Did Mrs. Child read her Bible? Wasn't she a hypocrite more concerned about slaves, who were well treated, than the workers up North? Child seemed to relish the argument. Abolitionists were not ignorant fanatics—not fanatics at all, she said—and then after listing the abuses of slavery, which included rape, torture, and murder, Child lectured Mrs. Mason. "In this enlightened age, all despotisms *ought* to come to an end by the agency of moral and rational minds. But if they resist such agencies, it is the order of Providence that they *must* come to an end by violence. History is full of such lessons."

That was the lesson of John Brown.

For in the North, as Child tartly noted, "after we have helped the mothers, *we do not sell the babies.*"

The letters were published the next year as a twenty-eight-page pamphlet, *The Correspondence between Lydia Maria Child and Governor Wise and Mrs. Mason, of Virginia.* It sold 300,000 copies, and made for as good a story as John Brown's.

ON DECEMBER 2, 1859, the morning of his execution, John Brown wore red carpet slippers, white socks, a black frock coat, and a black slouch hat. He pressed a note into the hand of the guard: "I John Brown am not quite *certain* that the crimes of this *guilty, land: will* never be purged *away*; but with Blood. I had *as I now think: vainly* flattered myself that without very much bloodshed; it might be done." He rode out to the gallows in an open wagon, and, seated on his own coffin, he looked out toward the field and observed, "This *is* a beautiful country. I never had the pleasure of seeing it before."

"JOHN BROWN MAY be a lunatic," commented *The Boston Post*, but if so "then one-fourth of the people of Massachusetts are madmen." Garrison's *Liberator*, which initially had distanced itself from Brown, now embraced him. "In firing his gun, he has merely told us what time of day it is. It is high noon, thank God!" And on the day of Brown's execution, the poet Henry Wadsworth Longfellow wrote in his diary, "This will be a great day in our history; the date of a new Revolution."

"I believe John Brown to be the representative man of this century, as Washington was of the last," said George Stearns. Ralph Waldo Emerson went even further. Brown's death, he supposedly said, "will make the gallows as glorious as the cross."

Many were able to defend Brown's position and his courage—even Governor Wise said he admired Brown's integrity—but they roundly condemned his violence. Courage and violence were two separate things. Yet it's hard not to suppose that some of the fascination with Brown and admiration for him implied a tacit acceptance of his violence, though many people refused to entertain or fathom or even hear of the violence in their own rhetoric. Nonetheless, when the church bells tolled on the day of Brown's execution, they did not toll "because the acts of Brown are generally approved, for they are not," explained Samuel Bowles, the editor of the powerful *Springfield Republican*. "It is because the nature and the spirit of the man are seen to be great and noble." Nathaniel Hawthorne's wife, the woman who had cringed when forced to dine with a black woman at Horace Mann's table, said she admired Brown. And she noted with pleasure that a clairvoyant had recently talked with the dead Brown, who had said he "condemned his past course saying that violence will never abolish slavery. The noble man is wiser now." Such contortions of logic were not unique.

But Hawthorne drily noted that "Nobody was ever more justly hanged . . . if only in requital of his preposterous miscalculation of possibilities." Hawthorne hit on an insight few contemporaries cared to see: Brown may have secretly wanted his raid to fail. True, he was more visionary than strategist, but friends such as Frederick Douglass had told him outright that the raid would fail, and Douglass's reasoning was as sound as Brown's was flawed. Brown had to have heard Douglass, but he had not listened. He had not wanted to listen. Instead, he had faced the court neither as a fanatic nor a madman but as a law abider who, by respecting the rule of law, was cultivating for the first time the wide audience he wanted. Thus, Brown's raid wasn't necessarily the preposterous tactical failure Hawthorne had observed, but in the long term Brown had foreseen a far more strategic victory.

To W. E. B. DuBois and several biographers, John Brown "sparked the Civil War and seeded civil rights." Brown did kindle in the South a shock and an anger that bordered on the irrational. "People of Virginia are still making themselves ridiculous by panic and bluster," George Templeton Strong commented. "Charlestown thrown into consternation by the mistake of a sentinel in taking a cow for an invading Abolitionist contemplating a rescue."

Not a few Southerners regarded the North's ability to separate Brown's action from his courage as specious and another instance of Northern arrogance. For on a rainy day in October, John Brown had demonstrated to many a Southerner what the upshot of Republicanism would be: invasion, insurrection, destruction. "This must open the eyes of the people of the South," noted Edmund Ruffin of Virginia, an ardent secessionist. Dressed in a long, eye-catching overcoat, Ruffin proudly stood next to the Virginia Military Institute's color guard during Brown's execution. Among the crowd were two other Virginians: one, a civilian, was John Wilkes Booth, and the other was Major Thomas J. Jackson (later known as the famous "Stonewall"), who taught at the Virginia Military Institute. Jackson was slightly shaken. "Before me stood a man," he said, "in the full vigor of health, who must in a few minutes be in eternity." He had hoped Brown would not be executed.

Unlike Jackson, Ruffin was so excited that afterward he managed to get hold of John Brown's pikes, which he distributed to various governors in the South. Those pikes, he declared, were the "abiding and impressive evidence of the fanatical hatred borne by the dominant Northern party to the institutions and the people of the Southern States."

Robert Toombs accused Republicans of being in moral collusion with Brown and declared all Black Republicans—a race-baiting name—to be "Brown" Republicans. Senator James Chesnut of South

Carolina blamed William Seward for Harpers Ferry. Seward may have said he repudiated John Brown, but Chesnut had gotten hold of a broadside that quoted Seward's Rochester speech about the irrepressible conflict and then said, "John Brown has only practiced what William H. Seward preaches."

Jefferson Davis was morose. Though he considered himself a moderate, he railed at his colleagues from the North. "You announce your determination to make war upon us; and in obedience to that declaration you have made war on us," he charged. "You have invaded us." Jefferson Davis also parsed every sentence of Seward's Rochester speech. Seward had pledged war, John Brown had declared it, and Brown and a thousand more Browns might well march into the South with pikes and spears and Sharpe's rifles should a Republican, any Republican, be elected president. "Thank God," he said, "there is no point left on which compromise can arise!"

"We are arming," Davis also said, "not against the Government. We are arming to put down rebellion against the Government."

(7)

THE IMPENDING CRISIS

There's a certain slant of light, late-winter afternoons. Heavy with the coming snow, the New England sky darkens at about four thirty. In the large mills of Lawrence, Massachusetts, the lamps are being lit because employees won't leave the premises for at least another hour. Outside, the streets are quiet. Inside, machinery is pounding, and the six-story brick Pemberton building actually rocks and sways while scutchers and spreaders and carders and huge looms turn cotton fiber into cambric, into denim, into flannel. Among the seven hundred or so workers, including machinists, seamstresses, and bobbin girls, many are likely now dreaming about what they'll do that evening when they return home.

One of those young women, Harriet Brackett, was leaning out of the window of the Duck Mill around a quarter to five on January 10, 1860. Matthew Ryan, a spinner, was at one of the third-floor windows in the Pemberton, a few yards to the east. To amuse her, he had made a mustache and beard out of cotton and put it on his face. And probably no one but the two of them would ever have known about his pantomime if the Pemberton Mill had not then tumbled to the ground in what was soon called the worst industrial disaster in U.S. history.

Gruesome news moves quickly, almost as quickly as the huge building's collapse. For in a matter of moments it was reported that the building had imploded, trapping most of its employees. Although the mill's agent and its treasurer had managed somehow to run out, one woman had tossed her bonnet and shawl from the tall fifth-floor window before jumping, Harriet watched in horror as Matthew clambered onto the windowsill and vaulted to his death.

As many as half the workers hurled themselves out of the building. Most of them were immigrants from Ireland and Scotland. They raced down stairwells if they could before the oak floors gave way, the walls collapsed, and the iron struts and massive machines fell inward and on top of them. More than three hundred workers lay trapped, dead, or dying. Seventy percent of them were women and girls.

About two thousand rescue workers, including volunteers from the high school, rushed to the Pemberton Mill, or what remained of it. Lugging ropes and picks, they lit huge bonfires so they might see through the tangled mess of machine, brick, and twisted metal. Fires were breaking out all over the place. The firefighters doused them with force pumps or carried whomever they could to safety: girls with missing arms, men with missing legs, women with faces mashed beyond recognition. Maurice Palmer, one of the foremen, managed to cut his own throat, assuming that a speedy death might spare him from knowing he was being roasted alive.

The mayor of Lawrence, meantime, had telegraphed the mayor in the nearby city of Lowell to ask for more firemen. The doctors had by then arrived, mostly to no avail. Freed from the rubble, workers were taken to the temporary hospital set up in City Hall, where part of the main room served as a makeshift morgue. At midnight, while rescue teams were still trying to put out the local fires and to pull women and men from the piles of debris, one man accidentally plunged his pick into a lantern, and a spark shot out, igniting the combustible piles of cotton and whooshing them into a wall of flame. Survivors screamed; one firefighter dropped dead; three young girls were later found incinerated, clutching one another. By daybreak, the place was a charred heap of black ash and bone.

Newspaper journalists reported by the hour, and magazines sent their reporters to the catastrophe. *Harper's Weekly* said the mill proprietors were "before God and man guilty of the deaths of some two hundred innocent creatures." Soon it was also claimed that the local residents, workers, and even engineers had long regarded the building, constructed in 1853, as poorly made. Presumably even before the machinery had been installed, the walls had begun to crack so badly that they had to be patched up with twenty-two tons of iron plates to prevent them from folding, which they did anyway.

"Of course, nobody will be hanged," George Templeton Strong noted glumly when he read of the disaster. "Somebody has murdered about two hundred people, many of them with hideous torture, in order to save money, but society has no avenging gibbet for the respectable millionaire and homicide." Long gone were the days of benevolent capitalism for which the textile factories of the Merrimack River Valley were known; Charles Dickens had heard so much about them he couldn't wait to see them, and after he had, during his American tour, he was so pleased that he suggested that comparing these Massachusetts factories with England's was like comparing "Good and Evil, the living light and deepest shadow."

Dickens had visited Lowell, the industrial city named for Francis Cabot Lowell, who had converted the family importing business into a lucrative manufacturer of textiles and created, along with Boston Associates (his holding company), a labor force of young, virtuous country women attracted to his eponymous city by high wages— more than they could earn as school teachers or unpaid domestic help but low enough to keep factory overhead down. These young women, girls frequently, would be kindly provided with wholesome lodging run by virtuous matrons in the long rows of brick boardinghouses not far from the mills.

Their wages (minus what they had to pay for the boardinghouse) were sent home to support their families or were used for their dowries; any money left over was theirs to spend as they saw fit. They were, in a way, independent. And nobody came to the mill, recalled Union general Benjamin F. Butler (whose mother ran a boarding-house there), "to become a resident operative as a life business." It was a temporary stop on the road to marriage. Or, in some few but significant cases, life in the mills led to a life in literature.

The farmers' daughters turned mill hands produced their own pe-riodical, *The Lowell Offering*, in which they wrote poetry, translated novels, and celebrated the nature they glimpsed from factory win-dows and remembered from home. The poet Lucy Larcom, formerly a *Lowell Offering* contributor, said, "The girls there were just such girls as are knocking at the doors of young women's colleges to-day." She had started working at the factory at the age of eleven.

Benevolent capitalism had seemed to succeed. No more, or not for long, if it ever really had. In the 1850s, costs rose and wages fell. The hours were long, the job hard.. If an employee took ill, she had to pay for the privilege of the company hospital. Soon fewer girls were coming to the mills. Life in the boardinghouse had changed. The girls who continued to work from dawn until dark were now packed together in overcrowded rooms, three in a bed; their private lives were constantly monitored. "They are bell'd from bed, bell'd to the mill, bell'd home, bell'd everywhere," sniped one observer. If they were dismissed without an honorable discharge, they could not be hired again in any factory.

These girls were soon replaced by the rising tide of immigrants who, unlike the country girls, could not return to a family farm. Mostly the immigrants were huddled together in wooden shanty towns on the edge of the city where their safety or virtue was of little concern to the overseers. And the number of factories continued to grow.

Swooping down on the Merrimack River Valley to build yet another industrial city was the manufacturer Abbott Lawrence. Yet despite the early success of the city of Lawrence, which doubled in population in the 1850s, and of the Essex Company, of which the

Pemberton Mill was a part, in the later 1850s, and especially after the Panic of 1857, unemployment skyrocketed, textile corporations went bankrupt, and the city lost a large chunk of its population. The Pemberton was then sold at auction to George Howe, an entrepreneur, and David Nevins, a banker, and with the price of cotton goods depressed at the time, they aimed to increase output by adding more heavy machinery: the Pemberton had more than 600 looms and some 30,000 spindles.

Yet the owners failed to notice that the upper floors of the structure simply could not support the extra weight and that the cast-iron pillars supporting the floor beams were of shoddy construction. Three years later, on January 10, the pillars snapped, said the *Boston Herald*, "like so many damnable sticks of sugar candy." When the columns crumbled, the upper two floors crashed, and in less than a minute the entire five-story building had toppled inward.

The night after the Pemberton fell to the ground, the New England Society for the Promotion of Manufacture and the Mechanic Arts deferentially postponed its annual dinner. The day after that, John Lowell, who had once owned the Pemberton, politely distanced himself from the disaster, declaring in a letter published in the *Boston Daily Advertiser* that he bore no responsibility for any of it. And in February the coroner's jury that had been instructed to investigate the reasons for the collapse eliminated natural causes, such as an earthquake, which everyone knew hadn't caused it anyway. A huge relief fund was immediately set up for Pemberton victims and their families.

The only person held accountable for the disaster was the architect Charles Henry Bigelow. A veteran of the Army Corps of Engineers, Bigelow was the former vice president of the New England Emigrant Aid Society, which had delivered antislavery settlers, along with Sharpe's rifles, into Kansas with the help of Abbott Lawrence's nephew Amos. But the merchants were closing ranks. Considered a rabid abolitionist by the proslavery press, Bigelow was a perfect scapegoat even if he had in fact been only partly responsible for not having inspected the pillars. George Howe and David Nevins were not held liable. As *Vanity Fair* proclaimed, there was "no one to blame" for a "Rotten old Factory, founded on sand."

The employees at the nearby Duck Mill briefly refused to go to work until their building was deemed safe, and Horace Greeley at the *New-York Tribune* called for more building inspections. Even Greeley's newspaper rival, James Gordon Bennett, called the textile industry soulless. But there was no legislation proposed, much less passed, that protected the safety of a worker. And why should there be? "Mankind has not yet learned," rationalized a writer for *Scientific American*, "that laws are not omnipotent."

In 1862, though no criminal charges against him had been filed, Charles Henry Bigelow died distraught. By then another Pemberton Mill, rebuilt by David Nevins, had already risen out of the ashes—and from the insurance payouts—of the first.

WHEN THE CORONER'S jury exonerated the owners of the Pemberton, the *New York Herald* called for Massachusetts to rise to the defense of its "white slaves." The Democratic press, especially in the South, excoriated the pious New England factory lords—the Lords of the Loom. To prevent workers from leaving the mill, they ritually padlocked the doors of the factory every morning, it was said. "That several hundred human beings have to be locked up in a great manufacturing establishment like the Pemberton Mills," sneered an Alabama writer, "is certainly the most convincing evidence of slavery—a slavery that we candidly believe a Southern negro would not submit to."

A Georgia writer wondered why the likes of the outspoken Lydia Maria Child did not raise her abolitionist voice either in protest of Pemberton or in human sympathy with its victims. There had probably been no "traitors taken red-handed in the act of inciting to civil and servile war among the victims of this appalling catastrophe. Perhaps not even a fragment [sic], intellectual, ideal Negro," the author sniped, referring to John Brown and Frederick Douglass. To him, Lydia Maria Child was a cold-blooded white racist. "Can she not for once forget her partialities and bear with the afflicted, whose only fault to her is their white complexion!"

In Congress, disgust over Pemberton crept into the battle being waged over the election of the Speaker of the House. With the Thirty-sixth Congress convening three days after John Brown's execution and about a month before the Pemberton disaster, the already irascible men of the House—101 Republicans, 109 Democrats, 26 Know-Nothings, and 1 lonely Whig—were edgy enough to wrangle for months over the Speaker's seat. Republicans were backing the thin, good-looking, tall Ohioan John Sherman (a brother of William Tecumseh Sherman), whom Southern congressmen regarded as neither conservative enough nor disinterested enough—which is to say he was a Republican. Far worse, along with sixty-seven other Republicans, Sherman had endorsed a shortened version of a highly controversial antislavery book, *The Impending Crisis of the South*.

Originally published in 1857, *The Impending Crisis* was a racist diatribe against slavery that argued that slavery was disastrous for the nonplanter, the non-slaveholding white men and women of the South. Dedicating the book to "my countrymen"—Hinton Helper, the author, was a native North Carolinian—and to "those of them who are non-slaveholders," Helper said slavery depleted natural resources, prevented free labor, impeded industrial growth, and advanced nothing more than illiteracy, poverty, and ignorance. Non-slaveholding Southern whites needed to overthrow the system that robbed them of prosperity and progress, which was their due.

After all, hadn't Abbott Lawrence come to Richmond with the "noble purpose" of erecting cotton mills and machine shops? asked Helper. "His mission was one of peace and promise," Helper explained; "others were to share the benefits of his laudable and concerted scheme; thousands of poor boys and girls in Virginia, instead of growing up in extreme poverty and ignorance, or of having to emigrate to the free States of the West, were to have avenues of profitable employment opened to them at home; thus they would be enabled to earn an honest and reputable living, to establish and sustain free schools, free libraries, free lectures, and free presses, to become useful and exemplary members of society, and to die fit candidates for heaven." What had happened? The South itself had sent Lawrence and his dream of an industrial utopia packing.

According to Helper, newspapers such as the *Richmond Enquirer* had destroyed the deal. "That negro-worshipping sheet, whose hireling policy, for the last four and twenty years, has been to support the worthless black slave and his tyrannical master at the expense of the free white laborer, wrote down the enterprise!" Helper fumed. Lawrence delicately apologized, saying he hadn't realized his plan would be "interfering with the beloved institutions of the South," or so Helper quoted him as saying. The "abused, insulted and disgusted" Lawrence then went home to New England, where, as Helper raged on, he constructed "the cities of Lowell and Lawrence, either of which, in all those elements of material and social prosperity that make up the greatness of States, is already far in advance of the most important of all the seedy and squalid niggervilles in the Old Dominion."

Abolitionists and Republicans alike praised Helper's denunciation of the South, of slavery, and of blacks—and its tribute to Northern capitalism. Republicans also regarded the book as an opportunity. By distributing a shortened version of *The Impending Crisis*, they hoped to tip the coming presidential election in 1860 to their side: "Testimony of a Southern man, born and reared under the influence of slavery," claimed a promotional circular, "will be more generally listened to and profoundly heeded, whether in the Slave or in the Free States, than an equally able and conclusive work written by a Northern man."

Democrats fought back, almost as if they had not read the book. Helper's volume was labeled a "John Brown text-book." "The Republican Party Abolitionized" ran a headline in the *New York Herald*. In early 1860, less than two weeks after Pemberton, Representative

Thomas C. Hindman of Arkansas said the Republican Party was synonymous with "sectionalism, with hostility to State rights, with disloyalty to the Constitution, with treason to the Government, and with civil war, bloodshed, murder, and rapine." His peevishness was typical.

And so Hilton Helper as well as the specter of John Brown entered the House chamber although, as the historian Allan Nevins has noted, Helper's book was about "as exciting as Euclid, and as fiery as a ledger." No matter. Like Harpers Ferry, *The Impending Crisis* helped rally Southern Democrats. Representative Hindman continued his speech: fanaticism blinded Republicans from seeing the very real wrongs on their own doorstep. Take the treatment of the Pemberton Mill operatives. "Judge between the slaveholders of the South," Hindman admonished, "who hold the negro in that subordination for which nature and nature's God intended him, and the false philanthropists of the North, who inflict, or consent to the infliction, on the white men and women of such intolerable outrages and grievances."

Hindman's racism notwithstanding, the Pemberton collapse had been preventable, and though most of the Lords of the Loom were pro-Southern or mildly conservative, some of them were pious, anti-slavery Republicans. Was the Free North, then, really so free? Wasn't its labor system a system of bondage, with the worker subjected to conditions far more horrible than that of the Southern slave, who was cared for, protected, even loved? ("What a glorious thing to man is slavery," the proslavery author George Fitzhugh had cried, "when want, misfortune, old age, debility and sickness overtake him.") What would happen to the Northern "free" worker when he or she could no longer work? So, like Seward, although from the opposite point of view, Hindman reminded Congress that the source of the conflict between North and South was the conflict between capital and labor.

Ralph Waldo Emerson said the Stars and Stripes was sewn with threads of cotton—cotton and complaisance held the Union together.

Though Thomas Hindman's argument was not original or unique, it was effective, especially coming from a man so well versed in politics. Born in Tennessee, raised in Mississippi, and from a politically minded family, Hindman was the son of Thomas, Sr., a prosperous slaveholder who once enjoyed a lucrative post as agent to the Cherokee nation. The younger Hindman, a diminutive and dapper man (five foot one), once derided as "sweet-smelling," was always ready to brawl. After the man who would be William Faulkner's great-grandfather stabbed Hindman's brother (albeit in self-defense), Hindman trailed this William Falkner (as the name was then spelled), hoping to kill him, but fortunately for both men, a friend intervened. And when the resolute Hindman wanted to marry a woman whose father, in protest, had dispatched her to a convent, Hindman simply scaled the convent wall.

None of that encumbered Hindman's political fortunes; likely his derring-do had helped him. Elected in 1853 to the Mississippi house as the protégé of John Quitman and Jefferson Davis, at the end of his term Hindman moved to Helena, Arkansas, a booming Mississippi River port and a better theater for his ambition. A diehard Democrat, an aggressive soldier during the Mexican War, and a virulent opponent of the Compromise of 1850, Hindman was also a ferocious opponent of the Know-Nothings and their xenophobia (to say nothing of their position on slavery). And he was enthralled by Quitman, who in 1855 had proposed yet again another filibustering expedition to Cuba which he wanted to staff, or at least finance, with gentlemen, not thugs. Ready to risk "reputation and life in the enterprise," as he declared with a flourish, Hindman rounded up a hundred men in Helena for the mission.

Hindman never boarded any of Quitman's ships, which were never launched in any case after Franklin Pierce shut the operation down. By that time, Hindman was already out of the picture. Brought to trial for a barroom brawl and a shooting, he had to forgo the filibuster. If he had joined up, he explained, he would be "a fugitive from justice." The distinction between manslaughter and barging his way into Cuba (both illegal acts) was lost on him.

The court found him innocent.

Borne on the tide of his eloquence—he was regarded as a brilliant speaker—and on his crusade against members of the Know-Nothing party, whom he considered Northerners, Hindman was elected to Congress from Arkansas in 1858. A secessionist, he loathed Hinton Helper, John Brown, and William Seward, whose "irrepressible conflict" speech in Rochester had been praised in *The Impending Crisis*. "Sewardism, Helperism, and Shermanism are identical," railed Hindman. "The black mantle of Republicanism covers them all."

That meant that John Sherman was not going to be elected Speaker of the House. Accused of endorsing Helper's book, Sherman disingenuously claimed not to remember. Just as lamely, he said he hadn't even read the book. After two months of wrangling during which time House members began arming themselves with revolvers and bowie knives—some congressmen said they would rather wade in blood than seat Representative Sherman—Sherman withdrew his name. Sales of *The Impending Crisis* soared. You could purchase the book and even receive, along with it, a picture of John Brown—though Brown would have despised Hinton's bigoted brand of abolition.

A compromise figure was elected Speaker by a narrow margin almost a month after Pemberton. He was New Jersey's freshman congressman but an old-time Whig, the sixty-three-year-old moderate Republican William Pennington, who had been a supporter of the Fugitive Slave Act.

THE MONTH OF MARCH was raw and cold in Lawrence, Massachusetts, but the lanky man from the West waiting at the depot didn't seem to mind. Like everyone else, Abraham Lincoln had heard about the Pemberton disaster, and during his four-hour layover may even have gone to see the mill's scorched ruin. But the main object of his trip was to deliver speeches in Concord and Manchester, New Hampshire, before returning to Exeter, where his son Robert was in school.

After his enormous success just a week earlier, on February 27, in the Great Hall of New York City's Cooper Institute (as Cooper Union was then called), Abraham Lincoln had been riding the rails to Providence, Rhode Island, and up to Massachusetts, for he was not one to squander an opportunity, and this was his chance to meet with New Englanders and capitalize on his spectacular triumph in New York. After all, 1,500 New Yorkers, including the Republican kingmakers in the East, had sat under 168 flickering crystal chandeliers and listened, rapt, to the ungainly Republican lawyer with the bristly hair speak for ninety minutes about politics, slavery, and the Republican mission.

He had not mentioned Pemberton. His aim was longer range— and presidential. Instead, he began his speech with a well-wrought repudiation of Stephen Douglas, which in this case, was a well-wrought repudiation of the notion of popular sovereignty. Douglas had just published a justification of it in *Harper's New Monthly Magazine*, and Lincoln had responded, even mimicking Douglas by describing popular sovereignty as the " 'gur-reat pur-rinciple' that 'if one man would enslave another, no third man should object.' "

Lincoln wasn't really joking, and his quip merely punctuated what was an adroit refutation of Douglas's and the Democrats' contention that the Constitution forbids the federal government to control (which is to say prohibit) slavery in the federal territories. "Our fathers, when they framed the government under which we now live, understood this question just as well, and even better, than we do now," Douglas had said, giving Lincoln his opening. With his own constructionist reading of the Constitution—and his unassailable logic—Lincoln demonstrated that the founding fathers, who well understood the issue of slavery, did *not* forbid the government to legislate it. Nor did they intend to foster its extension; rather they "left an irrefutable record of their conviction that slavery should be prohibited in the territories." Republicans were not the destructive extremists, outlaws, and reptiles (Lincoln's word) that the Southerners made them out to be. They were traditionalists.

After an unflappable rebuttal of the Democratic position without resorting to any notion of a higher law—that would have taken him beyond the limits of the Constitution—Lincoln boldly concluded: "I defy any man to show that any one of them [the founders who formed the government], in his whole life, declared that, in his understanding, any proper division of local from federal authority, or any part of the Constitution, forbade the Federal Government to control as to slavery the federal territories." [Loud applause.]

He then addressed himself to the "Southern people." He denied the charges that Republicans were sectional, radical, or incendiary. He said John Brown was no Republican. And, what was more, Lincoln pointed out, no Republican had been implicated in the Harpers Ferry attack; if Southerners insisted that Republicans were "guilty in the matter," then "you are inexcusable for not designating the man and proving the fact." Anything else was slander.

As to Hinton Helper's book, which Lincoln also mentioned, he wisely pointed out that "there is a judgment and a feeling against slavery in this nation, which cast at least a million and a half votes." One could not destroy that sentiment, or if one tried to destroy it— Lincoln had listened to the apocalyptic warnings of the fire-eaters— regardless of "the peaceful channel of the ballot-box," what would one gain? He knew: "You will break up the Union rather than submit to a denial of your Constitutional rights."

This was not bluster. This was Lincoln making perfectly clear to his listeners and those who could soon read his speech in the national newspapers that he knew the South had been threatening war. He called the bluff. "You will not abide the election of a Republican president! In that supposed event, you say, you will destroy the Union; and then, you say the great crime of having destroyed it will be upon us! [*Laughter.*] That is cool. [*Great laughter.*] A highway man holds a pistol to my ear, and mutters through his teeth, 'Stand and deliver, or I shall kill you, and then you will be a murderer!'"

Lincoln had not spoken of abolition. Nor would he belabor the notion of a divided house except insofar as he blamed Southern radicals for the division. Rather he was to be a man of the people—though far surpassing almost everyone in eloquence and logic—a champion of free labor who possessed the gift of humor. (Southerners such as Mary Chesnut said, "If this country can be joked and laughed out of its rights, he is the kind-hearted fellow to do it.") Yet his speech, though witty, was determined, unemotional, and moved incrementally and with oratorical skill into a stirring call to devotion and dedication, duty and defiance.

Concluding, Lincoln turned his attention—"a few words now"—to Republicans. For after defying the Democratic interpretation of the Constitution and denying with the same logic—and wit—the Southerners' characterization of the Republican Party, he reiterated the legal obligation to let slavery alone where it was "because that much is due to the necessity arising from its actual presence in the nation." Yet he also felt an obligation, the Republican obligation, to prevent slavery's spread into the territories, to prevent its overrunning the Free States, and to abide by the Constitution. "Never let us be slandered from our duty by false accusations against us, nor frightened from it by menaces of destruction to the Government nor of dungeons to ourselves. [*Applause.*] LET US HAVE FAITH THAT RIGHT MAKES MIGHT, AND IN THAT FAITH, LET US, TO THE END, DARE TO DO OUR DUTY AS WE UNDERSTAND IT."

"NO FORMER EFFORT in the line of speech-making had cost Lincoln so much time and thought," said Lincoln's law partner, William Herndon. No wonder.

Lincoln had initially been invited to New York to speak at Henry Ward Beecher's Plymouth Church in Brooklyn partly to diminish Seward's strength among eastern Republicans, for many of them felt Seward could not win a general election; or they supported candidates of their own, such as Salmon P. Chase of Ohio, another outspoken antislavery man, or even the more conservative Edward Bates of Missouri or Francis Preston Blair, Jr., of Maryland, a member of a powerful political family.

Lincoln doubtless knew all that, though he learned of the change of venue—from the church in Brooklyn to the Cooper Institute in Manhattan—only at the eleventh hour. He had settled into his room at the Astor House, near City Hall and New York's Park Row (where Greeley's *Tribune* was published) and diagonally across from the Barnum Museum. Those days, crowds were clustering around an exhibit Barnum called "the missing link." Building on the popularity of Charles Darwin's *Origin of Species*, Barnum had hired William Henry Johnson, a black man from New Jersey with an unusually small cranium (caused by a neurological disorder, microcephaly), and claimed to have "captured" this "creature" in Africa. Dressed in a fur suit, Johnson silently performed for Barnum—he was not allowed to talk—under the sign "WHAT IS IT?" The show was strategically placed near a wax statue of John Brown. One newspaper quipped that the person was "neither white man nor monkey, therefore Black Republican"—like Lincoln.

Appearances counted. Despite the change of its venue, Lincoln's speech had been heavily publicized, and Lincoln knew that the time had come, as John O'Sullivan once told Nathaniel Hawthorne, for him to be manufactured into a personage. So Lincoln went over to the studio of Mathew Brady. Brady too had learned that the public's appetite for images was insatiable. And since everyone craved the illusion of immortality, formerly conferred only on the aristocracy, he was profiting from the innovation that his brilliant assistant from Scotland, Alexander Gardner, had brought to the studio. Formerly a chemist, Gardner had introduced into the operation the *carte de visite*, a forerunner of the snapshot. These were made from the wet-plate collodion negatives Gardner had also brought to the business. Wildly successful because they were sturdier than the fragile daguerreotype, they were traded and exchanged among the hoi polloi, and households across America began stuffing albums with their own likenesses as well as those of the rich and the famous. The culture of celebrity—the cash-and-carry kind—was born.

"The sun is a faithful biographer, and no respecter of persons," the popular author Gail Hamilton had recently written. She was speaking of Brady's photographs. "He gives us men as he saw them, shining down on their faces at noonday." Hamilton was wrong. Full sunlight was no longer a requirement of photography, which was nothing if not artifice: to prevent the slightest movement that would spoil the picture, for instance, an iron clamp had to be locked into place to hold the sitter's head stock-still. The misery of the trapped sitter shows up on many an old portrait, including that of Abraham Lincoln.

On the day of the lecture, Lincoln sauntered into Brady's gallery. The maestro would typically usher his clients into a grand salon, an overstuffed pleasure-dome draped with velvet curtains and shrouded in gold paper where his subjects—whether poet, general, or gawky lawyer about to deliver an important speech—could feel, among the marble and bric-à-brac, insulated from the clang of the omnibus and the clamor of the dirty city.

Brady typically posed his subjects, iron clamp notwithstanding, among appropriate props to provide a desired effect. In the case of Lincoln, they included a stack of books and a movable pillar, suggesting firmness, tradition, and longevity. He then moved the camera back to accentuate Lincoln's height and, to hide his long neck, he pulled up Lincoln's collar.

Soon Lincoln's likeness appeared in *Harper's*, in *Frank Leslie's Illustrated Newspaper*, in popular magazines and journals, and in the campaign biographies soon to be celebrating Lincoln as a backwoods rail-splitter, sleeves rolled up. Currier & Ives brought out lithographic copies of the Brady image for home consumption, and even caricatures of Lincoln as a Republican "What Is It?" came from Brady's image. An intelligent friend of Lincoln's, looking at the proliferation of Lincolns, knew what had happened. That photograph guaranteed Lincoln's election, he said. A star was born.

(8)

A CLANK OF METAL

A clairvoyant told Tennessee senator Andrew Johnson that John Brown had sent her a message from Hell, where he now was: Brown said Johnson would be nominated for president. Old Brown didn't have his information quite right, but it didn't matter. Johnson would have been happy to settle for second place, as Stephen Douglas's running mate, for he supposed he and Douglas, as a team, could beat Lincoln, who was admittedly looking pretty strong these days. In May, Lincoln had nosed out Republican front runner William Seward along with Salmon Chase and Edward Bates when shrewd political operators descended on Chicago. In the huge, tentlike building dubbed the "Wigwam" (because the Republican "chiefs" met there), they nominated Lincoln on the third ballot. The wooden rafters shook with the sound of thundering applause.

The Democrats didn't choose Andrew Johnson. They didn't choose Stephen Douglas either, or at least not entirely. The matter was far more complicated, and the Democrats were far more divided than the Republicans had been. In April, at their convention in Charleston, South Carolina, the Democrats' Southern wing had put forward an "Alabama platform" authorizing a congressional slave code similar to the one Jefferson Davis had already introduced in Congress stipulating that slavery be protected in all territories. Infuriating the western states, the platform was a slap in the face to Douglas and popular sovereignty. Regardless, men such as Alabama's William L. Yancey would not compromise. Never one to forgo a fight and still outraged by Harpers Ferry, Yancey reminded Southern Democrats, "*Ours* is the property invaded; *ours* are the institutions which are at stake; *ours* is the peace which is to be destroyed; *ours* is the honor at stake." And when the convention began to tilt toward Douglas's more moderate platform, Yancey stalked out, "smiling like a bridegroom," as an observer noted. The Mississippi, Louisiana, South Carolina, Florida, and Texas delegations followed, along with part of the Delaware and Arkansas delegations. Georgia left too. The grand Democratic Party of Andrew Jackson was falling apart.

With Robert Toombs and Jefferson Davis quieting the hotheads, the convention was rescheduled. In June, a month after Lincoln's nomination, Democrats reconvened in Baltimore at the Front Street Theater. The second meeting didn't resolve a thing. There was an unfriendly debate about whether those who walked out of the Charleston convention should be seated and whether the minority would pledge to support a majority candidate. Then someone suggested that the slave trade be reopened, and soon the delegates from Virginia, North Carolina, and Tennessee, part of Maryland, California, Oregon, Kentucky, Missouri, and Arkansas bolted. So did Benjamin Butler of Massachusetts. "I will not sit in a convention where the African slave-trade—which is piracy by the laws of my country—is approvingly advocated." The rump convention nominated Stephen Douglas for president (by a vote of two-thirds of the delegates who stayed) on a popular sovereignty platform, which included a plank denouncing state legislatures as revolutionary if they refused to execute the Fugitive Slave Act and a plank in favor of the acquisition of Cuba. His running mate was the wealthy, moderate Herschel Johnson of Georgia.

Southern Democrats and Buchanan's followers—Buchanan despised Douglas as much as Douglas despised him—nominated Buchanan's vice president, John C. Breckinridge, to run for president, with Joseph Lane of Oregon as the vice presidential candidate. Perhaps those Southern radicals hoped that a three-way race would throw the election into the hands of the House of Representatives—or, if Lincoln won, they could keep battling for secession and perhaps achieve it. But the gnomelike, sickly Alexander Stephens, a Douglas supporter, despaired of his fellow Georgians, who seemed glad to sacrifice their party for an abstraction called the "full measure of Southern rights" and worked themselves into a lather over the territories, where the people were indifferent to slavery and the climate not conducive to it anyway. Stephens argued, without much success, that these radicals did not understand that Douglas was actually "safe on slavery" and that he believed that slavery was better off in the Union than out of it. Demoralized by Baltimore, Stephens confided to a friend that "selfishness and personal ambition had taken possession of all."

Retrospective analyses of the Charleston and Baltimore conventions are much too rational, for at those conventions, the delegates sweated and fulminated and worked each other up into a state of near frenzy. But Southern rights activists had not been bluffing. They truly did not want to compromise. They felt they had already compromised too much and that any more compromise was lily-livered submission to the North and, now, to Northern aggression. "Submission to the rule of a party who have openly declared themselves our enemies," declared a Southerner, "and that they intend to destroy our property and (what is worse that they intended to degrade us and our families to an equality with our slaves), submission I say, under such circumstances is a thought to be entertained not for a moment."

Yet compromisers had not entirely vanished, particularly among Border State Whigs. It was they who pulled together a Constitutional Union Party, one that represented the Constitution and "the Union as it is," which is to say the Union as it once might have been, without the slavery question dominating every discussion. An amalgam of Know-Nothings and former Whigs (including Amos Lawrence), the Constitutional Union Party nominated the colorless, grimacing former senator John Bell of Tennessee along with the prolix Cotton

Whig (that is, southerly inclined) Edward Everett of Massachusetts. As the historian Sean Wilentz has noted, there was something clubbish, vague, and antediluvian about this almost benighted party, nostalgically looking backward.

Democratic schisms and Constitutional Unionists boded well for Lincoln. "I think the chances were more than equal that we could have beaten the Democracy united," he said. "Divided, as it is, its chance appears indeed very slim."

IT WAS A grinding campaign. In New York and elsewhere, youths dressed in paramilitary costumes, with long capes and black squarish hats, carried torches on four-foot poles, singing songs and proclaiming their support of Lincoln while they marched through the streets. They were the members of the so-called Wide-Awakes, militant organizations of young men, as many as 70,000 from coast to coast, who supported Republican candidates and protected them after dark. Denounced by fire-eaters such as Louis Wigfall as a newfangled Praetorian Guard, these enthusiastic Republicans were tired of compromising with the South but willing to support the compromises Lincoln offered, which seemed to them not compromises at all. They weren't the only ones excited about Lincoln. Calling him the first workingman's candidate, the Prussian-born Carl Schurz, who had experienced firsthand the failure of the 1848 revolutions in Europe, energetically campaigned for Lincoln in the Midwest.

Stephen Douglas, who applied himself unstintingly, even obstinately, to whatever he chose to do, was also campaigning ceaselessly as if his decision to throw aside the reticence demanded from presidential candidates—the office was supposed to seek the man, not the other way around—released a new flood of venomous and self-destructive but indefatigable energy. Douglas called Lincoln a disunionist, a Black Republican, an amalgamationist, an insurrectionist, a crackpot, a monkey. Douglas was the Unionist (which he was) and the only one, he said, who could avert secession. He shouted until he was hoarse.

When Douglas realized that Lincoln might actually win, he realized what Republicans seemed not to acknowledge: the Union was in deep trouble. He hustled to the border states to campaign against secession and for one Union, indissoluble. As late as October and November, he was touring the Deep South to decry secession. While in Alabama, he and his wife suffered injuries when the upper deck of a steamboat collapsed in Montgomery, but though he had to hobble around on crutches, though he was exhausted, his voice was hoarse, and his health was not good, Douglas did not stop. Instead, he told increasingly irate audiences, some of whom pelted him with eggs, that a lawfully elected president, even a Lincoln, must lawfully resist secession. It was, as Allan Nevins wrote, his finest hour. And then, just seven months after the polls closed, the forty-eight-year-old Stephen Douglas was dead. The country had splintered, nothing was the same, the Little Giant had worn himself out.

Those seven months had been harrowing for everyone, not just Douglas. As election day approached, the Southern press, suspecting a Republican victory, issued threat after threat. "Whether there be secession, revolution, or what not, one thing is certain—*Lincoln can never be President of the Southern States*," thundered the *Weekly Montgomery Mail*. Said the *Lynchburg* [Virginia] *Republican*, "the moment the lightning flash shall convey the intelligence of the election of Lincoln, [we] will unfurl to the breeze the flag of Disunion." To a correspondent in Georgia, Lincoln's election would bring "an abolition party in the Southern states, who will distribute arms and strychnine with which to murder their masters. It will encourage abolition 'nigger' stealers to steal your property, and by repealing the fugitive slave law, leave you without the slightest redress." And a series of fires devastating large chunks of north Texas and downtown Dallas were immediately attributed to the abolitionists, who, it was said, had been recruiting black men. White vigilantes then murdered at least thirty and perhaps up to a hundred people, both black and white.

By promising a homestead act, a protective tariff, internal improvements, and even a railroad to the Pacific, Republicans were trying to appeal to westerners, to Pennsylvanians, and to antislavery men with a traditionalist bent, such as the poet James Russell Lowell. Formerly the editor of the recently established magazine *The Atlantic Monthly*, Lowell explained that Republicans were really "the only conservative party." True, for him, the signal issue of the day was slavery, but Republicans intended neither to overthrow the government nor disrupt extant institutions, as it had been alleged. Comforting fellow moderates who were jittery about Republicanism, he calmed them. "The administration of Mr. Lincoln will be conservative," he said, "because no government is ever intentionally otherwise, and because power never knowingly undermines the foundation on which it rests."

In November Lincoln won the presidency, but it was a victory without much of a mandate. He had received slightly less than 40 percent of the popular vote. And even though he received 180 out of the 183 electoral votes from the free states—Douglas had won three of New Jersey's seven—he couldn't touch the South, where he wasn't on the ballot in ten slave states. And because the Republicans won decisive congressional victories in the North, the South was fuming. The country was thus split sectionally—and tragically, as it would turn out. For Douglas had been the Union, or compromise, candidate after all: 58 percent of the popular vote had gone for Lincoln and Breckinridge combined, neither of whom represented, or so it was perceived, any compromise on slavery. (Douglas had won 29 percent of the popular vote and John Bell, of the Constitutional Union Party, 13 percent.)

Lincoln was a minority president.

Minutemen companies, clad in red shirts and dark pants, marched throughout the Southern states, volunteer soldiers placed blue cockades in their caps, and posses of white men scoured plantations to sniff out insurrections. Blacks were lynched, and suspected abolitionists were run out of town. "Passion is rash," warned Sam Houston, the governor of Texas. Robert Toombs, once a Unionist, said that the South must "strike, strike while is yet time."

"So we go," said Alexander Stephens bleakly. "Our destiny seems to be fixed."

THE SOUTHERN NOVELIST William Gilmore Simms gleefully wrote a friend, "Unionism is dead, and Conservative politicians dare not open their mouths."

Though Lincoln's election has been interpreted as driving the South headlong into secession, that is not the whole case. Before November, there were Southerners who considered the fire-eaters more menacing than any Republican. The *Nashville Banner and Whig* pointed out that while "gallant Northern Union men" had the "enemy" in their midst, "we, meanwhile, turn our attention to the sectional spirit which infests the Southern states, and which, under the lead of such restless spirits as Yancey, Keitt, Rhett, and Spratt, and their fellow disunionists threaten, equally with Republicans in the North, to prove a wedge to split the Union in twain."

There was the economy to consider; what would happen to trade in Northern markets should secession occur? Nor were all young Southern soldiers pleased by talk of war. "Believe me there will be no such issue as these extravagant fanatics prophesy," a young cadet at the Virginia Military Institute calmed his sister. "We consider it here as trifling talk." Yet the cadets continued to drill, and twenty-five hundred cartridges were distributed among them. Nonetheless, the anxious youth reassured both himself and his family when he insisted, "Believe me it will amount to nothing,"

When the secession convention convened in the elegant, commercial city of Charleston on December 17, the white population was certainly not of one mind. There were schisms among the various classes and interests: the slaveholding gentry, or planters, disagreed with the nonslaveholding yeoman farmers, whose interests differed from the common laborers. Dominated by planters, the South Carolina legislature did not therefore represent everyone since its seats went to the white population in proportion to taxes paid, and the planters were certainly going to protect their capital investment—slaves. These very divisions, in fact, had been the subject of Hinton Helper's *Impending Crisis*. Yet since the impending crisis was now, finally, impending—momentarily, it seemed—people formerly divided seemed to come together, at least in Charleston, where "the merchants & their clerks, the lawyers, the mechanics & all classes of business men," as one visitor reported, "after working all day for money to support their families, drill nearly half the night in order to defend them." South Carolina left the Union on December 20.

Southerners seemed not to consider that the federal government might try to force them back—or might declare war. Perhaps they were sanguine because the federal government had backed down in Utah, when Brigham Young and the Mormons had threatened to secede. And even without Utah, there seemed to be ample evidence that Republicans would let South Carolina go in peace, evidence that, as a matter of fact, came from the North. "The Union is unnatural, a scheme of man, not an ordinance of God," rationalized Nathaniel Hawthorne, "and as long as it continues, no American of either section will ever feel a genuine thrill of patriotism." Though he disagreed with Hawthorne, Horace Greeley also seemed to shrug. "If the Cotton States shall become satisfied that they can do better out of the Union than in it, we insist on letting them go," he wrote in his widely read *Tribune*. "We hope never to live in a republic whereof one section is pinned to the residue by bayonets."

Let South Carolina go; let the whole damned South go. There were disunionists even among the abolitionists. "If the Union can only be maintained by new concessions to the slaveholders; it can only be stuck together and held together by a new drain on the negro's blood," Frederick Douglass observed, "then will every right-minded man and woman in the land say, let the Union perish, and perish forever." Still, disunion would of necessity abandon the slaves to their Southern masters. As William Goodell, one of the founders of the Liberty Party, insisted, freeing slaves is "the religious and constitutional duty of the Union." But Goodell's was virtually a lone voice.

There were disunionists too among Northern Democrats. At a meeting of merchants and politicians on December 15 at Brooke's Hall in New York City, the suave New York lawyer Charles O'Conor called the institution of slavery just and benign; if a black man was sold from one master to another, he asked, "where is the ill in that?" O'Conor maintained that the South had done right in attempting to stanch the antislavery zealotry of the North; secession was as a matter of fact the right way for the South to preserve its (states') rights. "The only men who are dangerous to the Union," he said, "are the honest and conscientious men of the North, who have imbibed the dreadful error that it is their duty to crush out slavery in the Southern States." If anyone was at fault for a foundering country, that fault lay with the abolitionists. "Abolition Is Disunion," shouted the *Chicago Times*. "Strangle It."

Former president Franklin Pierce said that if more Southern states seceded from the Union, fighting would break out in the North, with Democrats lining up on the Southern side. "I have never believed that actual disruption of the Union can occur without blood," Pierce told his friend Jefferson Davis, "and if through the madness of northern abolitionists that dire calamity must come, the fighting will not be along Mason & Dixon's line merely. It will be within our own borders, in our own streets." While John O'Sullivan begged Pierce to get back into politics and work to rid the country of "this wicked & crazy Republicanism," the Democratic mayor of New York, Fernando Wood, said that in the event of a disunion crisis, New York would declare itself a free city and continue conducting business with both sides—which is to say that New York City would have to secede too. Judah Benjamin of Louisiana hoped that the lower South would follow South Carolina's lead; then the Middle States (and New York) would join the South, "and that New England will be left out to the Union to enjoy by herself her fanaticism and the blessings of such freedom as she prefers."

Yet not all Southerners were happy about the prospect of secession in South Carolina or elsewhere. Unionist newspapers, particularly in the upper South, wanted to give Lincoln a chance. "He is today, what he has always been," argued *Brownlow's Knoxville Whig*, "an OLD CLAY WHIG, differing in no respect—not even upon the subject of *Slavery*, from the Sage of Ashland." Herschel Johnson, who had run with Stephen Douglas, was willing to blame his own party, in part, for the crisis. "Hasty action is always unwise," he counseled. "It is superlative folly, when prompted by passion for which, our own discretion has created the existing occasion." And he added that though he didn't like Lincoln or the Republicans, Lincoln had been legitimately elected—and, besides, was nothing more than a Samson shorn of his locks; the man was powerless before Congress, Johnson pointed out, which was "friendly to the constitutional rights of the South."

Benjamin F. Perry of South Carolina was more direct; he thought his fellow citizens were going straight to the devil, "exulting over the destruction of the best and wisest form of government ever sacrificed by God to man," he wrote in his diary. "Fools & wicked fools they know what they do." Perry had been a Stephen Douglas supporter and a friend of Yancey but no longer spoke to the latter. And Judge James Petigru of South Carolina, the president of its Historical Society and also one of the state's few Unionists, surveyed the scene with dismay. "Whatever may be thought of the motives of the actors," he told Robert Winthrop of Massachusetts, "their folly will be as much the subject of wonder as of censure."

"South Carolina is too small for a republic," Petigru confided to another friend, "but too large for an insane asylum."

Many Southerners balked at the notion that South Carolina might actually be coerced back into the Union, and if it were to be so, they threatened retaliation. The *Arkansas State Gazette* warned, "South Carolina has gone; let her go; and wo [*sic*] to the administration, or the power, that attempts to force her back into the Union against her will! The Southern States may not be united now, but an attempt to coerce South Carolina will not only unite the Southern States, but the Southern people, as one man."

Yet South Carolina's secession radicalized many a conservative Northerner. "If these traitors succeed in dismembering the country, they will have a front place in the Historical Gallery of Celebrated Criminals," said George Templeton Strong. "Their suicidal frenzy tempts me to believe in Wendell Phillips and Captain John Brown." A temperate man who had never much liked abolitionists, Strong had voted for Lincoln. And he did not regret it now. Other stiff-spined Northern Republicans said that if the North armed itself and showed itself ready to fight, all would be well—or at least better than it was. In the *New-York Evening Post*, William Cullen Bryant could not have been clearer: "Peaceable Secession an Absurdity," he declared as early as six days after the election.

To these Republicans, secession was treason. Treason? Robert Toombs scoffed. John Brown's accomplices (whoever they might have been) were never punished, and citizens such as William Walker were labeled pirates; foreign nations were protected but the South left vulnerable, defenseless, desecrated. "We are worse off in the Union than if we were out of it," he cried. "Now you can come among us; raids may be made; you may put the incendiary's torch to our dwellings."

"Hence we are armed," he continued, "and hence we will stay so, until our rights are respected, and justice is done."

Abolitionists continued to be blamed for the crisis. In Boston, angry demonstrators pelted black men and women with stones after an abolitionist meeting in a Baptist church, and demonstrators chased the gadfly abolitionist Wendell Phillips after breaking up the annual Massachusetts Anti-Slavery Society meeting because, just days earlier, he had shouted, "All hail disunion." Afterward, Phillips packed a revolver whenever he walked out of his house.

"Events," wrote Herman Melville, "they make dreamers quail."

Melville called his poem "The Conflict of Convictions," which he concluded in a blast of capital letters:

YEA AND NAY—
EACH HATH HIS SAY;
BUT GOD HE KEEPS THE MIDDLE WAY.
NONE WAS BY
WHEN HE SPREAD THE SKY;
WISDOM IS VAIN, AND PROPHESY.

Many were confused, many played politics, many were indignant, everyone underestimated everyone else, few rose to the occasion, and no William Wilberforce had appeared, as Frederick Douglass had hoped, to free the slaves without bloodshed. "None can foresee the issues or how the coil of compromises is to be unraveled," noted Bronson Alcott. Henry Adams later remarked with disdain that "the southerners were beyond all imagination demented" and that the greatest danger was the government itself; Buchanan's lame-duck position would have been farcical if it hadn't been so tragic.

What *was* Buchanan's position? Old Buck had alienated westerners and northwesterners when he vetoed the Homestead Act, finally passed by Congress. Squelching land development in the West, he had revealed his partiality, once again, to the Southerners who feared the advent of more free states. He had also alienated many of his own supporters by allowing, if not condoning, rampant corruption in his administration, particularly in his cabinet, and by actually having offered bribes during the Kansas crisis in order to push forward the Lecompton constitution. He had alienated Republicans just for the sake of alienating them.

In his annual message to Congress that difficult December, Buchanan declared that no state had the right to secede. At the same time he also said that the federal government had no right to make war against seceding states, which is exactly what he had tried to do with the Mormons. He thus conciliated the South. He would let it secede. Newspapers such as *The Brooklyn Daily Eagle* took up Buchanan's position, such as it was: yes, secession was unlawful, true, but one could do little about it. (Later it was alleged that Buchanan's operational passivity provided the South with the time it needed to arm and to organize.)

As if that weren't enough, to appease the South further, Buchanan brought to Congress compromise measures in the form of constitutional amendments that protected slavery in the territories and also quashed the Northern personal liberty laws that had circumvented the Fugitive Slave Act. He also proposed the acquisition of Cuba so that the South would have itself a nice new slave state.

John Sherman would remark, "The Constitution provided against every probable vacancy in the office of President, but did not provide for utter imbecility."

By the time Congress opened its thirty-sixth session that December, the hysteria over Lincoln's election had risen to such a pitch that the House selected a Committee of Thirty-three (each state being represented) to effect some kind of compromise with the angry South. But the days of Henry Clay had long passed. Representatives from Florida and South Carolina refused to serve on the committee. Thomas Corwin, an energetic representative from Ohio, wrung his hands. "If the States are no more harmonious in their feelings and opinions than these thirty-three representative men, then, appalling as the idea is, we must dissolve, and a long and bloody war must follow," he cried. "I cannot comprehend the madness of the times. Southern men are theoretically crazy. Extreme Northern men are practical fools. The latter are really quite as mad as the former. Treason is in the air around us everywhere."

John J. Crittenden of Kentucky, the seventy-three-year-old Senate veteran, rose to the disastrous occasion just before Christmas. A friend of the great compromiser Henry Clay, Crittenden could take Clay's place, or so many hoped; he could be a savior. "The eyes of all good men in all sections are turned toward you," a minister in Maryland wrote the senator.

Mild-mannered, chivalrous, and generally well liked, though his sunken cheeks gave him the air of a stern schoolmaster, Crittenden wanted very much to preserve the Union—to save the country in which he fervently believed and which he'd faithfully served for forty years. With that in mind—and with an eloquence he rarely summoned—Crittenden proposed a parcel of constitutional amendments soon to be known as the Crittenden Compromise. The Missouri Compromise line would be extended at 36 degrees, 30 minutes latitude through the territories to the Pacific, which would protect slavery in the South and in any territories acquired south of the line. Congress would not be allowed to interfere with the interstate slave trade or to abolish slavery in the District of Columbia or to interdict slavery in slave states. The owners of escaped slaves would receive monetary compensation. Finally, Crittenden proposed that Congress never be able to abolish slavery or alter those amendments.

Visiting the United States at the time, the British novelist Anthony Trollope laughed humorlessly. "Mr. Crittenden's compromise was moonshine."

It was moonshine particularly to Republicans, who rightly understood that Crittenden's proposals effectively voided their platform. "If we surrender, it is the end of us," said Lincoln, the president-elect. Not only would Crittenden's proposal allow slavery into the territories, he said, but "a year will not pass, till we shall have to take Cuba as a condition upon which they [the South] will stay in the Union." As it happened, the compromise died in the hands of the Senate's Committee of Thirteen, which had been appointed to deal with the crisis. The committee, which included, along with Crittenden, William Seward, Stephen Douglas, Robert Toombs, Benjamin Wade, and Jefferson Davis, turned down the proposals. All five Republicans on the committee voted against Crittenden's so-called compromise, and the committee could agree on nothing.

Within six weeks of South Carolina's secession, the legislatures of Mississippi, Florida, Alabama, Georgia, and Louisiana passed ordinances of secession. Then Texas joined the exodus despite Governor

Sam Houston's warning that the South was plunging into anarchy: "Here is a constitutional party that intends to violate the Constitution because a man is constitutionally elected President," Houston protested. "If the people constitutionally elect a President, is the minority to resist him? Do they intend to carry that principle into their new Southern Confederacy? If they do, we can readily conceive how long it will last." Of all the seceding states, Texas was the only one that submitted the secession ordinance to popular vote. But it passed handily.

Andrew Johnson of Tennessee also opposed secession. His confidence in the Union unshaken, he firmly believed "in man's capability to govern himself. I will not give up this Government that is now called an experiment," he said in the Senate. "No: I intend to stand by it, and I entreat every man throughout the nation who is a patriot [to] . . . rally around the altar of our common country, and lay the Constitution upon it as our last libation, and swear by our God, and all that is sacred and holy, that the Constitution shall be saved, and the Union preserved."

"In the language of the departed Jackson," he stoutly declared, "let us exclaim that the Union, 'the Federal Union, it must be preserved.'"

Hailed to the skies as a reincarnation of Andrew Jackson, Johnson had crossed swords with a number of powerful Southern leaders over the Homestead Bill and now prudently threw in his lot with Unionists although he did believe what he was saying. Such are politics, a mixture of expedience and conviction. But this self-made son of a seamstress was the proslavery Unionist hero of a very short-lived hour; there was talk in the Tennessee legislature of removing him from the Senate, and in Memphis he was hung in effigy.

While Northerners dithered, according to Carl Schurz, the South grew stronger. "Action, action is the great secret of success, and if ever a time called for it, it is now," Schurz declared. "I do not understand the men who, when the decision of one of the vital questions of the age is within their grasp, stand there chicken-hearted and cast about for small contemptible expedients." These contemptible expedients were precisely the compromises that, as it happened, neither the North nor the South would accept; why they could not is another matter: pride to a degree—but mostly the reason was what the abolitionist Thomas Higginson rightly called "negrophobia." Southern radicals drew on their standard shibboleths: that Lincoln's election would inspire slave insurrections throughout the South; that Republicanism presaged a nation of black men and women with rights equal to those of the white population, social as well as legal; that Southern institutions would be denied the right to decide for themselves when and how to abolish slavery, if they should so desire. Fanatical, money-grubbing New Englanders would keep on leading them around by the nose.

Understandably, Southern secessionists also assumed that a political party committed to an antislavery platform would eventually want to abolish slavery everywhere. The very presence of such a platform, though it promised to protect slavery where it existed, was certainly implying that slavery was immoral. To maintain an immoral system was at best a contradiction, at worst an impossibility, and Southerners knew it. Their "peculiar institution" was lost—that is, in the "house divided" language of Lincoln, it was doomed to "ultimate extinction in all States, old as well as new, north as well as south." Said one weary observer, "It is this perpetual putting of each side in a false light toward the other which has brought us where we are."

So while men such as Seward edged toward a conciliatory Southern policy, more and more Southerners believed that the North, controlled by Republicans, could never truly compromise; they thus took no comfort in rhetoric about the protection of slavery where it was or about the vaunted inviolability of states' rights. And the Southerners were right: the Republicans (led by Lincoln) would not compromise over the extension of slavery. These same Southerners often failed to admit they too would not give an inch.

And their gospel of secession was not a new creed, not by any means. At least in South Carolina, it sprang from the sense of entitlement encapsulated in John C. Calhoun's nullification doctrine, espoused years earlier. Calhoun had asserted that a state had possessed the right to veto, or nullify, any federal law it found unconstitutional, which was what the South Carolina legislature had done in 1832 when it had deemed a federal tariff null and void. And the legislature had gone even further, saying that the federal government's failure to honor the state's action was grounds for secession. President Andrew Jackson had disagreed, claiming that under the Articles of Confederation, the nation had existed before the Constitution was ratified and that, in any case, the Constitution established a national government, not a series of independent, strutting states that could ignore the federal laws they had all made.

When South Carolina had lost that battle twenty-eight years before—no other state had supported its nullification lobby—it had nonetheless believed it had won the war. Secession came to be seen in South Carolina and then in the Deep South in general as a state's sovereign right. Alfred Iverson of Georgia put it this way: secession is "the right of revolution." He, among others, now reasoned that the 1860 presidential election elevated minority over majority rule. Secession was therefore a War of Independence against a brutal despot, the North. "I can't stand the idea of being domineered over by a set of Hypocritical scoundrels such as Sumner, Seward, Wilson, Hale, etc. etc.," he announced.

Though argued as a democratic right, secession was a slap to democratic government and of course to Stephen Douglas and the Douglas Democrats, for whom popular sovereignty was the consequence of democracy. Yet most secessionists saw themselves as protecting the Constitution, not tearing it apart; secession was their duty. "We are upholding the true doctrines of the Federal Constitution," cried Jefferson Davis. "We are conservative." For them the Constitution was a proslavery document and as such deserved protection. In fact, secessionists considered William Lloyd Garrison an unsuspecting ally, for when he called the Constitution a pact with the devil, he was saying what Southerners, especially Southern radicals, insisted all along: the

Constitution protected slavery. Snorted the clever Robert Toombs, Garrison was far more honest than that duplicitous, two-faced Black Republican, Abraham Lincoln.

But now, as it had been during the nullification crisis of 1832, the underlying issue was the North's increasing power. And that power endangered slavery. Secessionists worried that if slavery did not expand into the territories, the black population would stay where it was, bottled up and likely to explode. Fear motivated them. That is to say, racial anxiety was as pervasive as economic anxiety when it came to secession, though it was hard to separate the two, for they were threaded together with the rope that bound secessionists and many Southerners to their land, their way of life, their mint juleps, and their pride of race.

Lincoln's election was thus not so much the *cause* of secession as its excuse: institutional restraints (read: the federal government) had insulted Southerners, imperiled their way of life, undermined their moral structure, triggered their racial fears, and held them in thrall to Northern financiers who had forced planters to buy goods in a protected market. Even Hinton Helper, the voice of the yeoman, wanted the Southerner, especially the non-slaveholder, to walk tall or walk out. How could one resist? "On the 4th of March 1861, we are either slaves in the Union or freemen out of it," said a heated Georgian. "It's a revolution!" Judah Benjamin cried—a "prairie fire," unstoppable, unquenchable.

As if in reply, a disconsolate Alexander Stephens observed, "Revolutions are much easier started than controlled."

HAVING BEEN FOR years surrounded by Southern advisers such as Davis and Toombs, and with Southerners dominating his cabinet, Buchanan had supported secession by not opposing it. So when in late 1860 the Southern states began to seize federal property such as courthouses, post offices, customhouses, and forts, the dilatory Buchanan would be forced to take some action. Yet he did not reinforce

Forts Moultrie and Sumter, near the coast of South Carolina, with munitions and food, as General Winfield Scott had asked him to do. Lewis Cass, Buchanan's secretary of state, resigned in protest. To Cass the issue was plain: the government must defend federal property. Of course that was not so simple. Buchanan believed that reinforcing the forts implied military intervention, and if he intervened militarily, he would be stoking the secessionist fires.

In the meantime he was discredited by the discovery of corruption in his administration and, in particular, in the office of his secretary of war, John B. Floyd, a former governor of Virginia. A double-dealer who was either lazy or venal—no one ever knew which—but who definitely hated those Black Republicans, Floyd had been sending long-range artillery and thirty-two pounders (large cannon) to the South. In fact, Floyd had ordered Major Robert Anderson, a Kentucky-born Virginian, to Fort Moultrie, likely expecting that Anderson would do his bidding, which was to say do nothing—or, as Floyd put it, "to yield to necessity"—if Southerners tried to seize the fort.

Anderson was nervously awaiting reinforcements that never came.

The day after Christmas 1860, Major Anderson ordered his men to put on their knapsacks and paddle across the water from Fort Moultrie to Fort Sumter, the sturdier stronghold, where he could better protect his troops and defend the Stars and Stripes, if it should come to that. To Anderson, there was no choice; this move had to be made if he were to do his duty as he saw fit. South Carolinians were furious. Assuming that Buchanan had secretly told them, or at least had implied, that he wouldn't reinforce the forts or interfere with Charleston Harbor, Governor Pickens of South Carolina insisted that Anderson return to the weaker Fort Moultrie. Indeed, Buchanan too wanted to order Anderson to go back to Moultrie. Of course, that would leave Anderson and his men vulnerable to attack; in fact, it was a death warrant.

Fortunately for Major Anderson, though, several tough-minded Democrats had joined Buchanan's cabinet. Replacing Lewis Cass as secretary of state was a clear-eyed jurist, Attorney General Jeremiah

Black. Replacing John Floyd as secretary of war was the cantankerous but brilliant Edwin M. Stanton. And John Adams Dix had replaced Howell Cobb as secretary of the Treasury. Both Black and
Stanton were Unionists who knew that ordering Anderson back to
Moultrie—acceding to South Carolina's demands—was tantamount
to treason, if not out and out murder. And Dix declared that if anyone
tore down a U.S. flag, that traitor was to be shot on the spot.

Buchanan changed course. The federal government would defend
national property against possible attack and not remove its troops
from the harbor.

As expected, Southerners exploded in rage. When the unarmed
federal merchant ship *Star of the West*, loaded with provisions, tried
to reinforce Fort Sumter, Robert Toombs said he'd like to blow it
out of the water. The Yankees were invading. South Carolinian guns
opened fire on the *Star*, which, to keep the peace, steamed quietly out
of Charleston Harbor—and in so doing proved to angry Southerners
what they believed all along: under the pressure of iron, the North
would turn tail.

THOUGH PRESIDENT-ELECT LINCOLN was not cut from the same
cotton cloth as Buchanan, it's difficult to know what he was thinking
or planning to do as he bided his time before March, when he would
be inaugurated. An astute observer who met him during that troubled winter later noted that he seemed "crafty and sensible," which is
to say he would not show his hand.

Little word had come out of Springfield, where Lincoln waited,
other than the occasional announcement of names he was considering for his cabinet. Chief among them was that of William Seward,
the beak-nosed, stoop-shouldered, resilient politician whose dream
of occupying the White House had been thwarted by a prairie statesman. Lincoln shrewdly selected Seward to be his secretary of state.

Though devastated when he'd lost the Republican nomination,
Seward was an optimistic man and a professional who had campaigned

hard for the 1860 Republican ticket. (Hannibal Hamlin of Maine had
been Lincoln's running mate.) And during what seemed the inter-
minable four months between Lincoln's election and his inauguration, Seward, with supreme self-confidence, took on the mantle of
chief of state, or so thought young Henry Adams, who was serving as
his father's private secretary. Gimlet-eyed, Adams carefully observed
Seward and accorded him the respect later commentators denied him,
for to Adams, Seward was the great conciliator whose forbearance,
caution, and moderation may have saved the day, if it could be saved
at all—and without the loss of a single life. There was "no shake" in
Seward, said Adams; "he talks square up to the mark and beyond it."

With the crisis deepening and secessionist desperadoes (Carl
Schurz's term) trying to seduce Maryland and Virginia to join them,
Seward, along with Charles Francis Adams, Henry's father, drew up
another conciliatory plan: New Mexico could enter the Union, effectively as a slave state (albeit with very few slaves), which everyone
had assumed it would be anyway (under the terms of the Compromise of 1850). Northerners would go along because they knew that
slavery couldn't thrive there anyway, they reasoned, and Southerners
would get a slave state without troubling the North overmuch. It was
a plan, certainly, but one that again voided the Republican platform.
And it demonstrated how compromise had come to mean surrender
to the Southerners who were now overtly secessionist. Yet to Adams
and Seward, the South's rejection of the proposal demonstrated that it
was fire-eaters, not Republicans, who refused to negotiate. For what
Seward and Adams wanted above all was to mollify the border states
and the states of the upper South, neither of which had committed
itself to one side or another. And Seward wanted to believe that the
seceding states would come back to the Union, if coddled enough.

On Saturday, January 12—by then Mississippi, Florida, and Alabama had seceded—Seward dusted off the notion of compromise—
this, in spite of Lincoln's avowed insistence on hewing close to the
Republican platform, which is to say not extending slavery into the
territories. But Lincoln had been silent so far. Perhaps he would fold

after all or, as naysayers alleged, did not yet know what he wanted to do. In any case, in a speech before the Senate, Seward painstakingly outlined the dire effects of disunion on commerce, diplomatic relations, prestige, and peace. Insisting that the tried-and-true method of saving the Union—congressional compromise—would likely not work this time, Seward then reiterated that the Republicans (and he) wished only to defend the Constitution, not to threaten or abolish slavery where it already existed. Staying silent on higher laws, he hinted that he would happily repeal those personal liberty laws that circumvented the Fugitive Slave Act; and he readily admitted that he would uphold any law that prevented one state's invasion of another and thus indirectly addressed the fear sparked by John Brown's raid in Harpers Ferry.

Though he was aiming his proposals primarily at the border states and the Unionists of the upper South, to antislavery men, Seward's suggestions smacked of appeasement, as did, worse yet, his suggestion that when the situation calmed the country consider a constitutional amendment to forbid congressional interference with slavery forever. Perhaps as a sop to the South, he wanted to assure it that Republicans intended to protect slavery where it already existed. This had been Buchanan's idea as well as that of the New York political wire puller Thurlow Weed, who had over the years worked closely with Seward.

Seward concluded his speech with the benign benediction of a pie-eyed dreamer captivated by his own pie-eyed dream of a reconstructed America. "Soon, it will be seen that violence and sedition are only local and temporary," he said. "I feel sure that the hour has not come for this great nation to fall."

Tears welled up in the eyes of John Crittenden, but John Hale of New Hampshire fidgeted in his seat. Partially recovered from his beating by Preston Brooks, Charles Sumner glumly stroked his handsome head. Old Ben Wade twirled his large thumbs. Not long afterward, a Republican senator cried out, "God damn you, Seward, you've betrayed your principles and your party."

The abolitionist poet Whittier wondered if Seward was nothing more than an appeaser dressed in the dubious clothes of a compromiser. "If he yields the ground upon which the election was carried and consents to the further extension of slavery," Whittier remarked, "he will 'compromise' me as well as the country and himself." Similarly, Frederick Douglass thought Seward the typical enemy of slavery, willing to purchase peace at any price. Maybe so. Seward's wife, Frances, told him that he was sounding lamentably like the disgraced Daniel Webster. "Compromises based on the idea that the preservation of the Union is more important than the liberty of nearly 4,000,000 human beings," she said, "cannot be right."

Henry Wadsworth Longfellow thought so too. "With the human soul," he said, "there is no compromise."

THE COUNTRY WAS brutally, madly, perplexingly split.

Men in military uniform marched through Southern streets, and, as if they were headed for an unnamed battlefield, they lugged knapsacks and carried bayonets. Almost five hundred such men descended on Charleston. Near the military academy, the Citadel, artillery was being stockpiled, ready to be used immediately or transported where it was needed. In California, the *Sacramento Daily Union* lambasted Washington: "The Government, great overgrown giant as it is, must stand and let South Carolina cut off one arm, Alabama another, Mississippi slash away a leg, while Florida and Texas each gouge out an eye, and still the powerful giant must patiently endure the mutilation of his body."

Yet some in the cotton states thought that the North would peaceably acquiesce to secession after all. "Republicans are as much afraid of us as we are of them, and they are more impressed with the idea of our resources and our strength. And my opinion now is that if you can avoid a collision, assume towards old Lincoln an attitude of respectful determination," said a former Georgian congressman to Howell Cobb, "that we can so manage him as to get along till Congress meets, when they repeal all federal laws as far as they affect the seceding States."

Maybe the day could be saved; hope springs eternal. In February, the Virginia legislature sponsored a peace conference in Washington attended, as one might have guessed, by none of the cotton states. It dragged on for three weeks, went nowhere, accomplished nothing. And on the same day that the peace conference convened, the seceded cotton states met in Montgomery, Alabama, to organize their new nation, form a provisional government, and write a constitution. The delegates were efficient, dedicated, and inspired white supremacists, and when a band played "Dixie," Varina Davis, the wife of the Confederacy's provisional president, Jefferson Davis, dubbed the song the anthem of an independent South.

As William L. Yancey put it, "The hour and the man have met."

Tall and spare, colorless and rigid, his skin pulled tautly over his face, Jefferson Davis promised the South, "No compromise, no reconstruction, can now be entertained." And there was none. The provisional constitution, largely a copy of the U.S. Constitution, enacted such reforms as limiting the president to one six-year term. It also pledged itself to state sovereignty and guaranteed slavery in all new territories. And the Confederate Constitution did not spurn the word "slave" or "Negro," which it repeated over and over.

Accompanied by the provisional vice president, none other than the small-boned and unhappy Alexander Stephens, chosen in part as a counterweight, Davis rode forth with kingly pomp on inauguration day, Monday, February 18. Sitting in a barouche lined in yellow and white satin, decorated with silver, and pulled by six fine horses, Davis and the pasty Stephens were met with roars of approval from the crowd in front of the Alabama capitol. A brass band was playing, and militia companies decked out in blue trousers and red coats stood nearby. Besieged with flowers, Davis, wearing a plain gray suit, explained from the portico that the new Confederate nation "illustrates the American idea that governments rest upon the consent of the governed, and that it is the right of the people to alter or abolish them at will whenever they become destructive of the ends for which they were established."

As for slavery, it was the reluctant secessionist Alexander Stephens who emphatically made the case. The "corner-stone" of the Confederate States, he said, "rests upon the great truth, that the negro is not equal to the white man; that slavery—subordination to the superior race—is his natural and normal condition. [Applause.]" Speaking impromptu in Savannah, Georgia, a few weeks after the inauguration, he enthusiastically called the new Confederate government "the first, in the history of the world, based upon this great physical, philosophical, and moral truth." And, as he added, its constitution "has put at rest *forever*, all agitating questions relating to our peculiar institution—African slavery as it exists among us—the proper *status* of the negro in our form of civilization.

"This was the immediate cause of the late rupture and present revolution. Jefferson, in his forecast, had anticipated this as the 'rock upon which the old Union would split.' He was right. . . . The prevailing ideas entertained by him and by most of the leading statesmen of the time of the formation of the old constitution, were that the enslavement of the African was in violation of the laws of nature: that it was wrong in *principle*, socially, morally, and politically. It was an evil they knew not well how to deal with, but the general opinion of the men of that day was, that somehow or other, in the order of Providence, the institution would be evanescent and pass away."

To Stephens, however, those founding ideas were utterly wrong. "They rested upon the assumption of the equality of the races," he continued. "This was an error. It was a sandy foundation, and the idea of a government built upon it; when the 'storm came and the wind blew, it fell.' "

Stephens was reiterating the standard Southern rationale for slavery, as he'd done when he'd retired from Congress two years earlier: the Bible sanctioned slavery. "There is a hierarchy among human beings which is based on natural differences," he insisted, "and these differences have been ordained by God."

But Stephens had skipped a step in his argument. Even if you granted him his poor premise—the superiority of one race over another—you still could not justify the owning of human beings.

For, unlike Lincoln, with whom he had recently corresponded, Stephens did not bother to distinguish between slavery and race. To Stephens, they had become the same thing.

Lincoln had replied to Stephens, whom he otherwise admired, as directly as he'd answered Douglas. "You think slavery is *right*, and ought to be extended," Lincoln wrote in private, "while we think it is *wrong*, and ought to be abolished. That, I suppose, is the rub."

Whatever the rub, voters in North Carolina and Tennessee chose not to assemble secession conventions, and in Virginia, Arkansas, and Missouri, the voters sent Unionists to their respective conventions. By April, those states decided not to secede. And then they had to deal with Lincoln.

LINCOLN WAS NOT a sanctimonious Boston Brahmin protecting his factories or looking to turn the other cheek; nor was he a dispirited doughface like Buchanan, paralyzed by the situation he had inadvertently helped to create. Nor was he Stephen Douglas, who was fighting hard to save a Union in which he fervently believed—and to destroy the Buchanan minions who had destroyed him. No, Lincoln, with his fine-tuned political instincts, came from a part of the country where standing up to bullies was de rigueur. He also managed to temper anger with eloquence, outrage with magnanimity, and politics with principle. And he'd been legitimately elected.

"We have just carried an election on principles fairly stated to the people," Lincoln said. "Now we are told in advance, the government shall be broken up, unless we surrender to those we have beaten, before we take the offices. In this they are either attempting to play upon us, or they are in dead earnest. Either way, if we surrender, it is the end of us, and of the government."

If since November Lincoln seemed to fiddle while fire-eaters burned the Union, slaveholding state after slaveholding state leaving it, the president-elect had actually not been idle, for he would soon appoint a cabinet that included not only William Seward but also other Republicans, strange bedfellows who, like Seward, had sought the presidency: Edward Bates of Missouri for attorney general; the ex–Free Soiler Salmon P. Chase for Treasury, and Pennsylvania's allegedly crooked Simon Cameron, a controversial choice, to head the War Department. He also tapped Gideon Welles of Connecticut as secretary of the navy, Caleb B. Smith for Interior, and, as post-master general, Montgomery Blair, the scion of the well-connected and somewhat unpopular political family from the border state of Maryland. Charles Francis Adams called the group a "motley mix-ture, consisting of one statesman, one politician, two jobbers, one intriguer, and two respectable old gentlemen."

Lincoln had also been composing with great care an inaugural address that he ran by a number of men, such as Stephen Douglas, Carl Schurz, and the more pacific and bombastic Seward, plus his adviser and confidant from Illinois, Orville Browning. For Lincoln was confronting a dismal situation. During his twelve-day trip from Springfield to Washington, he had been assailed by reports of assas-sination attempts and, as Whitman put it, men with knives and pistols in hip or breast pocket, ready to fight when the riot started.

Though Seward suggested Lincoln revise the inaugural speech here and there, the result was utterly Lincoln's own: precise, exact, impas-sioned, and steeled with tough-minded phrases that clearly addressed the salient issues. His command of the crisis brooked no dillydallying, no hesitation, no equivocation. So he began mildly, reiterating that he had "no purpose, directly or indirectly, to interfere with the institu-tion of slavery in the States where it exists. I believe I have no lawful right to do so, and I have no inclination to do so." He supported the Fugitive Slave Act and all laws, as he said, "which stand unrepealed."

After offering these assurances, Lincoln cleaved to the Constitution—and, by so doing, implicitly discarded any suggestion that he adhered to any other higher law. Rather, his legal task was to support what he called "the fundamental law of all national governments," which was their perpetuity. "No government proper," he said with bite, "ever had a provision in its organic law for its own termination." The Union's

Constitution, in other words, did not provide an instrument of its own destruction, no matter what secessionists wanted to believe.

He also pointed out that the Union predated the Constitution; that, in fact, the Constitution had been established "to form a more perfect union." The destruction of one part of the Constitution rendered the Union less perfect. "It follows from these views that no State, upon its own mere motion, can lawfully get out of the Union." Make no mistake, he seemed to be saying, I am here to enforce the law and to safeguard the Union.

Further, Lincoln argued later in the speech in a less legalistic but no less ingenious way that the "central idea of secession," as he put it, is anarchy. "If a minority . . . will secede rather than acquiesce [in majority rule], they make a precedent which, in turn, will divide and ruin them; for a minority of their own will secede from them, whenever a majority refuses to be controlled by such minority. For instance, why may not any portion of a new confederacy, a year or two hence, arbitrarily secede again, precisely as portions of the present Union now claim to secede from it." The self-devouring logic of secession, as he had said before, contains its own destruction.

To maintain the Union, however, there need be no bloodshed—unless, he added, "it be forced upon the national authority." He was talking about the forts, particularly Moultrie and Sumter. Promising no invasion of the South—"the government will not assail you"—he said that the mails would continue. As to matters more grave than the delivery of letters, Lincoln reiterated what he'd said to Alexander Stephens. "One section of our country believes slavery is *right*, and ought to be extended, while the other believes it is *wrong*, and ought not to be extended." This was the heart of the matter, this had caused a separation that outran geography—and this separation was unlike that of a husband and wife who divorce and move far away. The homespun analogy made the point.

He also suggested considering lawful constitutional amendments—that is, via "the modes prescribed in the instrument itself." In the meantime, he asked for calm, time, deliberation, and reflection.

He delivered the speech on March 4, 1861. The windy, chilly, overcast morning visibly brightened at noontime when over twenty-five thousand, perhaps thirty thousand, men and women thronged the Capitol. But the event was as martial as it was celebratory. "It seemed more like escorting a prisoner to his doom than a President to his inauguration," said an onlooker.

Uniformed cavalry and armed regiments roamed the streets. Sharpshooters took aim from the tops of buildings in case of trouble. "I never expected to experience such a sense of mortification and shame in my own country as I felt to-day," said another spectator, "in entering the Capitol through hedges of marines armed to the teeth."

Lincoln seemed nervous. Recently, he'd grown a beard. Whiskers seemed dignified, or at least they helped cover his long neck. He wore a new cashmere suit, but the silk stovepipe hat—by now his signature—made him appear even taller and bonier. He clutched a gold-tipped ebony cane. And he sat uncomfortably in the four-horse carriage along with the tired, discredited James Buchanan. This was part of the ritual parade. What was different, though, was the huge float drawn by six white horses and decorated with a large gilt eagle. On top of it rode thirty-four young women representing each of the states.

When Lincoln unwound his long legs and stood up to speak, he could not find room for his silk hat on the rickety table in front of him. Stephen Douglas leaned forward and, with a smile, grabbed the hat, which he held in his lap all through Lincoln's speech, almost as if he were anticipating Lincoln's closing remark, "We are not enemies, but friends."

"We must not be enemies," Lincoln concluded. "Though passion may have strained, it must not break our bonds of affection. The mystic chords of memory, stretching from every battle-field, and patriot grave, to every living heart and hearthstone, all over this broad land, will yet swell the chorus of the Union, when again touched, as surely they will be, by the better angels of our nature."

Shared pasts cannot be forgotten. A family united by blood and kinship should not be torn asunder.

. . . .

ON THE DAY that Lincoln delivered his inaugural address, the gun manufacturer Samuel Colt sent Howell Cobb's wife a gift in a box shaped to look like a book. On the back of the box was an inscription: "Colt on the Constitution, Higher Law and Irrepressible Conflict, dedicated by the Author to Mrs. Howell Cobb."

Inside the box was a pistol case; inside that, a finely engraved, ivory-handled revolver.

The din in the country was such that no one could listen to Lincoln without hearing what they already believed. The *Charleston Mercury* said that Lincoln did not "grasp the circumstances of the momentous emergency," and Frederick Douglass said the inaugural was a "double-tongued document, capable of two constructions." Parsed by politicians and partisans alike, North and South, Republican and Democrat, Unionist and secessionist and everyone in between, the speech seemed to have something for everyone; it was a bit of a cipher, as was Lincoln.

The speech does show, though, that Lincoln knew what he was facing. His so-called indecisiveness or reticence during the previous months had been a strategic exercise in the noncommittal. "I claim not to have controlled events," he shrewdly noted three years later, "but confess plainly that events have controlled me." Lincoln possessed the master politician's knack for manipulating events while pretending to be mastered by them.

Though Lincoln could not have anticipated with any certainty the future course of these events, he did want to control them, yet he was also ready for the worst, should it come, and even should he help it come.

From his perch in New York, then, perhaps George Templeton Strong came closest to assessing the inaugural address, and Lincoln, correctly: "I think there's a clank of metal in it."

PART TWO
{ 1861—1865 }

(9)

On to Richmond

War came. Yet somehow those two words, accurate though they are, make the war seem inevitable: what came, had to have come. Perhaps, but perhaps not; for even with hindsight, it's hard to say that this or that would or could have stopped the war.

In the years prior to 1861, however, a certain sense of inevitability dominated the newspapers, diaries, letters, and broadsides; war seemed a foregone conclusion, almost a promise. Clearly, there were those who wanted it. And clearly there were those who failed to imagine it. And since the threatened showdown between South and North had not materialized, not after years of acrimony, why not continue acrimonious, each side boosting the volume, each side letting off steam even if that meant standing by while speakers were mobbed or lynched and if now and then some troublesome, know-it-all senator was caned? Where was the incentive to budge, to question one's own righteousness, to create the grounds on which a compromise might occur, if indeed it should? "We learned once for all that compromise makes a good umbrella but a poor roof," reflected James Russell Lowell, "that it is a temporary expedient, often wise in party politics, almost sure to be unwise in statesmanship." Compromise had become an anathema to people straddling one fence or another, whether Unionist or antislavery or just plain sick and tired of a problem that did not seem to go away and that admitted of no easy solution.

If conservative Republicans such as Lowell were willing to abandon compromise or the language of compromise and yet dismiss secessionists as mad, they were not heeding the rumble of hatred, fueled by anxiety, that lay beneath years of bluster. "Events are crowding in upon us in thick succession," warned Senator John Hale. "It does not become any of us, with rash and presumptuous courage or temerity, to shut our eyes to what is before us." What was before the country was desperation, fear, and fury; secessionists suspected their way of life was doomed: doomed economically, because their great prosperity depended not just on slavery but on an agrarian economy that needed expansion, particularly into the Caribbean; doomed by their devotion to a single crop; doomed morally. Despite the enduring racism in the North, in the South, slavery was a "moral anachronism," noted the historian Kenneth Stampp, who argued that the Confederacy unconsciously willed its own collapse. Defeat would rid the South of a moral burden too heavy, too out of step, too repulsive to shoulder any longer.

That did not cause secession or explain it. President Abraham Lincoln and the Republicans spelled the beginning of the end of slavery, and the South knew it. Without expansion, the slaveholding states would be hemmed in by the free states. Over time, they would lose the political numbers in Washington needed to block any constitutional amendment forbidding slavery. Such an amendment would in all likelihood appear sooner rather than later. And since slavery had been the prized cornerstone (to use Alexander Stephens's word) of Southern society and economics, as Stephens had made amply clear, the South would fight to the death, if need be, to protect it.

Both sides underrated their opponents, each side misread the other—and themselves—and both sides failed to imagine that mutual mistrust could bring on massive slaughter. That failure of imagination was not inevitable by any means. And its consequences were terrible. "War begins where reason ends," Frederick Douglass later said.

THE WAR: MERELY a day after his inauguration Lincoln had received word from Major Robert Anderson at Fort Sumter that he desperately needed supplies. What to do? Evacuate Sumter? That would confer a kind of legitimacy on the Confederacy, which Lincoln would not permit. Force South Carolina's hand by reinforcing Sumter and inevitably trigger a hostile confrontation? That might provoke states of the upper South, such as Virginia, to secede. Opposing the conciliation urged by General Winfield Scott and Secretary Seward, Postmaster General Montgomery Blair was adamant about not surrendering Sumter to the Confederacy, and Lincoln carefully listened to the advice of his Treasury secretary, Salmon Chase, who argued that if the troops, stationed in a federal fort, needed sustenance of any sort, then the administration must provide for them, even if the consequence of so doing was military resistance.

By that time, Fort Sumter was a name familiar to newspaper readers—or to the spectators at Barnum's Museum, who could see, for twenty-five cents, a dramatic performance of "Union Drama, Anderson and Patriots at Sumter in '61." Yet it seemed that few in the North expected a confrontation: Sumter would be evacuated, and Lincoln would cave in to the Confederacy, which had unfurled its new flag in Charleston Harbor.

Still, that Confederate flag was a symbol, one that must be considered treasonous—and so too was Sumter a symbol, though in this case a symbol of the federal government and its strength. Lincoln therefore decided to provision the fort. He would send only food, not soldiers or guns.

He notified Governor Francis Pickens of South Carolina of his plan to ship supplies to Sumter, and though he said the mission would be peaceful, Jefferson Davis didn't believe it. Lincoln was baiting the Confederacy into firing first—and firing on a couple of tugboats, no less, dispatched simply to feed a garrison of very hungry men. "They mean to compel us into a political servitude we disown and spurn," Davis cried.

José Gonzales, the Cuban émigré who had briefly stood behind Narciso Lopéz, joined his old friend the dashing Creole general Pierre

Gustave Toutant Beauregard in Charleston. Delivering an ultimatum to Major Anderson, Beauregard had been ordered to fire on Sumter if Major Anderson did not surrender it. Anderson said that unless he received supplies or instructions, he'd evacuate the fort, but since the Confederates knew that provisions were on their way, at three thirty in the morning Beauregard had to notify Anderson that should he not surrender, then he, General Beauregard, would open fire, which he did, exactly an hour later, at four thirty on April 12.

Fort Sumter surrendered on April 14. Lincoln pressed 75,000 state militia into service for three months. At hastily called town meetings, selectmen were authorized to borrow thousands of dollars for uniforms or to care for the families of needy volunteers; on college campuses in the North, Southern students packed their bags and once back home enlisted in the Confederate army; North and South, women began to sew and collect supplies for the soldiers. "I shall have no winter this year—on account of the soldiers—," Emily Dickinson slyly wrote. "Since I cannot weave Blankets, or Boots—I thought it best to omit the season." Young boys drilled on town squares. Whitman noted, "Squads gather everywhere by common consent, and arm / the new recruits, even boys—the old men show them how to wear their accoutrements—they buckle the straps carefully; / Outdoors arming—indoors arming—." Patriotic flags decorated the roofs of homes and offices in every town and hamlet in the North. The firing on Fort Sumter had infuriated the North and united it as nothing else had. Meantime, five ex-presidents—James Buchanan, Franklin Pierce, Millard Fillmore, John Tyler, and Martin Van Buren—met in Philadelphia to try to settle hostilities. As the *New York Herald* caustically noted, from that "fossil court of arbitration, we need hardly say, nothing is to be expected."

The next month, Lincoln called for 42,000 three-year volunteers and 18,000 sailors, and Congress, which approved the actions Lincoln had already taken, called for a million three-year volunteers. Though Delaware, Kentucky, Maryland, and Missouri had not joined the Confederacy (much to Lincoln's relief), right after Sumter,

Virginia, North Carolina, Tennessee, and Arkansas did. The issues were clear: honor, independence, and the refusal of what was called "subjugation." "Our cause is just and holy," Jefferson Davis declared to his Congress. "We protest solemnly in the face of mankind that we desire peace at any sacrifice save that of honor and independence; we seek no conquest, no aggrandizement, no concession of any kind from the States with which we were lately confederated; all we ask is to be let alone; that those who never held power over us shall not now attempt subjugation by arms."

War had come.

Davis moved the capital of the Confederacy to Richmond, which was closer to Washington than Montgomery. Richmond was a manufacturing center, and its Tredegar Iron Works produced locomotives, projectiles, and cannon. And Thomas Jefferson had designed the lovely and luminously white state capitol.

"On to Washington," cried the *Richmond Examiner* in April. "On to Richmond," answered the masthead of the *New-York Tribune* in June.

ON JULY 20, 1861, readers of Northern newspapers believed the North had just won a grand battle fought at Bull Run, near Manassas Junction, twenty-six miles southwest of Washington. "Great Battle: Brilliant Union Victory," blared the *New York Herald*—until, that is, journalists on the field during the next few days recounted for readers the ignominious and headlong rout: Federal troops stampeding along roads clogged with abandoned wagons, riderless horses galloping past wounded men, wounded men begging for help and ignored, mostly, by panic-stricken soldiers running for their lives. Soldiers tossed away their picks and shovels, knapsacks, blankets, cooking tins, bayonets, muskets, even belts, all to lighten their load as they ran as fast as they could. "The regular cavalry, I record it to their shame," wrote one correspondent, "joined in the mêlée, adding to its terrors, for they rode down footmen without mercy."

Four days earlier the Federal army had marched toward the

Confederates, entrenched beyond the town of Centreville, just past Bull Run Creek. Fighting them at Blackburn's Ford, the Confederates had initially repulsed the attack. By Sunday the twenty-first, the tide had turned. The Federals (as the Union forces were also called) were driving back Confederate forces. They were going to win, no doubt about it. So what had happened? Confederate reinforcements arrived, and their counterattack not only broke up the Federal defense but also turned its retreat into a stampede. Pausing near a stream, one reporter watched in disbelief as soldiers scurried past him. "Ayer's battery dashed down the turnpike," he wrote. "A baggage wagon was hurled into the ditch in a twinkling. A hack from Washington, which had brought out a party of congressmen, was splintered to kindling. Drivers cut their horses loose and fled in precipitate haste. Instinct is quick to act." The intrepid Ben Wade, a senator from Ohio, tried halting the retreat by blocking the road with his carriage and waving his rifle at the fleeing men.

A rout, pure and simple, had taken place, the morale of the army shattered, the ranks broken, "the dust, the grime and smoke, in layers, sweated in, follow'd by other layers again sweated in," recounted Walt Whitman, "absorb'd by those excited souls—their clothes all saturated with the clay-powder filling the air—stirr'd up everywhere on the dry roads and trodden fields by the regiments, swarming wagons, artillery, &c.—all the men with this coating of murk and sweat and rain, now recoiling back, pouring over the Long Bridge—a horrible march of twenty miles, returning to Washington baffled, humiliated, panic-struck."

The many eyewitness reports together told a story of shocked disbelief. Twenty-seven-year-old Edmund Clarence Stedman had caught the attention of fellow Northerners when he celebrated John Brown as brave and godly, if a bit crazy, in a poem that "rang like a reveille," or so said Lincoln's secretary John Hay. Later known as a lyricist of little power—and a successful financier—Stedman was also a critic whose anthologies of poetry, published at the turn of the century, virtually created the (much-derided) category of Victorian poetry. Born in Hartford, Connecticut, he entered Yale at sixteen; though he was expelled for dissipation two years later, Yale recanted, awarding Stedman, late in his life, an honorary degree.

Back in 1861, the long-faced, large-eyed Stedman was easily recognized by his mutton-chop beard. As a field journalist on the staff of the *New York World,* on the morning of July 21 Stedman was on the Bull Run battlefield, waving the standard of the 5th Massachusetts Infantry and begging its men to rally round him. He too pleaded to little avail, and in his newspaper dispatch, he pulled no punches: "a grand army, retreating before superior numbers, was never more disgracefully or needlessly disrupted, and blotted, as it were, out of existence in a single day," he wrote. "This is the truth, and why should it not be recorded?" As soldiers fled the field, one thousand wounded men were left behind. The long-limbed, lean, Bavarian-born Henry Villard, on assignment for the *New York Herald,* fell out of a tree he had climbed a that morning to try to get a better look at the battlefield. Villard, who years later would purchase *The Nation* magazine, landed with a thump near Stedman and the illustrator whom *Harper's* magazine had sent to sketch the battle. But as Villard said, "the scenes on the battlefield beggar description. . . . Here lay one man with his leg shot off, there another with a wound in the head, a third with an arm shot off, and hundreds of wounded in nearly all the various portions of the body."

It wasn't only the frightened soldiers who had run. After the battle began, around six in the morning, the sound of guns could be heard in Washington, where members of Congress and their families had filled their picnic baskets and piled them into carriages and hacks and ridden out to nearby fields to watch through opera glasses what was sure to be a victory. It was a sunny day, and the broad Potomac was curled like a silver ribbon, noted the celebrated William Howard Russell, a middle-aged British journalist for the London *Times* who had covered the Crimean War. Soon he heard shots and then a low dark boom from the cannon, and on his way to Centreville, where the picnickers had opened their baskets, he could see wagons, which he supposed were returning for more supplies. The crowd grew larger, and one man began to yell, "Turn back! Turn back! We are whipped." Russell almost laughed but was overcome by the vague sense that "something extraordinary [was] taking place which is experienced when a man sees a number of people acting as if driven by some unknown terror." He acidly noted that though Washingtonians had gathered "in the hope of seeing the Lord deliver the Philistines into his hands," what they actually saw was mayhem. Most of the spectators scurried back to Washington in confusion.

"Their hearts were all willing to witness the killing," a Boston versifier mocked them:

> When the jolly civilians had chosen their ground;
> They drank and they nibbled—reporters they scribbled,
> While shot from the cannon were flying around.
> But nearer the rattle and storm of the battle
> Approached the civilians who came to a show,
> The terrible thunder filled them with wonder
> And trembling, and quaking with fear of the foe.
> The hell's egg-shells flying, the groans of the dying,
> Soon banished their pleasure and ruined their fun;
> There was terrible slaughter—blood ran like water,
> When civilians were picnicking down at Bull Run.

The rout wasn't just a consequence of flying missiles, blue smoke, and crackling gunfire. It was one of arrogance.

The battle plan had been that of the forty-two-year-old General Irvin McDowell, a West Pointer who had never before led men in the field. He had aimed to attack the Confederate lines with three advancing columns of about 35,000 men each and then confront Brigadier General P. G. T. Beauregard's forces at Manassas Junction. Afterward, he intended to move south and seize the Confederate capital at Richmond. It was a bold and risky plan, and it was as much the result of the *Tribune*'s pugnacious prodding as of sound military logic. McDowell, for instance, wanted the reporters covering the battle to wear white uniforms, as if to indicate their purity of character—and as if battle would be a romantic, organized storybook affair.

But the militia was made of three-month men, green and poorly trained. Their officers were as yet unproven. And the plan didn't take into account that Confederate reinforcements could (and did) sweep down on them, many arriving by rail. McDowell had no reserves, and Union boys, tired, hot, and frightened, went up to the Confederate lines, cowered, and then ran away.

Nor did the North count on the ferocious tenacity of the Confederate soldiers. It did not count on such leaders as the thin-lipped, unflappable Brigadier General Thomas Jackson, the Confederate who earned his "Stonewall" sobriquet here at Bull Run. Urging his men forward, Confederate Brigadier General Barnard Bee shouted, "There is Jackson with his Virginians, standing like a stone wall! Rally behind the Virginians!" Bee was killed, but Jackson made a firm stand at Bull Run; he was an unrelenting man. Often compared with Oliver Cromwell, so ferocious was his belief that the Southern cause was divinely inspired, so flamboyantly humble was he in the face of providential destruction, Jackson was bent on invading the North to wreak unrelenting destruction. "For our people," Jackson said, the war was "a *struggle for life and death.*"

"THE VAUNTED UNION we thought so strong, so impregnable," said Walt Whitman, "seems already smash'd like a china plate." The Battle of Bull Run demolished the fantasy that the war would be bloodless or brief. But the fantasy of a short war hadn't yet disappeared for everyone. Howell Cobb, who joined the Confederate army, wrote his wife in August that from "the tone of the Northern papers I infer that the people there are getting sick of the war and since their disastrous defeat at Manassas they begin to talk of peace." The war wouldn't last past the next January, everyone thought.

. . . .

IN JULY, AFTER the Federals' rout from the plains of Manassas, Horace Greeley removed the "On to Richmond" command from the masthead of the *Tribune*, and the unhappy Lincoln, accompanied by Seward, decided to inspect the troops at Fort Corcoran. Things were a mess. The restless Colonel William Tecumseh Sherman was now barking that he'd shoot anyone who disobeyed his orders on the spot, for, according to him, the scared and hence unreliable privates—boys, really—had caused the rout. But the Battle of Bull Run was also, as Sherman would recall, "the best lesson a vain & conceited crowd ever got. Up to that time no one seemed to measure the danger, the necessity of prolonged preparation and infinite outlay of money."

"Youth must its ignorant impulse lend—," Melville wrote. "Age finds place in the rear. / All wars are boyish, and are fought by boys."

Lincoln dismissed the defeated McDowell and placed Major General George Brinton McClellan in charge of the Army of the Potomac. It seemed a good move. A West Point graduate and classmate of General Beauregard, McClellan had served in the Mexican War, where he was brevetted first lieutenant and captain. Afterward, he had superintended the Illinois Central Railroad and the Ohio & Mississippi before returning to the military. Handsome, his shock of reddish hair cut short, and with a thick, well-groomed mustache that bristled with charm, McClellan was a compact, broad-chested man never at a loss for words about his infallibility. He said he had led the Union to important (he called them brilliant) victories in western Virginia earlier that spring when he had guarded the strategically significant Baltimore and Ohio Railroad, which linked Washington to the Midwest. Though not on the battlefield himself, he had directed his troops to win skirmishes at Philippi, Rich Mountain, and Corrick's Ford—successes, he said, that had helped that area become a new state, West Virginia, the following year.

When he first arrived in Washington, the man already known as the Young Napoleon seemed fresh from the battlefield, eager for a fight, optimistic despite what he found: "no preparations whatever for defense, not even to the extent of putting the troops in military position," he said. "Not a regiment was properly encamped, not a single avenue of approach guarded. All was chaos, and the streets, hotels, and bar-rooms were filled with drunken officers and men, absent from their regiments without leave, a perfect pandemonium. Many had even gone to their homes, their flight from Bull Run terminating in New York, or even in New Hampshire and Maine." The thousands of thirty-day soldiers who had been coming to Washington since April had quickly learned that nothing much awaited them: there were scant food and water, few uniforms, makeshift quarters. Disorganization, then, could be seen not just in the poorly drilled soldier but on the faces of the befuddled, hungry men who stood around in blazing heat or driving rain, wandering the streets or dispatched to camps where rations were measly, blankets thin, and ill-fitting shoes falling apart.

Brimming with the sanguine confidence of the egoist, McClellan set about organizing the army, enlarging its staff, and overseeing the details of regimental life, everything from the stocking of the commissary to the counting of horses, harnesses, and wagons. His assessment of the army's unpreparedness was not wrong. Reporting to the newly formed Sanitary Commission, a private organization established to create field hospitals, to bring medical supplies, surgeons, and nurses to the army, and to coordinate casualty lists, the architect Frederick Law Olmsted wrote a blistering account of the army in his "Report on the Demoralization of the Volunteers," in which he accused the government of sending starving, thirsty, tired boys into battle without much of a plan, much organization, much discipline, or any awareness that this was not a temporary emergency but a long, hard war.

And according to William Henry Hurlbert, the Charleston-born Douglas Democrat now editing the *New York World*, the defeat at Bull Run had also been caused by "professional rivalry, jealousy, envy; the desire of promotion and of conspicuous command; in some cases a mere craving for the popularity to be so easily won by falling in with the public clamor of the hour." One of the volunteer officers testified that "the officers themselves did not know what to do; they were themselves raw and green. Every man went in to do his duty, and knew nothing about anybody else." George Templeton Strong, who visited Washington shortly after the Battle of Bull Run, noted, "The men have lost faith in their officers, and no wonder, when so many officers set the example of running away. Of the first three hundred fugitives that crossed the Long Bridge, two hundred had commissions. Two colonels were seen fleeing on the same horse." In addition, about a third of the country's officers had left the Union for the Confederacy.

Yet Northern poets reassured nervous readers of such reports that "Repulse may do us good, it should not harm; / Where work is to be done, 'tis well to know / Its full extent." Readers were also reminded that although volunteers were registering for service by state, they would soon enter a national army, where the term of service was now three years, not three months; and that though many officers would continue to be appointed only because of their political or social connections, more and more of them would be appointed because of their army training or experience. The Battle of Bull Run had wakened the North to the work that needed to be done, and now it would go, better prepared, to the war that had already come.

As LINCOLN REPUTEDLY remarked to the correspondent William Russell, the London *Times* "is one of the greatest powers in the world—in fact, I don't know anything which has much more power—except the Mississippi." Whether news came fast or slow, whether it urged armies forward or back, whether it praised or blamed or recounted, newsmen were very much part of the war.

Not only was news quickly disseminated by virtue of a steam-powered press and the steam-powered locomotive on which reporters could hop a ride, there was the telegraph. Simon Cameron, the secretary of war, had appointed the young Andrew Carnegie, superintendent of the Pittsburgh Division of the Pennsylvania Railroad, to the U.S. Military Telegraph Corps, for Cameron had foreseen in a flash the importance of both railroad and telegraph. Carnegie was commissioned to organize the military railroad and telegraph service. The government also took temporary possession of the American Telegraph Company, and thereby the War Department largely controlled the news. While a battle was in progress, Lincoln practically moved into the War Department's telegraph office to read the ciphered dispatches and rifle through the drawer in which they were kept.

Telegraph officers had been called to Washington to work for the Union shortly after the bombardment of Fort Sumter in April 1861, and they were under pressure for the duration of the war. "I have seen a telegraph-operator in a tent in a malarious locality shivering with ague, lying upon his camp cot with his ear near the instrument, listening for messages which might direct or arrest movements of military armies," Quartermaster General Montgomery C. Meigs would recall. "Night and day they are at their posts." During the Battle of Bull Run, battle news landed in the government's War Department telegraph office, sent from the village of Fairfax, Virginia (northeast of Bull Run). Since the telegraph lines did not go much farther south than Fairfax, information had to come first from the couriers who had rushed to the village with their dispatches. So, like many Northerners, Lincoln initially heard glowing reports of the battle; he had known of the delays but not the rout.

News was not belated for long. Soon telegraph operators tapped out messages to the War Department to notify various far-flung troops of one another's movements. After McClellan took over the command of the army, he wisely oversaw the development of insulated telegraph wire for a Signal Corps to organize communications, whether visual signs (flags and torches) or the electric telegraph. Of course, the telegraph worked for the Confederates too and, in the case of the Battle of Bull Run, better, for they were in close contact with Richmond and knew reinforcements were coming by rail.

When Sumter was bombarded, there was no ready-made apparatus for the gathering and distributing of eyewitness accounts of battles, even though papers such as the Democratic *New York Herald* had already identified strategic cities to which to send their correspondents. The *Tribune* posted two dozen men in or near Charleston. Soon every major city sent at least one reporter, called a "special," into the field. William Russell dressed in Union blue and joined Stedman and Villard. The only "special" correspondent from Boston, writing for the Boston *Journal*, was the genial Charles Carleton Coffin, grandson of a Revolutionary War veteran, who stuffed a watch, a pocket compass, a pair of binoculars, and several notebooks under his large coat and covered the entire war. And from Pennsylvania came twenty-four-year-old, tight-lipped Uriah Painter, a Quaker, who wrote for the *Philadelphia Inquirer*. Long on facts, short on description, Painter too had tried to rally the 5th Massachusetts at Manassas but, as he said, "we might as well have pleaded with the winds to stop blowing."

These were just a few of the correspondents, a motley crew—a "hybrid," said one of them, "neither a soldier nor a citizen; with the Army, but not of it; present at battles, and often participating in them, yet without any rank or recognized existence." Scribbling at night by the light of a candle stuck in a bottle, men such as George W. Smalley, Whitelaw Reid (later Greeley's successor at the *Tribune*), and Samuel Wilkeson of *The New York Times* were on site, calling themselves the Bohemian Brigade. They wandered wherever the war took them, writing their copy on their knees, often paying their own way or for their own horses, courting danger. At Antietam, Smalley had two horses shot out from under him, his clothes ripped by bullets, and he then rode six hours to Frederick, where he wrote his story in the telegraph office after convincing the operator to transmit it. (Usually the summary of the news, not the longer version, was sent over the wire. In Smalley's case, the reluctant operator finally relented but didn't send Smalley's dispatch to New York, as instructed, but to Washington and the president.) All this happened after General Hooker used Smalley to carry orders to a regiment that seemed to have fallen back. "Unthinkable," a later commentator said. At Gettysburg, Samuel Wilkeson filed his story soon after learning that his nineteen-year-old son, Bayard, an artillerist, had been "crushed by a shell," as he wrote, "in a position where a battery should never have been sent, and abandoned to death in a building where surgeons dared not to stay."

Correspondents were not always welcome in the field, especially when they were critical of officers or strategy. Tall, slender, and fine-looking, his bright blue eyes darkened with worry, Whitelaw Reid rode with fellow Ohioan general William Rosecrans as his aide-de-camp and later covered the two-day-long action at Shiloh for the Cincinnati *Gazette* in April 1862, a year after Sumter. But Reid's controversial allegation that Sherman was insane and that the Union victory had been a near disaster earned him Sherman's everlasting wrath. To Reid, Shiloh was not an unalloyed success—*not* because the total casualties (an unimaginable 24,000 dead or wounded) exceeded all losses in all U.S. wars until then but because the Union forces, taken by surprise, had almost bungled it. The battle had begun at sunrise when soldiers were bayoneted in their tents, alleged Reid in a claim as contentious as his suggestion that Union defeats were by and large caused by poor generalship. When the Confederates, yelling frantically, flew into the Union camp, "Many, particularly among our officers, were not yet out of bed," Reid scoffed. "Others were dressing, others washing, others cooking, a few eating their breakfasts. Many guns were unloaded, accoutrements lying pell-mell."

Thirty years later, in 1892, Reid ran for vice president on the Republican ticket, but in 1862, General Sherman would have been happy to see him hanged. A bunch of buzzards who undermined the Union war effort with their scurrilous falsehoods, their brainless criticism of strategies they knew nothing of, their leaking of sensitive military information, and their spreading the malicious slander that sold newspapers, said Sherman, reporters were "the most contemptible race of men that existed, cowardly, cringing, hanging around, gathering their material out of the most polluted sources." General

Henry W. Halleck, the commander of all the Union forces, called the press a hive of unauthorized parasites and ordered them (without success) to leave the field. When General Ambrose Burnside suppressed the Democratic *Chicago Times* for disloyalty, Lincoln had to intervene. In St. Louis, Major Justus McKinstry issued restrictions on the embedded press and briefly muffled the Unionist *St. Louis Republican*; that earned him little applause, especially in Washington, though in early 1862 Edwin Stanton, who replaced the far more incompetent Simon Cameron in the War Department, consolidated control over the telegraph lines and tried to censor the papers from time to time.

Ironically, Sherman's attack against the press showed that by the time of Shiloh, the press corps was no longer untested but ready to participate in the war effort as it saw fit—not as so-called objective reporters but as commentators, promoters, magpies, or boosters, depending on what they witnessed and their political point of view. The war hugely increased the profits of James Gordon Bennett's widely read *New York Herald*, a Democratic paper that had as many as sixty correspondents and "specials" covering the military. The Democrat William Henry Hurlbert, for one, said that the Battle of Bull Run had been a useless slaughter prompted by the irresponsible breast thumping of newspapers such as Greeley's (Republican) *Tribune* and newspapermen such as Greeley. He was not entirely wrong.

The idealistic Junius Henri Browne, who worked for the *Tribune* (and defended it), declared that a few bad war correspondents shouldn't tarnish the reputation of the whole profession. The reporter was the crucial link between the military and the public. "The misfortune is," he said, "that the unworthy, by their assurance, carelessness and lack of principle, give such false impressions of the entire tribe, that I marvel not a most wholesome prejudice exists against them on the part of many officers." Bitten by mosquitoes, doubled over with hunger, and decimated by disease, the correspondents rode long into the night to catch a train or a steamboat to get back to Washington as fast as they could in the hours before the news bureaus opened. Quick to deliver battle news to their newspapers, even if only a shortened version by telegram, special courier, or pony express before supplying a report far longer, far more descriptive, as if battle news were a serialized novel, they wrote in camp, at night, in the morning, they wrote in ambulance wagons and when half asleep, all to get their news to their readers. But communication could be slow—mercifully so. When Noah Brooks, the Washington correspondent for the *Sacramento Daily Union*, wanted to write about troop strength, Lincoln shrugged. "You can send that by letter to California, by and by, if you want. It can't get back there in time to do any harm."

As de facto combatants, correspondents were never out of harm's way. Junius Henri Browne spent nearly two years incarcerated in one Confederate prison after another. He and three other reporters were captured outside Vicksburg in May 1863. (Hearing rumors that they'd been killed, Sherman quipped, "That's good! We'll have three dispatches from hell before breakfast.") But danger and duty and the need for information notwithstanding, war meant commerce. The Northern press was adding morning and evening editions, even "extras," to feed the public appetite for news about their local men away at war. Already the *Tribune's* circulation had reached 200,000. In the Midwest, the *Chicago Tribune* published 36,000 of just its Battle of Bull Run edition. At the same time, the Associated Press, which had initially consolidated the New York dailies—there were seventeen papers in New York City alone and three in Brooklyn—collected news and dispatched it to far-flung places and also dispatched exclusive bulletins from the White House, which thus controlled some of what was deemed news. Yet readers knew that they were receiving skewed or partial reports. Besides, all newspapers were partisan; everyone knew that. So did Lincoln, who had secretly purchased the *Illinois Staats Anzeiger* in 1858 to promote Republicanism among German Americans. In his younger days an underpaid and disgruntled reporter for Greeley's *Tribune*, Henry Raymond, the conservative founder and editor of *The New York Times*, had formerly been a Whig member of the New York state legislature and a lieutenant governor, and now he chaired the national Republican Party. Yet Elizabeth Blair Lee, the daughter of the old-time Democratic journalist Francis Preston Blair, loyally declared, "This is the Peoples war & as such the Press is a channel of communication with the people." *Harper's Weekly* put it this way: "News of the War! We all live on it. Few of us but would prefer our newspaper in these times to our breakfast."

Often Southerners looked more favorably on the war correspondents than Sherman did, praising the "specials" as men possessed of a "personal courage often equal to their conceit, but who do not hesitate to attempt to make or mar the reputation of generals and admirals according to their fancy." But the situation of the press was different in the South—not in terms of partisan politics but in terms of finances. As time went on, most Southern papers, including the powerful *Richmond Examiner*, couldn't afford newsprint, ink, and postal expenses, never mind newfangled printing presses. Often Southern newspapers depended on rumor and hearsay. Yet the accounts of battle, atrocity, hysteria, and hardship were no less graphic than what was printed in the North. And nothing was more gripping, more suspenseful, more cruelly authentic than the rolls of the dead, the wounded, the missing. Men and women lived from edition to edition; the news was breathtaking, unbelievable, and very close at hand. Newspapers had become agents of elation and messengers of grief.

There were pictures, too. They rendered visible a war taking place in one's very own country: in 1851, Frederick Gleason and Maturin Ballou established one of the United States' first illustrated papers, *Gleason's Pictorial Drawing-Room Companion*; in 1854, *Graham's Magazine* offered woodcut illustrations based on Brady's work, and since 1855, *Frank Leslie's Illustrated News* had been touting pictures to supplement and ultimately supplant the written word. Ditto the *New-York Illustrated News* (1859) and *Harper's Weekly* (1857). After 1861, their circulations surged; posting a sketch-corps at the battlefronts, *Frank Leslie's Illustrated News* reached an audience of 150,000.

Though the front-page pictures of *Harper's Weekly* often displayed wood engravings copied from Mathew Brady ambrotypes (positive images on plates of glass), the magazine was sending its own illustrators into the field. Engravers in New York, who worked in wood, copied the artists' sketches and then made a metal impression for publication. Sometimes the sketches arrived in New York in a jumble, with just a few illegible notes attached, and what subsequently appeared had nothing to do with what the soldiers had seen or done. "If all the terrific hand-to-hand encounters which we have seen for two or three years displayed in the pages of our popular weeklies had occurred," said the *Army and Navy Journal* in 1864, "the combatants on each side would long ago have mutually annihilated each other."

The irascible Sherman did not like the artists any more than he liked the press. Not only did he typically refuse to pose for his portrait, he also tried to bar artists from tagging along with his men. "You fellows make the best spies that can be bought," he snapped. Eventually he relented, perhaps after hearing what his friend Ulysses S. Grant had reputedly told the illustrators. "We are the men who make history, but you are the men who perpetuate it." And, like soldiers, artists were not immune to pneumonia, smallpox, bullet holes, or capture. *Leslie's* John F. E. Hillen was caught by the Confederates at Chickamauga, and the ebullient Theodore Davis, who sketched the battle of the *Merrimack* and *Monitor*, had his horse shot out from under him at least once and was twice wounded, once at Shiloh and once at Antietam. When the surgeons wanted to amputate his legs, he slept with a pistol under his pillow.

The freelancer Winslow Homer had moved from Boston to New York, where *Harper's Weekly* hired him as an engraver and part-time illustrator. During the first year of the war, Homer sketched often for the magazine, and in late 1862 he eerily depicted a sharpshooter on picket duty, sitting on a pine tree branch, his canteen slung on a nearby limb, his long-range rifle aimed to fire, his eye bright. "The above impression struck me as being as near murder as anything I ever could think of in connection with the army & I always had a horror of that branch of the service," Homer would say. War was not faceless to him, and he did not sketch with the candy-box stock types. He showed murder up close, personal, even technological. The sharpshooter's rifle had a scope.

If technology would change war, with the invention of such weaponry as the Gatling gun, mounted on huge wheels for rapid firing, the minié ball, the torpedo, the underwater mine, and the ironclad warship, it also changed its depiction. This was the first war to be photographed from start to finish and the first to be photographed by individual entrepreneurs with a mission. For though the Crimean War had had its photographers, particularly Roger Fenton, they had been hired by the British government. In America, ambitious men such as the self-employed Mathew Brady were on the cusp of a remarkable change in the reproduction of war images.

In 1859, in addition to his New York gallery, where Lincoln would be photographed, Brady had opened another studio, Brady's National Photographic Art Gallery, in Washington, D.C., on Pennsylvania Avenue between Sixth and Seventh Streets. There Walt Whitman met Brady, who was promoting the photograph as history, saying, "How much better it would often be, rather than having a lot of contradictory records by witnesses or historians . . . if we could have three or four or half a dozen portraits—very accurate—of the men: that would be history—the best history—a history from which there could be no appeal."

War created that kind of history. After Sumter, soldiers flocked to Brady's before heading to the front lines. Photographs had superseded daguerreotypes in popularity, and those soldiers wanted to have their photographs taken. Neatly clad in their blue uniforms, their buttons glossy, their coats new, their belts buckled, they walked up three flights of stairs for their sitting. Enlisted men came, generals came. In his full-dress uniform Winfield Scott, at seventy-five years, looks the tired, stern old soldier that he was, a bit pompous, perhaps, but a war hero, having been in both the War of 1812 and the Mexican War. Scott is a decorated soldier, with sword and epaulets, but he seems out of place in a war of sharpshooters, bushwhackers, and appalling carnage.

Perhaps Brady guessed as much. As he later explained, pictures were events to him. Overcoming the objections of the military, Brady wheedled permission from General Scott to go to Bull Run with two wagons, as he later recalled, which he would use as portable darkrooms. Dressed in a long white linen dust coat and wearing a flat straw hat atop his curly head and carrying extra pairs of spectacles to aid his failing eyesight, Brady planned to photograph the landscape as it looked before the battle.

And when the army moved, before dawn, he moved too; he'd gotten as far as Blackburn's Ford, near Manassas, where he first witnessed a battle, and on July 18 and again on July 21, he soon abandoned his camera and helped the surgeons tend the wounded. Journalist Henry Villard thought Brady one of the most humane and energetic men on the field. But in the smoke and commotion, Brady lost his bearings and, according to one biographer, was likely caught up in the confusion of the Union panic. Presumably, he then wandered, alone and bewildered, near the creek, until a regiment of New York Fire Department Zouaves (named for a band of North African fighters), arrayed in flowing pants and red shirts, found him and his negatives. Along with the copy filed by Stedman and Villard, along with the sketches of the artists, along with the eyewitness accounts, Brady's assistants would soon portray a silent world of frayed landscape and broken trees.

Though shaken by the panic, the killing, the stench of the bodies, and the sound of whinnying and terrified horses, Brady continued to cover the war. "I felt that I had to go," he reminisced years later. "After that I had men in all parts of the army, like a rich newspaper." (Secretary of War Stanton allowed Brady to send his photographers to the front as long as Brady covered the expenses of his crew—he estimated them at more than $100,000—which eventually would bankrupt him.) Wearing signature dust coats, like Brady, his assistants (who took many of the pictures ascribed to him) rode out to the field with their mobile darkrooms, called "whatisit wagons," loaded with cameras, tripods, lenses, and bottles of chemicals. Considered combatants, they trekked through slimy mud to distant, dangerous locations. There were other photographers, but only Brady's operators had the moving darkrooms equipped to handle glass plates and so Brady seemed to hold a monopoly in the field.

"In every glade and by the roadsides of the camp, may be seen all kinds of covered carts and portable sheds," noted a correspondent. Whether for "the mighty tribe of cameraists," or for the newspapers, or for the makers of guns and boats and uniforms, or for the "manufacturers of Metallic air-tight coffins and embalmers of the dead," war was more than religion or rhetoric or representation; it was fast becoming business.

THE PHOTOGRAPHS TAKEN by Alexander Gardner, who managed Brady's Washington studio, shock the viewer even today with their graphic depictions of the unburied dead and the mortally wounded. Joining McClellan's staff, the Scottish-born Gardner and his assistant James Gibson photographed the burial crews and the corpses strewn on the rolling fields near Antietam Creek, not far from Sharpsburg, Maryland. McClellan's men had fought the Confederate general Robert E. Lee for two days there in September 1862, in a battle that resulted in more than 26,000 casualties, making it the single bloodiest day in the war. ·

"The hills were black with spectators," said the illustrator Edwin Forbes. War spectators had not yet learned what war was, what it would cost—or, if they had, they hardly believed the evidence of their own eyes. A young officer at Antietam said, "There were men in every state of mutilation, sans arms, sans legs, heads, and intestines, and in greater number than on any field we have seen before." When the thick smoke cleared, George Templeton Strong, come to inspect the battlefield for himself, witnessed, like the others, "dead horses, swollen, with their limbs protruding stiffly at strange angles, and the ground at their noses blackened with hemorrhage."

Gardner showed those images to the men and women who hadn't been at Antietam; he wanted to make sure they saw what he had seen and that they would not forget. For four days in late September, he and an assistant took pictures of the field, chronicling the dead and dying. The seventy resulting photographs, a mélange of historical document, sensationalistic detail, and commercial ingenuity, were displayed in October at Brady's studio in New York. "The Dead of Antietam," as the exhibit was called, dumbfounded the spectator who had scanned the morning newspaper before his morning coffee for bulletins of war: it was as if there was a funeral next door, said a reporter for *The New York Times*, as he looked into the "pale faces of the dead." The photographs then appeared as a series of woodcuts in *Harper's Weekly*: rows of dead bodies as far as the eye could see, the dead crumpled on the battlefield, the dead shoeless and in rags.

The newspaperman Frank Leslie had been disgusted by the callous indifference of the battlefield tourists, as he called them, sketched by his artist Frank Schell. No more: the picnic was over, and the cry of "On to Richmond" was bullying, dangerous propaganda at its worst. Gardner's photographs told the viewer how odd and grotesque that "the same sun that looked down on the faces of the slain, blistering them, blotting out from the bodies all semblance to humanity, and hastening corruption should have thus caught their features upon canvas, and given them perpetuity for ever. But so it is."

So it was.

IN RICHMOND, CONFEDERATE orators had applauded the victory at Manassas (as the South referred to Bull Run) in which their soldiers had so nobly fought. But Mary Chesnut, whose husband had been at the battlefield, looked out of her window at the jubilant crowds and wondered why the army hadn't chased those Yankees right into Washington and taken their city. Robert Hunter, secretary of state of the Confederate States of America, crossly replied, "Don't ask awkward questions."

The question wasn't just awkward; it was nagging. "Why did we not follow the flying foe across the Potomac?" If the decision not to follow, in retrospect, seems apt—the troops were exhausted, disorganized, low on ammunition, and would likely have met Union reserves—the question is one that will occur again and again in the annals of the Civil War, as similar questions do in any war. Earlier, on July 29, 1861, just weeks after the Confederate victory at Manassas, William Russell had disparagingly told readers of the usually sympathetic London *Times* that "On this day of the week the *Confederates could have marched into the capital of the United States.* They took no immediate steps to follow up their unexpected success. To this moment their movements have betrayed *no fixity of purpose* or settled plan to pursue an aggressive war." Even the soldiers dressed in gray or butternut brown wondered why they had not hounded the blue troops. "There is no legitimate excuse for our not following," decided one of them. "It is customary to say that 'Providence did not intend that we should win,' but I do not subscribe in the least to that doctrine. Providence did not care a row of pins about it. If it did it was a very unintelligent Providence not to bring the business to a close—the close it wanted—in less than four years of most terrible & bloody war."

Perhaps beyond good military reasoning, beyond luck, and beyond the inevitable fog of war, thick and fast as it had come, is another possibility: no one could quite countenance the destruction of the Union capital, which until recently had been theirs too. And though the numbers of casualties multiplied beyond what could—what can—be imagined, and though the vehemence of the men on the battlefield grew hotter and more ferocious with time and more blood, and though the women in Southern or Northern drawing rooms braced for the bad news that seemed to rain on them, and the politicians in Washington and Richmond bickered among themselves, so too did another quieter feeling stir, one that had been dormant these past years of war-mongering and invective and vitriol.

That was an aversion to killing one's own countrymen. Even as late as 1863, on the eve of battle, the Federals and the Confederates, at Stones River, Tennessee, went back and forth, one group singing "Yankee Doodle," the other replying with "Dixie," until one of the army bands changed the tune and began "Home Sweet Home." In moments, "Thousands of Yankees and Rebs, who tomorrow would kill each other," wrote the historian James McPherson, "were singing the familiar words together."

Although Stones River took place a year and a half after Manassas, the sentiment was doubtless long-standing. These countrymen in Tennessee and Virginia and Pennsylvania, countrymen from the backwoods of Missouri and Maine, had been rocked to sleep with stories about Washington or Jefferson; they had heard the same tales about Bunker Hill and Yorktown, the valor of Patrick Henry, and the flintiness of John Quincy Adams. Though they called their battles by different names—Confederates generally designating by towns, such as Manassas, and Federals referring to nearby streams or rivers, such as Bull Run—they spoke the same language, shared the same history. To be sure, families were dividing. The sons of John Crittenden, whose last-minute proposals to save the Union had failed, joined different sides: his eldest, George, joined the Confederate forces, and Thomas, the Union. Were they ambivalent about what they pledged to do—kill each other? Would they be reluctant?

If so, with reluctance came, almost in direct proportion, viciousness, brutality, rage. Regardless of sentiment—likely because of it—the two sides would indeed fight and fight hard. The sentiment of brotherhood and nationhood bred a sense of betrayal and with that, fury. And sentimentality masked the violence that women and men could not admit. There were 900 killed and 2,700 wounded at the First Battle of Bull Run/Manassas. And though higher and more stunning numbers of casualties were to come—at Stones River, of the 81,000 engaged, one-third were casualties (27 percent on the Confederate side, 29 percent on the Union)—the figures from the Battle of Bull Run stupefied both the North and the South.

Stonewall Jackson was not stupefied. He foresaw and welcomed death, and he appraised the Confederate victory at Bull Run as a warning. To this soldier, who had admired the courage with which John Brown faced the gallows, the Battle of Bull Run/Manassas had created a dangerous delusion. "The South was proud, jubilant, self-satisfied; it saw final success of easy attainment," Stonewall Jackson had reportedly said. "The North, mortified by defeat and stunned by ridicule, pulled itself together, raised armies, stirred up its people, and prepared for war in earnest."

(10)

BATTLE CRY OF FREEDOM

War in earnest: so it was. Corpses lay bloated by the hot sun, soldiers stepping over them, the wounded and the dying, thirsty and in pain, moans echoing through villages and towns, South and North.

Why was the war being fought? To some Northerners, the justification for men fallen on the battlefield was the abolition of slavery. "Either slavery is essential to a community, or it must be fatal to it,—there is no middle ground," declared Thomas Higginson in 1861. "Never, in modern days, has there been a conflict in which the contending principles were so clearly antagonistic." He was wrong. The contending principles were not clearly antagonistic, not to everyone.

Lincoln had promised to protect slavery where it existed; that had been the Republican platform. Now that a war was under way, Lincoln was vowing to preserve the Union, not to abolish slavery—as John Crittenden reminded his Senate colleagues after the disaster at Bull Run. The war was "not waged upon our part in any spirit of oppression, nor for any . . . purpose of overthrowing or interfering with rights or established institutions of those States," he said. The war was a war for the Union.

Yet some men embraced John Quincy Adams's argument about slavery: that in case of war, military emancipation of slaves was constitutional and proper: "From the instant your slave-holding states become a theater of war—civil, servile, or foreign," Adams had declared in 1836, "—from that instant the war powers of the Constitution extend interference with the institution of slavery in every way that it can be interfered with." Lincoln did not seize on Adams's idea, which would have been politically disastrous both for himself and the Union cause—and ultimately for abolition.

Major General Benjamin Butler seemed, at least superficially, to agree with Adams. Slightly corpulent and very smart and the son of a widow who had run one of the boardinghouses for the Lowell mills, Butler was a superb lawyer who had championed the factory workers, arguing for a ten-hour day, a blunt Massachusetts Democrat, and a delegate to the Democratic National Convention in 1860, where he'd backed his friend Jefferson Davis and voted for him more than fifty times. (Butler was subsequently hanged in effigy in Lowell.) After Sumter, though, the heavy-lidded man who had scorned abolitionists and was scorned in turn as disreputable underwent such a transformation that his brash and bold Unionism alarmed Winfield Scott, who urged Lincoln to restrain him a bit.

In actuality, Butler was a reed in the political wind, although a tough one. There were always rumors circulating around him about underhanded deals, though nothing was ever proved. The theatrical but perspicacious General P. G. T. Beauregard would call Benjamin Butler "the Beast," for while Major General Butler was military governor of Union-occupied Louisiana in 1862, he arrested the mayor of New Orleans, executed a man for pulling down the Stars and Stripes, imprisoned others (whom he released if bribed), and was said to have filled a coffin with stolen silver spoons. Worse, after his soldiers suffered ill-treatment at the hands of New Orleans women—they had presumably poured the contents of the chamber pot on the heads of Union men—Butler issued General Order No. 28, which promised to treat all females who harassed his troops as "women of the town plying their avocation."

In 1861, Butler was commander of Fortress Monroe, the federal stronghold in Virginia strategically located on the James River, when three black field hands, the "property" of the secessionist colonel Charles Mallory, took refuge there. Butler fed and clothed the three men, Frank Baker, Shepard Mallory, and James Townsend, and put them to work. The North could seize the South's labor force, he reckoned, and apply John Quincy Adams's injunction about abolishing slavery during wartime; and those slaves who had been picking cotton, digging trenches, and sustaining the Confederacy could just as well work for the North. "Shall they [Confederates] be allowed the use of this property against the United States," Butler asked, "and we not be allowed its use in aid of the United States?"

The question was direct enough, the consequences far-reaching. Butler felt that he was under no obligation to return fugitives to their masters. As far as he was concerned, the Fugitive Slave Act "did not affect a foreign country," which Virginia had, for the moment, become by seceding from the Union—and, moreover, the Fugitive Slave Law could not affect a foreign country at war with the United States. "Our troops could not act as a marshal's posse in catching runaway negroes to return them to their masters who were fighting us at the same time," he reasoned. (Unionists, of course, did not recognize the right of any state to secede, so Butler could not really have regarded Virginia as a foreign country; but Virginia was surely the enemy.) However, said Butler, if Colonel Mallory would come to Fortress Monroe and swear the oath of allegiance, Butler would hand over Baker, Mallory, and Townsend. (Butler probably knew that Colonel Mallory wouldn't show up.) Until that time, which never came, Butler considered the field hands to be "contraband of war"—a phrase he likely coined.

The abolitionist Wendell Phillips called the phrase a "bad one," for the term validated the claim that the runaways were possessions. Neither Butler nor the federal government had freed them. Yet Butler had pushed forward an important issue, which, as *Frank Leslie's Illustrated Newspaper* acknowledged, "increased the dilemma of the Secessionists to a remarkable degree, since it is at once equally hostile to both Abolitionism and Secession."

In a matter of days, black men and women were rushing to

Fortress Monroe, "$60,000 worth of them," Butler estimated without emotion. Having asked for instructions from Washington and having initially received none—though Secretary of War Cameron would cautiously approve his actions in August—Butler continued to employ the black men and women flocking to the fort. Whatever else to do with those hungry, ill-clad, homeless persons eager for freedom?

And what to do with their children? Calculating though he might have been, and never before remotely considered an abolitionist, Butler said he wouldn't take able-bodied men and women into his service and ignore their children. And what to do with them in the long term? To Butler "the slave question" had become a "stumbling-block" in the prosecution of the war, and it was a humanitarian issue: evident, unassailable, and poignant.

Congress both confronted and evaded the issue when it passed the first Confiscation Act of 1861, which authorized the federal govern-ment to seize the property of anyone directly rebelling against the government. The act began to chip away at the institution of slav-ery. But by codifying the idea of the fugitive as contraband, it also sustained the idea that people are property. And it protected slavery in the border states, which were not directly rebelling against the government. The thirty-two-year-old abolitionist lawyer Edward L. Pierce (formerly the private secretary of Salmon Chase) who had en-listed with the 3rd Massachusetts Volunteer Militia drily explained to readers of *The Atlantic Monthly* after he witnessed what had hap-pened at Fortress Monroe, "The venerable gentleman, who wears gold spectacles and reads a conservative daily, prefers confiscation to emancipation. He is reluctant to have slaves declared freemen, but has no objection to their being declared contrabands."

Abolitionists had taken note of Butler, and presumably Private Edward Pierce, in charge of the contrabands at Fortress Monroe, sug-gested to him that he not only employ the black men rushing to his camp but also arm them. For the abolitionists pushing for emancipa-tion decided that, for them, the defeat at Bull Run had been a victory of ideological sorts. Butler said in retrospect, "one might reverently believe that a special Providence ordered it, so that slavery might be wiped out. Because if we had beaten at Bull Run, I have no doubt the whole contest would have been patched up and healed over by concessions to slavery, as nobody in power was ready then for its abolition."

MEANWHILE, THE IMPETUOUS Pathfinder had again stepped onto the stage, this time in the theater of war. After losing, as expected, his bid for the presidency in 1856, John Frémont had returned to California to shore up his increasingly indebted gold mines. In 1861, he sent word to President Lincoln that he wouldn't mind being placed in the field, and in the summer of 1861, he accepted a commission as commander of the new Department of the West, a region that ran from the Mississippi to the Rocky Mountains and included the rough and poorly protected border state of Missouri, where secessionist guerrillas burned bridges and sharpshooters terrified settlers. The government and the press had been concentrating on the eastern theater of war, not the West, as Frémont noted when he arrived in St. Louis in July. "Our troops have not been paid," he complained, "and some regiments are in a state of mutiny, and the men whose term of service is expired generally refuse to re-enlist." It was a messy, explosive situation, but Major General Frémont would make it worse.

On August 30, Frémont shocked President Lincoln, he shocked conservative Republicans, and he shocked abolitionists, Democrats, and Southerners, by declaring martial law and—outdoing Butler—declaring free the slaves of anyone in his department who had taken up arms against the federal government.

Frémont's timing was poor. His own star had been falling. Accused of peremptoriness, imperiousness, and lavish living, Frémont had been rapidly losing the support of Missouri's Blair family in an internecine squabble that would have national implications, especially since the intelligent and voluble Montgomery Blair, formerly the counsel for Dred Scott, was now Lincoln's postmaster general, and his brother Frank Blair, a leading Missouri Republican, was the chair of the House Committee on Military Defense. Lincoln had been concerned about Frémont's military prowess anyway. When the redheaded, rash Brigadier General Nathaniel Lyon had been shot in the heart at the battle at Wilson's Creek, it was Frémont who had been blamed, even though he had urged Lyon to retreat until reinforcements arrived. But with casualties high and morale low, the press wanted to know why Frémont had not reinforced Lyon sooner. His answer was that he had fewer troops under his command than he had let on and that they were needed to defend St. Louis.

Lincoln, who had not been notified in advance of Frémont's proclamation, knew that if he permitted Frémont to free the slaves of Missouri rebels, he risked losing credibility with all the border states, and he needed them, if not on his side, to be neutral. As Lincoln's friend Joshua Speed (a Kentucky slaveholder) reminded the president, "You had as well attack the freedom of worship in the north or the right of a parent to teach his child to read—as to wage war in a slave state on such a principle." So in a private communication to Frémont, Lincoln requested that he revise the proclamation to conform to the Confiscation Act. In response, Frémont demanded Lincoln openly order him to do so, which would force Lincoln to suggest publicly that he was against emancipation.

Jessie Frémont went to Washington to deliver her husband's reply in person. As she recalled, she had rushed to the White House without changing out of her dusty clothes. Lincoln did not ask her to sit. Instead, he listened to her appeal and read the general's letter; later he said he had had to muster all his "awkward tact" just to be polite. He must have been furious at Frémont's cheek. When she again tried to argue with him about her husband's proclamation, he called her "quite a female politician"—not exactly a compliment—and told her "it was a war for a great national idea, the Union, and that General Frémont should not have dragged the negro into it—that he never would if he had consulted with Frank Blair." Refusing to grant her another interview, Lincoln ordered her husband to retract the proclamation.

A few days later, Frémont arrested Frank Blair for insubordination.

That was the final straw. Vilified as imperious, incompetent, a poor general, a corrupt administrator, and even as an opium eater, Frémont was forced out of the Department of the West.

Elizabeth Blair Lee, the sister of Montgomery and Frank, had already accused Frémont of playing to "the abolition horde in the north." There was a degree of truth in the charge. Northerners rallied round him. To John Greenleaf Whittier, Frémont appeared to be a brave man, albeit "without the statesman's tact," who would "strike at cause as well as consequence." Even the conservative Republican James Russell Lowell was moved to ask, "How many times we are to save Kentucky and lose our self-respect?" That is, how long will we perpetuate the horror of slavery just to coddle border states? The citizens of Hamburg, Ohio, sent the president a petition supporting Frémont and his proclamation, and so did a committee representing the German volunteer regiments in New York. The revocation of Frémont's proclamations will make abolitionists of us all, cried *Harper's Weekly.* And the more moderate Orville Hickman Browning of Illinois frankly told Lincoln that Frémont's proclamation "was accomplishing much good. Its revocation disheartens our friends, and represses their ardor." Yet whether Frémont was a hothead trying to reclaim his tattered reputation or whether he was sincerely trying to make emancipation the centerpiece of the war, his proclamation did invigorate the slavery debate.

Regardless, abolition was still unthinkable to many in the North or on the border, such as the Blair family, who hoped to revive the now moribund notion of colonization to rid the country of blacks altogether. So too did Lincoln—though he favored and put forward a plan of gradual emancipation whereby the loyal slave owner would be offered compensation for the freed slave. The freed slave would then be repatriated—to a colony called Lincolnia, sardonically suggested one newspaper—and slavery would be extinct in about twenty or thirty years.

Frederick Douglass pointedly asked, "Why, oh why, may not men of different races inhabit in peace and happiness this vast and wealthy country?"

Though Lincoln's plan, which he offered to the Delaware legislature in a test run, does seem unadventurous compared to Garrisonian abolitionism, no other president of the United States had gone as far. The proposal went too far and not far enough: too far, in that conservatives shuddered at the thought of a slippery slope—emancipated slaves might actually clamor for citizenship—and not far enough in that buying slaves in order to free them still presumed them to be nothing more than sticks of furniture.

In early 1862 the proposal died in Delaware's House of Representatives. Lincoln continued to pursue Congress with his idea of compensated emancipation, but it was an idea not supported in the border states in any case. The effort, however misguided, reveals and foreshadows one of the knottiest questions of the war and its aftermath: that of the meaning of full citizenship. Contraband, freed slave, freeman: "These terms are milestones in our progress," noted Edward Pierce; "and they are yet to be lost in the better and more comprehensive designation of 'citizens,' or, when discrimination is convenient, 'citizens of African descent.'"

THE POPULAR SINGERS from New Hampshire whose repertoire included such temperance favorites as "Father's a Drunkard and Mother Is Dead" entertained the Army of the Potomac near Washington with "Tenting on the Old Camp Ground" and "The Battle Cry of Freedom." But when they set to music Whittier's "Hymn to Liberty," inspired by Luther's hymn "Ein feste Burg ist unser Gott" ("A Mighty Fortress Is Our God") and sang to the soldiers about how slavery was destroying the nation, the Hutchinson Family Singers heard a rustle and then loud and long and angry boos. General McClellan promptly revoked the Hutchinsons' permit to sing in the army camps, reminding them with asperity that abolition was *not* the object of the war. "*I* am fighting to preserve the integrity of the Union & the power of the Govt—, on no other issue."

Regardless of what he said he was fighting for, by March 1862, seven months after McClellan had taken command, very little had happened. George B. McClellan could not or would not move his army. His troops might adore him, but the president was losing confidence in Young Napoleon. So was the new secretary of war, the aggressive and sometimes bullish Edwin Stanton. Horace Greeley, never one to mince words, called McClellan an outright Copperhead (as Northerners who opposed the war were called after a box of snakes, presumed to be poisonous, escaped from a package bound for Washington, D.C.). And few observers could understand the wisdom of McClellan's proposed "peninsular strategy" in which he would ship his huge army by sea to the tip of the York-James Peninsula and then fight westward, toward Richmond.

Beloved by his troops, insubordinate to the commander in chief, courted by Democrats, and despised by radicals, the handsome McClellan seemed to dillydally while, in the West, the unkempt, spare-spoken soldier with a reputation for drinking too much actually captured Fort Henry and Fort Donelson. That was in February 1862, and the general was Ulysses S. Grant. Grant, not McClellan, had won the first major Union victory. And it was the now-famous Grant who had told Confederate general Simon Buckner that "no terms except an unconditional and immediate surrender can be accepted." This was news, this was excitement, this was soldiering, yet all the while the Army of the Potomac had not budged.

Finally, after almost six months of delay, in early March 1862 McClellan and his huge army finally advanced toward Centreville, near the Bull Run battlefield, still covered with bones whitening in the spring sun. It was an inauspicious start. The Confederates had withdrawn—they had also left Yorktown—and McClellan and his men discovered not the huge fortifications he'd imagined but wooden logs painted black to resemble cannon. "It was as if General McClellan had thrust his sword into a gigantic enemy," scoffed Nathaniel Hawthorne, "and beholding him suddenly collapsed, had discovered to himself and the world that he had merely punctured an enormously swollen bladder." Besides, Washington learned with mounting dismay that the Confederates had fortified the peninsula and McClellan's maps were inaccurate. And that he had continued to delay, constructing earthworks and inflating the numbers of the enemy he said he would have to face.

Union armies were soon occupying Corinth, Mississippi, and they'd already taken Memphis. New Orleans had fallen into Union hands. But though McClellan's Army of the Potomac finally did advance close enough to Richmond—within five miles—to hear the clang of its church bells, it did not capture the Confederate capital. McClellan had remained cautious while Robert E. Lee—the new head of the Army of Northern Virginia—took the offensive, summoning Brigadier General J. E. B. Stuart, a fine soldier, blue-eyed, twenty-nine years old, and in command of the cavalry. Stuart, who liked to wear a red-lined cape, a large yellow sash, jack boots, and on his head, a soft broad hat with a footlong ostrich plume jutting out of it, rashly wanted to ride entirely around McClellan's large army to assess its position. Lee let him do it, and Stuart glamorously galloped into history for his successful expedition. Lee also summoned the inexorable Stonewall Jackson, who arrived fresh from his success in the Shenandoah Valley campaign, where he had defeated far larger forces than his own and sustained far fewer casualties than he inflicted. Lee also had in his command the combative Ambrose P. Hill, Daniel H. Hill (no relation), and General James Longstreet, the husky forty-one-year-old West Pointer whom Lee called his war horse; Longstreet was "the brain of Lee as Stonewall Jackson was his right arm," said Lincoln's secretary.

With a bold battle plan for direct assault—and the successful defense of Richmond—Lee took the offensive in what became known as the Seven Days battle. Yet despite crushing the Confederates who (foolishly) assaulted Malvern's Hill on July 1 and leaving more than 8,000 of them dead or wounded there, McClellan fell back to Harrison's Landing on the bank of the James, deluded, believing himself to be outnumbered and refusing to take the offensive even though he had defeated the Confederates assaulting Malvern Hill. The Seven

Days Battle was a protracted bloodletting of unthinkable proportion. More than 35,000 men were killed or wounded—more even than had fallen at Shiloh just six weeks earlier and more than would fall at Antietam in a few months. To Northerners, the battle was a bitter, exhausting, dispiriting, and perhaps even predictable fiasco. McClellan had failed.

"THE WATCHWORD 'IRREPRESSIBLE CONFLICT' only gave the key," wrote the optimistic Thomas Higginson, "but War has flung the door wide open, and four million slaves stand ready to file through." Well, the door wasn't as wide open as this abolitionist liked to think, but it had been pried ajar at least a crack by Generals Butler and Frémont—and by Major General David Hunter, who, in the matter of abolition, would make more of a stir.

With a complexion so dark that some of his West Point classmates called him "Black Dave," and though his brown hair was receding (it was sometimes said he wore a wig), Hunter when young had been rather handsome. A duelist who had once challenged a superior officer and a former friend of Jefferson Davis, he had since the 1860 presidential campaign served Abraham Lincoln, and, fearful for Lincoln's life, had accompanied him during the long ride from Illinois to Washington and the inaugural. At the time of Fort Sumter's bombardment, Hunter, then fifty-eight, was not well known outside of the military. By 1886, the year of his death, he was considered a war criminal by Southerners for his slash-and-burn Shenandoah campaign in Virginia in 1864—and, for that matter, for his radical abolitionism.

Wounded in the neck at Bull Run, Hunter had served briefly in the West, and in March 1862 he was appointed commander of the Union's Department of the South, which consisted of sections of South Carolina, Georgia, and Florida, as well as the tropical Sea Islands off the coast of South Carolina, which the Union forces had taken over. Treasury Secretary Chase dispatched government agents to extract the cotton crops (estimated at $2 million) and also appointed his friend Edward Pierce to superintend the former slaves. The wealthy white population had fled the Islands, leaving behind, in their hurry, the cutlery on the table, the linens in the cupboard, the pianos, the livestock, the cotton plantation—and the slaves, about ten thousand of them: more contraband. Pierce, however, refused to call those men and women "contraband." They were freedmen and ready to work, he said.

Would they fight? The topic of black volunteer regiments remained taboo. "Colored men were good enough to fight under Washington," scoffed Frederick Douglass, "but they are not good enough to fight under McClellan." As early as November 1861, Secretary of War Cameron had been advocating the arming of freed slaves. Like Frémont, Cameron had tried to circumvent Lincoln by releasing a report to the press before Lincoln could read it. "It is as clearly a right of the government to arm slaves, when it becomes necessary, as it is to use gunpowder taken from the enemy," he wrote. "Whether it is expedient to do so is purely a military question." Irate, Lincoln had ordered Cameron to retract the report, believing it to be premature, as he had told the Frémonts, and politically damaging. It was too late. Papers such as the *Chicago Tribune* said that arming slaves would be impolitic in Kentucky—but not arming them in Beaufort, South Carolina, was just plain stupid. And Henry James, Sr., declared, "Every negro ought to be armed; it is a crying shame that the Govnt. doesn't take the thing in hand more earnestly and devote itself to it." Cameron was asked to leave the cabinet six weeks later; his tenure at the War Department was known for incompetence, mismanagement, and possible corruption, but his release of the report played its part in the discussion of arming freed slaves.

For all Lincoln's seeming transparency, the tall man with the keen intelligence who sometimes looked like an undertaker and wielded his down-home humor kindly—and like a club—was, as one observer noted, as "deep as a well." He was in a thorny situation regarding emancipation in the border states. And there was the question of England and France to consider: would emancipation make them less likely to recognize the Confederacy? Lincoln was troubled, especially since recently there'd been a near disaster in international relations—and the horrific possibility of a war between the Union and Great Britain—when two Confederate agents had been arrested aboard a British ship.

The two envoys were James M. Mason of Virginia (whose wife had tangled publicly with Lydia Maria Child over John Brown) and Louisiana's John Slidell, the wealthy merchant from New Orleans who was partial to filibustering expeditions. On November 8, 1861, they were leaving Cuba on a special British packet, the *Trent*, bound for England, when Captain Charles Wilkes of the U.S. frigate *San Jacinto*, on blockade patrol, intercepted the *Trent* and, something of a bully, arrested Mason and Slidell. Incensed, the British accused the United States of violating neutrality laws and of insulting the British flag. The British War Office heatedly talked of reprisals, and British-leaning Confederates—there were many—noisily denounced the American North.

Aware that the United States was in the wrong and that the incident might damage the Union cause in any case, Secretary of State William Seward adroitly managed to defuse the matter. Insisting that Captain Wilkes had acted on his own recognizance, he made sure that Lincoln quickly released Mason and Slidell. Of course, they soon headed back to Europe in a long—and ultimately fruitless—attempt to secure recognition of the Confederacy. But knowing that he had to keep Britain and France out of this war, Lincoln also calculated that making emancipation an aim of the war might just do that.

Yet the time was still not right.

General David Hunter, on the other hand, did not care about politics. He needed more troops. Since his requests to Secretary of War Stanton had been ignored, and since the number of former slaves was very large, in frustration, on May 9, 1862, Hunter on his own initiative declared "forever free" *all* the slaves throughout the Department of the South. This might have been a military necessity, but it was emancipation nonetheless. "John Brown *IS* a-marching on," exulted the former moderate George Templeton Strong, "and with seven league boots." And, far more radical than the proclamations of Butler or of Frémont, Hunter's edict also authorized the conscription of all able-bodied black men ages eighteen to forty-five in the 1st South Carolina Volunteers.

Inspired by Hunter's proclamation, on the night of May 13, 1862, the young slave Robert Smalls, along with a few crewmen (fellow slaves), boarded the *Planter*, a Confederate gunboat owned by his master, and secretly piloted the boat out of Charleston Harbor and toward Port Royal. Well stocked with artillery and ammunition as well as Smalls's friends and family, the *Planter* sailed past Fort Sumter and Moultrie to freedom with Smalls at the helm. Then it headed to open seas. Hoisting up a bedsheet and a Federal flag, Smalls surrendered to the U.S. Navy. In the North, the courageous Smalls was hailed as a hero—and, thanks to Hunter, a free man.

But there was a problem. When the freedmen did not volunteer in droves, as Hunter had mistakenly assumed they would, the draconian general instructed his men to pull the former slaves out of their cabins under the cover of darkness, yank them by day from the cotton fields, tear them from their families, and bully them into uniform at the point of a gun. Five hundred black men were pressed into service and loaded upon a ship at Beaufort to be transported to Hilton Head. Issued certificates of freedom, the men, it was said, sighed "for the 'old fetters' as being better than the new liberty."

Lincoln closed Hunter down just eleven days later, on May 20. Rescinding the proclamation, he also halted the brutal impressment. But he stood by Hunter, a friend, who perhaps had launched the trial balloon on emancipation that Lincoln, this time, had already approved. "Gen. Hunter is an honest man," the president explained to a delegation representing the border states. "I valued him none the less for his agreeing with me in the general wish that all men everywhere could be free." Separating his personal belief from what was politically advisable, Lincoln said he had had no choice in the matter. The proclamation would at present do more harm than good.

Regardless, Hunter's impatience had one salutary effect in the North: the issue of whether to arm black men was again on the table, very plainly, for all to see.

THE ARMING OF black men was debated in Congress, to a degree. In March 1862, a new article of war had prohibited the army from returning fugitive slaves to their masters. In April, all slaves in the District of Columbia were freed. In June, slavery was prohibited in all U.S. territories (though slaves remained slaves in the states). In July 1862, Lincoln issued an order to enlist persons of "African descent" for war service, declaring that these persons would receive wages for their labor. That same month the radical majority now seated in Congress passed the Second Confiscation Act, which declared those slaves belonging to rebels and in Union lines to be captives of war but, nonetheless, "forever free."

The aim of the war was changing.

"Broken eggs cannot be mended," Lincoln said.

Part of the reason for the change—or the rationalization for it— was one of so-called military necessity, and military necessity, meaning the military itself, would help effect the major, most lasting social transformation caused by the war: the eradication of slavery. Still, General McClellan adamantly opposed any talk about abolition as a cause or a consequence of the war. "Neither confiscation of property, political executions of persons, territorial organization of States; or forcible abolition of slavery should be contemplated for a moment," McClellan wrote to Lincoln in July, adding that "a declaration of radical views, especially upon slavery, will rapidly disintegrate our present armies." Nonetheless, the war was pulling in a different direction.

Lincoln, who said very little about McClellan's letter, further annoyed the general by appointing the western commander, Henry W. Halleck (commonly known as "Old Brains") to head the Union forces as "General in Chief." Halleck ordered McClellan to withdraw from the peninsula southeast of Richmond and coordinate with

General John Pope along the Rappahannock River for the campaign that would become known as the Second Battle of Bull Run (or Second Battle of Manassas). McClellan, who still had his heart set on Richmond, protested, if for no other reason than that he objected to Pope's appointment. "Do you know Pope is a humbug," asked one soldier, "and known to be so by those who put him in his present place?" Ordered to leave the peninsula and return to northern Virginia, McClellan had moved slowly, far too slowly, suspiciously slowly, and by so doing, he'd effectively refused to reinforce Pope. The Federal army slunk back to Washington, said Charles Adams, "in danger of utter demoralization."

Rumors, jealousy, and dissension had spread while accusations of incompetence were whispered in Washington as well as on the field.

Besides, in early August 1862, Stonewall Jackson and his famous foot cavalry defeated the Massachusetts major general Nathaniel Banks north of Cedar Mountain, in Virginia, killing 30 percent of Banks's army. Jackson then marched his troops fifty miles to seize the depot at Manassas Junction, and together with Lee and Longstreet, had defeated Pope at the disastrous Second Battle of Bull Run.

This decisive and second thrashing of Union forces at Bull Run woke up those who still dreamed about a short war. This would be a long, aggressive war, a fight to the finish. William Tecumseh Sherman confided to his brother the senator that "I rather think many now see the character of the war in which we are engaged. I don't see the end or the beginning of the end, but suppose we must prevail and persist or perish. I don't believe that two nations can exist within our old limits, and therefore that war is on us and we must fight it out."

Two nations not existing within their old limits also implied the end of slavery, even if only out of necessity. Gideon Welles, Lincoln's secretary of the navy, where blacks were already serving, recalled that Lincoln had said, "We must free the slaves or be ourselves subdued." The Union could not be restored without the destruction of slavery; this was obvious from the start to many although few had been willing to admit it aloud. But times were changing.

Slowly. For not everyone agreed. "I think that the best way to settle the question of what to do with the darkies would be to shoot them," one Federal enlistee had declared. To McClellan abolition was "the perversion of the war for the Union into a war for the Negro." At the same time, abolitionists decried the notion of emancipation as "military necessity"—to damage the Confederacy while swelling Union ranks—because it ignored the real and human fact that a slave was entitled to freedom and nothing less. Freeing slaves as a "'military necessity,'" said Parker Pillsbury, would be "the most God-insulting doctrine ever proclaimed." Yet as James R. Gilmore, the editor of *The Continental Monthly* (a new journal devoted to national policy and literature), had pointed out, "All of that old abolition jargon went out and died with the present aspect of the war." Expedience was all—no longer could the abolitionist afford to wait for humanitarian or evangelical arguments to win hearts and minds. Likely, military arguments would be—had become—the more persuasive ones.

In all this discussion, some of it rancorous, Lincoln heeded himself. More than anything, he cared for the Union, which was facing defeat. Toward the end of July, after Hunter repeatedly asked to authorize enlisting more black troops, Lincoln called together his cabinet and announced his decision—to issue an emancipation proclamation and free all slaves within the rebellious states. (The proclamation would not touch slaves in the border states.) Secretary of State Seward counseled the president to wait before issuing the proclamation, for the North first needed a military victory; military necessity must trump higher law in order to enforce it.

The restive Horace Greeley, not privy to the inner workings of the administration but eager for attention—and emancipation—issued his own declaration in the *New-York Tribune* on August 19, 1862. In his "Prayer of Twenty Millions," Greeley reminded readers that "the Rebellion, if crushed out to-morrow, would be renewed within a year if Slavery were left in full vigor—that army officers, who remain to this day devoted to Slavery, can at best be but half-way loyal to the Union—and that every hour of deference to Slavery is an hour of added and deepened peril to the Union." Alert to the power of the press, Lincoln swiftly replied, and with political panache put his own inimitable rhetorical stamp on the question. He raised hope, he dashed it. He insinuated, he did not state. "My paramount object in this struggle *is* to save the Union, and is *not* either to save or to destroy slavery. If I could save the Union without freeing *any* slave I would do it, and if I could save it by freeing *all* the slaves I would do it, and if I could save it by freeing some and leaving others alone I would also do that. What I do about slavery, and the colored race, I do because I believe it helps to save the Union; and what I forbear, I forbear because I do *not* believe it would help to save the Union."

No compromiser on the matter of preserving the Union, for which too many men had already died, and which, for him, was an absolute, Lincoln would compromise on the issue of slavery, which he intimated was the negotiable part of his plan. Or so he said. He hinted something else: that he would in fact free all the slaves, some of whom had already been freed under the Confiscation Acts. What he intended, few knew, except of course it was clear that he could and would draw a line between his personal views and what he termed his "official duty." "I intend no modification of my oft-expressed personal wish that all men every where could be free," he insisted.

"Was ever a more heartless policy announced?" *The Liberator* scornfully responded. "With the President public policy is *everything*, humanity and justice nothing."

Yet Lincoln's reply was an eloquent lesson in responsibility—and a demonstration of the conflicts that beget compromise. If there were those so-called higher laws of freedom for all, there were also legal, even constitutional, issues to be considered as a means for achieving them and for achieving justice. And so if official duty clashed with what may have been his conscience, his conscience did not suffer defeat and it would not, for he knew how to wait, how to plan, how to deliberate, how to achieve—which so many others did not or could not. This didn't mean he had no plan in mind or that he had forgotten about justice. As it was, after all, the Union was not being saved and, as he must have known, would never be saved by perpetuating slavery in any form.

THE CHANGE HAD begun. On August 25, 1862, Secretary of War Edwin Stanton wrote to Brigadier General Rufus Saxton, the Massachusetts man assigned to the Sea Island plantations, who had recently requested authority to arm black men. Stanton told Saxton that he could "arm, uniform, equip, and receive into the service of the United States such number of volunteers of African descent as you may deem expedient, not exceeding 5000." Only five thousand, true, but at least the men would be paid. "You are therefore authorized by every means within your power to withdraw from the enemy their laboring force and population," he instructed Saxton, "and to spare no effort consistent with civilized warfare to weaken, harass, and annoy them." These men, along with wives, mothers, and children of all men enlisted in the service, would also, like them, be declared forever free.

Obtaining the official order David Hunter had requested, Saxton was in one way like Lincoln: he was a practical idealist. He was also a maverick among West Point graduates in that he was actually a committed antislavery man. And now he was to take possession of all plantations previously occupied by rebels and to feed, employ, and govern their remaining inhabitants, who had been left without shelter, clothing, provisions, or the wherewithal to buy any. This was an anomalous position, he ruefully admitted, one that straddled the gulf between civilian and soldier, slave driver and general, despot and humanitarian, so he reassured his troops, black troops, that no person serving under him would ever receive unjust treatment.

To recruit and train volunteers of African descent in what he called the 1st South Carolina Volunteers (Hunter's regiment had been disbanded), Saxton recruited the white abolitionist writer Thomas Higginson to command this, the first regiment of black troops ever regularly organized and mustered into the U.S. military. (The

Virginia writer James Branch Cabell was not impressed. All that had happened, he said, was that the slave had moved "from the dull and tedious drudgery of farm work in favor of a year or two's military service under the more noble excitements of gunfire.")

Since Hunter and Saxton and Higginson were convinced that the slaves could and would fight for their freedom, they knew it would be hypocritical not to allow them to do just that. But Northerners seemed to regard what was called the Port Royal experiment—not just the arming of men but the development in the Sea Island of a labor force, of cash crops, banks, and schools—as just another one of Barnum's exhibits. Many of them flocked there—government agents, teachers, hucksters, and just plain do-gooders—and pestered Saxton with insulting inquiries about what these freed blacks were really like. Saxton testily answered, without fail, that they were "intensely human."

THOUGH HE'D INITIALLY been reluctant, by the end of August 1862, Butler was also mustering a troop of free black men into service—and cleverly taking credit for a position he'd formerly opposed; no matter. Two regiments were quickly filled, a third followed. A regiment of black troops was formed in Kansas, too. The abolitionist senator James Lane was recruiting them (without authorization), and by early 1863, there were six companies serving as the 1st Regiment, Kansas Colored Volunteers.

The Union defeats of late summer and early fall had threatened to roll back the tide of emancipation, but on September 17, 1862, McClellan partially redeemed himself at the bloody battle near Sharpsburg, Maryland, along Antietam Creek, where twelve hours of fighting "sucks everything into its red vortex," said Oliver Wendell Holmes, who afterward went to find his son, who had been shot in the neck. The partial redemption came at a very high cost: another 26,000 casualties and a battlefield so deeply covered in corpses that horses couldn't cross it; men slept, exhausted, their heads resting on the inert bodies of other men, unable to distinguish the wounded from the dead. Outside the hospitals, there were stacks and stacks of amputated arms and legs piled high. Impossible to think that death had undone so many. That is what Gardner had come to photograph.

Pyrrhic victory? Lincoln's secretaries, Nicolay and Hay, thought so. "The carnage was frightful, the result in no proportion to the terrible expense." The field was left to McClellan, who had fought splendidly, or so he told his wife; the battle was his masterpiece. Yet he hadn't finished the job. He had not renewed the attack, and instead of crushing Lee the following morning, he weighed his options, allowing Lee's army to withdraw across the Potomac and back into Virginia.

Whatever held McClellan back—whether caution, exhaustion, or incompetence—he had given Lincoln the victory he needed, and Lincoln issued the preliminary Emancipation Proclamation on September 22: if the rebellious states did not return to the Union by January 1, 1863, their slaves would be pronounced forever free. Lincoln was basically annulling the Fugitive Slave Act—and doing much more, for though he did not mention the arming of black men, by virtue of the proclamation, the Union army would effectively become an army of liberation. Yet Lincoln did not free all slaves—just those in rebellious states. This was, after all, a war act; Lincoln did not have the power to abolish slavery in the loyal border states. To them (Maryland, Delaware, Missouri, Kentucky), he promised gradual and compensated emancipation. (He also continued to favor colonization, or what the former slave William Wells Brown aptly called deportation.)

In the South, members of the Confederate Congress fulminated, as of old, about slave insurrections: that Lincoln intended to foster uprisings among their slaves; that the slaves would kill white women and children when white men, absent from home, could not protect them. Federal soldiers harboring or employing slaves should therefore be considered criminals, not prisoners of war, and hanged. Senator Benjamin Hall of Georgia disagreed and saw Lincoln's purpose as more political than military or moral. With autumn elections upcoming and Democrats as well as radical Republicans fidgeting, Lincoln had needed to appease border states and to curry favor with Northern abolitionists at the same time. To conceive of his proclamation in any other way, said Hill, dignified it beyond importance.

Northern opinion was split. Though jubilant in public, William Lloyd Garrison complained in private, "The President can do nothing *for freedom* in a direct manner, but only by circumlocution and delay." General McClellan insisted yet again that the proclamation would demoralize the army, though the journalist George W. Smalley would point out that it wasn't the army that was demoralized, just certain generals. In Europe, the response was also mixed; those people already hostile to emancipation regarded the proclamation as a bid for international sympathy and support, which it was, yet frequently, like the Southerners, they regarded it as the prelude to the horrific slave insurrections that were bound to come. Nonetheless, the proclamation, following on the heels of Antietam, helped quash the idea of any involvement in the war or recognition for the Confederacy in sympathetic circles of the British government. Said Henry Adams, secretary to his father, Charles Francis Adams, who was now the U.S. minister to England, "the Emancipation Proclamation has done more for us here than all our former victories and all our diplomacy."

In Boston, where radicals argued that the scope of the proclamation was limited—it did not free all slaves—Ralph Waldo Emerson reminded people that it did not admit "of being taken back." That is, as he said, once "done, it cannot be undone by a new administration." As Lincoln had said, broken eggs cannot be mended. The country was headed toward true and uncompromising justice; it made "a victory of our defeats," Emerson continued, and guaranteed that those who died in this war would not die in vain. "We have recovered ourselves from our false position, and planted ourselves on a law of Nature." That law of Nature, that higher law, was freedom.

IT MAY HAVE become a different kind of war, though only up to a point. That point was racism. Yet if racism was pervasive in the North, which it largely was, its racism differed markedly from that of the South, which, as Alexander Stephens had explained, amply justified slavery—even celebrated it—as the core of the Confederacy.

By freeing slaves in that same Confederacy, the Emancipation Proclamation was thus recognized as changing the aim, if not the tide, of war. General Henry W. Halleck, who had once prohibited blacks from joining the Union lines, wrote to General Grant in early 1863, "There is now no possible hope of reconciliation with the rebels. The Union party in the South is virtually destroyed. There can be no peace but that which is forced by the sword."

In the South, General Saxton had hosted a grand celebration of the Emancipation Proclamation, which was to take effect on New Year's Day 1863. It was not the proclamation of the previous September but a more radical version, one that allayed the abolitionists' fear that Lincoln would renege on it: it authorized the recruitment of black soldiers, and even though for the present it exempted parts of Tennessee, of Louisiana and of Virginia, and the border states, it promised freedom to all once the Confederacy was crushed.

In Beaufort, South Carolina, in a grove of live oaks, black and white men and women congregated together, people arriving any way they could, on foot, in carriages, on horseback or mule back: cavalry officers, black women wearing brightly colored head scarves, teachers, superintendents, soldiers. William Henry Brisbane, a South Carolinian planter who earlier had freed his slaves, read from the proclamation, "On the 1st day of January, A.D. 1863, all persons held as slaves within any State or designated part of a State the people whereof shall then be in rebellion against the United States shall be then, thenceforward, and forever free." Men tossed their hats into the air, and women hugged one another. Spontaneously, an elderly man and two women, former slaves, burst into song, belting out "My Country, 'Tis of Thee."

As numbers of white enlistments had dropped, black regiments had become more acceptable to their detractors; they were essential to winning the war. But none of it came easily, proclamations notwithstanding. The capture of the Confederate post of Port Hudson,

Louisiana, by the 1st and 3rd Louisiana Native Guards and the 1st Louisiana Engineers, prompted one Union general to muster a backhanded compliment. "Our negro troops are splendid," said he. "Who would not be a Niggadier General?"

In Massachusetts, Governor John A. Andrew, a stalwart antislavery man with a pudgy face, obtained authorization to recruit a black regiment from his state, and soon men such as the black activist Lewis Hayden and the white activist George Stearns were recruiting free blacks into the ranks of the much-publicized 54th Regiment of Massachusetts Volunteer Infantry. Frederick Douglass published a broadside, *Men of Color, to Arms!,* and two of Douglass's sons, Charles and Lewis, enlisted. "In a struggle for freedom the race most directly interested in the achievement of freedom should be permitted to take a hand," recalled Garth Wilkinson "Wilkie" James, one of the sons of Henry James, Sr., and a soldier at seventeen.

Required by the federal government to commission white men as officers, Governor Andrew appointed two young abolitionists to head the "Bostons," as the 54th was nicknamed. One was Robert Gould Shaw, a fair-haired son of philanthropic Yankees and formerly a captain in the 2nd Massachusetts Infantry, a veteran of Cedar Mountain, and a survivor of Antietam. Second in command was the Philadelphia Quaker Norwood Penrose Hallowell. Hallowell would eventually lead the 55th Massachusetts, the regiment formed after recruitment efforts swelled the ranks of the 54th.

On May 18, 1863, the 54th received orders to report to General Hunter in Hilton Head, South Carolina. Ten days later, 3,000 men and women hailed the troops, 1,000 men strong, as they paraded through Boston. "At last the North consents to let the Negro fight for his freedom," cheered Henry Wadsworth Longfellow. And though Copperheads threw stones and scuffled with the police near Battery Wharf, the columns of young men were proudly reviewed by Governor Andrew, William Lloyd Garrison, Wendell Phillips, and Frederick Douglass. Shaw, riding at the head of the regiment, looked up, saw them, and kissed his sword with a flourish. At that moment, his sister Ellen, as she later recalled, knew she would never see him again. The Bostons were marching toward a staggering death at Battery Wagner, just outside Charleston.

In South Carolina, the regimental leader of the 2nd South Carolina Colored Volunteers, another black regiment, was Colonel James Montgomery, who had not long before fought slave owners in Missouri. A tall, thin man with slightly stooped shoulders and a hard-bitten face, Montgomery was a practiced avenger in the mold of John Brown. He believed that praying, pillaging, and burning were the only way to win the war. And he assumed that black soldiers should do his bidding. In the spring of 1863, shortly after the Massachusetts 54th arrived, Montgomery ordered the men to sail to the mouth of the Alameda River and shell plantations along the way, regardless of who might still be living there, and once they arrived in the undefended town of Darien, Georgia, Montgomery further insisted that Shaw's men load all furniture and movable goods onto their boats and burn the place to the ground. Montgomery himself set fire to the last buildings. "It was as abominable a job as I ever had a share in," said Shaw.

Montgomery exploited black troops to conduct guerrilla warfare, complained Colonel Higginson to Charles Sumner: "This indiscriminate burning & pillaging is savage warfare in itself—demoralizes the soldiers—& must produce reaction against arming the negroes." Montgomery persisted. Accusing a black man in his regiment of desertion, he asked if the man had anything to say in his own defense. The soldier answered "Nothing," and Montgomery, with nonchalance, replied, "Then you die at half past nine." "I accordingly shot and buried him at that hour," he told Brigadier General George Crockett Strong.

Years later, Higginson angrily remembered that if Montgomery "had done it to white soldiers, he would have been court martialed himself." The army was filled with Montgomerys, whether proslavery or antislavery men. "Do not think this rapid organization of colored regiments is to be an unmixed good to the negroes," he confided to a friend in the early summer of 1863. "There will be much &

terrible tyranny under military forms, for it is no easy thing to make their officers deal justly by them."

The soldier whom Montgomery shot had deserted because he had not been paid; the 1st South Carolina Volunteers had not received their wage of $13 a month. In fact, their salary had been cut to $10 per soldier a month. Higginson barraged the *New-York Tribune* and *The New York Times* with letters. "We presume too much on the supposed ignorance of those men," he fumed. "I have never yet found a man in my regiment so stupid as not to know when he was cheated." Higginson was also livid when, later, he learned that retroactive pay would be given only to "free colored regiments" and not those composed of fugitive slaves that had been "earlier in the field," namely the 1st South Carolina.

Moreover, the soldiers were aware that in the army or navy they were assigned the most menial jobs: digging ditches, cleaning latrines, hauling cargo. And, wasted by pleurisy, smallpox, and pneumonia, black troops had not received sufficient medical attention. The physician serving the 1st South Carolina Volunteers tried to prevent scurvy without vegetables, amputate limbs without knives, and was begrudgingly equipped with weapons. Higginson's and Montgomery's regiments were told, at one point, that their firearms would be replaced with pikes.

But they'd fight. Fully grasping the symbolic importance of the 54th, for instance, Colonel Shaw understood that to every commander of a black regiment was entrusted a chance to undo the racial prejudices that permitted slavery in the first place. So, eager to test the mettle of his black soldiers, who hadn't been tried in battle, Shaw pushed them forward into the front lines when he had the chance. For Brigadier General Quincy Adams Gillmore, Hunter's replacement, would call on the Massachusetts 54th, now in General Strong's brigade, in his attempt to advance slowly toward Charleston. "Well I guess we will let Strong put those d—d negroes from Massachusetts in the advance, we may as well get rid of them, one time as another," scoffed Brigadier General Truman Seymour. Seymour had opposed the enlistment of black troops; General Strong was a Democrat.

On the morning of July 18, 1863, the 54th Massachusetts landed on Morris Island to lead the column against an impregnable Fort Wagner in Charleston Harbor. Prepared for hand-to-hand combat, the men stole on foot across a narrow bar of sand until they were within musket-range of the daunting fort. The hour was late, about 7:45, and the skies were streaked with purple rays from a fading sun. Just as the 54th was about to rush across the ditch surrounding the fort, a sheet of fire from small arms lit the coming darkness. Men lurched across the ditch, staggered, and fell. Wilkie James was struck in the side. Reeling, he was hit again. Shaw scaled the ramparts and was shot through the heart. The sword sheath of Sergeant Major Lewis Douglass, Frederick Douglass's son, was blown away. General Strong went down. Hand grenades thrown from the parapet burst over them as the men scaled the face of the fort and, for a fleeting moment, one of them, Sergeant R. J. Simmons, planted their flag at its top. More than 1,500 Union men were killed.

Shaw's body, which had fallen inside the fort, was subsequently stripped naked and placed on display before being thrown into the bottom of a large pit, the corpses of his troops tossed on top of him. "Buried with his niggers," the victorious General Johnson Hagood had presumably said; but a Confederate officer, Lieutenant Iredell Jones, said the Negroes had fought valiantly. Shaw's father instructed General Gillmore not to remove his son's body, which should remain buried with his men, the black soldiers with whom he had fought. And there he remains.

(11)

THIS THING NOW
NEVER SEEMS TO STOP

When you meet people, sad and sorrowful is the greeting;" Mary Chesnut observed in the spring of 1862, "they press your hand, tears stand in their eyes or roll down their cheeks, as they happen to have more or less self-control. They have brothers, fathers, or sons—as the case may be—in the battle. And this thing now never seems to stop."

It did not stop and would not stop, not for three more long years. Despite desertions, despite bickering in the government, despite the odds, the Confederates continued to fight. And they fought for different reasons than those that inspired Northerners or those that were exploited to inspire them. The Confederacy was territory invaded and beleaguered even though, at Sumter, Governor Pickens had fired the first shot. And as a country beset and besieged, the Confederacy pledged to safeguard its way of life, its grace, its privilege and those gallant generals who did not fight in order to protect their men, as the vacillating McClellan had, but who fought hard to protect their homes and homeland against enemy invasion.

That was what the stalwart Robert E. Lee chose to do; that was the reasoning of the man later beloved by the South for his determination, moral rectitude, and sheer brilliance as a soldier. Lee didn't like slavery, and he didn't much like secession. He cared little for the so-called unity of Southern interests, and at first he believed that the Union might be disassembled amicably. But to that ramrod-straight, courteous Southern gentleman, the state of Virginia was home; it was family. He would not fail it.

On Lincoln's behalf, Francis Blair had asked Lee to command the U.S. Army with the rank of major general. "I could take no part in an invasion of the Southern States," Lee courteously declined. Six days after the surrender of Fort Sumter, he resigned his commission in the U.S. Army, and two days later he was bound for Richmond. His thin lips were set, his disciplined purpose unswerving, although, it was later alleged, he knew the South was weak, the road long, the outcome dubious at best. No matter; he was a professional soldier, a West Pointer, committed to doing what he had to do. "He moves his agencies like a god," it would be said of him, "—secret, complicated, vast, resistless, complete."

In the early years of the war, though, it was Stonewall Jackson, not Lee, who captured the imagination of men and women in the South as well as the North. Mary Chesnut called him the "Confederate hero par excellence," the man who did not hesitate to shoot deserters, arrest officers, or kill as many men, including his own, as possible. His dazzling campaign in the Shenandoah Valley in 1862 with its aggressive, lethal strikes against the enemy and his messianic commitment to winning the war won the hearts of his soldiers. "I always thought we ought to meet the Federal invaders on the outer verge of just right and defense," Jackson had said, "and raise at once the black flag, viz., 'No quarter to the violators of our homes and firesides!'"

As fanatical in his way as John Brown, Stonewall Jackson had long been looking for a religious cause, and he'd found one for which he could fight with all his discipline, zealotry, and ecstatic might. The Confederate States of America had been established to elude tyranny, assert the right of the individual state, and to safeguard that state's right to govern as it saw fit, to live free and protect itself against subjugation, despotism, and the moral condescension of the Northern industrial states. Its Constitution guaranteed the protection of its sovereign members, it ensured justice and the liberty of each state and each of its (white) citizens, and it defined citizens by refusing to sidestep such incendiary terms as "slave," as the earlier U.S. Constitution had done. It declared—without fear of reprisal—that it honored the "right of property in negro slaves," and the document repeated the phrase "the right of that property" three insistent times.

Non-slaveholders in the South—such as Stonewall Jackson—vehemently supported the Confederacy. So did those who had doubted the economic wisdom of slavery (such as Hilton Helper) or those who had doubted or even despaired of its (and their own) humanity, such as Lee. Why were all those people willing to fight? Why would they be willing to soak the land in blood, as Virginia governor John Letcher, a moderate Democrat, had glumly predicted? The putative answer: the righteous shaking off the yoke of the North, a foreign invader that intended to upturn homes and appropriate lands, to desecrate institutions and destroy tradition, to plunder and then profit from the theft. Foreigners, outsiders, call them what you would, had come to invade and ultimately to deracinate the white Southerner by accepting, perhaps even encouraging, the mingling of races. If they didn't fight to protect or to extend slavery, they did fight for what they considered purity, which at bottom amounted to fighting to preserve slavery.

In March 1862 Jefferson Davis told his Congress that he needed more men, more artillery, more small arms, and more ironclads along the lines of the *Virginia* (known in the North as the *Merrimack*), which had battered the Union's presumably invincible ironclad, the *Monitor*. But since the South was an agrarian economy and had depended on the North for its manufactured goods, little was forthcoming—not blankets, not shoes, not small arms, not ammunition. One historian said that in 1862 "otherwise rational men proposed arming Southern soldiers with pikes."

Morale too wavered. From the Sea Islands, Edward Pierce reported that when the Federal soldiers had taken over the plantations near Port Royal, South Carolina, they had found books denouncing slavery. "These people seem, indeed, to have had light enough to see the infinite wrong of the system, and it is difficult to believe them entirely sincere in their passionate defense of it," Pierce observed. "Their very violence, when the moral basis of slavery is assailed, seems to be that of a man who distrusts the rightfulness of his daily conduct, has resolved to persist in it, and therefore hates most of all the prophet who comes to confront him for his misdeeds, and, if need be, to publish them to mankind." Whether Southerners considered the invading Yankees to be prophets is debatable, but ambivalence about their peculiar institution doubtless increased Confederate ferocity. Mary Chesnut had read *Uncle Tom's Cabin* and more recently James Redpath's hagiographic biography of John Brown, and though she detested what she considered Stowe's and Redpath's fanaticism and thoroughly believed black people to be lazy, she also acknowledged that "we forget there is any wrong in slavery at all."

The war dragged on, bloodier and bloodier. And with low morale, scarce supplies, and ghastly death tolls came infighting. With Forts Henry and Donelson in Tennessee lost in early 1862; with the beautiful and rich New Orleans occupied by Union forces in the spring of 1862; with control of the valuable Mississippi River no longer certain; with much of eastern North Carolina under Union control; and with the hero of First Manassas, Albert Sidney Johnston, mortally wounded at Shiloh, where the casualties were staggering, Confederate politicians wondered if Jefferson Davis and his advisers were up to the job. Disgruntled about food shortages to his troops, General Beauregard breached military etiquette and publicly mocked Davis, his commander in chief. Vice President Alexander Stephens was disheartened as well, and Robert Toombs was carping about Davis's "lamentable incapacity." The interim secretary of war, Judah Benjamin, bore much of the brunt of their criticism—after all, he was a quarrelsome fellow and a Jew. (Mary Chesnut said "the mob" called him "Mr. Davis' 'pet Jew,' " but the unperturbed Davis placed him in the State Department when Robert M. T. Hunter left the cabinet.) In his paper, the *Charleston Mercury*, an angry Robert Barnwell Rhett called Davis an egomaniac, and the *Richmond Examiner* retracted its effervescent support: the president of the Confederate States of America was an autocrat. Like that gorilla Abe Lincoln, Jeff Davis had suspended the writ of habeas corpus. Though the Confederate Congress allowed Davis to declare martial law should he need to do so, in a new country fighting for self-determination, states' rights, and the sacrosanct white individual, those acts, real or potential, were no different from those of the tyrannical invader.

Was the exercise of leadership tyranny? The prosecution of the war demanded order, centralization, command. Passed in the spring of 1862 by the Confederate Congress on behalf of President Davis, the first Conscription Act required every white man between eighteen and thirty-five to join the army. There were some exceptions: those who had served in previous wars, those who occupied such professions as miners, telegraph operators, clergymen, or teachers; those who could hire a substitute for as much as the absurd price of $4,000. (By comparison, substitutes in the North cost $300—and even that was a significant sum.) And the Twenty Negro Act exempted from military service men who owned twenty or more slaves. This was a rich man's war, it was said over and over, and a poor man's fight.

Yet the poet Henry Timrod, himself a poor man, urged his fellow Southerners to put down the "bloodless spade," to torch "the books of trade," and to vanquish the Northern "despot." Timrod had enlisted. Said to be as delicate as a mimosa, the fragile Timrod was soon discharged from the army, and his stint as a correspondent was likewise short. He did continue to fight—in words, that is, praising the South as an "endless field" of white (cotton as well as men)—inviolable though violated. Soon Timrod was the unofficial poet laureate of the Confederacy.

Timrod had long complained that the Southern author was the pariah of contemporary literature, which, he insisted, was dominated by a Northern cabal. And though his poems had been published by Ticknor & Fields—the Boston house of Hawthorne and Longfellow—Timrod was calling for Southern independence from a Northern rule that extended even into the arts. Southerners needed to look to their own poets, not to those of the snooty North with its antislavery presumptions. As the Virginian secessionist Edward A. Pollard told Northerners, you "vaunt over our heads a rotten and phosphorescent literature, you even sneer at us over self-assertions of your puritanical virtues." And so, during the war, poems flooded the offices of magazines and newspapers, which began to print more and more original verse about homeland, triumph, and Northern aggression. "Are we to bend to slavish yoke?" asked the former editor John O'Sullivan, who became a Confederate poet. Not at all: "For home, for country, for truth and right / We stand or fall in freedom's fight."

Much of this poetry was a form of martial propaganda camouflaged as tributes to the agrarian ideal. Ruffians of the North had violated the "sacred sands," as Timrod had written, and if "ten times ten thousand men must fall," so be it. In his poem, "Maryland, My Maryland," the belligerent, Baltimore-born James Ryder Randall called his neighbors to "Avenge the patriot gore / That flecked the streets of Baltimore / And be the battle-queen of yore, / Maryland! My Maryland!" This was the bloody dawn of a new day; dally not. Northerners were "codfish poltroons." A very popular call to arms, published just days after Sumter in the New Orleans *Daily Delta*, "Maryland, My Maryland," was sung to the tune of "O Tannenbaum," and in 1939 the state of Maryland made Randall's poem its state song.

The unofficial anthem of the South, "Dixie," had originally been sung in a Northern minstrel show, and it too told of old times not forgotten and seeped with sentimental nostalgia about those old times, long before war's beginning; it looked back to what the war, presumably, was being fought for. But at night, it was "When This Cruel War Is Over" that Confederate soldiers sang. The Union soldiers sang it too, and so did those sitting at the piano back home.

· · · ·

ON MAY 6, 1862, just days before General David Hunter brashly issued his proclamation freeing the slaves of the Sea Islands, Henry David Thoreau died of consumption at age forty-four in Concord, Massachusetts. Three days later, a service was held in Concord's First Parish Church. Thoreau would have disliked that, for he'd spurned the church and all other institutions. But Emerson had insisted. He wanted as many people as possible to mourn Thoreau, for his friend's death marked the end of an era.

It was certainly the end of the kind of phosphorescent literature, transcendentally lit, that Pollard detested and had included the vatic poems of Jones Very, Hawthorne's haunted early tales, the exhortations of Margaret Fuller, and Thoreau's lapidary tale of an experiment in living at Walden Pond, away from mills and industrialists. Thoreau's was a life devoted to the higher laws incarnated in men such as John Brown—and Stonewall Jackson.

Northerners called Jackson a "species of demon." That was praise. He was the man who inflicted more damage than he sustained, who lifted Southern morale with his daring, capturing supplies and arms, easily it seemed, and outwitted large forces. At the Second Battle of Manassas (Bull Run), in August 1862, he had outflanked General Pope and cut the telegraph lines between the Union forces and Washington; at Antietam, he had again been firm and resolute: he was a hero, a legend, a star, indeed a demon.

Mythologized as a plain man (an orphan, no less) and a humble, God-fearing, modest one (which only increased his fame), Jackson was just the sort of man the North needed. "We should be, like the South, penetrated with an idea, and ready with fortitude and courage to sacrifice everything to that idea," Wendell Phillips goaded his Northern audiences. "No man can fight Stonewall Jackson, a sincere fanatic on the side of slavery, but John Brown, an equally honest fanatic on the other. They are only chemical equals, and will neutralize each other. You cannot neutralize nitric acid with cologne-water. You cannot hurl William H. Seward at Jeff Davis."

In his way, Stonewall Jackson was another transcendentalist, as

Thoreau had called John Brown—a hero ready for the times, especially since morale was sinking low in the North, too. Washington was flooded with wounded and half-dead soldiers in the aftermath of one or another battle. "Nothing here nowadays," reported Edmund Stedman, "but smallpox and congressmen, and mud." There were also soldiers and diplomats, war correspondents and spies, nurses, office seekers, wire pullers, traitors, parents looking for their sons, and men such as Hawthorne and his editor, who had come from Boston to see the war for themselves, jamming the cigar-smoked corridors of hotels. Generals vied with generals, the radical Republicans wanted to oust Seward, conservatives wanted to oust Chase, the Northern public craved scapegoats on whom they could blame military fiascos. Fat generals looked like stuffed fowls, said Louisa May Alcott. They seemed complacent, with nobody aggressing pursuing victory. In Europe, Friedrich Engels and Karl Marx had been monitoring events in America, with Marx often writing for Greeley's *Tribune*. But Engels wrote to Marx privately that "I must say I cannot work up any enthusiasm for a people which on such a colossal issue allows itself to be continually beaten by a fourth of its own population and which after eighteen months of war has achieved nothing more than the discovery that all its generals are idiots and all its officials rascals and traitors."

Elections in November 1862 had not gone well for Republicans. Anti-Lincoln Democrats such as New York's Horatio Seymour and Fernando Wood swept into office. Lincoln, vexed yet again at McClellan's caution, particularly after Antietam in September, seemed almost desperate when he chose Ambrose E. Burnside to replace him as commander of the Army of the Potomac.

Burnside was dubious about whether he could lead an army of more than 100,000 men, but since the popular, ruddy-faced general Joseph Hooker thought the honor should have gone to him instead, Burnside might have accepted the post partly to prevent Fighting Joe from getting it. Bewhiskered, bald, decent, and dignified, a West Pointer and an inventor of the breech-loading rifle, Burnside was a capable man. But the Army of the Potomac needed more than mere competence. And Burnside could be as reckless and stubborn as Mc-Clellan was cautious and slow.

Burnside wanted to prove himself, and to do so, he planned to take the huge Army of the Potomac to Fredericksburg, Virginia, after crossing the Rappahannock, and launch a surprise attack on Robert E. Lee's Army of Northern Virginia, which was located around Culpeper, from the east. To do this, he would build pontoon bridges somewhere near the city of Fredericksburg, and his army would cross the Rappahannock there—undetected, he hoped. ("It seemed foolhardy to attempt the passage of a river in the presence of such an antagonist as Lee, yet that was what our general decided to do," recalled one soldier.) The campaign went awry from the start. The bridge engineers and equipment were delayed. It rained and rained. The river rose, the roads grew impassably thick with ugly brown mud. The pontoons were delayed even longer. And Lee had a good idea of what was going on, so that by the time the pontoons were ready, so was he; Longstreet had arrived, and Stonewall Jackson, and A. P. Hill's and D. H. Hill's divisions.

As soon as they began constructing the bridges, the Union soldiers had been fired on ceaselessly by the Mississippi sharpshooters who had remained in Fredericksburg to protect it. Frustrated, Burnside reacted with overwhelming force, sending infantrymen over the newly erected bridges on December 11 and unleashing a cannonade that pounded the city into rubble. After the cannonade, the Union soldiers went into Fredericksburg like vandals, throwing chairs and sofas and cooking utensils into the front yards of the charred houses. They ripped keys from pianos and tore pages out of books, and, decked up in the clothes of Confederate women, they danced in the streets.

Why did the Union bombard this nearly undefended town? a correspondent asked a Union officer. There was no answer until a private piped up, "They want us to get in. Getting out won't be quite so smart and easy."

Burnside had made other mistakes. After the sacking of Fredericksburg, he did not attack the Confederates for two more days, during which Lee was able to bring Jackson's corps into position. He dispatched unclear orders to his men, and he divided his forces. When Burnside did finally order an attack, he sent seventeen brigades to storm the heavily fortified hill known as Marye's Heights. In front of the hill was a stone wall, about four feet in height; behind it were Longstreet's riflemen, waiting. "A chicken could not live on that field when we open on it," said one of Longstreet's men. The bluecoats walked into a killing field.

They never got within thirty yards of Lee's and Longstreet's men. "We might as well have tried to take Hell," said one Federal soldier. Union general Darius N. Couch recalled that under the pitiless fusillade, brigade after brigade "coming up in succession would do its duty and melt like snow coming down on warm ground." Each one bravely, tenaciously, hopelessly rushed into the wall of artillery fire regardless of who had fallen before their own eyes, assuming, that is, that they could see what was going on in the smoke and commotion. Fresh Union soldiers kept coming, per Burnside's orders, boys sent to the slaughter. General Longstreet later said, "The spectacle we saw on the battlefield was one of the most distressing I ever witnessed." General Hooker, who was waiting for a breach in the Confederate lines, wanted to stop the assault but didn't have the authority. "It can hardly be in human nature for men to show more valor," noted one war correspondent, "or generals to manifest less judgment, than were perceptible on our side that day."

This was no battle, said a nurse back at Union Hotel Hospital in Washington. This was murder. The cold field in front of the stone hill at Marye's Heights was carpeted with corpses, naked, their uniforms and shoes stolen by ill-clad Confederates. Over nine hundred men had been killed there, and in all there were more than 13,000 Federal casualties and about 5,000 on the Confederate side. Nothing had been accomplished. On December 15, Union troops withdrew to the northern side of the river. "If there is a worse place than Hell," Lincoln declared when he heard what had happened, "I am in it."

. . . .

MANY OF THE wounded soldiers were transported into Washington by steamer. At Union Hotel Hospital, a fetid, poorly ventilated tangle of noxious odors and noise, Louisa May Alcott waited.

Had she been a boy, she said, she would have marched off to war, shouldering a musket, but as it was, when she had insisted on leaving Concord to serve as an Army nurse, her father, Bronson, said he was losing his only son—and, as it happened, the family breadwinner. Louisa was thirty years old, competent, a plain young woman with luxurious chestnut hair, and she hadn't been in Washington long before the battered young men of Fredericksburg began to arrive. She washed young faces with brown soap, she dressed wounds, sang lullabies, wiped brows, and scribbled letters to the mothers and sweethearts of the damaged men, some without arms or legs, who lay in excruciating pain in the hotel's ballroom. "Horrid war," Bronson Alcott cried. "And one sees its horrors in hospitals, if anywhere."

Apathy, embezzlement, mismanagement—all plagued the Union Hotel Hospital. When Hannah Ropes, its head nurse, went to file a complaint, little was ever done. Women belonged in the kitchen. And when she discovered one of the stewards stealing, the male surgeons closed ranks. "I think through all this troubled water the men have been much less clear in the sense of right than the women have," Ropes said. "Is it that they hate to give up one of their club to the law?" She eventually had to apply to Secretary of War Edwin Stanton, who listened to her only because he disliked the hospital's chief surgeon.

Six weeks after Alcott's arrival in Washington, Hannah Ropes was dead of typhoid pneumonia, and Alcott herself, infected with the same illness, said her head felt as heavy as a cannonball. So sick was she that her father traveled to Washington to carry his delirious daughter home—when the nurses fell ill, said Alcott, the doctors departed. She woke up in Concord only to find that her beautiful hair had been lopped off. For the rest of her life, she suffered from headaches, stomach ailments, boils, and joint pain, possibly caused by the calomel (a mercury compound) administered during her recovery. But now, back with her family, she was writing about the boys cut to pieces at Fredericksburg and her experiences while nursing them in a series of stories, *Hospital Sketches.*

Most of the stories were moneymaking pabulum about the fortitude of the wounded knights who suffered in silence as they lay on their narrow iron cots, their faces damp, their legs roughly amputated—the boys who, "when the great muster roll was called," would bravely answer. Yet underneath the heroic glitter that Alcott sprinkled over what she'd seen, she recounted the desperate conditions that had made her, like many others, so sick: not just the fetid water and the poor ventilation and scant or inedible food, not just the clammy foreheads and agonized deaths, but also the inescapable racism of those, including her fellow nurses, who never thanked the black men or black women who served them their meals. When Alcott voluntarily touched a small black child, she was labeled a fanatic.

She also wrote about "the barren honors" that these dying boys had won. Such "carelessness of the value of life" astonished and dismayed people such as Alcott, who had devoted herself to abolition, as her family had done, and very much needed to believe no one had been sacrificed in vain.

THE WAR, AS Mary Chesnut had said, would not stop. Nor would the killing, the backbiting, the suffering, the grief, the hunger, the fear. Men deserted in droves from both the Union and Confederate forces. And those not killed on the battlefield were dying of scurvy, dysentery, malaria, or smallpox.

An indefatigable reformer of prisons and insane asylums, the small, energetic Dorothea Dix was appointed superintendent of nurses in 1861, and, when given authorization to recruit, she promptly advertised for homely white women over thirty who wore no jewelry and whose dresses were without bows and hoops. Surprisingly, Dix managed to appoint 3,200 nurses before the aggressive surgeon general took over their hiring and allowed women to enter the field regardless of age, size, or looks. Undefeated, Dix then turned her attention to the conditions faced by prisoners of war; the crusade for prison reform would occupy her long after the war.

Women wanted to serve the war effort. Working in the Patent Office in Washington, Clara Barton, when she first learned of the bombardment of Fort Sumter, went to a shooting range with her gun and put nine balls within six inches of a target at a distance of fifty feet. Distrusting bureaucracy, the compact Massachusetts woman not only did not wear hoopskirts but also wanted permission to go to the front, which was not easy to secure. (Some few females, dressed in blue or gray uniforms, had passed themselves off as soldiers in order to fight for their country.) "The field is no place for a woman," Barton had been told. Yet on the field there were no trained ambulance corps, few supplies or bandages, hardly any fresh water or clean surgical instruments, and no system of emergency relief.

Declining to join Dix's group of nurses, Barton decided to go out on her own and use her Massachusetts connections to collect money and supplies from charitable women's groups and then deliver food and medical equipment to the soldiers by herself. Soon she was sorting canned goods and clothes in her boardinghouse and then in rented warehouses, all the goods ready for distribution. Not until the next year, 1862, did she receive the coveted passes from the quartermaster's office to go to the front.

In her plain brown frock, she and several other volunteers boarded the railway cars for Culpeper, Virginia, near the site of the battle of Cedar Mountain, where in the summer heat the wounded were taken to private houses or the Main Street Hospital, their legs and arms blistered and broken, their jaws blown away. A few weeks later, on August 31, 1862, after the Second Battle of Bull Run, Barton clambered aboard a train to Fairfax Station to take the wounded whatever she could: brandy, wine, soup, jellies. She was not ready for what she encountered—a huge field of burnt-over grass blanketed with men, thousands of them. With little more than the sanction of the quartermaster's office and a chain of wagons stocked with candles, cotton bandages, lanterns, and bread—more goods donated from New England women—Barton trekked out to Sharpsburg, Maryland; she rode not far from the army and set up a crude hospital at the farm of a German immigrant near the battlefield. She brought drafts of water, she extracted a bullet, she held the tables so the patients wouldn't wiggle while the surgeons operated, she comforted the dying for twenty-four hours straight, and she returned to Washington with typhoid fever.

Yet in December Barton trekked out to Fredericksburg, where she could see for herself the slaughter from her perch on the second floor of the once gracious mansion, Lacy House, that was now a hospital. Leaving it, she crossed the river while under Confederate fire to attend the Union men lying in a heap near the stone wall. Burial had begun before the battle ended—although the air was so frigid, the earth so frozen, that the dead men's skin stuck to the ground. Lee had refused a truce, so that the dead hadn't been immediately collected, and the soldiers had to dig shallow graves in the hard soil with nothing more than the jagged pieces of exploded shell.

Lacy House was crammed with 1,200 men. "I wrung the blood from the bottom of my clothing, before I could step," Barton said, "for the weight about my feet."

"All that was elegant is shabby, all that was noble is shabby," said one of the surgeons. "All that once told of civilized elegance now speaks of ruthless barbarism."

Though assisted by the Sanitary Commission, Barton trusted few people. A loner, she felt she'd been thwarted too many times by well-intentioned folks. "My position is one of my own choosing," she boasted, "full of hardship and fraught with dangers." Aid societies and do-good chaplains, with their inexperienced, callous, or befuddled natures, were nuisances at best, and though the Sanitary Commission was large and moneyed, it was not hers. "I am singularly free," she said, "—there are few to mourn for me, and I take my life in my hand and go where men fall and die, to see if perchance I can render some little comfort." Of course she had to cultivate officials—men in high places, men such as Senator Henry Wilson of Massachusetts, who chaired the Military Committee—but Barton preferred direct action and not, as she later said, "the ordinary deliberations of organized bodies," which were of no use when it came to alleviating real and bloody anguish.

"I do not believe in missions," Barton explained, although she would go on to found the Red Cross. Unlike Dix, Barton had no grand scheme to revolutionize institutions or medical practice even though, as everyone knew, Florence Nightingale in the Crimea had been the doyenne of the battlefield, and until now, in America, nursing had been a male profession. No more. "This war of ours has developed scores of Florence Nightingales whose names no one knows but whose reward in the soldier's gratitude and Heaven's approval, is the highest woman can win," *Harper's Weekly* declared—though often women were not greeted with open arms. "Dr. Buck informed me that he didn't wish a woman in his military hospital," said Mary Ann Bickerdyke, the matron of nursing in Cairo, Missouri. "It was no place for a woman." Bickerdyke then asked the patients, most of them amputees, to vote on whether she should stay. The vote was unanimous. Yes.

THEY CAME TO look for the lost. A mother, a father, a brother, a sister, a young wife: they walked through the hospitals or picked through the scores of men who looked frighteningly alike as they lay in the tents hastily converted into makeshift hospitals. Walt Whitman was among them. The brassy poet had come from New York to Washington in search of his brother First Lieutenant George Whitman of the 51st New York Infantry. After the battle at Fredericksburg, Whitman rode out to the camp of Brigadier General Edward Ferrero, who had been a dancing master before the war. The camp wasn't too far from Washington, and as Whitman slowly walked through it, he noted with quiet despair the dismembered legs, arms, and feet piled high under a tree. George had not been badly hurt, thankfully, but the poet could not bring himself to return home to New York. He rented a room in the Washington house of a friend.

Like Barton, Whitman had found a job as a part-time copyist. Evenings, dressed in burgundy corduroy, he would leave the paymaster's office and mop the brows of feverish soldiers in the hospital wards, or he read to them or wrote their letters home. Distributing small amounts of change to them, he cheered them too with little gifts, such as apples, oranges, or sweet crackers. He went out to the regimental, brigade, and division hospitals, merely tents on the cracked field, where the injured men on the frozen ground were "lucky," he said, "if their blanket is spread on a layer of pine or hemlock twigs." Some of the boys, he later recalled, were no more than sixteen.

After the war, each in different ways, Alcott, Barton, and Whitman kept doing a version of what they had done: Barton would search for soldiers missing in action; Whitman would continue to write poetry and essays, and Alcott would transform her family into the March household of *Little Women*. They also published wartime recollections, as so many people would do that by the 1880s the public grew bored with them. In 1885, in *The Rise of Silas Lapham*, the novelist William Dean Howells created a Civil War veteran, the crude self-made millionaire Silas Lapham, who listens apprehensively while his dinner guests wax nostalgic about bygone days. "I don't want to see any more men killed in my time," Lapham says. His companions rustle uncomfortably and turn the discussion to other, pleasanter things.

CONFEDERATE WOMEN SERVED the machine that kept the war going, not necessarily to keep it going but to minister to the broken bodies on their doorsteps. Short on supplies, crippled by the Union blockade, the Confederacy often depended on women's ingenuity and hardiness. Anxious wives, mothers, and sisters stuffed boxes with

coarse pillowcases or handkerchiefs finished with a little bit of em-
broidery, mute and sad tokens of love and hardship, from the land
they were protecting. And not only did they sew flags and underwear
and collect money for such aid organizations as the Ladies' Gunboat
Societies, they smuggled necessary drugs to the front in the heads
of dolls, gave over their homes to the care of the wounded, or set
up extemporaneous hospitals near the battles, converting schools and
churches into relief stations staffed by local volunteers. No one had
special training, and without centralization, which didn't occur until
1862, the relief societies were mostly a federation of those who did
the best they could do.

After the Battle of Shiloh in the spring of 1862, Kate Cumming
managed to get herself from Mobile, Alabama, to Corinth, Mississippi (circa three hundred miles), where she pulled together a traveling hospital to follow the army. Like Barton, she was distributing the
supplies she'd gathered, caring for the wounded, and mobilizing other
women who, like Hannah Ropes, encountered "a great deal of opposition from surgeons," said Cumming, "as all of the ladies have who
desire to go into hospitals." Yet in late 1862, the widow Phoebe Yates
Levy Pember was named chief matron of Richmond's large Chimbo-
razo Hospital, where she too discovered jealousy and competition—
state against state, officer against enlisted man, doctors against nurses;
but the women shared a common emotion: hatred of Yankees. "The
women of the South had been openly and violently rebellious ever
since they thought their states' rights touched," Pember would write.
"They were the first to rebel, the last to succumb."

To Pember, the hospital served as an extension of the home,
where hard work did not, after all, detract from a lady's refinement.
When one of the wounded men, in the aftermath of Fredericksburg,
called out for his comrade at arms, she found the boy. "The results of
war are here to-day and gone tomorrow," she noted when the same
boy died. Another young man, maybe eighteen, asked her to tell his
widowed mother that her only son had perished "in what I consider
the defense of civil rights and liberties."

Home, husband, and country—those were the ideals that Confederate women embodied, or so they told themselves, or were told, and so they believed. Henry Timrod praised them in his poem "The Two Armies," published in the *Southern Illustrated News*. The women's army, "with a narrower scope,"

> Yet led by not less grand a hope,
> Hath won, perhaps, as proud a place,
> And wears its fame with meeker grace,
> Wives march beneath its glittering sign,
> Fond mothers swell the lovely line,
> And many a sweetheart hides her blush
> In the young patriot's generous flush.
> No breeze of battle ever fanned
> The colors of that tender band;
> Its office is beside the bed,
> Where throbs some sick or wounded head.
> It does not court the soldier's tomb,
> But plies the needle and the loom;
> And, by a thousand peaceful deeds,
> Supplies a struggling nation's needs.

And when William Gilmore Simms collected the war poetry of the South into a single volume after the war, he dedicated the book to "the women of the south," who lost a cause "but made a triumph! They have shown themselves worthy of any manhood."

DESPITE THE CONFEDERATES' victories at Fredericksburg and, in the spring of 1863, their success at Chancellorsville, where Stonewall Jackson smashed Fighting Joe Hooker's confused forces, there were hard losses. The beloved Stonewall Jackson was killed at Chancellorsville from wounds inflicted by friendly fire, and his death seemed to symbolize—or perhaps foretell—the doom of the Confederacy, slain by its own hand. The news of Jackson's death rocked the South. A volume of Confederate verse contained forty-seven elegies about Jackson, and Lee later lamented, "Had I Stonewall Jackson at Gettysburg, I would have won a great victory."

There were other hard changes brought on by war: the North's Emancipation Proclamation, and in the South, the Conscription Act as well as the new law authorizing the seizure of private property, which might include one's slaves, should one have any. There was the indignity of the Impressment Act. Passports were now needed to enter or leave a city such as Richmond. And Richmond, the once gleaming capital, was "crowded to suffocation," Mary Chesnut observed. Refugees, as well as thieves and prostitutes newly minted in order to pay the bills, were looking for food, for money, for jobs, and for housing, which, if they were lucky enough to find, they couldn't afford.

The winter of 1863 had been a tough one. It had been cold and snowy. There weren't enough men around to work the small farms. There wasn't enough to eat. Railroads carried men and munitions, not grain, and in any case no one could keep up with inflation. The Confederate currency was depreciating by the minute, it seemed. Hungry children scavenged for bread. Demoralized and destitute, the women of the working classes felt forgotten and forsaken.

On a warm April morning in the muddy, rainy spring of 1863, a crowd of women and boys—many of the women were wives of men who worked in the Tredegar Ironworks factory—congregated in Richmond's Capitol Square, near the statue of George Washington, to protest the devastating food shortages. Shouting "Bread! Bread!" or "Bread or blood!" they headed to the business district, Main and Cary Streets, looting stores, seizing with their skinny arms coffee and meat, hats and shoes. The leader was a tall woman with a feather in her hat, it was said, but, as another woman disdainfully noted, the mob was made up mostly of "women and children of the poorer class."

When the mayor couldn't do anything to quiet the crowd, Jefferson Davis mounted his horse and rode over to the square to beg the rioters to go home. Visibly upset—Davis was not a cruel man—he told the people: you do not have money, so here is all I have. He emptied his pockets and threw down some coins, as if that might help. According to eyewitnesses, the gaunt president then told the crowd to disperse or he would have to order the military to open fire. Other eyewitnesses said it was Governor Letcher who authorized the militia to load their muskets, which they did. People left quietly, their stomachs still empty.

In the coming weeks, forty-three women and twenty-five men were arrested for having fomented a riot. Confederate troops prowled the streets of Richmond to make sure there were no more outbreaks by half-starved women eager to protect their homes, not their home-land. James Seddon, the Confederate secretary of war, issued an order to suppress any mention of the disturbance in public papers to prevent the Yankees from "plying their lying arts," although the *New York Herald* and *New York Times* did run accounts, some contradictory, later in April, taken mainly from local papers: beggar women had been turned away from shops, they reported; women carrying hatch-ets and axes had smashed plate-glass windows and had beaten down locked doors; the rabble had instigated the riot, they said, but selfish, silly women who steal shoes and jewelry can never harm the Confed-eracy; greedy speculators had been hoarding goods to jack up prices.

The various conflicting accounts, observed *Harper's Weekly*, seemed fishy. "We had forgotten Yankees and were fighting each other," lamented Mary Chesnut, who was lucky, she knew, to have meat on her table.

RAISED IN THE border town of Wheeling, Virginia (later West Virginia), Rebecca Harding had published a novella, "Life in the Iron Mills," and then a serialized novel, *Margret Howth*, in *The Atlantic Monthly* during the earliest years of the war. Readers bred on roman-tic fancies found "Life in the Iron Mills" dark, elemental, gritty, and gruesome. Harding was a new voice, a woman's voice, a voice of the voiceless, the laborer, and the mill girl; she was a voice too of the border between North and South. "I write from the border of the battlefield," she said in *Margret Howth*, "and I find in it no themes for shallow argument or flimsy rhymes."

As she later recalled, "My family lived on the border of Virginia. We were, so to speak, on the fence, and could see the great question from both sides. It was a most unpleasant position." In nearby Pennsylvania, abolitionists called her slaveholding friends Simon Legree. At home, she argued with her slaveholding friends, who called abolitionists emissaries of Hell. "The man who sees both sides of the shield," she said, "may be right, but he is most uncomfortable."

In the summer of 1862, flush with the success of her *Atlantic* publications, the thirty-one-year-old Harding went to Boston to meet the reigning literati, or what was left of them, and in Concord, she was introduced to Emerson, Bronson Alcott, and the depressed Hawthorne. "While they thought they were guiding the real world, they stood quite outside of it," she later said, "and would never see it as it was." Alcott and Emerson talked of a war they knew nothing about; something was lacking: the backbone of fact. For she was witnessing "the actual war," she said, "the filthy spewings of it; the political jobbery in Union and Confederate camps; the malignant personal hatreds wearing political masks and glutted by burning homes and outraged women; the chances in it, improved on both sides, of brutish men to grow more brutish."

Neither sentimental nor chivalric, Harding's view of war, although written in retrospect, served as a corrective to the postwar sugarcoated paeans, the stories of gallant soldiers falling with grace for a glorious cause. For if men and women behaved with courage, they also acted in unthinkable ways. "A man cannot drink Bourbon long and remain in his normal condition," she noted. "We did not drink Bourbon, but blood." Soldiers did not enlist for patriotic reasons, or not patriotism alone; many of them had been recruited from jails and penitentiaries, especially in the border regions; and since war and its maintenance were the sole business of the country, men had to enlist or go hungry. The border was an armed camp with "right and wrong mixing each other inextricably together," as she wrote in one of her Civil War stories. So too for the country.

And death was everywhere, not just at Shiloh or Antietam or on the carpeted plain in front of Marye's Heights. "Does anybody wonder so many women die?" Mary Chesnut asked. "Grief and constant anxiety kill nearly as many women as men die on the battlefield."

Under those conditions, the ailing and aging Hawthorne could not squeeze out another romance. This was no time, he too discovered, for phosphorescent literature. Just a few months before Thoreau's death, he had boarded the series of trains that would take him to Washington, calling himself, when he wrote of his trip, a "peaceable man," to alert his *Atlantic* audience that he did not write as a partisan or Republican but as a Democrat who preferred peace to war and peace to the abolition of slavery. Disgusted by the waste, the inefficiency, the bloated lies, the ignorance, and the basic absurdities of the slaughter, Hawthorne remarked that the war had sprung from "the anomaly of two allegiances": the North devotes itself "to an airy mode of law, and has no symbol but a flag," he said, while the South fights state by state, which "comes nearest home to a man's feelings, and includes the altar and the hearth."

He may not have been wrong about the reasons Southerners said they were fighting, but his analysis did not warm Republican hearts. "What an extraordinary paper by Hawthorne in the *Atlantic*!" cried George W. Curtis, the antislavery editor of *Harper's Weekly*. "It is pure intellect, without emotion, without sympathy, without principle." Yet Hawthorne, like Rebecca Harding, deplored the poetic propaganda, North and South, written to boost flagging spirits, allay nagging doubts, or stifle the unstoppable screaming of the wounded in the night.

(12)

THE LAST FULL MEASURE
OF DEVOTION

The dead cannot bury themselves.

During the Civil War, more than 750,000 soldiers died, North and South combined, a dumbfounding number (recently revised upward) and far greater than the number of men who had perished or would perish in all other U.S. wars put together. They died from cannonades, from rifle fire, from exploding shells and minié balls; they died from typhoid fever, from pneumonia and gangrene, from infection, exposure, and sunstroke. At Antietam, as mentioned, in just one day, the number of casualties exceeded 26,000, and during the three-day battle at Gettysburg, Pennsylvania, in the summer of 1863, it rose to an unthinkable 51,000, which made Gettysburg the most shattering and destructive battle of the war to date. If an American sibyl had foretold that, no one would have believed her.

Assuming their chances of survival to be slim, soldiers often pinned their names to the insides of their uniforms so if their bodies were found, they could be identified. They carried pocket Bibles inscribed with directions on how to notify next of kin. Even so, the bewildering number of men missing in action—so many thousands of them—prompted Clara Barton to open an Office of Correspondence with the Friends of the Missing Men of the United States Army in the spring of 1865. In just a few months, she located as many as 20,000. By the time her bureau closed three years later, she'd received more than 60,000 letters from despairing men and women in search of their lost boys.

In 1862 Congress authorized the creation of national cemeteries for the men who died serving their country. Not churchyard burial plots, these secular cemeteries were to be located near the site of a battlefield. Though the national cemetery at Gettysburg would be no exception, there the interred soldiers were not to be divided by rank or status, as they had previously been, but to be buried with their regiment, row after row of them, as if in death—as in life—these men had been equals: equally brave, equally committed, equally frightened.

AFTER THE THREE days of carnage at Gettysburg, horses lay distended on the broad fields, and unrecognizable bodies putrefied in the summer sun. "The corpses seemed to be everywhere, for at times I could not put my foot to the ground without feeling some portion of a man's body beneath it," said one soldier. Thousands of bluebottle flies buzzed around them, and the stench was hard to believe; not even the kerosene-soaked fires burning the animals could block it. The smell rose right to the edge of the little college town, where the streets had been sprinkled with disinfecting lime to stave off disease and contagion. Private homes, as well as their barns and stables, and public spaces were filled with mortally wounded men—they numbered about ten times the 2,500 residents—for there was little or no provision for transporting them out of town by rail. The skies had opened, and it poured the day after the battle, but the surgeons, damp with rain and blood, performed amputations outdoors if they had to.

Members of the Sanitary Commission had come as quickly as they could to help tend the wounded. Alexander Gardner and his camera operators came too. Gardner believed the war to be a tragic waste. And so his pictures did not bury the dead—they revealed them to be grotesque and real. To heighten the effect of his grisly pictures, Gardner sometimes rearranged the bodies. Even today those photographs of mangled soldiers disturb the viewer. But already—in those images and elsewhere—there was a distancing at work, a detachment from a horror difficult, if not impossible, to understand. Regardless, the photos were for sale.

BRINGING THE WAR closer, keeping it at bay: had Lincoln not traveled to Gettysburg in November 1863 to commemorate the soldiers fallen there, we might remember the three-day battle as just another sickening site of Civil War slaughter, albeit one that afforded the Federals a much-needed victory after their defeats at Fredericksburg and then at Chancellorsville, where the new commander of the Army of the Potomac, General Joseph Hooker, had miscalculated, dallied, collapsed, and disgraced himself by falling back.

Or if Lincoln had not traveled to Gettysburg, we might remember how yet another new commanding general had been pushed into the Federal field right before a major battle: Burnside had replaced McClellan before Fredericksburg; Hooker had replaced Burnside before Chancellorsville; and now General George Gordon Meade was heading the Army of the Potomac less than a week before Gettysburg. One middling general after another, scoffed many a Confederate.

Lincoln had been disappointed with all of them, though disappointment is perhaps too mild a word. The president was baffled, frustrated, angered by the incompetence, paralysis, or whatever it was that transformed his top generals into reluctant warriors disinclined to fight (McClellan) or whatever it was that made them reckless (Burnside) or paralyzed them with last-minute battle fatigue (Hooker). Perhaps Meade would prove more capable. Tall and vitriolic—his nickname was "Old Snapping Turtle"—and another West Pointer (class of 1835) as well as a Mexican War veteran who had fought well at Second Manassas, Antietam, and Chancellorsville (where Hooker's inaction had troubled him), the forty-seven-year-old Meade had been awakened in the middle of the night on June 28, and before he'd had time to dress, he had been told of his promotion. There he stood in his nightshirt, incredulous.

Or had Lincoln not traveled to Gettysburg and spoken at the dedication of its national cemetery, we might remember the place principally as the site of General Robert E. Lee's canny and risky commitment to invading Pennsylvania, of striking hard into enemy territory to undermine enemy morale by seizing Northern territory at last. Jefferson Davis too had been eager for the invasion. A victory on Northern soil, particularly coming after the victory at Chancellorsville, might bring the Confederacy the foreign intervention it so badly needed. However, General James Longstreet, the burly head of the First Corps, wanted instead to reinforce the Confederate army in the West rather than invade the North; he could take his men to Tennessee and link up with Generals Bragg, Johnston, and Buckner in Murfreesboro to stop the Union's General William Rosecrans—and perhaps dislodge Grant from his stubborn position near Vicksburg. But Lee and Jefferson Davis were set.

Lee was marching his Army of Northern Virginia northward, across the Potomac River and into Pennsylvania, but before all his divided forces gathered—he couldn't be ready for battle until they'd all arrived—General Henry Heth, on June 30, sent Brigadier General James Pettigrew and his 2,584 men to the small, prosperous town of Gettysburg for supplies, particularly the stash of shoes said to be there. When Pettigrew learned that Union troops were near, he asked Heth for instructions; assuming their numbers were negligible, Heth obtained permission from his corps commander, General A. P. Hill, to get those shoes anyway. Heth took four brigades into Gettysburg to get rid of the Union troops and secure the footwear, which was far more important than a skirmish with a detachment of Federal cavalry. But Hill miscalculated their strength. He did not know that

Federal infantry was camped nearby. As Heth later recalled the battle the next day, "on July 1 was without order or system . . . [since] we accidentally *stumbled* into this fight." Lee had been blindsided.

Lee was blindsided partly because he hadn't heard from his trusted cavalryman and scout, the jaunty and vainglorious "Jeb" Stuart, with whom he'd captured John Brown. Stuart was delayed, missing, or dead. "Can you tell me where General Stuart is?" Lee's officers heard him ask over and over. According to one of those men, with Stuart's delay, Lee had no cavalry and poor reconnaissance in this unfamiliar terrain, two factors that led directly to his subsequent defeat at Gettysburg. So Lee did not know the size of the Federal army he would have to fight in this unexpected and horrid engagement. It was not what he'd had in mind.

Still, he trounced the Federals on July 1. But because he didn't yet know how large the Union forces were, he couldn't press his advantage far enough by day's end. He then sent instructions to General Richard Ewell, the commander of what had been Jackson's Second Corps, telling him "to carry the hill occupied by the enemy, if he found it practicable." Ewell, who had lost his leg at Second Manassas, didn't think it was practicable. Had he tried, however, the Confederates could very well have occupied Cemetery Hill, an impregnable position that the Federals secured that night. But it's possible Lee's gentlemanly and seemingly discretionary instructions had been unclear.

By daybreak on July 2, another hot day of furious fighting, Longstreet had again disagreed with Lee and suggested a defensive maneuver that would separate Meade from Washington and force Meade to attack. Or, if Lee insisted on continuing the Gettysburg battle, Longstreet wanted at least to wait for Pickett's division to arrive; he said he did not want to go into battle with "one boot off." Lee replied that "the enemy is here, and if we do not whip him, he will whip us." Dressed in his worn black felt hat and his long gray jacket with its collar decorated simply with three stars, Lee paced back and forth, field glasses in hand. He stuck to his plan, and Longstreet had to go along, but to some observers and, years later, angry commentators, Longstreet seemed to dawdle; was he deliberately slow, lacking confidence in Lee's orders? Critics later alleged that Longstreet's reluctance to execute Lee's plan had cost the Confederates a knockout victory on that second gruesome day, for despite their heavy losses the Union troops held on—and they had a strategic position on high ground at Little Round Top, which they defended against a brutal Confederate assault.

The casualties totaled a monstrous 35,000. Lee, having attacked on the left and the right of the Union line, decided that on the next day, July 3, he would cannonade its center with a fierce artillery assault commencing at one o'clock. There were fire and smoke, horses bursting open, metal flying; the noise was so loud, so terrifying, that the crashing was heard, it was said, as far away as Pittsburgh. Cannon thunder aside, the firing had been inaccurate and the missiles—about 10,000 rounds of ammunition, calculated one soldier—flew above the Federal line, missing it. And when the artillery stopped, about forty minutes later, there, coming out of the woods, appeared the glinting rifles and battle flags of what would become famous as Pickett's charge. General George Pickett's division led, rushing into the breach, if a breach there was, screaming the terrifying "rebel yell" for which the graycoats had become famous as they ran over open ground. The Federals opened fire from Cemetery Ridge. Pickett, his long ringlets flowing down the back of his neck, his high boots highly polished, struck one observer as a "desperate-looking character." He moved three brigades forward. They were joined by Hill's division. Two thousand men were killed or wounded in a matter of thirty minutes, yet the shelling continued. We mowed them down, recalled one Union soldier. "The execution of the fire must have been terrible, as it was over a level plain, and the effect was plain to be seen. In a few minutes, instead of a well-ordered line of battle, there were broken and confused masses, and fugitives fleeing in every direction." It was a massacre: more than 1,000 dead, 4,500 wounded.

The journalist Whitelaw Reid saw what happened: "The Rebels— three lines deep—came steadily up. They were in point-blank range. . . . At last, the order came! From thrice six thousand guns, there came a sheet of smoky flame, a crash, a rush of leaden death. . . . A storm of grape and canister tore its way from man to man, and marked its track with corpses straight down their line! They had exposed themselves to the enfilading fire of the guns on the western slope of Cemetery hill; that exposure sealed their fate."

The sacrifice was futile, Reid concluded. "Death! death everywhere, in all its horrid, awful forms!" exclaimed another war correspondent. "The swift bullet and the cruel shell both had been at work: and I realized what a price is paid for victories."

Longstreet had to agree. "That day at Gettysburg," he later said, "was one of the saddest of my life." Though he carried out Lee's orders, he considered Pickett's charge suicidal. "I thought it would not do," Longstreet would write; "that the point had been fully tested the day before, by more men, when all were fresh; that the enemy was there, looking for us; . . . that the conditions were different from those in the days of Napoleon, when field batteries had a range of six hundred yards and musketry about sixty yards." Longstreet had suggested that Lee go around Meade's left and attack him from the side, but Lee was adamant about staying put.

There was some small solace. "The rebels behaved with as much pluck as any men in the world could," noted a Union soldier; "they stood there, against the fence, until they were nearly all shot down." Their bravery was faultless, and it was heartbreaking, and Lee assumed full responsibility for their defeat. One officer approached him, nearly in tears, to say that his brigade had been slaughtered. "Never mind, General," Lee tried to console him. "*All this has been my fault*—it is *I* who have lost the fight and you must help me out of it in the best way you can."

AND HAD IT not been for Lincoln's speech almost four months later, we might remember Gettysburg as the site of other ceaselessly debated questions—not just about Lee and his strategy but about why the lantern-jawed, quick-tempered General Meade, the bags under his eyes deeper than they'd been just a few weeks earlier, had not pursued Lee and crushed the Army of Northern Virginia once and for all. Meade had not ordered his reserves forward to counterattack. If Meade had been aggressive, he would have prevented Lee and his remaining army (maybe 40,000) from crossing the river back to safety.

For one thing, Meade was wary of Lee. To the Federals, Lee was a magician who might reappear at any moment, his army refreshed, his terrifying calculus refurbished. Perhaps Lee's retreat to the other side of the Potomac was just a ruse to retest the mettle of Meade's army; perhaps the whole army had not retreated. What would happen then? But generals' not finishing the job tormented Lincoln: McClellan at Antietam, Rosecrans at Corinth, and now Meade. (For that matter, the same could be said of the Confederate generals Joe Johnston and P. G. T. Beauregard at the First Battle of Bull Run.) Did those men not want to push their luck and risk failure after succeeding? In sparing the soldier, as McClellan was apt to do, were they jeopardizing ultimate victory? Were they prolonging the war? Were they enacting some kind of strange, collective reluctance to defeat the army of their countrymen?

The next day, July 4, it rained. Torrential pounding rain, rain in sheets. Moving a huge army with wagon trains and heavy cannon off the high ground was difficult in the soppy mud. Heavy rains not only made roads impassable, they also caused the river to rise, which made it harder to cross. On July 6 Meade promised Henry Halleck, the general in chief of the Federal forces, that he would "proceed in search of the enemy," but the search was halfhearted if conducted at all. The rain stopped, the roads were drying, but the Federals moved slowly. By July 10, Lee was way ahead of Meade. Meade said he would pursue and attack but he never did. Lincoln wrung his hands. "They will be ready to fight a magnificent battle," he said of Meade and his men, "when there is no enemy to fight." On July 12, Meade took council with his corps commanders and Halleck, in frustration, sent a telegram to Meade, telling him to "act upon your own judgment and make your generals execute your orders. Call no council of war. It is proverbial that councils of war never fight." As Shelby Foote derisively noted, the council of war amounted "to an attempt to lock the stable after the pony had been stolen."

"We have certain information that Vicksburg surrendered to General Grant on the 4th of July," President Lincoln informed Halleck, who in turn forwarded the president's message to the dilatory Meade. "Now, if General Meade can complete his work, so gloriously prosecuted thus far, by the literal or substantial destruction of Lee's army, the rebellion will be over." Nothing happened. Halleck was peeved, Lincoln was incensed, Lee had departed. "The substantial destruction of his [Lee's] army would have ended the war," Lincoln complained, and "such destruction was perfectly easy."

"Your golden opportunity is gone," Lincoln upbraided Meade on July 14, "and I am distressed immeasurably because of it." Though Lincoln didn't send the letter, Meade, knowing Lincoln was angry, tendered his resignation. But Lincoln needed Meade, who was now widely applauded, and couldn't accept it. Meade withdrew it in any case.

As for Lee, he escaped but had lost seventeen generals and eighteen colonels. Anguished, he repeated over and over again, "It's all my fault."

THOUGH MEADE DID not complete his work, Grant had completed his. The soldier from Illinois who had been the best man at Longstreet's wedding back in 1848, the man who had smelled of failure and cigars and whose foreclosed home had been called "Hardscrabble," the general who had already tried once and failed to pry the strategically located city of Vicksburg from Confederate hands, in the summer of 1863, that man succeeded in raising the Stars and Stripes over the graceful Mississippi city on Independence Day. With the western states of the Confederacy finally severed from the east, the fall of Vicksburg sealed the "fate of the Confederacy," or so Grant would claim in an uncharacteristic display of pride.

Having failed to take Vicksburg earlier in the year, the dogged general had come up with a line of attack, one that depended on skill, luck, and the deft coordination of his forces with those of the naval fleet. Admiral David Dixon Porter would have to send his gunboats and transports down the river, south of Vicksburg, and past the batteries in order to meet with Grant's troops on the west bank of the river and haul them to the other shore so that they could march northward, up toward Vicksburg, and assault the city from the southeast. At the same time, Colonel Benjamin Grierson, a former music teacher from Illinois, and General William Tecumseh Sherman would be distracting the Confederates and letting them think that Grant's forces were even larger than they already were. The plan involved so many moving parts that even Grant's friend Sherman initially doubted its viability.

Once on the east side of the river in April—Porter had succeeded— Grant was able to deceive Confederate general John C. Pemberton, who assumed that Grant would attack from the north. Grant managed to get between Pemberton, near Vicksburg, and Joe Johnston, who was near Jackson, Mississippi. By the end of May, Pemberton had retreated to Vicksburg. Church bells rang, and, after the morning services, the women of the town were entreated to make bandages for the groups of dusty soldiers who soon appeared, "wan, hollow-eyed, ragged, footsore, bloody." "We are whipped," the soldiers said, "and the Federals are after us."

For the next several days, the Confederates pushed the Federals back while Grant kept up the assault, flinging his entire army at the enemy. Pemberton, who still had no reinforcements, resisted gallantly. If reinforcements did not come, he would be trapped in Vicksburg along with its 3,000 inhabitants, many of whom had initially rushed to the city for protection because the Federal cavalry, under Grierson's command, had been raiding the outlying towns. Meanwhile, in town, a band played "Dixie" while mortar shells, smaller so-called Parrott shells, and shrapnel fell on the city, crushing buildings, killing animals. The very air seemed dead.

Whinnying in terror, horses reared up at the sound of the shells. For months, the residents of Vicksburg had listened with dread to the slow, steady pounding of the city or watched in helpless disbelief as the night sky turned bright red, reflecting the flames. Noncombatants had been ordered to leave as early as March, but many stayed, taking refuge in small caves dug out of the hills near their homes. "Caves were the fashion—the rage—over besieged Vicksburg," wrote a woman survivor with a dash of mordant humor. Praying that they would not be buried alive, they listened to the report of guns and the loud rumble of the plummeting shells, and if they ventured out, they watched in awe "the burning matter and balls [that] fell like large, clear blue-and-amber stars, scattering hither and thither."

The garrison did not have sufficient provisions, and for a while families lived on corn bread and bacon. "We are utterly cut off from the world," said another woman, "surrounded by a circle of fire." That was at the end of May. In June the local newspaper was printed on wallpaper, and dogs and cats mysteriously disappeared, likely eaten by hungry civilians and soldiers. In July, the Federals entered the town. The siege was over; there was nothing more that Pemberton could do. General Johnston had never arrived with reinforcements. Instead, the Union men strode into the city with their "sleek horses, polished arms, bright plumes,—this was the pride and panoply of war," said a Vicksburg survivor. "The heart turned with throbs of added pity to the worn men in gray, who were being blindly dashed against this embodiment of modern power."

True, Grant had more men than Pemberton. True, Jefferson Davis had had no troops to send to Pemberton. But the Confederates were also divided against themselves. They had been defeated not by "modern power" as much as the difference of opinion between Pemberton, who wanted to defend Vicksburg, and Johnston, who preferred to defend the army now and recapture Vicksburg after destroying Grant. And there was Grant himself: implacable and relentless, the man who hated bloodshed so much that he could not stomach rare meat but who, after the heavy losses at Shiloh, was called a butcher.

In Washington, Halleck was mighty pleased by the news of Grant's victory. "In boldness of plan, rapidity of execution, and brilliancy of results," Halleck told Grant, "these operations will compare most favorably with those of Napoleon at Ulm." Lincoln too was relieved, at last. "I can't spare this man," he reportedly said. "He fights."

ABOVE VICKSBURG, AT a Federal post at Milliken's Bend, Louisiana, a Confederate brigade had attacked four regiments of black troops, including the 9th Louisiana Volunteers of African Descent and the 1st Mississippi Infantry, in June. The fighting was fierce especially since the black troops, armed with muskets that didn't work, had to take to hand-to-hand combat, using their guns as clubs. Yet their success, despite their heavy losses, helped dampen doubts about the black soldiers' ability on the battlefield. So too had the bravery of the black troops fighting under General Nathaniel P. Banks at Port Hudson, Louisiana, changed many minds—particularly that of Banks himself, who was no abolitionist. "I posted the First and Third Regiments of negro troops. The First Regiment of Louisiana Engineers, composed exclusively of colored men, excepting the officers, was also engaged in the operations of the day," Banks reported to Halleck. "The position occupied by these troops was one of importance, and called for the utmost steadiness and bravery in those to whom it was confided. It gives me pleasure to report that they answered every expectation. In many respects their conduct was heroic," Banks continued. "Whatever doubt may have existed heretofore as to the efficiency of organizations of this character, the history of this day proves conclusively to those who were in condition to observe the conduct of these regiments that the Government will find in this class of troops effective supporters and defenders."

Charles Dana was ecstatic. A member of the experimental commune Brook Farm in his early days, he'd been managing editor of the *New-York Tribune* and the man who had convinced Greeley to run the "On to Richmond" slogan. Stanton had hired him as assistant secretary of war, but in reality his job was to spy on Grant and report on the general's alleged drinking problem. From Milliken's Bend, he wrote with exultation that the battle there had "completely revolutionized the sentiment of the army with regard to the employment of negro troops. I heard prominent officers who formerly in private had sneered at the idea of the negroes fighting express themselves after that as heartily in favor of it."

That was only part of the story. A great number of soldiers, including officers, and citizens did not care what happened to the black soldier or, for that matter, to the slave. Those people supported and fought for the Union, and only the Union. To them, emancipation muddied or in fact subverted war aims. "The war is not waged by abolitionists, is not the result of abolitionism," Edmund Stedman had reassured his mother after the First Battle of Bull Run. *We are not fighting the negro's cause.*" Though Stedman later changed his mind, he was as hostile to abolitionists as were other Union supporters and soldiers. Hearing that Robert Gould Shaw and the Massachusetts 54th had been defeated at Fort Wagner that summer, Shaw's friend Major Henry Livermore Abbott remarked that Shaw "was too good a fellow to be sacrificed for an experiment, & an experiment that has demonstrated niggers won't fight as they ought." The black soldiers had indeed fought, and fought valiantly, but Major Abbott, among others, refused to believe it.

In the South, hatred of the Yankees competed for animosity against black soldiers; it was a tough call. That was true on the border, too. "We are for the Union, not for the Yankees," said one family member in the newly formed state of West Virginia. "Shall we sink down as serfs to the heartless, speculative Yankee for all time to come," asked a writer in *The Crisis* of Columbus, Ohio, "—swindled by his tariffs, robbed by his taxes, skinned by his railroad monopolies?" Doubtless anti-Yankee sentiment and racism—as well as resentment of the Lincoln administration and hostility to abolitionists—spurred men such as Ohio representative Clement Laird Vallandigham and his harebrained plan to unite the western states with Southern ones against New England. "[Horatio] Seymour, the New York *World*, Jeff. Davis, and [Samuel] Cox and Vallandigham, have taken advantage of the crisis to make a joint attack on New England, with a view to detach the West from the loyal cause and join her to the Gulf States, and leave New England in the cold," declared Edmund Stedman. "I think, to be sure," he added, "that our abolitionists are making idiots of themselves, . . . but the Northern copperheads . . . are our worst foes."

Copperheads: the name for those sympathizers with the South came not just from the snake but from the copper penny, with its picture of Liberty, that some of them wore as lapel pins. Clement Vallandigham was one of them. A silver-tongued man of many words, as early as 1855 he advised his fellow Democrats to tackle head-on the issue of slavery in the anti-abolition and antislavery terms of the day: "PATRIOTISM ABOVE MOCK PHILANTHROPY; THE CONSTITUTION ABOVE ANY MISCALLED HIGHER LAW OF MORALS OR RELIGION; AND THE UNION OF MORE VALUE THAN MANY NEGROES." The self-confident, oracular son of a Presbyterian minister, Vallandigham liked to preach politics, and a player in the Democratic Party, he'd been elected to the Ohio state legislature when he was only twenty-five. In Congress in 1858, he was repeatedly branded a secessionist and dug in his heels. He would not be stopped. With that telltale copper penny in his lapel, he called himself a westerner, not a Northerner, and announced he had very little sympathy with the North.

Any and all opposition provided Vallandigham with the publicity he liked, and after Fort Sumter he immediately accused Lincoln of "executive usurpation." "Every principal act of the Administration since has been a glaring usurpation of power, and a palpable and dangerous violation of that very Constitution which this civil war is professedly waged to support," Vallandigham spoke out in the House, accusing the government of despotism and tyranny. Newspaper editors had been seized and arrested in the dead of night, civil liberties had been trampled, and the poor Union soldier marched barefooted, bareheaded, and famished while "contrabands" and fugitive slaves filled their stomachs. Though he wanted to squelch the rebellion, to him there were actually two rebellions afoot, "the Secession Rebellion South and the Abolition Rebellion North and West. I am against both; for putting down both."

After losing his congressional seat by 600 votes in the fall of 1862—thanks to Republican gerrymandering—Vallandigham crusaded more brazenly than ever against continuing the war. As he explained before he left the House chamber for the last time, he had never supported the war and had consistently voted against appropriations—except of course when the "separate interests" of the soldier were involved. He respected the young man who had enlisted, and he praised anyone, unlike himself, who was committed to the war effort. But he would not join it. He could not. He deplored its death tolls, its barbarism, its basic violation of protected freedoms and the civil rights of white men. He loathed the nationalization of such institutions as banks—the National Banking Act (to organize a nationally chartered bank, create a federal banking system, and to issue notes to finance the war) became law in early 1863—and the monopolistic enterprise of the railroads. Above all, he utterly loathed what he called the Republicans' "enslavement of the white race, by debt and taxes and arbitrary power."

"Ought this war to continue?" he asked and answered his own question. "No—not a day, not an hour."

If Vallandigham had pacifistic points to make, his racism consistently undermined his position—his racism and his regionalism, which for him had become the same thing. Proposing "reunion," that is, union as it had been (his campaign slogan had been "The Constitution as it is, the Union as it is"), he wanted to turn back the clock, as if there had been no war, no Emancipation Proclamation, no black soldiers dying on the front, nothing. He was not an appeaser; he was a fantasist. As for slavery, he continued, that was not the cause of the war; abolition was, and it remained the culprit—ugly, creeping abolition. Reviving the old saw about how slavery could never take hold in the West anyway, he dismissed out of hand the territorial issues that had rattled the nation before and, tragically, after 1848. At stake were simply two systems of labor, slave and free, which had always existed compatibly in the South. Declare free trade between North and South. And remember: in the North, or in the West, free men should enjoy free soil, which is to say no competition from an influx of free blacks. As for the South, he continued, the Constitution protects slavery there and can do so again. Let slavery persist—in other words, protected where it is: keep the Union as it is now.

On January 14, 1863, Vallandigham spoke without notes to a packed House, and while Republicans were wont to label his long speech as brilliant treason, grinning Democrats rallied round him and shook his hand. Vallandigham soared to the top of the Peace Democrat ladder; newspaper editors in the Middle West joined the movement. *The Cincinnati Enquirer* claimed, "The real genuine Democracy of the country were never at heart for the war."

On May 1 Vallandigham opened his gubernatorial campaign in Mount Vernon, Ohio, speaking amid floats and flags about the unnecessary, wicked, and cruel war. It was a political ploy, this speech, not just because of what he said but because he was taunting the irritable, impetuous General Burnside, who was waiting nearby, ready to pounce. Assigned—demoted—to the Department of the Ohio, the truculent general precipitously issued a general military order (No. 38) that outlawed so-called seditious speech, which was to say such declarations as Vallandigham's about the war. And now there was this: Vallandigham, orating among the floats and flags, wondering aloud what purpose the dead of Fredericksburg had served. He was baiting Burnside.

At three o'clock in the morning on May 5, Burnside's soldiers broke down the door of Vallandigham's home in Dayton, Ohio, and arrested Vallandigham in his bedroom on the charge of publicly expressing "his sympathies for those in arms against the Government of the United States, declaring disloyal sentiments and opinions, with the object and purpose of weakening the power of the Government in its efforts to suppress an unlawful rebellion." Dragged before a kangaroo military tribunal that found him guilty, Vallandigham was sentenced to imprisonment for the duration of the war, which of course was a boost to his gubernatorial campaign. "I am a Democrat—for Constitution, for Law, for the Union, for Liberty—this is my only 'crime,'" he cried from jail, addressing himself to the "Democracy of Ohio." He was a happy martyr.

The arrest sparked a political firestorm. When Vallandigham applied for a writ of habeas corpus, the request was denied, and the issue—a serious constitutional one—fell right into Lincoln's lap. Though the arrest had occurred without the president's knowledge, Lincoln had to act quickly. Not wishing to undermine an order issued by one of his generals, he commuted Vallandigham's sentence to banishment. Regarded as an enemy of the state, the handsome, eloquent, ambitious Democrat was escorted to Murfreesboro, Tennessee, where he was met by General William Rosecrans and subsequently turned over to Confederate authorities. As an exile, he was remade, or so some hoped, into a "Man without a Country," which is what Edward Hale called him in the didactic and very popular story of that name, written that summer and based on the Vallandigham case. To throw away one's country was not just treason; it left one isolated, homeless, silent, adrift.

Lincoln appears in the backdrop of "Man without a Country" as the common man who rose to the country's highest office. Soon this common man, the president, dispatched two public letters, one to the New York Democrats and one to the Ohio Democrats, to explain his recent course of action in legalistic, rational, and comprehensive terms. Patiently noting that the Constitution allowed the suspension of the writ of habeas corpus in cases of rebellion, and declaring that "ours is a case of rebellion," he pointed out that public safety required such actions as the one he took. And in what was swiftly becoming Lincolnesque fashion—balancing unbalanced antithesis, posing abstract questions in plainspoken terms—the president prudently wondered whether he must "shoot a simple-minded soldier boy who deserts, while I must not touch a hair of a wily agitator who induces him to desert?"

Wily agitators: they were legion, or so it seemed, if one were to judge by such secret societies as the Knights of the Golden Circle, founded in the Midwest by members who swore secret oaths and recognized the special handshake or uttered secret codes. First organized in 1854, the Knights, their filibustering eye on Mexico, hoped to turn the Gulf (the Golden Circle) into one big slave plantation. By 1860 the secret organization was overtly secessionist, and after the outbreak of war, the Knights were presumably aiding and abetting the Confederates, perhaps by burning bridges or perhaps by intimidating blacks and Northern sympathizers. No one knew for sure; maybe Northerners were imagining things, though probably not. Doubtless the system of hand signals and passwords (for instance, Calhoun spelled backward), divulged under penalty of death, dismayed as many people as it titillated, which kept the rumor circulating: that Vallandigham was a grand commander of the Knights or some related society and in the summer or fall of 1863, the secret members, armed with revolvers, would welcome back Vallandigham, who would then foment a rebellion of free states. As it was, the Confederates had helped him flee to Canada, where he pursued, in absentia, the Ohio governorship.

Rumors of a conspiracy to overthrow the government reached Washington through Rosecrans in Missouri. The reports were too incendiary, thought Rosecrans, to be committed to paper, so Lincoln instructed John Hay to go to Missouri and talk directly to the general. Hay learned from the hearty, sociable blond Rosecrans that a group called the Order of American Knights, headed by Vallandigham in the North, planned to join guerrillas and rebels in the border states and harass, plunder, and even murder Unionists. It would be a campaign of terror to make sure Lincoln would not be reelected. To verify his claim, Rosecrans had discovered secret documents but wouldn't entrust them to Hay. Lincoln pooh-poohed the whole thing. The secret seemed out, and as far as he was concerned neither the Knights of the Golden Circle nor this group were "worth regarding."

The Copperhead mutiny may have been a muddled fantasy or a

very real and very sinister plan that failed. Whatever it was, the news in the summer of 1863 of Confederate corpses rotting on the Gettysburg battlefield and of Grant's taking Vicksburg checked the popularity of the Peace Democrats and forced the Knights to change course. Vicksburg and Gettysburg, despite the horrific numbers of dead and dying, spelled victory at last, victory incontrovertible. Morale skyrocketed. The Mississippi was open—"the Father of Waters again goes unvexed to the sea," Lincoln wrote in purple prose—and the once indestructible Lee no longer lived a charmed life.

THERE WAS UGLY rioting in the North but not because of any Copperhead mutiny, or at least not directly. The issue was the national draft, instituted the previous March.

More soldiers were needed. "The conscription is necessary," ran an editorial in *The New York Times* on Friday, July 10. "Even after the late great victories, a new army of 300,000 men must be got ready to move upon the confederacy." That Saturday, July 11, just a week after the Federals hauled their flag over Vicksburg and Lee retreated from Gettysburg, there was a draft lottery in New York City. It began quietly, and on Sunday, the newspapers published the names of the draftees.

On Monday, July 13, the city was in flames.

Governor Horatio Seymour was a Peace Democrat from upstate who opposed conscription. Temperate and dignified, well read, smooth-faced, and soulless, at least according to George Templeton Strong, Seymour was a firm advocate of states' rights, and, like Vallandigham, he believed that slavery had nothing to do with the war and should continue to have nothing to do with it. What had brought the nation to disaster were Southern fire-eaters and Northern abolitionists—and the present Republican administration. Seymour detested its emancipation policy; to him, emancipation was simply "a proposal for the butchery of women and children, for scenes of lust and rapine, and of arson and murder, which would invoke the interference of civilized Europe." For him, the national draft was yet

another unconstitutional means of freeing the slaves—at the expense
of the white worker.

The draft had taken recruitment out of local hands and had
opened the door to fraud, corruption, unfairness, and mishandling.
Men could buy their way out of conscription for $300, so the draft
seemed to fall disproportionately on poor and immigrant populations, and in New York Seymour alleged that Republicans had set
higher enrollment quotas for Democratic districts, which was also
to say for the Irish immigrants who lived there. But though Peace
Democrats were not averse to fomenting racism—let black men fight
for their own freedom, rioters viciously protested—the brutality of
the draft riots in New York brought them up short.

A mob had roared through the draft headquarters at Third Avenue
and 46th Street, and by Monday night, the Orphan Asylum for Colored Children on Fifth Avenue and 43rd Street, just above the reser-
voir, had been burned to the ground. There hadn't been a policeman
in sight. The office of the *Tribune* was set on fire, railroad tracks ripped
up, telegraph wires cut, streetcars toppled, paving stones flung, and
for the next four days, the city was bedlam. Still no police. "Men and
ladies attacked and plundered by daylight in the streets; private houses
suddenly invaded by gangs of a dozen ruffians and sacked, while the
women and children run off for their lives," wrote George Templeton
Strong. You could hear fire bells clanging day and night.

Most despicable was the hounding of the black community.
"They are the most peaceable, sober, and inoffensive of our poor,
and the outrages they have suffered during this last week are less
excusable—are founded on worse pretext and less provocation—than
St. Bartholomew's or the Jew-hunting of the Middle Ages," Strong
said. "How is one to deal with women who assemble around the
lamp-post to which a Negro had been hanged and cut off certain
parts of his body to keep as souvenirs?"

The rioting lasted four long days. Stores were locked tight. New
Yorkers huddled indoors. The agitated Governor Seymour gave a
speech outside City Hall, and when he reportedly called the rioters

"my friends," he offended almost all Republicans. He had refused to call for federal troops as a preventive measure, and the state militia hadn't stopped these "friends" of Seymour from looting, burning, pillaging, and killing. The riot had been sparked by the draft, no question, but there had been men who wanted it to happen, who had been stoking the class and racial divisions, and George Templeton Strong went so far as to think that the riot had been engineered by agents of Jefferson Davis. Mayor George Opdyke, a Republican, called on Stanton for troops. Now that Lee had retreated across the Potomac, the secretary of war was able to spare them. He dispatched them from Pennsylvania to New York. But many doubted their loyalty—would those soldiers really put down a riot of fellow citizens who were protesting an abolitionist war? David Dudley Field very much wanted the Federals to restore order—and to avenge themselves; he hoped that Beast Ben Butler would commandeer the New York traitors the way he had dispatched the women of New Orleans.

More than 100 people would be killed, more than 300 people injured or wounded. George Templeton Strong, with muted satisfaction, noted after the city quieted that "the Democratic Party is at a discount with all the people I meet."

Governor Seymour asked Lincoln to suspend the draft, which the president would not do, although he did promise districting reform. As for the constitutionality of the conscription law, Lincoln stood by it. So too did he stand by the Emancipation Proclamation, which Peace Democrats were hoping he would also retract.

Lincoln wouldn't do that either. Reassuring the dubious Frederick Douglass, who spoke with Lincoln in his office—a black man in the executive mansion, Douglass marveled, later recalling that "I at once felt myself in the presence of an honest man"—Lincoln subsequently inquired of Grant what he thought about arming black troops. Grant replied swiftly and to the point: "I have given the subject of arming the negro my hearty support. This, with the emancipation of the negro, is the heaviest blow yet given the Confederacy." Lincoln had what he needed for the public letter he was writing to his friend in Springfield, Illinois, James C. Conkling, to address Copperheads, conservative Republicans, and the Peace Democrats who looked forward to a reversal of the Emancipation Proclamation.

Conkling had invited Lincoln to speak at a mass Republican rally in September organized partly to counteract the peace meeting of the previous June in Springfield, when 40,000 people had protested Lincoln and the war. Though Lincoln had to decline Conkling's invitation, he delicately composed a response, to be read aloud. For he understood that behind all the criticism lay a fundamental distrust not of the war itself but of the war's aim insofar as that aim involved—indeed, depended on—emancipation of the slaves. "To be plain," he confronted the skeptics head-on, "you are dissatisfied with me about the negro." Wielding the balanced oppositions that came easily to him—though he reputedly worked hard on his speeches—Lincoln pitted himself against his critics, neutralizing them with logic, countering distrust with homespun homily, and concluding with an incantatory flourish, part apocalyptic and part conciliatory. He emphatically committed himself to the continuance of the war and its objectives, which was to say, at this point, not just the end of the rebellion but the end of slavery. He distilled his argument to its essence: "You dislike the emancipation proclamation; and, perhaps, would have it retracted. You say it is unconstitutional—I think differently. I think the Constitution invests its commander-in-chief, with the law of war, in time of war." That was the matter firmly put. As for its retraction, he concluded, "it can not be retracted, any more than the dead can be brought to life."

Nor could a man or woman, once free, return to slavery. He did not, he said, "believe any compromise, embracing the maintenance of the Union, is now possible." There was no turning back, and, as he even more plainly stated, "you say you will not fight to free negroes. Some of them seem willing to fight for you."

The use of black troops, as he further explained (quoting Grant), "constitute[s] the heaviest blow yet dealt to the rebellion." And so he made explicit what had been implicit, for those who chose to hear him. Emancipation was a military strategy, and the black man, if he were to be effective as a soldier, needed to fight for something. "I thought that whatever negroes can be got to do as soldiers leaves just so much less for white soldiers to do, in saving the Union. Does it appear otherwise to you?" he reasoned. "But negroes, like other people act upon motives," he added. "—Why should they do any thing for us, if we will do nothing for them? If they stake their lives for us, they must be prompted by the strongest motive—even the promise of freedom. And the promise being made, must be kept."

The promise being made, must be kept.

And with promises kept, peace might come; "Peace does not appear so distant as it did," the president concluded.

"I hope it will come soon, and come to stay; and so come as to be worth the keeping in all future time. It will then have been proved that, among free men, there can be no successful appeal from the ballot to the bullet; and that they who take such appeal are sure to lose their case, and pay the cost. And then, there will be some black men who can remember that, with silent tongue, and clenched teeth, and steady eye, and well-poised bayonet, they have helped mankind on to this great consummation; while, I fear there will be some white ones, unable to forget that, with malignant heart, and deceitful speech, they have strove to hinder it."

His was an incantatory, inspiring admonition from one who hoped—who imagined—he could see an end to all the bloodshed.

THE IMPLAUSIBLE SHOCK of it—countless graves lined up one after another—must have been dizzying to the thousands of people who went to Gettysburg in November to gather at the new national cemetery.

Andrew Curtin, the Republican governor of Pennsylvania, had been raising money for a national cemetery, some seventeen acres on Cemetery Hill. Soon the corpses left half buried or decomposing in the sun and even those that had been hastily covered with soil were exhumed and reburied, thanks to the combined efforts of a local lawyer, the governor, and Gettysburg civic leaders. Designed by the landscape architect William Saunders, who had designed the Mount Auburn Cemetery in Cambridge, Massachusetts, the National Cemetery at Gettysburg stretched wide, almost as far as the eye could see. Its consecration ceremony would feature, as the main speaker, Edward Everett, a gifted Harvard scholar and former secretary of state who, as a Constitutional Unionist, had run against Lincoln back in 1860 on John Bell's ticket. Many of the North's state governors would be there, as would President Lincoln, who would make a few short remarks, as he'd been asked to do, to solace widows and orphans and to assure them that the dead would not be forgotten.

On his tall black hat, Lincoln still wore a mourning band. It was for his young son Willie, who had died of a fever the year before. As the president sat on the raised platform, the mourning band was indistinguishable. When he rose to speak, he placed his reading glasses on his nose. Everett hadn't needed them. He had orated for almost two hours without spectacles or notes. But Lincoln held his speech in his hand. It was only nine sentences long.

The sky was clear, the trees empty of leaves, the marshals on their horses trotted slowly around the thick crowd.

The next day, Lincoln's speech was printed in the Republican newspapers. Some Democratic papers trimmed it. Copperheads complained. In the long run that hardly mattered. Schoolchildren in the next century and the one after would be made to memorize it.

Somber and gangly, President Abraham Lincoln had come to consecrate the ground, which he did, by commemorating those who had lost their lives there. He had come to mourn and to console and to remember those who gave the last full measure of devotion. He had come to convert a war of the states, among the states, into a mission, national and purposeful. And thus he resolved, as he said, "that these dead shall not have died in vain—that this nation, under God, shall have a new birth of freedom—and that government of the people, by the people, for the people, shall not perish from the earth."

(13)

FAIRLY WON

Salmon Portland Chase didn't much like his name. He said it sounded fishy, and that was all the more irksome because he knew he was reputed to be a political opportunist. Yet he looked like a solid statesman, which he very much prided himself on being. Six feet tall, he towered over many of his opponents, he was buttoned-up and staid, and if he lacked the oratorical charisma of a Wendell Phillips, he was no less an abolitionist. He had joined the Liberty Party in 1841, and four years later, when handed a sterling silver pitcher in honor of his support of fugitive slaves and free blacks, he firmly declared, "True Democracy makes no enquiry about the color of the skin, or the place of nativity."

One of the four senators, along with Charles Sumner, who had voted against the Fugitive Slave Act, Chase later helped found the Republican Party, for he had long studied the work of William Wilberforce ("How his example shames & humbles me"), and, like Wilberforce, he frequently drew a hard moral line. That was true even in church, where Chase refused to take the communion cup if he felt unworthy, which was often. He had been trained to be righteous, even self-righteous, by his uncle, the Episcopal bishop of Worthington in the new state of Ohio, and by the Congregationalism of Dartmouth College. He had a penchant for absolutes. His abolitionism too sprang from religious evangelism mixed with arrogant humility. Slavery was a moral evil, and Chase was a moral man, right down to his personal habits: he did not drink or smoke or for that matter read much fiction.

Chase was a disappointment to many, including himself, and he was understandably unhappy. (By the time Lincoln had appointed Chase as Treasury secretary, he had buried three wives and two children.) Cold, lonely, and humorless, he was also so nearsighted that he frequently failed to recognize friends on the street who, being sensitive, assumed they had been slighted, perhaps rightly in some cases. True, Chase might be a "man of mark," said Secretary of the Navy Gideon Welles, but he possessed an "inordinate ambition, intense selfishness for official distinction and power to do for the country, and considerable vanity. These traits impair his moral courage; they make him a sycophant with the truly great, and sometimes arrogant towards the humble."

The ambitious appetite of Salmon Portland Chase had been partly sated: before he entered Lincoln's cabinet, he'd been senator, governor, and presidential contender from Ohio, and after Lincoln accepted Chase's resignation in the spring of 1864, he would take the bench in 1865 as chief justice of the U.S. Supreme Court. But Chase had wanted to be president, and it seemed that nothing but that office would satisfy him. "He constantly indulged in hope and delusions that always proved deceptive," recalled Carl Schurz. "It was a pathetic spectacle." Chase's friend Senator Ben Wade put the matter more succinctly: "Chase is a good man, but his theology is unsound. He thinks there is a fourth person in the Trinity."

Lincoln knew that Chase, unlike the other members of his cabinet (William Seward, for instance), still harbored "fond dreams" of the presidency. And so Chase was a potential threat. He was the darling of the more radical wing of the Republican Party, and certain key War Democrats admired him. Even Noah Brooks, a journalist partial to Lincoln, publicly praised the secretary. "Chase keeps ahead of public sentiment," Brooks concluded, "Lincoln prefers to be led by it."

Maybe so; or perhaps Lincoln just wanted the press to believe he was directed by events, which, given the vagaries of the battlefields, was a reasonable position in wartime. It was also a useful hedge: belittling your power left you free to be subtle, to be more imaginative, and to manage people, if not events, more shrewdly. Lincoln supervised public sentiment far more delicately than his opponents did, and he outmaneuvered Chase, who had his own eager, conflicted self to deal with.

In the fall of 1863, just when Union fortunes seemed to be improving, given Gettysburg and Vicksburg, the fair-haired, well-liked General William S. Rosecrans and his Army of the Cumberland were roundly defeated at Chickamauga, south of Chattanooga, Tennessee: 16,000 Union casualties, 18,000 Confederates. Earlier, Rosecrans had tangled with the choleric Confederate general Braxton Bragg at Murfreesboro, which was another celebrated Union victory but another slaughter during which Rosecrans's closest friend had been decapitated before his eyes; by early September Rosecrans had seized eastern Tennessee and Chattanooga, a railroad center which he boasted he'd taken without spilling a drop of blood. But General Longstreet had come to reinforce Bragg with two of his battle-proven divisions, and near Chickamauga Creek (Chickamauga being a Cherokee word meaning "river of death"), Bragg pummeled Rosecrans while Longstreet efficiently exploited an inadvertent gap in the Federal line. The soldiers retreated, as did Rosecrans, leaving General George H. Thomas (soon dubbed the "Rock of Chickamauga") and his one brave corps to fight the onslaught of grim graycoats and provide cover until dusk.

Yet the Confederate victory was not exploited; this time a Southern general failed to pursue. Confounded by the huge numbers of dead and dying (including ten generals), the unpredictable Bragg refused to heed the urgings of Longstreet and those of the cavalry lieutenant general Nathan Bedford Forrest, both of whom wanted to fight to the finish and destroy the Army of the Cumberland the very next morning, once and for all. They did not, and Rosecrans was able to make it back to Chattanooga. Stanton's spy Charles Dana, who had been with Rosecrans, was calling the general a dolt—likely, Dana was influenced by Grant, who had never liked Old Rosy—and newspapers were reporting that the Rosecrans who had recently been hailed as a peerless strategist was actually an opium eater and religious maniac (Rosecrans was a Roman Catholic). What else could account for his being addled during such an important battle? Even the president said that Old Rosy was behaving "like a duck hit on the head."

Secretary of War Stanton, like the implacable man with a mission that he was, furiously organized the various railroad lines to make sure that Hooker and an expeditionary force could get to Chattanooga as quickly as possible—a record eleven days, as it happened—to reinforce Rosecrans, whose men had little food and scant ammunition. Lincoln, meanwhile, placed Grant in command of a newly created Division of the Mississippi (which included the Army of the Cumberland, the Army of the Ohio, and the Army of Kentucky), and at Grant's request he replaced Rosecrans with George Thomas.

On October 23, Grant rode into Chattanooga, and in November he was joined by his redheaded, testy friend William Tecumseh Sherman, who arrived with the Army of the Tennessee. Their combined forces—Grant, Hooker, Sherman, and Thomas—turned on Bragg. In the so-called Battle of the Clouds, Hooker attacked the Confederates on Lookout Mountain, and Sherman attacked Bragg's other side, less successfully than Hooker did. Grant sent Thomas to Missionary Ridge, whose steep incline he and his men spectacularly climbed, placing their flags at last on the ridge. Bragg and the Confederates fled. The Confederate lines of communication between the East and the Mississippi Valley had been broken. Bragg asked to be relieved of command. The mood in the North again brightened.

Replacing Rosecrans with George Thomas had made good military sense, but Rosecrans was a popular general—from Ohio, no less, Salmon Chase's home state. John Hay, Lincoln's young secretary, warned the president that Chase would doubtless "make capital" out of Rosecrans's demotion. Lincoln seemed unconcerned. "I suppose he will," he retorted, "like the bluebottle fly, lay his eggs in every rotten spot he can find." Still, since Clement Vallandigham, cracking his Copperhead whip from Canada, was running for governor of Ohio, Lincoln decided not to announce Rosecrans's replacement until after the election.

Chase hurried to Ohio to campaign hard against Vallandigham. Vallandigham lost, but Chase had, of course, been campaigning for Chase. Again Lincoln seemed to shrug. If Chase actually won the presidency in 1864, he said, "the country will never do worse." It's hard to know what he meant—unless he was referring to the country that might exist after the war. For the word "Reconstruction" was on everyone's lips: Arkansas had already been occupied by Federal troops, Nathaniel Banks was in Texas, and in early December, Sherman seized Knoxville. Lincoln had told Andrew Johnson, whom he'd appointed military governor of Tennessee, that it was time to reorganize a loyal state government there. Mindful as early as the fall of 1863 that there would be a presidential election the following year, Lincoln pointed out to Johnson that "it can not be known who is next to occupy the position I now hold, or what he will do."

In his annual message to Congress that December, Lincoln again brought up the subject of the future, promising not to "attempt to retract or modify the emancipation proclamation," as he said, "nor shall I return to slavery any person who is free by the terms of that proclamation, or by any of the acts of Congress." Yet there remained a host of worrisome questions: what about slaves in states not technically affected by the proclamation, such as Maryland and Missouri? What about states that had seceded and wanted to be readmitted to the Union; what would be the status of emancipation in those places? And what would happen after the war? Would slavery be abolished once and for all? If so, how?

Lincoln attempted to deal with some of those issues in the document he appended to his address. The Proclamation of Amnesty and Reconstruction offered full pardons to ex-Confederates and the restoration of all rights to property (except slaves) to those seeking

amnesty, providing they hadn't been Confederate government officials or high-ranking officers—and as long as they took an oath
of allegiance. In that oath, they would have to swear to respect and
defend the Constitution and all the laws of the United States, including laws passed during the existing rebellion with reference to slaves
and all proclamations of emancipation issued by the president. (That
provision circumvented any reversals by the Supreme Court, where
Chief Justice Roger Taney still presided.) In addition, if, in any of the
former rebel states, at least 10 percent of the voters in the 1860 presidential election took the oath, that state could be recognized by the
president. As the historian James McPherson wrote, in effect the amnesty proclamation was "a retail policy of unconditional surrender."

Lincoln concluded the proclamation of amnesty with characteristic aplomb. He thought it "the best the Executive can suggest," but,
he added, "it must not be understood that no other possible mode
would be acceptable." His door stood ajar.

For a fleeting moment, the Proclamation of Amnesty and Reconstruction pleased everyone, or so thought John Hay, who remembered
the dour, lordly Charles Sumner, the man who had been beaten senseless by Preston Brooks, beaming with pleasure as he listened. In New
York, George Templeton Strong also rejoiced. "President's message
and proclamation of conditional amnesty to the rebels, certain classes
excepted, finds very general favor," he crowed. "Uncle Abe is the
most popular man in America today." Yet the tall man with the regal
bearing, the New England abolitionist Wendell Phillips, considered
Lincoln's proposals unwise, unsafe, and unfeasible. The proclamation
could easily leave landed Confederates in power and make, as he said,
"the negro's freedom a mere sham." Yet despite his blunt criticism of
the administration, Phillips surmised that Lincoln did not expect the
proclamation to be accepted and in fact rather hoped that the president
was using it to make Confederates reveal their hand to the Democrats
who were campaigning for peace; Jefferson Davis and his ilk wanted
an independent Confederacy and had no intention of settling for less.
The war must, then, go on, and Phillips very much wanted it to go on.

In that, Phillips had an ally and protégé of sorts in the young, extraordinarily popular orator Anna E. Dickinson, a Quaker from Philadelphia. She was twenty-one years old, she was articulate, she was pretty, and she was possessed of a voice that listeners called musical. With her dark brunette hair arranged around her face in soft, flattering curls, she dressed in a plain gray dress, though sometimes she tied a red ribbon around her neck and wore a black velvet bonnet. When in later years she wore lace collars and gilt buttons, she said her audience demanded it. Perhaps they did; she was able to support herself and her family with her lecture fees, which often totaled $1,000 per appearance.

Dickinson had come to her lucrative vocation as an antislavery and women's rights activist after she had publicly called General George McClellan a traitor in late 1861 during the time he was being lionized by the press and the public. For such perfidy, she had lost her job at the U.S. Mint in Philadelphia, but William Lloyd Garrison, who had signed her as a speaker for the Massachusetts Anti-Slavery Society, requested that she address 4,000 people in Boston at the Music Hall. Invited to New Hampshire by the Republican State Central Committee, she stumped so long and hard that the bellwether Republican victories at the state polls in 1863—though hardly landslides—were credited to her. When she subsequently campaigned in Connecticut, again Republicans laid their victory at her feet. "The Goliath of the Connecticut Copperheads has been killed not by a stripling but by a Girl," said Wendell Phillips.

Phillips admired Dickinson, and those who heard her said that she was second only to Phillips, himself a great orator. Born in Boston in 1811 and the son of Boston's first mayor, Wendell Phillips had long been associated with the abolitionist movement, which he joined after marrying Ann Terry Greene, an heiress who had been active in the Boston Female Anti-Slavery Society. Greene was infirm, the victim of rheumatoid arthritis, and Phillips, a graduate of Harvard before he was twenty and then of Harvard Law School, proposed on what he thought was Ann's deathbed, so passionate were her courage and her convictions. Once married, the couple (when Ann was well) often appeared together at rallies. But not until the 1837 murder of the editor Elijah Lovejoy and the strong stand of John Quincy Adams for the right of petition did Phillips find his own eloquent, extemporaneous, and effective voice. He never lost it.

Slender, modest, graceful, and conversational in his speech, Phillips was not a Garrisonian pacifist, and though he respected Garrison, he had no problem using violence, if need be, to rescue a fugitive slave. "Ask no man to do for you anything that you are not able and willing to do for yourself," his father had told him. Tirelessly traveling from city to city (he was famous by the 1850s), he was a celebrity with a cause and a gift. (He seldom wrote out his speeches in advance.) His notoriety never went to his head, and he was not, like his friend Charles Sumner, pompous, although he was equally brilliant, impassioned, and well versed in history. Like Sumner, however, he seldom admitted he was wrong. Yet Phillips willingly gave up profession, friends, and social standing, for he regarded himself, as the historian Richard Hofstadter once observed, as a "counterweight to sloth and indifference." The inscription on his small white calling cards read, "Peace if possible. Justice at any rate. W. P."

Phillips distrusted Lincoln, but he liked Anna Dickinson, whose main talents were earnestness, seeming fearlessness, and an entertaining and withering sarcasm. Her buoyant youthfulness didn't hurt either—and partly because of it she could get away with stinging asides about the administration or the president, whom she likened to a slave catcher after he annulled General Hunter's early emancipation proclamation; that too had helped make her famous. She was not a silent Quaker, but, as Elizabeth Cady Stanton would later recollect, a self-made woman who "carved her way, with her own right hand, to fame and independence"; Wendell Phillips said she was "the young elephant sent forward to try the bridges to see if it were safe for older ones to cross." The Pennsylvania State Republican Party offered her the huge sum of $1,000 a day to campaign for twelve days and speak to the coal miners, who detested the conscription act and the war.

They often came to heckle and hiss and in one case fired a pistol at her, but she pushed on, fulfilling her commitment; the Pennsylvania State Republican Committee, on the other hand, never paid her. In the future, she insisted on written contracts.

Detractors carped that "what you brought away with you was not so much a remembrance of what she had said as it was of the manner in which she had said it," and later it was rumored that Wendell Phillips was either her lover or wrote her speeches; but such was her undeniable, alarming power: it had to be undermined. In 1886, the novelist Henry James would cast her as Verena Tarrant, the empty-headed and unlikable women's rights activist in his novel *The Bostonians*.

Though Dickinson agreed with Phillips that the Proclamation of Amnesty and Reconstruction was a sham, around the Christmas holidays, in 1863, she received an extraordinary letter signed by Vice President Hannibal Hamlin, twenty-three senators, and seventy-three representatives, including Thaddeus Stevens, James Garfield, John Sherman, Henry Wilson, and Charles Sumner. They were inviting her to speak to Congress in January. A woman, no less, had been called to the Capitol to talk one evening about black freedom; that would be unusual, to say the least, for it would be the first time a woman had ever addressed Congress. The house was crammed with spectators waiting for what one onlooker called "crazy Jane in a red jacket."

Ushered forward by Vice President Hamlin, who compared Dickinson to Joan of Arc—evidently not realizing that this standard comparison forecast an unhappy end—she summed up the divisive, hot issues of the day when she argued firmly for equal pay for black soldiers and for universal suffrage. The Lincolns, both the president and his wife, Mary, had softly stolen into the gallery at about eight o'clock, just in time to hear the young woman—a girl, really—criticize the Supreme Court and then the president and his amnesty program. "Let no man prate of compromise," Dickinson declared. "Defeated by ballots, the South had appealed to bullets. Let it stand by the appeal. There was no arm of compromise long enough to stretch over the sea of blood, and the mound of fallen heroes, to shake hands with their murderers." Then she surprised her audience with what seemed an about-face when she endorsed a second term for Lincoln. The crowd cheered. Lincoln bowed his head forward on his long neck.

Radical Republicans loved the speech. She supported the president while excoriating him. (Later she withdrew her endorsement of Lincoln and then at the last minute, before the 1864 election, changed her mind again.) She was also unambiguous about the fate of the freedman: burdened with a man's responsibilities, he should have a man's rights; in a land of traitors, he should have his share of the traitors' confiscated estates. A constitutional amendment should guarantee the rights of all slaves, former and newly freed, and shield them from any claims to the contrary.

Only John Quincy Adams had been bold enough to propose a constitutional amendment on abolition. That was in 1839, and it had failed. Lincoln knew this, of course. Perhaps with that in mind, his proclamation implied that the only way to protect emancipation from the courts—and, in particular, from the Supreme Court, which had passed Dred Scott—was with a constitutional amendment. For as a political tactician without peer, he knew that the specter of a hostile, activist court would spur the congressional Radicals to action.

In other words, let Congress take up the cause and place emancipation on the rock-solid ground of an amendment. James Ashley, an Ohio Republican, introduced a House bill in support of an amendment prohibiting slavery, and so had Representative James Wilson of Iowa. More significant still was the joint resolution proposed in the early winter of 1864 by Senator John Henderson of Missouri (formerly a Douglas Democrat): that "slavery or involuntary servitude, except as a punishment for a crime, shall not exist in the United States." The Senate Judiciary Committee, headed by Lyman Trumbull, discussed these measures and another proposed by Charles Sumner, who added the more radical proposal of guaranteeing equal rights under the law for black citizens. War Democrats and conservative Republicans would not hear of it: that dour, damnable Sumner liked to toss apples of discord into Congress, jeered Henry Raymond, the editor of *The New York Times*; and what could it accomplish anyway, except to show the South that Republicans were squabbling? Raymond didn't believe that the people wanted or would brook any change to the Constitution.

Racism too had to be reckoned with; it was no abstraction. "Let them be free as the beasts in the fields," intoned *The New Orleans Tribune* when speaking of former slaves. When a black officer with the rank of major was thrown off a streetcar in the District of Columbia and Sumner protested, one of his Senate colleagues wanted to know why the major hadn't been riding in the separate car provided for people of his color in the first place. Senator Henry Wilson immediately backed off. *He* had certainly never intended to foist "Negro equality" on anyone. And the black abolitionist James McCune Smith noted that even if Congress passed a constitutional amendment forbidding slavery, "the word *slavery* will, of course be wiped from the statute book, but the 'ancient relation' can be just as well maintained by cunningly devised laws."

So it wasn't too hard for conservative Republicans, such as Raymond, to find common ground with the War Democrats—including James Gordon Bennett of the rival paper, the *New York Herald*. Not only did they all oppose any constitutional amendment guaranteeing universal civil rights or anything that smacked of racial equality, they all hated Sumner. Aware that an amendment securing freedom for the slave would be easier to pass than one guaranteeing civil liberties, Trumbull cobbled together several proposals, including Ashley's and excluding Sumner's. But as one historian of the Thirteenth Amendment has cogently argued, "By rejecting Sumner's language"—that of equal rights under the law for black citizens—those Republicans "placed an effective cudgel in the hands of later jurists and legislators who beat down any attempt to broaden the amendment into a extension of civil equality for African Americans." Or women, for that matter.

. . . .

THERE WAS ALSO the matter of jurisdiction. Which branch of government should superintend this supposed reconstruction, should it come? Members of the Thirty-eighth Congress felt it to be their prerogative. The executive branch of government had already arrogated too much power to itself, appointing, for instance, military governors in the Union-held sections of Tennessee, Louisiana, Arkansas, and South Carolina. Though such appointments might be permissible in time of war, in time of peace, Charles Sumner had explained in the pages of *The Atlantic Monthly*, "if a new government is to be supplied, it should be supplied by Congress rather than by the president, and it should be according to established law rather than according to the mere will of any functionary, to the end that ours may be a government of laws and not of men."

Sumner also urged Congress to acknowledge that the rebel states could no longer exist as states since they had been "*vacated*," as he put it, " . . . by all local government which we are bound to recognize, so that the way is open to a rightful jurisdiction." Since the treasonous states were no longer states, they should be considered territories and, as such, subject to congressional control. Moreover, he said, the land owned by former Confederates should be divided among "patriotic soldiers, poor whites, and freedmen," a redistribution that would prevent the restoration of the planter class—the perfidious Confederates, that is, who had started the war and would want to stay in power.

Anxious that Lincoln's reelection would make the president's "manifest tendency toward compromises and temporary expedients of policy" stronger, three Radical congressmen decided that the redoubtable Salmon Chase, not Abraham Lincoln, would best be able to implement their plan for reconstruction. One of them, Representative Henry Winter Davis of Maryland, wasn't a personable man. He often seemed dogmatic and rubbed even his friends the wrong way. But he combined confidence, intelligence, and oratorical polish with an ability to question his earlier opinions. The son of a slaveholder and formerly a Know-Nothing who thought America should be governed only by bona fide Americans—not naturalized Germans or naturalized Irish—he was a loyal Unionist who had voted for John Bell and the Constitutional Union Party in 1860. After Fort Sumter, though, he had supported the recruitment of black soldiers and even emancipation in Maryland; after all, freeing the slaves was a matter that fell under the jurisdiction of the state. And he deeply resented Lincoln's suspension of habeas corpus as a usurpation of executive privilege.

Another of the men who thought Salmon Chase the man of the hour was Benjamin Wade. The chair of the powerful (and partisan) Committee on the Conduct of the War, Ben Wade had for a very long time criticized Lincoln as too cautious for prosecuting what Wade called "your rose-water war." By 1864 he was so furious that he joined forces with Davis and the far less savory character Samuel C. Pomeroy to topple the long-legged president. Formerly an agent of the Emigrant Aid Company in Kansas, Pomeroy, as president of the Atchison, Topeka, and Santa Fe Railroad, had failed to acknowledge any conflict of interest when he had been elected senator from Kansas. He'd also been accused of bribing the government agent of the Pottawatomie Indians, and after the war, his name was so synonymous with corruption (called "Pomeroyism") that in their aptly titled novel *The Gilded Age*, Mark Twain and Charles Dudley Warner caricatured him as the portly and sleazy Senator Abner Dilworthy, who read his Bible upside down.

Davis, Wade, and Pomeroy (John Hay called them the Jacobin Club) composed a putatively secret circular that urged like-minded folks to dump Lincoln and join in a campaign for Salmon P. Chase as president. Known as the "Pomeroy Circular" because Pomeroy alone had signed it, the document did not stay secret for very long, and when the *New York Herald* published it, astonished readers at first thought it was a hoax.

What was going on? Did Pomeroy intend to pit Salmon Chase against Lincoln and divide Republicans so that they would abandon the president, introduce a third candidate, and then throw the nomination back to Chase? "This is a very pretty game," snorted the Lincoln-leaning *Chicago Tribune*, "but it won't work." What did Chase know about all this? He was sitting in Lincoln's cabinet, after all, and stabbing the president in the back if he did know, which it seems he did.

Chase, Pomeroy, and whoever else was involved had overplayed their hand. Postmaster General Montgomery Blair's brother Frank, back in Congress, blasted Chase, charging that the Treasury Department was a den of fraud and corruption and that Chase was himself speculating and profiting on cotton from the Sea Islands. For Chase had been in an awkward position for a while. On his shoulders fell the responsibility of financing the war. Though a Democrat, a hard-money man, and a free trader, he issued legal tender notes ("greenbacks," so named because of the color of the ink with which they were printed) and oversaw a graduated income tax to help pay for the war. (Chase's own face was imprinted on the dollar bill, so everyone knew what he looked like. And as a pious man, he'd also added the pious phrase "IN GOD WE TRUST" to the tender.) Chase had also sought the assistance of the financier Jay Cooke to sell government bonds to the public but was criticized for allowing Cooke a monopoly on the sale of those bonds. Calling Chase corrupt and devious, Frank Blair accused him of receiving kickbacks from the sale.

Such allegations, along with a virulent backlash against the Pomeroy Circular, derailed Chase's presidential juggernaut. In early March, his reputation tarnished, the secretary irritably announced that he was not a candidate for the presidency after all. Embarrassed—and cravenly protesting that he was ignorant of his allies' machinations—he wrote a sniveling letter to Lincoln affirming his loyalty and offering to resign his post. "The Salmon is a queer fish," quipped the *New York Herald*, "very shy and very wary, often appearing to avoid the bait just before gulping it down." Lincoln replied in a short, unflappable way: he was not yet ready to accept the resignation. He wanted to keep an eye on Chase.

Since Chase had allowed his ambition to override his genuine zeal for reform, his presidential bid obscured the legitimate complaints of the Radical Republicans (as the radical wing of the Republican Party had been dubbed). They had passed the confiscation acts, repealed the Fugitive Slave Act, and at least on paper authorized equal pay for black regiments. And now they feared that a lenient Reconstruction would restore former rebels to power. To a Radical such as Wendell Phillips, for instance, Lincoln had been nothing but slow, untrustworthy, and vacillating. "What McClellan was on the battle-field—'Do as little hurt as possible!'—, Lincoln is in civil affairs—" Phillips charged. "'Make as little change as possible.'"

Radical Republicans were labeled fanatics in their own time and later. Regardless, as Rebecca Harding Davis observed, "fanatics must make history for conservative men to learn from."

This may or may not have been the case with John Frémont, if he actually was a Radical Republican. He was, more certainly, a man with a grudge who never forgave the president or the Blair family for the loss of his prestige and the loss of his command in Missouri and then in the Mountain Department (western Virginia, eastern Kentucky, and part of Tennessee), and he was ready for the spotlight once again. Some Radical Republicans, disappointed by Lincoln, were beguiled by Frémont. Wendell Phillips preferred him to the president; it seemed that the man who early on had declared the slaves free would do battle for civil rights—equality for all men under the law, without regard to race or color.

In May in Cleveland, at Cosmopolitan Hall, notorious abolitionists such as Frederick Douglass, Gerrit Smith, and Wendell Phillips, women's rights activists such as Elizabeth Cady Stanton, and disappointed Republicans such as the journalist James Redpath expected to patch together a third political party, which they called the Radical Democratic Party, in the hope of attracting disillusioned War Democrats as well as disillusioned Radical Republicans to a platform more radical than any offered by Lincoln and moderates. That is, their platform pledged to prosecute the war without compromise, to safeguard the First Amendment and the writ of habeas corpus, to push for constitutional amendments abolishing slavery and protecting civil rights, and to recommend a one-term presidency. Frémont accepted their nomination. Running with him was the New York War Democrat General John Cochrane. Frémont's political adviser was David Dudley Field, a brother of the man who had tried to lay the transatlantic telegraph cable.

A ragtag bunch, sneered General Halleck. "I don't believe there are bladders enough in this country, if every one should be inflated to its utmost capacity, to float such a mass of corruption and humbugs." And perhaps Frémont was a humbug after all, for in pandering to Democrats, he reneged on the equality platform. Disillusioned dissidents, such as Anna Dickinson, decided to support President Lincoln and his so-called compromises after all, and Radical Republicans of a practical bent, such as Zachariah Chandler, conferred with Ben Wade; if Lincoln would remove Montgomery Blair from the cabinet, they would back Lincoln.

Along with prominent abolitionists such as John Greenleaf Whittier, they asked Frémont to withdraw from the field, which he finally did in September, though not because he'd cut a deal. He believed that the Democratic nominee for president, George Brinton McClellan, if elected, would end the war—and restore slavery. That would be awful.

By THE SPRING of 1864, the country had seen the horrors of Antietam and Gettysburg firsthand in the photographs of Alexander Gardner; it had read with revulsion about the carnage at Shiloh, Cedar Mountain, Fredericksburg, Chancellorsville, Fort Wagner, and Murfreesboro, just to cite a few of the towns or places that had once been unknown by most people but had grown familiar. People now spoke knowingly of breech-loading muskets and grape shot and minié balls and Parrott guns, names of things that could tear through arms and legs and hearts.

Most recently, in April, Americans had learned of a place called
Fort Pillow. An earthwork located on a high bluff on the east bank of
the Mississippi and north of Memphis by about forty miles, it had been
captured by bluecoats in 1862. By the spring of 1864, more than 260
black soldiers and almost 300 white ones were occupying it, living,
eating, and sleeping within its thick walls: one battalion of the 6th U.S.
Colored Heavy Artillery, formerly the 1st Alabama Siege Artillery African Descent; one section of the 2nd U.S. Colored Light Artillery;
and one battalion of the 13th Tennessee Cavalry (white).

On the morning of April 12, 1864—which happened to be the
fourth anniversary of Fort Sumter—one of General Nathan Bedford Forrest's divisions surrounded Fort Pillow. Forrest arrived, demanded unconditional surrender, and when the fort's commander
refused, Forrest attacked. Union casualties numbered more than
three hundred dead or wounded.

There were ugly rumors about what had happened: atrocities, barbarities. Had the Confederates attacking Fort Pillow really
screamed, "No quarter! No quarter! Kill the damned niggers; shoot
them down!"? Why had black soldiers made up nearly two-thirds
of the dead? What had Forrest's men done? Had they burned black
soldiers in their barracks? Buried men alive? Had a black man really
been nailed to the side of a building outside of the fort and then
the building torched? After the Union soldiers fled to the riverbank,
where they vainly hoped that a gunboat would cover them, had they
thrown down their arms, putting their hands up in surrender, only to
be picked off by rifle fire? Had Forrest's men shot them at point-blank
range before throwing their bodies into the river? A surviving bluecoat told his family that a Rebel had found him on the ground and
yelled, " 'You'll never fight with niggers again, you d—ded yankee,'
and he snapped his revolver, but she wouldn't go off as he had shot the
last load out when he killed the soldier by my side."

To what extent was Nathan Bedford Forrest responsible? Did he
really leave Fort Pillow around six in the evening, unaware of the
atrocities—if, that is, they had even occurred? Did he try to stop

the shooting once it was clear he had won the day? Did he witness the murders—the atrocities—and do nothing to halt them? Should he be held accountable? Was he a soldier or a guerrilla? Was there a difference?

Forrest already had a reputation as a little bit of both. Familiarly called the Wizard of the Saddle, he was an expert horseman whose battle strategy was to get there first with the most men, shoot everything blue, and keep up the scare. Sixteen when his father died, he supported his large family by speculating in stocks, gambling, farming, and trading in horses and human flesh. By the age of twenty-five, he was a prosperous planter, married, and living in Memphis not too far from the slave pens he owned downtown. He claimed to be a millionaire. He was elected alderman. When Tennessee seceded, he enlisted and raised a cavalry regiment.

Audacious, brave, profane, and illiterate, with a white scar running down the side of his thin face, Forrest was an improvisatory soldier who did not work by the book. Nor did he need to. It was said that twenty-nine horses had been shot from beneath him, he was said to have killed thirty men with his own hands, and he liked to say that war means fighting and "fighting means killing." At Shiloh, wounded in the spine and coming on a regiment of blue skirmishers, he'd grabbed one hapless Union soldier by the collar and pulled him up onto his horse to use him as a human shield while he rode to safety. He was revered by his men. An increasingly anxious Confederacy considered him something of a savior. He was an electric storm, reminisced the writer George Washington Cable. Sherman called him the Devil.

Though Forrest did admit that, at Fort Pillow, "the river was dyed red with the blood of the slaughtered for 200 yards," the Confederate government contested the allegation of a massacre as a pack of propagandistic lies. Forrest's superior, General Stephen Dill Lee—a veteran of the peninsular campaign, the Second Battle of Manassas, and the Battle of Antietam—asserted unequivocally to the Union forces, "Your colors were never lowered, and your garrison never surrendered, but retreated under cover of a gun-boat with arms in their hands and constantly using them. This was true particularly of your colored troops, who had been firmly convinced by your teachings of the certainty of slaughter in case of capture."

General Lee backed Forrest without exactly denying what had happened. "The case under consideration is almost an extreme one," he explained. "You had a servile race armed against their masters, and in a country which had been desolated by almost unprecedented outrages. I assert that our officers, with all the circumstances against them, endeavored to prevent the effusion of blood, and as an evidence of this I refer you to the fact that both white and colored prisoners were taken, and are now in our hands." Similarly, the *Richmond Examiner* faulted the Union army's invasion of the South and its depredations of its people. "Our Northern brethren are in the position of burglars and brigands resisting the authorities; and the sheriff may do to the highwayman what the highwayman must not do to the sheriff. The constable may shoot, or starve out, or smoke out, or blow up, the resisting burglar, because he has a lawful warrant; but if the burglar perpetrates these enormities upon the constable, it chills the blood and sickens the heart."

A congressional committee was convened six days after Fort Pillow to investigate, and the Joint Committee on the Conduct of the War released a damning report—part propaganda, part fact—that ignited a storm of protest. Some of it was directed against Lincoln. "You, Abraham Lincoln," Henry Ward Beecher's radical newspaper, *The Independent*, accused, "you who have persistently withheld from the negro the protection of the flag for which you besought and compelled him to fight—you are the chief bearer of this great and awful responsibility. Shall we now have some action by the Government which will prevent a repetition of these atrocities?" Prevention, yes; not retaliation. But in what form could prevention come? The resilient abolitionist Gerrit Smith noted that if Lincoln did not recognize the right of black men to vote, he was contributing to the outrages perpetrated upon them.

Promising reprisals, at least at first, and no doubt responding to the heat of the hour, Lincoln consulted with his cabinet as to what he should do. The angry Stanton wanted to hold Confederate officers as hostages until the Confederates gave up Forrest and his officers for trial. Though somewhat milder in character, Secretary of the Navy Gideon Welles also felt that the officers in command at Fort Pillow should be held accountable. And if they weren't turned over to Washington, other Confederate troops should be punished accordingly. Secretary of State Seward agreed, but Attorney General Edward Bates and John Palmer Usher, the new secretary of the interior, would not go that far. Lincoln spoke with Frederick Douglass, but by the time he did, he seems to have decided against taking action. "Once begun," Lincoln told Douglass, "I do not know where such a measure would stop."

"Remember Fort Pillow!" cried black soldiers. If the cry went largely unheard, it also shaped the debate about emancipation and Reconstruction. In July, Senator Ben Wade and Representative Henry Winter Davis (the chairman of the House Reconstruction Committee) joined forces to sponsor a bill that differed from Lincoln's far milder Proclamation of Amnesty and Reconstruction. The Wade-Davis bill assuaged Radical Republicans, who feared that slavery would be allowed to persist if former Confederates, no matter what kind of loyalty oath they swore, were permitted to hold office. Under Wade-Davis, those with positions of power or authority in the Confederacy or those who had shouldered its muskets were forbidden to serve as delegates to state constitutional conventions or even to vote for the delegates who did. The Wade-Davis bill also required 50 percent of voters to swear an oath of allegiance before a rebel state could reenter the Union (instead of Lincoln's 10 percent); it demanded that a state constitutional convention occur before there could be an election of state officials (which had not occurred in Louisiana); it repudiated all public debt, such as Confederate bonds, held under the Confederacy; and it stipulated that to return to the Union, a state must abolish slavery.

The bill did not, however, require black suffrage. In that respect, it didn't greatly differ from Lincoln's plan. Yet Lincoln pocket-vetoed the bill—that is, he refused to sign it, and in not signing, he again asserted his executive power. Only a constitutional amendment could abolish slavery, he reasoned, not an act of Congress, which could easily be overturned by an unfriendly court.

Wade and Davis were furious, intemperately so. Carefully distinguishing between the Republican Party, which they supported, and the man at its helm, whom they volubly disliked, they published an ill-conceived manifesto in the *New-York Tribune* accusing Lincoln of despotically appropriating legislative authority to himself and scuttling the root-cause of the war: slavery. To them, Lincoln was refusing to "protect the loyal men of the nation against three great dangers: 1. The return to power of the guilty leaders of the rebellion. 2. The continuance of slavery, and 3, the burden of the rebel debt."

Republicans were again publicly turning on one another. Moderates were worried. "The radical Republicans, those who go for slave-suffrage and thorough confiscation, are those who will defeat him, if he is defeated," fretted one Lincoln supporter. The war dragged on, exhausted men and women were heartsore, the Union was frazzled and fractious. Henry Winter Davis said, "Everybody is looking for a new candidate."

But the intense indictment of Lincoln also backfired, to a degree: Lincoln wafflers now rallied to his side. New England abolitionists such as Charles Sumner and Governor John Andrew of Massachusetts did not want to split the party, and in Maryland, Henry Winter Davis lost the renomination for his congressional seat. Lincoln had affirmed his commitment to emancipation, if at his own pace. He did have his principles and still knew how to practice an art that bordered on compromise—and, as it would happen, without compromising his stand on emancipation.

BY THE TIME Lincoln stuffed the Wade-Davis bill deep into his pocket, he had already clinched the Republican nomination the preceding June. And he had strengthened the ticket, or so he hoped, by replacing his vice president, Hannibal Hamlin, with a War Democrat from Tennessee. That was Andrew Johnson, a man popular in the North ever since he'd declared himself a Jacksonian Unionist. His presence also had the advantage of reminding folks that Tennessee was still in the Union. (Not everyone agreed; Thaddeus Stevens, a Republican representative from Pennsylvania, was unhappy. "Can't you find a candidate for Vice President in the United States," he wanted to know, "without going down to one of those damned rebel provinces to pick one up?")

Lincoln also got rid of Salmon Chase. When the secretary tendered his resignation from the cabinet yet again—he'd done so three times already—Lincoln surprised him by accepting it. Chase had clashed with New York senator Edwin Morgan, who happened to be the national chairman of the Republican Party, and though Lincoln had bluntly told Chase that he needed Morgan's support, Chase had refused to back down. Lincoln had had enough—but he also knew that Chase would be the best man to replace Chief Justice Taney, who had died in October, and protect emancipation or civil rights legislation.

Despite the new ticket, the removal of Chase from the cabinet, the withdrawal of Frémont from the field, and even a presidential platform promising a constitutional amendment to end slavery, there was continued discontent, divisiveness, perfidy—and silliness—among Republicans, and some of the discontent now came from a different but no less annoying quarter: Horace Greeley.

Greeley was an American gladiator. He loved a good fight partly because he loved to place himself at its righteous center. Grandiose and humble, he was a man of mercurial temperament, of practicality and visionary foolhardiness, and known to be "the most hysterical man of genius America ever produced." Born in 1811 to a family of poor farmers in Amherst, New Hampshire, he too was a self-made man—"a self-made man," quipped a fellow journalist, "who worshipped his creator." Typesetter, printer, journalist, and then editor, with a smooth baby face, a disarming smile, a shambling gait,

and a feisty prose style, by the time he was thirty he'd founded the
New-York Tribune, whose circulation almost immediately rocketed to
11,000. His pungency was part of the reason. "Meek as he looks,"
said Harriet Beecher Stowe, "no man living is readier with a strong
sharp answer. Non-resistant as he is physically, there is not a more
uncompromising an opponent and intense combatant in these United
States." Greeley knew what he was about, at least journalistically, and
his successes in print often went to his conniving political head.

"He is ambitious, talented, but not considerate, persistent, or profound," Gideon Welles characterized Greeley. A contradictory man,
Greeley opposed women's suffrage but eagerly hired the women's
rights activist Margaret Fuller and made her his foreign correspondent; he urged international copyright (there was none) to protect
American authors; he suggested that young men go west to homestead the land; he promoted vegetarianism; and he deplored the
Mexican War and the Compromise of 1850. An early member of
the Republican Party and a backer of Lincoln in 1860, in 1858 he'd
swung his considerable journalistic weight behind Stephen Douglas. Initially, he had supported secession (let the erring sisters go),
but then he had urged in his paper that the untried bluecoats march
"On to Richmond" before the First Battle of Bull Run. Though not
directly responsible for the rallying cry—his associate Charles Dana
had approved the headline in Greeley's absence—Greeley acknowledged that the buck did stop with him.

He was thus a man of parts. His "Prayer of Twenty Millions,"
published in 1862, had been a plea for emancipation. He had supported the draft and bravely did not flee the *Tribune* offices during the
draft riot of 1863. Yet he also supported peace and never more so than
in the dark summer days of 1864, when Lincoln seemed to drift, or
so it was supposed, and Northerners grew wearier than ever, worried
about the war debt and darkly dubious about whether General Grant,
the newly appointed commander in chief of the entire Union army,
would make good on his expensive summer campaign, costly in dollars, costlier in men.

"I propose to fight it out on this line if takes all summer," Grant had said, and he continued to batter the Confederates—and his own army. As general in chief, the highest post possible, of the army, since March 1864, the quiet Grant had moved his headquarters east and planned to engage Lee's forces as long as possible and as fiercely as possible. But there had been 95,000 casualties between May and early July: the statistics defy comprehension. In the tangled, dark Wilderness of Virginia, for instance, the battle was long, fierce, and useless, said one of Grant's biographers. It resulted in 17,500 Union casualties, 7,000 Confederate. Near Spotsylvania Courthouse, at the so-called Bloody Angle, for eighteen hours men killed each other with bullets and bayonets, and waged what one scholar called an "atavistic territorial battle." The trench floors were slimy with blood; men stood on wounded men to fight hand to hand regardless of storms, mud, and the bodies of dismembered comrades lying nearby. And after the battle at the crossroads known as Cold Harbor, near the Chickahominy River, in early June, Grant threw so many men against the entrenched Confederates that even he would say, in sorrow, that no advantage whatever was gained. The losses had been insane. Mary Lincoln again thought Grant a butcher; she wasn't alone. The bone-tired Lincoln, lanky and funereal and slightly stooped, paraphrased *Henry IV, Part I,* saying that the "heavens are hung in black."

"Many a man has gone crazy since this campaign began from the terrible pressure on mind & body," wrote Oliver Wendell Holmes, Jr., who had already been wounded three times. "I hope for success strongly before the end of the summer," he said, "—but at what a cost." Grant's and Lee's armies prepared for a long siege outside Petersburg, twenty miles southeast of Richmond, in intricate, forbidding trenches. The Army of the Potomac was battle-weary; so many men had died, so many men were leaving, their term of enlistment coming due. Lincoln called for 500,000 volunteers: more men to be thrown on the pyre of dead men. If the men didn't show up, he'd authorize a new draft.

"Our bleeding, bankrupt, almost dying country also longs for peace—shudders at the prospect of fresh conscription, of further wholesale devastations, and of new rivers of human blood," Horace Greeley had assailed Lincoln. Greeley decided to take matters into his own hands. He thought he himself could broker peace with the Confederacy by meeting with Southern agents in Canada. Two emissaries from Richmond, who were ready to negotiate, he said, were waiting for him on the Canadian side of Niagara Falls. Not wishing to alienate Greeley or seem averse to peace, Lincoln cleverly told the editor he would meet with whatever bona fide commissioners, authorized by Jefferson Davis, that Greeley might find there and bring to Washington. The president was thereby able to placate Greeley, pretending to hear peace proposals while, once again, demonstrating that the Confederacy was not going to tender them. If Davis wanted peace, Lincoln knew, it would be peace with disunion.

Lincoln was right. For one thing, the men Greeley met were not at all authorized by Jefferson Davis. And, as Lincoln had rightly surmised, Davis would not settle for anything less than Southern independence. Plus, Lincoln had also sent his secretary John Hay to Niagara Falls. A good man for the job, courteous, keen-witted, and eminently loyal, Hay had carried a note from Lincoln promising safe passage to the alleged envoys, if indeed they were envoys, as long as their peace proposition embraced "the integrity of the whole Union, and the abandonment of slavery, and which comes by and with an authority that can control the armies now at war." But the envoys—Clement Clay, a former senator from Alabama, and James Holcombe, a man "tall spare false looking," as John Hay recalled, "with false teeth false eyes & false hair"—had no authority at all.

Outfoxed by the president, who had maneuvered him into making the foolish trip, Greeley returned in shame to New York City very much aware that he'd been duped: by the Confederate secret agents, by Copperheads and Peace Democrats trying to finagle Lincoln out of office, by his muddle-headed confidence in his own abilities, and not least by the president himself. "Greeley is an old shoe," Gideon Welles remembered Lincoln saying. "'In early life, and with few mechanics and but little means in the West, we used,' said he, 'to make our shoes last a great while with much mending, and sometimes, when far gone, we found the leather so rotten the stitches would not hold. Greeley is so rotten that nothing can be done with him. He is not truthful; the stitches all tear out.' "

Lincoln had defeated another foe within his own ranks.

Yet Greeley never gave up easily. Much to Lincoln's annoyance, he published his self-serving justifications in his widely read paper. Nor were the Confederate agents easy to slough off. In high dudgeon they also released to the papers a letter to Greeley in which they accused Lincoln of closing a door to negotiations that they had opened. What Lincoln had done, they opined, was to preclude negotiations—and to prescribe in advance "the terms and conditions of peace." That is, they continued, the president's letter returned to the "original policy of 'No bargaining, no negotiations, no truces with the rebels except to bury their dead, until every man shall have laid down his arms, submitted to the Government, and sued for mercy.' " What was left? they asked. Just the imperial will of Lincoln, fresh blasts of war to the bitter end, and the destruction of all hope.

Attempting to discredit Lincoln, to splinter Republicans further, and to hearten Copperheads and Peace Democrats, the Confederate agents were successful enough to make Lincoln amenable to the importuning of two other men: James R. Gilmore, an author who wrote under the name of Edmund Kirke, and Colonel James Jaquess, a Methodist clergyman presently on furlough from the 73rd Illinois Regiment. Lincoln granted the two agents from the North safe travel through Virginia, for they hoped to talk with Jefferson Davis— unofficially—and bring back news of the Southern president's point of view, which Lincoln knew would yet again strengthen his own hand. He also knew that Davis could not decline to meet with those backdoor emissaries, for Davis valued propaganda and the press as much as he did, and he knew that Davis would scuttle the benighted plan of those Union do-gooders who wanted to settle the war.

Lincoln was right—so he approved the publication of Gilmore's

account of the interview. Spare and iron-willed, Davis had predictably forbidden any talk of peace without Southern independence.
"Withdraw your armies, and peace will come of itself. We do not
seek to subjugate you," he had presumably said, reiterating the sentiments of his 1861 inaugural. "Let us alone, and peace will come
at once." As for emancipation, he scoffed at it. "Emancipation!" he
laughed. "You have already emancipated nearly two million of our
slaves, and if you take care of them, you may emancipate the rest."
That was the kind of battle cry that Lincoln could profitably use to
advantage. "You may emancipate every negro in the Confederacy,
but *we will be free!*" Davis stolidly concluded. "We will govern ourselves. We *will* do it, if we have to see every Southern plantation
sacked, and every Southern city in flames."

THOUGH THE REPUBLICANS had already nominated Lincoln for
a second term, Greeley was still sniping in August that "Mr. Lincoln
is already beaten. He cannot be elected. And we must have another
ticket to save us from utter overthrow." A Peace Republican, Greeley
was also arguing in tangled fashion for universal emancipation. That
the Union could never have peace, emancipation, and one united
country, given the intractable position of the Confederacy, was something he did not seem to understand. Lincoln did. Only a military
victory could preserve the Union, he believed. And he would not
renege on emancipation, which, as he further believed, only a constitutional amendment could guarantee.

On August 23, 1864, the day before the Democratic convention,
an exhausted and sallow president brought the members of his cabinet a piece of paper, its pages folded. Later it would be called his
"blind memorandum." He asked his cabinet to sign the paper without reading it.

"This morning, as for some days past, it seems exceedingly probable that this administration will not be re-elected," he had secretly written. "Then it will be my duty to so co-operate with the

President-elect as to save the Union between the election and the inauguration; as he will secure his election on such ground that he cannot possibly save it afterwards."

A FEDERAL SOLDIER promised his family that "Lincoln's re-election will end this war. You have no idea how hopeful the soldiers are. No croaking from them. None but non-combatants whine and find fault with the administration."

On November 11, Lincoln showed his cabinet the message they had signed the summer before. A dark and rainy election day had come and gone, with Lincoln winning the electoral vote decisively (221 to 21) and trouncing George B. McClellan.

Lincoln was able to lead a relatively undivided Republican Party to victory. To appease the party's Radical faction and recalibrate the cabinet now that Chase was gone, Lincoln had accepted Montgomery Blair's resignation as postmaster general. And though Wendell Phillips had counseled voting for neither Lincoln nor McClellan— two evils, he called them—the president had the support of William Lloyd Garrison, Salmon Chase, and Anna Dickinson. Campaigning against McClellan at Cooper Union, Dickinson had entertained a huge crowd with the anecdote of the old woman who asked, "Why will the people keep attacking poor, dear, little George McClellan? I'm sure *he* never attacked anybody."

Even the austere Henry Winter Davis, mustering his considerable eloquence, had explained what he—and all Republicans—must do: "The great mass of the American people having, as it were, been surprised into the renomination of the present candidate—then for a moment pausing, as if frightened at what they had done—then listening to the first echo from Chicago, and forgetting every doubt, throwing aside every hesitation, subjecting every criticism to the dictates of the highest reason and the highest statesmanship, as one man, turned to the candidate whom before they had doubted, with a resolution that they must make an election—not between two individuals, not between the personal qualities of Abraham Lincoln and George B. McClellan, not between the public services of the one or the other, but an election between the overthrow and the salvation of the Republic."

The issue was and remained the war. And since Rear Admiral David Farragut, lashed to the rigging on his flagship, had damned the torpedoes in Mobile Bay, smashing Confederate gunboats in August, the Union felt strong, stronger, more justified, emboldened. Farragut's victory had taken place just a few weeks before General William Tecumseh Sherman dispatched his famous telegram on September 3. "Atlanta is ours," the redheaded general cried, "and fairly won." Blood-dimmed though it was, the tide had turned again.

(14)

ARMED LIBERTY

Violence: it was lodged in the heart of the lone bandit and the vigilante, whether in Mississippi, Texas, California, or on the Great Plains, and the war had let it run free, often to the point of mass murder. Of course, the country had been born in revolution and war and before that had earned its stripes in the woods and on the plains, fighting tribes of Indians, claiming territory, hanging witches, and tarring and feathering Tories. The Reverend Cotton Mather had praised Hannah Dustin for ax-murdering the Indians, including young boys, who had killed her baby and kidnapped her, and the citizens of Salem, Massachusetts, had heard the sobs of their neighbors who were tortured in the name of religious purity. More recently, Nat Turner's 1831 rebellion in Virginia had taken the lives of about sixty men, women, and children, and it had unleashed a gory reign of terror afterward, with black men and women chased from the state or murdered, their heads left at the sides of roads or stuck on posts as a bleak rebuke and warning. Violence: it happened in the city. The Ursuline Convent near Boston was set afire in 1834 when a group of men disguised as monks, their faces painted, forced out the nuns and then sacked the place and torched it. No one was held accountable. A mob in Boston attacked William Lloyd Garrison, and in Illinois in 1837 a mob killed the abolitionist editor Elijah Lovejoy. He was shot five times while defending his fourth printing press, which was then smashed to pieces and tossed into the Mississippi River. The next year Pennsylvania Hall, built to house antislavery meetings, was burned to the ground just four days after its dedication. In 1844 the Mormon leader Joseph Smith and his brother were gunned down in a Carthage jail. That same year, workers, women, and children in Philadelphia mobbed the streets to protest the government's approving railroad construction down a main thoroughfare in the district of Kensington; they absconded with railroad ties, tore up a portion of the road, and burned the timber used to build it; for the moment, popular sovereignty won the day. Ten years later in Boston, when the self-appointed Vigilance Committee tried to free the fugitive slave Anthony Burns, a guard was mortally stabbed. In New York City, gangs of b'hoys, or working-class young men, were belligerent, armed, and dangerous, and in 1856 Democratic Party supporters gathered in Baltimore with guns and clubs. In Ohio, Margaret Garner, a fugitive slave from Kentucky, cut her two-year-old daughter's throat rather than see her sent back into slavery. In 1859 Congressman Daniel Sickles, later a Federal general, shot and killed Philip Barton Key, the son of Francis Scott Key, with a two-dollar pistol. His plea of temporary insanity worked, and one of his lawyers, Edwin Stanton, was later secretary of war. John Brown liked to kill in the name of justice. "It seems to me that every society rests on the death of men," Oliver Wendell Holmes, Jr., would say; wounded three times in three years, he had been at such killing fields as Ball's Bluff, Fair Oaks, Antietam, Chancellorsville, Spotsylvania, and Cold Harbor.

Justice, violence, and political expression: people taking the law into their own hands or stepping to their own drummer, as Thoreau had advised, although the naturalist also believed that no human being "past the thoughtless age of boyhood" would ever wantonly murder "any creature which holds its life by the same tenure that he does." Yet Alexander Stephens, the vice president of the Confederacy, had once said, "I have no objection to the liberty of speech, when the liberty of the cudgel is left free to combat it." Southerners and Northerners—not all, but certainly governors, senators, congressmen, lawyers, even a president—settled disagreements with pistol and balls, or they chose their seconds and named their weapons for their gentlemanly duels: Andrew Jackson, Henry Clay, Congressman John Randolph of Virginia, Hawthorne's friend Congressman Jonathan Cilley of Maine (who was killed), Sam Houston, Thomas Hart Benton, Henry Wise, and the fire-eater William Yancey, to say nothing of Alexander Hamilton and Aaron Burr. Ben Wade took his squirrel rifle to the Senate chamber and sometimes threatened to use it, and in 1842 Abraham Lincoln accepted a challenge from the Illinois state auditor, James Shields, a Democrat, who he'd intimated was a fool and a liar. Lincoln ingeniously wiggled out of the duel by outrageously selecting large cavalry broadswords as his weapon of choice. Though he was never proud of what had happened, always, for him and others, the issue at stake was honor, that ephemeral quality linked somehow to manhood, self-reliance, revenge, chivalry, and the pursuit of prosperity, all of which were connected by hostility and revenge to a country forging a tradition which, in part, was a tradition of violence. D. H. Lawrence commented, many years later, "The essential American soul is hard, isolate, stoic, and a killer."

Maybe so, maybe not. Throughout the North, armed vigilance committees protested the capture of fugitive slaves in their states and fought and killed to protect them. Violence in the streets too, as the New York draft riots painfully proved, and in the bush, and outside the so-called rules of engagement: that was what happened at Fort Pillow, for sure, when frustrated men murdered other men as the flag of truce reportedly waved overhead. "My life had stood—a loaded gun—," Emily Dickinson wrote during the war. A poem of murder, killing, rape, it jars the reader, any reader, especially those who know its author as a recluse living in a New England college town. But she was also a poet of violence: creativity is violence, sacramental and erotic, mystical and horrific, a scalping of the soul, as she wrote, that dances like a bomb—and has its bandaged moments. Dickinson refashioned aggression into poetry. The milder Stowe too had transformed it into her wildly successful—and brutal—*Uncle Tom's Cabin*, in which Uncle Tom is battered and slaves are roasted alive on blasted trees. So too did the stories of fugitive slaves, most notably by Frederick Douglass or Harriet Jacobs, chronicle the lives of men and women tracked by dogs and whipped, humiliated, hunted, and raped. So too did the final, echoing words of John Brown tell an American story: "I John Brown am now quite certain that the crimes of this guilty land: will never be purged away; but with Blood."

HIS NAME WAS William Clarke Quantrill. He said he was an abolitionist, but he sold the fugitive slaves he had presumably saved. He robbed mail trains, he stole horses, he ambushed Union soldiers, and he enjoyed killing. He was sandy-haired, thin, and soft-spoken and wore a smiling mustache; he was self-confident, enigmatic, and preternaturally calm—the calmer, the more dangerous, it was said. The son of a schoolteacher, he came from Ohio, and he too had taught school for a while. He went to Kansas, where he pretended to be a jayhawker—an abolitionist bandit along the lines of John Brown—but he was in fact the slaveholders' spy. Soon he was hailed as the bloodiest man in the annals of America, which is saying something, especially during the Civil War, when he had to vie for the title of "butcher" with Grant and Nathan Bedford Forrest.

Quantrill had formed a band of like-minded, pro-Confederate "irregulars," or guerrilla partisans, as they were also known, men and boys—Missouri boys, in this case—who fought outside the regular army, on their own, raiding and stealing and sowing terror. To join his particular and infamous band, all a boy had to do was answer one qualifying question Quantrill asked: "Will you follow orders, be true to your fellows, and kill those who served and support the Union?"

Wearing a loose, flowing shirt, Zouave-like, with a low-cut collar, the twenty-six-year-old Quantrill, in the summer of 1863, ordered his gang to saddle up and head toward that city of abolitionists, Lawrence, Kansas. Several women who had sheltered guerrillas such as Quantrill had been recently imprisoned in a rickety Kansas City jail, and when it suddenly collapsed, critically wounding them, Quantrill and his boys were set on revenge. Around sunup on August 21, 1863, a clear day, they rode into Lawrence, about four hundred of them; they'd attracted a good number of stragglers along the way. Quantrill was wearing a black slouch hat, his standard guerrilla shirt ballooning in the breeze, and gray pants tucked into his boots. He shouted his orders: torch every building, kill every male big enough to carry a gun, even the clergyman, who was milking his cow that morning, and even the twenty or so boys, teenagers or children as young as ten years old. When it was all over, more than 150 people lay dead, incinerated, shot, or mutilated.

Border warfare in Kansas and Missouri had not ended; it had been institutionalized by the larger war, and of course Washington knew that Missourians had mired themselves in what Lincoln sadly called a "pestilent factional quarrel amongst themselves." So it was, so it continued, lawless or with new laws concocted to mete out retribution in more orderly fashion. Union general Thomas Ewing, a brother-in-law of Sherman and the man responsible for imprisoning the wives and sisters of the guerrillas in Kansas City, issued the infamous General Order No. 11, which called for the compulsory removal, in fifteen days, of all citizens, whether adult or child, from four counties in western Missouri. Ewing assumed that they, like the women he'd jailed, were Confederate sympathizers. The 15th Kansas Cavalry then enforced the order with a burning spree that left the region, soon called the Burnt District, in smoldering ruins. A Union colonel told his wife, "It is heart sickening to see what I have seen since I have been back here. A desolated country and men & women and children, some of them allmost [sic] naked. Some on foot and some in old wagons. Oh God."

By the fall of 1863, Quantrill sometimes wore a Confederate uniform with three dark gold stars on the collar. Although living by conventional, or army, protocols had never much appealed to him, he had ridden all the way to Richmond to secure an official military appointment, and if Richmond demurred, it nonetheless recognized his effectiveness. After the sacking of Lawrence, Quantrill was heading south toward Texas when he happened on information that two companies of Federal troops were en route to Fort Baxter, Kansas. And since the wagon train and its escort happened to include General James Blunt, the new commander of the District of the Frontier, Quantrill changed into his other signature garb, a Union blue coat, and attacked. Taken unawares, Blunt's men were overwhelmed and most of them were killed. Their wagons were looted. Blunt escaped and was deprived of his command, and Quantrill calmly continued on to Texas.

BACK IN 1862, former congressman Thomas Hindman, the dapper Arkansan, then thirty-four years old, had capitalized on the readiness of partisans to plunder and pillage and retaliate against jayhawkers, thieves, and Union guerrillas. Fight fire with fire: that had always been Hindman's way. (Just three years after the war, he would be murdered in his home in Helena, Arkansas, when an assailant shot him through a window.)

Hindman had traded his patent-leather shoes for army boots, and as the fierce commander of the Confederacy's Trans-Mississippi District, he intended to clear the place, particularly Missouri, of Federals. After Jefferson Davis, who never much liked the guerrillas, nonetheless approved the Confederate Partisan Ranger Act, which allowed officers to form bands of partisan rangers, Hindman followed suit and welcomed Quantrill into his ranks. "With the view to revive the hopes of loyal men in Missouri and to get troops from that State," he declared, "I gave authority to various persons to raise companies and regiments there and to operate as guerrillas. They soon became exceedingly active and rendered important services, destroying wagon trains and transports, tearing up railways, breaking telegraph lines, capturing towns, and thus compelling the enemy to keep there a large force that might have been employed elsewhere."

What else could he do? Richmond had been ignoring the Trans-Mississippi for a very long time, and the Confederacy was short on manpower. According to one of Robert E. Lee's aides, Lee himself understood that "since the whole duty of the nation would be war until independence should be secured, the whole nation should for the time be converted into an army, the producers to feed and the soldiers to fight." In many cases, the irregular soldiers took the law into their own hands, which was what Quantrill had done. And especially during the months preceding the election of 1864, the partisans in Arkansas and Missouri hoped that the havoc they created and the blood they spilled might help elect a presidential candidate in the North willing to negotiate a peace, which is to say grant the Confederacy its independence.

Yet what exactly separated a partisan from a soldier from a bandit? In Missouri, on the border, the lines between Confederate sympathizer, Union loyalist, regular soldier, civilian, and desperado were blurry. Often it was difficult to distinguish irregulars from Confederate soldiers, which led many a soldier to despise them, for the guerrillas were often so indiscriminate—they didn't care whom they killed or what farm they destroyed—that they created a backlash against the graycoats. Confederate brigadier general Joseph Shelby angrily complained to one of his men that "if this detestable system of 'jayhawking' is not broken up they [citizens] will soon come to prefer the Federals to us."

"Arrest all bands of jayhawkers, whether Southern or Union, who may be committing outrages on the citizens," Shelby ordered, though he himself had welcomed the guerrillas into his column. "In all cases when the proof is sufficient against any person or persons who may be or who have committed depredations on the citizens of Arkansas, you will cause them to be shot," he continued. "All squads and unorganized bands must be broken up." Thomas Hindman, on the other hand, had been protesting against the fact that the Union treated Confederate guerrillas as if they were pirates. General Sherman was nonplussed. "Now, whether the guerrillas or partisan rangers, without uniform, without organization except on paper, wandering about the country plundering friend and foe, firing on unarmed boats filled with women and children and on small parties of soldiers, always from ambush, or where they have every advantage, are entitled to the protection and amenities of civilized warfare is a question which I think you would settle very quickly in the abstract," he said. "In practice we will promptly acknowledge the well-established rights of war to parties in uniform, but many gentlemen of the South have beseeched me to protect the people against the acts and inevitable result of this war of ununiformed bands, who, when dispersed, mingle with the people and draw on them the consequences of their individual acts. You know full well that it is to the interest of the people of the South that we should not disperse our troops as guerrillas," he added ominously, "but at that game your guerrillas would meet their equals, and the world would be shocked by the acts of atrocity resulting from such warfare."

By late 1863, after Sherman had seen too many irregulars fire at steamboats, he irritably declared, "To secure the safety of the navigation of the Mississippi River I would slay millions. On that point I am not only insane, but mad. Fortunately, the great West is with me there."

General Sherman, now the head of the Georgia campaign, intended to seize manufacturing areas and destroy the South's provisions and munitions as he and his army marched all the way from Vicksburg to Atlanta. In February 1864 he and about 25,000 of his men had moved southward from Vicksburg to Meridian, Mississippi, a small town of about 800 inhabitants and a supply center for the Confederates. From there he planned to trudge to Selma, Alabama, and blow up the cannon foundry. Along the way, as Sherman reported to General Halleck, "we lived off the country and made a swath of desolation 50 miles broad across the State of Mississippi, which the present generation will not forget." Jefferson Davis said that the Yankees were a cruel, traditionless, uncivilized people, "worse than vandal hordes."

When Sherman arrived in Meridian on Valentine's Day, the warehouses were empty, the town evacuated. Angry, his men tore

up the railroad tracks, and, in what became one of their most notorious actions, they heated the rails over bonfires and then twisted
them around trees or telegraph poles: those were the so-called Sherman neckties. They also destroyed the town—houses and warehouses
were pummeled with axes, crowbars, and sledges—and torched the
debris. When it was all over, Meridian was gone.

Sherman was a garrulous, intelligent, and candid man with decided points of view he very much wanted circulated, and since they
were well known—and have continued to be—and since the general,
and not Quantrill or Hindman, has come to best represent warfare
against civilians as it was practiced during the war, his comments are
worth quoting at length. "Should we treat as absolute enemies all in
the South who differ from us in opinion or prejudice, kill or banish
them, or should we give them time to think and gradually change
their conduct so as to conform to the new order of things which is
slowly and gradually creeping into their country?" he asked. And he
answered, "When men take up arms to resist a rightful authority,
we are compelled to use like force, because all reason and argument
cease when arms are resorted to. When the provisions, forage, horses,
mules, wagons, etc., are used by our enemy, it is clearly our duty and
right to take them also, because otherwise they might be used against
us. In like manner all houses left vacant by an inimical people are
clearly our right, and as such are needed as storehouses, hospitals, and
quarters. But the question arises as to dwellings used by women, children and non-combatants. So long as non-combatants remain in their
houses and keep to their accustomed peaceful business, their opinions
and prejudices can in no wise influence the war, and therefore should
not be noticed; but if any one comes out into the public streets and
creates disorder, he or she should be punished, restrained, or ban-
ished, either to the rear or front, as the officer in command adjudges.
If the people, or any of them, keep up a correspondence with parties
in hostility, they are spies, and can be punished according to law with
death or minor punishment. These are well-established principles of
war," he concluded, "and the people of the South having appealed

to war, are barred from appealing for protection to our constitution, which they have practically and publicly defied. They have appealed to war, and must abide *its* rules and laws."

As if to stave off the public outcry sure to come, before Meridian, Sherman had fervently broadcast his intentions in a long letter he wanted made public. "When the inhabitants persist too long in hostility it may be both politic and right we should banish them and appropriate their lands to a more loyal and useful population," he stated. "No man will deny that the United States would be benefited by dispossessing a rich, prejudiced, hard-headed, and disloyal planter, and substituting in his place a dozen or more patient, industrious, good families, even if they be of foreign birth."

Sherman was decided and impatient, as hard as his features—the pointed nose, the creased face, the close-cropped reddish hair, the unblinking eyes. His son had recently died of typhoid. But the man did not stop for death; he sublimated. He was heated, intense, quick, a warrior, and now, writing for himself and strangers—and his superiors—about war and peace, he explained why he was about to do what he did: "I believe that war is the result of false political doctrine, for which we all as a people are responsible; that any and every people have a natural right to self-government, and I would give all a chance to reflect and when in error to recant. . . . In this belief, whilst I assert for our Government the highest military prerogatives, I am willing to bear in patience that political nonsense of slave rights, States' rights, freedom of conscience, freedom of the press, and such other trash as have deluded the Southern people into war, anarchy, bloodshed, and the foulest crimes that have disgraced any time or any people."

He also promised "gentleness and forbearance" to those people who "submit to the rightful law and authority." He would not handle Confederates—whether or not they wore a uniform—with the same gentleness and forbearance: "to the petulant and persistent secessionists, why death is mercy, and the quicker he or she is disposed of the better."

Publish this letter, he said, and "let them use it so as to prepare for my coming."

Those who broke the law, who waged war and caused war and would not stop, must be held to account, even if the accounting abrogated a moral law. Sherman knew that he would transgress the code of the professional soldier, but he had a reason, which he articulated over and over: the Southern secessionists who caused the war must suffer the consequences of what they had wrought. Even those who had not directly caused it but who stood by and let it happen or aided and abetted it and their comrades, they too were part of the problem, and if it took violence and deportation and despoliation to stop them, so be it. As far as he was concerned, they were guerrillas, all of those so-called noncombatants. He never intended to take the practices of warfare into peacetime but rather to end the war and restore the peace.

"To make war," Sherman had told Charles Dana, "we must & will harden our hearts."

General Grant did not disagree with the plans of his redheaded friend. After the carnage at Spotsylvania, in the spring of 1864, a reporter visited Grant's tent hoping for a comment. Grant admitted that the hard fighting of that day had not accomplished much. He paused for a moment. Then he spoke again. "I do not know of any way to put down this Rebellion and restore the authority of the Government except by fighting, and fighting means that men must be killed."

At Kennesaw Mountain, near Marietta, Georgia, Sherman had launched an indecisive, gruesome frontal attack against General Joseph E. Johnston (who had replaced Braxton Bragg) and his Army of Tennessee; when the Federals charged uphill, said a Confederate soldier, "we mowed them down like hay." Sherman did enter Marietta in July, and though he kept advancing, neither he nor Johnston engaged in a conclusive battle; Johnston had far fewer men and was careful not to lose them. Impatient, Jefferson Davis suddenly replaced Johnston with the aggressive John Bell Hood, who had lost the use of his left arm at Gettysburg and lost his right leg at Chickamauga. Hood finally attacked Sherman, east of Atlanta, late in July, but at one crucial point misconstrued Sherman's actions. Sherman had been shelling the city—sometimes as often as every fifteen minutes; when he stopped, Hood thought Sherman's army had left, which was far from the case. Hood had evacuated Atlanta on September 1, and Sherman telegraphed General Halleck his famous "Atlanta is ours."

As is well known, before Sherman left Atlanta, he ordered all the public buildings set afire. A high wind accomplished even more destruction than Sherman had perhaps anticipated. Soldiers a mile away presumably read their letters from home by the light of the awful blaze, as Atlanta burned brightly in the distance. One reporter noted how the city's blackened chimneys stood quiet as gravestones.

In November Sherman and his men began their equally infamous eastward march to the sea, covering nearly 300 miles in twenty-six days, foraging along the way, bayoneting hogs, chicken, geese, anything they could lay their hands on, and blowing up track along the Georgia Central Railroad. Severing Lee's vital connection with the lower South, Sherman had moved from Atlanta to Savannah and then marched his troops northward through South Carolina. Savannah surrendered unconditionally in late December rather than see itself ablaze, like Atlanta, and from there Sherman—after awarding the city to Lincoln as a Christmas gift—kept pressing on, northward up through the Carolinas. His men waded through thick swamps, bridged swollen creeks, marched over muddy roads in shoes worn and thin; they clobbered these states, cutting railroad lines and capturing locomotives, cotton, and 25,000 animals, or so one correspondent calculated, all the while drinking, dancing, looting, and torching cotton and cotton gins. Another reporter said that the sun was red with a garish afterglow. "A garden was before them," the author Joel Headley wrote, "a desert behind them." As Federal soldiers passed Southern homes, women hung out white tablecloths, as if in surrender, trying to protect what they had loved, sometimes to no avail. According to one soldier, wealthy residents fled and then fled again as the Yankees advanced, but though their homes were burned, their pianos taken, their libraries pilfered, and their linens shredded, the property of poorer folk was respected. From the roads you could see Sherman's monuments: chimneys without houses. But the army also fed about 15,000 refugees, mostly dispossessed former slaves. The Union army was an army of both devastation and emancipation.

On February 17, 1865, the Union soldiers were in Columbia, South Carolina, where, intoxicated as much by victory as by alcohol, they ran loose all over town, stealing what they could carry and sending men and women and children, some half naked, from their beds into the streets as their houses went up in smoke. Many could find shelter only in the lunatic asylum or the churches. Appalled, Sherman gave orders to put out the fires while the men apparently kept setting them. By morning, the streets, the gardens, and the large ash trees were smoldering. "War, after all, has horrors even greater than the battle-field," cried one witness. Called "Sherman's Brick Yard," the city lay in ruins, though it remains unclear whether it was because Sherman's men had drunk too much confiscated whiskey or because the Confederates, on the orders of General Wade Hampton, had actually burned their own cotton before riding out of town. John Bell Hood had no doubt; the fire was Sherman, all Sherman. "This unprecedented measure transcends in studied and ingenious cruelty, all acts ever brought to my attention in the dark history of war," Hood exclaimed. "In the name of God and humanity, I protest."

Sherman answered quickly; war was cruelty, as he had said; peace was the higher law justifying what he'd had to do. The Confederacy had declared war, not peace, and should therefore expect cruelty. He had no hand in making the war, he continued, which was founded in error and perpetuated in pride, but he would sacrifice as much, if not more, than anyone, to secure peace. Peace was what he was after.

THE "GRAY GHOST" who struck in the early-morning fog and then vanished into the haze was John Singleton Mosby, who, with his Partisan Rangers, cast a spell over the Virginia countryside. Herman Melville visited the Federal troops in Virginia in what he called Mosby territory, where it was unsafe to travel without a Union escort, and

he saw Union soldiers capture several of Mosby's "wandering brood."
Mosby "seems a satyr's child——," he later wrote in "The Scout toward
Aldie," which Edmund Wilson said romanticized Mosby a little too
much. Many a writer did romanticize him, though Walt Whitman
sharply observed that Mosby's men "would run a knife through the
wounded, the aged, the children, without compunction."

Before Virginia seceded, Mosby had been opposed to slavery, and
though he was not in favor of secession, he cleaved to his Virginia,
much as Robert E. Lee had. But his predilection for violence was
long-standing. While a student at the University of Virginia, he'd
shot a man during a quarrel. He was expelled, but the governor eventually pardoned him, for Mosby, who weighed under 130 pounds,
was said to be so frail he simply had to carry a gun in self-defense.

Trained as a lawyer, well read, interested in antiquity, quiet, gray-
eyed, wiry, and smart, Mosby had enlisted in the Confederate army
in 1861 and soon joined the staff of Jeb Stuart's command as a skilled
scout with a fondness for irregular action. It was his reconnaissance
that allowed Stuart to ride successfully around McClellan's army
during the peninsular campaign. But he resigned his formal commission and in Virginia formed his own band of brothers, wore a feather
in his cap, carried two pistols at his side, and so riled General Grant
in August 1864 that Grant gave orders to hang, if captured, any of
Mosby's guerrillas without trial.

Mosby's tactics were to a certain extent sanctioned by Richmond,
though General Lee believed all irregulars should be eliminated. "I
regard the whole system," he told the Confederate secretary of war,
"as an unmixed evil." Yet there was no denying Mosby was good at
what he did: seizing horses, robbing trains, capturing guns and rations and other loot, and wounding or killing Union soldiers, especially stragglers. Mosby hanged so many Federal stragglers that it was
said that Union desertions actually decreased; no bluecoat wanted to
meet up with him, and northern Virginia became known as "Mosby's Confederacy," for, among other things, its citizens offered him
intelligence and shelter.

Earlier, Mosby's enemy had been Union major general David Hunter, who had been sent to the Shenandoah Valley to replace Franz Sigel. Hunter was also the man who had issued his own early version of an Emancipation Proclamation in the Sea Islands, annoying Lincoln. Removed from the Carolina coast and needing to burnish his reputation, Hunter became notorious in the Shenandoah Valley for an unwonted ruthlessness that pushed those formerly sympathetic to the Union into the arms of the Confederacy.

In June 1864, for instance, Hunter's troops had broken into the home of Stonewall Jackson's Pennsylvania-born sister-in-law, ransacked the cellar, slaughtered the sheep, and stole the horses. At Virginia Institute, they stripped the laboratories of equipment, looted the classrooms, and then set fire to every building except the superintendent's quarters. They plundered the library at Washington College, they razed the home of Virginia governor John Letcher. And all that took place before Grant said that if Hunter couldn't cut the rail lines, he should devastate the valley—turn it into a wasteland so that, as Grant graphically put it, "crows flying over it for the balance of this season will have to carry their provender with them." As if reconsidering what he had said, he backed off a little and added, "I do not mean that houses should be burned, but all provisions and stock should be removed, and the people notified to move out."

Nestled between the Allegheny and the Blue Ridge Mountains, the opalescent Shenandoah Valley was of significant strategic importance to the Confederacy: it led right to Washington and, with its yellow grain, fertile soil, and plentiful livestock, it operated as a rich breadbasket for Lee's army. Grant knew that; capturing the valley and destroying its provisions would help defeat the Army of North Virginia as much if not more than the taking of Richmond. At the same time he would try to prevent Lee's army from getting its supplies from points south of Richmond by seizing Petersburg, a rail center, located on the Appomattox River about twenty miles below the Confederacy's capital.

War was no longer confined to the battlefields of Bull Run,

Antietam, or Gettysburg; it had spilled into hearts and homes, with
Union soldiers avenging themselves and guerrillas avenging the avengers: soldiers such as Mosby had become the raiders and pirates of war.
The men of the 2nd U.S. Cavalry—or perhaps Custer's men—captured
several of Mosby's rangers and hanged them when they refused to di-
vulge Mosby's hideaway. "I was sorry enough the other day that my
Brigade should have had a part in the hanging and shooting of some of
Mosby's men who were taken," observed the Harvard-educated Union
soldier Charles Russell Lowell. "—I believe that some punishment was
deserved—but I hardly think we were within the laws of war, and any
violation of them opens the door for all sorts of barbarity." Yet what
were the rules of modern warfare? Were there rules at all? Sherman
had thought so but then saw what war did to people, so he reframed his
question—and his answer—in order to simplify its moral complexity.
War is cruelty. Better avoid war; once war came, there was no turning
back: raze the city and sow it with salt.

Hunter's philosophical outlook on war, whatever it may have
been, was not so boldly stated as Sherman's. The behavior of his
men seems entirely without purpose. Moreover, Hunter had been
a disappointment to Lincoln and Grant. For weeks he avoided the
single-minded Confederate general Jubal Early, come to stanch—
and avenge—Hunter's destruction of the countryside. Uneasy, Grant
replaced Hunter with the thirty-three-year-old Philip Sheridan, the
head of the Cavalry Corps of the Potomac, and sent him to command
the newly formed Army of the Shenandoah. In the Shenandoah,
Sheridan was to place himself south of the enemy and then follow
that enemy "to the death." As Sheridan explained to another officer, his instructions were to make the valley "untenable." No more
grain and food for Lee's army; no more planting; no more irregular
recruits, many of whom (including Mosby's men) came from there.
Quakers, however, were to be left alone, as well as loyal citizens such
as Mennonites and "Dunkers" (Baptist Brethren). And if the loyal
citizens objected to the necessary destruction, they could take their
complaints to Washington.

Grant needed to distinguish between combatants and noncombatants, Union sympathizers and Confederates. It would not be easy, and soldiers such as Grant, as even-tempered as he had often seemed, were pushed to the limit. Major General Sheridan was just the man for the job. Short—only five feet, four inches, if that, and weighing 115 pounds—he was bandy-legged, his face narrow, his mustache long and bushy. But "Little Phil," as he was known, was a crack horseman and a hard fighter, and was taken aback slightly when Lincoln repeated to him the old joke about no one ever seeing a dead cavalryman (implying that cavalrymen didn't fight).

The former West Pointer never slept and never got angry, at least according to a young officer who fought with him, and he liked to ride at the front of his troops both to encourage his men and to keep a lookout up ahead. "With forehead of no promise and hair so short that it looks like a coat of black paint," remarked George Templeton Strong, "of all our chieftains he alone has displayed the capacity of handling men in actual shock of battle, turning defeat into victory." Strong noted this in the fall of 1864, after the rout at Cedar Creek, where Jubal Early had launched a surprise attack so devastating that the Union troops had retreated quickly to Winchester. Sheridan, who had been in Washington conferring with higher-ups, arrived in Winchester, put his ear to the ground, and, hearing the rumble of what was clearly a fight, rode his soon-to-be-famous black horse, Rienzi, twelve miles to Cedar Creek, yelling at the defeated soldiers who lined the road to "Face the other way, boys. We are going back to our camps. We are going to lick them out of their boots." The soldiers followed him back to the "slaughter," said one of them, "as hounds follow their master." The battle was then won by the very men who had lost it, recalled John De Forest, a soldier from Connecticut who would live to write a novel of the war. Sheridan's ride was celebrated far and wide in Thomas Buchanan Read's poem: "The first that the general saw were the groups / Of stragglers, and then the retreating troops. / What was done? what to do? a glance told him both; / Then, striking his spurs, with a terrible oath, / He dashed down the line, 'mid a storm of huzzas, / And the wave of retreat checked its course there, because / The fight of the master compelled it to pause."

Sheridan earned a reputation for destruction in the valley that outstripped even that of Hunter and his brigands. Barns filled with hay and straw, gristmills and fences and corncribs, gardens and cornfields—all of them went up in columns of dark smoke. "Relentless, merciless," said an onlooker, "the terrible torch has done its work in the centre and on either side of the valley." The gleaming light of distant fire could be seen for miles and miles. "The time had fully come to peel this land and put an end of the long strife for its possession," a chaplain from the 1st Rhode Island Cavalry later wrote. "Sheridan was to do for the valley what Grant was doing for Richmond—clean it out. The flames here shortened the work of war, and so were a mercy. Loss of property is nothing as measured with blood. The order led to the destruction of about two thousand barns, seventy mills, and other property, valued in all at twenty-five millions of dollars." Women and children looked for places to hide. Refugees piled into trains—if they could find them.

Sheridan: by his own unapologetic account, he took war right up to the door of the civilian. Up to the door, but not inside in that he didn't wish to make wholesale arrests, and he did not. Years later, he reportedly told Otto von Bismarck that "the people must be left with nothing but their eyes to see and lament the war."

Sheridan estimated that he had burned 2,000 barns and 70 mills in only one month in the Shenandoah. "Death is popularly considered the maximum of punishment in war, but it is not," he observed. "Reduction to poverty brings prayers for peace more surely and more quickly than does the destruction of human life, as the selfishness of man has demonstrated in more than one great conflict."

MARCH 4, 1865, Inauguration Day: Much had happened. Charleston, South Carolina, the city where the war had begun, had been evacuated, and the day after Columbia burned, the Union army had taken back Fort Sumter. Twenty-five cannon, captured from Charleston, were fired in salute, and Federal soldiers drank to the health of the president in the tumblers of wine they had confiscated.

Sheridan had more or less finished laying waste to the Shenandoah Valley, having defeated Early's men at Waynesborough, and he would meet up with Grant near Petersburg, the city Grant still had under siege. The war could not last much longer, or so many Northerners began to believe, especially since Lee's army was dwindling and stretched too thinly. In Washington, the Radical Republicans were in a good mood. And Lincoln had been courting Democrats, hoping they would support the new constitutional amendment outlawing slavery throughout the United States.

"There is a hope felt here of disposing of the Negro question in a constitutional way this session," Elizabeth Blair Lee reported. "A large number of Democrats are willing to vote for it now—Our people are working hard for it."

Two months before the inauguration, in early January, James Ashley was again managing the amendment to abolish slavery turned down by the House the previous spring but that had passed the Senate. Abolition had been on the minds of many—for years. In early 1864, the leaders of the Women's National Loyal League, Elizabeth Cady Stanton and Susan B. Anthony, had collected the signatures of 100,000 women on a petition for an amendment to free the slaves. And now Representative Green Clay Smith of Kentucky, an unconditional Unionist, was declaring that "we should destroy slavery, root and branch, as soon as possible. We must have the Union without slavery." Smith believed the amendment would ensure a permanent peace because abolition would remove the war's most "distracting cause." Frederick E. Woodbridge, a Republican from Vermont, called slavery a relic of barbarism. Promised patronage for his brother by Ashley, Anson Herrick, a Democrat from New York, changed his vote from the "nay" of the previous spring and explained, "I think such action on my behalf is best calculated to assist in the maintenance of the Government, the preservation of the Union, and the perpetu-ation of the free institutions which we inherited from our fathers."

Yet there were those, such as George Pendleton of Ohio, McClel-lan's running mate, who challenged the constitutionality of the pro-posed amendment, arguing that such an amendment violated states' rights. Aghast at the specter of states' rights again raising its ugly head, particularly after the bloodshed of recent years, Ashley pushed back. He condemned the "defending [of] the State sovereignty dogmas, and claiming that the national constitution cannot be so amended as to prohibit slavery." If the Constitution could not be amended, he inveighed, then it was nothing more than "a dead letter, the States sovereign, the Government a confederation, and the United States not a nation."

Samuel S. Cox, a Democrat from Ohio, feared that abolishing slav-ery might prolong the war. On the fence, he withheld his affirmative vote when he heard rumors that three Confederate peace commis-sioners, Alexander Stephens, R. M. T. Hunter, and John Archibald Campbell, were en route to Washington. The president denied that any envoys had come to the city, which was technically true; they were coming to talk about peace, but they were headed to Fortress Monroe in Hampton, Virginia, not Washington. Cox held firm.

Yet technicalities and arm-twisting carried the day. The Blair family vigorously worked to wrest votes for the amendment from Democrats. So did William Seward, who presumably promised to hand out offices or other bonuses as a reward for voting with the administration. Allegations of corruption swirled around Seward, ac-cused sub rosa of bribing congressmen for their votes. Lincoln too had actively worked to convert moderate Democrats and lukewarm Republicans to his side, making the legislative process his business. In his annual message the previous December, he had informed Con-gress that the time for an amendment banning slavery had come at last; recent elections had suggested as much, and the amendment would be passed sooner or later. And, he added, almost as a warning, that while he was president of the United States, he would not retract or modify the Emancipation Proclamation or return any person to slavery who had been made free by it. What he implied was that the country had an obligation—for the sake of the war effort, for the sake of the nation, for the sake of justice—to protect the freedom of all men and women.

Whatever had happened behind closed doors in Washington, whatever patronage plums were offered or accepted, in January fifteen Democrats who had earlier opposed the amendment now voted to pass it, and when James English of Connecticut voted "aye," the chamber's members broke into applause. Speaker Schuyler Colfax finished calling the roll, then announced that there were 119 yeas—all Republicans were in favor—and 56 nays, and that the joint resolution amending the Constitution had passed.

Stunned silence filled the room before it erupted into hurrahs and hugs, congressmen throwing their arms around each other. Grown men wept. On the balcony, women waved their handkerchiefs, and though one congressman proposed adjourning in honor of the tremendous event, the Copperheads insisted on a recalling of names. The names were recalled amid the pandemonium. The cannon of Washington fired in triumph and relief. Said Carl Schurz, "It is worth while to live in these days."

On February 1, Lincoln signed the amendment, although, by law, the president's signature was unnecessary. He wanted to sign. As the jubilant Elizabeth Lee put it, the amendment "has laid nearest to his & somebody elses heart." The somebody else was herself.

The amendment was on its way to the states for the requisite three-fourths ratification, which it could achieve since most of the slave states were not in the Union. Ten months later, the Thirteenth Amendment to the U.S. Constitution became law: "Neither slavery nor involuntary servitude, except as a punishment for crime whereof the party shall have been duly convicted, shall exist within the United States, or any place subject to their jurisdiction."

Then, on March 3, the day before the inauguration, Congress also passed the Freedmen's Bureau Act of 1865, which established for one year a government agency, the Bureau of Refugees, Freedmen, and Abandoned Lands, to assist in the placement of freedmen and refugees and to oversee abandoned or confiscated land. Perhaps the war was really ending; one could almost taste the future.

By the next day, the city was ready for a celebration. The hotels were jammed, and travelers who couldn't find a room slept in one of the capital's firehouses. But there were also rumors that the president would be kidnapped, maybe killed. Violence would not really surprise anyone. Stanton ordered sharpshooters to be stationed on top of the buildings near the Capitol, where the second inauguration of Lincoln would take place.

On March 4, the weather was uncooperative. That morning, a torrential downpour rendered impassable streets more treacherous than ever, with thick wads of ankle-deep mud clinging to the wheels of the slow-moving omnibuses. There was a parade, of course, though the day was also cold and terribly windy, yet, even with that relentless rain, as many as 30,000 spectators showed up. At least "half the multitude" reported the London *Times*, "were colored people." Never before. The mile-long procession, which included floats and all kinds of marching bands, also flexed military muscle with two regiments of the Invalid Corps, a squadron of cavalry, a battery of artillery—and four companies of troops from the 45th Regiment U.S. Colored Troops. Never before had that happened.

The inauguration ceremony took place outdoors on the eastern portico of the Capitol, where a temporary platform had been built. Above and behind it loomed the Capitol's iron dome, completed at last, and on top of that was a nineteen-foot statue known as *Armed Liberty*: a militant Minerva, cast in bronze, holding a sword in one hand and an olive branch and shield in the other. Jefferson Davis might have been somewhat pleased. Years earlier, as Pierce's secretary of war, Davis had protested the sculptor Thomas Crawford's first design, in which Minerva wore atop her head the liberty cap that symbolized the emancipation of the Roman slave. Davis wanted her to wear a helmet, signifying war, which she now did. But Davis likely would also know that when the martial Minerva was finally installed in 1863, just after the Emancipation Proclamation had been announced, it faced the South.

The swearing-in ceremony of Vice President Johnson had taken place inside the Senate chamber. Johnson, who had been ill, had evidently taken more than a medicinal draft of whiskey to help him get through the event, and he delivered a long-winded, incoherent speech while gesturing lavishly with the Bible and then planting a wet kiss on it. Edwin Stanton whispered to the embarrassed Gideon Welles, "Johnson is either drunk or crazy," and when he saw him later, in the crowd outdoors, Frederick Douglass also thought him inebriated. Lincoln had already told a marshal not to let Johnson speak to the crowd.

The rain had finally subsided when the presidential party appeared at about one o'clock on the platform, and just as the tired president stepped forward from the shelter of the Capitol building, the sun began to shine, as if on cue. A man in the crowd could see that Lincoln's beard was trimmed, his head uncovered and slightly bowed; but it was the man's silent strength and the eloquence of that silence that were dazzling—as well as the scriptural beauty of the speech he read in that high-pitched voice of his.

Lincoln's brief address, all 700 or so words of it, began with a backward look to his first inaugural, when the nation had stood, or so it seemed, on the brink of a war that was then waged, more and more brutally, throughout his entire administration. "While the inaugural address was being delivered from this place, devoted altogether to saving the Union without war," he reminisced, "insurgent agents were in the city, seeking to destroy it with war—seeking to dissolve the Union, and divide the effects by negotiation. Both parties deprecated war," he continued, "but one of them would make war rather than let the nation survive, and the other would accept war rather than let it perish; and the war came." Both parties, in other words, embraced war without comprehending, it seemed, its contradictory and irreversible pain.

"And the war came": the monosyllables were flat and—because understated—ominous. One side would make war, one side would accept war, and so the war came, as if no one could have prevented · it. ("I claim not to have controlled events," as he'd said the previous spring, "but confess plainly that events have controlled me.") And the war came: the spectators stood quiet; their eyes brimmed with tears. Lincoln continued, his rhythms perfect, his comparisons apt and heart-rending. "Both read the same Bible, and pray to the same God, and each invokes his aid against the other. It may seem strange that any men should dare to ask a just God's assistance in wringing their bread from the sweat of other men's faces; but let us judge not, that we be not judged. The prayers of both could not be answered. That of neither has been answered fully. The Almighty has his own purposes." Such purposes—the purpose of all that slaughter, all that suffering—are beyond the reach or knowledge of humankind, and seen, if seen at all, through a glass darkly. Or so Lincoln seemed to be saying. The self-righteousness, the commitment to higher laws, the pride, the scruples, and the suspicions: all those had brought on the war, and he would not deign to pass final judgment on either the South or the North for the slaughter.

Yet he knew what lay underneath, what had caused the war: slavery. Slavery, slavery as scourge, slavery as an *American* institution, not just a Southern one; and so Lincoln invoked both the New and Old Testaments, for he too could harden his charitable heart, much as Sherman had fixed his own moral compass. Grant, Sherman, Sheridan: they were hired hands, employed by the government of the United States and its president, the man who now cried, "Woe unto the world because of offences! for it must needs be that offences come; but woe to that man by whom the offence cometh! If we shall suppose that American slavery is one of these offences, which in the providence of God must needs come, but which, having continued through his appointed time, he now wills to remove, and that he gives to both North and South this terrible war as the woe due to those by whom the offence came, shall we discern there is any departure from those divine attributes which the believers in a living God always ascribe to him?"

Not at all. God is vengeful and merciful, both at the same time. And this terrible war must be fought; it was being fought. "Fondly do we hope, fervently do we pray, that this mighty scourge of war may speedily pass away," Lincoln resumed. "Yet if God wills that it continue until all the wealth piled by the bondman's two hundred and fifty years of unrequited toil shall be sunk, and until every drop of blood drawn with the lash shall be paid by another drawn by the sword, as was said three thousand years ago, so still it must be said, the judgments of the Lord are true and righteous altogether."

We will fight until the finish, he was saying. Yet as he looked beyond the present war, he asked, If the Union wins, what then? To finish the work that we began, Lincoln said. He spoke less, now, of vengeance than of mercy: such would be the peace. But how could mercy supersede vengeance, supplanting it, and could the moral guilt of slavery be washed away while the nation's wounds were being bound up? To do that, to start to do that, he offered a generous home-coming to those who had fought and all of those who had, as he said, borne the battle. And so the most famous and frequently quoted part of his speech was its conclusion: "With malice towards none, with charity for all, with firmness in the right as God gives us to see the right, let us strive on to finish the work we are in; to bind up the na-tion's wound; to care for him who shall have borne the battle, and for his widow and orphans; to do all which may achieve and cherish a just and lasting peace among ourselves and with all nations."

The new chief justice, Salmon Chase, administered the oath of office to the eloquent but weary president, who then began his second term.

REACTION TO THE speech was predictably partisan. The *New York World* dismissed it as a prose parody of John Brown's hymn. And *The Liberator* gently chided the president for not adding "a few words of friendly encouragement and assurance in a direct address to the freedmen, or even the incidental mention, in the Inaugural Address, of a duty due to them from the nation, and of the President's desire that this duty be discharged." Lydia Maria Child admired the speech, mainly; though it represented Lincoln's moral growth and basic kind-heartedness, she also warned "that the newly-emancipated will need vigilant watchmen on the towers for one generation more, at least." As she put it, the "pro-slavery devil, after he has come out, with such terrible rending and tearing, will assume all manner of Protean shapes for mischief."

Lincoln thought he had done pretty well. The speech would "wear as well as—perhaps better than—any thing I have produced," he said. Still, he could guess why it wasn't "immediately popular": "Men are not flattered by being shown that there has been a differ-ence of purpose between the Almighty and them. To deny it, how-ever, in this case, is to deny that there is a God governing the world. It is a truth which I thought needed to be told."

Temporarily barred from the White House reception—because he was black and had been, momentarily, unrecognized—Frederick Douglass did manage to attend and to talk to Lincoln, who asked for his opinion of the speech. Douglass told the gratified president that it had been a "sacred effort."

Lincoln did not know, though, of the tired Confederate war clerk in Richmond who in the privacy of his diary summarized the speech with resigned perspicacity. "It is filled with texts from the Bible. He says both sides pray to the same God for aid—one upholding and the other destroying African slavery," he observed. "In short, he 'quotes Scripture for the deed' quite as fluently as our President; and since both presidents resort to religious justification, it may be feared the war is about to assume a more sanguinary aspect and a more cruel nature than ever before. God help us! The history of man, even in the Bible, is but a series of bloody wars."

(15)

AND THIS IS RICHMOND

If the war would soon be over, the sorrows of it might disarm, in every sense of the word, all animosity, or so Herman Melville hoped. So too Abraham Lincoln fervently prayed.

The Confederate States of America was exhausted; its people and its army were starving, its currency was nearly worthless. In Baton Rouge, flour was not to be had at any price; neither were soap, candles, matches, coffee. Coal sold for $90 a load (circa the equivalent of $1,267 in 2013). In Richmond, wood cost $50 per cord (circa the equivalent of $704) before the price doubled; two chickens cost $30 ($422 in 2013). President Davis and his wife ate mainly rice and cornmeal. Many men, knowing their families were in dire straits, deserted from the army to return to their homes and farms. Those who stayed in the army were hungry. "Our rations have been shorter than ever; no meat at all, a small quantity of sour meal and one roll per day," wrote a soldier in Georgia in January 1865. "It appears as if we are to be starved to death." And in Richmond, a staff officer remarked, "The wolf is at the door here. We dread starvation far more than we do Grant or Sherman. Famine—that is the word now."

A woman in Winnsboro, South Carolina, reflected, "The Confederacy seemed suddenly to have changed, a glory had passed from it, and, without acknowledging it, we felt the end was near."

In January the Federals had pounded Fort Fisher in North Carolina with the full force of the fleet and with 8,000 troops. Wilmington, North Carolina, the last major Confederate seaport, fell into Union hands. Later that month, Confederate secretary of war James A. Seddon resigned. The Confederate Congress promoted Robert E. Lee to general in chief, which was a vote of no confidence in Jefferson Davis. "He has not the broad intellect requisite for the gigantic measures needed in such a crisis, nor the health and physique for the labors devolving on him," a war clerk close to the administration grumbled. "Disaffection is intense and widespread," said General Josiah Gorgas, a Confederate ordnance officer. "Lee is about all we have."

Though Judah Benjamin denounced as traitors and cowards anyone who wanted to end the war, there were rumors, half welcome, about peace negotiations. The venerable newspaperman and family patriarch Francis Preston Blair, Sr., undertook his own harebrained plan: unite the South with the North by waging war against Mexico. He secured a pass from Lincoln to travel to Richmond and talk to his old friend Jefferson Davis; Lincoln knew that the plan was misguided—and violated the Monroe Doctrine—but he permitted Blair to go ahead and arrange a meeting of Federal and Confederate peace commissioners. Neither Lincoln nor Davis wished to appear unwilling to discuss terms.

On January 29, 1865, the commissioners descended on Petersburg, Virginia. A white flag flapped in the winter breeze. Diminutive and pale, the vice president of the Confederacy, Alexander H. Stephens, had arrived, flanked by the Confederacy's former secretary of state, R. M. T. Hunter, and Assistant Secretary of War James A. Campbell. Although Secretary of the Navy Gideon Welles thought it a bad idea for Lincoln to attend, Lincoln wanted to go, and he did, along with Secretary of State Seward. For four hours on February 3, 1865, they met with the Southerners on General Grant's flagship, the *River Queen*, at anchor near Fortress Monroe, in what became known as the Hampton Roads Conference.

The meeting predictably concluded without any treaty, and since no reporters or stenographers were allowed aboard, what we know about the conference are oft-told anecdotes (the men had also agreed that no one should take notes). Lincoln had presumably declared that he wouldn't parley with "rebels"—that is, he refused to recognize the Confederacy as an independent entity. Robert Hunter replied that during the English Civil War even Charles I had negotiated with the rebels. "I do not profess to be posted in history," Lincoln dryly retorted. "All I distinctly recollect about the case of Charles I, is, that he lost his head."

As unwavering as Lincoln, Jefferson Davis used the conference's failure as propaganda. The intransigent North, he told his Congress, refused "to give to our people any other terms or guarantees than those which the conqueror may grant, or to permit us to have on any other basis than our unconditional submission to their rule." Then a large band played as some 10,000 men and women trudged on a snowy day to the African Church near Capitol Square, the only building large enough to accommodate the huge white population jostling inside to hear Davis, though feeble, roundly spurn Lincoln as His Majesty Abraham the First and passionately declare that he, Davis, would live and die with the Confederacy, which would survive, victorious and grand.

Old-time revivalism and a cheering band could not get Richmond very far. People were hungry and frightened, and they teetered on the edge of hopelessness. Yet it was not a revival meeting; Secretary of State Judah Benjamin was also going to speak—with a particular purpose in mind, one that had been on Davis's mind too, but that Benjamin would voice aloud. "War is a game that cannot be played without men!" the pudgy secretary shouted. By men, Benjamin meant soldiers, and since soldiers were scarce, the time had come to enlist able-bodied slaves. "Is it not a shame that men who have sacrificed all in our defense should not be reinforced by all the means in our power?" he asked. "Is it any time now for antiquated patriotism to argue a refusal to send them aid, be it white or black?"

The audience caught his drift, and someone yelled out, "Put in the niggers."

The secretary ventured a step further. The Negro, he said, would not fight without being emancipated. "If we impress them," he warned, "they will go against us."

Benjamin had gone too far. "There is much excitement among the slaveowners, caused by Mr. B's speech," recorded a spectator. "They must either fight themselves or let the slaves fight." Benjamin was willing to give up slavery in order to win; it was a pragmatic position at odds with those who believed in unqualified, unalloyed sacrifice to the cause, all the way to the bitter end.

Already disliked by several cabinet members and censured by the Senate, Benjamin offered to resign from the cabinet, so unpopular was his position, but Davis kept him on, hoping against hope that at this eleventh hour he could pull a different rabbit out of the hat: Europe. "Intervention on the part of European powers is the only hope of many," groaned a despondent war clerk. "Failing that, no doubt a negro army will be organized—and it might be too late!"

Davis had already sent Duncan F. Kenner to France and Britain on a diplomatic mission geared to snagging their aid at last. A wealthy sugar planter who in 1860 owned 473 slaves, the suave Kenner had been a member of the Confederate Congress and chair of its Ways and Means Committee. A protégé of Louisiana's John Slidell (the Confederate envoy arrested on the *Trent*), a breeder of racehorses, and a close personal friend of Benjamin, who had shared a house with him when the two Louisianans had first come to Richmond, Kenner had for a long time favored a policy of gradual emancipation. And now Kenner agreed with Benjamin that the Confederacy's independence as a sovereign nation was far more important than the preservation of slavery. They had brought the idea to President Davis. Kenner argued that his family owned more slaves than all the members of the Confederate Congress put together and he was therefore not asking anyone to give up more than he was.

Davis authorized Kenner to go incognito to Europe and to offer

France and England, in return for recognition and aid, the promise to end slavery. Mary Chesnut scoffed. "Abolish slavery to propitiate England. What does she care?"

Wearing a fake beard and a chocolate-colored wig to cover his light hair and perceptible baldness, under the name of A. B. Kinglake, Kenner made his way to New York, where he boarded a German ship. Bearing false papers and coded messages and speaking only French, he presented Emperor Napoleon III his offer, but the monarch wasn't interested in the issue of slavery; nor would France act alone—and Britain's prime minister, Lord Palmerston, had already turned Kenner down. Britain did not want a war with the United States. The United States was obviously winning its own war—news of Sherman taking Atlanta had reached London—and in any case it had just passed the Thirteenth Amendment.

Slavery's death knell was ringing.

DOUBTLESS THE PASSAGE of the Thirteenth Amendment had increased the pressure on the wan and fretful Jefferson Davis. "Send us protection in the shape of our sons & husbands and we will send you able bodied negroes," Southern women begged him. With desertions rising and morale falling, with men so malnourished that a slight wound would kill them, with wives and sisters left to tend what was left of shuttered homes and neglected fields, by the middle of March even the Richmond papers were running advertisements for the recruiting of black troops.

Perhaps more than anyone, Robert E. Lee understood the need. He was on the field, and, as in the North, on the field, numbers mattered. The Federal army could and did recruit former slaves—whom it freed—and in so doing increased its size, while Lee's army was growing smaller, thinner, frailer. "I think, therefore, we must decide whether slavery shall be extinguished by our enemies and the slaves be used against us," Lee reasoned, "or use them ourselves at the risk of the effects which may be produced upon our social institutions.

My own opinion is that we should employ them without delay." The enlistment of black soldiers, Lee concluded, would revitalize the military and would give the South, at last, a political advantage over the North "that would result to our cause from the adoption of a system of emancipation." Freedom should thus be granted those black men—and their immediate families—who fought for the Confederacy.

Charleston Mercury editor Robert Barnwell Rhett might lampoon General Lee as a closet abolitionist, but the issue of impressing black troops really did cut to the heart of the Confederate cause. Representative Thomas S. Gholson of Virginia, a member of the Second Confederate Congress (it was seated in the spring of 1864), bluntly declared, "By the conscription of slaves, we shall surrender every ground, assumed by us on the subject, at the commencement of the war." Warren Akin, also a member of the Second Confederate Congress, wondered whether calling "forth the negroes into the army, with the promise of freedom, will . . . not be giving up the great question involved by doing the very thing Lincoln is now doing." It was a serious problem.

Howell Cobb was in a rage. "The proposition to make soldiers of our slaves is the most pernicious idea that has been suggested since the war began," he said. Promoted to major general in the Confederate army, he was organizing volunteers—white volunteers, not black—in Georgia. "It is to me a source of deep mortification and regret to see the name of that good and great man and soldier, General R. E. Lee, given as authority for such a policy." Presciently, he added, "The day you make soldiers of them is the beginning of the end of the revolution. If slaves will make good soldiers our whole theory of slavery is wrong."

"It is the desperate remedy for the very desperate case," sighed a clerk in the Confederate War Department. Increasingly frantic—after all, the institution of slavery had been written into their constitution—the Confederacy had to confront the unthinkable at last. For the issue of enlisting slaves as soldiers had come up before. It had been proposed by Kenner himself and also by Thomas Hindman's law partner and friend, Major General Patrick Cleburne, the well-respected Irish-born soldier regarded—in the North as well as the South—as one of the finest division commanders in the Army of the Tennessee. In late 1863, Cleburne had written a memorandum, signed by several brigade and regimental commanders, recommending that slaves be enlisted in the armed forces and that, further, any slave who fought for the Confederacy until the end of the war should be freed and that his family be freed. Such a step would bring to the Confederate army the increased manpower it badly needed, he reasoned. In fact, it might even shorten the duration of the war once the Confederacy clearly and without ambivalence fought for nationhood and not to perpetuate slavery. "Slavery, from being one of our chief sources of strength at the commencement of the war," he had cogently argued, "has now become, in a military point of view, one of our chief sources of weakness."

Cleburne also thought that enlisting black men as soldiers with the promise of their future freedom would strengthen the position of those Copperheads in the North weary of the war and ready for peace. But he encountered virulent opposition from division commanders, who called his idea, as one of them stormed, "revolting to Southern sentiment, Southern pride, and Southern honor." Cleburne's memorandum was forwarded to Jefferson Davis, who ignored it, and Cleburne, despite his demonstrated skill as a leader, was quietly denied promotion.

Years later, Cleburne's commanding officer, John Bell Hood, praised him as being "in advance of many of our people. He possessed the boldness and the wisdom to earnestly advocate, at an early period of the war, the freedom of the negro and the enrollment of the young and able-bodied men of that race. This stroke of policy and additional source of strength to our Armies, would, in my opinion, have given us our independence."

Cleburne was killed in the fall of 1864 while fighting under Hood in the futile and horrific Battle of Franklin, Tennessee, during which there were almost 7,000 Confederate casualties—and five generals lost. (He'd opposed the attack as suicidal.) "And how could man die better / Than facing fearful odds," Mary Chesnut wrote, quoting Thomas Macaulay's "Horatius at the Bridge," on learning of Cleburne's death. "The deep waters are closing over us," she shuddered.

FORMER FIRE-EATERS, SLAVEHOLDERS, and many of those committed to the peculiar institution remained indignant. Yet as the proslavery Warren Akin acidly noted, those who opposed arming the slaves were mainly the planters. "Have you ever noticed the strange conduct of our people during this war? They give up their sons, husbands, brothers & friends, and often without murmuring, to the army; but let one of their negroes be taken, and what a howl you will hear. The love of money has been the greatest difficulty in our way to independence."

Yet the die was cast. So Jefferson Davis, along with Lee, urged the governor of Virginia to raise black troops by promising "to seek legislation to secure unmistakable freedom to the slave, who shall enter the army, with a right to return to his old home when he shall have been honorably discharged from military service." Fort Fisher had fallen, Sherman was relentless, Grant was single-minded, Lee's forces were shrinking, peace efforts had failed, Europe had turned its back. On March 13, 1865, the Confederate Congress passed a Negro enlisting bill, authorizing what had been unthinkable even just a few months earlier, the recruitment of able-bodied black men into the military—with the permission of their owners, of course—for the duration of the war.

Though the law pointedly did not mention freedom or gradual emancipation for the black man or his immediate family, congressmen such as Gholson of Virginia continued to oppose the measure. "What is this but abolition?" he fumed. He was not wrong. Making a slave a soldier would create, as it had in the North, a revolution. "You may make a soldier out of a slave, very readily," Thomas Higginson had recently said, "but you can no more make a slave out of a soldier than you can replace a bird in the egg."

Jefferson Davis promised putative freedom to those who enlisted—as if to say, grudgingly, that slaves were not property but human beings who needed to be treated as such or at least to be treated as such until the war ended. On March 23, Davis signed the army's General Order No. 14, maintaining, "No slave will be accepted as a recruit unless with his own consent and with the approbation of his master by a written instrument conferring, as far as he may, the rights of a freedman." Davis called on the states for 300,000 more soldiers. Few came, and none of the black soldiers fought; the war would end too soon for that. Regardless, the linchpin of the Confederate cause—as it had been articulated in 1861—could no longer be slavery. As the *Charleston Mercury* observed, "Assert the right in the Confederate Government to emancipate slaves, and it is stone dead."

That meant Howell Cobb had been right—if slaves make good soldiers, the whole theory of slavery is wrong. Cobb's point must be that only men can be good soldiers, and if a slave can be a soldier, he must be a man, a person. The Confederacy was proving just that— that slaves were persons—by turning to them and asking for their assistance, although the request came mostly in the form of a demand.

By admitting that the slave could fight and die for a cause and that if he did so he deserved to be free, the Confederacy could no longer logically argue that it fought to defend slavery. Neither could it fall back on the ideology of states' rights. If the individual Confederate states didn't fill enlistment quotas, President Davis was authorized to "call on each State, whenever he thinks it expedient, for her quota of 300,000 troops, in addition to those subject to military service under existing laws." By doing that, though, the president was overreaching his authority, wasn't he? The struggle between local and centralized power had long unsettled the Confederacy, and it opened Davis to criticism, condemnation, hostility, and intrigue.

So now the Confederate States of America was running headlong into the question of how it might endure or prevail. No one knew. As

Sherman marched inexorably eastward to meet the obdurate Grant, the South's "peculiar institution" was doomed from within and perhaps so too the very notion of the Confederacy as a group of independent states.

THE TEXAS CAVALRY in Virginia, once 5,000 men strong, now numbered only 180. Varina Davis, the president's wife, sold the family furniture at auction and left the city with her children. Certain Richmond ladies offered their silver and their jewelry to raise money for the troops. Bridesmaids wore black. On Clay Street in Richmond the residents hung out red banners to indicate that their belongings were for sale or their houses could be rented by the highest bidder. Bacon sold for $20 a pound; ditto butter. New black troops marched through the city as if on display. And the chilly rumor about town was that Grant had a total of 200,000 men under the commands of Sherman, Thomas, Sheridan, and himself, and they were soon to converge on Richmond.

On the evening of March 24, the Confederates were preparing to break the Union line around Petersburg by attacking Fort Stedman. It was another of Lee's bold assaults. He hoped that he could withdraw some of his entrenched troops from Petersburg and send them to reinforce Joe Johnston in the North Carolina hills so that Johnston might attack Sherman before Sherman reached Grant. It was the desperate measure of desperate men. The night before the attack, to be led by General John B. Gordon, Gordon's wife stayed up late tearing strips of white cloth so the soldiers could identify each other during the confusing fog of battle, when blues and grays and butternut brown all merged together in the haze. The next day, Gordon's men hurled themselves at Fort Stedman. The Union line stayed intact. Lee lost 5,000 soldiers he could not spare as well as General A. P. Hill, who was killed. A few days later, on April 1, in the battles that culminated at the intersection called Five Forks, Sheridan and his 12,000 cavalrymen helped deliver a blow to Confederate forces under General George Pickett, who, because he and several other officers had been to a traditional Virginian shad bake, arrived late on the scene. One Southern cavalry officer called Five Forks the Waterloo of the Confederacy.

Grant, who had 120,000 troops outside Petersburg, had effectively sliced what was left of Lee's brave army in half. Lee ordered an evacuation of the city and on April 2 telegraphed Davis that Richmond also had to be evacuated.

On that mild Sunday morning, Davis was sitting in his pew at the fashionable St. Paul's Episcopal. Guns boomed in the distance as the pale man with the sunken face solemnly walked out of the church, saying nothing, after reading the telegram from Lee. By afternoon, word was all over town. Women dressed in black stood in doorways and wept. At about eleven that night, bound for Danville, Virginia, Davis and members of his government boarded special trains at the depot. Always effervescent and waving his cigar, Judah Benjamin tried to cheer his friends by talking about other great causes that had seemed lost—but that had, at the last minute, been rescued by the unforeseen. Some chance event or deus ex machina would save the Confederacy yet.

The exodus from Richmond told a different story. People fled the city on horses, on mules, on foot. Those who stayed ran through the streets, clutching one another as the air turned blue-black, Mary Chesnut wrote. Tobacco warehouses, public buildings, flour mills had all burst into flame, set afire by retreating graycoats headed by the one-legged General Ewell. Federal soldiers not far from the Confederate capital heard a sound like thunder just seconds before the blaze lit the darkness and rockets shot deep into the night sky. Exploding magazines destroyed what was left of the armory building. A south wind fanned the flames. Newspaper offices and banks were burned to a crisp. Piles of brick and broken glass cluttered the streets. "Secession was burned out," said Thomas Morris Chester, the thirty-year-old black war correspondent who wrote for *The Philadelphia Press*, "and the city purified as far as fire could accomplish it."

Union troops riding into the city the next morning felt as though they were entering the crater of an active volcano. Their mission was to save the burning city from itself—from the mobs of stragglers and escaped convicts and now-freed slaves roaming the streets, looting what was left of stores and homes, swiping cotton goods and tobacco, shoes, furniture, military clothing, whatever could be carried. Reporters coming into the city noted that Capitol Square "was filled with furniture, beds, clothing, crockery, chairs, tables, looking-glasses. Women were weeping, children crying. Men stood speechless, haggard, woebegone." The journalist George Alfred Townsend, who ambled through the devastated Richmond at twilight, wrote, "There is no sound of life, but the stillness of the catacomb, only as our footsteps fall dull on the deserted sidewalk, and a funeral troop of echoes bump their elfin heads against the dead walls and closed shutters to reply, and this is Richmond. Says a melancholy voice: 'And this is Richmond.'"

One Federal brigade, along with a black drum corps, had played "Yankee Doodle" and "The Battle Cry of Freedom," and black men and women cried "Glory to God! Glory to God!" or "You've come at last" and "Have you come to stay?" Still, one Federal officer told a Richmond resident that Northerners did not like Negroes any more than he did.

While struggling to put out the fires and establish some sense of order, Richmond's mayor, Joseph Mayo, surrendered the keys to the city to Generals Charles Devens and Godfrey Weitzel. It was an ironic moment: as a soldier, Devens had fought bravely at Ball's Bluff, Fair Oaks, and Chancellorsville and during the battle of Cold Harbor commanded his troops from a stretcher, but in 1851, Devens, then a federal marshal in Boston, had returned Thomas Sims, a fugitive slave, to captivity, earning the scorn of the abolitionists.

A teacher at West Point before the war, Godfrey Weitzel was in charge of the 25th Corps (Colored) Infantry; Richmond citizens thought it impolitic to have so many black troops in their city.

Lincoln had to see it all for himself. He talked with Grant the next day, April 3, in the splintered city of Petersburg, and he visited the fallen capital of the Confederacy twice. Though Admiral David Porter was on the lookout for snipers, thousands of black men and women greeted him. Doffing his big hat, he bowed to the black population thronging about him. The owners of the Richmond slave pens had thrown open the doors and told the men and women they were free, but they couldn't believe it until they saw the president with their own eyes. "I know I am free," said one elderly woman, "for I have seen Father Abraham and felt him." Later, the new military governor of Richmond recalled how sad the president had looked, touched and sorrowful, at the outpouring of gratitude and relief—and commenting on how many black men and women "bore the traces of a mixed lineage," he saw as if for the first time that black and white were not easily separated and had never been.

WITH LITTLE TO eat but parched corn, Lee still hoped to join General Johnston, whose ranks had shrunk to 16,000. Lee was grim. In the scurry of departure, he'd taken no supply trains with him and hoped against hope to find food and ammunition for his men at Amelia Court House, thirty-five miles west of Richmond, when they arrived on April 4. There was virtually none of either.

Sheridan had ridden south of the Appomattox River to cut off Lee and his men from the railroad, and two days later, he hit Lee. On April 6, at Sayler's Creek, located midway between Petersburg and Appomattox Court House, the cavalryman George Armstrong Custer of the wide-rimmed hat captured more than 6,000 of Lee's small force, including General Ewell. "The Confederate rear was crushed to fragments," recalled General Longstreet. When Lee heard the news, Longstreet remembered, Lee cried out, "My God! Has the Army been dissolved?"

At Appomattox Court House, John B. Gordon and his tattered troops valiantly—and fruitlessly—tried to stop Sheridan.

The Confederate situation was hopeless, Grant reckoned. He wrote to Lee on April 7 to say that he wished "to shift from myself the responsibility of any further effusion of blood, by asking of you the surrender of that portion of the C. S. Army known as the Army of Northern Virginia." Longstreet was with Lee when the latter read the note. Lee passed it to him. "Not yet," replied Longstreet. Lee answered Grant, asking what terms he was offering. Grant said that there were none save giving up arms against the U.S. government. The two generals were circling each other. Lee would talk peace but not surrender; Grant had no authority to talk anything but surrender. Grant sent another note while General Meade battered the Confederate rear guard. Sheridan struck the railroad at Appomattox station and seized four supply trains. Lee's horses were by then so weak they couldn't haul guns.

Lee met with his officers the next day. John B. Gordon remembered staff officers hunkered down on the ground on blankets or on their saddles near a low-burning campfire. There were no camp stools, tents, or tables. Lee rose. One more time they would try to break through Grant's lines and try to reach Joe Johnston in North Carolina.

That was a pipe dream. Grant had repelled Gordon's column, which, according to Gordon, had fought to a frazzle. It was finally over. Gordon's and Longstreet's forces at Appomattox numbered fewer than 8,000, a skeleton crew of emaciated, worn-out men and boys. "There is nothing left me but to go and see General Grant," concluded General Lee, "and I had rather die a thousand deaths."

It had taken twelve days, from the beginning of Grant's campaign, on March 29, to April 9, to maneuver Lee into a position where he had no other available options.

Lee and Grant met on the ninth at Wilbur McLean's small brick house, located a little back from the street, near the village of Appomattox. Having exchanged brief notes, the men had come together at last, each of them playing himself to the hilt, the way thousands of newspaper readers and reporters had come to think of them and as the general public would think of them long after their meeting that day passed into legend. The silver-haired Robert E. Lee wore a crisp new full-dress uniform. His boots were shined and decorated with handsome spurs. He sat at an oval table near the front window, his jewel-handled sword, said to be a gift from the state of Virginia, at his side. On the table lay his long buckskin gloves and his gray felt hat, which matched the color of his uniform. Grant was swordless. His trousers were tucked inside mud-spattered top boots. His shoulder straps were the only designation of his rank. He sat at a marble-topped table in the center of the room. "A stranger, unacquainted with the situation," said John B. Gordon, "would have selected Lee for the conqueror and Grant for the vanquished hero." Their faces were expressionless. They exchanged a few pleasantries before getting down to business.

The terms of surrender were simple and generous: Lee and his men were to lay down their arms and return home; they were not under any form of arrest as long as they did not take up arms again to fight the United States or disobey its laws; the officers could keep their sidearms and their baggage. When Lee reportedly asked that his soldiers be able to keep their mules or horses for plowing and Grant agreed, Lee said, "This will have the best possible effect on my army. It will be very gratifying and do much towards conciliating our people." Lee suggested that his army be given rations, and again Grant complied, ordering enough for 25,000 men, a number that included soldiers too ill to fight.

Lee left the house at four o'clock. He paused on the front step before mounting his beloved horse, Traveler. Grant and his men saluted Lee, raising their hats, and Lee returned the gesture before riding off, erect and tall. Grant did not permit his troops to cheer or gloat. "The war is over," he said, "the rebels are our countrymen again, and the best sign of rejoicing after the victory will be to abstain from all demonstrations in the field."

A Confederate soldier devoted to Lee recalled, "When our idolized leader sheathed his sword at Appomattox the world grew dark to us. We felt as if the sun had set in blood to rise no more. . . . But that same stainless hero whom we had followed with unquestioning devotion taught us not to despair. He told us it was the part of brave men to accept defeat without repining. 'Human virtue,' he said, 'should be equal to human calamity.'"

The news of his surrender had reached the Confederate government in exile in Danville. No one said a word, and the cabinet officers, along with Jefferson Davis, prepared to board trains yet again in the damp night, this time for Greensboro, North Carolina. The Confederate secretary of the navy said the times were out of joint. In Richmond, at the huge African church where no one of African descent had previously dared speak from the pulpit, black men and women filled every seat; if they couldn't find a seat, they perched on the windows and stood in the doorway, and the hundreds who couldn't enter the packed hall at all gathered outside to listen to their black minister speak at last of full freedom.

On the twelfth, the Army of Northern Virginia marched to the Appomattox Court House, where they stacked their arms and folded their regimental flag. Years later, General Longstreet recalled, with sadness and with pride, that the young men then "walked empty-handed to their distant, blighted homes."

(16)

THE SIMPLE, FIERCE DEED

Identifying themselves as the nonexistent 4th Missouri Cavalry, William Quantrill and thirty-three men, disguised in blue uniforms, set out on New Year's Day 1865 and rode east. Quantrill's intention: to assassinate the president.

Ever since Lincoln's election, the grandiose guerrilla had been plotting to save the Confederacy. He would reconstitute his band of Missouri outlaws; they would saddle their horses, gallop into Washington, and shoot Lincoln dead. The Federal army would collapse, the Confederacy would rise, and Quantrill, to whom fame mattered more than country, would be hailed a hero forever.

Calling himself Captain William Clarke of the 4th Missouri, Quantrill moved slowly. Frequently sidetracked by the joy of highway murder, he and his men hung around Kentucky, where people hid in the brush when they heard Quantrill was coming. In Danville, Kentucky, he and his boys lined up the citizens, robbed the local stores, and gutted the telegraph office. At New Market, they captured and burned nine army wagons and killed three guards. Near Hartford, Kentucky, Quantrill rode into a Federal camp and tricked two Federal officers with whom he'd chatted confidentially, convincing them that he and his gang needed guides to the Ohio River. The Federal officers helpfully suggested one of their men, who knew the country well, and another enlisted man. A third Federal soldier volunteered to help out as well. A few miles from the Union encampment, Quantrill shot two of the bluebellies and hanged the third.

Quantrill and his gang still intended to make their way to Washington, but they were too late. On the evening of April 14, 1865, Good Friday, at ten o'clock, while Abraham Lincoln and his wife were sitting in the upstairs box at Ford's Theatre watching a performance of the comedy *Our American Cousin*, John Wilkes Booth slipped into the box, pointed his small single-shot derringer at the back of Lincoln's head, and pulled the trigger. The simple, fierce deed: that's what the bereaved poet Walt Whitman would call the assassination of this president.

BOOTH'S SIMPLE, FIERCE deed encapsulated all the brutality, all the gore, all the hatred of the past four years, all the contradictions and confusions and sorrow; it was the culmination of war and the consequence. And funneling the horror of those four years into the tragedy of one man's death, this simple, fierce deed seemed more than people could bear. It was as if there had been a death in every home, wrote *New York Times* editor Henry Raymond. Every family folded in sorrow, many of them for the second or third time. The reporter Noah Brooks said that men and women and children wandered the streets of Washington on the morning of April 15, tears streaming down their faces, while the bells were tolling and with the flags lowered to half-mast, it almost seemed, at the very same time. The simple, fierce deed: the North was stupefied, and the South too, albeit for somewhat different reasons.

There had been four years of unaccountable, untold violence that no one could have prepared for; now no one was prepared for this, never this, the assassination that Lincoln had been warned of and that he, for some reason, had shrugged away, as if he had almost sought it out. He'd been having a strange recurring dream about seeing himself mourned in the East Room after his assassination; it was half a foreboding, half a wish. Acquainted with death, too much death, perhaps he had assumed that he had already imbibed it during this great war—when he walked through devastated Richmond or stood, the summer before, on the parapet at Fort Stevens, his tall stovepipe hat an easy target. Oliver Wendell Holmes, Jr., had yelled for him to get down, damned fool. Not long afterward, a soldier standing near Lincoln had been shot.

Quantrill and his boys heard the news the day after the assassination when they had stopped for a few drinks as they wended their slow, murderous way to Washington. Quantrill, already in his cups, raised another glass. Less than a month later, on May 10, he was fatally shot in the back by Federal guerrillas who stormed James Wakefield's barn in Spencer Country, near Taylorsville, Kentucky, where he and his men were sleeping in the hayloft. He died less than three weeks later in a Louisville military hospital.

"THE HEAVIEST BLOW which has ever fallen on the people of the South has descended," lamented *The Richmond Whig*, mourning less for Lincoln than for its shattered country. General Joe Johnston, who would soon surrender to Sherman (he had continued fighting for some days after Appomattox), also thought the assassination a calamity for the South. And Confederate general Richard Ewell wrote to Grant saying that he and his officers had been shocked by the "appalling crime"—as well as the tendency to connect the South with it. "Need we say that we are not assassins," Ewell archly declared, "nor the allies of assassins, be they from the North or from the South, and that coming as we do from most of the States of the South we would be ashamed of our own people, were we not assured that they will reprobate the crime." But in Louisiana, Sarah Dawson noted that "the more violently 'Secesh' the inmates, the more thankful they are for Lincoln's death, the more profusely the houses are decked with the emblems of woe. They all look to me like 'not sorry for him, but dreadfully grieved to be forced to this demonstration.'"

Among the surgeons and members of the cabinet gathered at Lincoln's deathbed, it had been the gruff secretary of war, Edwin Stanton, who had been at Lincoln's side immediately after the president had been moved from Ford's Theatre to a boardinghouse nearby. Lincoln lay diagonally across a bed far too short for his long body. The pillow was soaked with dark blood. And when he was pronounced dead just eight minutes before seven-thirty in the morning, it was Stanton who, tears spilling down his cheeks, uttered the memorable words: now he belongs to the angels, or ages; no one is quite sure which, but either worked poignantly well.

Stanton, who needed to bring the war to a conclusion, also needed to bring the assassin or assassins to quick justice. So too the cantankerous vice president, Andrew Johnson, who wondered if the actor Booth could have managed the horrid act himself, particularly since more than one foul deed had been perpetrated the night before. At his home in Lafayette Square, Secretary of State Seward had been recovering from injuries recently sustained in a carriage accident when a man, posing as a doctor or someone bringing medicine, had rushed into his room and slashed the secretary with his knife in the neck and face. The assailant had also fractured the skull of Seward's son Frederick with a pistol that had misfired and wounded the secretary's nurse, the convalescent soldier Private George Robinson, before fleeing the premises.

Who knew, then, how many people were involved, how many officials had been targeted? It was rumored that Jefferson Davis was part of the conspiracy; perhaps General Ewell had heard that or just assumed that the North would look to the South for the culprits. Stanton had straightaway begun interviewing witnesses, dictating orders, telegraphing for more detectives, updating generals. For he knew that by calling the Emancipation Proclamation treason, Jeff Davis had put a price on Lincoln's head, since treason was a capital crime. But it couldn't be proved that Davis or other Confederate leaders had had anything to do with this dreadful thing, and besides it was easier, more comforting, and less incendiary to assume that the assassination had been the brainchild of the actor John Wilkes Booth, a man sometimes called the flower of the Confederacy.

Booth was the son of the great and famous Junius Brutus Booth, an erratic actor of enormous talent with an affection for alcohol who by the end of his life was known as Crazy Booth, the Mad Tragedian. Booth was also the younger brother of Edwin, himself an actor since his teens; by his twenties, Edwin's rendition of Richard III rivaled that of his father, and eventually his huge celebrity eclipsed that of the Mad Tragedian. But the notoriety of John Wilkes would far exceed either Edwin's or his father's.

During his youth on the family farm in Maryland, John Wilkes felt constrained and abandoned; he tried the stage but didn't share his father or brother's talent or their fame (not yet anyway). The critics were harsh; "He would have flashes, passages, I thought of real genius," said Walt Whitman, but they were only flashes. Yet he was so good-looking, with his dark hair, white skin, and magnificent mustache, that he was soon called the handsomest man in America. But like his father, John Wilkes was unreliable. He preferred self-dramatizing to losing himself in a role: at twenty-six, the young dandy draped himself in a long black greatcoat, oozed chivalry and savoir-faire, and invited—indeed, required—a measure of adoration.

He was also a good shot, a good horseman, and a ladies' man singularly fixated on Lincoln, whom he despised. His root and branch were Southern, and, like William Quantrill, he saw himself as the South's savior—a leading man who would preserve its whiteness, its honor, and its future. Persuasive, he presumably drafted several men, among them the Confederate courier John Surratt—though it's also possible that Surratt may have drafted Booth. Surratt was a known agent who traveled often between Richmond and Montreal at the behest of Judah Benjamin and the Confederate Secret Service. He packed stolen goods in his wagon, stuffed secret messages in his boot heel, or lined the pages of James Redpath's *Life of John Brown* with Confederate dispatches on his runs up to Canada and back. About a week before Lincoln's assassination, Benjamin had evidently given

Surratt several such dispatches to take to Montreal and paid him $200 in gold for his expenses. From Montreal, Surratt had gone to Elmira, New York, also in the service of the Confederacy. That's where he had been, he later said, when he had learned of Lincoln's death.

The shady Surratt claimed that Booth had approached him with a plan. "I was led on by a sincere desire to assist the South in gaining her independence," he explained. "I had no hesitation in taking part in anything honorable that might tend towards the accomplishment of that object." That honorable plan involved kidnapping the president and whisking him off to Richmond, where Booth would ransom him for Confederate prisoners of war.

Booth often met Surratt at the boardinghouse in Washington, D.C., that his profligate and recently deceased father had purchased for his mother some years earlier. On the night of March 17, about a month before the assassination, Surratt had left the boardinghouse, unhitched his horse, and raced off with six other men. When he returned, he was clasping his pistol so tightly that his knuckles had turned white. "My hopes are gone," he had moaned. Pale and glum, Booth followed him into the parlor and quickly closed the door behind him. Lincoln's schedule had changed. There had been no kidnapping.

Disappointing as that night had been, the next weeks were worse: the fall of Richmond; Appomattox; and during Holy Week, on Fat Tuesday, April 11, to be exact, Lincoln had stood on the second-floor balcony of the White House and read from a carefully prepared text. Tall and magnanimous, he said he favored giving the vote to certain black men—the soldiers and the smart ones—now that victory clearly belonged to the Union. Booth heard the speech. "That means nigger citizenship," he said. "Now, by God, I'll put him through. This is the last speech he will ever make."

On Good Friday, Booth went to the Surratt place on H Street, handed John's mother, Mary Surratt, a parcel—it looked like a few saucers wrapped together in brown paper—and asked her to carry it out to Surrattsville, the place named for her deceased husband's post office and tavern. The tavern was also locally known as a safe house for Confederate couriers and spies. Mrs. Surratt later claimed she had been going to Surrattsville that very afternoon to collect a debt, but when she arrived, she reputedly told the tavern keeper, an unreliable boozer named John Lloyd, to keep "those shooting-irons ready." The shooting irons were the carbines her son had concealed behind the wall upstairs, the same carbines that Booth and another accomplice had fetched just hours after the president was murdered. That would be the evidence marshaled against her thanks in part to the testimony of Lloyd, who was eager to save his own neck. It would send her to the gallows.

John Lloyd wasn't charged, and John Surratt was headed to Rome, where, known as John Watson, he joined the Zouaves stationed at the Vatican. But others—namely, George Atzerodt and Lewis Powell (aka Lewis Payne)—were arrested. For, according to Booth's diary, Atzerodt was to kill Vice President Johnson and Lewis Powell (formerly one of Mosby's rangers) was to assassinate Seward. Atzerodt had gotten cold feet, though Powell had done his best. Also arrested were Michael O'Laughlen and Samuel Arnold, both of them boyhood friends of Booth. Each had served as a Confederate soldier for a brief period and had signed on to the foiled March kidnapping plot. Edmund "Ned" Spangler was a carpenter who worked at Ford's Theatre and presumably had Booth's horse ready for his escape. Spangler too was arrested, and so was Mary Surratt.

Unfortunately for Mrs. Surratt, while the police were interrogating her, Powell had showed up at her door at midnight. Carrying a pickax, he claimed he'd come to dig a gutter at the widow's request, although she said she didn't know him. That didn't look good. Nor did the photograph of Booth hidden on her mantelpiece. Nor did the situation look good for Dr. Samuel A. Mudd, the physician who had attended to the leg Booth had fractured when he had jumped from the president's box onto the stage below, crying *sic semper tyrannis* ("Thus always to tyrants").

After shooting the president and getting out of the theater as quickly as possible, Booth had managed to cross the bridge over the

Potomac near the navy yard. Joined by David Herold, he eluded the federal troops for twelve days, but on April 26, in Caroline County, Virginia, the soldiers discovered Booth hiding in a tobacco barn owned by Richard Garrett. Garrett's barn was burned, Herold surrendered, and Booth was mortally shot in the neck by a skittish soldier, Sergeant Boston Corbett, who hit the actor through a hole in the barn's wall. A few hours later, Booth muttered, "Tell my mother I die for my country."

ARNOLD, O'LAUGHLEN, SPANGLER, Powell, Atzerodt, Herold, Mudd, and Mrs. Surratt: the eight of them were held in irons at the Old Arsenal Penitentiary. They had been accused of maliciously, unlawfully, and traitorously conspiring to murder the president, the vice president, the secretary of state, and General Grant, who, on that fateful night, had decided not to attend the theater.

They had also sabotaged the peace and undermined the war, and because Lincoln, as president, was commander in chief and thus a military personage whose assassination was a military crime—not a mere criminal offense—Andrew Johnson decided that the eight alleged conspirators should be tried by a military court. The decision was controversial. This was no time for either vengeance or military despotism, former attorney general Edward Bates angrily wrote in his diary. The suspects were not military personnel, for one thing. And they were charged with murder or conspiracy to commit murder, not with treason. Plus, with the civil courts in Washington open, there was no constitutional reason for a military trial. "Ours is a government of *Law*," he declared, "and that the law is strong enough, to rule the people wisely and well." Unconstitutional *and* unlawful *and* an overreach of government: it was a disastrous policy. The public cried out against the tribunal. In haste, Johnson instructed the attorney general, James Speed, to defend the constitutionality of his decision, but Bates considered Speed nothing more than a lackey and an imbecile.

Just as controversial was the decision of the military court to hold its trial in secret. Reporters were not to be admitted; the court's proceedings would be communicated by one man, Judge Advocate General Joseph Holt, who was presiding, to a single representative of the press at the end of each day. This too seemed an unconstitutional muzzling of the freedom of the press, particularly since the country was no longer at war. Holt reversed this ruling—and only this ruling.

Yet, as expected, the testimony darkened the already dark mood of the country, especially in the North, where it was rumored that the assassination had been a Confederate plot to create anarchy in the North and prepare the way for a dictator, or so said Benjamin Perley Poore, the journalist who edited the *Congressional Directory* and the *Congressional Record* and who, as a court reporter, published the trial proceedings. The simple, fierce deed could not have been simple. It was unthinkable that a U.S. president, even during wartime, could actually be killed by a lone assassin—never mind by a mediocre actor flanked by a cadre of ne'er-do-wells. But had they acted alone? Weren't they connected to Confederate officials or spies?

Even if it wasn't a conspiracy, Lincoln's murder was yet another consequence of the South's benighted institution of slavery, which lay at the heart of everything that had happened during the last four years. "It is not simply the death of a man, however high his station, however great his attributes, however foully murdered, that tortures us today," Anna Dickinson told a crowd of 3,000 at Cooper Union, where Lincoln had spoken so memorably during his 1860 election campaign. "It is liberty that was assailed in the person of our Chief—it is the country that bleeds and put it how we will, it is slavery that inflicts the blow."

Still, for all practical purposes, the war against slavery was over. The Thirteenth Amendment, having passed both houses, had already been ratified by twenty-one states; it was well on its way to the necessary three-quarters. Jefferson Davis was on the run; General Joe Johnston had surrendered to General Sherman. And yet there was something undeniably personal about the assassination of a president—the murder of the country's titular father—that the country took personally, holding its collective breath as Lincoln's funeral train retraced in reverse the route he'd taken before his first inaugural, when he had ridden to Washington from Springfield, Illinois. Lincoln was to be buried in Springfield. As the nine cars of the so-called Lincoln Special slowly chugged along the tracks, more than seven million men and women stood dumbstruck. George Templeton Strong heard how some solitary farmer might lay down his hoe or stop his team, take off his hat, and stand stock-still, his head uncovered, while the train passed by. "When lilacs last in the door-yard bloom'd," Whitman wrote in his great elegy. "I mourn'd—and yet shall mourn with ever-returning spring."

ON MAY 10, less than a month after the assassination, Jefferson Davis was captured in Irwinsville, Georgia, by soldiers in the 4th Michigan Cavalry, who reputedly saw his boots underneath the hoopskirt he was wearing while trying to escape. "The news of the capture of Jeff. Davis falls quietly upon the public ear," noted *The New York Times*, "so much is the universal eye and ear turned toward the great assassination trial." The trial had begun the same day Davis was caught, on the third floor of the Old Arsenal Penitentiary, where the eight defendants were accused of conspiring to kill President Lincoln and of conspiring with Jefferson Davis—in other words, of a general conspiracy, which was in effect the Confederacy itself.

THE TRIAL WAS the most exciting tourist attraction in Washington that spring—the trial of the century for the crime of the century. Marian "Clover" Hooper (later Mrs. Henry Adams), one of the many ticket holders crammed into the courtroom, carefully examined Mary Surratt for signs of guilt or innocence, but, disappointed, she couldn't settle on either. Mrs. Surratt seldom raised her eyes, though one could see they were iron gray—a slightly darker shade of gray than a Confederate private's spanking new uniform. Dressed in black, she wore her dark brown hair parted in the middle and tied in the back. She fingered her rosary and in an unflattering photograph, clutched a New Testament with a large gilt cross on its cover. Nearly forty, large-sized, shabbily dressed, and with a coarse expression was how the usually sedate *New York Times* described her.

Surratt was seated not far from the panel of nine handpicked judges, combat generals and colonels, all military men presided over by Judge Advocate General Holt, the Kentucky Unionist who had been Buchanan's attorney general and one of the cabinet members who had stood firm while Buchanan hemmed and hawed over the supplying of Fort Sumter. A friend of Edwin Stanton, Holt had been serving as judge advocate general under him since 1862. The judges included Major General David Hunter, the man who had issued his own peremptory emancipation declaration in the Sea Islands in 1862 and then gone on to uncertain fame as a Shenandoah Valley burner. More recently, his hair now white, he had accompanied the late president's body as it traveled to its final resting place in Springfield. He was joined by Major General Lewis "Lew" Wallace, a small, pale, lithe man who wore a long, dark mustache. Formerly a lawyer from Indiana, Wallace would later become governor of New Mexico—and the author of the wildly popular novel *Ben-Hur*. Another commissioner was Major General August V. Kautz, a cavalry officer. None of the men had legal training.

Under the rules of martial law, the judge advocate operated both as prosecutor and judge. What's more, a military court would not have to bother with the rules of evidence that had to be carefully laid out in civil trials. Nor were the suspected conspirators informed of their right to counsel, although Senator Reverdy Johnson of Maryland, a Unionist, briefly served as attorney for Mrs. Surratt, as did Brigadier General Thomas Ewing, Jr., General Sherman's stepbrother. During the length of the trial, which lasted fifty days, they heard 360 witnesses tell the truth as they had seen or remembered it. Twenty-nine of them were former slaves who testified both for and against the defendants. But whatever anyone—black or white—alleged, or whatever the presumed innocence or the guilt of the defendants, the Northern public wanted convictions, and the government wanted to show that Booth's single bullet could not undo what so many soldiers had died for.

During fifty days of testimony, the public heard depositions that extended far beyond the defendants and John Wilkes Booth; they heard about Canadian Confederates who had planned irregular war-fare, about vials of smallpox smuggled over the border in suitcases by Confederate agents hoping to infect the North, and about the horrific conditions at the notorious prisons, Libby in Richmond and Andersonville in Georgia, where, at the latter, in just one year 13,000 Yankees had been left to starve or rot or die of dysentery, gangrene, and scurvy if they hadn't been lucky enough to be killed. Somehow the eight defendants who shuffled into the makeshift courtroom, their legs in irons, and wearing hoods over their heads (except for the woman, Mary Surratt), were accused of more than conspiring to kill the president; they were guilty of war crimes.

On Wednesday, July 5, 1865, Judge Advocate General Holt handed down guilty verdicts for all eight defendants. Four of them, including Surratt, were sentenced to hang; O'Laughlen, Mudd, Arnold, to life in prison; Ned Spangler, to six years in prison. Mary Surratt wept. The execution would take place in just two days. Her attorneys asked for a postponement, claiming that she needed time to see her priest—she was Catholic—and prepare for death. They applied for a writ of habeas corpus. The public suddenly seemed sympathetic to her; the idea of hanging a woman was repugnant. Five of the commissioners who had convicted her—one of them was David Hunter—petitioned for executive clemency for Mrs. Surratt. Stephen Douglas's hand-some widow went straight to the White House to plead for mercy for Surratt. But to grant the writ would have been to interfere with a military trial; to accede to Mrs. Douglas's demands would have been to tie oneself to a petticoat. Even the commissioners' petition recommending clemency fell on deaf ears. Mrs. Surratt had kept the nest that had hatched the plot, Andrew Johnson said; and besides, he grumbled, there hadn't been enough women hanged in this war.

The execution took place on schedule early in the afternoon of July 7. It was a sweltering day. As the unofficial government photographer, Alexander Gardner had already photographed Ford's Theatre inside and out, and aboard the *Montauk* and the USS *Saugus*, where the accused conspirators were initially held, Gardner took stark photographs of the men: two views, one front-faced and one in profile in the prototype of what would become the conventional mug shot. He also photographed the execution. Even today, the photographs seem astounding, horrible, and prurient. Yet, anticipating Gardner, Nathaniel Hawthorne's daguerreotypist in *The House of the Seven Gables* had claimed that pictures might well serve "as a point of evidence that may be useful . . . and also as a memorial."

THE FOUR CONVICTED conspirators were executed for plotting to assassinate President Lincoln; but the only man executed as a war criminal was Commandant Heinrich Hartmann "Henry" Wirz of the Andersonville (aka Camp Sumter) prison, a hellhole in rural southwest Georgia and a symbol of cruelty, neglect, and bureaucratic failure.

A peevish martinet with blood on his hands, the Swiss-born Wirz was also a scapegoat.

Born in Zurich, he'd emigrated in 1849 to the United States and for a while had worked as a weaver in one of the mills of Lawrence, Massachusetts, before moving to Kentucky and then to Louisiana, where he had found employment as a physician on a plantation despite the fact that he wasn't a doctor. In 1861, he had enlisted in the Confederate army; badly wounded in the right arm during the Seven Days' Battle, after his recovery he had been posted at a military prison in Alabama. In the spring of 1864 he had taken charge of Andersonville.

Wirz firmly believed that he should not be blamed for the cruel corollaries of war, such as the condition of prisons. But at the trial of the Lincoln conspirators, men and women heard harrowing stories about men left for dead or gagged and dumped outside in the cold, or chased by bloodhounds and torn apart, their bodies piled onto wagons and flung into trenches, or of old Captain Wirz telling his guards that if a Yankee prisoner crossed a line and was shot, the shooter would receive a forty-day furlough. Yet, as a former prisoner recalled, Wirz was no villain, just "gnat-brained, cowardly, and feeble-natured" and not particularly troubled by good intentions.

Wirz presented himself as a functionary whose hands were tied. His superior officer had just died. His requests for shoes or the materials to make them, or for rations, went unanswered by a beleaguered Richmond. Besides, Wirz suggested, were the prisons in the South, of which Andersonville was the most chilling example, really more lethal and disgraceful than those in the North?

For example, in the summer of 1864, Grant had ordered General Butler to stop allowing the exchange of prisoners even though Grant, like Lincoln, was aware of Andersonville's squalor: the miserable deaths from exposure or disease that numbered anywhere from thirty to seventy a day; the vermin, the ignominy. "It is hard on our men held in Southern prisons not to exchange them," Grant had explained, "but it is humanity to those left in the ranks to fight our battles. Every man we hold, when released on parole or otherwise, becomes an active soldier against us at once either directly or indirectly." At the same time Grant also told Secretary Seward, "We ought not to make a single exchange nor release a prisoner on any pretext whatever until the war closes. We have got to fight until the military power of the South is exhausted, and if we release or exchange prisoners captured it simply becomes a war of extermination." Paroled Confederates frequently rejoined their army, while paroled Federals often deserted.

By not exchanging soldiers, the Federals had guaranteed overcrowding in Confederate jails—and the likely death of their soldiers, who frequently believed that they'd been abandoned by the government. At Andersonville, they had been forced to drink from the clotted stream that served as the prison's sewer system and, as one of them testified, were given a whole day's ration of a half-pint of corn-meal ground with cobs and stones, two ounces of rotten bacon, and a spoonful of salt. Who was to blame?

In a large, well-carpeted room in the Court of Claims Hall, the sickly Wirz, guarded by eight soldiers, faced a military tribunal, as the Lincoln conspirators had, and, much agitated, listened while Colonel Chipman, the presiding judge advocate, read the charges against him: conspiracy to destroy the lives of Union soldiers; and murder, in violation of the laws or customs of war. *The New York Times*, in an article called "The Rebel Assassins," which linked him with Booth, condemned Wirz as "a man of iron will, determined in purpose, and heartless in the execution of it." Wirz pleaded not guilty.

Angular, slender, stooped, and penniless, Wirz protested that he should not have been arrested at all but should have been paroled under the terms of surrender agreed upon by Generals Johnston and Sherman. Before a packed courtroom, for two months Wirz heard testimony that was vicious, uncontested, heartbreaking, and in many cases highly impeachable: Wirz was said to have killed men even though he could not have been present at the time of the killing; he had murdered prisoners who had never been prisoners. Testimony on his behalf was routinely disallowed. Southerners believed that the trial was engineered to deflect attention away from the Union's refusal to exchange prisoners.

Sentenced to hang, Wirz was said to be responsible for the death of ten thousand men. And in his synopsis of the trial, Judge Advocate Holt declared the atrocities at Andersonville, "accomplished by the rebel authorities and their brutal underlings," to be part of a "monstrous conspiracy." Wirz was then the sole person in a conspiracy that neither Holt nor Stanton could prove, much as they would have liked to impugn Jefferson Davis, James Seddon, or Howell Cobb—and Davis, in his own defense, later claimed that a member of Johnson's cabinet had promised Wirz a pardon if he would implicate Davis in the cruelties of Andersonville. If Wirz had been so approached, he had turned down the offer.

President Johnson refused to hear any plea of clemency, and Wirz was hanged on Friday, November 10, in the morning, about four months after the Lincoln assassination conspirators were executed, probably for some of the same reasons: horror, grief, vengeance, and an odd form of relief. "Talk about liberty in this country," Wirz scoffed, and then was said to pray for his prosecutors' souls.

The two hundred or so spectators—a thousand had applied for admission tickets—who hoped that Wirz might yell, cry, or repent were disappointed. From the tops of their homes or perched on tall trees, they saw a man who seemed braver, or so wrote one reporter, than the Lincoln conspirators. Alexander Gardner photographed Wirz, his head lowered, at the gallows, erected on what would be the site of the Supreme Court of the United States. He also photographed the autopsy conducted on Wirz's body even though the War Department, which had authorized the photograph, later suppressed it. The taking of it—and those of Booth's autopsy—was again strange. Meanwhile, relic hunters cut off splinters from the scaffold and spirited away about a dozen feet of rope.

ON APRIL 11, two days after Appomattox and just four days before he was shot at point-blank range, Abraham Lincoln had addressed a roaring, interracial crowd about the work that lay ahead. The nation's capital had been exuberant for two days. The buildings were lit with candles, bonfires were blazing, and the front of the War Department was decorated with flags and evergreens. Across the Potomac, the Custis-Lee Mansion, where General Lee had once lived, now confiscated, was brightly illuminated with blinking colored lights on the vast lawn. Cheering loudly, the crowd was expecting a different speech that misty evening from the one they heard.

The war may have been won, Lincoln said from the balcony of the executive mansion, but the devastated South would need reconstruction. The consequences of emancipation would have to be met head-on. That was the speech that Booth, too, had heard.

"The whole subject of what is called Reconstruction is beset with difficulty," Gideon Welles had worried a year earlier. In Syracuse, New York, with delegates coming from as far away as North and South Carolina and Louisiana, a national black convention called for universal suffrage and equality before the law. But Republicans were divided. After the Thirteenth Amendment was ratified in December 1865, William Lloyd Garrison stopped the presses of *The Liberator*. His object—emancipation—was attained, and he was far less sure about universal suffrage than he had been about abolition. Not so Senator Charles Sumner. "Liberty has been won," he remarked. "The battle for Equality is still pending." And Frederick Douglass said that without suffrage, "we should have slavery back again, in spirit if not in form."

Republicans and Democrats were at the same time trying to figure out where Lincoln's thinking had been headed before his death. Recollecting the Hampton Roads conference, Admiral Porter claimed that the president possessed "the most liberal views toward the rebels"; Sherman too, in his memoirs, remembered that the president said that as soon as the rebels surrendered, "they would be at once guaranteed all their rights as citizens of a common country." But all that was recalled after the fact. Similarly, Lincoln's last speech was and has been parsed over and over. Nonetheless, when he spoke from the balcony of the White House on April 11 to the large crowd of black and white listeners, he declared that "we, the loyal people" were not of one mind about what he called Reconstruction, or the "re-inauguration of the national authority." It could be "fraught with great difficulty." He repeated that he was open to more plans than his own. And as for the recent controversy over Louisiana (where only 10 percent of eligible voters had elected the new state government), Lincoln admitted he would not at all mind enfranchising black men who were "very intelligent" or who had served "our cause as soldiers." It was an astonishing event: as the historian Eric Foner noted, no other U.S. president had ever even hinted at the possibility of black suffrage.

NO ONE REALLY knew what Lincoln had intended or where his Reconstruction policies might have led, especially in peacetime. Lincoln was a brilliant man and master politician comfortable with restraint as well as risk and capable of change and reflection.

At fifty-six years old, Andrew Johnson seemed ready for the difficulties that lay ahead when Chief Justice Salmon Chase administered the oath of office just a few hours after Lincoln had been pronounced dead on that doleful and rainy morning of April 15. The poor white man from North Carolina who had walked all the way to Tennessee to build a life there, the man who seemed to frown perpetually and whom Washington snobs had thought a vulgar drunk ever since his unfortunate behavior at Lincoln's second inauguration, the man whom, it was rumored, Lincoln had not much liked, never mind taken into his confidence—Johnson nonetheless inspired measured optimism. He kept his poise. He grasped the reins of power reassuringly and without hesitation. He appeared disciplined and calm. George Templeton Strong, who once had considered Johnson ungenteel and low, remarked that the new president seemed "dignified, urbane, and self-possessed." The reporter Noah Brooks was relieved not just by Johnson's demeanor but also by the way his administration seamlessly followed Lincoln's. "It was a remarkable illustration," Brooks said, "of the elasticity and steadiness of our form of government that its machinery moved on without a jar, without tumult, when the head was suddenly stricken down."

In the wake of the country's terrible loss, Johnson promised continuity. He would keep the members of Lincoln's cabinet as his own, at least at first. He reassured Republicans, particularly Radicals, that he was "clearly" of the opinion "that those who are good enough to fight for the Government are good enough to vote for it; and that a black heart is a more serious defect in an American citizen than a black face." Senator Ben Wade greeted him with a hearty "We have faith in you," and Representative George W. Julian of Indiana announced that Johnson "would prove a godsend to the country." He would not coddle former Confederates. Treason is a crime and will be punished, Johnson had said, although he had been referring to assassination conspirators. Still, former Confederates were being put on notice, it seemed.

So when Sherman offered General Johnston terms of surrender that far exceeded Sherman's authority, President Johnson acted quickly to reject them. Sherman had offered Johnston a general amnesty, recognition of existing Confederate states, and a restoration of property and political rights. Better than anyone, Sherman knew what devastation he had caused, what wasteland he had helped to create, and he naively hoped these magnanimous terms would bring not just an end to the war but would guarantee law and order. What he feared most, he said, were roaming guerrilla bands who would never capitulate.

Johnson not only cast aside Sherman's so-called armistice but also authorized the pursuit of Jefferson Davis, assuming that Davis, among others, had been involved in the assassination. Of course Johnson and Davis had been bitter enemies, which may also account for his offer of an enormous sum, $100,000 reward, for his capture. Yet to many Republicans there seemed no reason to question his resolve to punish the South or at least hold it far more accountable than he would in the months to come.

ON A SUNNY, warm Wednesday, May 23, Washington decked itself out for a two-day victory parade during which General Meade's Army of the Potomac and Sherman's Army of the Tennessee and Army of Georgia would march before the crowds, reportedly 75,000 strong, that lined Pennsylvania Avenue. Though the public buildings were still wreathed in mourning ribbons of black crepe, the flags no longer flew at half-mast, and there was plenty of bunting and bold-colored streamers to welcome home the heroes of the republic, the gallant defenders of the nation. There were people perched on the roof of one building or another. Landlords rented out windows that overlooked Pennsylvania Avenue, which had been cleaned by the fire department, but so many visitors descended on Washington that some of them had to sleep in horsecars or on park benches. Fortunately, the weather was mild, and although it had rained for two days earlier in the week, the streets were relatively dry.

The commissioner of public buildings placed a gleaming gilded eagle over his front door, then climbed the stairs inside the Capitol dome to get a better view. Men and women wore their Sunday best, and many of them waved small flags. Young girls carried roses and others threw flowers from the tops of the houses and cheered although, technically, the war had not yet ended, even if most of the seaports were already open to commerce.

This grand review was the frenzy of jubilation that followed the frenzy of mourning. Flanked by generals and members of his cabinet, President Andrew Johnson was on the covered stand located in front of the executive mansion. As the armies passed it, they lowered their regimental flags—many of them riddled with bullet holes—and President Andrew Johnson, ramrod straight, saluted them or shook the outstretched hands of the victors. On Wednesday came the Army of the Potomac, all of it, the horses clattering, bugles blowing, the cavalry and the mounted artillery and the engineering brigades. Walt Whitman was there, watching and taking notes, and on the second day he spotted the self-possessed Sherman and his proud western army.

Sherman passed by rapidly, ignoring the shouting crowd, his face twitching. Behind him was a tight column. "The glittering muskets looked like a solid mass of steel," he recalled, "moving with the regularity of a pendulum." Near Sherman rode the one-armed major general Oliver Otis Howard, wounded at Fair Oaks and the new head of the Freedmen's Bureau. When a young girl offered Howard a wreath, he couldn't manage it with only one arm, so he just smiled and rode on.

Clover Hooper had a seat on the congressional platform, roofed over to keep the spectators from the sun. It was the most perfect day, she said; there were Zouaves, brightly dressed in their baggy scarlet trousers and dark blue jackets, red fezzes on their heads, and the Irish brigade wore green. Most of the officers in the parade carried roses, and many of the horses had wreaths around their necks. Onlookers could see the artillery, ambulances, and army wagons. Mother Bickerdyke, who had nursed the western fighters, rode sidesaddle with the Fifteenth Corps. All the noise spooked General Custer's stallion, which dashed up Pennsylvania Avenue at top speed, and though Custer lost his hat in the wind, the blond soldier, his troops swathed in scarlet scarves, saluted the president with his hand touching the place where his hat would have been.

The two-day parade was like inauguration day, General Grant later reminisced, recalling the tumult and the waving flags—and the doorsteps and sidewalks "crowded with colored people and poor whites who did not succeed in securing better quarters from which to view the grand armies." Missing was Philip Sheridan, who didn't ride in the review, much to his disappointment and that of the crowd; he would be en route to Texas to make sure that General Edmund Kirby Smith's Confederate army surrendered, which they had yet to do. And spectators saw no black troops, for they too remained in the field—although the 22nd U.S. Colored Infantry had marched in Lincoln's funeral procession just weeks before. It was said that they were being sent, along with Sheridan, to the Southwest. Instead, there were black laborers—black men without threatening muskets—and a dozen or so black women in bandannas along with a few children, a goat, and a couple of gamecocks.

Missing too was the commander in chief, who for four years had steered the war as best he could, each year deepening the lines on his bony face and showing sorrow in his melancholy eyes, the man who promised justice and mercy and also the avenging sword, if need be, and who proved himself as good as his promise. Abraham Lincoln should have been in the reviewing stand. "All felt this," Gideon Welles said—yet it could almost seem as if he were. Clover Hooper said, "It was a strange feeling to be so intensely happy and triumphant, and yet to feel like crying." Amid the patriotism and cheer, amid the rugged display of nationalism and wreaths and fluttering banners, amid the clatter of horses' hooves and the blare of "John Brown's Body," amid all of it there had to be a sadness, a loneliness, an anxiety about the future and the haunting memory of dead comrades and bloody bodies left to rot atop one another on a faceless field: "The martyred heroes of Malvern Hill," wrote the transplanted westerner Bret Harte, "Of Gettysburg and Chancellorsville / The men whose wasted figures fill / The patriot graves of the nation."

And then there were the crossed or overlapping purposes for which the war had been fought—the preservation of the Union, the freeing of the slaves—that were somehow waved away for two days of celebration and forgetfulness, the flip side of mourning and dread.

There were so many unknowns. One of the largest was Reconstruction.

"Did I ever think to live to see this day," said a Southern refugee in despair and anger after she learned that Joe Johnston had surrendered. "After all the misery and anguish of the four past years—," she cried. "Think of all our sacrifices—of broken hearts, and desolated homes—or our *noble, glorious dead*—, and say for what? *Reconstruction!* how the very word galls."

PART THREE

{ 1865—1876 }

(17)

But Half Accomplished

Rufus Saxton was solid; he followed orders, he fulfilled pledges, he defended with dignity whatever and whomever he believed to be right, regardless of color. And if the journalist Whitelaw Reid patronizingly called him a dull but well-meaning functionary ("not very profound in seeing the right but energetic in doing it when seen"), Saxton had been charged with a seemingly impossible function: the supervision—no, the care—of the 20,000 or so former slaves who had remained in the South Carolina Sea Islands after the arrival of the Union fleet in late 1861. He performed his job well—so well, that he would anger his superiors.

A Massachusetts native, Saxton was the son of a radical Unitarian who had very much wanted his sons to attend the experimental school at Brook Farm. Only one of them had, and it hadn't been Rufus. He'd preferred the rigors of West Point to the radicalism of West Roxbury. After graduating in 1849, he commanded an expedition to survey a route through the Rocky Mountains for the Northern Pacific Railroad, taught military tactics at West Point, headed the drawing and engraving division of the U.S. Coast Survey, and patented a self-registering thermostat for deep-sea soundings, which earned him an honorary degree from Amherst College. During the war, he served on the staffs of Generals Lyon, McClellan, and

Thomas W. Sherman as chief quartermaster. In 1862 he defended the strategic and now symbolic Harpers Ferry against Stonewall Jackson, for which he later received the Medal of Honor. Stanton and Lincoln then wanted him to leave the field to become military governor in the Department of the South, where he would supervise the former slaves to whom he would issue rations and clothes and supplies—and from whose population he would recruit and train soldiers.

Short, compactly built, with deep-set eyes and curly black side whiskers ("what ladies would call a handsome man," Reid said), General Saxton had likely earned the appointment because he believed that slavery was wrong and that not only would black men fight to end it, they would fight well. Headquartered in Beaufort, South Carolina, in late 1862, he recruited and trained black soldiers, and he organized the freedmen who were too old or who were unable to serve, setting them to work on abandoned plantations to harvest the cotton—about $2 million worth—which he turned over to the U.S. Treasury. In a way, he was hoping to create another Brook Farm— but in the South, among blacks, so that freedmen could achieve economic independence and prove to former Confederates at home and racists everywhere that black men and women were competent, ready to fight, ready to farm, desirous of freedom, and fully deserving of it.

Saxton visited General William Tecumseh Sherman in Savannah not long after the city's surrender in late December 1864. He was surprised by what he found. Charities were being distributed to "rank secesh women, in silks, while poor whites & destitute negroes are turned away & told to go to work," said Captain Samuel Willard Saxton, his brother's aide-de-camp. And with new fortunes to be made in cotton, opportunistic Northerners were coming to do just that—with the help of former Confederate planters. "The heads of that army don't care much about humanitarian labors," noted Willard Saxton.

Rufus Saxton was more encouraged when the crusty secretary of war, Edwin Stanton, went to Savannah and the Sea Islands the next month. Stanton said he wanted General Saxton to remain where he was. As a matter of fact, he'd brought papers confirming Saxton's promotion to brevet major general, which meant, in addition to the military honor, that Washington (Lincoln's Washington) was committed to continuing Saxton's work with former slaves in South Carolina. The two men, along with General Sherman, also talked with twenty black clergymen and local leaders, and on January 16, 1865—three months before Appomattox—Sherman issued his famous Special Field Order No. 15, which gave land confiscated by the Union to the freedmen.

Land: Special Field Order No. 15 designated a specific belt of abandoned land, extending along the coast from Charleston to Jacksonville, on which freedmen could settle. The head of each black family would obtain not more than "forty acres of land and a mule." Sherman wanted to help black families become independent, though not necessarily for altruistic reasons; the army had over 80,000 black refugees to house and feed, and the sooner they could take care of themselves, the better. Whatever the motive, the order implied a radical land redistribution, which upended the propertied class system in the South and gave the gift of home and property to those who had been denied both. And so, as in the case of emancipation, a military strategy was forcing a political and social sea change—but only up to a point. Special Field Order No. 15 could not stipulate that these black families would actually own the land they were given.

Appointed Inspector of Settlements and Plantations in South Carolina, Georgia, and Florida, General Saxton faced the giant task of resettling the freedmen and then protecting their claim to the land, pending the passage of a bill in Congress to that effect. Saxton didn't relish the assignment. He had been asked to enforce an order that might not be enforceable, and later he remembered arguing with Stanton, telling him that "former promises which I had made to the freedmen with reference to the occupancy of land had been broken, and I feared that in the enforcement of that order they would be disappointed—again. I begged the Secretary of War, therefore, to relieve me from the duty of carrying it out. He ordered me, with great emphasis, to enforce it to its fullest extent, and I promised him that I would do so."

Misgivings aside, Saxton intended to fulfill Sherman's promise. He wished, he said, "every colored man, every head of a family, to acquire a freehold, a little place he can call his own," to work his own farm with dignity—and to save money in locally established banks. By June, General Saxton had resettled 40,000 black men and women on about 400,000 acres of land, presumably issuing what Sherman had called "possessory" titles to that, since no one yet knew who legally owned it. The resolution of that question—who had legal title to the land—would become a core feature of Reconstruction.

Despite his promotion, Saxton may have secretly hankered after a different appointment: that of heading the newly formed Freedmen's Bureau, organized shortly before Lincoln's death. For one year, the Bureau was to oversee all aspects of the freedmen's lives—everything from aid to education to the adjudication of disputes, which was what Saxton had been doing. And though the Bureau had been organized without reference to Sherman's Special Field Order No. 15, its mandate also included the apportionment of confiscated land into forty-acre plots, which were to be leased to freedmen and refugees and then sold to them, assuming that the government had title to the land, a detail that still remained unclear.

Certainly General Saxton was well suited to run the Bureau—except that to some he was a bit too "ultra." Not so General Howard, a man of narrow though well-meaning views, a penchant for platitudes, and a belated and befuddled conversion to antislavery. Named the head of the Freedmen's Bureau, he would manage affairs from faraway Washington while Rufus Saxton, who gracefully accepted an appointment as assistant commissioner, would stay in South Carolina. The government thought Howard the better choice. He was not an abolitionist but rather a pious Christian whose conversion experience in

1857 did not preclude him from shouldering a rifle. Familiarly known as "the Christian soldier," Howard would presumably appeal to civilian philanthropic organizations. He did not drink or swear and, like John Brown and Stonewall Jackson, though of a milder temperament, the devout Howard optimistically believed in the moral righteousness of his cause, which was the restoration of the Union first and emancipation second. Educated at West Point (graduating fourth in the class of 1854) and at Bowdoin College in Maine, he had fought at the First Battle of Bull Run and lost his arm at Fair Oaks. He had seen action at Antietam, Fredericksburg, and Chancellorsville, where his troops were routed by Stonewall Jackson, and at Gettysburg he had faltered so badly that Joe Hooker had said that if Howard hadn't been "born in petticoats he ought to have been, and ought to wear them." Regardless, Sherman had selected him to lead the Army of the Tennessee, which, headed by this one-armed Christian soldier, had marched through Georgia and the Carolinas savagely burning what they could not carry.

Though he had fired his Christian gun in a cause that also included emancipation, Howard's commitment to universal suffrage and equal protection of blacks under the law was lukewarm. Radical Republicans were disappointed. Sure, Howard was "a man of pure purposes, unspoiled integrity, and undoubted singleness of aim," they said. "But his mind is neither so broad, so penetrating, nor so aspiring as his work demands." Plus, as his friend General Sherman reminded him, when it came to a freedman, be a realist, not a New Englander; keep your expectations low. And that he seemed to do. He embraced the advice of well-wishers such as the preeminent man of the cloth, Henry Ward Beecher. Urging peace and reconciliation at the Union flag-raising ceremony at Fort Sumter in April 1865, Beecher counseled against "*too much* Northern management of the Negro." Beyond a "small *start*, in tools, seed, etc.," Beecher cautioned, nothing more should be given the freedman, particularly because the North harbored that frequent, misguided tendency "to dandle the black man, or at least, to recite his suffering."

No one need have worried. Oliver Otis Howard would not mollycoddle anyone, least of all Rufus Saxton.

THOUGH HORATIO ALGER, JR., would not invent Ragged Dick until 1867, the tale of rags to riches was already a mainstay of American folklore, at least in the North. Southern planters were less enthralled, and Edward Pollard, the fire-eating editor of the *Richmond Examiner*, cast a very cold eye on the self-made man—or what was known in his circle as a "scrub." Andy Johnson was a scrub: impeccable clothes couldn't conceal the gaucheness of that backwoods Tennessee tailor given to malapropisms. Johnson knew what the planters thought of him; in turn, he hated the Southern elite and their condescension. He hated their sense of superiority. He had fought them when they spouted off about secession. A Jacksonian Democrat, he had even joined up with Lincoln and the Republicans to defeat them, to preserve the Union, and, not coincidentally, to advance his career.

It wasn't long after Johnson took the oath of office, though, that the Republicans realized that the new president wasn't one of them either. When they requested a special session of Congress to deal with Reconstruction—Congress was not due to convene until the December after Lincoln's assassination, almost seven months away—Johnson rebuffed them, and he took Reconstruction into his own hands. His plan for Reconstruction was a restoration—a restoration of the Union exactly as it was, just without slavery. He wouldn't hear of rights of the freedmen and women. For Johnson made no secret of his racism. While seeming to conciliate the Republicans and to praise black troops, he was also heard to have said, "This is a country for white men and, by G–d, as long as I am president it shall be a government for white men."

In May 1865 Johnson proclaimed a general and generous amnesty to Southerners willing to take the oath of allegiance; he excluded Confederate government and military leaders and those rich rebels whose taxable net worth exceeded $20,000 (he still hated the

Southern aristocracy). Yet any of them could ask for a presidential pardon, and soon the White House teemed with supplicants looking not just for pardons but patronage, which Johnson regally dispensed. By the following year, Secretary of State Seward reported 7,197 pardons with an additional 707 on the way. Johnson also called for a convention of loyal citizens (a citizen was anyone who had been eligible to vote in 1860, so freedmen were excluded) to be held in North Carolina, and he appointed William Holden as the state's governor. He appointed governors in Georgia, Alabama, Mississippi, Florida, and Texas. In South Carolina, he put Benjamin Perry into the governor's seat even though Perry had been in the Confederate legislature during the war.

Though Johnson remained leery of federal control and was a firm advocate of states' rights, he had never acknowledged secession. As far as he was concerned, the eleven states of the Confederacy had not legally seceded, which also meant that the Southern states had not left the Union nor relinquished their right to govern themselves as they wished. For instance, in Mississippi, when the state legislature had recently convened, it had passed a set of ordinances known as the Black Codes, which effectively limited or took away the rights of the freedmen: it rewrote vagrancy laws to prevent freedmen and women moving from place to place in search of work; it mandated that former slaves prove residence and occupation by showing their contracts with employers or their licenses for self-employment; it consigned black orphans to unpaid labor; it outlawed ownership of any kind of weapon; it outlawed freedmen's leasing farmland. Johnson also permitted the Mississippi legislature to raise a state militia (likely composed of Confederate veterans) to help enforce those codes, which in effect forced freedmen and women to return to the plantations where they were once enslaved, presumably as workers. Said a member of the 5th U.S. Colored Heavy Artillery, "They are doing all they can to prevent free labor and create a kind of secondary slavery."

Mississippi wasn't alone in creating codes designed to rob the rights of the freedmen. Sidney Andrews, a Northern reporter, said,

"The whites seem wholly unable to comprehend that freedom for
the negro means the same thing as freedom for them." A chaplain
in Beaufort, South Carolina, complained that the planters regarded
the Emancipation Proclamation as a wartime—not a peacetime—
measure and so rejected the very idea of free labor, undermining it
however and wherever they could, with taxes, for example, levied on
blacks who chose any occupation other than farming.

The Black Codes were but one form of social control. Violence
and the threat of violence were another. In South Carolina more
than a dozen Union men, black and white, had been killed in two
months. Saxton reported that in the spring of 1865 the sons of some
of the "first families" around Augusta, Georgia, had formed bands of
guerrillas committed to the summary murder of freedmen not working on a nearby plantation. "We heard that a negro had been *killed*
in town. Taken out by a band of disguised men at midnight," a distressed South Carolina woman said. "An innocent, peaceable negro,
taken from his frightened wife, taken out, tied, the house searched &
then he was shot & left lying in the street next morning. The intention being to warn other negroes of danger perhaps." When black
soldiers, as well as some white ones, were also killed, the culprits
were not pursued. In the meantime several states in addition to Mississippi formed their own (white) local militias with former Confederate soldiers among their ranks, their putative task to restore law and
order and prevent uprisings—a Southern bogeyman—although the
freedmen (and General Saxton) believed these so-called regulators
were simply the bullying patrols of slavery days, now regrouped to
subjugate and intimidate the black population.

Saxton guessed that those well-armed, well-organized regulators
wanted him to disarm the freedmen (which Saxton would not do)
in order to "have the whole black population unarmed and defenseless." As it was, black troops lacked officers and were in any case being
discharged from service, all the more so since Southerners had been
complaining about their presence. "The Government is now pressed
by the ex-Rebels to disband its Black soldiers forthwith," explained

the *New-York Tribune.* "But what is to become of these soldiers? Many if not most of them dare not return to the homes they left to enter the Union service. They know they would be hunted down and killed by their badly reconstructed White neighbors." And as far as Saxton was concerned, the agents of the Freedmen's Bureau were in danger too. "There are large numbers in South Carolina who would consider it no greater crime to kill an agent of the Freedmen's Bureau, who claims justice for those committed to his charge, than to kill a negro."

Yet Saxton persisted in helping the freedmen settle on land, start farms, create new colonies, and organize town governments. At a mass meeting in Savannah, he explained the meaning of titles, and afterward, in just one day, there were 5,000 acres assigned to the freedmen. Soon 40,000 people could be resettled on the property allotted them. "It was Plymouth colony repeating itself," exulted a sympathetic reporter.

Meanwhile, former planters had been lobbying Johnson to return land confiscated by the federal government and nullify Sherman's orders. Of course, the issue was not a simple one in any case: the question of whether confiscated land fell under the temporary or permanent jurisdiction of the federal government had not been resolved. To whom did the land belong? To the white planters who had abandoned it? What was the status of those planters? Had they been fullfledged citizens of the Union all along, or were they traitors who, once pardoned, were enfranchised members of the body politic? The freedmen were of course not any of those things; but did they have a moral claim and legal right to the land that they had worked for generations and that had been granted homesteading freedmen and women per Sherman's Special Field Order No. 15?

No friend to the freedman, President Johnson ordered General Howard to return the territory confiscated by the Treasury Department during the war, some 450,000 acres in all, to pardoned former Confederates even though freedmen had recently been resettled on much of it. Initially refusing to surrender abandoned or confiscated property to former rebels, even pardoned ones, Howard responded to Johnson's Amnesty Proclamation with Circular No. 13. It urged Bureau commissioners to exclude the forty-acre tracts already given to the freedmen. Johnson rescinded Howard's circular and again mandated that the land be restored to the now-pardoned former owners.

Saxton begrudgingly carried out the president's directive where the lands were unoccupied or on the mainland under his jurisdiction (particularly in upcountry South Carolina and Georgia), but he refused to dispossess the freedmen of their property in the Sea Islands. "I should break faith with the freedmen now by recommending the restoration of these lands," he hotly declared. "In my view, this order of General Sherman [Special Field Order No. 15] is as binding as a statute." Without a special order from Washington, he therefore refused the peremptory demands of former Charleston rebels to restore their land, and he protested to Howard, pointing out that the freedmen of the Sea Islands had raised more than $300,000 worth of cotton and had deposited almost $250,000 in the Freedmen's Savings Bank.

Over Saxton's protests, the cotton crop had been shipped to New York to be sold by the Treasury Department, which retained the proceeds from its sale. And with lands being returned to the former white owners, Saxton had no more sources of income with which to staff his huge district with agents or buy provisions, whether blankets, shoes, food, or medicine. One physician commented in anger that he thought the military "have conspired together not to furnish us but to drive us away." In Georgia, Saxton's agent, John Emory Bryant, who superintended the freedmen in the Augusta area, said that no doctors would staff the hospital he'd set up. Many freedmen of the Sea Islands were fleeing to places such as Savannah, which already teemed with refugees who had no clothes, no shelter, no work, no prospects.

More soldiers were going home, leaving General Saxton understaffed. Besides, many of the military men now sent South were far more prejudiced than the former rebels. So it also seemed to Laura Towne, a teacher in the Sea Islands, who noted that they "only care to make the blacks work—being quite unconcerned about making the employers pay."

White folk who had supported the Union weren't much better off. "Yankees and negroes are all the rage," a former planter from Hilton Head spat out in disgust. Traveling south after the war, Whitelaw Reid listened to Unionists in Atlanta explain, "We are in no sense upheld or encouraged by the Government. Public sentiment is against us because we opposed the war; or, as they said, because we were tories; but, when the Government triumphed, we were secure because we were on the winning side. But you pardon Howell Cobb and every other leading secessionist; they at once become the natural leaders in an overwhelmingly secessionist community; and we, through mistaken kindness of our own Government, are worse ostracized to-day, in the new order of things, than we were during the war."

On October 19, 1865, General Saxton had to give up his fight against the government and "break the sad news to the people that they must lose their lands." Before the week was out, it was rumored that the "high-toned chivalry" of South Carolina had gone so far as to pressure Johnson to get rid of Saxton, which Johnson was happy to do although, for the moment, Stanton was backing him. Other military brass closely allied with the president, such as General James Fullerton, soon won Howard and Stanton to their side by inveighing against Saxton and others who worked with him in the Bureau. It was said that the black leader Martin Delany, for instance, had recently called a meeting to tell "the negroes in public speeches that the lands that they have been working upon belong to them and they should have it." Saxton and such men, it was said, were rabble-rousers who not only wanted to redistribute land to the freedmen but, even more dangerously, advocated radical measures such as universal suffrage.

For a short while General Howard tried to conciliate everyone, but he couldn't do it, for he had acceded to the Johnsonian idea that freedmen should go back to work for their former masters under lopsided employment contracts that bound them to a form of servitude not unlike slavery. The freedmen were punished if they broke the contracts; the white men were not. (In Mississippi, freedmen were not permitted to buy land.) And so with no land forthcoming (or having been taken away) and no jobs, they did return to work for the planters and, at best, became sharecroppers in the new labor system.

When, in 1866, Congress passed the Southern Homestead Act, it did set aside 40 million acres of poor soil in five Southern states for purchase by loyal whites or freed blacks; but former slaves had no money to buy the land, so they often had to work other people's farms. Corralled into gangs not unlike what men and women endured during slavery, they received, instead of wages, a tiny share of the crops—to be divided among the entire labor force. In addition, all too frequently planters or merchants extended credit at high interest to the sharecropper for supplies or equipment or took a lien on the coming crop; the lien only perpetuated a cycle of indebtedness and poverty, generation after generation.

To a Southerner writing in *DeBow's Review*, however, these freedmen were a lazy bunch, mostly drunk, defiant, and well armed—as well as deluded by the promises of such men as General Saxton. Thwarted in his efforts to redistribute land (particularly on the mainland) and painfully aware that pardoned Southerners were flocking back to it, Saxton had instituted a system of short-term labor contracts to protect the freedmen from exploitation. But freedmen often refused to work for the planters for fear they would not be paid and worse: "The negro believes that his former master wishes to make him a slave again, and has no confidence in his promises," he pointed out. "He desires particularly not to make any contract or to work for his old master, preferring to work for northern men. Northern men can get all the labor they require, with capital; but not so with the former slaveholders; the only way this feeling can be broken down and a mutual confidence restored is to give the negro all his rights." Yet according to the Southerner, by providing the Sea Islanders with land and then employment contracts, Saxton had sowed discontent among them; they now petulantly refused to sign contracts or to work: such was the result of "this unnecessary and unnatural disturbance of their proper [black and white] relations."

In December 1865 the weary but determined Saxton proposed that Congress appropriate sufficient funds to purchase all the estates seized under Sherman's Special Field Order No. 15 and that it offer the former white owners a choice of receiving a fair price for the property or the property itself; if the latter, congressional funds should be given as long-term loans to freedmen wishing to purchase farmland elsewhere. His proposal was ignored. Commanded to set up a board of white men to oversee contractual arrangements between landowners and freedmen, Saxton then outraged the whites by appointing a black man, who declared that he wouldn't approve any contracts and nothing but ownership of land would satisfy the freedmen. The lawyer and former Confederate officer William Whaley loudly declared he would rather his lands "sink to perdition than a black man compose one of the Board." Other white men, among them former governor William Aiken (once a major slave owner), Benjamin Perry (the present governor), and a planter and former slave owner, William Henry Trescot, lobbied President Johnson to fire Saxton. "Here is the proof," said Trescot, "of the utter impossibility of doing anything as long as he controls the department of the bureau."

Saxton was offered another position but said he "would not touch [it] with a thousand foot pole." Rumors flew: General Howard had advised Saxton to resign because Saxton's radical views stood in the way of Johnson's—and Howard's—Reconstruction policies. ("O that we had Ben Butler at the head of the Bureau," cried Saxton's brother.) Saxton was offered a promotion. He refused. He said he preferred "loss of rank to loss of honor."

On January 22, 1866, Saxton was relieved of his duties in the Sea Islands. "It is a triumph of the rebels, which they have long labored to attain," said his brother, "—one of the 'compromises' which have been the bane of the nation for years past." Before he left, he restored no land to former rebels; after he left, he learned that the freedmen had been turned out of their houses, and in a matter of months

430,104 acres of land previously under the jurisdiction of the Freed-men's Bureau had been surrendered to pardoned owners. Trescot had worked hard to block any validation of the Sherman land titles and was largely successful. Ultimately, freedmen holding titles received from the government nothing more than the right to rent or pur-chase twenty-acre plots on government-held land. "All subsequent attempts to define the personal rights of the negro to the land were fated to come to naught," wrote a commissioner after the fact, "by the final policy of the Government, on the return of the Southern people to their old possessions."

Collecting their pennies to buy Saxton a farewell gift, the freed-men of the Sea Islands protested his dismissal. Had he been sacked, they wanted to know, "because he delivered the poor that cried, the fatherless, and him that had none to help him? Was it because the blessing of the poor, him that was ready to perish, came upon this Christian soldier, and he caused the widow's heart to sing for joy? Was it because he was eyes to the blind and feet to the lame?" They respected him, his patience, his solicitude, and his perseverance in "securing to every man the benefit of law and order; our schools, printing-press, churches, our bank at Beaufort, with a deposit today of $240,000, and his impartial decisions on the labor questions, vs., a fair day's work for a fair day's labor, stand as constant memorials before us of his actual worth, as a civil and military ruler."

But Saxton was flayed in the press—the Northern press. He and his administration were lambasted by two of Howard's subordi-nates and Johnson allies, Generals Fullerton and James B. Steedman, the latter "a rough character with no sympathy for the negroes," as Howard later recalled. Because neither man agreed with Saxton or cared for the Freedmen's Bureau, Johnson had sent them south on a fact-finding mission during which they had learned that blacks vigor-ously supported the Bureau. "If the Freedman Bureau was removed, a colored man would have better sense than to speak a word in behalf of the colored man's rights, for fear of his life," said a black leader in Wilmington, North Carolina. That didn't matter to Steedman or Fullerton. They alleged widespread corruption and malfeasance among Bureau commissioners from Virginia to Texas (though they did not visit Kentucky, Tennessee, or Arkansas and did not report on the successes in Alabama). And as for General Saxton, they were damning. "The result of Gen. Saxton's administration, at any rate, based as it was on such a mistaken policy, was meretricious in the extreme," concluded the Johnson-sympathizing *New York Times*, "and well nigh disastrous to the interests of both races."

His dander up, Saxton fought back publicly—a way to secure equality for the freedmen by other means. Fullerton and Steedman had spent a mere twenty-four hours in the Sea Islands, Saxton charged; they interviewed mainly half-reconstructed rebels and in their final report made no mention of the regiments of black soldiers he had organized and who demonstrated that former slaves could and would fight; no mention of the cotton he had raised to finance his administration; no mention of the revenue he had sent to the Treasury; no mention of the savings bank he had established where the freedmen deposited their earnings; no mention of the schools he had started. And as he would explain to the joint Committee on Reconstruction, there was no real reformation among Southerners—"that, in their own words, they are overpowered, not conquered, and that they regard their treason as a virtue, and loyalty as dishonorable."

It was too late. Replacing Saxton was the bushy-haired general Robert Kingston Scott, formerly a feverish gold seeker, both in Mexico and in South America, who had prospected with little success. Scott had then moved on to speculation in real estate, and when the war began, he raised a regiment. Like Howard, he rode with Sherman through Georgia and the Carolinas, leaving destruction and a displaced refugee population in his path. Now, these underfed refugees—the lands once promised them repossessed—were piling up their household goods in heaps and tying their smaller goods in blankets. They were often homeless, their cows and goats wandering the countryside and stalked by guerrillas with blackened faces wearing Union uniforms.

Wendell Phillips was angry. The South was victorious: we may have conquered Southern armies, he said, but we have not conquered Southern values, Southern prejudice, or Southern determination. The freedman was not free. "After earning a dollar, may he keep it and invest it in land? That is for the white man to say. May he testify in court? Perhaps. May he sit in the jury box? It is not certain. May he marry with the common solemnity of that sacrament? Well, we do not know. May he learn to read a Bible? Well, we'll see. May he hear the dirge of his own children? Perhaps. May he go to the ballot box? Certainly not."

ANDREW JOHNSON HAD also asked General Grant to gather information about conditions in the South during a hasty five-day trip in December 1865, just before the Thirty-ninth Congress was to reconvene. When Grant returned to Washington—after one day in Raleigh, two in Charleston, and a day each in Savannah and Augusta—he submitted a bland, brief report. He advised against removing the military presence from the region although he did think that keeping black troops was inflammatory—and demoralizing (to the whites). And he steered clear of the controversies surrounding the Freedmen's Bureau except to say that giving confiscated land to former slaves had been a mistake, which is what men of property and standing in Charleston and Savannah and Augusta had told him.

The French correspondent Georges Clemenceau called Grant's milquetoast report nothing more than a prop in Johnson's theater of restoration.

It was a prop that Johnson sorely needed. He had already asked Major General Carl Schurz to travel to the former Confederacy to investigate the results of Reconstruction. When Johnson read Schurz's eloquent—and utterly scathing—report, Johnson supposedly quipped that his only error as president so far had been sending Schurz to the South. Grant's report was supposed to be the antidote to that of Schurz, but the damage had already been done.

Carl Schurz was a powerful antislavery leader determined to accomplish in America what he'd failed to do in Germany: fight successfully for democracy. Born in 1829 near Cologne, the brilliant émigré arrived in the United States from Paris, where he briefly worked as a correspondent after the failure of the German revolution and his near capture in 1848 by the Prussians against whom he'd been fighting. He temporarily returned to Germany, though, to mastermind the successful escape of a former teacher from prison, whom he spirited to England. He then sailed to America, married a wealthy Hamburg-born wife, and, after learning to speak and write flawless English, settled in Wisconsin in 1852, where he was admitted to the bar. Five years later, he was an antislavery candidate for lieutenant governor fluent in two languages, which made him an asset to German Americans and their spokesman. Losing by a tiny margin (200 votes), he remained active in politics, chaired the Wisconsin delegation to the Republican national convention in 1860, and so impressed Lincoln that he appointed Schurz minister to Spain. More important, the thin, wiry, intense Schurz became Lincoln's confidant.

After Fort Sumter, Schurz resigned his diplomatic post in order to join the Union army. He fought at the Second Battle of Bull Run, at Chancellorsville, and at Gettysburg, earning an uncertain reputation in the field but all the while believing the war must be fought for abolition as well as for the Union. Devastated by Lincoln's assassination, he held out hope for Johnson's administration, but his report on the conditions of the South was not what the new president wanted to hear.

Having traveled extensively throughout South Carolina, Georgia, Mississippi, Alabama, and the Gulf, Schurz produced a report of forty-six eloquent, well-reasoned, and well-corroborated arguments that thoroughly condemned Johnson's Reconstruction policies. He told of the unreconstructed Southerner who had apprehensively waited for reprisals but who had grown strong and defiant when none came. He told of the countless Southerners who still believed in the right of secession despite their swearing of loyalty oaths; treason did not seem odious to these men, who possessed no real national allegiance. He told how Yankees and, in particular, Union soldiers were still considered enemies, how acknowledged Southern Unionists lived a precarious life, how bands of highwaymen ruled the roads, and how cotton, horse, and cattle stealing went unchecked. Large numbers of freedmen still worked on plantations but were not remunerated; they were subject to unfair contracts, poor working conditions, and physical force. The white planters thought, in any case, that the system of free labor would never work—one Georgia planter, to prove his case, said that his black employee had actually refused to submit to a whipping. Other freedmen flocked to cities and seaports, where they were penniless, unemployed, and reviled. Codes and ordinances deprived the black population of the freedom of movement, the freedom to carry arms, the freedom to testify against accusers, the freedom to open a business, and in one strange case the ability to buy or sell goods without written consent. In more instances than one knew, black people were hanged, drowned, stabbed, or shot dead, though in South Carolina, at least, General Saxton had stood up to the planters who perpetrated violence against the freedmen. Non-slaveholding and landless whites were bitter and vindictive against the freedman and -woman, and if only certain people acted out their hatred by killing and maiming, those who did not kill or maim refused to stop those who did.

Still, Schurz was not unsympathetic to the white people he found in the South, a people stripped of means of self-support—particularly those who lost their plantations or whose farms were heavily mortgaged. He was aware of the many people, now insolvent, who had indirectly depended on these farms and plantations to keep their own businesses afloat since so much of the South's commerce was agriculture-based. He was aware too that the returning Confederate soldier did not find, as did his counterpart in the North, jobs or prosperity. He saw a carnival of ruin: homesteads destroyed, blackened chimneys aloft in open fields, farms devastated, families dressed in rags, boys and girls shoeless, entire communities exhausted. And these white communities were understandably suspicious of the change from slave to free labor.

Schurz then asked what he considered an eminently practical question: "If, as long as the change from slavery to free labor is known to the Southern people only by its destructive results, these people must be expected to throw obstacles in its way, would it not seem necessary that the movement of social 'reconstruction' be kept in the right channel by the hand of the power which originated the change, until that change can have disclosed some of its beneficial effects?"

Johnson answered no. Give the South back to the Southerners, he said.

As for the white population's complaints against the freedmen, Schurz laboriously countered such grievances about their refusal to work, their vagrancy, insolence, and their inability to honor contracts. Schurz paternalistically noted, with as much wonder as condescension, "Centuries of slavery have not been sufficient to make them the enemies of the white race. If in the future a feeling of mutual hostility should develop itself between the races, it will probably not be the fault of those who have shown such an inexhaustible patience under the most adverse and trying circumstances."

Schurz's conclusions—the ones that most angered President Johnson—were simple: "unadulterated free labor cannot be had at present, unless the national government holds its protective and controlling hand over it." And unadulterated free labor was essential to dignity and a new social order. This new order was one of human rights—which was to say suffrage: "A voter is a man of influence," the freedom-loving Schurz ardently declared; "small as that influence may be in the single individual, it becomes larger when that individual belongs to a numerous class of voters who are ready to make common cause with him for the protection of his rights."

Andrew Johnson refused to publish the report, most of which appeared in the *Boston Daily Advertiser* anyway and so pleased Charles Sumner that he arranged to have it appended to the same congressional document as Grant's report. For Schurz confirmed the worst fears of Sumner and those Republicans growing disenchanted, if not outright hostile, to what one of them called Johnson's proslavery policies. "*I* did think it was good policy to place some one living in a Southern state—who had been true—on the ticket and favored Johnson," said one early backer, "—for which the Lord forgive me." Said another, "A disastrous eclipse will come over affairs, & . . . he will bring the nation to shame."

And so Congress reconvened, Carl Schurz reminding its members a revolution was at hand. He may have lost the one in Germany, but his adopted country was the land of possibility, founded in the name of liberty. Yet he wasn't naive. Change would not come easily. "The power which originated the revolution," he said, "is expected to turn over its whole future development to another power which from the beginning was hostile to it and has never yet entered into its spirit, leaving the class in whose favor it was made completely without power to protect itself and to take an influential part in that development."

Power and powerlessness: the North needed to maintain and sustain the victory hard won on a four-year battlefield. "Nothing renders society more restless," Schurz warned, "than a social revolution but half accomplished."

(18)

AMPHITHEATRUM JOHNSONIANUM

Muggy weather in New Orleans in summer isn't particularly unusual, but the thickness in the air this morning comes from tension. It's Monday, July 30, 1866. Twenty-six members of a newly called Constitutional Convention will be meeting at the Mechanics' Institute at noon. They will talk about a new state constitution, one that might include black male suffrage. That makes people uneasy. Three days ago, at an interracial rally of some 1,500 people, speakers were calling for black male suffrage, which the conservative press reported as a call for revolution. It said that the dentist Anthony Dostie, a Radical Republican originally from Chicago, was telling the crowd to cover the streets in blood.

Something had to be done. And it had to be done that day.

THE CONSTITUTIONAL CONVENTION slated for July 30 was actually a reconvening of the Unionist one that had adjourned two years before, in 1864. That seemed extraordinary, especially to the New Orleans Democrats. But since a loophole in the state constitution allowed the convention's president to recall it, the convention would technically be legal. And Rufus K. Howell, a Louisiana Supreme Court associate justice and convention president pro tem, had issued the call because Louisiana governor J. Madison Wells very much wanted him to do just that.

Of course, the convention would need a quorum, which no one expected there would be—why would conservatives come to the convention, especially since they suspected its motives? To them, the convention was being recalled mainly to give black men the vote and to abolish the Black Codes: ratifying the Thirteenth Amendment for the purpose of reentering the Union had been one thing, they'd conceded, but enfranchising black men would be quite another. So the mayor of New Orleans, John T. Monroe, who had been elected while an unpardoned rebel (Johnson had quickly pardoned him), promised to break up the convention and arrest the delegates and charge them with subversion. What's more, Mayor Monroe had the support of the commanding officer in the Gulf, Major General Philip Sheridan, who regarded the planners of the convention as "political agitators and revolutionary men."

On July 30, while Sheridan was in Texas, around nine o'clock in the morning, one hundred fifty freedmen, many of them war veterans, marched up Burgundy Street and across Canal Street to the Mechanics' Institute on Dryades. Waving the Stars and Stripes, they pounded drums, and someone played the fife. Several of them had brought canes or walking sticks, and some were said to have pistols. On the side of the streets, police and spectators, perhaps 1,500 in number, were milling. The police, who ordinarily carried just nightsticks, were heavily armed.

With Sheridan away, General Absalom Baird was in charge. An elegant West Pointer from Pennsylvania, before the war Baird had been a teacher at his alma mater, where one of his favorite students had been the painter James McNeill Whistler. A veteran of the First Battle of Bull Run, the peninsular campaign, and Chickamauga, Baird had also fought at Chattanooga and in Sherman's Atlanta campaign. Worried, he'd heard from Mayor Monroe that the convention was going to disturb the peace, and though he didn't think the army should be directly involved, he had wired Stanton to ask for instructions. Stanton didn't answer. The only man to reply to Baird's request for instructions was Lieutenant Governor Albert Voorhies, a former Confederate official, who said that though no arrests should be made, General Baird should place troops on Dryades Street, outside the Mechanics' Institute, about an hour before the convention. Baird later claimed that he was told the convention would start at six in the evening—not at noon—so when the shooting started, he had no troops nearby. They were about three miles away.

Maybe Baird had been intentionally misinformed. It's hard to know. Information about what happened that day was contradictory. Twenty-six delegates did assemble at noon. The Reverend Dr. Horton opened the meeting with a prayer, but since there wasn't a quorum, the delegates decided to recess, hoping more of them would show up before long. Then they heard the popping sound of gunfire from outside.

There had evidently been a skirmish. One journalist later reported that he had seen "several negroes lying dead" on the sidewalk.

Someone had fired a weapon—a black man in the procession that had marched to the Mechanics' Institute? A policeman nearby? All of a sudden, it seemed, a dense white mob had formed. Wearing white handkerchiefs tied round their necks or their hats facing backward so they could recognize one another, the police and the white mob attacked the black marchers, firing at them and kicking and clubbing them where they fell. The marchers ran toward the Mechanics' Institute, hoping to take shelter there. The firemen arrived. They too attacked the marchers.

"I'll shoot down every damned son of a bitch in the building!" a white man yelled. "We'll go and tear down the Institute, and we'll get a cannon." The police in front of the Mechanics' Institute blasted out the windows, and together, the mob, the police, and the firefighters pushed open the doors of the building. The delegates inside picked up whatever they could lay their hands on. "It seemed ridiculous to me that men should with chairs, battings, and pieces of railings contend against an armed force, regularly organized," recalled one of the delegates. Black men scrambled up to the second story, but the police followed them, and soon more than two inches of blood were congealing on the floor. The uninjured jumped out of windows and were shot when they landed. The wounded were stabbed, their heads beaten with clubs.

The Reverend Dr. Horton waved the white handkerchief he'd tied on one of the little flags in the room. "Stop firing; we are non-combatants; if you want to arrest us, make any arrest you please, we are not prepared to defend ourselves," he shouted. "God damn you," replied one of the men in the mob. "Not one of you will escape from here alive." The reverend was shot in the arm, one of his fingers was broken, his skull was crushed by a brick, and he died the next day.

Later, when a congressional committee investigated the New Orleans mêlee, they heard that some men were shot while kneeling and praying for their lives; others were kicked, cudgeled, and stabbed after they were already dead. One old, gray-haired man walking at a distance from the Institute was shot through the head when a policeman riding in a buggy fired his gun from the carriage into a crowd of black men. Another policeman boarded a streetcar on Canal Street, aimed his gun at a black boy, and then dragged him onto the street, where he beat him. Bodies were stacked in carts. Whites and blacks were hauled off to jail in wagons and then thrown into small, rancid cells with the wounded, the dead, and the dying. That night, drunken white boys prowled the streets, breaking into homes. A son of former vice president Hannibal Hamlin, who happened to be in New Orleans that day, said, "I have seen death on the battlefield but time will erase the effects of that, the wholesale slaughter and the little regard paid to human life I witnessed here on the 30 of July I shall never forget." A reporter cried in horror, "It is 'Memphis'" all over again.

Memphis, early May, same year, 1866: During three days of violence, forty-six black men and women and two white men had been killed, and five black women had been raped, during an unmitigated assault on the black community by white mobs and white policemen. Homes, businesses, and churches had gone up in flames.

But cosmopolitan New Orleans? With its lacelike iron balustrades and narrow streets, its shuttered courtyards and courtly palms, its Acadians and Irish and its mixed-race elite, its commerce and its urbanity, its vast numbers of former slaves, its free people of color, and its lively and strategically significant port, New Orleans seemed a place of grace and pleasure. But it was a place of crime too, as well as simmering resentment: under Federal control since 1862, it was the city that Beast Butler had ruled with his crooked and steely fist.

Then, in 1864, Lincoln had contacted Michael Hahn, the Unionist governor of Louisiana, to ask him confidentially whether "some of the colored people may not be let in—as, for instance, the very intelligent, and especially those who have fought gallantly in our ranks." Not only did Lincoln wish to keep a Republican base of power in the South; he had begun a kind of reconstruction of his own. The "colored people," Lincoln had said, "would probably help, in some trying time to come, to keep the jewel of liberty within the family of freedom." The next year, and just days before his assassination, Lincoln had stood on the second-story balcony of the White House and told his audience—John Wilkes Booth included—in public what he'd told Hahn in private: that certain Louisiana blacks should be enfranchised.

After the war, Louisianans had been among the Confederates headed for Mexico, their filibustering dreams of yesteryear transformed but not quite dead; they hoped to acquire land, and some hoped to go to Brazil, where they could resurrect their shattered Southern way of life. A number of former slaveholders had stayed put, however, and by 1866, the state legislature was so full of ex-Confederates and secessionists that it was often called the "Rebel Legislature." Members included Duncan Kenner, the man who had traveled to Europe at Jefferson Davis's behest in a last-minute effort to save the Confederacy. President Johnson had issued a special pardon to Kenner, who, by the fall of 1865, had repossessed his plantation, recouped his war losses, including his sleek racehorses, and, sitting in

the state legislature, had sponsored bills regulating (black) labor. In-
vesting in sulfur mines, levee construction, banks, railroads, and real
estate, by the year of his death, 1887, Kenner was again one of the
wealthiest men in the South.

To mollify men such as Kenner and bolster the ancien régime,
Johnson had also ousted the assistant superintendent of the Freedmen's Bureau in Louisiana, a man who supported black suffrage, and
installed General Joseph S. Fullerton. Fullerton, one of the men who
had denounced Rufus Saxton, was charged with returning confiscated lands to pardoned Confederates and enforcing vagrancy laws
to keep freedmen from rural areas out of New Orleans. It was bad
enough to have black soldiers walking along the streets in their blue
uniforms; Fullerton didn't want poor, hungry, unemployed blacks
hanging around. The returning and embittered Confederate soldiers
hated them—and hated the government that had occupied their city
for so long. The Confederate veterans were welcomed, however, by
the police force, and by the time of the July 1866 riot, two-thirds of
the 550-man force were Confederate veterans.

The man who replaced Michael Hahn as governor, J. Madison
Wells, was a conservative Unionist who had campaigned for Stephen
Douglas in 1860, opposed secession, and served as lieutenant governor under Hahn, whose policies he would reverse, or so former Confederates believed, when Wells was elected governor in 1865. But
he swiftly lost the support of the rebel legislature, whose members
wanted to get rid of him and eliminate the Unionist state constitution of 1864. The legislature offered to nominate Wells for the U.S.
Senate and pack him off to Washington, but Wells refused.

Currying favor with the more radical Republicans, Wells decided
to back the idea of a new convention. It was he who had appointed
Judge R. K. Howell president pro tem so that the 1864 Constitutional Convention could be reconvened in 1866. After all, Wells reasoned, during the 1864 convention, the country had been at war and
many of the state's parishes hadn't been represented. He also said he
would issue writs of election for new delegates who advocated black

suffrage. This was their chance to pass it. He thus had two motives: to preserve the Republican Party in Louisiana, which was in danger of extinction, and to preserve the rights of the black population, which would in turn sustain the Republican Party.

So when black leaders and Republicans decided to reconvene the 1864 state Constitutional Convention, the Democrats of New Orleans were hostile, rancorous, edgy, and spoiling for a fight. The *New Orleans Daily Crescent* firmly declared, "It is our general belief, fixed and unalterable, that this country was discovered by white men, peopled by white men, defended by white men, and owned by white men, and it is our settled purpose that none but white men shall participate in its government." And those white men would stop, by force if need be, any convention bent on ousting them.

Which is what happened. On July 30, if federal troops had not arrived when they did—even as late as they did—the rioters would likely have killed all the freedmen and Union supporters in the city. The historian W. E. B. DuBois later concluded, "Reconstruction in Louisiana was a continuation of the Civil War."

General Sheridan rushed back to New Orleans. President Johnson let it be known that he wanted the mob to be found innocent of wrongdoing, which Sheridan could not in good conscience do. For within three hours, over one hundred men and women lay dead or dying and as many as three hundred were wounded, perhaps more. Grimly, Sheridan wrote a long telegram to General Grant, which the president released to the press—omitting a key passage in which Sheridan said that what had happened in New Orleans was unnecessary and atrocious murder. It had been "no riot," he had already told Grant. "It was an absolute massacre which was not excelled in murderous cruelty by that of Fort Pillow."

IN WASHINGTON, AT the opening of the Thirty-ninth Congress in December 1865, just seven months before the riot, Republicans had refused to seat the representatives from the former Confederate states.

Those states had to be "reconstructed," to use the Republican term; yet no one could quite define what the term meant, and no person or agency had been given the authority to define it. With more than a three-to-one majority in both houses, Republicans in Congress believed that they and not the president possessed that authority—especially since, to them, Johnson had been restoring the Confederacy, not reconstructing the Union.

Johnson continued to insist that the seceded states never actually seceded because they never had the right to do so. That's like saying a murderer could not kill because killing was against the law, quipped Thaddeus Stevens. But Johnson was intent on pursing his own course, which included his argument for states' rights. To Republicans, of course, states' rights was what the war had been fought to prevent: slavery packaged as a state prerogative. Inflexible, Johnson also insisted that civil rights fell under the purview of the state and not the federal government—and he bolstered his argument, paradoxically, by pardoning high-ranking ex-Confederates, restoring rebel property, appointing governors, and dispensing patronage. He wanted the reconstruction policy implemented to be his, or none at all.

And so he would not relent on the matter of citizenship for black men and women. The Thirteenth Amendment had not addressed the issue; in fact, by not granting blacks the right of citizenship, the Thirteenth Amendment left the door wide open for the Black Codes that soon followed, which prevented the almost four million freedmen and -women from making contracts, filing lawsuits, appearing in courts as plaintiffs, assembling—and, of course, voting. Thus the constitutional amendment that abolished slavery also managed to perpetuate the fatal compromise of the Constitution, which had counted the slave as only three-fifths of a person, and that is no person at all.

The Radicals in Congress approached the president privately, but to no avail. Johnson would not take suggestions about civil rights from the likes of Charles Sumner, a pretentious Boston intellectual who counted Longfellow among his close friends. Before Sumner left the president's office, Johnson had made his feelings clear by using

Sumner's hat as a spittoon. Johnson also met with a delegation of blacks, including Frederick Douglass, to talk about universal suffrage. That did not go well either. His racism unabating and unapologetic, the president afterward railed that Douglass was "just like any nigger, & he would sooner cut a white man's throat than not."

Johnson vetoed a bill to renew the Freedmen's Bureau in February 1866. He was on the attack. He declared he wouldn't sign a bill negatively affecting the South since the South was not represented in Congress, and since he was elected by all the people, North and South, he represented all of them, which was to say he also represented the South. In March, when Congress passed a civil rights bill intended to block the Black Codes by granting former slaves such rights as renting or owning property or making and enforcing contracts, Johnson again vetoed the bill. Congress overrode Johnson's veto, but it was clear that the Joint Committee on Reconstruction, formed in January, had to hammer out an amendment to define and protect citizenship constitutionally.

Duplicating the civil rights bill, the Fourteenth Amendment conferred citizenship (but not suffrage) on all those people born or naturalized in the United States, and it guaranteed these citizens due process. The amendment also reduced Southern representation in the House of Representatives—unless, that is, a state was to enfranchise black men. For though the amendment was intended to appease all the factions within the Republican Party (not everyone had agreed that suffrage could or should be mandated by the federal government), it also encouraged each state to grant suffrage to black males for the purposes of representation in Congress, which was of course based on the number of men allowed to vote.

The amendment's third section denied the vote to Confederate military personnel and former officeholders in the Confederacy until 1870. That too was a compromise measure, for a two-thirds vote of Congress could reinstate those former Confederates. The fourth section of the amendment declared Confederate debts null and void.

True, the amendment ignored the question of the confiscated land

and sidestepped the issue of universal suffrage—but did not preclude it, or so Republicans hoped. The amendment passed both houses of Congress in June. And in July, over the president's objection, Congress passed a new Freedmen's Bureau bill that extended and shored up the initial Freedmen's Bureau Act.

All that legislation meant that Congress was instituting its own plan of reconstruction by working out compromises between the radical and moderate Republicans—and in spite of the vetoes and the ire of the president.

"We have at last agreed upon a plan of reconstruction," Senator Grimes of Iowa sighed in relief. "It is not exactly what any of us wanted; but we were each compelled to surrender some of our individual preferences in order to secure anything, and by doing so became unexpectedly harmonious."

HARMONY SEEMED TO be the great theme of John Greenleaf Whittier's poem "Snow-bound: A Winter Idyll," which was published in early 1866 and, by the time of the New Orleans massacre, had sold an impressive 20,000 copies.

Though Whittier had written such popular wartime ballads as "Barbara Frietchie," the abolitionist Quaker seemed now to conceal the war and its complicated aftermath under a blanket of forgetful snow. "Snow-bound" was a mawkish hymn to childlike innocence—or so critics later interpreted the poem. But Whittier, born in poverty, knew that childhood bliss had never existed—it certainly hadn't for the slave—and knew too that there was much work to be done. "There is no possibility of a safe reconstruction of the States," he declared, "without his [the black man's] vote."

Rather than an exercise in escapism, "Snow-bound" is an elegiac postwar meditation on loss: the loss of friends, the loss of youth, the loss of blinkered innocence. It is also a statement of faith that a new generation

Shall Freedom's young apostles be,
Who, following in War's bloody trail,
Shall every lingering wrong assail;
All chains from limb and spirit strike,
Uplift the black and white alike.
Scatter before their swift advance
The darkness and the ignorance,
The pride, the lust, the squalid sloth,
Which nurtured Treason's monstrous growth,
Made murder pastime, and the hell
Of prison–torture possible.

Whittier had not forgotten the darkness, ignorance, and pride that had caused the war, and he too was disgusted with the president and the president's fantasy of a prelapsarian white America. "I have been opposed to impeachment hitherto," said Whittier, "but it may be necessary yet." And then there was the president's embarrassing, Barnum–like stumping tour, an unprecedented spectacle of self-promotion widely known as a "Swing Around the Circle." In the late summer, Johnson traveled across the country to campaign for himself and against the Fourteenth Amendment. "If he left Washington the ninth part of a man," Whittier remarked, "what a pitiful decimal fraction he brings back."

General Grant and Admiral David Farragut, along with Gideon Welles and William Seward, had accompanied Johnson in his Swing. Uncomfortable and pleading illness, which detractors took to mean that he was drunk, Grant often declined to appear on the platform with the president. Wanting to distance himself from Johnson, the popular general reportedly said that he "didn't like attending a man who was making speeches at his own funeral." And though he tried to stay nonpartisan, he told his wife that he considered Johnson and his speeches "a National disgrace."

The appearance of such heroes as Grant at his side was of no help to Johnson, who anyway compared himself to Jesus Christ (they both pardoned sinners) and who answered hecklers yelling out "New Orleans!" that the blood of the New Orleans dead wasn't on his hands but on those of Thad Stevens, Charles Sumner, and Wendell Phillips. And again, in Cleveland, when someone shouted, "Hang Jeff Davis," the president shouted back, "Why not hang Thad. Stevens and Wendell Phillips?"

Johnson was turning himself into a buffoon. "If there is any man that ought to hang," Carl Schurz said, "it is Andrew Johnson." Senator John Sherman told his brother that the president had "sunk the Presidential office to the level of a grog-house." Democrats shuddered too. "Does Seward mean to kill him off by this tour?" asked one of them.

Johnson was doing the job himself. Three members of his cabinet resigned their posts after he approved the formation of a new National Union Party (the "coppery" party, as one magazine writer called it) with Democrats such as Clement Vallandigham. The party was the intended antidote for Radical Republicanism, and though it attracted conservative Republicans such as Henry Raymond of *The New York Times* to its Philadelphia convention—Vallandigham stayed away—one of the vice presidents of that convention was the former Confederate general Nathan Bedford Forrest of Fort Pillow infamy.

No new national party was formed. New Orleans and the "Swing Around the Circle" had irreparably damaged Johnson. Republicans swept into office in the congressional elections in November, gaining a two-thirds majority in the House and the Senate. New Orleans had been proof that his policy had failed, was failing, would fail. He was weak, vain, and vulgar. The London *Spectator* called him blind and crazy. James Gordon Bennett and his conservative *New York Herald* abandoned him. He was a bully, a fool, an autocrat. He had usurped power not delegated to him by appointing provisional Southern governors, for instance, and prescribing the terms of reconstruction, such as pardons for former rebels. These were misdemeanors if not high crimes, and the man was responsible for the New Orleans massacre, make no mistake. The noisy Beast, Benjamin Butler, began to call for the president's impeachment.

Thomas Nast, the popular caricaturist for the widely circulating *Harper's Weekly*, lambasted Johnson as "King Andy," the regent presiding over the promised execution of Thaddeus Stevens, whose head is on the chopping block. Waiting in line behind him are such other leaders as Wendell Phillips, Charles Sumner, Benjamin Butler, and Anna Dickinson. At the end of the line is Nast himself and his sketchbook.

Born in Germany in 1840, the rather dapper and plump idealist had been hired by *Harper's Weekly* in 1862 as an illustrator, and though he had also been drawing for magazines such as *Frank Leslie's Illustrated News*, *Harper's Weekly* would be his main forum. During the war, he was befriended by officers such as Philip Sheridan, who invited him to set up shop in his headquarters, and he drew warm campfires and domestic scenes intended to bolster the morale of both soldier and civilian. "Thomas Nast has been our best recruiting agent," Lincoln reputedly said. He invented Santa Claus in 1862 as a jolly fat man draped in the Stars and Stripes.

After the war, combining coruscating satire with a bit less patriotic corn, Nast often referred in his cartoons to the New Orleans bloodbath. In a cartoon he called "The Massacre of the Innocents," the imperial Andy, wrapped in a ceremonial toga, impassively watches the slaughter below from his balcony seat in the "Amphitheatrum Johnsonianum." A hawk-nosed Secretary Seward bends over him, his minister-in-waiting. Secretary of the Navy Welles leans over the balustrade, and with his long curls partly concealed under his helmet, General George Armstrong Custer looks on. In the lower left hand of the cartoon, General Ulysses Grant holds back General Philip Sheridan, who seems to want to help.

Nast joined forces with the humorist writer David Ross Locke, better known to newspaper readers as Petroleum Vesuvius Nasby, to publish *Andy's Trip to the West, Together with a Life of Its Hero*. Nast and Locke together ridiculed Johnson as the president who throws the Constitution out the window while a citizen asks, in one cartoon, "How about New Orleans?" As Nasby's Johnson explained, "I have great confidence in the American people, all except Members of Congress, Unionists and Niggers; they are all traitors, and I mean to fight them with the help of General Grant."

WHETHER THE TAILOR from Tennessee had been seduced by the planter class he had despised, whether his racism had upended his judgment, whether his Democratic animus against the Republican Party was deep-rooted and long-standing, whether he was trying to do right by the light in which he saw it, or whether his combination of obstinacy, paranoia, and vanity had prevented him from working with Congress is difficult to say.

Yet the matter went deeper than petty policies, personalities, or any strict constructionist reading of the Constitution. Those were important issues, to be sure, but there was also a feeling of postwar disquiet. The corpses had been tallied, or they were being tallied. The figures were horrifying. Clara Barton was looking for missing soldiers. Hundreds of thousands of unknown soldiers lay in undocumented, unknown places. "These poor men have lost not only their lives," said Barton, "but the very record of their death."

Those in the North who had fought in the war, those who had sewn for it and made bandages and scoured the bloody fields for their loved ones, or those who had just supported it needed to feel the war had meaning. And for the sake of those who perished in unmarked graves, it was necessary to verify again that theirs had been a great cause, a real cause, an important and just cause. "What like a bullet," Melville exclaimed, "can undeceive!" To James Russell Lowell, then, the war had been fought—it had had to be fought—"as an effort of the ideal America."

"If we had looked upon the war as a mere trial of physical strength between two rival sections of the country," Lowell said, "we should have been the first to oppose it, as a wicked waste of treasure and blood. But it was something much deeper than this."

Johnson had spoiled that, what "with his paltry offer of 'my policy,' in exchange for the logical consequences of all this devotion and this sacrifice. What is any one man's policy," Lowell continued, "and especially any one weak man's policy, against the settled drift of a nation's conviction, conscience, and instinct?" Even the veteran Oliver Wendell Holmes, Jr., the person most often associated with postwar skepticism, could lace his cynicism with nostalgia. War had been fought by men touched with fire. "To fight out a war," Holmes said, "you must believe in something and want something with all your might."

Conviction in the rightness of the cause despite the carnage and cruelty that resulted had to be an article of faith maintained, and Johnson seemed to undermine the very reasons for the war. That was intolerable. And it might account for why certain Republicans began to seek the inexpedient expedient of pushing him out of office when another presidential election would soon be on the horizon.

Thaddeus Stevens, the acerbic congressman from Pennsylvania, who hurled epithet after cutting epithet at Johnson then and later, became the poster boy for Radical Republican obduracy. A clever parliamentarian with an acid tongue, a sincere abolitionist who believed secession to be treason and slavery a moral outrage, Stevens had in his long career favored colonization, but he deplored the Fugitive Slave Act and fought it with force and rigor. He unfailingly protected runaway men and women in his native Pennsylvania and in the 1852 Christiana case had courageously defended the men charged with killing and wounding would-be captors of runaways. For that apostasy, he had briefly lost his congressional seat. But when he returned to the House of Representatives during the war, he was the chairman of the powerful Ways and Means Committee, which oversaw the difficult task of financing the war, and as its chair, worked hard to make sure that former slaves were armed—and freed.

Afterward, he was the first chairman of the Appropriations Committee, which monitored Reconstruction expenditures, and later, as a member of the Joint Committee on Reconstruction, he fought hard and consistently for black suffrage and equal rights. As a result, he was the butt of a great deal of ridicule and opprobrium. Considered the kind of ideologue whose bleak face, Lincoln once said, was always "set Zionsward," Stevens was certain of himself and also an unafraid, unprejudiced, formidable, and farsighted leader. He insisted on black suffrage, on the distribution of confiscated land to the freedmen, and on Southern economic development—and not necessarily for the benefit of the Northern speculator or entrepreneur, though he was accused of that. When his colleague from Pennsylvania William Kelley importuned Congress to aid a Northern railroad, claiming that it would help impoverished freedmen, Stevens tartly asked, "May I ask my friend how many of these starving people he thinks are stockholders in this road?"

Stevens continued to press the issue of land redistribution regardless of opposition from the more moderate members of his own party. The redistribution of land was a radical measure, for it would drastically realign the propertied classes in the South. *The New York Times* protested that land redistribution would also "strip the Southern [white] people of the little property the war has left them" and "prolong the derangements of industry, the suspension of business and the general prostration and suffering of the Southern states." Stevens believed, however, that racism motivated such arguments. "A deep-seated prejudice against races has disfigured the human mind for ages," he said. "For two centuries it has oppressed the black man and held him in bondage after white slavery had ceased to exist. Now it deprives him of every right in the Southern States. We have joined in inflicting these wrongs."

No more. "This doctrine of human equality may be unpopular with besotted ignorance," he declared. "But, popular or unpopular, I shall stand by it until I am relieved of the unprofitable labors of earth." He was true to his word. As one historian later noted, when Stevens died, so did an abiding commitment to racial justice.

Because of that commitment, Stevens was described as a ferocious character straight out of Hawthorne, his "whole countenance," said one contemporary, "from the grand arched forehead to the hard chin . . . the very ideal of cold, pitiless intellect." And in spite of his great commitment to social justice and a better life for the poor, powerless and abused, his prevailing mood was one of hopelessness. Just before his death, when he learned that the cemetery plot he had purchased in Lancaster, Pennsylvania, did not allow black men and women to be buried there, he sold the plot and bought one in the integrated Schreiner Cemetery near Lancaster, stipulating that the inscription on his gravestone read "I repose in this quiet and secluded spot, not from any natural preference for solitude, but finding other cemeteries limited by charter rules as to race, I have chosen it that I might be enabled to illustrate in my death the principles which I advocated through a long life— equality of man before his Creator."

Yet for years Stevens would be remembered as a diabolical revolutionary who, along with radical senators such as Ben Wade, waged a fanatic's campaign against property owners in an effort to unite blacks and poor whites against the planter class. The mixed-race (then called mulatto) woman living with him could not have been his housekeeper but must have been his mistress; and his clubfoot, a birth defect, was surely the sign of the devil. When the novelist Thomas Dixon and the filmmaker D. W. Griffith portrayed him, thinly disguised, in *The Clansman* and in *The Birth of a Nation*, he appeared as a scowling cripple of lascivious tastes and pernicious intent who wore an awful wig atop his tyrannical head.

ALTERNATIONS OF GRIEF and jubilation, disillusion and high moral purpose—what Melville called wail and triumph in his poetic *Battle-Pieces*, published in 1866—surged through the North after Appomattox and Lincoln's death. Whitman recalled the white skeletons of young men, "debris and debris of all the slain soldiers of the war," but he also remembered them in the "glad serenades" of meaning, eternity, nature, regeneration. It was not senseless death if meaning could be wrested from it—first, in retribution, with the executions of the alleged Lincoln conspirators and the Andersonville prison commandant, Captain Wirz.

The craving for such overt retribution did not last, and in fact, Andrew Johnson and opponents of the Radical Republicans accused the friends of the freedmen of desiring only vengeance, not justice. Meaning had to be found elsewhere. For Johnson, it was in a restored white Union. For the Radicals, it was in Reconstruction, suffrage, fairness.

In the South, where there was little jubilation, meaning would be located elsewhere: in the return of home rule. For in the South there was poverty and untold distress among white and black, and with such poverty and distress came anger, violence, the blood on the streets of Memphis and New Orleans, the bashed heads, the hardened hearts. In Columbia, South Carolina, which had been burned, the poet Henry Timrod told a friend in 1866 that for the last year his life had been one of *"beggary, starvation, death, bitter grief, utter want of hope!"* He had been selling furniture and heirlooms to buy food: "we have eaten two silver pitchers, one or two dozen silver forks, several sofas, innumerable chairs, and a huge—bedstead!!" The next year, just months before he died of tuberculosis, he wrote the ode to the Confederate dead recited at Magnolia Cemetery in Charleston, a poem commemorating the valorous "martyrs of a fallen cause," never to be forgotten.

The elegiac Timrod was not alone in sprinkling perfume over the defeated South. The former secessionist and prolific writer Edward Pollard produced his best-selling version of what had happened in *The Lost Cause*, explaining how the garish and clattering North had coveted power and wealth while the South had defended liberty, individuality, honor. And slavery? It had been nothing more than a pretext for war, Pollard claimed; the war's real cause had been the incompatibility of separate civilizations.

To Pollard that remained the case: the North seeking power, the South a stalwart champion of liberty. "The extreme Black Republican party" aimed "to disfranchise the whole Southern people, to force negro suffrage upon the South, to prevent the South from being represented in Congress so as to perpetuate the power of the

Radicals, and afford them the means of governing the Southern States as conquered and subjugated territories." As Henry Timrod had said, Thaddeus Stevens, if he could, would outlaw the changing seasons.

For Pollard and the others who would write magnolia-scented history, Lee had been nobler in defeat than Grant in his victory, Lincoln's assassin had been indefensible but brave, the Confederates were the finer men and, best of all, the South had abandoned the contest of the last four years only to resume it in a wider arena: in its literature, manners, intellect, refinement, in its very civilization. Defeat was victory, failure the measure of grace, fortitude the hope and watchword of the future. As James Branch Cabell would say, "No history is a matter of record; it is a matter of faith."

With Pollard succoring the destitute and defeated Southerner, the Confederacy and its cause were now writing history. Meanwhile, Pollard gave the Northerner a warning. "Civil wars, like private quarrels," he cautioned, "are likely to repeat themselves."

(19)

POWER

ociety in America was always trying, almost as blindly as an earthworm, to realize and understand itself," Henry Adams would reflect in old age. Certainly it was true in 1868, when Adams was thirty: a protracted war had freed the slaves, cost 750,000 people their lives, killed one president, and triggered an acrimonious debate about the concept of citizenship. The devastated South had been partitioned into military districts, which were policed by federal generals. A sitting president was facing impeachment charges. All that had been unthinkable back in 1861, when Adams had been headed for the Court of St. James's in London, where his father, Charles, Sr., was the U.S. ambassador for the duration of the war.

At the time, Fort Sumter had just been fired upon, but young Adams and his father, the descendants of two presidents, had assumed that the war would be of short duration and the earth would not shake. After all, the United States was still largely an agrarian nation ruled by men of goodwill, like themselves; its industry was respectable and profitable but not ostentatious, like themselves; the railway system was regional and unexceptional, the South was strong, everyone knew his place, and Boston was the hub of the cultural universe, at least according to its residents. Adams and his father were wrong, all wrong.

The war lasted four years and changed everything. Carl Schurz measured the change in terms of freedom for the former slave, but Henry Adams would say that he weighed change in terms of power, raw power, the power of coal, of iron, of steam. In places such as Lawrence, Massachusetts, the drab brick factories near the Merrimack River produced man-made shoes by the hundreds each day; the stockyards of Chicago were famous for their prosperous stench, and the mining camps in the new state of Nevada seemed to gush gold and silver. Ships, firearms, textiles, wheat, corn, beef, railroads, and railroad lines, as well as copper and quartz and coal; massive oil production, steel manufacture and the discovery of new ore deposits, the burgeoning meatpacking and agricultural industries, to say nothing of powerful industrialists and financiers: the war had created a huge demand for all kinds of items, from uniforms and boots to bullets and boats, and though those items had been manufactured before the war, the war had created new, ravenous markets, new inventions, new forms of standardization in production, and new entrepreneurs and swindlers.

Adams realized that he was out of place in this new world. His inheritance had been political power, which he understood as moral power, and here he now was, small and fastidious and confronting a world not of moral force or of what he considered moral force but of material might. "The truth is," Senator John Sherman had told his brother the general in 1865, "the close of the war with our resources unimpaired gives an elevation, a scope to the ideas of leading capitalists, far higher than anything ever undertaken in this country before. They talk of millions as confidently as formerly of thousands."

If a civil war had divided the country, it had also united it. In 1862 Congress chartered the Union Pacific Railroad with the Pacific Railway Act, and it finally passed the Homestead Act, which set aside 160 acres of surveyed land, per applicant, in the western territories for purposes of settlement and improvement. That was a boon to a population made increasingly mobile by the new railroads. Two years later, in 1864, Lincoln reported that twenty miles of track for a transcontinental railroad had just been laid in California; it wasn't much, but it was the beginning of what would be a national bonanza, particularly because a second Pacific Railway Act, in 1864, allocated $50 million worth of guaranteed government bonds to the railroads for thirty years and also provided the railways with land grants. That the donated land often belonged to the Indians was a question that would cause more war, but for now, it all looked good to financiers, land developers, and territorial governments.

With the bygone imperative "Go west, young man," made far easier by the 35,000 miles of track taking that young man wherever he wished to go, to Henry Adams the railroad had changed everything. "The generation between 1865 and 1895 was already mortgaged to the railways," Adams said, "and no one knew it better than the generation itself." Henry's brother Charles Francis, Jr., a veteran of Antietam and Gettysburg who had also served under Rufus Saxton in South Carolina, turned his attention to the railroad, first in terms of reform and then as president of the Union Pacific, in which he owned a great deal of stock; by the end of his life he had amassed a small fortune from the railroad and related industries. The multimillionaire Cornelius Vanderbilt, the steamship magnate, began to consolidate railroad lines between New York and Buffalo along the old Erie Canal and then moved them farther west, to Illinois and Michigan. Later he could transport his passengers from New York to Omaha, and eventually he controlled more than four thousand miles, having graduated from commodore to railroad baron. Henry Villard, the journalist who had climbed a tree to see the action at the Battle of Bull Run, acquired the Northern Pacific in later years after gobbling up the Oregon Steam Navigation Company and the Oregon Steamship Company; he too built an empire. Retired general George B. McClellan lived on his income from stock in the Ohio & Mississippi Railroad. In 1865 the former Confederate P. G. T. Beauregard became president of the New Orleans, Jackson & Mississippi Railroad. With far less success, William Rosecrans invested in Mexican railroads, and John Frémont, dreaming of a Southern transcontinental line, invested heavily in several railroad lines over which he soon lost control.

As early as 1843, with his deep-dyed pessimism, Nathaniel Hawthorne had satirized the railroad as the nice new conveyance that lightened the pilgrim's heavy load and let everyone live everywhere and nowhere, both at the same time. Henry David Thoreau was quick to notice that the tracks of the railroad in Concord, Massachusetts, lay perilously close to the gemlike Walden Pond. "By means of railroads and steamboats and telegraphs," he wrote in his journal, "the country is denaturalized—farmer becomes a market capitalist," and in *Walden* he wondered, "But if we stay at home, and mind our business, who will need railroads? We do not ride upon the railroad; it rides upon us."

Yet Walt Whitman's great poem "Song of Myself," published the same year as *Walden*, was a railroading of people, place, and time, all crisscrossed in the poet's capacious imagination. Railroads put people back on track too, uniting us. "We have bound the sister-states together with innumerable iron-bound railways," the poet exulted in 1858, and in his poem "Passage to India," written after the war, he celebrated "the Pacific railroad surmounting every barrier" and the "continual trains of cars winding along the Platte carrying freight and passengers." It was a new day, a postwar day of national promise.

And not just metaphorically: on May 10, 1869, at Promontory Summit, Utah, the Central Pacific Railroad met the Union Pacific Railroad, and their president, Leland Stanford, drove a special spike into the last rail tie with a silver hammer. "May God continue the unity of our Country as this Railroad unites the two great Oceans of the world" were the words inscribed on the Golden Spike, which was wired to telegraph lines so the nation could hear the sound of silver and golden unity, east coast to west.

But the railroad had also helped sunder the country, albeit indirectly. The idea of a transcontinental railroad had motivated Stephen Douglas. Known as a steam engine in breeches, Douglas had been angling for a route through his home state of Illinois; its terminus would be Chicago, once, that is, the Nebraska Territory was organized into states, which Douglas naively thought could happen without a hitch—hence, his ill-conceived, self-interested Kansas-Nebraska bill. The passage of that bill, which he promoted with his passion for popular sovereignty, helped divide the country, doom the Democrats, spawn Republicans, and propel the country into war. And certainly the railroad had been essential to that war, facilitating the movement of huge numbers of troops and munitions and supplies, particularly in the North. Though railroads were destroyed, mainly in the South—Sherman's neckties the sorry symbols of their destruction—and not quite 7,000 miles of track were laid down there after the war, the federal government amply helped Northern railroads, according to one historian, breed like rabbits.

Charles Francis Adams, Jr., pointed out that since "trade dominates the world, and the railroads dominate trade," the railroad tycoon's "object has been to make himself the virtual master of all by making himself absolute lord of the railways." Why not? With the railroad came capital, banks, the manufacture of iron and steel, technicians, engineers, new shipping and distribution networks, and inevitably more than a tad of corruption. Huge land grants, charters, military contracts, and a great deal of money were made available to the railroads, resulting in what became, as Vernon Parrington would later call it, a "Great Barbecue."

A barbecue, yes; but the making of money wasn't the sole great expectation. "I am duly thanking Heaven that I live here and in this age," said the journalist Edwin L. Godkin, editor in chief of the weekly magazine *The Nation*, whose first issue had appeared on July 6, 1865. Brave young warriors, recently discharged from the military, thought they could "do their country a great deal of good," said Henry James's sister, Alice—especially in the South. Northern philanthropists encouraged these young warriors: go South, young man, you who fought in the war and do not now know what to do. Go South, and we will capitalize you, and you will grow rich. Prosperity was power, declared John Andrew, the wartime governor of

Massachusetts. Prosperity would convince the Southerner, as only money could, to guarantee black men and women their rights; prosperity would protect the black worker against Southern supremacists. Andrew established the American Land Company and Agency to supply Northern capital to the South; he and other like-minded Northern philanthropist entrepreneurs firmly believed that the South simply needed "the emigration of the Yankees and Yankee energy."

As many as 30,000 young men went South to manage, lease, or buy plantations to make money, to help the freedmen, or both. Despite having encountered unreconstructed rebels during his postwar southern tour, the journalist Whitelaw Reid leased three plantations in Louisiana and Alabama and hired at least 150 freedmen. Harriet Beecher Stowe sank $10,000 into a freedmen's colony, a former cotton plantation called Laurel Grove, in Florida, south of Jacksonville, to be run by her son Frederick, who had been wounded at Gettysburg. But Frederick had recovered from his injury slowly, if at all, and, addicted to alcohol and morphine, he walked off the plantation one day. After heading out to San Francisco, he disappeared, never to be heard from again. Whitelaw Reid gave up too, although more profitably, for during his Southern stay he wrote two books, and when he went back east, he returned to Greeley's *Tribune*, which he would someday run.

Then there was Garth Wilkinson "Wilkie" James, a brother of William, Henry, and Alice, a veteran of the 54th Massachusetts, the black regiment under the command of Robert Gould Shaw. Gentle and genial, Wilkie had attended school at Concord Academy, which was run by Franklin Sanborn (the Sanborn who had been one of John Brown's not-so-secret Secret Six) and where his classmates included two of John Brown's daughters. Wilkie had left school at the age of seventeen to enlist in the Massachusetts 54th. Wounded badly in his side and left foot at Fort Wagner, where he was one of the few survivors, the idealistic teenager had nonetheless rejoined his unit and managed to march victoriously into Charleston in 1865. After the war, he and his brother Robertson ("Bob"), a veteran of another

black regiment, moved to Florida, about ten miles north of Gainesville. With several other veterans, they formed a colony named for
George H. Gordon, a Massachusetts general; they had no experience
in managing a community, much less in farming—they had been too
young for Brook Farm—but they planned to run a plantation with a
labor force of freedmen.

Financed by his father and with the assistance of such Boston
businessmen as John Murray Forbes, Wilkie eventually invested
more than $40,000 in land and cotton. Employing thirty ex-slaves,
he helped build a schoolhouse, hired a teacher, sent for Bibles, bought
cattle and tools, and set up a post office. "We came down and settled
in a region where many of the inhabitants have never seen a Yankee,
where the population though sparse was ignorant, rude, and lawless.
None of them had faith in negro labor," he wrote his family in the
spring of 1866. He intended to change all of that, partly by winning
the friendship of his new white neighbors, so when he was elected
postmaster, he gave the business over to a local man.

Optimistic by nature, Wilkie remained cheerful, or he feigned
good cheer, as long as he could. "We are at the mercy of the elements, frost and fire and secession may injure us," he told his parents, "but we have fully vindicated the principle we started on, that
the freed negro under decent and just treatment can be worked to
profit to employer and employee." Yet Wilkie's locution—that the
freed Negro "can be worked"—suggests what went wrong with his
scheme beyond the heavy rains, the greedy caterpillars, the plummeting prices, and the inevitable animadversion of hostile neighbors who
grew more and more resentful of this naive Yankee. Idealistic pater-
nalism could not alter the racial or economic or political conditions
in the South. The freedman could not vote; neither could he own his
own land nor make enough money to buy it, which many of the in-
vesting philanthropists, such as Governor Andrew, had hoped might
be the case. Nor could the freedman choose which crops to grow or
set his own wages. Wilkie's black laborers grew restive and wanted
more money, which Wilkie could not afford to pay them. Sufficient

quantities of cotton could not be harvested until "the freedmen who labor in the field are paid *fairly* and *frequently*," a former agent of the Freedmen's Bureau declared.

Governor Andrew folded the American Land Company in 1867. And when many Northerners began returning home, they left behind the thieves and crooks labeled carpetbaggers and scalawags. These were the ugly terms that for a century schoolchildren learned, instructed that those denizens of corruption had bled the already depleted South, depriving it of resources, integrity, and public office. Because of them, the story went, the Civil War had ended not with a bang but with the jingle of coins fast lining the felonious pockets of unscrupulous rascals in the South (Unionists, mainly, who supported Reconstruction) and crooked capitalists from the North (Republicans, mainly). Certainly, many Northerners did regard the South as a business venture; as one of the men who worked in the Freedmen's Bureau in Louisiana explained, "Cotton is gold." And Wilkie James told his father that "politically and privately, all men, with but few exceptions down here, are working for but one object, namely, that of cheating every one else in order to add a few dollars to their own possession."

"The persons mainly responsible for the misdeeds of the so-called 'carpet-baggers' were the people of the South themselves," Thomas Higginson noted. To this veteran of the 1st South Carolina Volunteers, another black regiment, Southerners had made conditions impossible for Northerners of goodwill. "The men of the better class who would have been useful citizens more commonly sold out their purchases at a sacrifice and went North again," he concluded. "The cheats and bullies, on the other hand, were less scrupulous, and stayed to revenge themselves amply on their persecutors."

Affairs in Washington weren't much better. Higginson wrote scornfully, "What most men mean to-day by the 'president's plan of reconstruction' is the pardon of every rebel for the crime of rebellion, and the utter refusal to pardon a single black loyalist for the crime of being black."

. . . .

WITH ITS REPUBLICAN majority, Congress fought back. In March 1867 it passed a new Reconstruction Act, which temporarily divided all the Southern states, except Tennessee, into five military districts and placed each one under the jurisdiction of a military commander appointed by Congress. The districts could not be readmitted to the Union until they held new Constitutional Conventions whose delegates were voted on by both white and black men. Each state needed to ratify the Fourteenth Amendment, and each state needed to adopt a constitution guaranteeing universal male suffrage, although, more controversially, former Confederates not permitted to vote under the Fourteenth Amendment were still disqualified from voting.

"What a bitter dose for their arrogant aristocracy of only seven years ago!" George Templeton Strong gloated. "Was there ever a more tremendous and searching social revolution?"

Defying Congress, President Johnson had issued a second general amnesty. He ignored a Senate resolution that required pardoned landowners to provide homesteads for their former slaves. He replaced Republican military personnel with Democrats, and he urged whites to obstruct voter registration in the South. He removed General Sheridan from his command because Sheridan had dismissed Mayor Monroe of New Orleans for failing to prevent the riots in the summer of 1866. Johnson removed General Sickles as commander of the North and South Carolina district. ("The President . . . musters out all my officers," General Howard of the Freedmen's Bureau would complain. "Measures are on foot . . . which are doubtless intended to utterly defeat reconstruction.") "I fear he is among the worse men we have ever had in high place," Strong confided to his diary. By refusing to execute congressional legislation, Johnson was essentially nullifying parts of the Reconstruction Act.

Plus, in the summer of 1867, Johnson demanded Stanton's resignation from the War Department. The recently passed Tenure of Office Act, though, required Senate approval for the sacking of

government employees appointed to high office. To Johnson, however, the act had been passed solely to hamstring him. By suspending
Stanton, an outspoken critic, and replacing him with General Grant,
Johnson was presumably testing the constitutionality of the act—as
well as tarnishing Grant's reputation among Republicans. (Johnson
feared that the popular general might be the party's next presidential
nominee.) But thus far Johnson was obeying the Tenure of Office
Act by merely suspending Stanton and seeking the consent of the
Senate—until, that is, the Senate Military Committee overruled
Stanton's suspension.

Distancing himself from Johnson, Grant then declared he would
not remain as secretary of war; he had never intended to violate any
law or assume the secretaryship, he explained, except on an interim
basis and to keep someone worse from filling the office. Furious,
Johnson accused Grant of lying; Grant most certainly had accepted the
position. Grant retaliated. "I can but regard this whole matter, from
beginning to end," he told Johnson, "as an attempt to involve me in
the resistance to the law." Vindicating his honor, the popular Grant
boosted his reputation higher, even among Radical Republicans.

In early 1868 Stanton returned to his post, which he had left only
out of respect for Grant. Then Johnson openly defied the Senate and
violated the terms of the Tenure of Office Act: he fired Stanton, who
locked himself in his office and refused to give up his key. Charles
Sumner sent Stanton a simple one-word telegram: "Stick." The new
interim secretary of war, General Lorenzo Thomas, went to Stanton's
office to try to evict him, but he arrived with a hangover. Bleakly
amused, Stanton offered him a stiff shot of whiskey, which the men
tossed down together. It was opera buffa—though deadly serious.
Stanton stayed put.

Moderates as well as Radicals were outraged. Talk started again
about impeaching the president. The president had flagrantly broken
the law. And so on a snowy Monday, February 25, 1868, the House
of Representatives, led by Thaddeus Stevens, voted to present articles
of impeachment to the Senate. Never before had anything like that

happened in the country's short history; then again, never before had it fought a Civil War.

That was the country to which Henry Adams returned.

THE CONSTITUTION OF the United States stipulates that a federal officer can be impeached for a high crime or a misdemeanor, and Johnson had done much more than just violate the Tenure of Office Act, or so the Radicals argued, though that was bad enough. When broadly construed, Johnson's actions constituted an abuse of power: he had wielded his authority to contravene the will of Congress and nullify its legislation; he had meddled with the Freedmen's Bureau; he'd returned land to Southern slave owners; he'd not required provisional governors to swear they'd never aided the Confederacy; and he'd fired military men. Johnson was fomenting resistance to the cause Northerners had fought for, and he had abetted Southern resistance to that cause.

This had been the argument of the Radical Republicans. But until the eruption over the Tenure of Office Act, both conservatives and moderates had wondered if those were really impeachable offenses. They had claimed that a president should be arraigned for a specific crime, not a "bundle of generalities," as the chairman of the Judiciary Committee put it, since Johnson had not violated a criminal statute or law. After all, weren't the Radicals braying about impeachment merely to advance their agenda? And in so doing, weren't they threatening the stability of the country? Shouldn't one proceed slowly—in all things and, in particular, in matters of Reconstruction, land distribution, and black suffrage, never mind the unseating of a president? Wasn't compromise the art of the politics? Senator Sumner thought not. "A moral principle cannot be compromised," he had already insisted. Or, as Theodore Tilton, the editor of the radical New York *Independent*, had sarcastically said, "If the great culprit [Johnson] . . . had forged a check; he could have been indicted, prosecuted, condemned, sentenced, and punished. But the evidence shows that he only oppressed the Negro; that he only conspired with the rebel; that he only betrayed the Union party, that he only attempted to overthrow the Republic."

Then came the brouhaha with the secretary of war, which left moderate and conservative Republicans no choice but to join with their more radical counterparts, for it seemed that the president was deliberately flouting their authority and, to some, taking their earlier unwillingness to impeach as a sign of their weakness. As one moderate explained, reluctance was "construed by him as a license to trample on even the penal statutes of the nation." After a terrible war and a terrible assassination, with this flagrant lawbreaking, Congress could no longer allow Johnson to pursue his brash and defiant course.

Johnson's defense ably questioned the constitutionality of the Tenure of Office Act and also argued that, regardless of its legitimacy, it did not protect Lincoln's cabinet appointments, such as Stanton (even though Johnson had kept Stanton in the cabinet and treated him as if he were his own cabinet appointee). While the legal issues were being debated, Johnson may also have cut a few deals behind the scenes—seven Republican senators voted for his acquittal—assuring moderate Republicans such as Senator James Grimes of Iowa that he would no longer obstruct Congress and promising to appoint the conservative General John Schofield, with Grant's permission, as secretary of war. Moderates wanted those assurances: impeachment was an unprecedented and grave legal step as well as a political one, as war had been and as the assassination had been and as Reconstruction was proving to be. "The dignity of the nation is at stake," *The New York Times* intoned, "and all feel that a great event is at hand which is pregnant with serious consequents, for good or evil, in regard to which passion is folly."

Moderates thus made certain that Johnson's impeachment embraced a narrow definition of the grounds necessary for such an historic undertaking, and partly on that basis—regardless of whether or not Johnson had committed a specific crime, what his intentions were, and what constituted impeachable offenses—Johnson was acquitted by the Senate. There were other reasons, too. Republicans had not been faring as well in recent elections, and conservative Republicans knew that if Johnson were convicted, the passionate president pro tempore of the Senate, Old Benjamin Wade, would become president of the United States. Republicans might lose more seats because of him, for Wade was as contentious and problematic as Johnson; Representative James Garfield speculated that many of his colleagues were more afraid of Ben Wade than of the president. A longtime antislavery man loudly committed to civil rights and impartial suffrage, Wade believed in women's suffrage, high tariffs, and the rights of labor.

And Wade had been one of the senators who had refused to seat the elected officials from the South under the terms of the president's Reconstruction.

To many moderates, then, the Radicals were much too radical—but not to Thaddeus Stevens, who called the reluctant Republicans spineless. "I see little hope for the Republic," he cried when he learned Johnson had been acquitted by a vote of 35 to 19, which was only one vote shy of the two-thirds majority needed for conviction. To the ailing Stevens, Republicans in the South and black men and women all faced a real and imminent danger. "May God save our country from the consuming conflagration," a Republican from Florida agreed. "The eyes of the rebels sparkle like those of the firey [sic] serpent."

Johnson's vindication did warm the hearts of his supporters in the South, where fireworks brightened many a night sky. "Safe deliverance out of the hands of the Radical Philistines," exulted a former Confederate officer. "Radicalism has gone to h—, and the country is safe," rejoiced the *Memphis Daily Avalanche*. And the Richmond *Daily Dispatch* said that Johnson's acquittal "will only be to inflict a terrible rebuke on the radical party, and diminish its physical force (it never had any other)."

Yet Johnson had become an albatross even to admiring Democrats, who knew the unpleasant man couldn't possibly win a national election, which he nonetheless hoped to do. "What can we do with him?" asked a party member. The answer was obvious: unload him.

Republicans too had been mindful of the upcoming election—and mindful of the acrimony that the impeachment trial had created in their own ranks. As the radical financier John Murray Forbes admitted to the moderate Republican William Pitt Fessenden, one of the senators who had voted against impeachment, "Nobody feels more deeply than I do the misfortune of seeing impeachment fail; but it is sheer madness to add to this great disaster the risk of splitting up the Republican party, now the only bulwark of freedom." So, who might better secure the bulwark than the hero who had fought for it—General Ulysses S. Grant?

AS CHIEF JUSTICE of the Supreme Court, Salmon Chase had presided over the impeachment trial of President Johnson with visions of the presidency still dancing in his head. But Chase was not comfortable with the Republicans, nor they with him. He hadn't been in favor of Johnson's impeachment, and though he had been an ardent abolitionist before the war and supported universal suffrage after it, he hated how the Republicans had moved to centralize and consolidate federal power, particularly with their Military Reconstruction Act. He opposed what he called arbitrary military governments and military trials for civilians in peacetime, as was made evident in his support of the 1866 *ex parte Milligan* decision, which declared that in a state where the courts were open, even if habeas corpus had been suspended, a resident citizen could not be tried, convicted, or sentenced by a military tribunal. Chase also disagreed with the Radicals about disfranchising former Confederate military and political personnel. All that made him attractive to moderate Republicans and, perhaps, he hoped, to Democrats: he represented constitutional law, not military power.

The Republicans were rejecting him. Chase is "on every man's tongue, but in no man's heart," said one Republican, who felt that

Chase had betrayed the party. Even his friend the financier Jay Cooke observed, "People don't like the Chief Justice and his last position in the impeachment business has effectually squelched out all his claims upon the Republicans."

There was another issue too on which he differed from most of his party. On the question of the currency, hotly debated since the end of the war, Salmon Chase was a free trader who believed in hard money (payment in gold or silver). Yes, as secretary of the Treasury under Lincoln, he had approved, although reluctantly, the circulation of paper currency, which was supposed to be only a wartime measure. Now he wanted the government to return to an economic policy that included the retirement of the greenbacks issued during the war and the resumption of the use of specie (gold and silver).

Moderate Republicans agreed with Chase on this and on the matter of free trade. Henry Adams and Carl Schurz, both free traders, believed that the protective tariff favored special interests, inhibited laissez-faire capitalism, and promoted the gargantuan growth of corporations. But Radical Republicans such as Thaddeus Stevens, a protectionist, remembered that the South had argued for free trade. To Stevens, the protective tariff not only shielded industry from foreign competition but kept the South at bay; yet it was said he was merely sheltering the iron foundries of Pennsylvania, his home state, in which he allegedly had an economic share.

So Chase reminded the Democratic National Committee that regarding the tariff and finance, he was still one of them, a Democrat, and he let it be known he would not be averse to accepting the Democratic Party's nomination, should it be offered. But no Democrat could ever endorse a man who supported the Fourteenth Amendment and universal male suffrage, even if the South and the West seemed to approve of him. "C. is as radical as ever," warned one. "Chase is out of the question," the Democratic delegate Sanford E. Church told Samuel J. Tilden of New York. "We will use him well, but must not think of nominating him."

Instead, Democrats nominated the courtly Horatio Seymour,

the wartime governor of New York who had opposed conscription and been forever stained by his coppery behavior during the New York City draft riots. Standing near "Boss" Tweed, Seymour had attempted to pacify the rioters and took his time calling for federal troops. But with Seymour, the Democrats hoped to squelch the Radicals once and for all, which they believed the progressive Chase might not have done.

A surprised Seymour reportedly wept on hearing of his nomination, either out of joy or fear. Charles Dana of the New York *Sun* deeply regretted the choice. Chase would have saved the party, renewed it, strengthened it. Seymour's nomination was party politics as usual. He would hand the election to Grant by reducing it to a fight between a former disunionist and a man who had put his life on the line.

AFTER THE ASSASSINATION of a president who had spoken of charity and the better angels of our nature, and after three years of an unyielding president whose idea of charity was Southern appeasement in a spectacle of spite, the country listened to General Grant. General Grant was no longer associated with the lame-duck Andy Johnson. Grant could unite the Republican Party. Grant had saved the Union. And Grant promised peace, not war. "Let us have peace": the general did not want peace at any price; he wanted the peace promised by the North's victory.

Still, his slogan was sometimes regarded as a sop to people frustrated with Reconstruction, weary of it, or who had just grown indifferent. "Everybody is heartily tired of discussing [the Negro's] rights," *The Nation* had declared in its very first issue, back in 1865.

Or, as Henry Adams would cynically say, the general's "let us have peace" meant nothing more than—leave me alone.

The presidential election of 1868 did not bring peace to Wilkie James in Florida. Bands of white men, guns raised, prevented black men from voting there. The day before the election, five whites rode up to a black man's cabin and shot at him through the door and windows, and then they chucked a fiery knot of wood into the place. The man ran out, whereupon the five white men, Wilkie said, "put eight holes through his body with their rifles."

"There is going on a fierce and most relentless war," said Frederick Douglass, who cautioned voters not to be gulled by the South's peaceful facade. The black men near Wilkie's colony armed themselves. Wilkie advised them not to seek more bloodshed but to join him though his own life was at risk. He wouldn't scare off, he said. Instead, he rebaptized himself in his father's secular religion, which included trust in the goodness of mankind and a commitment to brotherhood and equality. "To tell the plain truth," he said, "I feel that any moment I may be called upon to give up my life for the faith of the principle I professed when I was a soldier in the open field."

Confiscated lands were being handed back to their former white owners; men such as Nathan Bedford Forrest, after presiding over the capture—and massacre—of black troops at Fort Pillow, was leading the newly founded Ku Klux Klan, and when the farms of Unionists in the South weren't being robbed at gunpoint, they were laid waste by inclement weather or falling prices (though falling prices are the result of the other two). Property was losing its value everywhere in the South, and the Ku Klux Klan, spreading from Tennessee to every Southern state, was specifically targeting blacks and their white Republican friends. Klansmen visited them in the middle of the night, dragged them from their beds and whipped them with hickory switches, and then rode off laughing. Blacks and whites were lynched, raped, burned to death, kidnapped, mutilated. Schools were torched. Klansmen even appeared in the broad light of day. John Stephens, a North Carolina state senator, was murdered in the grand jury room of the court house in Greensboro, North Carolina, where he was stabbed on a Saturday afternoon and then hanged on a hook. According to the Radical Republican judge Albion Tourgée, himself a carpetbagger from Ohio living in North Carolina, the Ku Klux Klan would soon murder more men in the state than there were members of the legislature. The Ku

Klux Klan also killed hundreds of black men and women in Louisiana and Georgia.

Wilkie James might have wanted to make a difference, but he had no organization and no economic or political power beyond the money donated by a solicitous parent. He was not nominated as a delegate to the Florida Constitutional Convention, as he'd hoped to be, and in any case the polls near him had been barred. He possessed only personal charisma and principled tenacity, but he was growing tired. One of Wilkie's best friends refused to talk to him again after learning that Wilkie had enlisted to fight with a Negro regiment. And a group of armed men prowled around the Gordon colony at night, pistols cocked. "Do not understand me as backing out of the enterprise," Wilkie assured his father.

"No Northern man likes to bring his family into such a nation of fighters," said Charles Stearns, a Garrisonian abolitionist gone South to try his hand at cooperative farming. Stearns had purchased a 1,500-acre plantation in Georgia and planned eventually to sell off parcels to his black labor force. In a matter of weeks, though, he was sleeping with a revolver under his pillow and had to take his breech-loading rifle to church. "This is about as bad as it used to be in Kansas in border ruffian times," he said, "and I feel even more insecure than I did then, for we have no friends but the blacks, and they are very poorly armed."

Although the conditions in Florida as well as much of the South had worsened, Wilkie James held on for another three years. Facing bankruptcy, he was able to raise money in Massachusetts and turn his plantation into an agricultural colony. Not until the country's financial crisis in 1873 did he have to close down his operation for good. The experiment had failed.

Wilkie James eventually settled in Milwaukee, Wisconsin, near his brother Bob, who had found employment there as a clerk for the St. Paul Railway. Meantime, his father, citing his losses in the Florida venture, excluded Wilkie from his will. Wilkie James died in 1883 at the age of thirty-eight.

. . . .

GRANT POSSESSED MORE power than any other man in the United States, though he shunned any outward show of it. At first he claimed he didn't want the nomination, and after he accepted it, he claimed he'd been "forced into it in spite of myself." "Backing down would leave the election to be contested between mere trading politicians," he sheepishly explained his about-face to Sherman, "the elevation of whom, no matter which party won, would lose us, largely, the results of the costly war which we have just gone through." He meant what he said, in part at least, but his motives weren't always clear. Ulysses S. Grant was a cipher. "It is difficult to comprehend the qualities of a man who could be moved by a narrative of individual suffering," said Massachusetts congressman George Boutwell, "and who yet could sleep while surrounded by the horrors of the battles of the Wilderness."

Running against Grant and Schuyler Colfax (the speaker of the House) was the Democratic ticket of Horatio Seymour and that resilient politician Frank Blair, who had been General Frémont's nemesis, had served under General Sherman, liked Lincoln, and had supported Andrew Johnson to the hilt. With a campaign motto of "This is a white man's country, let white men rule," they declared all Reconstruction acts null and void. Dourly, Frederick Douglass wondered, "Does anybody want a revised and corrected edition of Andrew Johnson in the presidential chair for the next four years?" He endorsed Grant.

Yet Democrats rightly noted—with some aspersion—that while Republicans had mandated universal male suffrage in the South, black men still could not vote in the North.

In November Grant won the presidency with a sizable electoral count—214 electoral votes from twenty-six states for Grant versus 80 electoral votes from eight states for Seymour—but he received only 52 percent of the popular vote; the margin of victory was but 300,000 ballots—and since 500,000 black men in the South had voted for

Grant, that meant white men overwhelmingly hadn't. Yet the country had made a choice. It did not want a politician or an ideologue. It preferred a winner: a manager of huge armies who adroitly handled tough generals and stubborn government men, who preserved law and order, which he could enforce with unswerving might, but who also spoke, when he spoke at all, of peace. The taciturn Grant had won with silence. Saying very little, he revealed nothing of what he thought. "He could depend on that countenance of his in all emergencies," Mark Twain would later remark. "It never betrayed him."

Grant was a drunk, Grant was a butcher, cried the Democratic opposition. All war is butchery, was the reply. Let us not look further. Let us read Whittier's "Snow-bound" as comforting us. Let us forget. Let Wilkie James go back North. Let us make money. Let us have peace.

(20)

DEEP WATER

R emember the ladies," Abigail Adams had said, but it seemed that no one had. "I have argued with [Wendell] Phillips and the whole fraternity and all will favor enfranchising the negro without us," Elizabeth Cady Stanton told Susan B. Anthony as soon as the war was over. "Woman's cause is in deep water."

For almost two decades Stanton had been passionately committed to securing equal rights for American women. The author of the Declaration of Rights and Sentiments that had been read at the Seneca Falls woman's rights convention in 1848, which she had helped to organize, Stanton had been married for twenty-five years to Henry Brewster Stanton, a well-known abolitionist whom she had met at the home of her cousin Gerrit Smith. Defying stereotypes about women activists being mean, mannish, and unmarried, she had given birth to seven children; she was round and rosy; her hair was snow white, her manner amiable, her dress an unoffending and forgettable calico. Said a friend of the fossilized men who sat open-mouthed when Stanton appeared in public, "Our fossil is first amazed—next bewildered—then fascinated—then convinced—not exactly of the doctrine of woman's suffrage, perhaps—but at any rate that a woman to be an advocate of that doctrine need neither be a fright nor a fury."

As a girl, she had been accomplished in chess, horseback riding, Greek, and the law (her father was a judge), and now, at fifty years old, she had not forgotten being told she should study only French, music, and dance—or that her father wished she had been a boy. She hadn't wanted to be a boy; she just wanted to be a person who enjoyed the same privileges.

Growing up in Johnstown, New York, she had been influenced by the remarkable evangelist Charles Grandison Finney, one of the burned-over district's most charismatic preachers. At twenty-nine, while practicing law in Adams, New York, Finney had undergone a conversion experience during which he committed himself to teaching the Gospels. He was ordained three years later, in 1824. In cities such as Utica, Auburn, and Troy and then Boston and New York, he sermonized in a plain but vigorous evangelical style that galvanized listeners; speaking at a giant revival in Rochester, New York, he told his audience that each individual was a moral agent, that slavery was wrong—he refused to give communion to slaveholders—that liquor, tobacco, and caffeine were pernicious, and that men, and women too, could relinquish sin, renew themselves, and love God without intermediaries. He actually welcomed women into the prayer meeting, where they were invited to testify, and took his sense of equal rights to Oberlin College, a pioneering institution in coeducation that, regardless of race, admitted women as well as men. "Men came to Oberlin for various reasons," the activist Lucy Stone would say, "women, because they had nowhere else to go."

In 1840, while on her honeymoon, Stanton had been excluded from the World's Anti-Slavery Convention in London, and from then on, her commitment to abolition had included or been superseded by her commitment to women's rights. Along with Susan B. Anthony, during the war she had established the Women's National Loyal League, a political organization like the male-only Union League, which had been founded to preserve the Union, but had also gathered support for emancipation, the Republican Party, the Thirteenth Amendment, *and* equal rights.

Stanton and Anthony hadn't met until 1851, when the two women quickly discovered that they complemented each other perfectly; they remained political partners in the fight for women's suffrage and equal rights for fifty years. "I forged the thunderbolts," said Stanton, "and she fired them." Stanton possessed a tremendous legal intelligence, Anthony a Herculean endurance, especially for those long trips on the road, riding in sooty trains, eating bad food, sleeping on hard beds in faraway places.

"No matter what is done or is not done, how you are criticized or misunderstood, or what efforts are made to block your path," Anthony counseled a new generation of women, "remember that the only fear you need have is the fear of not standing by the thing you believe to be right." That encouragement meant a great deal to the 1,500 persons gathered in Washington to listen to Anthony's last public speech, delivered on her last birthday, and hear her firmly declare, "Failure is impossible." Not long after Anthony died, in 1906, at the age of eighty-six, Gertrude Stein called her "the mother of us all."

Yet failure was very possible, and she'd become accustomed to it. Unlike Stanton, Anthony did not come from wealth; just the opposite. Born in western Massachusetts in 1820, she moved with her Quaker family to upstate New York, where her father managed a cotton mill. During the Panic of 1837, he lost his job and just about everything else. Anthony, who had been in school near Philadelphia, came home to support her large family (she had seven siblings) by teaching. In 1845, after her father's financial condition had improved and he bought a farm, she moved with her family to Rochester, New York, where she continued to teach in one school after another, earning less money than the male instructors.

While in Rochester, Anthony met the abolitionists Amy and Isaac Post and Frederick Douglass, people who fought not just for abolition but for women's rights and equality for all. As a temperance reformer, she learned early on that though women were invited to meetings, they were told not to speak. So she spoke. Barbed and sarcastic, she made her positions clear: respect for woman's work, equal opportunity and equal pay, liberalized divorce laws, and the ballot. Because she was a merciless organizer, she circulated petitions, she scheduled meetings to coincide with legislative events, she wrote pamphlets and traveled from county to county and state to state; it was easy to spot her in her gold-framed spectacles. She preferred to be photographed only in profile because of a wandering eye; she was not conventionally pretty or conventionally charming or conventionally dependent on anything or anyone.

In the last few years, the matter of rights for black people, for Southern poor whites, and for ex-Confederates—but not for women—was on the table, and by the spring of 1866, the women's cause, as Stanton had said, was in deep water. So Anthony and Stanton, along with their allies in the abolitionist movement—including Frederick Douglass, Henry Ward Beecher, and the radical editor Theodore Tilton—formed the American Equal Rights Association for white and black men and women to lobby the government for universal equal rights for all, male and female, black and white. Eloquent as ever, Douglass declared, "The right of woman to vote is as sacred in my judgment as that of man, and I am quite willing at any time to hold up both hands in favor of this right."

The path to securing that right had just been made more difficult, though: the Fourteenth Amendment had introduced the category of "male" into the Constitution, where it had never been used before. "If that word 'male' be inserted," Stanton gloomily warned, "it will take us at least a century to get it out."

Why not guarantee voting rights to *all* adult persons—or, better yet, to citizens? she wanted to know. "The disfranchised all make the same demand, and the same logic and justice which secures suffrage for one class gives it to all," Stanton explained. She and Anthony hoped to have another friend in the popular orator Anna Dickinson. Douglass credited Dickinson, along with Theodore Tilton, for articulating what would become the Fifteenth Amendment, guaranteeing black male suffrage, and she was also praised for educating the public about it. But Dickinson linked arms with moderate Republicans, who, along with many former abolitionists, unceremoniously reminded Stanton and Anthony that this was the "Negro's hour." This was the *nation's* hour, Stanton replied.

Everyone walks through the door or no one walks through the door, she said. Wendell Phillips disagreed with Stanton. The spokesman for the independent voter, the disenfranchised, and the cause of black equality, Phillips was not ready to speak up for women; he reiterated that the ladies' turn would come; they just needed to wait. He did not object to the enfranchisement of women per se, he said, but he thought that campaigning for "woman suffrage" (as it was called) undercut the case for black males. One reform at a time. Stanton was furious. "If the two millions of southern black women are not to be secured in their rights of person, property, wages, and children," she said, "then their emancipation is but another form of slavery."

Horace Greeley too, once a supporter of woman suffrage, took a step back. "The ballot and the bullet go together," he said, waving Stanton away. "If you vote, are you ready to fight?"

Stanton answered, "Yes, we are ready to fight, sir, just as you did in the late war, by sending our substitutes."

Greeley was silent but never for long. "Public sentiment," the editor soon explained more temperately, "would not sustain an innovation so revolutionary and sweeping." The Negro's hour would swiftly pass if nothing were done; Stanton should know that. Charles Sumner felt the same way. Her timing was "most inopportune," he coldly explained. He categorically refused to have a black male voting bill "clogged, burdened, or embarrassed" by the likes of woman suffrage. The war had been fought for the enfranchisement of black men, not for women. True, many former slaves were women. Since making her famous speech, known popularly as "Ain't I a Woman?," that marvelous orator Sojourner Truth had been the representative of all blacks and especially of women; true, there were free black women such as Frances Watkins Harper, whose speeches had kept morale high during the war. That was irrelevant now. This was the

Negro's hour, which was to say the black man's hour, even if black women would be doubly disenfranchised.

In the spring of 1867, at the first anniversary of the American Equal Rights Association in New York City, George T. Downing, an entrepreneur and leading black activist, asked Mrs. Stanton if she really believed that black men shouldn't have the vote until women did. Everyone should have the ballot, she replied; Reconstruction without universal suffrage did not interest her. Equal rights for all. Frankly, she continued, she didn't trust the "colored man" to safeguard her, a woman's, rights. "Degraded, oppressed himself, he would be more despotic with the governing power than even our Saxon rulers are," she explained. "I declare that we go into the kingdom together."

Annoyed, Downing asked his question a different way: whether Mrs. Stanton would really reject half a good result—the enfranchising of men regardless of color—if women didn't get the vote. Digging in her heels, she retorted with an argument that alienated some of her supporters, both then and now. "The wisest order of enfranchisement is to take the educated classes first," she said. That is, why allow uneducated men to govern women? "Would Horace Greeley, Wendell Phillips, Gerrit Smith or Theodore Tilton be willing to stand aside and trust their individual interests, and the whole welfare of the nation to the lowest strata of manhood?" she asked. "If not, why ask educated women, who love their country, who desire to mould its institutions to the highest idea of justice and equality, who feel that their enfranchisement is of vital importance to this end, why ask them to stand aside while two million ignorant men are ushered into the halls of legislation?"

It was not her best moment. From the crowd, a woman's voice shouted out, "Shame! Shame! Shame!"

WHILE THE MEMBERS of the American Equal Rights Association were meeting in New York, Lucy Stone and her husband, Henry Blackwell, were in Kansas stumping for universal suffrage. The

Kansas legislature had proposed two separate but related referenda to the state Constitution: one would grant black men the vote by removing the word "white" from the Constitution; the other would grant the vote to women by removing the word "male." If both referenda passed in the fall of 1867, impartial suffrage, as it was called, would prevail on the Kansas plains—and from there, the sky was the limit. "Success in Kansas means success everywhere," cried Blackwell.

Canvassing the entire state in the winter and spring of 1867, Stone and Blackwell were bumping along in oxcarts and open wagons—with or without springs—and traveling for as many as forty miles a day. It was hard work, but their spirits were high. "We climb hills and dash down ravines, ford creeks, and ferry over rivers," Blackwell cheerily exclaimed, "rattle across limestone ledges, struggle through muddy bottoms, fight the high winds on the high rolling upland prairies, and address the most astonishing (and astonished) audiences in the most extraordinary places." Stone excitedly telegraphed the members of the American Equal Rights Association meeting back in New York: "Kansas rules the world!"

But all was not well. "A persistent effort has been made by the enemies of female suffrage," commented a Kansas newspaper editor, "to get up a fight between that and negro suffrage." Pitting women against black men seemed a ploy engineered by the enemies of both movements, even though, it was true, there was already friction between them, and Kansans who openly opposed giving the vote to women had already formed an anti-woman suffrage league. And that league sought help from the Republican State Committee, which sent out speakers to defeat the women—including one man who stood up at a woman suffrage meeting to ask whether men really wanted old maids to vote.

This sort of prejudice was not confined to Kansas. Women agitating for the right to vote had to be crabby spinsters without the power that was a woman's true strength. "I do not believe in suffrage for women," said Jessie Benton Frémont. "I think women in their present position manage men better." Anyway, didn't women acquire power from some separate and higher sphere? Wouldn't voting therefore demean women? "As to woman's rights, I have always found privileges much better things," Nathaniel Hawthorne's sister chastised his daughter. "I do not like your saying that you 'suppose many women would vote as well as most men,'" she continued. "It is placing women whose mental endowments make them the eminent and enviable few, put on a level with the herd of mediocre men."

When Stone and Blackwell left Kansas and returned to the East, Olympia Brown, the country's first female minister, took their place. So did Stanton and Anthony. They too traveled as many as twenty-five or thirty miles daily, speaking in every county and every school district, sometimes twice a day. They slept in farmhouses, drank sorghum instead of coffee, chewed moldy green biscuits, and hauled with them speeches, documents, tracts. Their male allies in the American Equal Rights Association—Phillips, Beecher, Tilton—did not join them. "I have often found men who, if you could believe their words, were ready to die for the negro," Olympia Brown grimly reflected, "but would at the same time oppose bitterly any engagement of women's opportunity or sphere." Tilton offered to print only one editorial in *The Independent*. Beecher was busy writing a novel for which he had been paid a $30,000 advance. Phillips was on vacation. The men signed a petition on the women's behalf; that was all.

Anthony tried Anna Dickinson. She was home in Philadelphia, sick. "If only Anna E. Dickinson could make ten or 15 of the strong points—we should feel sure," Anthony tried again. Dickinson did not budge. Recalled the rueful Olympia Brown, "We had no party, no organization, no money." Until, that is, the ostentatiously rich George Francis Train blew into town in October, offered to fund the campaign, hop on the Kansas trail, and save the day.

A colorful and very controversial man, the Boston-born Train had been orphaned at four years old, in 1833, after his father, mother, and three sisters had died of yellow fever. Raised by his grandparents in Waltham, Massachusetts, Train, as a boy, had heard the esteemed master of self-reliance, Ralph Waldo Emerson, deliver one of his rousing speeches, and taking to heart Emerson's injunction to build your own world, he had gone to work for a relative in the shipping business in Liverpool. That didn't satisfy him, so he made his way to the gold rush town of Melbourne, Australia, where he started his own firm, dispatched the first clipper ships to California, served champagne in his office, and frequently sent off vivid journalistic reports to the *Boston Post* about commerce—and about his travels to Java, Singapore, and Shanghai.

Back in America, after speculating in contraband cotton during the war, Train bought shares in the Union Pacific Railroad and concocted a system, which he called the Crédit Mobilier of America, to capitalize the Union Pacific and secure land rights from the government for its expansion. He grew even wealthier. By 1868, at the age of thirty-eight, he had built the Train Villa in Newport, Rhode Island. It contained several green-tinted billiard rooms, bowling alleys, sumptuously sculpted flower gardens, and a huge guesthouse for his father-in-law. He drew the line at the six carriages his family used when driving around town, which he considered wasteful. The upkeep of the showplace cost $2,000 a week. The Gilded Age was well under way.

And he was its barker, "an American in excess," said a contemporary.

Part Emerson and part P. T. Barnum, Train possessed a gift for platform histrionics that turned staid New England rectitude on its head. Wearing lavender kid gloves, a blue dress coat with brass buttons, white vests, and shiny patent-leather shoes, he rambled, he clowned, he cajoled, he blustered, and he mesmerized his audience for as many as two and a half hours with his jokes and his causes: Irish home rule, soft (paper) money, eight-hour working days—and woman suffrage. He was a madman, a mountebank, a cracked crusader. He vied with Mark Twain for the stage—their names were occasionally confused, much to Twain's annoyance. "The same God that made George Francis Train made also the mosquitoes and the rats," Twain remarked. But Train believed himself destined to become president of the United States.

"He is a highly exaggerated type of our people and country," an acquaintance said, "and has all the energy, boldness, independence, irrepressibleness, that are popularly supposed to belong to the Anglo-Saxon race." True enough, Train was an American of his time and place. And accordingly, he was a robust racist. Years earlier, at Faneuil Hall, while Charles Sumner was praising Lincoln's preliminary emancipation proclamation, Train interrupted to harangue Sumner, who, Train said, "could speak of nothing but the 'sublime nigger.'"

Train thus seemed an unlikely—if not horrible—choice to help Stanton and Anthony in Kansas. But Stanton did not care if Train was a bigot or a boob. He put his money and his showmanship at suffrage's disposal. "If the Devil steps forward to help," she declared, "I shall say good fellow come on!" The Republicans had sabotaged women. Train understood that. "The Garrisons, Phillipses, Greeleys, and Beechers," he sang, "False prophets, false guides, false teachers and preachers, / Left Mrs. Stanton, Miss Anthony, Brown, and Stone / To fight the Kansas battles alone."

Why, then, shouldn't she seek help from Train? Stanton's friends were appalled. Train was a Copperhead with a reputation as a huckster who entertained audiences by pandering to their basest fears, warning them that with black male Negro suffrage, "we shall see some white woman in a case of negro rape being tried by 12 negro jurymen." Stanton replied, "Suppose George Francis Train had devoted his time & money for three months to the negro as he has to the woman, would not the abolitionist on all sides be ready to eulogize & accept him, of course they would. Do they ignore everyone who is false to woman? By no means." To her, those former abolitionists who hugged the higher law failed to admit how they'd been willing to compromise; let him who was without sin cast the first stone. "I would not talk of negroes or women," she also pointed out. "I would talk of citizens. That is where Wendell Phillips failed; he should have passed from the abolitionist into the statesman, instead of falling back to the Republican platform."

Though Train may have damaged the Kansas campaign, it's likely that neither referendum would have won in any case, and neither did. "It was not the woman suffrage question that killed the negro question," Susan B. Anthony summed up. "It was the Republican leaders—the Republican party leaders, who killed negro suffrage, and woman suffrage, too. Had these men been true and brave, had they been willing to have carried out their principles, and made an application of these principles to women as well as to the black men in the State of Kansas, neither the black man's question nor the woman's question would have been defeated." As far as Anthony was concerned, the Republicans had thrown the black man overboard, and the female rats had known when to leave a sinking ship.

In other words, there was plenty of blame to go around.

WITH TRAIN COVERING their expenses, Anthony and Stanton went back east, delivering speeches all the way from Omaha to Boston. Once in New York, they launched a weekly newspaper, *The Revolution*, again with Train's money, to be edited by the abolitionist Parker Pillsbury. Train's subsidy didn't last long, but his racism continued to alienate former friends and delight enemies.

Still, Anthony and Stanton had refused to denounce him. Nor did they, as it turned out, move from suffrage to statesmanship. Their rhetoric was disconcerting, patronizing, xenophobic. In St. Louis, Anthony told an audience, "When you propose to elevate the lowest and most degraded classes of men to an even platform with white men—with cultivated, educated, wealthy white men of the State—it is certainly time for you to begin to think at least whether it might not be proper to lift the wives, daughters, and mothers of your State to an even pedestal." The next year, Stanton said without compunction, "Think of Patrick and Sambo and Hans and Yung Tung, who do not know the difference between a Monarchy and a Republic, who never read the Declaration of Independence or Webster's spelling book, making laws for Lydia Maria Child, Lucretia Mott, or Fanny Kemble.

"Would these gentlemen who, on all sides, are telling us 'to wait until the negro is safe' be willing to stand aside and trust all *their* interests in hands like these?"

Such an argument played into the hands of the most bigoted of the Democrats, for sure, but Stanton and Anthony were angry, resentful, indignant. Frederick Douglass tried to smooth out relations with them in New York in the spring of 1869. Speaking before a crowd in Steinway Hall at the American Equal Rights Association annual meeting, he affirmed his friendship for Stanton and his respect for her—there was no greater advocate of equal rights, he said—but he just could not embrace her use of such unfortunate terms as "Sambo."

Moreover, he could not see how anyone could pretend that giving the vote to women was as urgent as it was to black men. "When women, because they are women, are hunted down through the cities of New York and New Orleans," he said, "when they are dragged from their houses and hung upon lamp-posts; when their children are torn from their arms, and their brains dashed out upon the pavement; when they are objects of insult and outrage at every turn; when they are in danger of having their homes burnt down over their heads; when their children are not allowed to enter schools; then they will have an urgency to obtain the ballot equal to our own."

The leonine-headed Douglass ardently made his points. Then a woman shouted from the back of the hall, "Is that not all true about black women?"

"Yes, yes, yes; it is true of the black woman," he answered, "but not because she is a woman, but because she is black."

Such was the argument, the quandary, the political koan: was it fair, right, practical to put black men ahead of women, all women, if one had to choose? Did one have to choose? Could fairness, justice, and expedience be separated? Should they? The dilemma split men and women of goodwill, it ruffled feathers and assumptions. Clara Barton, who had worked without stop during the war and afterward, taking medicine and succor and information to the wounded and their families, believed women should vote, yet she too felt obliged to put black men ahead of women; how not? There were "thousands of hungry Negroes men & women & children at our doors," she explained, "thousands upon thousands waiting in fear, trembling and uncertainty all through the South, surrounded by an enemy as implacable as death, and cold as the grave." To her, giving the black men the vote might stop the brutal murders and beatings inflicted on the entire black population.

Then there was, yet again, the matter of politics. In 1868 General Grant had been elected president, but he'd won by only 300,000 votes. Both moderate and Radical Republicans saw the Democratic handwriting on the wall. If they did not pass federal legislation to secure the black man the vote, the Republicans would lose elections—and fail to complete the work that the war had begun: not just to save the Union but to reconstruct it. The ladies had to wait, and ladies, ladylike, should do so.

THOUGH THE PASSAGE of the Fifteenth Amendment in 1870 did enfranchise the black man—"The right of citizens of the United States to vote shall not be denied or abridged by the United States or by any state on account of race, color, or previous condition of servitude"—the amendment said nothing about protecting or enforcing that right. It did not prevent any state from adopting restrictions that might deprive the freedman of his ability to cast his ballot. Nor did its language acknowledge the terrorist techniques, the murders, the beatings, and the threats already used to frighten black voters in the South. The freedman could be asked whether he owned property, whether he could read or write, whether he knew how many bubbles were contained in a bar of soap. Yet Wendell Phillips, for one, realized that a broader amendment was further than most people were willing to go. Compromising, Phillips urged his radical friends not to oppose the Fifteenth Amendment if for no other reason than as an act of common political sense.

After the Fifteenth Amendment passed both houses, establishing the right to vote "regardless of race, color, or previous condition of servitude," the American Anti-Slavery Society disbanded. In May 1870 Congress did try to look after the black voter with an enforcement bill aimed to safeguard him and his right to vote, and Phillips promised he'd keep up the good fight to ensure black men their rights. And to work for women.

But because the Fifteenth Amendment had excluded them, Elizabeth Cady Stanton denounced it as enacting what she called "an aristocracy of sex." The amendment might be hailed as creating a national citizenship—a national citizen—in a unified nation, but women had been specifically discounted by that body politic. She and Anthony therefore moved in a different direction that, though it included the ballot, also projected a reconstructed American society: where women and men could be treated equally, where women could earn the same wages for the same work, where they could go to college if they wanted or, as Margaret Fuller had put it so many years before, become sea captains if they wished.

For a short time, they embraced the National Labor Union, a reform organization founded in 1866, and hoped that together they might work outside the Republican Party and outside the Democratic Party too, if necessary, and link up with working-class women. "We think our national life does not depend on any party but on the safety, sobriety and education of its citizens," Stanton declared. In addition, she and Anthony organized the New York–based National Woman Suffrage Association, with herself as its initial president and its membership mainly educated (white) women.

Its membership did not include Lucy Stone. She disagreed with Stanton, disliked Anthony, and hated to discuss such distracting topics as labor laws or divorce, especially before black men had the vote. Yet she too was an indefatigable activist, the first woman in Massachusetts to earn a bachelor's degree—at Oberlin College—and a superlative organizer and marvelous orator with a low, pleasing voice. She had insisted on keeping her name in marriage—she had consulted Salmon Chase about the legal ramifications—but she was more conservative on social issues than either Stanton or Anthony. She believed that changing the divorce laws, for instance, would permit men to abandon women. And she'd been completely scandalized by Stanton and Anthony's alliance with George Francis Train.

Calculating the harm done by Train's involvement in woman suffrage and, worse, by Stanton's opposition to the Fifteenth Amendment, and furious when she learned that the National Woman Suffrage Association had been formed behind her back, as it seemed to her, Stone established a dissident movement, initially in New England, that included the notables of the abolition movement, such as William Lloyd Garrison and Thomas Higginson as well as the lively journalist Mary Livermore and new convert Julia Ward Howe, still famous as the author of the "Battle-hymn of the Republic." That was the core of the American Woman Suffrage Association. As its executive committee disingenuously said, it had been organized "without depreciating the value of Associations already existing." But its very existence did deprecate Stanton and Anthony.

Unlike the rival organization, the American Woman Suffrage Association did not push for restructuring the relationship between men and women; ultimately and despite their very real, deep, and utter commitment to woman suffrage and civil rights, those liberal white men and women were reformers, not radicals. They wanted to create a broad-based national alliance focusing mainly on the ballot box and steering clear of such polemical topics as divorce, prostitution, contraception, and women's control over their own bodies. Yet the two groups did share a great deal, as Theodore Tilton knew, and in the spring of 1870, when he proposed their merger, many well-known white and black advocates of woman suffrage such as Lucretia Mott, Gerrit Smith, Samuel May, and Harriet Tubman met the proposal with what seemed like relief. But James Redpath, the veteran of Bleeding Kansas who now ran a Boston lecture agency, wryly noted, "The attempt to reform reformers is a hopeless one." Whittier too was dubious. No good comes of meddling, he reminded Tilton; that was too bad, he continued, since all the strife just made sport for the Philistines.

Whittier and Redpath turned out to be right. The Boston secessionists, as Stanton privately called Stone's group, would never agree to any merger, and as it happened the two factions wouldn't unite for another twenty years. For his pains, Tilton was called a busybody. And the Philistines did in fact begin to gather, particularly once the accusation of free love was hurled at the woman's movement—which made Stone all the more eager to separate herself from the National Woman Suffrage Association.

The question batted about ever since was whether the rupture in the suffrage movement cost women the vote, which they would not receive for another fifty years. Perhaps; but the call for equal rights for women, like so much other reform, had already lost steam in the aftermath of war. Higginson, who had joined the Boston group, might foolishly call the nineteenth the woman's century, and Tilton may have declared in *The Independent* that after abolition, woman suffrage was the next great movement, but the fact was that people were tired of causes, tired of speeches, tired of platforms and planks. The hour was not the Negro's or the woman's; it belonged to retrenchment.

Men who supported women's suffrage were called long-haired "Aunt Nancys." "*The Revolution*," carped one journalist, "is edited by two old and ugly ladies, *Mr.* Elizabeth Cady Stanton and *Mrs.* Parker Pillsbury, and published by *Mr.* Susan B. Anthony."

Yet a black man voting seemed a far less dumbfounding spectacle than a woman doing so. Stanton was not wrong about this; the so-called aristocracy of sex did exist. Since free black men had been walking on the streets of Boston, New York, and Brattleboro, riding the streetcars in Washington, working on the docks of Baltimore and San Francisco, the idea of those men voting, despite the color of their skin, was not as alarming as that of a woman with political power. They were, after all, men. So Stanton tried to reassure the critics. Giving women the ballot did not sully women, demoralize marriage, or wreck the home, she said; it did not render men an appendage of the dinner pot and washtub. But not many people wanted to listen.

. . . .

WOMEN ALREADY POSSESSED the right to vote: so said Mrs. Satan, an extraordinary individual from Ohio who, married at fifteen to an alcoholic, was a faith healer, a fortune-teller, a vagabond, a seller of patent medicines and contraception, a stockbroker, and the mother of two. With insouciance, she declared, "A woman is just as capable of making a living as a man"—and just as capable of running a banking house as selling ribbons and thread. It was Thomas Nast who caricatured Victoria Woodhull as Mrs. Satan, the female devil; that's how powerful, for a brief time, she seemed.

Neither maternal and brainy like Elizabeth Cady Stanton nor a small workhorse like Lucy Stone, Victoria Claflin Woodhull was another grandiose American, excessive and homegrown: she was a proud, sexy, modern woman who resembled the dynamo that Henry Adams would later use to represent the era and not the Virgin with which he romanticized it. "In this age of rapid thought and action, of telegraphs and railways," acknowledged Susan B. Anthony, "the old stage coach won't do." Woodhull was a steam engine, slick and smart and determined to get wherever she wanted to go. She also had the help, she said, of friendly spirits—one of whom, the Greek orator Demosthenes, provided her with stock tips.

While Theodore Tilton was ineffectually trying to arrange a marriage between the two suffrage groups, Woodhull said she was running for president of the United States, and she wasn't joking any more than George Francis Train had been; the United States seemed up for grabs. Like Train, Woodhull was no stranger either to controversy or dissent or self-invention. She and her attractive sister Tennessee "Tennie" had already opened a brokerage firm on Wall Street, presumably with the financial assistance of the powerful, lonely tycoon Commodore Cornelius Vanderbilt, who reputedly visited Woodhull to make contact with the spirit world.

To Isabella Beecher Hooker, a sister of the Reverend Beecher, Woodhull seemed "heaven sent for the rescue of woman from her pit of subjection." When the more squeamish took offense at Wood-hull's cheek, Elizabeth Cady Stanton told Lucretia Mott, "We have had enough women sacrificed to this sentimental, hypocritical prating about purity." If Victoria Woodhull be brash, so be it; if she be crucified, Stanton said, it wouldn't be by women: "Let men drive the spikes." Which they would—with Woodhull's help.

In the winter of 1871, the glamorous, wealthy Woodhull delivered a paper, reputedly written by Benjamin Butler, in Washington that claimed that women already had the right to vote. Butler, who had labeled the hostile women of New Orleans prostitutes, was the Republican congressman of uncertain reputation who had spearheaded the impeachment charges against Johnson and, after the death of Thaddeus Stevens, had assumed the Radicals' mantle. Brilliant if often unscrupulous, meretricious, and untrustworthy, he may also have been Woodhull's lover. In any case, he was her advocate and helped her snag a face-to-face meeting with the House Judiciary Committee; Woodhull was the very first woman to appear there.

She was modishly clad in a navy blue cloth jacket and skirt and a steeple-crowned hat with a "brigandish dash to it," as a journalist reported. Thanks to the Fourteenth Amendment, Woodhull cogently argued, woman could vote; the Fourteenth Amendment had declared all persons born or naturalized in the United States to be citizens, and all citizens have a constitutional right to vote protected by that amendment. Under the Fourteenth *and* Fifteenth Amendments, the thirty-two-year-old Woodhull continued, women were citizens, and no distinction between citizens was made on account of sex. It was a good argument.

The Judiciary Committee wouldn't touch it and decided instead that such issues should be settled by the courts and the states, not by the federal government. The buck was passed, ironically so; the committee invoked the doctrine of states' rights, which had become Reconstruction's fallback strategy. Yet if the issue lay dormant, Woodhull was not without recourse. She and her sister were publishing *Woodhull & Claflin's Weekly*, a newspaper—reportedly funded by Commodore Vanderbilt—to discuss politics, finance, and women's rights. It serialized a novel by George Sand, published the first U.S. edition of *The Communist Manifesto* in 1871, and talked about abortion, divorce, prostitution, and free love with a brashness that reached far beyond the radicalism of *The Revolution*, which was broke and would soon cease publication. A cross between a scandal sheet, a penny dreadful, a revolutionary tract, and a literary and political journal of serious intent, *Woodhull & Claflin's Weekly* had within its first year a circulation of 20,000. Detractors said there was nothing in it but "the fraudulent, the rotten, the mushroom and the speculative."

In addition to the paper, Woodhull had Woodhull. A confident, galvanizing speaker in the manner of Anna Dickinson, whether addressing congressmen or a large crowd, she appeared composed, well dressed, well spoken. Her comportment, in fact, surprised those who came to gawk at the lascivious radical who was acquiring a controversial reputation as a free-loving renegade so outré that some women would not share a stage with her at a women's suffrage meeting. Yet she gamely expounded her views. "She who marries for support and not for love, is a lazy pauper, coward, and prostitute," she wrote. Women, she said, should be able to control their own bodies. Women should be able to love whom they pleased. "To love is a right *higher* than Constitution or laws," she proclaimed. Invoking the language of higher laws, she claimed sexual freedom to be the new abolition. "Sexual freedom means the abolition of prostitution both in and out of marriage," she said, "the emancipation of woman from sexual slavery and her coming into ownership and control of her own body."

Actually, the doctrine of the higher law had already reentered the public conversation in similar dress when Henry Ward Beecher himself had been accused of endorsing it after he had presided at the deathbed wedding of Abby Sage McFarland and her lover, Albert Richardson. A war correspondent, Richardson had been shot at close range in the *Tribune* office by Daniel McFarland, Abby McFarland's abusive husband, whom she'd divorced in Indiana. But since New

York State did not recognize Indiana's so-called quickie divorces, Abby McFarland was a bigamist in the eyes of the press and Beecher an enabler, a man as guilty of a crime as she was. "Beecherism—or the higher law," sneered *The Brooklyn Daily Eagle*, "means merely that each man is to believe and do in all things about as he feels like doing, regardless of all recognized moral codes or legal provisions."

Moral codes and legal provisions buttressed assumptions about women's place in the home, the body politic, the world. But, asked the radicals, were these assumptions divinely ordained? The freedom to love was a human right, wasn't it, and as such, greater than statutes devised by fallible men eager to preserve the status quo? Lucy Stone and the American Woman Suffrage Association wanted to sidestep the issue and distance themselves at all costs from Woodhull and the specter of free love. "Be not deceived," the *Woman's Journal* admonished in 1870, "—*free love means free lust*."

Free love routed the church, the state, the home, the family— although when Woodhull rose to speak at a National Woman Suffrage Meeting, she assured her listeners that "I have asked for equality, nothing more." Again Woodhull was clear, unfaltering, and strong, but the audience outside Steinway Hall in New York, where she spoke, was not ready for her or the resolution read aloud after she left the stage: "All laws shall be repealed which are made by Government to interfere with the rights of adult individuals to pursue happiness as they may choose."

That statement was evidently written by Woodhull's friend or lover, the anarchist Stephen Pearl Andrews. An abolitionist and pioneering free-love radical who supposedly invented the word "scientology" in 1871, Andrews had once run a commune in a New York City brownstone where Edmund Stedman, the war journalist and poet (now a banker) had briefly lived. He had also presided over a free-love discussion in antebellum New York and had crossed swords on the topic with Horace Greeley and Henry James, Sr., who, despite their own radicalism, were bested by this progressive and amazing man, whose views were considered noxious.

Andrews and Woodhull would not be silenced. As seductive as she was lucid and poised, Woodhull announced in *The New York Times* in the spring of 1871, "I advocate free love in the highest, purest sense, as the only cure for the immorality, the deep damnation by which men corrupt and disfigure God's most holy institution of sexual relations." Republicans were fast falling away, again accusing women who agreed with her as unsexed suffrage shriekers or of being as uncouth and uncultivated as Woodhull. Former supporters such as Republican representative James A. Garfield made sure to distance themselves from suffrage. Horace Greeley advised dumping "the Woodhull," as his *Tribune* called her. "Sooner or later she will resign the craft to the bottom," the paper said, "if she is not thrown overboard." The *San Francisco Chronicle*, usually temperate in its disagreement with "those respectable women who spend their lives in agitation for political privileges," exploded in a white heat: "For these brazen Amazons of the Victoria Woodhull type," the paper fulminated, "we have only the contempt and disgust which is due the exhibition of their vile doctrines and worse practices."

Sexuality had been a troubling issue for reformers, who had nonetheless been adept at using it strategically. Abolitionists had publicized the rape of black women by their white masters to inflame the North and more recently white supremacists (and George Train) claimed that in a free society black men would be free to rape white women. Lucy Stone, who believed the mere mention of sex could bring down the suffrage movement, sought to keep it locked in her bourgeois house. She knew her enemies: not just male egoists or defenders of the status quo but women like another of the reverend's sisters, Catharine Beecher, who for years taught women the art of genteel domesticity to keep them safe from the suffrage movement and all its nasty, undomestic, sexually powerful implications.

Catharine Beecher happily signed a petition against female suffrage and asked "is woman suffrage contrary to common sense?" to which she replied with a resounding yes. Harriet Beecher Stowe, her sister, was also offended by Woodhull, whom she mocked as the

short-haired, loudmouthed character in her novel, *My Wife and I.*
Woodhull was Audacia Dangyereyes, a bully who "cuts the very
ground from under the whole woman movement; for the main argument for proposing it was to introduce into politics that superior
delicacy and purity which women manifest in public life."

Woodhull refused to be intimidated. And she was happy to retaliate. "Two of your sisters have gone out of their way to assail my
character both by means of the public press and by numerous private
letters," she notified the Reverend Beecher. "You doubtless know
that it is in my power to strike back." She made her meaning quite
clear in her paper. "One man, a public teacher of eminence, lives in
concubinage with the wife of another public teacher of almost equal
eminence," she wrote. "All three concur in denouncing offenses
against morality." She could incriminate the lot of them.

Woodhull had learned that Beecher had been having a protracted
affair with his parishioner the petite and pious Elizabeth Tilton, who
happened to be the wife of Theodore Tilton. Mrs. Tilton had confessed the two-year-long adultery to her astonished husband back in
the summer of 1870. Reeling, Tilton had told several friends, including Elizabeth Cady Stanton. Recriminations, confessions, and retrac-
tions were lobbed back and forth between the Tiltons and Beecher.
Then the affair was more or less hushed up. But Theodore Tilton,
who evidently learned that Woodhull knew of the affair, tried to
keep her quiet by writing a biographical panegyric about her of ri-
diculously flattering proportions. "Such a book is a tomb from which
no author again rises," laughed Julia Ward Howe when the puff piece
appeared. It was true; subscriptions to *The Independent*, his paper,
melted away.

But Woodhull hadn't sufficiently frightened Beecher, and when
he refused to introduce her before one of her lectures, she took aim.
On October 28, 1872, she and her sister published a special edition of
Woodhull & Claflin's Weekly and blew the lid off the affair. Woodhull
was declaring aggressive moral warfare against such phony reformers
as Tilton and Beecher, who, as she said, were really free-lovers.

After Commodore Vanderbilt had presumably stopped supporting it—assuming he ever had—*Woodhull & Claflin's Weekly* had barely limped along. But now readers were paying as much as forty dollars for one copy of the salacious "Beecher-Tilton Scandal Case," and by the end of the week more than 150,000 copies of Woodhull's paper had been sold. Beecher's Plymouth Church, on the Sunday after the story broke, was brimming with so-called worshippers.

Then down came Anthony Comstock on the sisters. A rising star in the antipornographic crusade that would take hold at the end of the century, Comstock had been a Civil War veteran and loner whose celebrated name would become synonymous with moral priggishness. (George Bernard Shaw, in 1905, said that Comstock would likely ban his play *Mrs. Warren's Profession* from the stage because Comstock cringed even at the site of a naked baby.) A New Englander in New York City, among its prostitutes and vile weekly newspapers, only ten cents a copy, and the saloons and bordellos that were, to him, eroding the moral fabric of the city, Comstock was placed at the head of a secret committee for the suppression of vice at the Young Men's Christian Association, funded in part by the banker and philanthropist Morris K. Jesup. In that capacity, Comstock was able to have Victoria Woodhull and her sister arrested for sending obscene literature through the U.S. mail. George Francis Train rushed to pay the sisters' bail, but they declined his offer. Woodhull said that from the first she had known that she must suffer for the sake of her conscience, and bail would spoil that.

Though Woodhull and Claflin were exonerated, the scandal further stigmatized the cause of woman's suffrage as located somewhere between degradation and tomfoolery but something nonetheless to be punished, banned, censored, and at all costs avoided. Even so, in large part *The Woman's Journal*, the newspaper of the American Woman Suffrage Association, continued its campaign. Still, when one of its contributors was later invited to write a column about women's issues for *Harper's Bazaar*, he was explicitly told not to mention suffrage.

The Woodhull–Beecher scandal hurt both the National and the American Woman Suffrage Associations; Beecher had been president of the latter, Tilton president of the former, and worse yet, in 1872 Woodhull had campaigned for president of the entire United States on a woman suffrage ticket. Yet while women from both organizations, including Susan B. Anthony, wondered if Woodhull was a confidence artist who had exploited suffrage to aggrandize herself, Elizabeth Cady Stanton noted, with a light touch of irony, that "all the agitation has helped in some way. The free love scandal has made suffrage respectable."

It did not make it respectable enough. Woodhull continued to supply more grist for the journalists' mill. Publicized for weeks in Woodhull's own newspaper as well as papers nationwide, the scandal and its aftereffects precipitated a major retreat from the suffrage ranks. "We *need* every clean soul to help us, now when such a flood of what is fatal to the peace, and purity of the family, is rolled in on our question," said the frustrated Lucy Stone. "My one wish in regard to Mrs. Woodhull is, that [neither] she nor her ideas, may be so much as heard at our meeting." That time Stone's reason was not prudery, or at least not prudery alone; she knew she had to dissociate suffrage from the inevitable Woodhull backlash to save the cause. "Died of Free Love," one newspaper announced, "The Woman Suffrage Movement."

In 1874 a desperate Tilton sued Beecher for alienating his wife's affections. After a trial that lasted for six gossipy, hysterical months, with the national papers incessantly hawking the story of failed friendship and of free love and lawlessness, the jury could reach no verdict. Tilton moved to France. Elizabeth Tilton was left alone with her children, without money, growing blind, and clinging to spiritualism to see what she could no longer physically see. Beecher returned to the pulpit. Lucy Stone focused most of her attention on the *Woman's Journal* though she continued to lecture. In 1879 she registered to vote under the Massachusetts law that allowed women to vote in school elections, but because she registered as Lucy Stone, not Mrs. Lucy Blackwell, her name was erased from the rolls.

Embroiled in lawsuits and evicted from their luxurious East 38th Street townhouse, in 1876 the sisters Woodhull and Claflin sailed to England, where both of them successfully remarried—Victoria Woodhull to a conservative British banker.

Like Lucy Stone, Elizabeth Cady Stanton continued to lecture, but mainly she wrote; she composed a history of the entire suffrage movement and a monumental two-volume *Women's Bible*. Susan B. Anthony kept traveling across America as a suffrage speaker. In Rochester, in the fall of 1872, she tried to cast her ballot in the presidential election. Arrested, convicted, and fined, she never served a day in jail and never paid the fine; rather, she trooped on, becoming the mother of us all.

(21)

RUNNING FROM THE PAST

That Susan B. Anthony insisted on voting in the 1872 presidential election could surprise no one who had taken seriously Victoria Woodhull's argument before the House Judiciary Committee that women already had the vote. Anthony's subsequent arrest could have come as no surprise either. Nor was Victoria Woodhull's declaring herself a presidential candidate that year on the short-lived Equal Rights Party ticket a startling event, at least not to anyone who knew Woodhull as an able, strong-minded woman determined to be seen, heard, and counted.

That Horace Greeley would run for president and help to splinter the Republican Party, that he would turn his back not just on women but also on the depredations against the black population of Tennessee, Georgia, Mississippi, and Louisiana, where blacks were being slaughtered and the whites who sympathized with them were being driven away: that was a surprise. Public schools for black children had been closed, churches and homes set ablaze, poll taxes instituted, and in Georgia, black members of the legislature had been thrown out. In South Carolina, the black legislator Benjamin Randolph was murdered in broad daylight while he waited on a railroad platform one afternoon, and the white ex-Confederate George Garner had been flogged in the middle of the night because he'd taken a job as deputy sheriff for the local Republicans.

Greeley's candidacy surprised even Democrats, one of whom, the banker August Belmont, called the nomination "one of the most stupendous mistakes which it is difficult even to comprehend."

Greeley was running as a candidate put forward by Democrats and Liberal Republicans, as they were called, on a platform promising lower tariffs, hard money, limited government, and civil service reform. It was the last—civil service reform—that had moved those Republicans to break with Grant and the regular Republicans. For the country had grown unrecognizable to those men—the elite "best men," as Carl Schurz called them—the only men fit to govern, who represented rectitude and moral value, who loathed government activism and large corporations and the sticky frauds of the times, and who were willing to reach out to the Southerner and to the Democrat in amity and friendship, letting bygones be bygones. Otherwise, there would be nothing left in America but bread, circuses, and money-grubbing.

"WHAT IS THE chief end of man?" asked Mark Twain in 1871. "To get rich. In what way?—dishonestly if we can; honestly if we must." Even the broadly optimistic Walt Whitman shook his shaggy head at an America "saturated in corruption, bribery, falsehood, mal-administration." Its great cities, he continued, "reeked with respectable as much as non-respectable robbery and scoundrelism," its public officials were hypocrites or liars, and no one trusted anyone. "The men believe not in the women," Whitman lamented, "nor the women in the men." Everywhere people were chasing after the almighty dollar, especially in New York City, a place that reflected in miniature much of contemporary America. There, extreme poverty rubbed shoulders with vast wealth, and tricksters and immigrants and gentry walked side by side on city streets where Victoria Woodhull

and William Magear "Boss" Tweed had set up shop, the former reading futures and the latter plundering government coffers to the tune
of $30 million. "The power of 'Rings' in our politics is becoming
enormous," said James Russell Lowell. "Men buy their seats in the
Senate, and, of course, expect a profit on their investment." Bleakly,
he added, "We are becoming a huge stock-jobbery, and Republicans
and Democrats are names for bulls and bears."

Lowell's observation never seemed more accurate than on Friday,
September 24, 1869.

The national debt stood at an enormous $2.5 billion. During the
war, the government had issued paper greenbacks, or soft money,
to fund itself and permit deficit spending. After the war, the Grant
administration and especially George Boutwell, its Treasury secretary, were committed to retiring greenbacks by buying them at a
discounted rate and thereby returning the country to a specie (coin)-
based economy. As a result, Boutwell authorized weekly auctions of
the government's surplus gold to increase revenue and reduce the
debt without shrinking the supply of gold. Because the government
held a good deal of gold in reserve, the amount of it in circulation was
limited. So Boutwell kept secret the amount of gold to be sold, and
no one could predict beforehand what the price might be.

The situation attracted a pair of brilliant gamblers who plotted to
corner the gold market by learning in advance how much gold Boutwell intended to sell that week. The mastermind of the plan was the
undersized, quiet Jay Gould, who had been a schoolmate of the poet
naturalist John Burroughs but who, to Henry Adams, "suggested
survival from the family of spiders. He spun webs, in corners and in
the dark." (An anti-Semite, Adams also called Gould "dark, sallow,
reticent, and stealthy, with a trace of Jewish origin.") Yet whatever
one thought of him, Gould was a financial wizard. With his partners
James "Jubilee Jim" Fisk and the financier Daniel Drew, he had already wrested control of the Erie Railroad from Cornelius Vanderbilt
with watered stock; the battle between them involved unparalleled

shenanigans in the market as well as the bribing of state legislators and judges, and when the buccaneers finished, they were not only in charge of the Erie, they soon managed to expand it.

Gould was far more modest in personal habits than his bravado sidekick, the speculator Jubilee Jim Fisk (also called the Barnum of Wall Street), an outsized peddler and dry goods merchant from Vermont with a long waxed blond mustache and a penchant for prostitutes and dissembling. To Henry Adams, Fisk, with his fat fingers ringed with diamonds, was the more despicable of the pair: "noisy, boastful, ignorant, the type of a young butcher in appearance and mind."

To pull off their scheme, Gould and Fisk needed inside men. Fortunately for them, enlisting Abel Rathbone Corbin, President Grant's brother-in-law, was not hard to do. A speculator and lawyer, Corbin enjoyed Grant's confidence although, as one of the president's biographers pointed out, "Grant rarely met a businessman he did not trust." Corbin's job was simple; he merely had to provide Gould and Fisk with access to Grant. Gould also enlisted the head of the U.S. subtreasury in New York, Daniel Butterfield. A former Union general with a spotty military record who was best remembered as the creator of the bugle call "Taps" (he'd actually just revised a lights-out bugle call), Butterfield had come recommended by Corbin. He would apparently be paid $10,000 to obtain information about the government's monetary policy and, in particular, how much gold the government would auction each week. Gould and Fish would buy it and hoard it. Next, if Gould could persuade the Treasury to sell less gold than usual, forcing up its price, he could sell his own stash at a huge profit. To do that, he needed the president's ear.

Corbin, as planned, arranged social occasions where Grant would happen to be in the company of Gould and Fisk. The men met on one of Fisk's steamers, the *Providence*, which was awash in gilded furniture and sparkling mirrors. Fisk wore his diamond breast pin, as big as a cherry, it was reported, and Gould spent the supper hour talking about finance, arguing that the government should not be buying back all the greenbacks but rather should keep gold selling at a high price. That would stimulate trade and in particular help the American farmer, who was paid in gold on the international market. Not coincidentally, farmers would then have to ship their lucrative grain on the Erie Railway.

Grant was noncommittal but seemed to approve. Gould was satisfied.

By the middle of September, while Fisk and Gould were buying as much gold as they could—it was selling at about $134 an ounce— Horace Greeley and a few others became suspicious of what Greeley called a conspiracy at the Gold Exchange Bank, the clearinghouse for gold brokers, located on the corner of Broad Street and Exchange Place. There was excitement in the Gold Room, in the middle of which was a large fountain of a Cupid holding a dolphin. The price of gold was climbing; it had risen to $138, then to $140. That was what Gould had wanted. But worrying that Grant might change his mind and sell off more gold, he persuaded Corbin to write the president to remind him of their earlier conversation about not depressing the market.

On vacation with his wife in western Pennsylvania, Grant received the letter, read it, and told the messenger, who had delivered it in person, that everything was all right; yes, he had read the letter. "Letter delivered all right," the messenger wired New York. The telegraph operator sent a slightly different version of what Grant had said: "Letter received. All right."

Gould understood the reply to mean that Grant had agreed not to put any more gold onto the market. But Grant, learning that Corbin had sent the letter by special messenger, had grown suspicious. He made his wife write to his sister. "Tell your husband that my husband is very much annoyed by your speculations," she said. "You must close them as quick as you can!" Corbin was continuing to buy. The price had reached $162 an ounce by eleven in the morning on that sunny day, September 24, soon to be known as Black Friday. The price kept shooting upward. Fisk kept buying. Brokers crowded into the Gold Room.

When Corbin received the letter Julia Grant had written his wife, he showed it to Gould, and Gould, smart man that he was, secretly began to dump much of his gold. By then, frantic telegrams had been reaching Washington about the hysterical surge in the price. Back in Washington the night before, Grant had sprung into action. Finally, he had seen the whole fraud clearly. Conferring with Boutwell, the president had ordered him to sell $4 million worth of gold the next day if the price continued to climb.

When Boutwell's telegram arrived at the Gold Room, the price dipped to $133 in a matter of minutes as investors hurried to get rid of their gold stock and then splashed water from the fountain onto their burning foreheads. Foreign trade virtually came to a standstill. Stocks fell as much as 50 percent in some cases. Several banking houses had to suspend payments. Men wept; one man fainted, and at least one man killed himself. The streets around the Exchange were blocked off, but Jay Gould still made $11 million.

"Wall Street still panting," noted George Templeton Strong a few days later, "like a man convalescing from tetanus, or delirium tremens." Strong and others blamed the shifty Fisk, who after the price of gold plunged couldn't show his face on Wall Street without risking bodily harm and hid in the Opera House at 23rd Street. Butterfield resigned from the subtreasury. Gould and Fisk hired excellent lawyers who argued their case in front of bribed judges.

George Templeton Strong did not blame Fisk or Gould alone. He blamed the "Railroad Kings" and other "Vikings of the stock market," as he called them, who had already been involved in widespread and runaway speculation. He also believed, as did the Adams brothers, Henry and Charles Francis, that the railroads had grown too big, too corporate, too monolithic, too capable of trampling on "law, custom, decency, and every restraint known to society," as Henry Adams put it, "without scruple, and as yet without check."

Congress investigated. There were no reprisals.

Something had to be done. Many scandalized Republicans decided that Grant was not the man to do it.

Certainly Charles Sumner didn't think Grant up to that or any other task. Brimming with wounded self-regard, the dignified if arrogant Sumner had been terribly insulted when Grant had not consulted him about his choice for secretary of state. And that insult had barely concealed the profounder and festering injury of Grant's not having appointed Sumner himself to that or any other cabinet post.

Hamilton Fish, the man Grant did finally name (after one person left the post and another declined), was a very capable man and a good choice. But Sumner, who had been passed over twice and who learned that several diplomatic appointments would not be going to his friends, at least had been able to secure the appointment of John Lothrop Motley, the writer and diplomat, as ambassador to the Court of St. James's. That was especially important to Sumner, who wanted Great Britain to pay war reparations. Despite claiming neutrality, the British had indirectly sustained the Confederacy by building and outfitting such ships as the *Alabama*, which had captured fifty-eight Union merchant ships. The British had therefore prolonged the war, claimed Sumner, and had cost the United States more than $2 billion.

The so-called *Alabama* claims galled the British government. Sumner was "a Fanatic," said his friend the Duchess of Argyll, "and never did see more than one side, which was well enough when he had to fight the deviltry of American Slavery." The British foreign secretary, the experienced Lord Clarendon, thought Sumner was breathing the "most extravagant hostility to England." Fortunately, Clarendon's son, who had just been visiting the United States, told his father that Sumner's saber rattling meant very little; in America, he said, "nothing but money making is really cared about." Prime Minister William Gladstone was satisfied for the time being; not only was Sumner's bark worse than his bite, he was a "man of huge and distempered vanity."

Unrealistic as well as overbearing, Sumner was hoping that as restitution the British might offer to hand over Canada. Certainly he wasn't opposed to extending the U.S. boundary northward. More to the point, though, was his need to assert himself as the man directing

U.S. foreign policy. It's true that both Grant and Secretary of State Fish would have liked an apology from Great Britain, a reexamination of international law, and the gift of Canada. But Grant was preoccupied with the Caribbean. In Cuba, insurgents were rebelling against Spanish rule. Refugees were flocking into Florida with stories of horror. With his faithful friend the tubercular John Rawlins as secretary of war and his moral compass, Grant considered aiding the rebels. But since intervention might seem similar to what the British had done with the Confederates, Grant realized he could not assist or even recognize the Cuban insurgents.

With Rawlins's tuberculosis worsening and then his untimely death in September 1869, and with Hamilton Fish urging reconciliation with Spain, Grant looked toward Santo Domingo (today's Dominican Republic). Though not an expansionist per se, he did recognize the island's favorable location, both commercially and militarily: Samana Bay, for instance, could serve as a port for ships on their way to the Isthmus of Panama, and the country was rich in natural resources. Plus, it might welcome the black men and women of the South, where the Ku Klux Klan seemed to grow stronger daily. Men cloaked in long robes burned down homes and schoolhouses, they fired guns into the houses of the men who tried to stop them, and, if put on trial, they assassinated key witnesses. They hit, they ran, they used the guerrilla tactics they had honed during the war. Grant knew it, and he deplored it. As he later said, "What I desired above all, was to secure a retreat for that portion of the laboring classes of our former slave states, who might find themselves under unbelievable pressure."

True, the idea of resettling black people in Santo Domingo was just another watered-down colonization fantasy—the fantasy that first slavery and now its aftermath could be swept under the rug. Still, the idea appealed to Grant for another reason: the island could become a beacon of freedom for Cuba, where slavery, under Spanish rule, was still legal. As unrealistic about annexing Santo Domingo as Sumner had been about annexing Canada, the president might also have been intrigued by what his biographer William McFeely called "the steamy pursuit of empire," although it's also possible that Grant's purposes were more complex: that the emigration of black workers to Santo Domingo would push the South to recognize and respect its black workforce.

Of course, Grant outlined the commercial reasons for annexation as they had been outlined to him by his shady personal secretary, Orville E. Babcock. An engineer and graduate of West Point (near the top of his class), the slim Babcock was affable and crafty. Grant believed him to be a dependable friend although Babcock more generally inspired little trust and far less admiration. But Babcock had Grant's ear, he lived in the White House, and he had served Grant well during the war as his aide-de-camp. Babcock had been by Grant's side at Appomattox, and Grant repaid loyalty, even to a fault.

Grant had sent Babcock, in the summer of 1869, to Santo Domingo to assess the feasibility of annexation. Accompanying him were two other shady American speculators, William L. Cazneau and Joseph W. Fabens. Those men, who owned a great deal of land in Santo Domingo and happened to be friends of Buenaventura Báez, Santo Domingo's president, were motivated to find the island ready to be annexed. And they saw what they wanted to see. Grant was likely unaware of that when the enthusiastic Babcock returned to Washington with terms laid out in an early draft of a treaty, also called a protocol. Annexation would cost the United States $1.5 million, a sum to be applied to the Dominican national debt, and the promise of statehood.

Babcock's trip and his negotiations with Báez had taken place without the knowledge of Congress, and Grant realized that nothing would go forward without the support of the chairman of the Senate Foreign Relations Committee. That man was Charles Sumner.

Grant and Sumner did not like each other. To Grant, Sumner was a puffed-up Boston prig taken with his own high-mindedness; when told that Sumner "had no faith in the Bible," Grant slyly answered, "Well, he didn't write it." For his part, Sumner saw Grant as a boorish soldier whose brain had been dimmed by the smoke he inhaled from his ever-present cigar. And he had, of course, been too witless to have appointed Sumner to his cabinet.

But Grant respected and understood power, and so, on January 2, 1870, he took the unprecedented step of walking across Lafayette Square to knock on Sumner's door. He was, he explained, asking for the senator's support for the annexation treaty he was about to submit to the Senate. Grant thought the meeting had gone well, but what he did not understand was the senator's carefully chosen send-off. Assuring Grant that he, Sumner, was "an Administration man, and whatever you do, you will always find in me the most careful and candid consideration"—or words to that effect—he closed the door on Grant. Rightly, he assumed that Grant would take the farewell as literally meaning that he would support the treaty—and Grant told his cabinet that Sumner would. The cunning senator had not however meant he would support the treaty; he hadn't even bothered to read it yet, as he told his colleagues, and would never assent to approving something he had not seen.

Sumner wanted to defeat the president at all costs. (Already he had averted intervention in Cuba, which would have weakened his demand for war reparations from Great Britain.) Sumner stalled; then he investigated; then he spoke dramatically and at length against the treaty. Not only was the price of annexation too high—could the United States really afford such a purchase during these rocky economic times?—but, he hinted, Babcock was receiving favors from the Dominican dictator, whose faltering regime was being propped up by American money.

Sumner concluded that Báez and American speculators, not the Dominican people, were pushing for the treaty's ratification, and he also surmised that annexation, if successful, wouldn't stop with Santo Domingo. The speculator Fabens had foolishly confided as much to him. He and his fellow knaves were also hankering after Puerto Rico, Jamaica, Cuba, the Windward Islands—and the free black republic of Haiti. To Sumner, it was simply the filibustering banditry of yesteryear. He would have no part of it. The treaty was wicked. Of course, as the imposing senator added, President Grant was "entirely honest." Sumner came to bury Caesar by praising him.

Though Grant supporters and Radical Republicans such as Zachariah Chandler fought Sumner, the annexation treaty failed to pass the Senate on June 30, 1870 (the Senate had divided 28 to 28, with Republicans joining Democrats). A tenacious man, Grant would not let it go. In retaliation against Sumner, he fired John Motley, and in his annual address to Congress, delivered the following December, he repeated again all the good reasons for annexation: Santo Domingo was rich in resources; its geographical position was important militarily; and if backed by a stable government (that of the United States), it would provide new markets for U.S. products. Annexation would help pay the national debt without overtaxing the American people. And unlike Mexico's, the Santo Domingo government was actively and voluntarily seeking annexation; this was not an imperial takeover. The people of Santo Domingo "yearn for the protection of our free institutions and laws, our progress and civilization," he declared. "Shall we refuse them?"

Not only that: again, he insisted that annexation would "settle the unhappy condition of Cuba and end an exterminating conflict." Now Grant, unusual for him, was venturing into the realm of the quixotic. Workers would flock to Santo Domingo from neighboring islands, he said, to "seek the blessings of freedom and its sequence—each inhabitant receiving the reward of his own labor." That was the truly idealistic, if credulous, reverie of a man branded, at times, a military martinet. "Porto Rico and Cuba will have to abolish slavery," he went on, "as a measure of self-preservation, to retain their laborers." Santo Domingo would also be able to give American blacks that which was being denied to them at home: "a free exercise of the elective franchise."

Sumner was as stubborn as Grant. He too repeated his reasons for quashing the treaty. Báez was no friend to Haiti; beware his intentions and those of the United States, which would likely absorb Haiti, the only black republic in the world, whose weak and humble people, as Sumner called them, were glad the Senate had turned the treaty down. In fact, by pushing annexation, Grant was threatening Haiti in the same way Pierce and Buchanan had heartlessly intimidated Free Soil Kansans in the 1850s.

No president would want to be compared to Pierce or Buchanan, least of all one who had fought in the bloody war that they had helped, in their way, to bring about. But Sumner intended to hurt Grant—and at the same time deprive him of any claim to his own well-earned title as a defender of freedom and human rights.

Senator James Nye of Nevada took the Senate floor. At five foot ten and weighing two hundred pounds, the easygoing Nye was well liked by his colleagues and known for his learning, although Sumner thought his anecdotes coarse. He and Sumner sat next to each other at their mahogany desks. Now Nye castigated Sumner, saying he'd been shocked by the vitriol of Sumner's attack. He turned directly to his colleague. "I lit my youthful candle at your lamp," he said. "What are you doing? Why vilify the president?"

Sumner was not the only Republican slamming the president. Former Radicals were lining up against Grant—and against Radical Republicanism, despite Sumner's continued commitment to it. They were tired of tales of bribery and fraud; they were disgusted by what they considered government expansion; they were wary of the black Republican legislators and unrest in the South. And Santo Domingo offered them an opportunity to rebuke the executive. Carl Schurz, recently elected senator from Missouri, argued against annexation. Also a member of the Foreign Relations Committee, Schurz took the floor on January 11, 1871. If the United States annexed Santo Domingo, the lean senator wanted to know, would Cuba be far behind? If we annexed Cuba, then why not Puerto Rico and every other West Indian island, and then everything down to the Isthmus of Darien? "The Anglo-Saxon race is somewhat notorious for its land hunger," Schurz scoffed, "and such appetites are always morbidly stimulated by eating."

It was not imperialism per se that turned Schurz's stomach.

Though the Senate had balked at Secretary of State Seward's plan to purchase Alaska in 1867, its hesitation had then come mainly from those who hated anything Andrew Johnson and his administration wanted to do. Sumner himself was an expansionist, and though he felt Seward had sprung the Alaska deal on him, he had endorsed the acquisition. And he had published a monograph in *The Atlantic Monthly*, "Prophetic Voices About America," to hail the U.S. empire. He quoted Bishop George Berkeley ("that empire is traveling westward"), John Adams ("Canada and Nova Scotia must be ours"); the Spanish diplomat Count d'Aranda ("the day will come when it will become a giant, even a colossus formidable"). Flanked by such company, Sumner concluded that, in time and with peace, "the name of the Republic will be exalted, until every neighbor, yielding to irresistible attraction, will seek a new life in becoming part of the great whole; and the national example will be more puissant than any army or navy for the conquest of the world." In other words, everyone is welcome to join the United States, except Santo Domingo.

Sumner's friend Schurz provided an argument different from Sumner's against the annexation of Santo Domingo, one that reflected his disillusion with Reconstruction. If you annex these tropical countries, he pointed out, you'll have to incorporate their people—black people—and those black people are not "quite compatible with the integrity, safety, perpetuity, and progressive development of our institutions." He continued, "Show me a single instance in any tropical country where labor when it was left free did not exhibit a strong tendency to run into shiftlessness, and where practical attempts to organize labor did not run in the direction of slavery." The tropics, his argument went, were similar to the American South; annex them, and you would have another South on your hands and another shiftless population, which is what he was implicitly calling American blacks.

The spirited Republican senator from Indiana, formerly its war governor, was Oliver Perry Morton, the son of a shoemaker. An antislavery Unionist who had been partly paralyzed by a cerebral hemorrhage in 1865, he had been converted to Radical Republicanism—some critics thought his conversion a gesture of political opportunism—and had helped secure the ratification of the Fifteenth Amendment in Indiana. Pointedly, he asked Schurz an elemental question: Weren't Schurz's arguments the same proslavery ones made for fifty years before the abolition of slavery? Brushing aside the question, Schurz claimed no knowledge of that. He would not budge. Anglo-Saxon vigor might be more powerful than that of the "mixed Latin, Indian, and African races," but since those mixed races are indigenous to tropical soil, imagine what would happen to the poor Anglo-Saxon in that climate: soil and shiftlessness would absorb the alien Anglo-Saxon in "assimilation downward." Thus had Darwin entered the conversation.

Sumner sat by, saying little. He wanted the annexation question defeated far more, apparently, than he wanted to refute Schurz, whose argument flouted Sumner's long-standing commitment to equality.

Grant had set up a commission of inquiry and sent several men, including Frederick Douglass, to Santo Domingo to continue to study the island. Though they made a favorable report to Congress in the spring of 1871, with Sumner and Schurz blocking Grant in the Senate, and with public opinion turning against the plan, the annexation question was dead. Sumner had won, though not entirely. With Grant's covert assistance, Secretary of State Fish engineered the senator's removal from his powerful position as chairman of the Senate Foreign Relations Committee. As a consequence, the Washington Treaty, which resolved the *Alabama* dispute, did not give him what he wanted. England acknowledged its culpability, and the matter of reparations was directed to an international tribunal in Geneva, which eventually ordered Britain to pay the United States $15.5 million, but there would be no annexation of Canada then or ever.

THE COUNTRY WAS soaked in sleaze. "Here are the believers in brazen mediocrity," *The Galaxy* magazine protested, "the admirers of smart rascality, the disciples of the creed that the test of merit is success, the fanatics in the faith that success in life means simply to make money, the preachers of the doctrine, 'Every man his price!' " P. T. Barnum had recently opened his "Grand Traveling Museum, Menagerie, Caravan and Circus," and gamblers and impostors and confidence men preyed on the gullible, the needy, and the men and women yearning to get rich quick. But the Cardiff giant, a petrified mummy in upstate New York, was a ten-foot hoax, and in New York City, after years and years of bilking the state and the city of about $30 million, Boss Tweed and his "ring" were, in 1871, finally on the ropes. Thomas Nast was partly responsible, what with more than 150 caricatures in *Harper's Weekly*: the Boss as a vulture, the Boss as a fat man with a moneybag for a head.

Readers across the country were more interested in the precipitate, if long-awaited, fall of Tweed than news of the impoverished and unstable South. Yet Southern black congressmen had come to Washington. The first black member of the Senate, the thickset Hiram Rhodes Revels, a minister, had been representing Mississippi since the state had accepted the terms of Reconstruction and after Charles Sumner had defeated the opposition to his being seated. Revels, Sumner, and other Republicans were receiving letter after letter about the Ku Klux Klan. Robert Brown Elliott, a black congressman from South Carolina, alleged that former Confederates, now considered respectable men, were encouraging and applauding the murderous Klan and its whippings, maimings, bombings, and executions of black men and women, Republicans, and former Union soldiers. Those former Confederates used anything at their disposal: their influence, their money, their open disdain of the federal government. Elliott went so far as to accuse Tammany Hall of circulating cash in the South to keep up the violence and get the Democrats back into power.

Elliott took his grievances to the public in a letter that Horace Greeley printed in the *Tribune* in March 1871. However, though Greeley publicized Elliott's position, he dismissed it by saying that

Klansmen were nothing but rowdy youngsters (boys will be boys) not to be taken too seriously. What the South needed—what would help conditions—was amnesty for the planter class.

"Those loyal men who dwell among the scenes of violence now being enacted in South Carolina, in momentary expectation of murder, exile, or the lash," Elliott drily replied, "will deem amnesty an untimely grace."

Northern Republicans such as Greeley wanted to be left alone, or so it seemed, and resented the expenditure of more money in the South. But Grant, who had failed to find a solution to the problem of violence there with his pipe dream about Santo Domingo, was working with his new attorney general, Amos Akerman, on the passage of a Third Enforcement Act, known as the Ku Klux Klan Act, which would implement more vigorously the equal rights provisions of two earlier enforcement acts. The two earlier acts had been designed to protect the Fourteenth and Fifteenth Amendments: the first levied federal penalties against anyone or any group who prevented the exercise of civil rights, such as the right to vote, and provided federal supervisors to monitor elections; the second act strengthened the provisions of the first, particularly in large cities. For the situation had been deteriorating, the violence escalating, and Grant would not let the South win the war after the fact. Securing Northern victory meant securing black suffrage. The third enforcement bill therefore authorized the president to dispatch federal troops wherever he thought necessary in order to protect the right to vote, and it allowed him to suspend the writ of habeas corpus wherever the equal rights protections of citizens had been obstructed. Such obstructions were considered rebellions against the government of the United States.

Southern Democrats sneered at the bill as a cynical attempt to bolster Republicans in the South, nullify states' rights, and establish martial law. But it wasn't just Southern Democrats, or Democrats in general, who chafed at the vigorous Ku Klux Klan Act. Republican representative James Garfield, a rising power, barely concealed his conservative impulses when he asked a host of questions about the act's constitutionality. Did it usurp the state's authority? Surely he would not want to do that. Still the head of the Judiciary Committee, Illinois senator Lyman Trumbull (one of the seven Republicans who had voted to acquit Johnson) also expressed his doubts about government intervention in affairs of the South. What *was* the role of state governments? he wanted to know. Could the federal government punish murder, for example? Carl Schurz thought the act "insane." Leave the citizen alone; leave the state alone. To interfere is to tyrannize.

Yet Grant took another unprecedented step, appearing in person before Congress to urge the bill's passage. And it did pass, in April 1871. To execute the law, Attorney General Akerman, a New Hampshire Yankee transplanted years earlier to Georgia, organized a team of lawyers and federal marshals in the newly founded Justice Department. There were arrests, trials, and prison sentences. In Mississippi, for example, the Justice Department indicted about seven hundred persons—and although the sentences were not harsh, it did obtain convictions in more than half of them. Federal troops and U.S. marshals hit areas of South Carolina hard. In October Grant had suspended the writ of habeas corpus in nine counties of South Carolina, and by the end of November Justice Department officials had made about six hundred arrests in South Carolina alone.

The Ku Klux Klan's power was effectively shattered, which was an enormous accomplishment. Akerman credited Grant with having brought such effective federal force to bear on these outlaws. But Akerman knew what he was facing. "Though rejoiced at the suppression of KuKluxery, even in one neighborhood," he told a friend, "I feel greatly saddened by the business. It has revealed a perversion of moral sentiment among the Southern whites which bodes ill to that part of the country for a generation."

Perhaps Akerman had an inkling of his future. He had been in office only eighteen months, when, two weeks before Christmas, Grant abruptly asked for his resignation. Grant seemed sorry. Evidently, Akerman had angered such railroad magnates as Collis

Huntington and Jay Gould when he had insisted that railroads pay interest on the subsidies granted them by the government, and they were angry that he wanted to regulate their access to western lands. Hamilton Fish hated the way Akerman insisted on recounting Klan atrocities at cabinet meetings. And though Akerman had successfully prosecuted the Klan, railroad men were powerful, as was Fish. More and more men in Grant's own party were sick of all the Southern fuss.

"The Northern mind," Akerman ruefully concluded, "being full of what is called progress runs away from the past."

CHEATS AND TRICKSTERS: they needed to be eliminated. How? Leapfrog the immediate past, the war, the hardship, and the often difficult violent peace, and get back to a golden era populated by farmers, artisans, and merchants virtuously working together in a Jeffersonian democracy. Ignore the railroads, the corporations, even the centralizing power of government. Reconcile North and South, wipe out old animosities, bury bloody shirts. Clasp hands. Bring together intellectuals such as the Adams brothers and dispossessed politicians ignored or humiliated by Grant with laissez-faire capitalists. Reconcile former Radicals with former rebels.

That was the reform movement spearheaded by Carl Schurz and Missouri governor Benjamin Gratz Brown, a Kentucky native, who had been elected to office by a coalition of Democrats and disaffected Republicans. Both men approved of a general amnesty for the Southern leaders who had been excluded from holding office under the terms of the Fourteenth Amendment; both men called for civil service reform, tariff reduction, universal amnesty, and the protection of states' rights. They shied away from federal interference in local affairs—and they shrank from further Reconstruction legislation, which, they claimed, had spawned such organizations as the Ku Klux Klan in the first place.

Although those Liberal Republicans had battled slavery and fought for passage of the Fifteenth Amendment, they concluded that they'd done what they could for black men and women. Black people were now on their own. Northern Democrats—and more and more Republicans—portrayed blacks as crooked, inept opportunists manipulated by greedy, power-hungry, whining whites. As early as 1871, Greeley's *Tribune* had complained of Southern Republicans running through the halls of the Capitol with their "same old, old story of murder, intimidation, and proscriptive oppression." To him, their grievances against secret organizations, miscounted votes, intimidated voters, and former Confederates unfairly unseated in government were just tired tales, full of sound and fury, signifying nothing. Rather, the black men in the South Carolina legislature, for example, were at fault; they were a "mass of ignorance and barbarism" who, despite the existence of a "few intelligent colored people," were basically thieves and ignoramuses who would sell their vote as easily as a mule or a chicken. Yet black men held no more than 20 percent of the offices in the South, and only in South Carolina were they proportionally elected.

More to the point, the time had come for the Southern white to take control of his homeland, which, as Carl Schurz insisted, he would manage with intelligence and vision. Samuel Bowles, the powerful editor of the *Springfield Republican*, agreed. "Of all the mistakes," Bowles wrote, "of General Grant's administration, the grand, cardinal mistake, so far as the future of the country is concerned, has been his neglect to do anything important for the restoration of good feelings and loyalty at the South." Bowles meant, of course, the white South. Franklin Sanborn, formerly one of the uncompromising Secret Six, joined the Liberal Republicans. So did Congressman James Ashley, the man who had steered the Thirteenth Amendment through the House and had introduced articles of impeachment against President Johnson. (Ashley harbored a grudge against Grant, who had not renewed his term as Montana's territorial governor.) Theodore Tilton joined. So did Whitelaw Reid, who worked for Horace Greeley, and Murat Halstead of the Cincinnati *Commercial*, and even old William Cullen Bryant of the *New-York Evening Post*. Grant's former secretary of the interior, Jacob D. Cox of Ohio, along with Lyman Trumbull, and Gideon Welles, Lincoln's secretary of the navy, joined the Liberals. After much waffling, Anna Dickinson too enlisted. Speaking at Cooper Union in a crowded hall whose audience included Susan B. Anthony and Elizabeth Cady Stanton, she wondered why, if the war had in fact ended, the government insisted on its military occupation of the South. The war was over, the freedmen were citizens. "Before the law they stand on a level with the whitest man here. [Applause.] That being the case there is no need and there should be no excuse for special legislation for any special class of people, since there is none such in the Republic." Applause, again.

Wendell Phillips would have none of it. "Liberal Republicanism is nothing but Ku-Klux-Klanism disguised," he declared.

With the support of so many journalists and editors, the call for reform echoed through major newspapers. And if only the kindly, benevolent Democrats, who meant well, would unite with these (uncorrupt) Liberal Republicans, they might forge a new relationship based on reconciliation. "What the South wants now is not military commanders, and carpet-bag Congressmen, and stump orators, and collectors of internal revenue, but missionaries," the *Tribune* helpfully suggested. Those missionaries would be the Liberal Republicans linked with the Democrats.

Objections to the rising Southern debt and accusations that money had been stolen further smeared the Republican state governments in the South. With property taxes plummeting throughout the Southern states, the tax base had shrunk. (And of course the state governments could no longer depend on revenue from a tax on the number of owned slaves.) "The increase in the debts in the Southern States under carpet-bag rule has been simply appalling," scolded the *Chicago Tribune*, which believed that the abuses of "carpet-bag rule," not economic reality, must be the sole cause of depleted coffers. Take South Carolina, it argued: of the 155 legislators, 80 paid no taxes. Instead, Brussels carpets, mirrors, "plush sofas," and porcelain spittoons were handed out to those legislators to furnish their private apartments. "A year's legislation of such a nest of thieves has proved not less destructive to the State," concluded the paper, "than the march through it of Sherman's legions, burning as they went."

This was a jaundiced view of Reconstruction that took little account of such improvements as rebuilt bridges and roads, the reorganization of judicial systems, and the ambitious establishing of schools. Nor did it take into account Grant's suppression of the Klan. But the South was in debt, ravaged, and distraught, and its conditions were laid at the feet of the Republicans. Allegations of corruption were taken as fact, particularly because the political ascent of blacks in state after Southern state worried Democrats, the planters, and the white yeomen. Still, corruption did exist: bribes, kickbacks, inflated bills, huge expense accounts, and, yes, votes for sale. "I don't pretend to be honest," said Henry Clay Warmoth, the Republican governor of Louisiana since 1868. "I only pretend to be as honest as anybody in politics."

"Why, damn it, everybody is demoralized down here," Warmoth continued. "Corruption is the fashion." Louisiana was no different from the rest of the country except perhaps louder. Republicans had turned against Republicans. The handsome governor Warmoth, originally from Illinois, was a centrist who had been cooperating with Democrats—as well as reneging on his Republican commitments, or so it was said, to build a strong Republican Party. Allegations flew thick and fast. Look what Warmoth had done: he'd vetoed the law forbidding discrimination against black men and women in hotels; he'd alienated Creole and black leaders in his stupid attempt to win over white businessmen and supremacists, which he could never hope to do. He'd appointed Confederate general James Longstreet to command the state militia. So what that it was a biracial militia, and so what that the job had cost Longstreet his stature among former Confederates, who were idolizing the recently deceased Lee and calling Longstreet, born in South Carolina and raised in Georgia, a scalawag?

Warmoth was not fit for the Republican Party, that was clear. Or at least it was clear to Oscar J. Dunn, Louisiana's black lieutenant governor, who was calling for Warmoth's impeachment. Dunn had formed a coalition of disgruntled Republicans, called the Custom-House group because they were backed by Grant's brother-in-law James F. Casey, the untrustworthy collector of customs. But Dunn, though Republican, was hardly Casey's tool. The son of a free woman and stepson of a black stage carpenter, Dunn had been apprenticed to a plasterer, run away, and then worked as a barber on Mississippi steamboats. During the war, he'd enlisted with the Union army but was disgusted by the army's racial discrimination; his promotion went to a white man. Employed by the Freedmen's Bureau after the New Orleans riot of 1866, Dunn was appointed by General Philip Sheridan to head the metropolitan police board and in 1868 became lieutenant governor, the first black man in U.S. history to hold that post. Known for his own irreproachable integrity, Dunn was said to have been considered by Grant as a possible running mate in 1872, which is likely not true although the rumor speaks its own kind of truth.

Dunn broke with Warmoth when the governor vetoed a civil rights bill. Accusing Warmoth of wanting to build a white man's party, Dunn denounced Warmoth's appointing several white Democrats to office. Warmoth argued that he was trying to protect black suffrage by bringing whites into an integrated government; perhaps he could protect black suffrage by keeping whites happy, which they wouldn't be if too many blacks received government appointments. The result was that everyone was unhappy. In the summer of 1871, anti-Warmoth delegates went to the state nominating convention in New Orleans, which was held in the U.S. Circuit Court room of the Customs House—and which was protected by federal troops carrying Gatling guns. Dunn and the Custom-House group wanted to impeach Warmoth, who had been denied entrance to the meeting. Warmoth took his men to another hall.

In November Dunn suddenly became ill. He complained of a cough, then of muscle spasms, then he vomited until he lost consciousness. In a matter of days, he was dead. Likely Dunn had been poisoned with arsenic, or so it was rumored. The matter had been hushed up, it was said, and the perpetrators allowed to go free. Nothing was proved, much was alleged, and Warmoth replaced Dunn as lieutenant governor with his ally P. B. S. Pinchback, a dapper black man known as a political operative with an abiding passion for political and civil rights.

Pinchback was similar to Dunn in some respects. The son of a Mississippi plantation owner and a former slave, Pinchback was born free in Georgia, then educated in Cincinnati, and as a boy he too worked on Mississippi steamboats. After enlisting with a company of black men during the war—the Louisiana Native Guards—he resigned when he was refused promotion. Pinchback was also a street brawler and a shrewd political operator. When he lost the race for state senator after the war, he complained of election fraud. Governor Warmoth investigated, the results were reversed, and Pinchback took his seat. Warmoth may have manipulated the result; Pinchback's reputation was damaged. Yet he had attended the Republican National Convention in Chicago as a delegate, and in 1871 he became president pro tempore of the Louisiana Senate, a position that allowed him to become lieutenant governor after Dunn died.

With Warmoth and Pinchback back in power, Louisiana seemed to symbolize corruption over honesty, backroom dealing over public probity, patronage and nepotism over civil sense and justice—and black men in high governmental positions. It was said Warmoth had his hand in the till, though it was also said that if he was corrupt, Louisiana had likely corrupted Warmoth more than he had corrupted it. Despite the honesty of such governors as Adelbert Ames of Mississippi, there were double-dealing and deception on both sides of a fractious divide. In 1870 Governor William Holden of North Carolina, who had been linked to railroad fraud, was impeached mainly for trying to defeat the Ku Klux Klan. In Florida, the conservative Republican governor, Harrison Reed, a supporter of Andrew Johnson, was roundly disliked by the Radical Republicans, whom he had ousted; by the black population, whom he believed to be inferior; by the Democrats, whom he offended; and by the Klan, which he deplored. Night after night, guns were fired near his home; and, charged with malfeasance and high crimes, he was said to be so corrupt that "he would not hesitate to sell his Country for a mess of pottage."

THE DISGUSTED CARL SCHURZ led the Liberal Republicans at a national convention in Cincinnati in the spring of 1872, and under his leadership and that of B. Gratz Brown, they brought together malcontent Republicans and Democrats in what Copperhead Clement Vallandigham, of all people, called a "New Departure."

Gratz Brown (he had shelved his first name) was in many ways the archetypical Liberal Republican, a man of diverse background whose radical views had grown less radical. Born in 1826 in Lexington, Kentucky, to a slaveholding family, he had been educated at Yale. A cousin of the Blair family, he and Frank Blair had purchased and edited the *Daily Missouri Democrat* after he moved to St. Louis in 1849. In 1852, at the age of twenty-six, he had served in the state legislature; in 1856 he had been shot in the knee during a duel with a proslavery Democrat and walked with a limp for the rest of his life. He hated slavery, he had opposed the Kansas-Nebraska bill, and during the war he had raised a regiment of volunteers in Missouri. Though a strong-willed, controversial figure in that obstreperous state, he was elected its Radical Republican senator in 1863. Claiming poor health, he resigned four years later.

By that time, the stout, broad-shouldered Brown was saying that all former Confederates deserved general amnesty. Nonetheless, he advocated universal suffrage—for black men and all women, white or black. In 1870, he was elected governor of Missouri by a coalition of Republicans and Democrats hospitable to his forgiving position toward the South and his demand for civil service reforms, a reduced tariff, and an eight-hour working day. That Brown had been accused of heavy drinking—he had buttered a watermelon during one alcoholic spree and vomited all over the streets of Jefferson City—made no difference to voters, who went to the polls in such large numbers that Brown began to ogle the White House.

Above all else, the Liberal Republicans wanted Grant out of office; as one of Grant's biographers observed, their convention rhetoric sounded like a denunciation of King George III. After castigating Grant as corrupt, unworthy, arrogant, and torpid, they called for civil service reform, tariff reform, an end to land grants for railroads—and political amnesty for the South. Though they embraced the Thirteenth, Fourteenth, and Fifteenth Amendments, they deplored the Ku Klux Klan Act as federal interference in the states; it offered guns instead of olive branches to those Southerners, intransigent or not, who had been deprived of office far too long. Be nice to them, it was suggested, and they would be nice to the black man. Henry Clay Warmoth of Louisiana led a delegation.

The German-born Carl Schurz, the chair of the convention, told a friend, "I cannot become President indeed, but confidentially, it is up to me to make the next one and I can do it, too." Schurz considered the scholarly iceberg Charles Francis Adams, Jr., the most principled, best respected, and most experienced contender for the Liberals' presidential nomination, but Gratz Brown wanted the job. Having fallen out with Schurz over the question of welcoming Democrats to the new party, Brown suddenly withdrew his name in return for the vice presidency. He backed Horace Greeley, whom Whitelaw Reid had put forward. To the shock of the Adams supporters such as Schurz, Greeley won on the sixth ballot.

And why not Greeley? Here was the man who, with Cornelius Vanderbilt and Gerrit Smith, had put up the bail for the ghostlike Jefferson Davis two years after his imprisonment at Fortress Monroe; here was a man who believed in a better society—during his socialist phase—and who believed in education, hard work, the dispersion of public lands ("Go west, young man"); here was a man of the present and future who after the war had then encouraged the young man to go south—just as soon as the federal government left it alone—and someone who believed in the transcontinental railroad and the virtues of civic morality as practiced by those best men, who, according to the Liberal Republicans, had been in scant supply.

The members of the convention were said to have burst into laughter on hearing of Greeley's nomination. It was, however, no laughing matter. E. L. Godkin, who was sympathetic to the Liberal Republicans, warned Schurz that the election of Greeley would be a national calamity. "I don't know whether you are aware what a conceited, ignorant, half-cracked, obstinate old creature he is." Godkin threw his support to Grant. It was bad enough to have Theodore Tilton, the biographer of Mrs. Woodhull, touting himself as a Liberal Republican, said Godkin; Greeley was the last straw. William Cullen Bryant, long esteemed as a spokesman of reform, refused to endorse Greeley. Schurz felt humiliated. Backroom dealing had undermined the very cause of reform, he said, and without compunction, he angrily told Greeley that his nomination was nothing more than "a successful piece of political hucksterism." Worse yet, the sixty-one-year-old editor was a diehard protectionist, and most of the Liberal Republicans were free traders. For a brief moment, Schurz actually considered resigning from his own newly formed party to nominate Adams, but he knew the broadcasting of internal divisions was not a good idea, and besides he realized Adams wasn't popular enough in the West to win an election.

In July, at their convention, the Democrats took Greeley as their candidate too—although, as George Templeton Strong drolly noted, they took him with "a few wry faces, but with less fuss than was to have been expected; and Horace Greeley (!!!) is Democratic (!!!) candidate for the presidency." Yet the depth of the animosity toward Grant surprised Strong. "Mere coldness and hardness of manner, ungeniality, and taciturnity," he said, "do not justify or account for active and savage hostilities."

A case in point was the sixty-one-year-old Charles Sumner, whose hatred for Grant was still so intense that even he, once the stately abolitionist of sterling mettle, decided to support Greeley. Sumner had been arguing for a new civil rights bill that would outlaw segregated schools, guarantee equal access to cemeteries and churches, and prevent racial discrimination in jury selection. After Greeley's nomination, Republicans joined forces with Democrats to pass a diluted form of Sumner's bill—without mention of equal rights, schools, cemeteries, churches, or juries—as soon as the senator went home for a nap. "Sir, I sound the cry," Sumner roared when he learned what had happened in his absence. "The Rights of the colored race have been sacrificed." Instead, the Senate had passed the General Amnesty Act of 1872, which allowed former Confederates to hold office.

Sumner's vote for Greeley left him to stand alone without the aid or approbation of former friends and abolitionists, many of whom, such as Gerrit Smith, labeled him a traitor. Smith charged that Sumner's aversion to Grant was irrational—and that of the rich man of the poor. Other Republicans and Radicals thought Sumner insane or vindictive or both. William Lloyd Garrison charged him with allying himself with all those who had long been his enemies. Lydia Maria Child was angry, and Wendell Phillips was stricken by Sumner's choice. "What could lead you," he sorrowfully asked, "to form such an estimate of the Northern Copperhead & the Southern Secessionist & to be willing they should come into power?"

He might not like Grant, but John Greenleaf Whittier was also upset on reading Sumner's four-hour diatribe in the Senate against the president during which Sumner called him "first in nepotism, first in gift-taking repaid by official patronage, first in presidential pretensions, and first in quarrel with his countrymen." When asked to comment publicly, Whittier was circumspect. "I regret his late speech," said the Quaker poet, "as it exposes the author to the charge of personal resentment, and because it seems to me unduly severe in its tone and temper." Yet Whittier was not the firebrand of old. "The colored man is to-day the master of his own destiny," he declared, sounding like a Liberal Republican. "Nearly all that legislation can do for them has already been done. We can now only help them to help themselves. Industry, economy, temperance, self-culture, education for their children,—these things, indispensable to their elevation and progress, are in a great measure in their own hands."

Grant or Greeley: neither would send the country to the dogs, Whittier concluded. And neither of them should be running at all. He quietly voted for Grant.

Frederick Douglass said he would rather blow his brains out than work to defeat General Grant. Though he might have appointed relatives to office and snubbed Douglass when Douglass returned from Santo Domingo (Grant had invited all the fact-finding commissioners except Douglass to dinner), Douglass said that Grant, who had crushed the Klan, was the best advocate black men and women had in the South. "The Republican party is the ship and all else is the sea," Douglass said. For the Liberal Republicans were righteous about financial corruption while discounting the political corruption of racial politics. Take civil service reform: what was that? It would keep competent blacks out of office. "You tell us that all the honors of the nation are open to us," said a Mississippi freedman, "yet you exclude us by ordeals that none of us can pass." Congressman Robert Brown Elliott was unequivocal too. "We hold our rights by no perpetual or irrevocable charter," he warned. "They are confronted by constant hazards." In other words, vote for Grant.

The contest between Greeley and Grant was in effect a referendum on Reconstruction. Despite the civil service reform dear to the heart of many Liberal Republicans, their choice of Greeley had tabled that question, more or less, along with issues such as tariff reform and hard money. Rather, Greeley promised not to trample on constitutional authority, which is to say not to send federal troops to the South or enforce the Ku Klux Klan Act, and in a campaign slogan that would come back to haunt him, Greeley asked his constituents to clasp hands over the bloody chasm which had too long divided the country.

Thomas Nast took up his pen. He lampooned Carl Schurz and he belittled Charles Sumner, whom he portrayed as Robinson Crusoe abandoning his man Friday (the black population). But mostly Nast ridiculed Greeley as a dissembling, disheveled figure who clasped hands with a Klansman or reached out over the huge field of Union graves at Andersonville Prison. Greeley clasped hands with other

pilloried characters such as Boss Tweed, or, dressed in a coat tat-
tooed with Democratic and Republican promises, he stands next to
P. T. Barnum; the cartoon's caption is "Barnum's New 'What Is It.'"
Greeley climbs to the top of a huge monument, "The Whited Sepul-
chre," inscribed with such maxims as "This is a white man's government," "A negro has no rights / which a white man is / bound to
respect," "New Orleans and Memphis/massacres," "Fort Pillow massacre, approved / by Congress of Confederate States / of America,"
and "KU-KLUX."

During a punishing campaign, Greeley often appeared as disorganized, addled, and as touchy as Nast depicted him. And few people
forgot, or were allowed to forget, that Greeley was the man who had
offended Unionists, saying he thought the rebel states should go in
peace. He had called "on to Richmond" before the army was ready.
He had bungled the attempt, foolish in any case, to make peace with
Copperheads, and he had damned Southerners as thieves and murderers, drunkards and adulterers. Southerners did not resent what
Grant had done as a soldier, said one observer, as much as what Greeley had said as a politician.

JUST BEFORE THE election, the New York *Sun* broke the story
of the Crédit Mobilier. Established during the Johnson administration, the Crédit Mobilier was a dummy construction company created by the Union Pacific Railway, whose directors were also Union
Pacific executives. Able, then, to charge whatever rates it wanted,
"They receive money into one hand as a corporation, and pay it out
into the other as a contractor," said Charles Francis Adams, Jr. That
is, they were contracting with themselves.

One of the chiefs of the scheme was Oakes Ames, a shovel manufacturer and Republican congressman who sold stock in the Crédit
Mobilier at a discount (or gave it away) to his congressional colleagues.
The stock rose; the men got rich. They were scoring profits—and
reselling their stock on the open market. Such men as Grant's vice

president, Schuyler Colfax, were tainted by the scandal, as well as such congressmen as the upstanding James Garfield and the less redoubtable James G. Blaine. They escaped prosecution, although Oakes Ames was censured and the intimations of corruption cost Schuyler Colfax his position as Grant's vice presidential candidate in 1872.

Despite the scandal, Grant won by a landslide on November 4. Blacks overwhelmingly voted for Grant and Henry Wilson, his running mate from Massachusetts (chosen partly as a rebuke to Sumner), in a relatively peaceful election during which Grant carried every state north of the Mason-Dixon Line. Veterans voted for him, a number of Democrats stayed home, and Grant remained popular, if pilloried. And after the election, in his remarkable second inaugural address, Grant bluntly and proudly defended himself. "I did not ask for place or position, and was entirely without influence or the acquaintance of persons of influence, but was resolved to perform my part in a struggle threatening the very existence of the nation," he declared. "I performed a conscientious duty, without asking for promotion or command, and without a revengeful feeling toward any section or individual."

Stonily, he continued, "Notwithstanding this, throughout the war, and from my candidacy for my present office in 1868 to the close of the last presidential campaign, I have been the subject of abuse and slander scarcely every equaled in political history."

If Grant was abused, he was temporarily vindicated by his victory. For Greeley, there was no victory and no vindication, least of all from the Furies now plaguing him. His wife, Mary, to whom he'd been married for thirty-six years, had died just six days before the election. Bereft, battered, and humiliated, he could not forgive himself—for what, it was not clear. His idealism? His vacillations? His ambition? His long career as reformer, crank, brilliant editor, and man of his time? It's difficult to know. "I have done more harm and wrong than any man who ever saw the light of day," he moaned. "And yet I take God to witness that I have never intended to injure or harm anyone. But this is no excuse."

. . . .

UNSUCCESSFUL IN THEIR temporary alliance and in their attempt to dislodge Grant, Liberal Republicans and Democrats were working and would continue to work to bury the past. Yet no matter how much the country seemed now to care only for material gain—or civil service reform, which, as a cause, took precedence over equal rights and social reform—Grant would not let his countrymen forget his sacrifice or that of anyone else. He would not forget. But for Horace Greeley, remembering was an affliction. His health failing, the famous editor of an infamous era was also half mad, and on November 29, 1872, just a few weeks after the election, as if he could no longer tolerate himself, this far-seeing, shortsighted man fell dead.

(22)

WESTWARD THE COURSE
OF EMPIRE

Americans were still obsessed with place, their place, the place they wanted to call America, the territory they appropriated for the sake of manifest destiny, as John O'Sullivan memorably dubbed the country's expansionist right to have more and more land, whether that land was bought or snatched. The country fought a war for Texas, Seward purchased Alaska, Grant eyed Santo Domingo, and Sumner set his sights on Canada.

The filibusterer of the 1840s and 1850s had looked southward toward Cuba or Nicaragua, lands of sugarcane and slavery, while the whiff of gold lured fortune seekers to the West, soon the fabled place of *Westward Ho!* "The Western spirit, is, or will yet be (for no other is, or can be), the true American one," Melville had written in 1855. The historian Francis Parkman, in his hugely popular and vivid *The Oregon Trail* and *The Conspiracy of Pontiac*, told stories about wagon trains stuffed with the pots and pans of emigrants who camped out on the bank of the Missouri River and of the doomed buffalo in the Wyoming Territory—and of Indians "hewn out of rock," whom the white settler inevitably and without regret "will sweep from the face of the earth." The Indian will not, alas, "learn the arts of civilization," wrote Parkman, "and he and his forest must perish together." Civilization marches relentlessly on.

Heroic, beautiful, and bold, the West conjured up images of landscape: open plains, empty deserts, and rugged mountains that renew the sorry soul. In the West, Parkman managed to recover from too much study, too many migraines, and a bad case of nerves. Amid buffalo and antelope, hawk and rattlesnake, and the grayish green sagebrush that sprouts up in barren rock, where nothing else will grow, the easterner is reborn, redeemed, and revived by strapping scouts and natives, gamblers, trappers, miners, derringers, and derring-do, for the westerner is that "solid personality," cried Whitman, "with blood and brawn, and the deep quality of all-accepting fusion." As another of the West's propagandists, Joaquin Miller, put it, the West is a land of space and dreams.

And boodle. "The West is the place for a young fellow of spirit to pick up a fortune, simply pick it up; it's laying around loose there," Twain slyly noted in *The Gilded Age*. So too natural resources: in 1853, several Americans cut down a three-thousand-year-old sequoia in California, a magnificent tree that measured ninety-six feet in circumference; then they polished the stump, turned it into a dance floor, and hollowed out the trunk for a two-lane bowling alley. The next year, in the Calaveras Grove, an enterprising miner named George Gale took twenty-two days and four men to cut down another giant sequoia, called the "Mother of the Forest." They shaved its bark to a height of 116 feet to ship it to New York, where it was reassembled and paraded, for a price, before the public. "This is what the scamps did in California," said Thoreau in disgust. "The trees were so grand and venerable, that they could not afford to let them grow a hair's breadth bigger, or live a moment longer, to reproach themselves."

James Mason Hutchings, an English gold miner turned publisher and western promoter, was enamored of the trees and not the tree cutters. Hoping to share one of the most beautiful places on the planet, Hutchings advertised Yosemite as a hot spot for tourists in his eponymous magazine, *Hutchings' Illustrated California Magazine*, which he founded in 1856. He also hired a San Francisco photographer, Carleton Watkins, to take pictures of Yosemite that he then transformed into wood-engraved illustrations to show what he was talking about, and he purchased the valley's first hotel so that pilgrims, as visitors were called, might have a place to stay when they came to call. Ralph Waldo Emerson was one of them. In 1871 he stayed at Hutchings's hotel. "These trees," commented the transcendentalist, "have a monstrous talent for being tall."

Almost a decade before Emerson saw the ancient sequoia, the renowned preacher Thomas Starr King had come from Boston to San Francisco and applied the full force of his Unitarian energy to saving the trees from the fate of their Calaveras siblings. Cutting, carving, or boring holes into those trees was sacrilege, he said; it defiled something fundamentally American, he wrote to the widely circulated *Boston Evening Transcript*. At the same time, Watkins, another eastern transplant, was again hired to photograph Yosemite, perhaps by Trenor Park, who owned mines nearby. For Watkins the job would be more difficult this time; he wanted to capture the physical magnitude described by King. He commissioned a cabinetmaker to fashion a huge camera for his oversized huge negatives, and with those large glass plates, lenses, tripods, and chemicals in tow, he headed out from the village of Mariposa, hauling his equipment up and down the steep trails.

The results were spectacular. Half Dome, Cathedral Rocks, Grizzly Giant, and El Capitan: even the names of the pictures were larger than life. The giant photographs, shown at the Goupil Gallery on Broadway in New York the next year, 1862, were such a hit that Watkins subsequently sent several to Emerson and twelve of them to Oliver Wendell Holmes, who marveled over them in *The Atlantic*, hailing them as art, though he seemed more stunned by the trees themselves.

In the same essay, Holmes also praised, if praise be the correct word, the photographs taken at Antietam as "terrible mementoes of one of the most sanguinary conflicts of the war." Yet photography was not just cultural documentation now; more and more, its purpose was to preserve America. With Watkins's Yosemite photographs of an idealized and undisturbed landscape—set against the unseen, unspoken backdrop of war—Yosemite represented an America unscathed by battles. It was that America that the Union had been fighting to save.

Watkins's pictures of Yosemite presumably helped persuade California's senator, John Conness—and then President Abraham Lincoln—to protect the now iconic Yosemite Valley and Mariposa Big Tree Grove from further desecration. In 1864 Lincoln signed the bill that converted Yosemite and the Mariposa grove into a national park "for public use, resort and recreation." Josiah Whitney, the state geologist, breathed a sigh of relief. Yosemite would not become, like Niagara Falls, "a gigantic institution for fleecing the public," he said. No, this was a national park and, like the nation, "inalienable for all time!"

Whitney had long been trying to protect the trees. A Yankee graduate of Yale University and well trained in America, France, and Germany as a chemist, he had worked on a survey in Michigan before publishing a highly regarded book on what he called the country's metallic wealth in 1854. Long intrigued by California, where a sister had settled, Whitney presumably wrote the bill that appointed him state geologist. And so dedicated was he to surveying California land that even when the state ran out of cash, he continued to work without pay and took out personal loans to keep going. After the landscape architect Frederick Law Olmsted, who had recently resigned as head of the Sanitary Commission, was stymied in his plans for New York City's Central Park, he went out to California to manage the Mariposa mines and make a little money. As chairman of the commission in charge of Yosemite and the Big Trees, he was able to loan Whitney twelve mules so that he could extend his geological survey into the valley.

Whitney took Carleton Watkins with him. In 1869, to "give satisfaction to those who are themselves unable to visit the scenes which they represent," Whitney and Watkins together produced the handsome *Yosemite Book: A Description of the Yosemite Valley and the Adjacent*

Region of the Sierra Nevada, and of the Big Trees of California, illustrated by
maps and twenty-four of Watkins's panoramic photographs. The result
was dramatic, visually precise, spellbinding. Whitney also understood
the value of publicity. He named a mountain after Watkins, and as
for the trees, they too were named: Andrew Jackson, Daniel Webster,
Thomas Starr King, and General Sherman. For Whitney hoped that
the photographs would help create a passion for American art and the
vastness of the American landscape, which was not just mammoth in
the size of its trees, mountains, and deserts but also, more implicitly,
gigantic in opportunities for greatness.

Watkins had arrived in San Francisco in 1851, long before photographers such as Alexander Gardner and Timothy O'Sullivan, who
had gone west after the war as if fleeing the corpse-studded battlefields they'd painstakingly photographed. But all of them were part
of the national postwar need to celebrate a transnational America.
They were converting the anguish of war and Reconstruction into
something that symbolized hope, unity, and progress—a renewed
country. Gardner did so by tying his fortunes to the railroad, pho-
tographing the construction of the Union Pacific Railroad, and in
1867 he published an album of more than a hundred photos, *Across
the Continent with the Kansas Pacific Railroad, Eastern Division*. One of
Gardner's photographs, aptly called "Westward the Course of Empire
Takes Its Way" (after the mural by Emanuel Leutze, which had been
painted during the war and was hanging in the Capitol), showed railroad workers laying track for the line and standing against an open
sky. That empty foreground, symbolizing promise, is not far from the
locomotive, which will bring them to a new age.

Images of the West also filled the pages of the colorful new dime
novels published by Erastus Beadle and the travelogue of the newspaper editor Samuel Bowles, who recounted his trip West in *The
Switzerland of America: A Summer Vacation in the Parks and Mountains of
Colorado*. Traveling in style in the new Pullman cars hired for the occasion, he and fellow Liberal Republicans could sit and smoke in their
parlor and then enjoy a good meal in the dining room before retiring

comfortably for the night. During the day, they watched the waving cornfields, and in makeshift towns of tents and shanties, such as the one called "Hell on Wheels," they could see bustling desperadoes, outcasts, immigrants, and speculators. This was a brand-new world, raw, and with its own problems, one of them (the biggest) being the indigenous people already living there. Learning that the Cheyenne, Arapaho, and Sioux were raiding the makeshift towns, Bowles assumed nonchalance. "The earth is the Lord's; it is given by Him to the Saints for its improvement and development," he told his readers, "and we are the Saints. . . . Let us hesitate no longer to avow it and act it to the Indian. Let us say to him, you are our ward, our child, the victim of our destiny, ours to displace, ours to protect. We want your hunting-grounds to dig gold from, to raise grain on, and you must 'move on.'" Bowles's book was a best seller.

The great showman P. T. Barnum, an expert in marketing the unknown and the exotic, also knew where the next nickel lay. Since the completion of the transcontinental railroad in 1869, men and women were pouring into the West, Barnum included. In September 1872 he rode out to Kansas by railroad for a grand buffalo hunt. His sponsor was none other than the yellow-haired, dashing Colonel George Armstrong Custer, who was the commanding officer at Fort Hays, on the Smoky Hill River in Kansas. "He received us like princes," Barnum later recollected. The gallant Custer supplied Barnum and his party with horses, guns, and fifty men from his 7th Cavalry Regiment. Barnum managed to kill at least two buffalo among the twenty or so that were slaughtered by his party on the open plain. They might have killed even more, he admitted, "had we not considered it wanton butchery."

ALMOST A DECADE before Barnum went west to shoot buffalo, another eccentric Yankee, named Clarence King, neared the Platte River not far from Fort Kearny in Nebraska and hired a local settler to ride with him in the direction of a large herd not far away. It was the summer of 1863, and King, a young scientist, was hunting for meat. After two weeks of hard travel, King and his classmate from Yale, James Terry Gardiner, wanted to eat something more appetizing than beans and corn bread.

King rode after a bull for about two miles until, close enough, he raised his Colt revolver, took aim, and fired, and though his aim was pretty good, he only hit the bull near the shoulder. The bull swerved, lowered his head, and charged at the terrified King, smashing into King's horse, which fell on top of King's leg. Somersaulting over the downed horse and rider, the buffalo then lay dead. King killed his injured horse with a single bullet to the head, but the herd of which the young bull was a part now charged toward him. The earth rumbled under the hooves of the stampeding buffalo while he lay as still as possible. The buffalo stormed past. King was a lucky man, said the plainsman who found him.

King did seem to live a charmed life. After the army doctor at the fort treated his leg, he was able to rejoin Gardiner, and the two youths continued on their journey to California. Like many travelers to the golden land, the twenty-one-year-old King was in search of something ineffable, something different from politics and certainly different from war, and something that might be found in nature, which to him meant the West. "It must have been a sense of the coming development of this continent," Gardiner later wrote, "and a desire to be part of it that led him to plan, when we were twenty-one, our trip to the West across the Plains."

King was not a settler. Nor was he, at the time, a gold digger. He was a trained scientist with a passion for the writings of John Ruskin and a weakness for mountain climbing and the study of rocks. Standing about five foot six, he was thickly built, athletic, and good-looking. His complexion was ruddy, his hair light. He was keen and genial, and he possessed a talent for drawing people to him and keeping them close although he revealed very little about himself. Henry Adams, who met him in 1871, adored him. John Hay, once Lincoln's secretary and a future secretary of state, thought King simply the "best and brightest man of his generation."

Born in Newport, Rhode Island, in 1842, King was the son of an affluent China trader who had died when King was just six; his mother, a teenage bride, eventually remarried but for the rest of her life depended on Clarence for emotional and material support, which he unstintingly provided. In 1860, just before the start of the war, King had entered the fairly new Sheffield Scientific School at Yale and in just two years had graduated from its three-year program. One of his biographers said that King had subsequently dodged the war, but it's also true that he'd been profoundly influenced by his abolitionist grandmother, a pacifist. In any event, King told a friend that he could not bring himself to killing, buffaloes excepted.

After leaving Yale, King briefly attended Louis Agassiz's lectures in glaciology at Harvard. No wonder: the foremost zoologist and geologist of his time, a world expert on fossil fishes, this Swiss-born naturalist had mapped out the Ice Age and scaled the Jungfrau before arriving in America in 1846 to deliver the prestigious Lowell Lectures in Boston. He was then appointed to Harvard's new Lawrence Scientific School, funded by the textile industrialist Abbott Lawrence. Beloved as a transcendentalist who could find God in every pebble, Agassiz told his eager students that "facts are stupid things unless brought in conjunction with some general law." A theatrical and popular lecturer, part serious scientist and, to his detractors, part plagiarizing confidence man, the ambidextrous Agassiz entertained his standing-room-only audiences with tales of the wonders of the natural world, while writing with both hands on the chalkboard or pulling a little specimen out of his pocket. The slightly dyspeptic chronicler of New England, Van Wyck Brooks, would call Agassiz the Johnny Appleseed of American science.

Broad and square, his hands large, his dark chestnut hair falling back from his forehead but long on the sides and the back, Agassiz was debonair, charismatic, irresistible. A prolific writer, he was also a Barnum-like collector of the zoological specimens that became the basis of Harvard's Museum of Comparative Zoology, which he helped fund with the proceeds of the school for young women run in his Cambridge home by Elizabeth Cabot Cary, his second wife, his first having died of tuberculosis shortly after she left him. (Elizabeth Agassiz's school was a forerunner of the Harvard Annex, which became Radcliffe; Elizabeth Agassiz was its first president.)

By the time King went to hear him lecture, however, Agassiz had become a rather dogmatic proponent of inferior and superior races. Caucasians were decidedly superior; "the brain of the Negro," he said, "is that of the imperfect brain of a 7 month's infant in the womb of a White." Agassiz's confirmed prejudice did not endear him to abolitionists (whom he considered misguided philanthropists); they accused him of supporting slavery. (After Fort Sumter had been fired upon, Agassiz wept. "They will Mexicanize the country," he cried. "They" were the abolitionists, who were bound to destroy "our civilization" with the "effeminate progeny of mixed races, half indian, half negro, sprinkled with white blood. . . . I shudder at the consequences.") Agassiz's racial theories were bound to comfort slaveholders, Charles Darwin noted.

Agassiz was a frank and unqualified disbeliever in Darwin's theories of evolution, which to him ranged much too far from the handiwork of God. To Agassiz, species did not mutate or adapt or change, not ever; every now and then, a catastrophe extinguished life as it then existed, which God replaced with a new and better version. Thus the naturalist's job was but to uncover what was already there. Agassiz's student William James (the brother of Henry, Wilkie, Robertson, and Alice) admired Agassiz but said he was also a great deal of claptrap.

No doubt Agassiz greatly influenced King. Self-assured, self-regarding, stubborn, larger than life, and with unbounded enthusiasm, Agassiz planned enormous works, monuments, collections; he loved an audience, he loved good living, he relished and cultivated his celebrity. So would King. Science could be grand, it could be made popular, and the scientist could be an athletic, even heroic,

man of the world, a friend, as Agassiz was, of both Emerson and fossil
fishes. As for Darwinism, while extreme, it was not to be completely
ignored by men such as King, who hoped to bridge the widening
gulf between empirical science and faith that had been pried open by
On the Origin of Species, published in 1859, when King was seventeen.

Like many men of his generation, King hoped to yoke his belief
in God to his belief in science and rid science of the pessimistic implications of Darwinian thought, particularly as articulated by Darwin's defender, the biologist Thomas Henry Huxley, the man known
as "Darwin's Bulldog," who coined the term "agnostic" and during
a well-publicized debate on evolution said, "I would rather be the
offspring of two apes than be a man and afraid to face the truth."
King hoped to replace Huxley's more materialist world of chance
by searching for the underlying laws of nature. And what better
place than the grand West to look for the spiritual in the empirical?
Of course, the romance of the wide-open West had also motivated
King's journey. "Better far that he should be a cowboy, with the
Bible and Shakespeare in his saddle-bags, the constellations his tent,
the horse his brother, than to have life, originality, and the bounding
spirit of youthful imagination stamped out of him," he rhapsodized
in later years. So when one of his Yale professors read aloud a letter
from William Brewer, the field director of the California Geological Survey, in which Brewer fervently described Mount Shasta, "that
settled it," King said: he was going to California.

After their long cross-country trek, King and Gardiner had
boarded a paddleboat chugging from Sacramento down the Sacramento River toward San Francisco when King took notice of a sun-
burned fellow wearing an old felt hat, a gray flannel shirt, and a
heavy revolver belt. King guessed that the man was Brewer, and it
was. King introduced himself, and after they talked together, Brewer
was so impressed with King that once in San Francisco he introduced
King to Josiah Whitney. So irresistible, apparently, were King's intelligence, ebullience, eagerness to work, and scientific background
and contacts—even though King's letters of introduction, along with

his clothes, had gone up in smoke in a fire near Virginia City, where he'd stayed en route—Brewer and Whitney invited King to join the Survey as an unpaid volunteer. (Gardiner worked for the U.S. Engineer Corps until he too joined the California Geological Survey as assistant topographer.)

King stayed in the field for three years. By the time he was twenty-five, in 1867, with his flair for getting people to believe in him, he had gone to Washington, D.C., with an inventive idea for a wide-ranging scientific survey of the West, and he managed to convince Secretary of War Stanton that one was needed. It had to be conducted by civilians, too; West Pointers were just not trained to carry out what he had in mind: a survey of the 800-mile stretch of land, from eastern Wyoming to the eastern slope of the Sierra Nevada along the 40th parallel, which would include the route of the Central and Union Pacific railroads, soon to be merged. King proposed to map out this area, fundamentally unknown terrain to anyone but the native population, but he wanted to do more than that. He also proposed that he and a corps of scientists take samples of plants and animals, and study and describe rock formations, mountain ranges, plains, saline and alkaline deposits, coal deposits (an important resource for fuel for railroads), and minerals. Of course, he would prepare maps of the chief mining districts and a topographical map of the whole region.

King was a practical man. Beyond the sound scientific justification for the survey were political and commercial interests, and he understood that to tease funding out of the government he would have to prove the survey would be as profitable in financial as in quantitative terms. He would ascertain whether the Comstock Lode mines could or would yield more silver. And he later made sure that the book he wrote, *Mining Industry*, appeared first in the series of seven volumes published from the survey's results so as to keep his backers economically motivated.

Recognizing the value of King's proposal—and fully aware that only surveyed land could be homesteaded—Stanton signed on. King also lobbied Senator John Conness of California, who introduced legislation authorizing the survey. Henry Adams called the bill the first modern act of legislation. Modern it was, for the survey came under federal, not state or purely military, jurisdiction. Appointed head of the newly formed U.S. Geological Exploration of the 40th Parallel, King would have to report to General Andrew Atkinson Humphreys, the chief of army engineers, but King's appointment as a civilian represented a major shift toward the formation of such national institutions as the National Park Service, the Coast and Geodetic Survey, and the Weather Bureau. (After the bill passed, Stanton reportedly said to King, "Now, Mr. King, the sooner you get out of Washington, the better—you are too young a man to be seen about town with this appointment in your pocket—there are four major-generals who want your place.") Actually, the timing couldn't have been better, for this federally authorized, centralized mapping of a national domain would bring together East and West geologically and symbolically, with word of the country's natural resources and prospects for settlement replacing news of the Ku Klux Klan or presidential impeachment.

Though capable of surveying the West in both scientific and commercial terms, King was pleased just to marvel at its raw beauty. "What would Ruskin have said," King exclaimed after climbing Lassen Peak, "if he had seen *this*!" (Years later, at a picture dealer's, King accidentally met Ruskin and so impressed the art critic that he later gave King the choice of the two best Turner watercolors in the collection he was selling. "One good Turner," replied King, "deserves another." King bought both of them.) King's mission, as he saw it, was to link science and the sublime and bring together the objective fact-gathering mission to which he was committed with his romantic response to nature—or with those emotions he ambivalently called indescribable. "Am I really fallen to the level of a mere nature-lover?" he once chided himself. Yet in writing about his adventures, which he did in a series of essays for *The Atlantic Monthly*, he best reconciled the mission of the scrupulous geologist with that of the impressionable nature lover who climbed to a mountaintop to breathe clean, free air—and to be alone.

King too was a man of his time and of his country, which meant that he shared its longing for land, for expansion and exploration, for revitalization and profit. And, like his country, King was created in conflict: between discovery and acquisition, between pure science and applied or moneymaking science, between the study of minerals and the development of means for their extraction, between the rough-and-tumble West and the clubby East, where King's charming presence was frequently sought. He was a man of eminently mixed motives in a nation of the same. Something of a dandy, he pulled on his doeskin trousers and lemon-colored gloves for dinner in the wilderness. His bright gold watch chain glimmered on his natty vest, and he sported a cane, which, as an agile mountain climber, he didn't need. He loved the figurative no less than the scientific, the transcendent no less than the factual, the glorious no less than the mundane, the romantic past no less than the practical present. In the Sierra Nevada, he observed Mount Whitney "as it really is—a splendid mass of granite 14,887 feet high, ice-chiseled and storm-tinted" and at the same time saw it as "a great monolith left standing amid the ruins of a bygone geological empire."

King was also of two minds about the indigenous or native populations, the Indians, though, like Parkman, he became convinced that they would, one way or another, inevitably disappear. (The 40th parallel survey ignored ethnology and did not include native populations in its studies.) "However complex and subtle the cause of this strange, swift extinction, however guilty enlightened society may be, the fact remains," he wrote in 1875, "civilization, flashing around the world like the advancing sun, discovers a savage tribe, only that we may see it stagger under the blinding focus, fall to the earth, and perish." Just a few years earlier, he had witnessed the funeral of an old Indian woman, mourned by her despairing husband of many years, and he'd been deeply moved when, racked by grief, the husband had tried to throw himself onto the pyre. Two old women had to drag him back to his children. "Didn't I tell you Injuns has feelings inside of 'em?" King's guide chastised him. The next day King couldn't find the husband. When he asked where he was, King was told that the man was "whiskey drunk"—and that he'd spent the night with his "new squaw." King abruptly changed the subject. No more softheartedness or Indian question for him. "The Quakers will have to work a great reformation in the Indian," he condescendingly said, "before he is really fit to be exterminated."

THE 40TH PARALLEL survey was carried out by a corps of men that included topographers and geologists as well as a botanist and an ornithologist. King hired men like himself, confident men, well trained and committed to science and hard work, who met together in Sacramento in the spring of 1867 to break in the mules. "I take a little ride every day on mule back," wrote the botanist in the group, "and am at present afflicted with a most grievous tail." That July, the caravan of eleven explorer-scientists, two freight wagons, an instrument cart, and extra mules and horses set off.

The days and months ahead were not easy; several of the men came down with malaria, and King himself was struck by lightning atop a mountain named Job's Peak. Yet, despite illnesses, the hazards of the great outdoors, the sore backsides, and the stifling weather, the expedition overall was an epic feat, as one historian called it. Its rigorous execution and precise results surpassed everything—in scope, result, clarity, and rigor—previously accomplished, and after its first two-year term, King managed to get Congress to renew the appropriations. His standards for fieldwork were high, his reputation for integrity spotless, particularly after he prevented the swindle famously known as the "Diamond Hoax" from wiping out many an investor. In 1872, a mysterious field, its whereabouts vague, was reputedly saturated with gemstones. That was geologically impossible. Determined to get to the bottom of it, King put together a series of tips and rumors, and, ascertaining that the diamond field probably fell under his jurisdiction—within the 40th parallel in northwest Colorado—he secretly rode out to the area and pried loose a couple of stones that clearly had been recently planted. He didn't hesitate to let everyone know about the scam to head off the ruination of the newly formed San Francisco and New York Mining and Commercial Company. One of its investigators, who went out to the diamond field in King's wake, admitted, "It would have been as impossible for Nature to have deposited them [the diamonds] as for a person standing in San Francisco to toss a marble in the air and have it fall on Bunker Hill Monument."

A celebrity for having exposed the hoax, King the geologist and raconteur was soon an estimable man of letters whose popular essays about the West were collected in 1872 in the volume *Mountaineering in the Sierra Nevada*. (William Dean Howells, then the assistant editor of *The Atlantic Monthly*, later remembered that King read the proofs with a pith helmet at his side.) A latter-day explorer like John Frémont but with a more literary bent, or at least more talent, King represented a new Californian type of writing: graphic and, well, exhilarating, said Howells. King's tale of mountain climbing in the West is the story of a man reaching beyond where it's safe for him to go, rising to a physical and spiritual summit where silence and solitude reign. "I have lain and listened through the heavy calm of a tropical voyage, hour after hour, longing for a sound," he wrote, "and in desert nights the dead stillness has many a time awakened me from sleep. For moments, too, in my forest life, the groves made absolutely no breath of movement; but there is around these summits the soundlessness of a vacuum. The sea stillness is that of sleep; the desert, of death—this silence is like the waveless calm of space."

That waveless calm of space had nonetheless betrayed many a traveler, and King was not naive. "The brave spirit of Westward Ho!" he wrote, "the weary march of progress over stretches of desert, lining the way with graves of strong men; of new-born lives; of sad, patient mothers, whose pathetic longing for the new home died with them; of the thousand old and young whose last agony came to them as they marched with eyes strained on after the sunken sun, and whose shallow barrows scarcely lift over the drifting dust of the desert; . . . but when urging on to wresting from new lands something better than old can give, it [the brave spirit of Westward Ho] degenerates into mere weak-minded restlessness . . . it results in that race of perpetual emigrants who roam as dreary waifs over the West, losing possessions, love of life, love of God, slowly dragging from valley to valley, till they fall by the wayside, happy if some chance stranger performs for them the last rites,—often less fortunate, as blanched bones and fluttering rags upon too many hillsides plainly tell."

Bones on the hillside: beware the race of the perpetual emigrant. Beware the romance of Westward Ho and of the writers who sentimentalize it. "'Tis wonderful how soon a piano gets into a log-hut on the frontier," wrote the ever-optimistic Emerson. "You would think they found it under a pine-stump. With it comes a Latin grammar." Bret Harte, the author of "The Outcasts of Poker Flat," gently laughed. There were pianos in the saloon, he said, not in the parlor, and the owner of the log cabin, by the way, won't be wanting any Latin grammar.

"Romance like this would undoubtedly provoke the applause of lyceum-halls in the wild fastnesses of Roxbury (Mass.), or on the savage frontiers of Brooklyn (NY)," Harte teased, "but a philosopher ought to know that, usually, only civilization begets civilization, and that the pioneer is apt to be always the pioneer."

Emerson's was the sweetened romance of a bygone era. Younger writers saluted Harte's unfrilly point of view as realism.

FOR THE 40TH parallel survey, Clarence King had also hired the Irish-born photographer Timothy O'Sullivan, who had gotten his start at the tender age of eighteen with Mathew Brady before he joined Alexander Gardner in Washington. Though very little is known about O'Sullivan's life, he was considered one of most prolific photographers at the front during the war, and afterward he worked for a while with the U.S. Army Corps of Topographical Engineers, which certainly helped bring him to King's attention.

For King, O'Sullivan produced a series of landscape photographs utterly unlike his dramatic pictures of war. Perhaps he intended as much. He talked about the war compulsively, reminisced one of the men on the 40th parallel survey. "One would think he had slept with Grant and Meade, and was the direct confidant of Stanton." But instead of generals, soldiers, and corpses, O'Sullivan's landscapes hovered just beyond articulate meaning and seem to capture silence, solitude, and space. Therein lies their aesthetic power, and because of that, they seem to wriggle free of the context in which they were made. Yet context there was. King had commissioned O'Sullivan to describe the area. And because the survey was a declaration of American natural resources and American hardiness, O'Sullivan's pictures of the land present a rugged and purportedly untouched, natural environment worthy of preservation and of conquest: the pursuit of a truly geological history of the earth's origins and development, and the stalking of mammon in the hills and mines of America.

Setting out with the King expedition with two mules and a packer, O'Sullivan photographed the huge volcanic tufa rock formations at Pyramid Lake in Nevada that seemed to change color, depending on one's perspective. This unsigned picture was included, in lithograph form, with an article in *Harper's New Monthly Magazine* in 1869, evidently by O'Sullivan himself, about the surveyors' adventures among rattlesnakes, disease-carrying mosquitoes, and white pelicans beating their wings so hard that the men couldn't hear one another.

Also reproduced in the magazine were O'Sullivan's photographs of the almost abstract geometrics of the canyon in the Ruby Range. And after he rode in an ambulance wagon drawn by a team of four mules to the Great Basin, where the mounds of sparkling sands, as tall as 500 feet, looked to him like undulating snowdrifts, he made the now-famous picture *Sand Dunes, Carson Desert, Nevada, 1867.* The photograph, spare and elegant, radiates with a light that seems to come from the dunes themselves. Against them, the ambulance wagon that O'Sullivan used to cart around his photographic supplies looks dark, small, and almost inconsequential. So does his mule team.

Nature dwarfs the human, but the human is decidedly there, if only passing through.

Though he mainly ignored people—except members of the survey—O'Sullivan also descended deep into the Comstock Lode mines sunk several hundred feet into the earth, a burning magnesium wire lighting his way. His was dangerous work, as hazardous as what the miners faced as they worked below ground in cramped space, breathing poisoned air. Those mute and hallucinatory photographs do show people, miners in small, dark spaces, but they were not used in any of the published volumes produced by the survey.

Except when they were reproduced as lithographs for those volumes, O'Sullivan's photographs were not widely distributed. King had commissioned them only for internal use and put them into three volumes of his reports; they were not, it seems, offered independently for sale. But O'Sullivan may have given a set to the French Geographical Society, and he sent a set to the 1873 World's Fair in Vienna. And at the nation's Centennial International Exhibition in Philadelphia in 1876, several editions of O'Sullivan's photographs were displayed, as if to celebrate the reunited United States, and when King's own volume from the survey, *Systematic Geology*, appeared in 1878, it contained monochromes of O'Sullivan photographs, hailed as classics in their field.

"IT IS ONLY lesser men who bang all the doors, shout out all doubts," said Clarence King. Suspicious of received wisdom, whether from the scientific or the religious community, he hoped to square Darwinism with the religious beliefs he refused to abandon. That is, though the scientists of his day—Louis Agassiz being the great exception—were looking to geology to confirm Darwin's theory of biological evolution, King was not marching to that particular drummer. Rather, he had not entirely relinquished the theory of catastrophism, the pre-Darwinian notion that cataclysmic events (floods, earthquakes, volcanic eruptions) had created the features of the earth's surface and not the slow, gradual evolution, or uniformitarianism, theorized by Sir Charles Lyell.

To catastrophists such as Agassiz, cataclysmic events do occur, they destroy life, and the Creator then starts all over again. But neither was that quite what King had in mind. For though he disagreed with Lyell that natural causes operated through time and that first causes, divine or otherwise, lay beyond the reach of geological inquiry, he wasn't entirely abandoning Darwin or the idea of evolution and natural selection. Rather, he was saying that the uniformitarians ignored the geological record—the physical, inorganic conditions of the environment—in their calculations. "Has environment, with all the catastrophic changes, been merely passive as regards life?" he asked. Not at all, he answered. Evolution might occur for a while, but "then," he continued, "all at once a part of the earth suffered short, sharp, destructive revolution unheralded as an earthquake or volcanic eruptions."

Delivering a well-publicized speech at Yale's Sheffield Scientific School in 1877, he suggested that evolution be understood in a context that included rapid acceleration and sudden climactic changes. For instance, huge volcanic eruptions and glacial floods had helped create the American West, he said, in a far faster manner than could be explained by a strict belief in gradual evolution. Uniformitarians failed to see that because they drew conclusions from Europe, with its "poor, puny little Vesuvius" and "the feeble energy of a Lisbon earthquake." Europe couldn't provide the dramatic geological data that was, of course, uniquely and exceptionally American.

"In the dominant philosophy of the modern biologist," King lamented, "there is no admission of a middle ground between these two theories." Even Darwin's theories, he pointed out, include the possibility of sudden great changes in the earth's history; the rate of biological adaptation was not uniform.

The time had come to reconcile.

While cataclysms could snuff out whole populations, the flora or fauna that did adapt could survive. "Plasticity," he said, implied an "accommodation between the individual organism and [the] organic environment," not a "Malthusian death struggle in which only the victor survives." Something more meaningful than blind chance, the survival of the fittest, and war rules the cosmos. "He who brought to bear that mysterious energy we call life upon primeval matter bestowed at the same time a power of development by change," he finished his speech, "arranging that the interaction of energy and matter which make up environment should, from time to time, burst in upon the current of life and sweep it onward and upward to ever higher and better manifestations.

"Moments of great catastrophe, thus translated into the language of life, become moments of creation, when out of plastic organisms something newer and nobler is called into being."

Squaring Darwinism with the divine, King tamed calamitous change. Catastrophe, particularly in America, had a purpose.

"YOU MAY DIVIDE THE RACE," King wrote, "into imaginative people who believe in all sorts of impending crises,—physical, social, political—and others who anchor their very souls in status quo." King's theory of catastrophism ("impending crises," in Hilton Helper's controversial term) nicely suited a postwar world racked by the recent American catastrophe, and, according to King, ensured a future of survival, adaptation, recovery, and value. Two years after speaking at Yale, King became the founding director of another centralized institution, the U.S. Geological and Geographical Survey of the Territories, which brought together under one roof various and sometimes competing surveys and field groups.

But King's theory pleased neither uniformitarians nor catastrophists, and his years in the West had taken their toll.

Suffering from recurrent bouts of malaria, he resigned from the U.S. Geological Service in 1881—he was thirty-nine—but not before he spent months whoring, as Wallace Stegner wrote, after Mexican gold mines, whose glitter lured him away from science and in pursuit of the meretricious that he increasingly scorned. "Size, brute mass, the big figures of the census are our pride," King complained bitterly in 1885. Ultimately dissatisfied with science and likely with himself, he declared that the scientific brain contained about as much passion as a wrought-iron derrick. He invested in large mining ventures, he served as an expert witness for mining litigation, he traveled to Mexico and Cuba and the Caribbean, and for a while he took up residence in one or another expensive resident hotel in Manhattan. And though he still intended to work on his theories of catastrophic geology, more to his fancy were treasures in the Sierra Madre and women of color—archaic women, Henry Adams called them—with whom he often fell in love. According to Henry Adams's wife, Clover, King seemed reckless of life and strength.

He also inveigled the biologist and entrepreneur Alexander Agassiz, the son of the famed Louis, to invest in several mines in Mexico whose prospects turned sour. King's "optimism," remembered Agassiz, "was greater than his judgment."

Nor was he luckier in his literary ventures. His manuscripts were accidentally tossed out from the Brunswick Hotel by a chambermaid; his business ventures were failing; and his health was precarious. He no longer fit into the life he lived, though his peers certainly believed he did. Unbeknownst to those friends who gathered at the Pacific Union Club in San Francisco and the Century Club in New York, King had introduced himself as a Pullman porter named James Todd when he met Ada Copeland, a black nursemaid almost twenty years younger than he. Ada Copeland became his secret common-law wife, with whom King, disguised as James Todd, had five children.

In 1893, as if the pressure of secrets, financial failures, and unfulfilled literary promise were all too much for him, he picked a violent fight at New York's Central Park Zoo, and he was arrested for disorderly conduct. He was willingly institutionalized for two months in the Bloomingdale Lunatic Asylum in Manhattan.

By 1901 King was also deteriorating physically. Restless and reckless, as Clover Adams had said, he went to Colorado, Arizona,

Montana, the Klondike, and Missouri, where, despite a lung ailment, he evaluated a lead mine. Diagnosed with tuberculosis, he suggested that Ada move herself and their children to Toronto, where they would encounter less racism, while he went to California to recuperate. His condition grew worse. During his last days, he tried to make sense of his life from a cottage in Arizona. He could not. "I have been trying to understand why a man as well endowed with intelligence as I," he wrote to his friend John Hay, "should have made such a failure of many matters as I have." He then revealed his real name to Ada so that her letters might not go astray.

On Christmas Eve 1901, the nomadic Clarence King died, not yet sixty years old. His fall from grace, or what his friends considered grace, seemed shocking to those who thought they knew him well. But perhaps he was too superlatively American to be known by this small cadre of accomplished men. Perhaps King embodied in a tragic way the America still riven by a series of internal wars, the America that had mistaken a grand destiny for a pot of gold and that sought to bury its peevish, ambivalent feelings about race and so-called civilization under the cracking veneer of Gilded Age gentility.

WHEN HENRY ADAMS, at the end of his life, wrote a book about failure, although he was ostensibly writing about his anachronistic self and the fact that, despite advantages of birth and education, he was out of place in the modern world, Adams was probably thinking about Clarence King. Though, to Adams, King was the consummately American and formidably strong paragon of physical energy, mental range, wit, grace, and science, Adams had to see him too as a paradigm of American failure: a man of great promise whose life unaccountably sputtered out in the American West, a man unfit for the modern world of raw power.

Adams may have been wrong—not in his anatomy of failure but in his assessment of its cause. King's life implied a failure of vision and of imagination, and his double life suggests that the white America of Adams and, in part, of King, fatally denied the country's true breadth and fortune—that is, it denied the varied, native, and multicolored cultures it was hell-bent on removing from its collective white memory.

For no matter how the penny press marketed the West, no matter how fluently Emerson philosophized its future, no matter that Bret Harte laughed at Emersonian hoopla; no matter that Barnum exploited it; no matter that Clarence King tried to grasp, explore, and whore after it: it was also the homeland of thousands of people who had been ignored—and then, catastrophically, shoved aside.

(23)

WITH THE TEN
COMMANDMENTS IN ONE HAND

The war had ended, or so it seemed, when Grant met Lee at Appomattox, yet wars were still being fought—undeclared wars, wars that didn't entail a draft or deadly confusions in the Wilderness or three days of fury at Gettysburg. The wars were fought on Dryades Street in New Orleans and in the black township of Colfax, Louisiana, where on Easter Sunday 1873, more than eighty black and white Republicans were killed by paramilitary whites. And wars were fought on that grand expanse of land stretching beyond the Mississippi to the Pacific, from the vast plains to the Rockies and the Sierras and to the north in the wide Montana Territory. These were the wars waged against tribe after tribe of Indians and wars that a century later would be called nation-building.

These wars killed people of all races. These were the Indian wars, a "subject," said General William Tecumseh Sherman, "as important as Reconstruction." These wars dragged on and on.

After Appomattox, General Sherman had left Washington for his home in St. Louis; he stayed there until Ulysses S. Grant appointed him head of the vast Military Division of the Mississippi, which extended to the Rockies and from Canada to Mexico. The area also happened to include land the federal government had donated to the railroads—although, technically and morally, it really belonged to the Indians.

"Possession is half the law: that is, regardless of how the thing came into possession?" Herman Melville had wondered in *Moby-Dick*. The railroad and the federal government both claimed ownership of the western lands, and the four million men heading west in the two decades after the war hoped to own some of that land too, but, whether seeking fortunes or staking out homesteads, they were all lighting out to territory already possessed by the various tribes living there. On the Great Plains, for instance, there were the Sioux, Cheyenne, Arapaho, Kiowa, and Comanche; in the Rocky Mountains, the Nez Perce, Ute, and Bannock, to name just a few.

Their numbers, though, had grown smaller. Reporting on the Ute, General Sherman noticed that they'd been reduced to a state of poverty "painful to behold." Their food supply (the buffalo) had been depleted by disease, drought, and slaughter—buffalo hides made the best robes and belts—and by the sporting pleasure of men such as P. T. Barnum. And whereas the buffalo had once roamed freely in search of their food, after 1874, after the invention of barbed wire cordoned off the prairie into ranches and farms, they were no longer able to do so. Soon they would be virtually extinct.

Often western settlers said they wouldn't mind if the Indians could be similarly removed; they blocked the way of new homes and fresh starts. And settlers wouldn't or shouldn't be stopped by uncivilized savages, especially when shiny metals were at stake. "If the whole Army of the United States stood in the way," said Senator John Sherman, "the wave of emigration would pass over it to seek the valley where gold was to be found."

The way west was fraught with danger, some real and some imagined and often exaggerated by the press, which recounted tales of babies brained in front of their petrified mothers and pioneers captured and roasted alive. Yet in 1864, during the war, it was the atrocities committed by white soldiers that grabbed headlines. Colonel

John Chivington, the Methodist minister known as "the Fighting Parson," was bucking for a place in the government should Colorado be granted statehood. In the meantime, he had been authorized by Colorado's territorial governor, John Evans, to raise a 100-days' regiment, the 3rd Colorado Cavalry, to fight Indians—regardless of the fact that the Southern Cheyenne chief, Black Kettle, was a peaceful man who had been urging his people not to engage the white soldiers. Along with several other Cheyenne and Arapaho chiefs, Black Kettle had signed a treaty relinquishing their land in Colorado. For that, he had received assurances from the U.S. government that if they gave up their arms, which they did, he and his people could migrate in peace to the Oklahoma reservation, which is where they were heading.

What happened next would happen again and again in the next decade. In the fall of 1864, Major Edward Wynkoop, the Indian agent whom the Cheyenne affectionately called "Tall Chief," had been relieved of his command at Fort Lyon in Colorado Territory. Nervous before he left the fort in November, he explicitly instructed Chivington not to disturb the Indians who lived nearby. But Chivington, the Fighting Parson, did not care for such minutiae as directives or treaties. "On the 27th day of November, 1864," Wynkoop later reported, "Colonel J. M. Chivington, with the Third Regiment of Colorado Cavalry (100-days' men) and a battalion of the First Colorado Cavalry, arrived at Fort Lyon, ordered a portion of the garrison to join him under the command of Major Scott J. Anthony, and against the remonstrance of the officers of the post, who stated to him the circumstances of which he was well aware, attacked the camp of friendly Indians, the major portion of which were composed of women and children."

The attack occurred at Sand Creek on November 29, at dawn. The young men of the village were away hunting when Chivington and his soldiers rode into the camp and killed almost two hundred of the remaining Cheyenne and Arapaho. Black Kettle, hearing the sound of the oncoming horses, had rushed out to hang a U.S. flag as well as a flag of truce on a pole in front of his tipi, but Chivington and his men were stalking the Indians like wolves, said one observer, and they shot them in cold blood as they tried to flee. White Antelope, another Cheyenne chief, stood with his arms folded, signifying peace. He was gunned down where he stood.

That wasn't all. "Bucks, women and children were scalped, fingers cut off to get the rings on them," reported a horrified soldier who had refused to fire his gun. "A squaw ripped open and a child taken from her, little children shot, while begging for their lives, many shot while on their knees, and with their arms around soldiers a begging for their lives."

The Denver press congratulated Colonel Chivington and his men even though—or likely because—they had hauled an array of Indian scalps and mutilated body parts back to Denver, where they were exhibited as trophies to loud applause at the Apollo Theatre.

Silas Soule was a twenty-six-year-old soldier from Massachusetts and an abolitionist who had roamed the Kansas border as a jayhawker. Not only had he known John Brown, he had tried to break Brown's accomplices out of jail, and he was a friend of Walt Whitman. At Fort Lyon that November, he hadn't been told where he was going—just to fight "hostile" Indians—and when he learned of the plan to raid the sleeping Sand Creek village, he protested to his commanding officer that Black Kettle had been promised protection. "Any man who would take part in the murder, knowing the circumstances as we did," Soule said, "was a low lived son of a bitch."

Soule had refused to fire his weapon at Sand Creek and the following February willingly testified before Congress, recounting what he'd seen happen there. Two months later, he was shot in the back on a Denver street, purportedly by a soldier acting on behalf of Chivington, though that was never proved. In Washington, the congressional investigating committee condemned the massacre, and though Benjamin Wade said it demonstrated "the worst passions that ever cursed the heart of man," Chivington was never indicted on any charges. Sioux, Cheyenne, and Arapaho Indians retaliated by cutting telegraph wires, setting fire to ranches and stagecoach stations, plundering wagon trains, and murdering settlers.

Sherman faced an infuriated, fearful public—and a difficult situation. He had taken up his post as head of the Division of the Mississippi believing that the Indians were "pure beggars and poor devils more to be pitied than dreaded," as he said. In 1865 he informed Grant that he was bound to honor the treaties with the Indians—and that "our plans for protecting the whites must be modified to conform to these treaties." But Indians and settlers alike disregarded treaties whenever it suited them, and settlers often wanted the troops to police the tiniest of infractions, such as an Indian's stealing a cow. "Our soldiers are not to be used against cattle thieves," growled Sherman. Plus, during a tour of the West, he came to the conclusion that the settlers wanted mainly to kill Indians—and do so indiscriminately—which he would not allow them to do.

Rather, the Indians should be absorbed into white civilization, he believed, where they would come under the jurisdiction of constables, not soldiers. The truth was that the government had so often backed out of its commitment to the Indians that it was in effect goading the Indians into war. The only solution that Sherman could see was to confine the Indians to reservations; otherwise they were sure to be annihilated. Senator Lot M. Morrill of Maine had to agree, at least in part. "We have come to this point in the history of the country that there is no place beyond population to which you can remove the Indian," he said, "and the precise question is, will you exterminate him, or will you fix an abiding place for him?" In the meantime Sherman ordered his troops to kill Indians only to scare them—so they would stop raiding white settlements.

For the railroads were coming. "Whether right or wrong, those roads will be built," Sherman said, "and everybody knows that Congress, after granting the charts and fixing the routes, cannot now back out and surrender the country to a few bands of roving Indians." The railroad, he calculated, could solve the Indian problem: by ferrying more and more settlers to the West, it would force the Indians to assimilate—and if the Indians resisted, the railroad could transport more and more soldiers west as well.

Yet by funding the railroads, the government was tacitly promising to protect its financiers, its builders, and its riders. There was the rub for Sherman: he didn't have enough soldiers. The regular army was diminishing—in the next year, it would have only 55,000 enlisted men and soon after that as few as 30,000. Regardless, blue-clad soldiers had been putting up forts along the Bozeman Trail, which cut right through the heart of the Powder River hunting grounds. And that meant trouble. In late 1866, for instance, not long after Fort Phil Kearny was built in present-day Wyoming, the Oglala Sioux, under their chief, Red Cloud, ambushed a group of eighty soldiers. Red Cloud had obviously planned well, having sent ten warriors ahead as decoys, including the young, sandy-haired Crazy Horse, to lure Captain William J. Fetterman and his troops out of the fort. Almost two thousand Sioux, Miniconjou, and Cheyenne, concealed behind the slope of the nearby hills and in the tall grass, wiped out the soldiers in a hailstorm of arrows. The Sioux then took the soldiers' shoes, rifled their pockets for coins, and dismembered their bodies.

Known as the Fetterman massacre, the attack was another headliner. "Now and then you will hear a chicken-hearted historian, who knows nothing of the red savage, extolling his noble characteristics and prizing his natural knightly endowments," railed the *Kearney* [Nebraska] *Herald*. "The best and only way to reconcile the blood-washed animal will be to impose upon him a worse schooling than has ever befallen the inferior races."

MAYBE NOT SO FAST: in the summer of 1867, after the release of a report, *Condition of the Indian Tribes*, Congress authorized a Peace Commission to discover the causes of the Indian wars, to investigate the well-being of various tribes, to negotiate treaties, and then to place Indians in reservations, where they could weave, learn to farm, and take English lessons. If that didn't work, the secretary of war could call for army volunteers; the implicit threat was clear.

The commissioners consisted of four civilians and four military men, including General Sherman, who together tried to convince the Indians to resettle on assigned reservations and to reassure them and the public that the Indian agents appointed to oversee Indian affairs would be honest. In fact, that had already been the plan for decades, so this new commission appeased eastern reformers, who had been complaining about a nefarious Indian Ring made up of unnamed agents, politicians, contractors, and double dealers who presumably bribed, bamboozled, intimidated and cheated both the Indian and the public. (Sherman's solution was for the military to take over all Indian affairs, but that wasn't going to happen.)

In October the commissioners met with a delegation of Kiowa, Arapaho, Southern Cheyenne, Plains Apache, and Comanche at Medicine Lodge Creek in Kansas to work out a new set of agreements. Known as the Medicine Lodge Treaty, it stipulated that the Indians would leave the Pacific railroads in peace and abandon their claim to the land between the Platte River and the Arkansas. For its part, the government promised to resettle the southern plains tribes on reservations, either north of the Red River or in Indian Territory (present-day Oklahoma), although the Indians would be able to hunt south of the Arkansas River as long as water ran and grass grew, the treaty promised. The southern plains Indians were also to receive an annual annuity payment, provisions, and army protection from unfriendly settlers.

By the first of the year 1868, the commissioners also produced a report that pulled no punches in its condemnation of white behavior. It pointed out that the government had made promises it had not kept, signed bogus treaties, stolen land, and dispatched corrupt agents to the reservations. No wonder the Indian had fought back. "If the lands of the white man are taken," the report explained, "civilization justifies him in resisting the invader. Civilization does more than this:

it brands him [the white man] as a coward and a slave if he submits to the wrong." When the Indian protests, the report starkly continued, "civilization with the ten commandments in one hand and the sword in the other, demands his immediate extermination."

A few months later, in April, at Fort Laramie (in present-day Wyoming), the Fort Laramie Treaty was signed, and the peace commissioners seemed to succeed again. Eventually endorsed even by the wary Red Cloud and a number of other Sioux leaders, the treaty ostensibly gave the Sioux what they wanted: a pledge to take down the forts built along the Bozeman Trail. (Of course, since the railroad would soon offer a different and faster way west, the federal government's agreeing to close the forts wasn't much of a victory for the Indians or much of a sacrifice for the whites.) The government also promised the Sioux a large reservation, the Great Sioux Reservation in the Black Hills, to be held in perpetuity, west of the Missouri in what today are the western half and southern parts of South Dakota. Whites would not be permitted to settle there, nor would they be allowed to cross into the territory along the Yellowstone River. Finally, the government recognized the Indians' right to hunt buffalo in the area of the North Platte—an easy concession for the government as it felt that the buffalo would soon disappear anyway.

As far as Sherman was concerned, a sustained war against the Indian would be "a sort of predatory war for years," he declared with typical amoral clarity. "The country is so large, and the advantage of the Indians so great, that we cannot make a single war and end it. From the nature of things we must take chances and clean out Indians as we encounter them."

"Clean out Indians": the phrase is startling but not limited to Sherman. That is, neither the army nor the Interior Department was willing, nor perhaps able, to distinguish hostile from friendly Indians, never mind one tribe and its culture from another, because Indian tribes and their way of life were not for a moment respected. All Indians were savages or barbarians, capable of improvement but not by much; "The red man," said Francis Amasa Walker, is "the most commonplace person imaginable, of very simple nature, limited aspirations, and enormous appetites." Walker served as commissioner in the government's Bureau of Indian Affairs in 1871–1872; he was also a well-known economist and eugenicist and later the president of the Massachusetts Institute of Technology. He said he spoke from experience: "The Indian is unfortunately disposed to submit himself to the lower and baser elements of civilized society, and to acquire the vices and not the virtues of the whites."

The matter of race: there it was again. "The great poison of the age is race hatred," Wendell Phillips declared. For the war against slavery was now ironically being waged against the Indians in rhetorical terms—and with rifles and knives. It's hard not to suppose that Indians served as substitute black (another "inferior race") against whom people afraid of change were raging, people afraid of people who looked, prayed, dressed, and buried their dead differently than they did—or even smelled different. "Most Indians have a personal exhalation, a sort of characteristic halo of atmosphere," said one soldier, "entirely unlike that which marks a negro, but in it was just as strong, though less offensive, and which a government mule will tremblingly detect at a great distance."

The men and women defending the Indian against the incursion of whites were abolitionists of a new order, or so it seemed. "Wendell Phillips' new nigger is the 'noble red man,'" the *New York Herald* contemptuously declared. "To talk of the rights of the Indian today requires the same nerve and moral courage and conscientiousness it did twenty years ago to talk of the rights of the slave," said another, less patronizing journalist, "and the man who asserts them is considered just as mad, foolish and visionary as were the Abolitionists of 1840 or 1850."

Wendell Phillips did not consider himself mad or foolish. He simply wanted to know why citizenship wasn't conferred on the Indian as well as the black man. What about the Fourteenth Amendment? he asked. Why weren't civil rights extended to Indians? Other reformers replied that the Indians should be "civilized" first; then citizenship could follow. But he again said that the issue was plain: "All the great points of the epoch have arisen out of this hatred between the races."

Race was, had been, and would continue to be the issue dividing the United States. "We shall never be able to be just to other races, or reap the full benefit of their neighborhood," he continued, "till we 'unlearn contempt.' "

Unlearning contempt was not going to happen. Neither was citizenship; maybe that was for the better, he reasoned. "Heaven forbid that we should betray the Indian to such protection as 'citizenship' gives to the Georgia negro and loyalist," Phillips scoffed. "No, we are thankful the Indian has one defense that the negro never had. He is no citizen and has the right to make war."

ALL OF THOSE negotiations had taken place during the administration of Andrew Johnson. Plagued more by the South than the West and exasperated by Philip Sheridan's commitment to enfranchising black men in Louisiana, Johnson had peremptorily reassigned Sheridan to the Department of Missouri, where he could battle Indians instead of unreconstructed whites. Johnson had thus hoped to solve the Indian problem and be rid of Sheridan in the bargain.

In March 1868 Sheridan took up his new post with a vengeance. There had been raids in violation of the Medicine Lodge Treaty. Many of the Indian signatories had had no authorization to sign in the first place, or so several warriors believed, and when appropriations for annuities and rations were hamstrung in Congress, a group of irate Kiowa, Southern Cheyenne, and Arapaho, fed up with false assurances and furious that buffalo were being killed or driven away, raided settlers in northwestern Kansas and Colorado. Indians were ransacking freight trains and mail stations, they were stealing horses and robbing stagecoaches, they were capturing women and children. Regarding those actions as a declaration of war, Sherman ordered the army to strike at the Indians without hesitation—if it was war the Indians wanted, he said, "I propose to give them enough of it to satisfy them to their hearts' content."

Sheridan did just that, taking a page from the campaign he had waged in the Shenandoah Valley: make the Indians, all of them, experience war in its full, unremitting, indiscriminate horror. "I hope to do much damage to the Indians before I get through," he told the governor of Kansas, "and have ordered the destruction of their ponies, lodges, and men, so that the border may never again be in danger."

"What I want now, and what the people of your State want," he continued, "is to chastise the Indians so that they will not again be troubled with murders and marauding. This can only be accomplished by killing as many as we can, by destroying their stock, hanging the ring-leaders, and by making them poor."

"The only good Indians I know," Sheridan would say, "are dead." (The inelegant phrase came to be quoted as "The only good Indian is a dead Indian.") But to his commander, General Sherman, an Indian war was an inglorious war; there was no honor in it. Though disheartened, his face furrowed with deep lines, William Tecumseh Sherman was a man of iron will. The military had not wanted to wage war, he had made that clear—and despite his own brass and bluster, he didn't really want another war either. He had thought he could just wait and let the railroads take care of the Indians. But he would do what he had to do. He told Sheridan he would back him to the hilt.

George Armstrong Custer was partial to bright white sombrerolike hats and velvet shirts, and though he perfumed his long golden hair with cinnamon oil, he had not lost his fondness for a fight. Vain and in some ways talented, he believed in himself, but he hadn't been handling the broad, treeless West very well.

Discharged from the volunteer army at the end of the war, the man formerly known as the Boy General in the regular army could claim only the rank of captain. Fortunately, Sheridan was Custer's friend—he'd even gone so far as to give Custer's wife, Elizabeth "Libbie," the table on which Grant and Lee had signed their peace agreement. Sheridan managed Custer's promotion to lieutenant colonel of the 7th Cavalry. Yet despite those tokens of confidence, Custer seemed to have lost his footing. In the West, there was little glamour for the likes of him. Soldiers traveled from one forsaken outpost to another. They drank too much, they mutilated corpses, they seemed bored and without purpose, and they were not swelled by a noble cause; often they were wanderers, veterans, or derelicts who just liked to kill.

In the summer of 1867 Custer wasn't finding any Sioux or Cheyenne, and he was behaving strangely. He was sullen and mean. He would ride off, leaving his men, to take his dogs out for a run, and on one such occasion he chased a buffalo and instead of killing it managed to shoot his own horse in the head, an achievement that left him alone on the plain, without a horse, and in full view of the buffalo, which fortunately for Custer decided not to charge. He humiliated his men, ordering their heads shaved when they bought supplies at Fort Hays without permission. His men began to desert in droves, sometimes in broad daylight. He marched his troops into Colorado, and when more of his men sneaked off, he ordered them rounded up and shot on sight. Three were found, shot, and wounded; one died. That July he'd also forced seventy-six of his soldiers, already exhausted, to travel east, all the way across Kansas to Fort Harker; they covered 150 miles in just four days—and he wasn't even looking for Indians. He had become so intent on seeing Libbie at Fort Riley that he pushed aside whatever or whoever might get in his way. Several of his men went on a scouting expedition, and when word came back that two of them had been killed by Indians, Custer refused to retrieve them or pursue the Indians.

Arrested by his commanding officer, Custer was charged with displaying conduct unbecoming an officer, leaving his post, using the army for his own private ends, and ordering deserters shot as well as abandoning the two men who had been killed. Found guilty on all counts that October, the Boy General was deprived of his rank, his command, and his pay for a full year.

Sherman certainly thought Custer irresponsible, but when Sheridan pleaded on Custer's behalf, Sherman said all right, Custer is a fighter; he needed fighters in the West, especially since Sheridan was bent on hitting Indian villages from several directions in the dead of winter in order to terrorize them. Custer was perfect for that. For Sherman had warned the Indians that if they did not go to the reservations, where, he said, they would be fed and protected, he would wage war. (But when more than 8,000 Indians arrived at Fort Cobb, which was under the command of General William B. Hazen, Hazen could barely feed or clothe the lot of them.)

Before his probation ended, Custer went back into the army, and on November 27, 1868, almost four years to the day since the Sand Creek Massacre, he was again astride his horse. At dawn, he and the 7th Cavalry attacked the village of Black Kettle, the same Black Kettle who had escaped from Sand Creek and was now camped near the Washita River for the winter. But Custer didn't know and couldn't have cared who those Indians were, and he didn't know that Black Kettle had already informed Hazen that the Indians rampaging north of the Arkansas River were not his people. Instead, after ordering the regimental band to strike up the jolly tune "Garry Owen," Custer and eight hundred soldiers obliterated the sleeping village, slaughtering men, women, and children, including Black Kettle and his wife, who were shot in the back as they tried to run. More than a hundred Cheyenne died. Custer's men set the tipis on fire and threw into the flames food, clothing, weapons, buffalo robes, anything they could find.

Custer's attack on Black Kettle's camp was a roaring success, or so he thought, and it redeemed him as a fighter and a crack Indian fighter to boot, which was how he was subsequently known. In the East, however, the destruction of the village on the Washita River sounded to many—and not just Wendell Phillips—like pure murder.

That's what Major Wynkoop called it, and, suspecting another Sand Creek, for which he still felt responsible, he tendered his resignation in protest. For Custer, however, the battle near the Washita meant something far different: he seemed to have found himself.

DESPITE HIS REPUTATION as a butcher, President Grant had little taste for killing and less for extermination. The victorious general who had used peace as a campaign slogan brought to the executive mansion an intense desire to prevent a war in the plains, and in his first inaugural address, delivered in March 1869, he vowed to find some sort of vaguely pacific solution to the conflicts. "The proper treatment of the original occupants of this land—the Indians—is one deserving of careful study," he said. "I will favor any course toward them which tends to their civilization and ultimate citizenship." Grant was therefore receptive to the humanitarians who desired a more peaceful Indian policy. For in his younger days, while stationed in Washington Territory, he had seen, as he said, "a once powerful tribe . . . fast wasting away from those blessings of civilization, 'whisky and Small pox," and he had told his wife, "It really is my opinion that the whole race would be harmless and peaceable if they were not put upon by whites."

Shortly after Grant's inauguration, Congress did pass the Indian Appropriations Act, which authorized the president to create a Board of Indian Commissioners. (The words "commission" and "commissioner" were often and confusingly used; this board, however, is not to be mistaken for the Indian Peace Commission of 1867, authorized by Congress during the Johnson administration.) Rather, Grant's Board of Indian Commissioners was the offspring of his new policy toward the Indians, which was not really new but rather codified the government practice of steering Indians into reservations and urging their domestication—the substituting of ceremonial paint and headdress with trousers and skirts—and transforming them into Jeffersonian farmers. Grant also wanted to end the treaty making, which had not been working in any case, to disrupt the tribal system at the heart of various Indian cultures and to deny the various Indian groups anything like nationhood. Also, he intended to replace the generally crooked Indian agents, whose jobs were the fruit of the patronage system, with missionaries.

The board would not be a government agency per se but rather a group of ten civilians, mostly philanthropists. Nicknamed "Grant's Quaker Policy" because the Society of Friends (Quakers) had been urging the government to treat the Indians more fairly, this evangelizing group of men would be selected not just from the Society of Friends but from all Protestant sects and would include Roman Catholics too (no Jews were represented). The missionaries would take religion, reform, agricultural implements, and ultimately assimilation to a specific reservation, and they would serve the government without pay. With the secretary of the interior, they would also oversee the disbursement of funds allotted by the act (including $2 million earmarked for "civilizing," educating, and Christianizing), and they would tour the West to report back on the conditions of the Indians.

Not one of the commissioners was a westerner or a military man. The only Indian was Ely Parker, Grant's adviser on Indian affairs. And good-hearted though they were, believers in reform, Christianity, confinement, and—in some cases—citizenship, they did not respect the various cultures, religious practices, or social organization of the Indians. Further, the head of the board, the Episcopalian sugar trader William Welsh, hated Parker for reasons that almost seemed personal.

The son of a Seneca chief who had fought the British during the War of 1812, Ely Parker had been born in 1828. Called Ha-sa-no-an-da ("Leading Name"), he had been educated in a Baptist mission school, had taken the name of its minister, and, as a young multilingual and determined man, had lobbied the government on behalf of his home, the Tonawanda Reservation in western New York. By 1851 he had been elected a Sachem of the Six Nations (or Iroquois) Confederacy and managed to help the Tonawanda Seneca

reclaim much of their land. Also, having been a civil engineer, he had
first met Grant in Galena, Illinois, where he had been working on
the new customhouse, and after he had enlisted in the army, he had
joined Grant's staff as an aide. The stocky, smart, and reliable Parker
had been at Grant's side at Vicksburg, and at Appomattox, it had
been Parker who had copied out the terms of surrender that Grant
dictated. And since Grant kept the men he trusted close by, he had
brought Parker with him to the White House.

Despite the friction on the board, Grant's first attempts at instituting his new policy inspired confidence—at least among the reformers. There was no talk of savages. There was much less talk of
extermination. But the policy was more improvisational than fixed;
it groped toward a solution rather than specifying one. And if the
road to peace was paved with good intentions, there was controversy
about who should regulate Indian affairs: the House and Senate were
competing for control over it, and the executive branch was divided
over whether the Department of the Interior or the War Department
should have jurisdiction over the board and Indian affairs generally.
Parker favored transferring Indian affairs to the War Department,
assuming that it could and would operate much like the Freedmen's
Bureau. Sherman too wanted Indian affairs kept at the War Department; men who had to fight were more motivated to keep the peace,
he thought, and certainly would be more motivated than the crooked
traders and Indian agents who, under the umbrella of the Department
of the Interior, supplied Indians with whiskey and Winchester repeating rifles, indifferent to how they might be used. Muzzle-loading
muskets bartered for buffalo robes had killed soldiers such as Captain
Fetterman, whiskey helped no one, and those seamy transactions disgusted Sherman, who argued that Indians toting American firearms
undercut his power to police the frontier.

Yet while the military considered all Indians not rustled onto
reservations as hostile—many of them were, in fact, hostile, particularly those in the northern plains—the reformers leaned in the other
direction and failed to understand the anger of young warriors such

as Crazy Horse, who loathed the reservation system and had no intention of giving up his or his people's freedom. Neither did the brilliant Sitting Bull, a medicine man and the chief of the Hunkpapa Sioux. Sitting Bull scorned "agency Indians," as those who had gone to the reservations were called. Better to have his skin pierced with bullet holes, he said, than to starve like them. "You are fools to make yourselves slaves to a piece of fat bacon, some hardtack, and a little sugar and coffee."

With bands of Indians continuing to attack settlers and travelers, the army was striking back hard—and indiscriminately. In January 1870, just as President Grant was beginning to implement the new peace policy, Colonel Eugene Baker of the 2nd Cavalry, along with two companies of mounted infantry, launched a surprise attack in Montana Territory, near the Marias River, against Piegan Indians, a band of the Blackfoot tribe. Baker and his men killed 173 of them, most of them women and children.

The story subsequently reported in the East about the Piegan massacre was all too familiar to reformers: Chief Heavy Runner had waved a piece of paper certifying him as a peaceful Indian and been gunned down in cold blood; of all the Indians killed, only fifteen were men; the rest were children under twelve, women, and old people; soldiers had fired into the lodges, where women and children were quietly sleeping; soldiers torched tipis, trapping the occupants inside as they screamed and burned; and when they realized that their captives were infected with smallpox, they abandoned them on the trail in forty-degree-below-zero temperatures without blankets or food. The captives froze or starved to death. It was worse than a massacre; it was a humanitarian disaster.

Still, it was part of Sheridan's overall strategy to terrify Indians, although, in his zeal, Colonel Baker had attacked the wrong village and in any case had been already ordered to leave Heavy Runner and his people alone. All those facts enraged Congress and the reformers, many of whom wrote editorials or poems or remonstrated at public meetings. Lydia Maria Child compared what was happening to the

Indians to what had happened to the slaves: "the whip was more efficient than wages to get work out of the black man; and now the
approved method of teaching red men not to commit murder is to
slaughter their wives and children!" In Boston, at the first meeting
of the New-England Labor Reform League (which had replaced the
American Anti-Slavery Society) Wendell Phillips again said that Indians should have the ballot. All men were created equal—*all* men,
whether the Chinese immigrant or the black man, the white man, or
(as he was known) the red man. Savages? The only savages, he said,
were Colonel Baker, General Custer, and General Sheridan.

Indian affairs would certainly not be transferred to the War
Department.

In May, the philanthropist Peter Cooper, the industrialist entrepreneur for whom Cooper Institute in New York City had been named,
called together a meeting of his own organization, the United States
Indian Commission. (The terms are still confusing. Peter Cooper's
group sounds like the Board of Indian Commissioners, which in turn
sounds like the peace commission, and it was neither; Cooper's commission had been founded two years earlier by himself and a group of
private philanthropists and radicals who were bent on defending the
Indians from predatory settlers.) His long, kindly face surrounded by
a fringe of white beard that made him look like a Dutch burgher, if
only he had been plumper, Cooper read from his prepared remarks
about the way the white man had been nothing but illegal, immoral
freebooters to an audience that included William Lloyd Garrison and
representatives from the Board of Indian Commissioners as well as
from the Cherokee and the Creek. Secretary of the Interior Jacob
Cox sent Cooper's organization a letter in which he said he hoped
the Indian Bureau could be another benevolent group, as effective as
the Sanitary Commission. General Sherman, who had been invited
to the gathering, sent the group a letter in which he declared that
meetings like this "accomplish little or no good." Hold the meetings
out West, where the Indians were, he advised. It wasn't stupid advice.

As a matter of fact, a number of Indians were coming to them.

Temporarily joining Chief Spotted Tail of the Brulé, Chief Red Cloud of the Oglala arrived in Washington in June. A good negotiator, Red Cloud was protesting, among other things, the building of Fort Fetterman in Sioux territory. He demanded that whites leave the Powder River country. Accompanied by other chiefs and several women from his tribe, he met with the "Great Father," Grant himself, with Interior Secretary Cox, and with Ely Parker, and he told those bald, gray men, as he called them, that "the Great Spirit did not tell us we are slaves," he said. "We have been driven far enough; we want what we ask for." Patiently explaining himself, as if he were talking to children, Red Cloud said that treaties had been broken, promises not kept, Indians deceived, and that he'd never received a brass pin for letting the railroad pass through his country. "The Great Father may be good and kind, but I can't see it," he continued. "Our nation is melting away like the snow on the sides of the hills where the sun is warm; while your people are like the blades of grass in the Spring when the summer is coming."

Despite his determination and diplomatic panache, Red Cloud did not achieve much except in the way of a publicity tour, for what that was worth. As Sherman had pointed out, nothing could be done anyway. The Indians weren't meeting with Congress. And Red Cloud, who could plainly see that he had gotten nowhere, wanted to go home; he'd had enough of the gray men who had hustled him onto a train bound for New York, where he had not wanted to go. He had been duped and disrespected yet again.

If anyone had thought about who and what Red Cloud was, they would have realized that he would not be impressed by the lights of Broadway, the black-hatted bustle of Wall Street, or the long, bright dresses that fashionable women wore on the crooked streets of lower Manhattan. "I came from where the sun sets," he told the New York delegation sent to meet him. "You were raised on chairs." Yet the chief dutifully appeared (in a starched white shirt) at Cooper Union—after, that is, Peter Cooper promised to donate to Red Cloud the seventeen horses President Grant had failed to give him.

Lining Fifth Avenue, thousands of men and women swarmed the sidewalks to catch a glimpse of the exotic Indians on their way to Cooper Union, where Red Cloud graciously accepted a tall silk hat before he and the other chiefs, along with their interpreters, mounted the stage on which Abraham Lincoln had forcefully spoken a decade earlier. It was a huge crowd pressed together, expectant and momentarily hushed. The auditorium was hot. Red Cloud refused to take a chair at center stage. He and the other Sioux chiefs preferred to sit near the end of the platform, which surprised his hosts. For them, being the center of attention was an achievement in itself.

To great applause, Red Cloud rose. Grave, dignified, and indifferent to the clapping and cheering, he called himself a representative of the original American race—the first people of the continent—and said that the white man had deceived the Indian with treaties misrepresented by the commissioners who asked the Indian to sign then. He and his people could not trust agents or traders. "I don't want any more such men sent out there, who are so poor that when they come out there their first thoughts are how to fill their own pockets," he declared. "We want honest men and we want you to help to keep us in the lands that belong to us so that we may not be a prey to those who are viciously disposed."

Another tribal chief, Red Dog of the Hunkpapa, told the audience he was so fat because he was stuffed with lies. There were more clapping and cheers, for the audience thought him very witty, and at least in the East and at least for a time, public opinion wafted to the side of the Indian.

RELUCTANT TO SHED more blood, Grant attempted to steer a middle course between the humanitarian reformers and the military and between the easterners and the westerners. Westerners often jeered at easterners as "Indian lovers" who imagined Indians as springing from the (wooden) pages of James Fenimore Cooper, who had given them Chingachgook, an Indian with the good grace to disappear in the vanishing wilderness. To westerners, though, as one Nebraska paper put it, the Indian was a "red savage," a "barbarian monster," a "blood-washed animal." In Montana, local residents felt justified in killing the Indians who had unsuccessfully attacked a trading post; they then cut off their heads, boiled them, and carved on the skulls such mottos as "I am on the Reservation at Last." Representative Thomas Fitch of Nevada, an otherwise tolerant man, nonetheless wanted to kill all such hostile tribes as the Apache. "Extinction," he demanded. "And I say that with a full sense of the meaning conveyed by that word." Republican representative Edward Degener of Texas reminded Congress of the forward march of civilization: "He who resists gets crushed. That is the history of the wild Indian." As for a more humane Quaker policy toward the "savage fiends" (not, he added, the Cherokee, the Chippewa, or other "tame tribes"), he contemptuously turned to the representative from Massachusetts, Henry Dawes. "The curse under which our frontier is now groaning was planted into our system years ago by the peaceful men of Massachusetts," he contended. "You were the cause, we suffer the effect."

Summing up the eastern and western views of the Indian, the Missouri-born Mark Twain craftily branded himself an "Indian worshipper"—until he encountered the (fictional) Goshoot Indians, he said, who "set me to examining authorities, to see if perchance I had been overestimating the Red Man while viewing him through the mellow moonshine of romance." Clarence King had written with mellow moonshine of the Indian, with his "spare, bronze face, upon which was written the burden of a hundred dark and gloomy superstitions," although, as he walked away, King remembered with relief the "liberating power of modern culture," which was to say white culture. White culture was the future; with it came progress. The Indian way of life was a thing of the past, romantic and unmodern, and, as Twain suggested, all the romance and moonshine was the flip side of wanting to "go shoot" Indians.

With that kind of anticipatory nostalgia, the Board of Indian Commissioners set about Christianizing and civilizing whatever tribes they could. The one-armed general Oliver Otis Howard, fresh from the Freedmen's Bureau, rode into Arizona and successfully negotiated, for a time, with the Apache chief, Cochise, while Red Cloud successfully negotiated for a reservation for the Oglala in northwestern Nebraska, near the Great Sioux Reservation, and one for the Brulé. But the peace policy was soon entangled in red tape and the chronic squabbles of Capitol Hill, especially because of the acrid charges of corruption that so often fouled Grant's administration and anything it hoped to accomplish. William Welsh resigned as the head of the Indian Bureau after serving for only one month and accused Ely Parker of being part of the "Indian Ring." Pleading innocent, Parker nonetheless left his job in 1871, suspected of having purchased cattle and supplies without advertising for bids, and Interior Secretary Cox, a civil service reformer who disapproved of the spoilsmen lurking around the White House, also resigned. Cox's replacement, Columbus Delano, was soon accused of selling inferior goods to the Indians, and he resigned in 1875. Then Secretary of War William W. Belknap was impeached by the House of Representatives for influence peddling in the West.

Bureaucracy, dishonesty, and empty promises: the Modoc chief, Kintpuash, known by whites as Captain Jack, had had enough. An 1864 treaty with his tribe had not been ratified by Congress for five years, and when it was, Captain Jack protested that it was not the one he had originally signed. Besides, not only had the Modoc been put into a cramped reservation with scant rations, shoddy clothes, tattered blankets, and with the money promised by the government not forthcoming, they had to share the reservation with their enemies the Klamath, who harassed them even after the Modoc were moved to yet another location. Infuriated, the Modoc sequestered themselves in the lava beds near Tule Lake, their former home, and, by refusing to return to the reservation, openly forced the U.S. Army into another war.

But Grant really did want peace. There was a parley in the spring of 1873, a meeting between Captain Jack and General Edward R. S. Canby. During it, Captain Jack, under pressure from rival leaders, signaled to his men, who opened fire on Canby, killing him and the

Methodist preacher Reverend Eleazer Thomas. Three other peace commissioners were also hit.

It was just this kind of treachery that justified exterminating the Indians, exclaimed George Templeton Strong, a New Yorker not of the peace persuasion. To him, all talk of peace had become just "the rosewater Quaker philanthrope policy."

"Our noble savages can be 'improved,' I think," he declared, "only by removal to a better world."

In the West, the editor of a Wyoming paper cried, "Let sniveling quakers give place to bluff soldiers."

Sherman, tolerant at first, could not have agreed more. "Treachery is inherent in the Indian character," he said. Even the liberal-minded *Harper's New Monthly Magazine* began to label the Indian with the same epithets used on the freed blacks of the South: "It is evident they are idle and shiftless, and unable to take care of themselves."

Captured in June, Captain Jack was tried by a military commission; he had no lawyer and no interpreter. In October he was hanged in Oregon, his head cut off and transported to Washington, while the rest of the captured Modoc—those not executed, that is, for Grant commuted two sentences—were shipped off to a reservation in Indian Territory.

THE POSTWAR BOOM went bust. In the fall of 1873, a panic on Wall Street sparked a dire financial crisis the likes of which the country hadn't seen since before the war. Banks failed, trade in securities companies was suspended, and then the invincible Jay Cooke & Co. collapsed; that was the house that had largely financed the war and was underwriting another transcontinental railroad, the Northern Pacific, headed straight toward the Indian Territory. Railroad men had overbuilt, farmers had overproduced, industrial manufacturers were overextended. In the next few years, railroad construction halted, and various roads went bankrupt. As many as 18,000 businesses folded—textile factories, iron mills, and small companies—and men took to the streets in protest as unemployment ran to 14 percent and destroyed the high hopes of the million new immigrants who had flocked into the country. Poverty swept through the nation like a cholera epidemic, while in the West, swarming grasshoppers descended like a plague and chewed through anything, it was said, that looked green.

A labor movement was forming, and Wendell Phillips had already become part of it. Finance robs labor, he said; it gorges capital. And though "labor, the creator of wealth, is entitled to all it creates," the Republican Party, the party of the Gilded Age, with its oligarchies and monopolies, makes "the rich richer, and the poor poorer, and turns a republic into an aristocracy of capital."

There was no money for the Indian, for sure, and certainly not for the South or even the white man—until, that is, there was talk of glittering gold in the dark Black Hills of Indian country. That put a gleam in the government's eye.

THEIR RIFLES GLINTING in the western sun, soldiers in blue had come to the Black Hills to make war on the Sioux, whose rich lands looked good to them.

The Indians would not cede what had been promised in the Fort Laramie Treaty even if the U.S. government was willing to renege and pretend that the army galloping into the hills was doing nothing more than making maps.

In the summer of 1874, heading a huge column of about a thousand men, a hundred wagons, cannon, three Gatling guns, a host of scouts, scientists, two miners, and newspapermen—all good for the publicity he was sure to exploit—Custer with the yellow hair (now shorn) was after gold, and gold was the word bouncing from west to east. "From the grass roots down," said one journalist, "it was 'pay dirt.'"

Though Grant had ordered the Black Hills closed to white settlers, he was soon offering to buy the hills, which were sacred to the Sioux, for $6 million. That is, though the hills were off limits to

whites (by treaty, actually), the army was there, pressuring the Indians; the back-and-forth demonstrates an inconsistent, unclear definition of ownership and possession, which was at the core of the peace
policy, for in the final analysis, to the government, the Indian really
owned nothing.

In the spring of 1875, Red Cloud returned to Washington with
a retinue of chiefs and interpreters to hear the government's terms:
sell the land or suffer the consequence—war—and if war, no more
beef would be delivered to the reservations. Red Cloud would not
yield. He said he needed to take the proposal (really, a threat) home
to a council of tribal leaders. After the leaders passed around the
ceremonial pipe, they mostly concurred with Red Cloud: hold on
to the Black Hills and do not abandon the hunting grounds near the
Tongue River. The Sioux were not a sedentary people; theirs was
a life of freedom, the freedom to hunt, to roam, to live as they had
been living before the white men had slaughtered the buffalo herds.

A congressional commission traveled West to cajole the chiefs.
Sitting Bull was unmoved.

"I want you to go and tell the Great Father that I do not want to
sell or lease any land to the government," he said, picking up a smid-
gen of dirt with his fingers, "—not even as much as this."

IN THE FALL of 1875, Grant consulted with his generals and decided to reverse his policy. He would allow miners into the Black
Hills. He knew that that meant war. And it almost seems as though
the government wanted one. Calling any Indian not on a reservation a
hostile Indian, the government ordered Indians of any band or tribe to
move to a reservation by January 31, 1876. Otherwise, they would be
crushed. But it was winter, and word traveled slowly. The Sioux may
not have heard of the new conditions being imposed on them, and
even if they had and had been willing to comply, how could they ride
through the blinding snow of the Dakota winter to arrive at the reservation on time? Sheridan didn't care. Roaming Indians were the enemy.

Yet when Custer smoked a peace pipe with the Southern Cheyenne after the Washita battle, he had sworn not to attack them again.
Taking no chances, Chief Medicine Arrows sprinkled tobacco ashes
into the bowl of Custer's pipe when it was almost empty to make
sure Custer kept his word. If he didn't, he would be "destroyed like
ashes."

And so he would be. Before that, though, he had been removed
from his command again, this time for failing to call on President
Grant before he rode out west again in 1876. Truth be told, Grant
hadn't actually wanted to see Custer, who had recently testified before
Congress that Secretary of War Belknap had received kickbacks;
what's more, he had implicated Grant's brother Orvil in the sleazy
business. Though Grant wasn't close to Orvil, he stood by friends
and family, all the more so when their reputations were impugned.

Once more Sheridan interceded on Custer's behalf, for Custer was
essential to the three-pronged campaign with which he intended to
demolish the Sioux, who, he believed, were encamped on the Little
Bighorn River, also known as the Greasy Grass. Custer returned to
service and though General Alfred Terry, not Custer, was placed in
charge of the Dakota column—Custer still had his 7th Cavalry—they
planned to advance on the encampment from the east. Leading the
Montana column, Colonel John Gibbon, with seven companies of
infantry, would approach from the west, and General George Crook,
a renowned Apache fighter in the Southwest, would come up from
the south with his Wyoming column, some 1,200 men.

General Terry intended to meet up with Gibbon's column on the
Yellowstone River, at the mouth of the Rosebud River, while Custer
followed the Rosebud; then Terry and Gibbon together would go
along the Yellowstone to approach Little Bighorn River, near where
they believed the Sioux were encamped, and strike the Indians—if,
that is, Custer had by then pinpointed their whereabouts. For Terry
had ordered Custer to follow a southward trail that had been recently
discovered and then join him and Gibbon; that way Custer would
be attacking from both the east and the south. Meantime, if Custer

encountered Indians along the way, he was to use his own judgment about whether to engage them.

Custer vastly underestimated the grit and the canniness of the Sioux. He also had no idea that Sitting Bull had amassed a coalition of about 2,000 warriors and was preparing to fight. With word spreading of the soldiers' advance, with the miserable conditions in the reservations, and with their mounting anger, more and more agency Indians had been swelling the ranks of the Sioux hunting bands, which had already been joined by such tribes as the Northern Cheyenne and the Miniconjou and Blackfoot. The Indians refused to give up their land whether or not the Great Father threatened them.

On June 17, Cheyenne and Sioux horsemen, led by Crazy Horse, attacked General Crook's Wyoming column on the Rosebud River. Riding up close, knocking the soldiers from their horses with their lances and firing their rifles for six ferocious hours, the warriors had stopped Crook's advance cold. Said one white soldier in retrospect, "the Indians were always scientific fighters. When . . . they succeeded in arming themselves with breechloaders and magazine rifles, the Sioux of the northern plains became foemen far more to be dreaded than any European cavalry."

A week later, around noon on June 25, Custer discovered what turned out to be a recently abandoned camp, the campfires still warm. The inhabitants had fled, leaving only a single tipi. Inside was a Lakota warrior, killed during the battle with Crook. Custer had not yet heard of the defeat and could not, in all likelihood, have imagined it. He decided to press forward with five companies in the afternoon.

What Custer then decided to do and when he decided to do it— and the outcome of his decisions—would be discussed for generations.

BACK EAST, THE country was celebrating its Centennial in Philadelphia with an exuberant display of unity and strength and modern technology. The fairgrounds stretched over 236 acres, and almost 200,000 people had come to the opening ceremonies in May, whether in the special trains built for the occasion or in their milk wagons: working women, cooks, servants, dandies, western farmers dressed in homespun. In Machinery Hall, President Grant himself had set into motion the gigantic Corliss engine that supplied power to the entire fairground. "Rich men and poor men," reported a special correspondent for *The New York Times*. "The crowd was nothing if not American." The Americans ogled the newfangled telephone or watched as bricks were fired, or they visited in droves the quaint, souvenirlike Indian tipis, located in the newly erected U.S. Government Building. They were not thinking about Custer.

News that Custer had gone down to certain death—and, as it would turn out, conspicuous celebrity—reached Philadelphia on July 4 in detailed accounts of the two hours of combat soon known as the "Last Stand." On Sunday, June 25, 1876, Custer had divided his men into three battalions, and by late afternoon, he and his battalion were under fierce attack. Leading his warriors, Crazy Horse had painted his face and dusted his horse with dirt before dashing past the soldiers to draw their fire. Crazy Horse was not hit—it was said that no bullet could kill him—and he broke the soldiers' line in two. In the smoke and dust, the shouting and the confusion, mortally wounded bluecoats tumbled from their horses; they were clubbed and shot and slashed with tomahawks; and in the end, nothing remained of Custer's battalion in the 7th Cavalry, no wounded, just dead ponies and saddles and corpses, 225 of them. "Our young men rained lead across the river and drove the white braves back," Sitting Bull recalled.

Two warm and sunny days later, on June 27, General Terry arrived at the battlefield where his lieutenants found the swollen bodies of some 210 dead soldiers, stripped and scalped and torn by scavenging animals. They seemed to have died in clusters, or some of them had; the rest were scattered all over the field. Naked but unmolested, Custer had been hit in the temple and near the heart.

The great Indian victory was a Pyrrhic one. Custer's defeat emboldened western Indian haters, it silenced eastern philanthropists, and it shook the already shaken peace policy. Indian killing was now an act of principled patriotism that united North and South. "As this is the centennial year of American independence," wrote an ex-Confederate to Representative Thomas L. Jones of Kentucky, "I desire to let the world see that we who were once soldiers of the 'lost cause' are not deficient in patriotism. Will you be kind enough to intimate to the President that I offer him the services of a full regiment, composed exclusively of ex-Confederates, to avenge Custer's death."

The Sioux and Cheyenne would succumb to Ranald Mackenzie's cavalrymen, and by the next year, after a winter of plunging temperatures and biting hunger, and with Colonel Nelson Miles and General Crook in pursuit, the Sioux were losing heart. Riding a spotted pony on the stage road from Fort Laramie to the Black Hills, in May 1877 the proud and silent Crazy Horse met with a delegation of U.S. soldiers at the Red Cloud Agency and placed his weapons on the ground. His people had little ammunition, food, or hope. With the promise of a reservation in Powder Hill country, he surrendered. The rest is uncertain. The army arrested him. On the way to the guardhouse, on September 5, 1877, he was mortally stabbed by a soldier. He was thirty-seven. His parents took his body and never told anyone where they buried him.

MINERS, PROSPECTORS, AND unwitting or witting settlers were soon swarming over the Black Hills, buoyed by "manifest destiny."

The Sioux had been reduced to helpless dispossession, for dispossession had been the true center both of the peace policy and of the war policy. But to the white settlers, ranchers and prospectors, to the magnates and to the men seated at their hardwood desks in the Capitol, to the readers of newspapers, the illustrators of magazines, and the investors on Wall Street, to all of them, westward settlement indicated progress—imperial progress, evolutionary progress, material progress. In the year of Custer's defeat, almost $2 million worth of gold was taken out of the Black Hills.

General Sherman had scanned the West and had seen the future: those iron rails stretching from Atlantic to Pacific, the sooty locomotives, their whistles shrieking across the grasslands where the buffalo hardly roamed. In 1880, the six-year-old Gertrude Stein would travel with her family on one of those grand locomotives, bound from the East to Oakland, California, and from the window of the train she saw something quaint, as if out of a storybook—what she called "red Indians"—scattered along what was for her, but not for them, a very exciting way.

(24)

CONCILIATION; OR, THE LIVING

Nathan Bedford Forrest carefully trimmed his mustache and the chin whiskers that had grown as lead gray as his thinning hair. He wore civilian clothes, also grayish, but the buttons of his vest were polished. He stood over six feet tall on small feet. He didn't know the difference between whiskey and brandy, he didn't use tobacco, he didn't eat much. He hated whistling, he hated dirt, he hated disorder. He liked to curse but never told a smutty story. No one wanted to see him angry. There were tales about how he had plunged his bowie knife into an army insubordinate, wiped off the blood, and then casually walked away as the man fell to the ground. He was born a soldier, it was said, the way some people are born poets. But now, in the fall of 1877, the fearsome general once known as the Wizard of the Saddle weighed a skeletal one hundred pounds. His flesh was stretched over his long frame, his face the waxy color of magnolia. Eager to recoup his fortune and assuming he was physically invincible, he had leased 1,800 acres on President's Island in the Mississippi River, and it was there, on his plantation, that he contracted malaria.

At the end of October, Nathan Bedford Forrest was dead. He was fifty-six years old.

When it came time to bury Forrest, some 20,000 people lined the streets of Memphis to watch a three-mile-long procession: two hundred mounted men from Forrest's cavalry, a brass band and ex-Confederate riflemen, still more ex-Confederates, a sprinkling of men dressed in Union blue, and black convicts who worked Forrest's plantation. All had followed the coal-colored hearse pulled by four sleek horses and the retinue of carriages that carried family and city officials. In one of them rode the gaunt former president of the former Confederacy, Jefferson Davis, along with the Tennessee governor, James D. Porter, who were pallbearers.

In the casket lay General Forrest dressed in his Confederate uniform.

Nathan Bedford Forrest was gone, but he had already become the stuff of myth: an audacious cavalry commander and ferocious guerrilla warrior, the illiterate backwoodsman responsible for Fort Pillow, a former slave trader and one of the richest men in Tennessee. General Sherman had said that Forrest possessed a genius for strategy—although Forrest had operated mainly on the margins of the major campaigns and, as one detractor noted, had never faced a really good officer, and he had rarely attacked unless he outnumbered his enemy. Still, there was something timeless about the man who remained incapable of pity or fear, or that's at least how he struck the writer Lafcadio Hearn, who observed the funeral procession with a mixture of horror and awe.

Hearn saw Forrest as "a typical pioneer, one of those fierce and terrible men, who form in themselves a kind of protecting fringe to the borders of white civilization." Defender of his beloved Tennessee and his beloved South, Forrest was one of the last Confederates to surrender—not until May 1865 did he admit defeat—and after the war, still defending his homeland, he was apparently the first grand wizard of the Ku Klux Klan, although when questioned by Congress he disingenuously denied having had any part of it. Denials notwithstanding, Forrest told friends, "If they send the black men to hunt those confederate soldiers whom they call kuklux, then I say to you, 'Go out and shoot the radicals.'"

Yes, there *was* something timeless—and infamous—about Nathan Bedford Forrest. For one thing, he was known far and wide as the Butcher of Fort Pillow although there too he had refused responsibility for what had happened back in the spring of '64. It didn't matter. Let Northerners scowl. General Forrest was also the consummate self-made man: from the rural South, not well born by any means, he had remade himself in true American fashion, converting the boy with the hardscrabble background and an aptitude for violence first into a millionaire and then into a glorious commander who knew that to win, you had to get there first, with the most men. He had survived the death of the thirty or so horses shot from beneath him, and he had survived the war, and though he had unsuccessfully invested in railroads and construction, he was surviving Reconstruction. He had reinvented slavery, after a fashion, by negotiating with local prisons for inmates to work on his malaria-infested plantation, which began to produce, it was said, more than 400 bales of cotton a year. The inmates received a measly 10 cents an hour.

Fortune had been kind to Forrest. Had he died sooner, he might have been remembered as a fighter for a bad cause, said a sarcastic reporter in an article called "Conciliation." He might have been remembered as the man responsible for the massacre at Fort Pillow. Yet by 1877 Forrest could be hailed as the noble defender of his homeland who had bravely resisted interlopers and invaders. Of course, that those invaders just happened to be Union men preserving the country from traitors was of no moment now. All had been forgotten, all forgiven. Even calling what had happened at Fort Pillow a massacre was a quarrelsome exaggeration. "Nothing interferes more with conciliation than to charge those who are to be conciliated with participating in revolting crimes," concluded the mordant reporter. Had dear General Forrest lived longer, he might even have entered the cabinet—or, better yet, taken a seat on the Supreme Court.

On Decoration Day, which had recently become an official holiday, Forrest liked to sprinkle flowers on the graves of the Union dead;

in 1877, when he appeared during the Fourth of July celebrations in Memphis, a group of black men and women was said to have handed him a bouquet of reuniting blossoms.

ON THE NIGHT of his burial, the rains came, heavy, gray, leaden rains, and a wild and howling wind.

Was Nathan Bedford Forrest, outfitted in the regalia of intransigence, again shouting the old Rebel yell and beckoning fellow Southerners to rise, reclaim their heritage and recommit to the peculiar institution, though far changed, for which they had fought? Or was the sound of the wind the sound of the death knell for the Confederacy and the Old South?

Perhaps both.

It was 1877, time for a renewed compromise—called "conciliation."

THE FUNERAL OF Nathan Bedford Forrest did not at all resemble the national funeral of John Quincy Adams, twenty-nine years earlier, when the momentary coming together of North and South had also marked the end of an era. And Old Adams had foretold, Cassandra-like, a future no one wanted to imagine: a divisive and brutal war, if nothing was done about slavery, if no one listened, if temperatures—like his own—climbed too high and minds stayed too made up. Slavery was "a deep-seated disease," he had told Whittier, "preying upon the vitals of this Union." He had foretold war, and war there had been.

Its effects were still being felt, especially in a South confounded by poverty, violence, and resentment. The previous year, during the Fourth of July celebrations, while Northerners had marked the Centennial in Philadelphia and digested the news of Custer's defeat, in the small, predominantly black town of Hamburg, South Carolina, there had been a parade. Company A of the 18th Regiment, National Guard—a black company—was marching on Market Street when two white men had suddenly appeared, driving a one-horse buggy and demanding to pass right through the center of the procession. They were told they would have to wait for the parade to pass or to drive on the side of the street, where there was apparently more room to maneuver. They refused. According to Daniel Lucius "Doc" Adams, the head of Company A, they had no intention of getting out of the way "for no d—d niggers."

A relative of one of the men in the buggy was soon insisting that Doc Adams be arrested for obstructing the road. Adams was served with a warrant, and when he appeared before the black trial justice, Prince Rivers, who had issued it, Adams reputedly ridiculed the complaint. (Newspapers would later complain that Adams had been "insolent.") The distinguished-looking Judge Rivers, who had stolen his master's horse during the war and ridden it across Confederate lines to join Thomas Higginson's Union regiment, cited Adams for contempt of court. He scheduled a trial date for July 8, a Saturday. By that time, though, about 100 white men, many of them drunk, most of them armed with pistols, rifles, hatchets, and clubs, were gathering. Afraid for his life, Adams told Rivers that he couldn't show up for his trial because he had overheard them saying they were going to kill him.

A local Democratic politician, General Matthew C. Butler, a Confederate general who had lost his leg in the war and had reportedly once been a pillar of the Ku Klux Klan, was selected to prosecute Adams. Butler offered a deal: the whole matter could be settled if Adams ordered his National Guard regiment to surrender its arms. Adams said he would do no such thing, and anyway, since the weapons belonged to the state, he had no authority to turn them over to Butler, a civilian. Judge Rivers offered what he thought was a peaceable compromise: box up the militia's arms and send them to Governor Daniel Chamberlain. Butler rejected the suggestion. He wanted those guns out of the hands of Company A, and he wouldn't believe they were unless they were delivered to him personally.

The number of white men in town was growing. They were

coming from Augusta, Georgia, just across the Savannah River, as well as from nearby Edgefield County, where Butler lived. And the white men had brought a cannon. "We are going to redeem South Carolina," Adams heard them sing in the streets. Adams and his company, armed, took shelter in a small brick armory.

The crowd, now a mob, surrounded it. Some were on horseback, their pistols raised. They shot out nearly all the windows in the building. Adams and his men returned fire, killing a white man in the crowd. When Adams's men heard someone outside call for two kegs of powder, they began jumping out of the windows, hoping to run to safety in the woods or down by the river.

There was mayhem in the town. Henry Purvis, a state representative, later said that almost every black man's house was looted (including his); furniture was broken, clothes stolen. Hiding in a neighbor's backyard, Adams said he saw a group of whites shoot James Cook, the black town marshal, then bash his head in with muskets and remove his boots and watch. He saw other white men fire at black people or beat them with sticks. Of the men fleeing the armory, twenty-five were captured before daylight while the moon shone as bright, said Adams, "as ever you seen it shine."

Allan Attaway, David Phillips, Albert Miniart, Moses Parks, and Hampton Stephens were shot in cold blood in a nearby hayfield, said Adams, because they were the town's leading Republicans; Pompey Curry was also shot, but he survived. Adams later explained to a Senate investigating committee that local Democrats had been joining with the various rifle clubs formed to intimidate Republicans, particularly black Republicans, and prevent them from going to the polls. They had begun their campaign in Hamburg. "There had to be a certain number of niggers killed, leading men," Adams said, "and if they found out after the leading men was killed that they couldn't carry the State that way, they were going to kill enough so they could carry the majority."

"The white men have declared that the State has got to be ruled by white men," he continued, "we have got to have just such a government as we had before the war, and when we get it all the poor men and the niggers will be disfranchised, and the rich men would rule."

The Senate investigating committee also heard testimony from a number of witnesses—Democrats—who impeached Doc Adams as a loafer, a trifler, a liar, and a man apt to pick a fight. After the riot, one white man and at least six or seven black men were dead. Congressman Robert Brown Elliott, who had returned from Washington to serve in the South Carolina legislature, helped organize a rally, and black men and women gathered in Charleston at Citadel Square, collecting money for the widows and orphans of the victims and demanding that Matthew Butler be arrested, tried, convicted, and punished. The Reverend Richard Harvey Cain of the African Methodist Church asked if blacks should give up their arms, and the crowd yelled that no, they knew how to use their Winchester rifles, and the 200,000 black women in the state knew how to use a knife. Daniel Chamberlain, the Republican governor of South Carolina, figured nothing would happen to Butler; moreover, he knew what lay ahead: Hamburg presaged the campaign of blood and violence that in the coming months would be directed against Republicans generally and him in particular.

Yet Chamberlain had enjoyed the support of moderate South Carolina Democrats even if some regarded this Massachusetts man a carpetbagger. ("Who is Mr. Chamberlain," jeered a native South Carolinian. "Is he a citizen of the State? and if so, how long?") The son of a farmer, Chamberlain as a youth had taught school in order to earn enough money to go to Yale, and he had been an early abolitionist who had heard Wendell Phillips speak about fifty times. Then, while he was studying law at Harvard, the war broke out. Chamberlain enlisted in 1864 and served as an adjutant under Colonel Charles Francis Adams, Jr., in the 5th Massachusetts Cavalry, a regiment of black soldiers in South Carolina. After the war, he had stayed in South Carolina and started his own cotton plantation. Employing the freedmen, he was hopeful as the idealistic Wilkie James had been. His plantation had gone nowhere—but not so his vision of an integrated, fair government in the South. In 1868 he had served as a delegate to the state constitutional convention from a black district and subsequently was elected for two terms as the Palmetto State's attorney general.

He was bald, he wore a long mustache, he looked directly at you when he spoke, and by 1874 he had been elected governor. Supported by such powerful black leaders as the recently elected war hero Congressman Robert Smalls (the "boat thief" who had stolen the rebel *Planter*) and Robert Brown Elliott, Chamberlain had nonetheless agreed with Democrats that the Republican legislature had been unfairly and disproportionately levying taxes, and he promised to reduce taxes, curtail government expenditures, and reduce state debt—that pleased conservatives—as well as to provide public services, improve public education, and to protect civil and political rights for everyone, which pleased Republicans. It seemed a partnership was actually possible.

Though Chamberlain did reduce taxes and defray the state debt, he also slashed the salaries of public officials and cut funding for schools. Plus, lowering taxes meant that he could not provide services desperately needed by poor whites and the black community, whose support he was beginning to lose. And there were other problems. When he refused to ratify the Republican legislature's appointment of two black circuit trial justices on the grounds that they were corrupt, he alienated his Republican allies. Chamberlain held his ground. Nominating two men known to be dishonest would play right into the hands of the state Democratic Party, which had begun to reorganize itself. Of course, Chamberlain did not help his own cause, either with blacks or other Republican supporters—or, later, with historians—when he told the New England Society of Charleston, "The civilization of the Puritan and the Cavalier, of the Roundhead and the Huguenot, is in peril."

Throughout the South, all-white Democratic administrations known as "redeemer" governments had been undoing the work of

Radical Reconstructionists. They were, by their own description, "redeeming" their states—that is, they were the self-appointed harbingers of a new era, which was the old era in slightly different garb. Slavery was not coming back, to be sure, but the Redeemers planned to restore white rule, and, as the Radical editor George William Curtis, writing in *Harper's Weekly*, put it, they saw "the possible return of the Democratic Party to power as an opportunity of 'putting the negro into his place.'"

In that they had help from Northern journalists. In 1874, James Shepherd Pike's *Prostrate State: South Carolina under Negro Government* ripped through the country with a lurid tale of how carpetbaggers and ignorant blacks—whom carpetbaggers were said to manipulate—were condemning the once grand state of South Carolina to a future of anarchy and theft. "Sambo takes naturally to stealing," Pike explained. "Seven years ago these men were raising corn and cotton under the whip of the overseer," he scoffed. "Today they are raising points of order and questions of privilege."

Charles Nordhoff, another respected Northern journalist—who, like Pike, had been a Greeley supporter—also traveled south to confirm his prejudices and those of his readers in his *The Cotton States in the Spring and Summer of 1875*. It too was a blistering appraisal of Reconstruction, which he too called a failure. Corrupt, carpetbagging whites had manipulated the infantile black population while together they raided the strongboxes, munching peanuts all the while.

Though South Carolina had been the particular target of such animus, Governor Chamberlain had won approval, at least at first, from Northerners. Liberal Republicans praised the cultured Yankee who had attended Harvard, *The Nation* momentarily declaring him "one who is really defending civilization itself against barbarism in its worst form." Since the terms "civilization" and "barbarism" implied "white" and "black," it's no surprise that the editor of the Charleston *News and Courier*, a Chamberlain fan, also hailed him as standing "like a wall of adamant between the public robbers and the honest and law-abiding people of this state." But by pleasing both Republican and Democrat moderates, Chamberlain was alienating the "straight-out" conservative Democrats (or "Stalwarts") who, made anxious by blacks in the legislature and the military, had been forming paramilitary rifle clubs to combat what they called a cringing compromising with principle. That principle was white supremacy—civilization. "Let the last Southern State, one of the thirteen that declared herself free one hundred years ago," railed one newspaper, "be again a white man's State."

When the Stalwart Democrats and the Republicans finally came to bloody collision in Hamburg in the summer of 1876, Chamberlain declared the killings to be far worse than "the slaughter" of Custer and his soldiers, who had at least been killed "in open battle." By contrast, the Hamburg victims were defenseless men gunned down in cold blood. Telegraphing Grant as soon as he heard of the killings, Chamberlain went to Washington, presumably at Grant's invitation, and met with the president, who told him to write a formal letter requesting troops.

In the letter, Governor Chamberlain explained how the massacre had caused "widespread terror among the Colored race and the Republicans of this state," for, as he pointed out, though many whites—Democrats and Republicans—had denounced the violence, they couldn't put a stop to it. Only the president could do that. "Will the general Government take such precautions as may be suitable, in view of the feeling of alarm already referred to, to restore confidence to the poor people of both races and political parties in the State," Chamberlain asked, "by such a distribution of the military forces now here as will render the intervention of the general Government prompt and effective, if it shall become necessary, in restoring peace and order?" He wanted troops.

Since Grant was out of town when Chamberlain's letter reached the White House, Secretary of State Hamilton Fish answered him—and refused the request. Sending troops was unconstitutional. Grant, when he returned, wouldn't disagree. Calling Hamburg "a barbarous massacre, cruel, bloodthirsty, wanton, unprovoked," as well as "a repetition of the curse that has been pursued in other Southern States," the president nonetheless equivocated; he would give Chamberlain the assistance "for which I can find law, or constitutional power." In other words, he wouldn't be able to do much.

Grant did not want to be seen as an autocrat. Democrats and some Republicans had been accusing him of Caesarism, particularly after he had sent troops to New Orleans during a riot on the eve of the 1874 elections; supremacist organizations known as the White Leagues and the White Lines had shot six Radical Republican officials—men from the North—that August, and in September they had staged an armed rebellion outside the Custom House and taken possession of the statehouse. The Republican governor, William Pitt Kellogg, had had to flee. There had been about a hundred casualties. "To say that the murder of a negro or a white Republican is not considered a crime in Louisiana would probably be unjust," said Grant—though he quickly noted that the perpetrators had gone free. Grant sent General Sheridan to Louisiana to look into the matter (and to bolster the Kellogg administration). After the election produced a predictably disputed outcome, with the Democratic and Republican election boards each returning different results, on January 4, 1875, with bayonets fixed, soldiers removed five Democratic members from the Louisiana House for taking their seats illegally. There are instances, said Grant, when the military and federal government simply have to interfere with wanton murder.

Democrats were, of course, furious. So was General Sheridan, who blasted "the terrorism now existing in Louisiana, Mississippi, and Arkansas." If Congress would pass a bill "declaring the ringleaders of the armed White Leagues . . . banditti, they could be tried by a military commission," he fumed. "The ringleaders of this banditti, who murdered men here . . . , should, in justice to law and order, and the peace and prosperity of this southern part of the country, be punished."

Banditti? Sheridan's letter sparked a firestorm of protest. Those good men protecting their homes had been vulgarly compared to wild and marauding Indians (also called banditti). At Faneuil Hall in Boston, Liberal Republicans and Democrats called for Sheridan's removal. They condemned Grant and praised the White Leaguers. When Wendell Phillips, hat in hand, made his way to the platform, he was shouted down, heckled, and hissed. Grant and Sheridan, the crowd yelled, had acted unconstitutionally. Phillips said he wasn't there to defend the administration but the black people of Louisiana. *Wendell Phillips is still on the warpath*, said a Montana paper. William Lloyd Garrison took up his pen to write a letter to the *Boston Daily Journal*. "Lawless and defiant White League organizations," he wrote, "are accurately described by General Sheridan (himself no sentimentalist) and without any sympathetic leaning either toward negroes or Indians) as 'a banditti.'" To those organizations, he noted, "the end sanctifies the means, however desperate and bloody; and that end is first, midst, last, and always, 'A WHITE MAN'S GOVERNMENT.'"

The New York Times was unruffled. "Wendell Phillips and William Lloyd Garrison are not exactly extinct from American politics," it said, "but they represent ideas in regard to the South which the majority of the Republican party have outgrown." What the majority of the Republican Party had "outgrown" was the rhetoric of the higher law—and it had outgrown Reconstruction. No one better espoused the need to bury the latter than the tall, spare, ever loquacious Senator Carl Schurz. In a long, repetitive, and sometimes supercilious speech, he too claimed the use of federal troops in Louisiana unconstitutional, a grave violation of the laws of the republic, and an infringement on the liberty and autonomy of a state government. "If this can be done in Louisiana," he warned, "and if such things be sustained by Congress, how long will it be before it can be done in Massachusetts and Ohio?" As for the ceaseless rash of bloodletting in Louisiana and elsewhere in the South, the fault lay with the federal government and its support of every vagabond—Schurz's term—or rapacious crook who declared himself a Republican and descended on Washington with a sob story about some offense or another. The good men of the South "are not a people of murderers and banditti," he cried. "Only the most morbid fanaticism, will call them so."

His hackles raised, Grant nonetheless heeded men such as Schurz insofar as he claimed not to wish to interfere in local politics. But he was blunt and direct about the need for federal troops in the South. "To the extent that Congress has conferred power upon me to prevent it, neither Kuklux Klans, White Leagues, nor any other associations using arms and violence can be permitted to govern any part of this country," he told the Senate. "Nor can I see with indifference Union men or Republicans ostracized, persecuted, and murdered on account of their opinions, as they now are in some localities." Inaction produces evil, he said. He could not have made his case any clearer.

Calm and almost bullish in his confidence as general during the war, Grant was calm and almost bullish now. Yet he had to retreat to a certain extent, lest he too be called a morbid fanatic who further endangered the Republican Party. A compromise was reached: Louisiana Republicans would control the state Senate and Democrats the House; and Governor Kellogg, though virtually ineffective, would keep his office.

For in the last year, the political climate had drastically changed. After the Panic of 1873, when Democrats had seized control of the House of Representatives, partly as a result of the depression, it had become difficult if not impossible for Grant to buttress Reconstruction—or to stem the withdrawal from it. Already skittish, congressional Republicans, particularly the Liberals, were retrenching. And though Grant publicly backed Charles Sumner's own last stand, his civil rights bill, which prohibited racial discrimination in such public places as schools, churches, hotels, burial grounds, and also in jury selection, faced severe opposition. A rules change allowed it to pass, albeit without the clause mandating integrated schools and without corresponding enforcement legislation.

Grant signed the Civil Rights Act of 1875. Declared unconstitutional in 1883, it was nonetheless a forerunner of the Civil Rights Act of 1964, historic legislation that did not, however, pass for almost a century. And the civil rights legislation went more or less unnoticed in the South, where in 1875, fully aware of Reconstruction's congressional twilight, Mississippi supremacists killed and expelled Northern men and Republicans, to say nothing of black Republican leaders: rallies were broken up; people ran for their lives; Charles Caldwell, once a slave and then a delegate to the state's constitutional convention, was shot in the back on Christmas Day. Republican governor Adelbert Ames, a brave West Pointer highly decorated during the war—who happened to be the son-in-law of the Radical and much-hated Ben "Beast" Butler—almost begged for federal troops to stop the killings. Grant refused, even though the Stalwarts were sweeping Democrats into county and state office. Democrats "support or oppose men, advocate or denounce politics, flatter or murder, just as such action will help them as far as possible to recover their old power over the negro," Ames protested, "and to do this they must disfranchise the negro, not necessarily by law, but practically." "Practically" meant by show of force, and that brutal show of force was called the "Mississippi plan."

The "Mississippi plan," said James Redpath, was "nothing more than a reign of terror."

The "Mississippi plan" had come to South Carolina, with Hamburg its first stop and Matthew Butler calling the "collision" between the races "the culmination of the system of insulting and outraging of white people which the negroes have adopted there for several years." A Georgia newspaper reported with satisfaction that "Negroes defy the civil power and are whipped into obedience." But in Congress, South Carolina representative Joseph Rainey, a black man, asked his colleagues if they "expect my race to submit meekly to continual persecution and massacre by these people in the South? In the name of my race and my people, in the name of humanity, in the name of God, I ask you whether we are to be American citizens?"

Some Northerners were overtly disgusted. Thomas Nast

published a cartoon in *Harper's* in which six black men lie in front of a cluster of inscribed tombstones: "Niggers Reformed at Hamburg, S.C.—All Quiet in Town—A Reform Victory Is Sure, says 'Gen.' M. C. Butler." On another, "Impudent Niggers Daring to Celebrate the 4th." Still another: "Reform Is Necessary in Nigger Killing." Thomas Higginson recalled how in Kansas in 1856 squads of border ruffians from Missouri had crossed the border to vote in the Kansas elections; now white men from Georgia were crossing the Savannah River into Hamburg. "Then the contest was to sustain slavery; now it is for white supremacy," he complained. "Then it was only the armed invasion of a territory; now it is the armed invasion of a state." John M. Carter of New York City directly petitioned Grant. "We black men in the northern states due [sic] feel most deeply for our people in the southern states . . . will the president of the United States Please for God sake look into this mater [sic] and stop the butchery of our people in the South."

Grant dodged the question. He had to adhere to the law. He referred the matter to the Senate and the House. But there the debate stalled. Representative Robert Smalls asked that federal troops remain in his state of South Carolina. In reply, Samuel Cox, Democrat of New York, read aloud from James Pike's *Prostrate State: South Carolina under Negro Government*—about a government of pickpockets and highwaymen who robbed black and white alike; that was the rotten government of South Carolina. Objecting, Smalls asked where Cox had gotten his idea about history—from the history of Tweed's New York? Cox sneeringly asked Smalls who had vouched for him. To which Small quickly replied, "Thirteen thousand majority of the voters of my district in my native State of South Carolina." Flushed, the representative from Mississippi, a man named Lucius Quintus Cincinnatus Lamar II, said, yes, yes, and alas the Hamburg massacre had been a disgrace, there were bad people in the South and in the North, but none of it was legitimate grist for the House mill; let's just move on.

. . . .

BY THE TIME Grant did send troops to South Carolina, in the fall of
1876, the damage had already been done. In Ellenton, about twenty
miles from Hamburg, the local rifle club had murdered as many as
150 blacks, likely more, during a frenzied week in September when
around 800 white men had gone on a rampage. Again joined by vigilantes from Augusta, Georgia, they were shooting blacks by the railroad (in full view of the passengers), in the fields, and in the swamp.
Nearby residents were afraid to bury them.

A relatively small contingent of federal troops arrived in South
Carolina on Tuesday, September 19. "The Yankees had saved them
this time," a white man said with a shrug, "but we would get them
the next time." The Democratic derringer, said a Republican, will
control the coming elections.

But a strapping white man decided to hold out an olive branch to
everyone, black and white. General Wade Hampton was back. This
gentleman of great property (at least before the war) and great standing, descended from men also of great property and standing, including one who had fought in the American Revolution and another
who had fought by Andrew Jackson in the Battle of New Orleans,
was going to run for governor. And though his family had owned
slaves, a good many of them, who had worked on its profitable and
elegant plantations, Wade Hampton had not been a fire-eating secessionist. Yet when South Carolina had seceded, he had entered the
Confederate army as a skilled cavalry officer (he'd been an outstanding horseman) and, with much of his own money, had put together
an aristocratic outfit of young South Carolinians known as Hampton's Legion. Fearlessly, he had fought at the First Battle of Bull Run
(Manassas), where he had been wounded; at Seven Pines, where he
had been wounded; at Antietam and Gettysburg, where he had been
wounded again. But he had continued to fight, though he couldn't
save Columbia, South Carolina, from Sherman, though Sherman
blamed Hampton for ordering the fires that had destroyed that city.

Hampton's own plantations had been torched by Sherman's men, so it's no wonder that when General Joseph E. Johnston gave up his arms, Hampton wasn't quite ready to surrender. His brother had been killed during the war, and his son had died in his arms.

Since Hampton was no longer a major landowner and was unable to afford the taxes on the property he still did own, he had retired from public life. He had invested in an insurance company and was trying to make ends meet. But in 1876, the indomitable, gracious General Hampton was the Democratic gubernatorial candidate who would face down the harried Daniel Chamberlain. For Hampton was a man of capacity and generosity come to rescue his state and to restore the benign, benighted relation between master and slave that he believed to be right, fair, just, and open-minded. The poet Paul Hayne praised Hampton to John Greenleaf Whittier: "If ever a statesman of enlightened views & far-reaching sagacity, of unimpeachable honor existed in this land, that Statesman is Hampton." Hampton very much supported black male suffrage, he said, if it was based on literacy and property. He was no unwashed, trashy racist capable of shooting a black man on sight just for being black. No, he would protect the freedmen—if only they would join him and the Democrats. His arms were open. He would be a very good master, and he would defend, shield, and educate his black brethren, for he firmly believed that "as the Negro becomes more intelligent, he actually allies himself with the more conservative of the whites."

That was the view of Carl Schurz as well.

Besides, Chamberlain's coalition was falling apart. The fact that he'd asked Grant for federal troops had not pleased his allies among moderate Democrats; federal intervention in state affairs was anathema to the sons and daughters of John Calhoun, the man who had fought to his last breath against such a violation of the state's rights. They also accused Chamberlain of using Hamburg to "prop up the waning fortunes of South Carolina Republicanism." Francis W. Dawson, the influential Democratic editor of the *Charleston News and Courier*, once a Chamberlain supporter, slid over into Hampton's camp. Chamberlain had also lost the confidence of many Republicans. Black Republicans accused him of selling out, and Dr. Martin Delany, the outspoken black abolitionist, also endorsed Hampton, believing that reconciliation with whites would prove economically beneficial to blacks—and that Black Republicans, such as those who had spoken against Hamburg in Charleston, were actually stoking racial tensions. "When my race were in bondage I did not hesitate in using my judgment in aiding to free them," Delany said. "Now that they are free I shall not hesitate in using that judgment in aiding to preserve that freedom and promote their happiness." Voting for General Wade Hampton would be the best way to preserve that freedom. Hampton had promised to adhere to the law, "the thirteenth, fourteenth, and fifteenth amendments and keep them in good faith, also pledging that no single right enjoyed by the colored people shall be taken from them," Delany continued. "They shall be the equals, under the law, of any man in South Carolina."

Though Hampton aimed to wash the state of Republican and Radical Republican rule, the Democrats had also chosen three black men as nominees for state positions. That was smart. Hampton was smart. At his rallies, he made sure that prominent blacks sat near him on the stage, and he kept his own campaign appearances free of explicit violence; symbolic power worked well enough. You could hear it when the cannon boomed as ex-Confederate horsemen charged into town, and, like a Roman gladiator, Hampton rode in a chariot festooned with roses and laurel. Said one South Carolinian, who watched in disbelief, "Such delirium as they aroused can be paralleled only by itself even in this delirious state." Ladies and gentlemen turned out in huge numbers to hear the gallant old aristocrat talk in the open air. Brass bands played and the mounted men, rifles ominously dangling from their saddles, sat ramrod straight astride their horses and warily scanned the crowd. They paraded up and down thoroughfares, the meaning of their weaponry very clear. Hampton was also careful to keep his distance from the armed whites who sat in trees, rifles ready, or who crashed several of Chamberlain's rallies.

Chamberlain said that when he opened his mouth to speak, he could hear the click of pistols.

Hampton wanted peace. Shrewdly he welcomed the federal troops ordered to his state with open arms. They were there to protect him, he said, against the black men and women he pretended to fear.

White Republicans who endorsed Hampton, as some of them did, were said to have "crossed Jordan." They may have been as intimidated as the black population, who often voted for Hampton to save their skins and their jobs and what little land they had. (However, by voting for a Democrat, they faced harassment from the other side—from their Republican neighbors.) On election day, there was little overt violence. Then again there was no need. "We kept away fifty or sixty [Negroes] from voting and got about a dozen to vote with us," the Stalwarts bragged. "Why, I carried one negro to the polls myself, and saw him put in his ballot all right, and his two brothers stayed at home all day, for I told them if they voted against us I would turn them off."

Hearing what they wanted to hear, many Northerners remained aloof, having declared a pox on both Republicans and Democrats: Chamberlain's supporters were sincere, decent reformers, it was said, and also pocket-lining scalawags and scoundrels; Wade Hampton was backed by intelligent, educated, and patriotic men like himself—and also by desperadoes and hooligans happy to slit black throats and blow men's heads off.

There was some truth in all of that, but mostly the North's fatalistic attitude became an excuse for ignoring the entire region.

Chamberlain had been abandoned, and he knew it. Republicans preferred political servitude, he said, to the real battle that emancipation entailed—and the very difficult task of reconstructing states poisoned for a century by racism, inequality, hatred, and a pervasive sense of white entitlement. He wasn't talking about this or that corrupt official or this or that legislative infraction or the cloaked night riders and martial men decked out in red blouses, which indicated their keenness to wave a shirt that was literally covered in blood. He was referring to the way that the Republicans had abandoned Reconstruction.

In November Chamberlain and Hampton both pronounced themselves the winner of the election, and Democrats and Republicans in the legislature lined up behind their respective governor. Federal troops were posted around the statehouse, and in a matter of days, both the Democrats and the Republicans were afraid to leave the hall and lose their places, for unauthorized personnel had been barred from the building and once outside, they could have trouble reentering. Hampton tried to keep the peace. He addressed the mob hanging about the Capitol and took his supporters over to Carolina Hall, where they organized themselves into their own legislative body. Then each group turned to the courts, which came up with conflicting results.

As weeks passed, Chamberlain's rump government, which had not been able to draw on public funds, fell into arrears. Its main support came from the federal troops, which, as it happened, were not really protecting him at all; they were guarding the political interests of the national Republicans and another contested race—the one for the president of the United States.

Despite a turbulent second term, Ulysses S. Grant remained hugely popular. Yet he had not run again for president even though his name was seriously and for a brief moment suggested. He was not the darling of the Republicans, certainly not Liberal Republicans in quest of what they considered the best, most genteel men. So he had stepped aside for Rutherford B. Hayes, who became the Republican nominee, and on the night of the election actually went to bed believing that a New York Democrat, Samuel Jones Tilden, was now the nineteenth president of the United States. Tilden had won the popular vote.

The next morning, Republican operatives told Grant that the Republican-appointed election boards in Florida, Louisiana, and South Carolina were contesting the returns. It seemed that blacks had been kept from the polls. White supremacists had ridden through

Florida warning men at gunpoint not to vote Republican, and they had policed the roads to polling places to prevent black men from getting there. One Louisiana parish after another reported similar and appalling conditions: men whipped if they said they were Republicans; if they weren't home, their wives were beaten. There were killing and disemboweling, and one black legislator had been "shot to pieces." In Augusta, Georgia, across the river from beleaguered Hamburg, white men could vote without proving they'd paid their taxes, but a black man had to show his tax receipt and answer as many as a dozen questions before he could vote. About half of those who showed up were not allowed to cast a ballot. "And this is equal rights!" wrote a Northern journalist who covered the election. "The whole thing looks like a farce."

Perhaps, then, Rutherford B. Hayes had won the White House after all. A nondescript congressman from Ohio, Hayes had joined the army after Fort Sumter and, promoted to major general for gallantry, had been wounded five times during the war. Afterward, in Washington, he had joined with the Radical Republicans and voted for Johnson's impeachment even though his major concern was making the Library of Congress into a first-rate institution. In 1868 he had returned to Ohio, and during his four years as governor there, he had worked hard for the ratification of the Fifteenth Amendment. A loyal Grant supporter in 1872, he had again run for Congress, and when he had lost, he had left public service—until 1875, that is, when he had squeaked back into the governor's seat.

An honest man, slightly colorless, Hayes was resolute but not stubborn, and that was appealing, as was the character of his running mate, William A. Wheeler, fifty-seven, who had been serving as a congressional representative from New York for five terms. ("Who is Wheeler?" Hayes had asked when he'd heard he'd be running with him.) Nominated mainly because the other contending candidates had canceled one another out—and it looked as though the front runner, Congressman James G. Blaine of Maine, had had some shady dealings with railroads—Hayes was a safe choice. He had even promised he wouldn't run for a second term to show he was no Caesar and had no thought of personal gain. His son-in-law, the novelist William Dean Howells, produced a campaign biography in which he praised Hayes's refusal to distinguish himself as a sign of his modesty, his courage, and his heroism—and the fact that when he had served on the committee to purchase items for the Smithsonian Institution, "no vote of his ever favored the purchase of trashy pictures or sculptures." Hayes, he said, also believed in the "blessings of honest and capable local government." That meant he was promising the Southern states home and not federal rule.

Samuel Tilden, however, was a formidable New York politician, famous for having taken down the Tweed Ring. But he needed 185 electoral votes to win and so far had gotten only 184. "The result: what is it?" asked the *New York Herald*. Republicans estimated that if they could secure the electoral votes in South Carolina, Florida, and Louisiana—if those states could be said to have gone for Hayes—a Republican would be the next president. (On the other hand, if the new elector in Oregon, where the previous one had been disqualified for being a government employee, went for Tilden, Tilden would win.) It was a tight spot for both men and both parties. Northerners hurried south to take testimony about the election and tabulate votes. John Sherman rushed to New Orleans. So did James Garfield.

The election was being stolen, Democrats charged. In Louisiana, for instance, the election board threw out a number of votes from parishes where blacks had been kept from the polls, and by December the Republican election boards in the three disputed Southern states were declaring Hayes the winner. Yet Democrats had come up with different results and demanded that the electoral votes be tallied in full view of Congress, as prescribed by the Constitution. But if two sets of returns were submitted, one by Republicans, one by Democrats, which slate of electoral ballots should be counted? Furthermore, the House of Representatives was controlled by Democrats, the Senate by Republicans, and no one could agree on which chamber of Congress should open the returns.

The unprecedented situation was so confused and so tense that people in Washington and throughout the nation began to fear the outbreak of another civil war. Grant certainly did not want anything of the kind, and he did not want to sit, Buchanan-like, on his hands. So in January, with the help of both the Republican and the Democratic leadership, he brokered a solution, an electoral commission charged with counting the electoral votes from the three contested Southern states.

With five senators, five representatives, and five Supreme Court justices, the commission was composed of seven Democrats and seven Republicans plus a political independent who soon disqualified himself because he had been elected to the Senate by Illinois Democrats. His replacement, a Republican, voted with his party not to dispute the official state returns, which meant that the election went to Hayes. In truth, though, the commissioners never really investigated voter fraud or the legality of the disputed states' returns; instead, they ratified the certificates entrusted to them by the unredeemed states (South Carolina, Louisiana) where Grant had made sure that federal troops protected the Republican legislatures. As a result, in the end, the Republicans did steal the national election; but Southern white Democrats had in fact suppressed the vote, which made them thieves as well.

According to the historian C. Vann Woodward, Southern Democrats in the Senate had decided not to filibuster (in the modern sense of the word) but to go along with the findings of the federal electoral commission in return for unwritten concessions: that Hayes would remove federal troops from South Carolina and Louisiana and in so doing effectively end what the South regarded as the military occupation that had helped hamstring the region's development. Hayes allegedly also promised to give Southerners more patronage positions, to appoint a Southerner to the cabinet, to shift more appropriations southward, to secure James Garfield the position of Speaker of the House, and to provide the Texas and Pacific Railroad with federal subsidies. In the end, Garfield did not get the job as speaker and the railroad wasn't built, but apparently Hayes hoped that his other unwritten concessions to white Southerners would generally bolster the fortunes of the Republicans, who had been losing seats in the House to the Democrats, and would further undermine the power of the Radicals left in the party.

Rumors of a deal notwithstanding, there were more important reasons for Democrats to accede to the electoral commission's judgment: many Southerners believed it was simply too dangerous not to comply. For what choice did they have? Having just fought a major war, leaders such as Lucius Lamar said he certainly would not take to the streets against Republicans merely to seat Tilden. Southern Democrats had little confidence in their temporizing Northern counterparts, whom they considered too weak and far too devoted to the almighty dollar to stand firmly by them, should they become belligerent. And they were more concerned about home rule and local self-government than about who won the White House. In the North, Hayes supporters such as Carl Schurz had been promising them just that: home rule and federal noninterference. As far as Hayes was concerned, that was no concession; it was the course he preferred.

The bargain struck became known as the Compromise of 1877, and if it was a compromise at all, it implied, among other things, the abandonment of Southern Republicans and blacks and hence the end of Reconstruction—though Reconstruction had been tottering for a very long time.

IN SOUTH CAROLINA, during the gubernatorial standoff, Wade Hampton hedged his bets. He wrote identical letters to Hayes and to Tilden. The solicitous Hampton said he wanted the matter of his own contested election—although he assumed himself the winner—to honor "the constitutional safeguards of popular rights."

The term "constitutional safeguards" was a euphemism: Hampton wanted the army pulled smack out of his state.

So did president-elect Hayes. The day before his inauguration, a friend of Hayes wrote to Daniel Chamberlain to suggest that federal troops now leave South Carolina. In other words, he was saying Chamberlain should step aside, hand the state seal to Hampton, and thereby earn the gratitude of the party, the president, and the country. But the Daniel Chamberlain who read that letter was not the Liberal Republican whom even Carl Schurz had wanted to court before the election. He had seen too much violence and too much chicanery in the past months to brook any compromise, so when the friend proposed a settlement of the gubernatorial dispute that didn't involve federal troops, Chamberlain blew up. "To permit Hampton to reap the fruits of a campaign of murder, and fraud," he fumed, "so long as there remains power to prevent it, is to sanction such methods."

Hayes did not agree. "It is not the duty of the President of the United States to use the military power of the Nation to decide contested elections in the States," he confided to his diary. That federal troops could go—had gone, would go—west to bully Mormons or rob the Sioux: those were different issues. There was gold in the West. There was nothing but poverty and dissension in the South.

On April 10 Hayes ordered federal troops out of Columbia. By May all federal troops had left the South.

"I am confident this is a good work," he told William Dean Howells. "Time will tell."

Time told. A Republican had been installed in the White House, and in the Southern state capitols the Redeemers were in charge. Chamberlain surrendered the state seal to General Hampton, and he soon went north, leaving South Carolina for good. He'd been sold out, he said; the president had made a bargain with the devil.

HAYES'S ELECTION ULTIMATELY disenfranchised the black voter. Hankering after the palmy days of the antebellum South, as one South Carolinian put it, the white Redeemers could use such legal tactics as poll taxes to prevent blacks from voting, or they could redistrict neighborhoods, or, when all legal measures failed, they could make use of the terror they had wielded so well. Writing in the *North American Review*, Governor Chamberlain remonstrated against such "violent exclusion and fraudulent suppression of the colored vote." Few people wanted to listen.

Yet Hayes and the so-called Compromise of 1877 did not cause the end of Reconstruction. After the death of Thaddeus Stevens in 1868, of Stanton in 1869 (at age fifty-five), just after Grant had appointed him to the Supreme Court, and of Sumner in 1874—and the failure of Ben Wade's reelection campaign—there were very few men in government of the old Radical guard pushing for equal rights under the law or willing to change the law to protect all citizens, all of them, or to enforce the civil rights laws as they existed. Liberal Republicans, who had been nibbling away at the foundations of Radical Reconstruction, had no heart or stomach left for the freedmen and freedwomen. The bloodshed in the South seemed the propaganda of old troublemakers. Carl Schurz took Hayes aside to remind him that the Republican parties in the South were dishonest (he made no mention of Democrats and their coercive tactics). Like most Liberal Republicans, Schurz was more interested in civil service reform and western wealth than righting Redeemer wrongs. Righteous indignation about slavery had given way to righteous indignation about alleged political corruption, and the complexities of principled compromise—and of principle—had subsided into a largely bombastic politics of conciliation.

Besides, the Supreme Court had been gutting enforcement legislation. In the Slaughterhouse Cases of 1873, a New Orleans butchers' association had sued Louisiana when the state government had relocated its slaughterhouses to the outskirts of the city, and it used the Fourteenth Amendment to claim it was being denied its rights without due process. The Supreme Court decided that the federal government had no jurisdiction over where butchers slaughtered their animals; that was for the state to decide. In other words, the Fourteenth Amendment could protect only the right of *citizenship*; it couldn't protect other rights, which were the state's prerogative. In one of his last acts, Salmon Chase dissented; the Fourteenth Amendment's equal protection clause, he said, allowed the federal government to shield individuals from discrimination by the state.

Then in 1876, in *United States v. Cruikshank*, the Supreme Court whittled away even more civil rights legislation. The matter at hand was the Colfax massacre: on Easter Sunday, three years earlier, a white paramilitary group had killed more than eighty black men in Grant Parish, Louisiana, where black men legitimately controlled the local government. Using the Fourteenth Amendment, the Justice Department had charged nine of the white ringleaders with conspiring to deprive the Colfax victims of their civil rights; three of them were convicted. But the Supreme Court decided, as in the case of the Slaughterhouse ruling, that the Fourteenth Amendment (and the Enforcement Act passed to protect it) had no dominion over the actions of private individuals. The men accused of the Colfax murders went free, a legitimate government had been overturned, and the white supremacists in the South knew they'd likely never face prosecution if they murdered black men and women.

Grant had not wanted to isolate himself further from his party or from the Liberal Republicans hounding him. To be sure, he was willing to fight to keep what he had recently fought and sacrificed so many men for, but he had been burned by Washington, blunted by criticism, and betrayed by a culture of corruption that he could not or did not want to understand and may, in willful ignorance, have fostered. In December 1876, in his annual message to Congress—which he delivered before the results of the presidential election were finally decided—he again spoke directly, sincerely, and without apology. "It was my fortune, or misfortune, to be called to the office of the chief executive without any previous political training," he said. "Under such circumstances it is but reasonable to suppose that errors of judgment must have occurred."

Mistakes had been made. Grant used the passive voice, as if he had not been responsible or at least not fully so. That was one of the hallmarks of his presidency and his prose: lucidity, candor, and shimmering opacity with a hint of deep loneliness, all at the same time. Yet clearly Grant suffered the burden—the anguish—of Reconstruction undone. And though he was exonerating himself, he shouldered some of the blame. "History shows that no Administration from the time of Washington to the present has been free from these mistakes," he continued. "But I leave comparisons to history, claiming only that I have acted in every instance from a conscientious desire to do what was right, constitutional, within the law, and for the very best interests of the whole people. Failures have been errors of judgment, not of intent."

In its way, his last annual message was heartbreaking: to see the right and, away from the battlefield, be incapable of achieving it.

RUTHERFORD B. HAYES tried to conciliate the factions that had placed him in the White House, but in many quarters he wasn't taken very seriously. Democrats called him "His Fraudulency," and though the Liberal Republican salonista Clover Adams thought him amiable enough, she didn't see any force of intellect in his eyes. As to be expected, the Radicals were harsher. Wendell Phillips dubbed Hayes "the gift Northern blundering has made to the South." Yet to many Republicans, Hayes seemed the solid choice, the inoffensive choice, the choice that spelled continuity, security, hard money and a stable currency, railroads, the safekeeping of beloved Southern institutions, and the protection of civil liberties nationwide. That such a tall order was impossible to fill and had been impossible for Grant, a stronger man despite his weaknesses, did not escape the notice of Phillips. "Half of what Grant gained at Appomattox," he said, "Hayes surrendered for us on the 5th of March."

As of old, William Lloyd Garrison scoffed. Conciliation was but another form of compromise, "meaning thereby," he said, "a truckling to the South as in the days of yore, and a stolid indifference to the fate of her colored population." Liberty and the franchise were being delivered back to the planters and that which seeks to " 'conciliate,' " he cried, "is devoid of all sense of honor, every pulsation of patriotism, every feeling of nationality." To Garrison, compromise had always been acquiescence. He did not see that men such as Chamberlain, however flawed, Robert Elliott, Governor Adelbert Ames, Frederick Douglass, and Chief Red Cloud had been working toward fair compromise—interracial coalitions, whether of Democrats, Republicans, or both. That those men had failed did not undermine their efforts, though their fallibility may have rendered those efforts futile, even tragic. However, Garrison was quite right about conciliation; that was another word for abased appeasement and the suppression of voters' and equal rights.

Yet time and tide flow wide, as Melville had written, though not with much hope. John Greenleaf Whittier ruefully admitted, "I see no better course." All else had foundered. "The colored people have not been saved from suffering between the upper millstone of 'White Leagues' and the nether one of unprincipled 'carpet-baggers,' " he sighed.

The aging, melancholic Quaker poet had grown tired of the Great Cause—though not as tired as the Liberal Republicans had. "The negro will disappear from the field of national politics," said *The Nation* with relief. "Henceforth the nation, as a nation, will have nothing to do with him." The time had come for consolidation, big business, a nation appeased and united in the pursuit of wealth and forgetfulness, secure nonetheless that it had once fought with ecstatic might for freedom and fairness.

Himself a conciliator, Hayes was the convenient tool of conciliators. That was the shrewd assessment of the newly seated Democratic senator from Mississippi, Lucius Quintus Cincinnatus Lamar II. Sizing Hayes up, Lamar called him "well meaning"—but ignorant about the South. "His ideas of the negro are what he gets from Whittier & Uncle Tom's Cabin."

Whittier and Uncle Tom had lost their sting.

· · · ·

LAMAR WAS KEEN, he was courteous, and he spoke in a low, seductive voice. His brown hair covered his earlobes, but he listened very carefully when anyone talked. His head was large, his shoulders were broad, and he had a certain imposing quality. In the fire-eating days before the war, he had approved when the delegates from Mississippi had walked out of the 1860 Democratic convention. Soon after, he had drafted Mississippi's ordinance of secession. But in 1874 it was Lamar who delivered the eulogy for Charles Sumner, a man reviled in the South: "Would that the spirit of the illustrious dead, whom we lament today," he mourned, "speak from the grave to both parties in this deplorable discord in tones which should reach each and every heart throughout this broad territory: 'My countrymen, know one another, and you will love one another!'"

Such astonishing words of conciliation, spoken by a white Southerner as influential and prominent as Lamar, were reprinted in almost every newspaper in the country.

Henry Adams would call Lamar charming, amiable, and reasonable. Mary Chesnut once said that Lamar was the cleverest man she knew, and his startling eulogy of Sumner was clever indeed. It boosted his political capital and handed him a national forum, both at the same time—and for a very long time. In the future, he would be remembered and praised, even by John F. Kennedy, as having inaugurated an era of reconciliation and peace between North and South, although at the time, and according to Governor Adelbert Ames, Lamar said one thing in the North and another in the South. Nor did Wendell Phillips think himself fooled by Lamar. "Drops of rose-water flung on the mad surface of Southern hate," Phillips called Lamar's speeches. W. E. B. DuBois said years later, "Lamar of Mississippi, fraudulently elected to Congress, unctuously praised Sumner with his tongue in his cheek."

Lamar was born in Georgia in 1825 to a family admired for its chivalry, its intelligence, and its Huguenot ancestry. The son of a state judge, he was educated at Emory University, founded in 1838, and then practiced law in Georgia, but after his marriage he eventually settled in Oxford, Mississippi, where his father-in-law (who happened to be the uncle of General James Longstreet) had gone from being president of Emory to president of the University of Mississippi. Lamar taught mathematics there, opened a law office, and in 1855 bought a plantation run by twenty slaves. Two years later, he was elected to Congress as a states' rights advocate come to defend Southern honor, and though he hadn't been a fire-eater himself, the planter-lawyer forcefully argued that secession was a revolutionary movement not unlike the one that had motivated the founding fathers.

Lamar enlisted in the army but after suffering a minor stroke, he resigned from active duty and briefly served Jefferson Davis as a foreign diplomat (although the Confederacy was never recognized abroad) and went to Georgia to counter, if he could, the animosity growing there against Davis. In Richmond, he was a judge advocate for a military court, which he later said was one of the most unpleasant experiences of his life.

After the war he went back to teaching at the University of Mississippi—until he was pardoned. He then returned to Congress as the respected, genteel, wily representative from Mississippi who managed to thwart any passage of legislation that protected blacks' civil rights. In 1876, once the Republican governor, Ames, was out of office, he was able to take a seat in the U.S. Senate. And there, thanks to his eulogy for Sumner, so great was his reputation as the Great Pacificator that by 1884, Grover Cleveland, the first Democrat to be elected president since the war, named Lamar secretary of the interior. Nathan Bedford Forrest could never really have been a Supreme Court justice—but Lamar could; in 1887, Cleveland appointed Lamar to the high court.

Lamar charmed Northern Liberal Republicans bent on rapprochement with the South, particularly during the contested battle for the presidency in 1876. That had been the strategy too of Governor Wade Hampton, who, after the election was decided in Hayes's favor, sidled up to the newly inaugurated president. The two reconcilers had met in Kentucky during the president's southern goodwill tour. "The country is again one and united!" Hayes enthused in his diary. For to him and other Liberal Republicans, the Democratic gentry in the South were as devoted to civil rights as they were—that is to say, in the same limited way—and with such reasonable men as Lamar in government, Hayes could remove troops from the South, which is what everyone wanted, with a clear conscience.

Some of those reasonable men would soon discuss the South's future in a symposium sponsored by the moderate magazine *North American Review*. The topic was "Ought the Negro Be Disfranchised? Ought He to Have Been Enfranchised?" Governor Hampton, Senator Lamar, Representative James G. Blaine, James A. Garfield, Alexander Stephens, and Montgomery Blair (Lincoln's postmaster general, a Tilden supporter) responded sensibly to the subject at hand. Wendell Phillips, also invited to speak, was as usual the odd man out.

Ought the Negro Be Disfranchised? Ought He to Have Been Enfranchised? The questions, of course, smack of reaction, repression, regression. Yet those men considered themselves to be without prejudice. Wade Hampton, for instance, had no intention of going back to anything like slavery. Keep black male suffrage, by all means, he said. "Whatever may have been the policy of conferring right of voting upon the negro, ignorant and incompetent as he was to comprehend the high responsibility thrust upon him, and whatever may have been the reasons which dictated this dangerous experiment, the deed has been done and it is irrevocable."

Lamar agreed. Those two courteous gentlemen—though Lamar was the craftier—would never think of disenfranchising black men. But Lamar did rue the day Republicans had taken office. "By a system, not one whit less a system of force or of fraud than that alleged to exist now, he [the Negro] was taken away from his natural leaders at the South"—such as himself—"and held to a compact Republican vote." Yet, alluding to the recent election of Hayes, he observed with a certain satisfaction that at least the Radical Republican misrule was a thing of the past. In the future, "whenever political issues arise which divide the white men of the South, the negro will divide too," he predicted. "The use of his vote will then be the exercise of his individual intelligence, and he will find friends on all sides willing and anxious to enlighten and influence him, and to sustain him in his decisions." He did not mention the many ways the black man had been prevented from casting that vote.

Wendell Phillips would. At sixty-six, he was slightly stooped, but his arguments were straight and strong. The *success* of black men and women was what the South had most feared, he said. "The negro wielded his vote so bravely and intelligently as to make the enemies of the Union tremble," he declared. No matter what race-baiting Republicans such as James Pike or Charles Nordhoff had written, or what Governor Hampton or Senators Lamar and Schurz might claim, the Fifteenth Amendment had once and for all "scattered the fogs about negro inferiority."

The failure of Reconstruction—if it could be said to have failed—had ironically been its achievement, he continued. Failed? he asked. If so, it had failed only because the Northern Republicans had sold out the Southern Republicans and abandoned the entire black population. "We have believed every lie against them; fraternized with unrepentant rebels; and on the Senate floor clasped hands dripping with the negro's blood," he declared. "While squabbling over the loaves and fishes of office," he continued, "we have allowed our only friends and allies to face the fearful dangers of their situation—into which we called them in order to save the Union—without the protection of public opinion, or the arm of Government itself."

To Phillips, equal rights for all (even women) was a principle important enough and large enough to contain multitudes, black, white, immigrant, laborer, rich, poor, Native Americans. Each could and should possess a part of a more perfect union. But he was still dismissed as a fanatic, and this was no time for fanatics.

Yet if the crusade seemed to have ended, a few of the crusaders were as fervent and as fit as ever, and they staunchly looked forward to the future. Congressman Robert Smalls was facing charges of corruption, likely bogus, not long after he had mocked Samuel Cox on the House floor. He had endured slavery, he had endured military action, and he would endure the U.S. Congress. Battling white supremacists years later, in the 1890s, he announced, with characteristic courage, "I stand here the equal of any man."

In 1876, on the anniversary of Lincoln's assassination, Frederick Douglass again had something to say. He who had once asked "What, to the slave, is the Fourth of July?" pointedly reminded his audience that black people are but the stepchildren—not the children—of Abraham Lincoln. He said that at the unveiling of the Freedmen's Memorial Monument at Lincoln Park in Washington, D.C.; he didn't much like the sculpture, a supplicant black man kneeling before the benevolent president. It was at that unveiling, also, that he called Lincoln tardy, cold, and dull—when, that is, "viewed from the genuine abolition ground." Yet this was not the only way to view Lincoln, he astutely added. "Measuring him by the sentiment of his country, a sentiment he was bound as a statesman to consult," Douglass said, "he was swift, zealous, radical, and determined." Lincoln knew how to straddle, how to wait, how to win, how to work within the law; for all that, he was tardy and swift, cold and zealous, like Douglass himself.

"Though justice moves slowly," Harriet Jacobs, once a slave, had told the longtime abolitionist Lydia Maria Child, "it will come at last." It had not come easily or quickly or fully. Child, who had written *An Appeal in Favor of That Class of Americans Called Africans* back in 1833, knew that. But to the reasonable men in power—from those who had met in a paper symposium about whether black men should have been enfranchised to those gathered in the halls of Congress— justice had been served. The slaves were free and black men might vote, and there were two amendments to the Constitution to prove it. That was that. No longer wielding the absolutist rhetoric of higher laws or the outmoded rhetoric of compromise, which was in any case tainted, these men clasped hands. The time had come for forgetting and healing, erasing and conciliating.

"The past is never dead," the Mississippi novelist William Faulkner would write. "It's not even past." Wendell Phillips would have agreed. He was not going to conciliate, shake hands, or silently walk away. Maybe the white South would never again leave the Union or take up arms against it, but it would rule from within, he said, and preserve as much of its past for as long as it could. His was another warning, milder than that of John Quincy Adams, but a warning nonetheless about the future of freedom and civil rights in America.

Phillips continued to write and lecture. He spoke of labor reform, Native Americans, the persistent depredations in the South, the wars in the West, bottomless greed, and, more recently and to come, the struggle between capital and labor in factories and coal mines. For the gadfly held on to what Emerson so many years before had called the party of hope, composed of those who boldly believed the impossible to be possible. That's why, to Phillips, despite some of his corkscrew logic, Reconstruction had been a success. In subsequent years, of course, it would be dismissed derisively as an abysmal failure—and the fault of the Phillipses and Douglasses, the Radical Republicans and inept blacks, and especially those in government who had bullied and cruelly occupied the South with military force and unforgiving venality. But, anticipating a view that wouldn't surface until the late twentieth century, Phillips understood that, regardless of Reconstruction's failures—and there were many—freedom and the ballot were no trivial achievements.

To him, or to a Robert Smalls, Reconstruction was ongoing. It had to be. They had seen too much and had lived too long to believe that, after all the country had suffered, this was the best it could do.

On a crisp October day in 1880, Phillips rode out from Boston to Wayland, Massachusetts, to the small home of Lydia Maria Child, who had just died. He told her friends what she, this stouthearted woman, wanted carved on her tombstone.

"You think us dead," she would say to future generations. "We are not dead; we are the living."

ACKNOWLEDGMENTS

A very long time in the making, this book would not have existed in the very first place without Sean Wilentz and James Atlas, who in the winter of 2005 encouraged me to take on the formidable task of writing it and the over the next eight years consistently and generously provided encouragement and support.

During those years, I also accumulated unpayable debts, firstly to the many librarians and archivists who unfailingly assist scholars and writers. Among them, I'm grateful for their permission to quote from various archival material: In particular, thanks to Richard Lindemann, curator, and Daniel Hope, assistant, George J. Mitchell Department of Special Collections and Archives, Bowdoin College; Dr. Isaac Gewirtz, curator, and Rebecca Filner, librarian, at the Berg Collection of American and English Literature at the New York Public Library; Susan Glover, keeper of special collections, Kimberly Reynolds, curator of manuscripts, and Sean Casey, reference librarian, at the Boston Public Library, Susan Severtson at *HarpWeek*; Tal Nadan, reference archivist, and David Rosado, at the Manuscript and Archives Division, the New York Public Library; Nancy Kandoian, map cataloguer at the Lionel Pincus and Princess Firyal Map Division, the New York Public Library; Colonel Diane Jacob, head of Archives and Records Management, and Mary Laura Kludy, Archives and Records management assistant, at the Virginia Military Institute; and Christine Weideman, head of the Manuscripts and Archives Division, as well as Diane E. Kaplan, head of Public Services, Cynthia Ostroff, manager of Public Services, Judith Ann Schiff, chief research archivist, and Steve Ross at Manuscripts and Archives, Yale University Library. I also thank Manuscripts and Archives, the Boston Public Library; the Library of Congress; the New York Public Library; the Virginia Military Institute; and the Sterling Library, Yale University, for permission to publish materials from their archives, as indicated in the notes.

I am also grateful to the Hertog Fellows Program at Columbia University, ably administered by Patricia O'Toole, and the excellent work of Elizabeth Redden, my fine former student at Columbia University's School of the Arts. I've also been superbly assisted in research by Columbia graduate students Abigail Rabinowitz, Kim Tingley, and Montana Wojczuk, as well as the distinguished Ph.D. candidate at the CUNY Graduate Center, Cambridge Ridley Lynch. Many thanks to my friend Dan Max, who introduced me to the wonders of Jonah Furman, an early and perspicacious copy editor of my manuscript. Thanks, too, to Fran Kiernan and Benjamin Taylor, who highly recommended Patrick Callihan, a model of diligence, conscientiousness, and calm, particularly when it came time to correcting notes and running down permissions.

While at the Leon Levy Center for Biography at the Graduate Center, City University of New York, where for two years I served as Distinguished writer-in-residence and Director, I had the privilege to work with the remarkable Shelby White, trustee of the Leon Levy Foundation, as well as with Judith Dobrzynski and Jon Bernstein of the Foundation; ditto, at the Graduate Center, President William Kelly and Professor David Nasaw. Most of all, it was a pleasure to know and learn from the fine fellows at the Center.

I am also very proud to teach in the Writing Division of the New School University and even prouder to have worked alongside my colleague and friend, Robert Polito, the program's director. I'm also grateful for the collegiality and kindness of Lori Lynn Turner. At Columbia, my fine colleagues include Binnie Kirshenbaum, Ben Marcus, Lis Harris, Richard Locke, and Phillip Lopate, to whom I'm indebted in a variety of ways, and at Union College, I'm deeply obliged to Dean Therese McCarty, whom I've admired and respected for many years, and to the recent chair of the English department, Kara Doyle, as well as its former chair, Jordan Smith.

Early and very generous readers of this book on whom I've imposed include Christopher Bram, who, with his acute eye and copious knowledge of American history, again offered both suggestions and succor. Rochelle Gurstein kindly insisted on reading an early draft and brought her fine-tuned sensitivity to language. And the generous Sean Wilentz, as mentioned, not only meticulously scoured the manuscript with vigor and typical brilliance, he also improved it; again, I'm grateful for his encouragement—and for his acute historical imagination. Then, too, I profited beyond price from the estimable Robert Gottlieb's meticulous and justly famous editing, the scrupulousness with which he reads, the clarity of his thinking, and the passion with which he discusses both restrictive commas and Henry Adams. I am honored, and this book, like so many others, is far the better for him.

Of course I could not have written this book without relying on the deep research and stunning insights of novelists, poets, historians, critics, and autobiographers—and, years ago, I was also fortunate enough to be introduced to their work by two unusual teachers: Sacvan Bercovitch and George L. Mosse. Each in a different way demonstrated how literature, culture, politics, and people intersect in what was once called the history of ideas, and each of these special teachers committed himself to work that continues to inspire, and from which I continue to learn.

To friends not already mentioned, I owe much more than a simple acknowledgment; but, in brief, I salute the outstanding poet and translator Richard Howard for decades of priceless loyalty, intelligent charm, copious reading, and wit; Larry Ziff for his many kindnesses;

the late John Patrick Diggins, whom I often bombarded with questions; and the incomparable Ina and Robert A. Caro for their thoughtfulness—and their dedication to making history come alive. I'm also grateful beyond words to those other friends and acquaintances who have sustained me with cheer and sympathy, patience and advice, recently and over the years: David Alexander, Alida Becker, Rachel Cohen, David Ebershoff, Benita Eisler, Ellen Feldman, Michele Fron, Wendy Gimbel, Brad Gooch, Molly Haskell, Rick Hamlin, Peter and Rosemarie Heinegg, Virginia Jonas, Wendy Lesser, Paul Levy, Doug Liebhofsky, Michael Massing, Daphne Merkin, Honor Moore, Geoffrey O'Brien, John Palattella, Jed Perl, Robert D. Richardson, Deborah Rosenthal, Helen Schulman, Kurt Silverman, Ileene Smith, Domna Stanton, Catharine R. Stimpson, Paul Underwood, Robert Weil, Robert Wilson, and the very special Victoria Wilson.

Lynn Nesbit, my agent, deserves her own paragraph, to thank her for consistent good sense, her reliability, her marvelous honesty and confidence, and her terrific charm.

Tim Duggan, my talented editor at HarperCollins, has been unfailingly kind, unfailingly efficient, unfailingly good-humored, and preternaturally sharp. With polish and patience, he too improved the manuscript by his careful editing and with his infallible advice. His wonderful associate editor, Emily Cunningham, is similarly a person of grace and reassuring proficiency. Thanks, too, to Lynn Anderson, copy editor; to David Koral in production; to Leah Carlson-Stanisic, who designed the book's interiors; and to Richard Ljoenes, who designed the jacket.

My ceaselessly amazing mother is a woman of rare resourcefulness, rare bravery, and incredible imagination, and I am sure that this book has been influenced by her in countless ways, as is so very much in my life. My father, a veteran of the Second World War and a career military (USNR) officer, with whom I affably argued over the years about military and political affairs, and from whom I learned a great deal, and from whom I continue to learn, unfortunately did not live to read this book. The acute suffering of his last months was relieved somewhat by my extraordinary husband, the composer Michael Del-laira, to whom I dedicate this book. A man of many wondrous and brilliant parts, he read every word of it countless times; discussed with me every phrase, sentence, and concept; stood by me every step of the way. He has brought light into my life, and this book is his as much as mine.

Brenda Wineapple, New York City, 2013

NOTES

COMMONLY USED ABBREVIATIONS

BPL: Rare Books and Manuscripts Department, Boston Public Library, Boston, Massachusetts.

CG: *Congressional Globe: Debates and Proceedings, 1833–1873*. Washington, D.C.: Blaire and Rives, 1834–1873.

LC: Library of Congress, Washington, D.C.

OR: *The War of the Rebellion: A Compilation of the Official Records of the Union and Confederate Armies*. Washington, D.C.: U.S. Government Printing Office, 1880–1901.

NYPL: The New York Public Library, Manuscripts and Archives Division (unless otherwise noted). Astor, Lenox and Tilden Foundations, New York, New York.

Yale: Archives and Manuscripts, Sterling Memorial Library, Yale University, New Haven, Connecticut.

PROLOGUE: THE END OF EARTH

2 "Public buildings that need": See Charles Dickens, *American Notes* (New York: Penguin, 2000), 125.

4 "This is the end of earth": Samuel Flagg Bemis, *John Quincy Adams and the Union*, vol. 2 (New York: Knopf, 1956), 536.

4 The passionate antislavery representative: Quoted in Allan Nevins, *Ordeal of the Union*, vol. 1, *Fruits of Manifest Destiny, 1847–1852* (New York: Charles Scribner's Sons, 1947), 20.

5 "What's the use": Quoted in John Wentworth, *Congressional Reminiscences* (Chicago: Fergus, 1882), 14.

5 "a stout heart": Bemis, *John Quincy Adams and the Union*, vol. 2, 531.

5 "We cannot find": Robert C. Winthrop, in *Token of a Nation's Sorrow: Addresses in the Congress of the United States, and Funeral Solemnities on the Death of John Quincy Adams* (Washington, D.C.: J. and G. S. Gideon, 1848), 8; see also Lynn Hudson Parsons, "The 'Splendid Pageant': Observations on the Death of John Quincy Adams," *The New England Quarterly* 53 (December 1980), 464–82.

5 "There have been": See Robert C. Winthrop, *A Memoir of Robert C. Winthrop* (Boston: Little, Brown, 1897), 81.

6 "battled for a common cause": *Token of a Nation's Sorrow*, 11.

6 "unapproachable by all others:" Ibid., 14.

8 "The last relic": "Ex-President Adams," *New-York Tribune*, Feb. 25, 1848, 2.

9 "Good-bye, Old Man!": Bemis, *John Quincy Adams and the Union*, vol. 2, 544.

9 "knew that the only danger": William Henry Seward, *The Life and Public Services of John Quincy Adams, Sixth President of the United States* (Auburn, N.Y.: Derby, Miller and Company, 1849), 392.

10 "all idealism is compromised": David Brion Davis, "Slavery and the American Mind," in *Perspectives on American Slavery: Essays*, ed. John Blassingame et al. (Jackson: University Press of Mississippi, 1971), 52.

10 "America is the country": Ralph Waldo Emerson, "The Young American," in *Emerson: Essays and Lectures*, ed. Joel Porte (New York: Library of America, 1983), 217.

CHAPTER 1: HIGHER LAWS

15 It is the third of August: This paragraph depends on Louis Schlesinger, "Personal Narrative of Louis Schlesinger, of Adventures in Cuba and Ceuta," *The United States Democratic Review* 31 (September 1852), esp. 212–14.

16 "strong negro or mongrel empire": Quoted in Eric H. Walther, *The Fire-Eaters* (Baton Rouge: Louisiana State University Press, 1992), 107; see also Leonard L. Richards, *The California Gold Rush and the Coming of the Civil War* (New York: Vintage, 2008), 120–21; and Samuel Flagg Bemis, *John Quincy Adams and the Union*, vol. 2 (New York: Knopf, 1956), 338.

16 it would be good: See Philip Foner, *A History of Cuba*, vol. 2 (New York: International Publishers, 1963), 10–33.

17 "every fool declared": Thomas William Wilson, *An Authentic Narrative of the Piratical Descents upon Cuba Made by Hordes from the United States* (Havana, 1851), 14.

17 "we find him in hostile array": "The Invasion of Cuba," *The Southern Quarterly Review* 21 (January 1852), 32

18 "The annexation of Cuba": Quoted in Tom Chaffin, "Filibustering and U.S. Nationalism," *Journal of the Early Republic* 15 (Spring 1995), 94.

18 "López was not particularly interested": Hugh Thomas, *Cuba: The Pursuit of Freedom* (New York: Da Capo, 1998), 213.

19 "You have my best wishes": Quoted in U. R. Brooks, ed., *Stories of the Confederacy* (Columbia, S.C.: State Company, 1912), 312.

20 "We should remember": Quoted in Chaffin, "Filibustering and U.S. Nationalism," 89.

21 "I feel it in my finger ends": James Buchanan, *The Works of James Buchanan*, vol. 8, ed. John Bassett Moore (Philadelphia: J. B. Lippincott & Co., 1909), 362.

21 "Cuba Is Free": Quoted in the fine, comprehensive Tom Chaffin, *Fatal Glory: Narciso López and the First Clandestine American War* (Charlottesville: University of Virginia Press, 1996), 37.

21 "I possess absolute power": Quoted in Walther, *The Fire-Eaters*, 97.

22 "the honor of the Government": Quoted in Chaffin, *Fatal Glory*, 171.

22 "If it be a crime": Quoted in Brooks, *Stories of the Confederacy*, 288.

23 "If the evidence": Quoted in James McPherson, *Battle Cry of Freedom: The Civil War Era* (New York: Oxford University Press, 1988), 106.

24 like dogs: See Louis Schlesinger, "The Personal Narrative of Louis Schlesinger, of Adventures in Cuba and Ceuta," *The United States Democratic Review* 31 (September 1852), 567.

24 "When I was attacked": Quoted in Robert Granville Caldwell, *The Lopez Excursions to Cuba, 1848–1851* (Princeton, N.J.: Princeton University Press, 1915), 105.

24 "He had not courage": Wilson, *An Authentic Narrative of the Piratical Descents upon Cuba Made by Hordes from the United States*, 24.

25 "the infant nation": Quoted in the excellent Daniel Walker Howe, *The Political Culture of the American Whigs* (Chicago: University of Chicago Press, 1979), 123.

27 "twenty years": James Madison, *The Papers of James Madison*, vol. 3, ed. Henry Gilpin (Washington, D.C.: Langtree & O'Sullivan, 1840), 1427.

27 "Great prudence and caution": Quoted in Bemis, *John Quincy Adams and the Union*, vol. 2, 350.

28 "preserve free white labor": Quoted in Charles Going, *David Wilmot, Free Soiler: A Biography of the Great Advocate of the Wilmot Proviso* (New York: D. Appleton and Company, 1924), 174.

28 "The day that balance": *CG*, 29th Congress, 2nd Session, Feb. 19, 1847, 454.

29 "If you seek to": *CG*, 31st Congress, 1st Session, Dec. 13, 1849, 28.

29 "so furious, so bloody": Henry Clay, *Speech of the Hon. Henry Clay, of Kentucky on Taking Up His Compromise Resolutions* (New York: Springer and Townsend, 1850), 32.

29 "years of piecemeal concessions": Quoted in Martin Duberman, *1807–1886* (Boston: Houghton Mifflin, 1961), 165.

29 "The fever of party spirit": Philip Hone, *The Diary of Philip Hone*, ed. Allan Nevins, vol. 2 (New York: Dodd, Mead, 1927), 885.

29 "If it will save the Union": Thaddeus Stevens, *The Selected Papers of Thaddeus Stevens*, ed. Beverly Wilson Palmer (Pittsburgh: University of Pittsburgh Press, 1993), 118.

30 "The slave trade": Quoted in Fawn Brodie, *Thaddeus Stevens: Scourge of the South* (New York: W. W. Norton, 1966), 108.

30 "The most majestic champion": David M. Potter, *The Impending Crisis, America Before the Civil War, 1848–1861*, completed and edited by Don E. Fehrenbacher (New York: HarperCollins, 1976), 98.

30 "has no compromise to offer": *CG*, 31st Congress, 1st Session, March 4, 1850, 455.

30 It was therefore a measure: Merrill Peterson, *The Great Triumvirate: Webster, Clay, and Calhoun* (New York: Oxford University Press, 1987), 458.

30 "sentiment, dear to every true": Quoted in Fergus M. Bordewich, *America's Great Debate: Henry Clay, Stephen A. Douglas, and the Compromise That Preserved the Union* (New York: Simon & Schuster, 2012), 130–31.

31 "The south does not like the north": Ralph Waldo Emerson, "Address to the Citizens of Concord on the Fugitive Slave Law, 3 May 1851," in *The Later Lectures of Ralph Waldo Emerson, 1843–1871*, ed. Ronald A. Bosco and Joel Myerson (Athens: University of Georgia Press, 2001), 272.

31 "head like a wise macaw": Henry Adams, *The Education of Henry Adams*, in *Novels*, ed. Ernest Samuels and Jayne N. Samuels (New York: Library of America, 1983), 814.

32 "We make fables": Ralph Waldo Emerson, *Nature*, in *Emerson: Essays and Lectures*, ed. Joel Porte (New York: Library of America, 1983), 48.

32 "The law of God is supreme": Orestes A. Brownson, "The Higher Law," *Brownson's Quarterly Review*, January 1851, 55.

32 "Mr. Seward had no right": Ibid., 86.

32 "doctrines were to be endorsed": "Washington Correspondence," *New Hampshire Patriot and State Gazette* (March 16, 1850), 2.

32 "sent me to bed": Quoted in Holman Hamilton, *Prologue to Conflict: The Crisis and Compromise of 1850* (Lexington: University of Kentucky Press, 1964), 85–86.

32 In Georgia, a newspaper: *The Georgia Telegraph*, March 26, 1850, 2.

33 "Who are they who venture": Quoted in Allan Nevins, *Ordeal of the Union: Fruits of Manifest Destiny, 1847–1852*, vol. 1 (New York: Charles Scribner's Sons, 1947), 301.

33 "A Kentuckian kneels only to God": Quoted in Caldwell, *The Lopez Expeditions to Cuba*, 103.

33 "I hate to see the poor creatures": Quoted in Abraham Lincoln, *Lincoln: Speeches and Writings, 1832–1858*, ed. Don E. Fehrenbacher (New York: Library of America, 1989), 360.

33 "A people capable of originating": Quoted in Martin Delany, *Martin R. Delany: A Documentary Reader*, ed. Robert S. Levine (Chapel Hill: University of North Carolina Press, 2003), 201.

34 "There is no effectual remedy": J. F. H. Claiborne, *The Life and Correspondence of John A. Quitman*, vol. 2 (New York: Harper & Bros., 1860), 44.

34 "The burning of powder": Quoted in Hamilton, *Prologue to Conflict*, 167

35 "and show our good citizenship": Quoted in the excellent Albert J. Von Frank, *The Trials of Anthony Burns: Freedom and Slavery in Emerson's Boston* (Cambridge, Mass.: Harvard University Press, 1998), 26.

35 "Let the men who would execute": Philip Foner, *History of Black Americans*, vol. 3 (Westport, Conn.: Greenwood Press, 1975), 20.

35 "I don't respect this law": Jermain W. Loguen, *The Rev. J. W. Loguen, as a Slave and as a Freeman: A Narrative of Real Life* (Syracuse, N.Y.: J. G. K. Truair & Co., 1859), 393.

36 "glorious, a holy mission": Lucy Holcombe Pickens, *The Free Flag of Cuba; or the Martyrdom of Lopez* (New York: DeWitt & Davenport, 1854); reprinted with an introduction by Orville Vernon Burton and Georgeanne B. Burton (Baton Rouge: Louisiana State University Press, 2002), 118.

36 Under the pseudonym: See Georganne B. Burton and Orville Vernon Burton, "Lucy Holcombe Pickens, Southern Writer," *The South Carolina Historical Magazine* 103 (October 2002), 298.

36 "Don't say Filibusters!": Pickens, *The Free Flag of Cuba*, 108.

37 Joining the campaign: See, e.g., the discussion of the filibusters and Cuba; see also Chaffin, *Fatal Glory*, and Caldwell, *The Lopez Excursions to Cuba*, as well as the very good Basil Rauch, *American Interest in Cuba, 1848–1855* (New York: Columbia University Press, 1948).

37 "'The revolution in Cuba' proposes": Quoted in Tom Chaffin, "'Sons of Washington': Narciso López, Filibustering, and U.S. Nationalism, 1848–1851," *Journal of the Early Republic* 15 (Spring 1995), 90–91.

37 "to keep in check": Martin Delany, *Blake: or; The Huts of America* (Boston: Beacon Press, 1970), 184.

CHAPTER 2: WHO AIN'T A SLAVE?

39 "In the midst of a world": Thomas Wentworth Higginson, *The Rationale of Spiritualism: Being Two Extemporaneous Lectures Delivered at Dodworth's Hall, December 5, 1858* (New York: T. J. Ellinwood, 1859), 7.

40 When Louis-Jacques-Mandé Daguerre: See the excellent Rebecca Solnit, "The Annihilation of Time and Space," *New England Review* 24 (Winter 2003), 5–19.

40 Formerly a jewel case manufacturer: See Alan Trachtenberg, *Reading American Photographs: Images as History, Mathew Brady to Walker Evans* (New York: Hill and Wang, 1989).

41 "By manufacturing you thus": Quoted in Brenda Wineapple, *Hawthorne: A Life* (New York: Alfred A. Knopf, 2003), 184.

42 "They have no heart": Nathaniel Hawthorne, *The Blithedale Romance*, in *The Collected Novels: The Blithedale Romance*, ed. Millicent Bell (New York: Library of America, 1983), 693.

43 "Thought would preside": Henry Sams, *Autobiography of Brook Farm* (Englewood Cliffs, N.J.: Prentice-Hall, 1958), 6.

43 "We should have": Ibid., 8.

43 "No sagacious man": Hawthorne, *The Blithedale Romance*, 755.

43 "authority from above": Ibid., 678.

44 "This Fugitive Law": Nathaniel Hawthorne to Henry Wadsworth Longfellow, May 8, 1851, *Centenary Editions of the Work of Nathaniel Hawthorne: The Letters, 1843–1853* (Columbus: Ohio State University Press, 1985), vol. 16, 431, ed. Thomas Woodson et al.

44 "We are rapidly preparing": Herman Melville, "Hawthorne and His Mosses," in *The Piazza Tales and Other Prose Pieces, 1839–1860*, ed. Harrison Hayford, Alma MacDougall, and G. Thomas Tanselle (Evanston, Ill.: Northwestern University Press and the Newberry Library, 1987), 248.

45 "Who ain't a slave": Herman Melville, *Moby-Dick* (New York: Library of America College Editions, 2000), 28.

45 "Let America add Mexico to Texas": Ibid., 91.

45 "We can't afford": Ibid., 465.

45 "I feel prouder": Ibid., 580.

46 "in fighting a fish": Ibid., 145.

46 "'Vengeance on a dumb brute'": Ibid., 197.

46 "Is there no other way": Ibid., 572.

46 "the incompetence of mere unaided virtue": Ibid., 222.

46 "If man will strike": Ibid., 197.

47 "So you're the little woman": See Joan Hedrick, *Harriet Beecher Stowe* (New York: Oxford University Press, 1994), vii.

47 "irresistible cause": Henry James, *A Small Boy and Others* (New York: Charles Scribner's Sons, 1913), 158; see also George Orwell, *All Art Is Propaganda: Critical Essays*, compiled by George Packer (Boston: Houghton Mifflin Harcourt, 2008), 252.

47 "Let us hope": Quoted in Wineapple, *Hawthorne: A Life*, 255.

47 "*heart's blood*": Quoted in Hedrick, *Harriet Beecher Stowe*, 231.

48 "I have felt all along": Quoted in Wineapple, *Hawthorne: A Life*, 255.

48 even the Christian slave: For a fine discussion, see Joan Hedrick, *Harriet Beecher Stowe: A Life*.

48 "When I thought": William Wells Brown, *Narrative of William W. Brown, a Fugitive Slave* (Boston: Anti-Slavery Office, 1847), 70

49 "It is a melancholy exemplification": "Southern Slavery and Its Assailants: *The Key to Uncle Tom's Cabin," DeBow's Review* (November 1853), 487–88.

49 "what becomes of her modesty": Quoted in Thomas W. Higginson, "Woman and Her Wishes," *The Una* (Boston: Robert F. Walcutt, 1853), 22.

49 "It does seem to me": Nathaniel Hawthorne to Sophia Hawthorne, March 18, 1856, in *Centenary Edition of the Works of Nathaniel Hawthorne: The Letters, 1853–1856,* ed. Thomas Woodson et al., vol. 17 (Columbus: Ohio State University Press, 1987), 457.

49 "If it should prevail": Quoted in Higginson, "Woman and Her Wishes," 25.

50 "The anti-slavery movement": Ibid., 25.

50 "Of course, in a novel": Harriet Beecher Stowe, *Uncle Tom's Cabin,* in *Three Novels* (New York: Library of America, 1982), 185.

50 "would grace one of the tallest trees": *CG,* 30th Congress, 1st Session, April 20, 1848, 502.

51 "the spirit of a Martyr": Elizabeth Peabody to Elizabeth Palmer Peabody, March 20 [1848], The Henry W. and Albert A. Berg Collection of English and American Literature, NYPL, Astor, Lenox and Tilden Foundations.

51 "A partisan cannot be": Mary Tyler Peabody Mann, *Life of Horace Mann* (Boston: Walker, Fuller and Company, 1865), 285.

52 "No man in the country": Quoted in Josephine Pacheco, *The Pearl: A Failed Slave Escape on the Potomac* (Chapel Hill: University of North Carolina Press, 2005), 147.

52 "Believing that the extinction": "Thoughts of the Week," *National Era,* April 27, 1848, 66.

53 "I feel in this case": Mann, *Life of Horace Mann,* 270–71.

53 "get the principles on record": Quoted in ibid., 269.

53 The convictions of Drayton and Sayres: See, e.g., Mann, *Life of Horace Mann,* 400; also David Herbert Donald, *Charles Sumner and the Coming of the Civil War* (New York: Alfred A. Knopf, 1960), 221.

53 "I shall be abused": Quoted in Richard C. Rohrs, "Anti-slavery Politics and the *Pearl* Incident of 1848," *The Historian* 56 (Summer 1994), 722.

54 And what had happened: See John H. Painter, "The Fugitives of the Pearl," *The Journal of Negro History* 1, no. 3 (June 1916), 243–64.

54 "knew how he could transmute": Horace Mann, *Slavery: Letters and Speeches* (Boston: B. B. Mussey & Co., 1853), 511.

55 "A thousand—fifteen hundred": William Beecher and Samuel Scoville, *A Biography of Rev. Henry Ward Beecher* (New York: Charles Webster, 1988), 293.

55 "were, under God, secured": William Parker, "The Freedman's Story, Part I," *The Atlantic Monthly* 17 (February 1866), 154.

56 "in liberating every one": Ibid., 160.

56 Carrying arrest warrants: For fine accounts of the Christiana resistance, see Jonathan Katz, *Resistance at Christiana: The Fugitive Slave Rebellion, Christiana, Pennsylvania, September 11, 1851, A Documentary Account* (New York: Thomas Y. Crowell Company, 1974); see also Thomas P. Slaughter, *Bloody Dawn: The Christiana Riot and Racial Violence in the Antebellum North* (New York: Oxford University Press, 1991).

56 "I am the United States marshal": Parker, "The Freedman's Story, Part II," 283.

56 "Leader, what do you say": Ibid., 285.

56 "at the risk of our own lives": Ibid., 160.

57 "take all this from a nigger": Ibid., 286.

57 "How many times": Ibid., 280.

57 "All you colored people": Ibid., 290.

CHAPTER 3: ONE AGGRESSES

58 "talent for silence": George Templeton Strong, *The Diary of George Templeton Strong*, vol. 2, ed. Allan Nevins and Milton Halsey Thomas (New York: Macmillan, 1952), 106.

58 Disgusted: Horace Mann's letters to his wife, Mary Mann, July–August 1852, Mann Collection, Massachusetts Historical Society.

59 "just an average man": Quoted in Brenda Wineapple, *Hawthorne: A Life* (New York: Alfred A. Knopf, 2003), 256–57.

59 "a thorough, unmitigated": Quoted in ibid., 262.

59 "If the Federal Government": Franklin Pierce, inaugural address, in James D. Richardson, ed., *A Compilation of the Messages and Papers of the Presidents*, vol. 5 (Washington, D.C.: U.S. Government Printing Office, 1897), 198.

60 "It is not to be disguised": Ibid., 201.

60 "General Pierce is not the equal": "Cuba! The Philosophy of the Ostende Correspondence," *Democratic Review* 35 (June 1855), 457.

60 "What possible interest": "The Cuban Question—Important Letter from Mr. Everett," *The New York Times*, Sept. 22, 1853, 3.

61 "only required having his stomach": "Recollections of an Old Stager," *Harper's New Monthly Magazine* 58 (January 1874), 254.

62 "wanton injury": *CG*, 33rd Congress, 1st Session, Exec. Doc. 76, March 15, 1854, 2.

63 "to detach that island": Henry B. Learned, "William L. March," in *American Secretaries of State*, vol. 6, ed. Samuel Flagg Bemis (New York: Alfred A. Knopf, 1928), 193–95.

63 "Judge Mason can scarcely": Don Piatt, "Cuba and the Ostend Manifesto," *Harper's New Monthly Magazine* 40 (May 1870), 901.

64 "It is said that the collision": *Boston Daily Atlas*, March 9, 1855, quoted in Amos Aschbach Ettinger, *The Mission to Spain of Pierre Soulé, 1853–1855: A Study in the Cuban Diplomacy of the United States* (New Haven, Conn.: Yale University Press, 1932), 403.

64 "Your money or your life": Quoted in Frederick Moore Binder, *James Buchanan and the American Empire* (Selinsgrove, Pa.: Susquehanna University Press, 1994), 216.

65 "higher and a more solemn obligation": Quoted in Robert Walter Johannsen, *Stephen A. Douglas* (Urbana: University of Illinois Press, 1997), 421.

66 "The Nebraska question": Quoted in Lars Schoultz, *Beneath the United States: A History of U.S. Policy toward Latin America* (Cambridge, Mass.: Harvard University Press, 1998), 54.

66 "this momentous question": Thomas Jefferson to John Holmes, April 22, 1820, Library of Congress.

66 "slaveholding despotism": Quoted in Johannsen, *Stephen A. Douglas*, 418.

66 "the pure unadulterated representatives": Quoted in Allan Nevins, *The Ordeal of the Union*, vol. 2 (New York: Charles Scribner's Sons, 1947), 114.

67 "the old policy": Quoted in Robert D. Samson, *John L. O'Sullivan and His Times* (Kent, Ohio: Kent State University Press, 2003), 223.

67 "abolition party": Stephen A. Douglas, *The Nebraska Question, Comprising Speeches in the United States Senate* (New York: Redfield, 1854), 46.

67 "this cruel attempt": M. A. DeWolfe Howe, *The Life and Letters of George Bancroft*, vol. 2 (New York: Scribner's, 1908), 124.

68 "It is now Sunday morning": J. Madison Cutts, ed., *A Brief Treatise upon Constitutional and Party Questions, and the History of Political Parties* (New York: D. Appleton, 1866), 100; but see also Gerald M. Capers, *Stephen A. Douglas: Defender of the Union* (Boston: Little, Brown, 1959), 120.

69 "When the white man governs": Abraham Lincoln, "Speech on Kansas-Nebraska Act," in *Lincoln: Speeches and Writings, 1832–1858*, ed. Don E. Fehrenbacher (New York: Library of America, 1989), 328.

70 "viewed from the genuine": Frederick Douglass, *Frederick Douglass: Selected Speeches and Writings*, ed. Philip Foner (Chicago: Lawrence Hill Books, 1999), 621.

70 "Slave States are places": Lincoln, *Lincoln: Speeches and Writings*, 331.

70 "Necessity drove them": Ibid., 338.

70 "Ask us not to repeal": Ibid., 320–21.

71 "Is it not probable that": Ibid., 335.

71 "For who after this": Ibid.

72 "We went to bed": Quoted in the fine account of Albert J. Von Frank, *The Trials of Anthony Burns: Freedom and Slavery in Emerson's Boston* (Cambridge, Mass.: Harvard University Press, 1998), 207.   .

72 "covenant with death": William Lloyd Garrison, "The Covenant with Death," *The Liberator*, July 21, 1854, 24.

73 "The white people owed": Quoted in Nell Irvin Painter, *Sojourner Truth: A Life, a Symbol* (New York: W. W. Norton, 1996), 137.

73 "Who can be serene": Henry David Thoreau, "Slavery in Massachusetts," in *Collected Essays and Poems* (New York: Library of America, 2001), 346.

73 "Let us teach, urge, encourage": James Redpath, *The Roving Editor: or, Talks with Slaves in the Southern States* (New York: A. B. Burdick, 1859), 84.

74 "to kill every God-damned abolitionist": Quoted in David M. Potter, *The Impending Crisis: America before the Civil War, 1848–1861*, completed and edited by Don E. Fehrenbacher (New York: HarperCollins, 1976), 203.

74 "I say let the Indians": Quoted in the fine T. J. Stiles, *Jesse James: Last Rebel of the Civil War* (New York: Vintage, 2003), 47.

74 "full of whiskey and resentment": Potter, *The Impending Crisis*, 201.

75 "The territory was covered": Redpath, *The Roving Editor*, 341.

76 "that the military authority": Quoted in "John Quincy Adams on Slavery Emancipation as Affected by War," *New-York Tribune*, September 1, 1861; see also John Fiske and John B. McMaster, *A History of All Nations*, vol. 23 (Philadelphia: Lea Brothers, 1905), 106.

76 "liberty and slavery are eternally": John W. Blassingame, ed., *The Frederick Douglass Papers*, ser. 1, vol. 2 (New Haven, Conn.: Yale University Press, 1979–1992), 482; see also Benjamin Quarles, *Frederick Douglass* (Washington, D.C.: Associated Publishers, 1948), 61–163.

76 "silently epitomized": William W. Freehling, *The Road to Disunion: Secessionists Triumphant, 1854–1861*, vol. 2 (New York: Oxford University Press, 2007), 79.

76 "But the reckless": Strong, *The Diary of George Templeton Strong*, vol. 2, 273.

CHAPTER 4: DEMOCRACY

78 "love Yankeedom less": Quoted in Theodore A. Zunder, "Whitman Interviews Barnum," *Modern Language Notes* 48 (January 1933), 40.

79 "of the good little girl": Quoted in A. H. Saxon, *P. T. Barnum: The Legend and the Man* (New York: Columbia University Press, 1989), 175.

80 "sensible Dramatic version": Edward Kahn, "Creator of Compromise: William Henry Sedley Smith and the Boston Museum's *Uncle Tom's Cabin*," *Theatre Survey* 48 (2000), 72.

80 By the time he published: For information on Barnum, see *Struggles and Triumphs; or, Forty Years' Recollections of P. T. Barnum*, ed. with introduction by Carl Bode (New York: Penguin, 1981), 23; Saxton, *P. T. Barnum*; Bluford Adams, *E Pluribus Barnum: The Great Showman and the Making of U.S. Popular Culture* (Minneapolis: University of Minnesota Press, 1997); Neil Harris, *Humbug: The Art of P. T. Barnum* (Chicago: University of Chicago Press, 1981).

80 "Our life is an apprenticeship": Ralph Waldo Emerson, "Circles," in *Emerson: Essays and Lectures*, ed. Joel Porte (New York: Library of America, 1983), 403.

80 "We had ceased": Milton Hindus, ed., *Walt Whitman: The Critical Heritage* (New York: Barnes & Noble, 1971), 56.

82 "the very God Pan": Bronson Alcott, *The Letters of Bronson Alcott*, ed. Richard L. Hernstadt (New York and Iowa City: University of Iowa Press, 1969), 211.

82 "heartiness & broad generalities": Henry David Thoreau, *The Correspondence of Thoreau*, ed. Walter Harding and Carl Bode (New York: New York University Press), 444–45.

82 "What is there in the people": Horace Traubel, *With Walt Whitman in Camden*, vol. 1 (Boston: Small, Maynard and Company, 1906), 212.

82 "Thoreau's great fault": Ibid.

83 "The best writing": Ibid., 374.

83 "I greet you": See the excellent David S. Reynolds, *Walt Whitman's America: A Cultural Biography* (New York: Alfred A. Knopf, 1995), 341–42.

83 "priapic": Thomas Higginson, *Contemporaries* (Boston: Houghton Mifflin, 1900), 77.

83 "I look in vain": Ralph Waldo Emerson, "The Poet," in *Emerson: Essays and Lectures*, 465.

83 "Mr. Walt Whitman": Quoted in Justin Kaplan, *Walt Whitman: A Life* (New York: Simon & Schuster, 1980), 209.

84 "In every department": Walt Whitman, *Complete Poetry and Collected Prose*, ed. Justin Kaplan (New York: Library of America, 1982), 1330.

84 "Yes, the world's a ship": Herman Melville, *Moby-Dick* (New York: Library of America College Editions, 2000), 66.

85 "The West": Adam Goodheart, *1861: The Civil War Awakening* (New York: Alfred A. Knopf, 2011), 222.

85 John C. Frémont was: See Richard Slotkin's fine *The Fatal Environment: The Myth of the Frontier in the Age of Industrialization, 1800–1890* (New York: Athenaeum, 1985), 199, and more generally, Tom Chaffin, *Pathfinder: John Charles Frémont and the Course of American Empire* (New York: Hill & Wang, 2002), and Allan S. Nevins, *Frémont: Pathmaker of the West* (Lincoln, Nebr.: Bison Books, 1983).

87 "The merest baby": Quoted in Allen C. Guelzo, *Lincoln's Emancipation Proclamation: The End of Slavery in America* (New York: Simon & Schuster, 2004), 47.

87 "Whether or not Frémont won": Evert Duyckinck to George Duyckinck, Oct. 20, 1856, Duyckinck Family Papers, NYPL.

88 the antislavery Republicans won: The voter turnout and the election results encouraged Republicans, who won 1,336,924 votes in the free states, versus 1,222,066 for Buchanan and 394,647 for Millard Fillmore, as Whig. In the free and slave states, the vote was 1,338,171 for Frémont; 1,863,991 for Buchanan; and 892,659 for Fillmore. See Lewis Clephane, *Birth of the Republican Party* (Washington, D.C.: Gibson Bros., 1889).

88 "the negroes received an idea": Sophia Hawthorne to Mary Mann, Dec. 30 [1856]–Jan. 2 [1857], Berg Collection, NYPL.

88 "to consider the practicality": Quoted in Brenda Wineapple, *White Heat: The Friendship of Emily Dickinson and Thomas Wentworth Higginson* (New York: Alfred A. Knopf, 2009), 89. The original source is the pamphlet advertising the Worcester Disunion Convention at the Houghton Library, Higginson Collection, Harvard University.

89 "We are treading": Quoted in Allan Nevins, *Ordeal of the Union: A House Dividing, 1852–1857*, vol. 2 (New York: Charles Scribner's Sons, 1947), 494.

90 "safely say": For an excellent summary of these issues, see Kenneth Stampp, *America in 1857: A Nation on the Brink* (New York: Oxford University Press, 1990), 92–109.

90 "secretly made a pawn": Ibid., 92.

90 In the stunning 7–2 decision: The literature on the Dred Scott case is voluminous. Among other sources, I have depended on the invaluable Don E. Fehrenbacher, *The Dred Scott Case: Its Significance in American Law and Politics* (New York: Oxford University Press, 1979).

91 "Man cannot hold": Frederick Douglass, "Two Speeches by Frederick Douglass: one on West India emancipation, delivered at Canandaigua, Aug. 4th, and the other on the Dred Scott decision, delivered in New York on the occasion of the Anniversary of the American Abolition Society, May, 1857": Frederick Douglass Papers, LC, 30.

91 "The sun in the sky": Ibid., 31–32.

91 "did not mean to say all were equal": Abraham Lincoln, "Speech on Dred Scott Decision, June 26, 1857," in *Lincoln: Speeches and Writings, 1832–1858*, ed. Don E. Fehrenbacher (New York: Library of America, 1989), 398.

92 Again, the Dred Scott decision: See again the important arguments of David M. Potter, *The Impending Crisis, America Before the Civil War, 1848–1861*, completed and ed. Don E. Fehrenbacher (New York: Harper & Row, 1976), 290, which I am summarizing here.

92 "you noticed that the time": Horace Traubel, *With Walt Whitman in Camden*, vol. 2 (Boston: Small, Maynard & Company, 1915), 382.

93 "Land! Land! is the cry": Quoted in Allan Nevins, *The Emergence of Lincoln: Prologue to Civil War, 1859–1861*, vol. 2 (New York: Charles Scribner's Sons, 1950), 157.

94 "Walker is all things to all men": Quoted in John McKivigin, *Forgotten Firebrand: James Redpath and the Making of Nineteenth-Century America* (Ithaca, N.Y.: Cornell University Press, 2008), 35.

94 "By God, sir": Quoted in Nevins, *The Emergence of Lincoln*, vol. 2, 250.

94 "broken-down political hacks": Quoted in ibid., 230.

95 as one Kansan noted: See ibid., 236.

95 "Cuba! Cuba!": "The Covode Investigation," 36th Congress, 1st Session, Report No. 648, 119.

95 "The fractious cabal": George Templeton Strong, *The Diary of George Templeton Strong: 1835–1875*, vol. 2, ed. Allan Nevins and Milton Halsey Thomas (New York: Macmillan, 1952), 381.

96 "I am sick to death": Quoted in Eric H. Walther, *The Fire-Eaters* (Baton Rouge: Louisiana State University Press, 1992), 110.

97 "When I am on one": Quoted in Daniel Walker Howe, *The Political Culture of the American Whigs* (Chicago: University of Chicago Press, 1979), 251.

CHAPTER 5: SOVEREIGNTY

99 "The end of the cable": "The Telegraph Celebration. Military and Civic Parade. Speech of David Dudley Field," *New York Herald Tribune*, Sept. 2, 1858, 8.

100 "American Mind, American Opinions": "Speeches of Gov. King and Senator Seward," *The New York Times*, Aug. 16, 1858, 3.

100 "two continents have been penetrated": Quoted in *Frank Leslie's Illustrated Newspaper*, Aug. 21, 1858, 1.

101 "Yesterday's *Herald* said": George Templeton Strong, *The Diary of George Templeton Strong: 1835–1875*, vol. 2, ed. Allan Nevins and Milton Halsey Thomas (New York: Macmillan Company, 1952), 408.

101 "There is no such thing": *Savannah Morning News*, Aug. 31, 1858, 1.

104 "They instituted among themselves": Quoted in David L. Bigler, "A Lion in the Path: Genesis of the Utah War, 1857–1858," *Utah Historical Quarterly* 76 (Winter 2008), 6.

104 "In temporal things": Quoted in Larry Schweikart, "The Mormon Connection: Lincoln, the Saints, and the Crisis of Equality," *Western Humanities Review* 34 (Winter 1980), 16.

106 "they desire a kingly government": "The Mormons and Their Doings," *DeBow's Review* 22 (May 1857), 491–92.

107 "Religion of Sensuality": Strong, *The Diary of George Templeton Strong*: 1835–1875, vol. 2, 376.

107 "those twin relics of barbarism": *Proceedings of the First Three Republican National Conventions* (Minneapolis: C. W. Johnson, 1893), 43.

107 "At whatever cost": "The Mormons," *Harper's Weekly*, April 25, 1857, 1.

108 "loathsome, disgusting ulcer": Quoted in "Kansas—The Mormons—Slavery: Speech of Senator Douglas, Delivered at Springfield, Ill., June 12, 1857," *The New York Times*, June 23, 1857, 1.

108 "upon the ground": Ibid.

108 "Why deprive the Mormons": "Lincoln's Springfield Speech," *Chicago Daily Tribune*, June 19, 1857, 2.

108 "Supersede the Negro-Mania": Quoted in Philip G. Auchampaugh, *Robert Tyler, Southern Rights Champion, 1847–1866: A Documentary Study Chiefly of Antebellum Politics* (Duluth, Minn.: H. Stein, 1934), 180–81.

109 "At the present moment": Buchanan quotations are from James Buchanan, "Message from the President of the United States to the Two Houses of Congress at the Commencement of the First Session of the Thirty-Fifth Congress" (Washington, D.C.: Cornelius Wendell, 1857).

109 "lie in the grand pathway": Quoted in Bigler, "A Lion in the Path," 4.

110 Young's replacement: Wallace Stegner, *The Gathering of Zion: The Story of the Mormon Trail* (New York: McGraw-Hill, 1964), 286. I have taken certain details about the Mormon evacuation of Salt Lake City in the previous paragraphs from this fine volume.

111 "The eyes of the whole Union": Quoted in *Dallas Herald,* August 1, 1858, 2.

111 "You are like Byron": Quoted in Don E. Fehrenbacher, *Prelude to Greatness: Lincoln in the 1850s* (Palo Alto, Calif.: Stanford University Press, 1962), 98.

111 "Let Mr. Douglas and Mr. Lincoln": Abraham Lincoln and Stephen A. Douglas, *The Lincoln-Douglas Debates: The First Complete, Unexpurgated Text*, ed. Harold Holzer (New York: Fordham University Press, 2004), 3.

112 "He is the strong man": Quoted in Ronald C. White, Jr., *A. Lincoln: A Biography* (New York: Random House, 2009), 258.

112 "If slavery be a blessing": Quoted in Avery Craven, *The Coming of the Civil War* (Chicago: University of Chicago Press, 1957), 320.

113 "The general recognition": "The Political Future," *The New York Times*, March 5, 1858, 4.

113 "He has shown": "Stephen A. Douglas," *The Portsmouth Journal of Literature & Politics,* June 5, 1858, 1.

114 "In my opinion": Paul M. Angle, ed., *The Complete Lincoln-Douglas Debates of 1858* (Chicago: University of Chicago Press, 1958), 22; see also "Senator Douglas at Home; Triumphant Demonstration!," *The* [Cleveland] *Plain Dealer*, July 12, 1858, 2.

114 "diversity, dissimilarity, variety": Lincoln and Douglas, *The Complete Lincoln-Douglas Debates of 1858*, 18, 20. See also Kenneth M. Stampp, *The Imperiled Union: Essays on the Background of the Civil War* (New York: Oxford University Press, 1980), for a brilliant analysis of the Douglas position and its moral shortcomings.

117 "I am not nor ever have been": Abraham Lincoln, *Abraham Lincoln: Complete Works, Comprising His Speeches, Letters, State Papers, and Miscellaneous Writings*, ed. John G. Nicolay and John Hay, vol. 1 (New York: Century Company, 1894), 370.

118 "Does he [Douglas] mean": Lincoln and Douglas, *The Complete Lincoln-Douglas Debates of 1858*, 68.

119 "If the slaveholding citizens": Fehrenbacher, *Prelude to Greatness*, 140–41; see also Harry V. Jaffa, *Crisis of the House Divided: An Interpretation of the Issues in the Lincoln-Douglas Debates* (Chicago: University of Chicago Press, 1959), 352–59, for a good overview and analysis of the matter.

119 "Compared with this": John G. Nicolay and John M. Hay, *Abraham Lincoln: A History*, vol. 2 (New York: Century Company, 1890), 163.

119 Gone too was his hope: In "'Buchanan's Blunder': The Utah War, 1857–1858," *Military Affairs* 25 (Fall 1961), 122–23, Richard D. Poll and Ralph W. Hansen interestingly argue that "inadequate communications" were in part responsible for misunderstanding both on the part of the Buchanan administration, although it did not investigate the allegations against the Mormons, and on the part of the Mormons, whose mail was put under embargo; "the facts did not support the alarms of either party to the conflict."

119 "glorious destiny": Quoted in Robert W. Johannsen, *Stephen A. Douglas* (Urbana: University of Illinois Press, 1997), 683.

119 "We live in a rapid age": Ibid., 684.

120 "the Senator from Illinois": Judah P. Benjamin, *CG*, 36th Congress, 1st Session, May 22, 1860, 2241.

121 "an independent foreign policy": See T. J. Stiles, *The First Tycoon: The Epic Life of Cornelius Vanderbilt* (New York: Alfred A. Knopf, 2009), 281; in fact, chap. 11 of

this book is a fine summary of the relationships among Vanderbilt, Walker, and the U.S. government.

122 "As soon as the Cuba question": *CG*, 35th Congress, 2nd Session, Feb. 25, 1859, 1352.

122 But Republicans such as: See Frederic Bancroft, *The Life of William H. Seward* (New York: Harper & Company, 1900) 1, 472–78.

122 "The Senate is the propagandist": *CG*, 35th Congress, 2nd Session, Feb. 25, 1859, 1355.

123 "Shall we give niggers": Ibid., 1354.

123 "The injustice and despotism": Pleasant H. Stovall, *Robert Toombs: Statesman, Speaker, Soldier, Sage* (New York: Cassell Publishing Company, 1892), 137.

123 "He may go tell": *CG*, 35th Congress, 2nd Session, Feb. 25, 1859, 1356.

124 "The social intercourse": Robert Toombs, Alexander H. Stephens, and Howell Cobb, *The Correspondence of Robert Toombs, Alexander H. Stephens, and Howell Cobb: Annual Report of the American Historical Association for the Year 1911*, vol. 2, ed. Ulrich B. Phillips (Washington, D.C.: U.S. Government Printing Office, 1913), 453.

124 "If you will stand with me": Quoted in William Y. Thomson, *Robert Toombs of Georgia* (Baton Rouge: Louisiana State University Press, 1966), 132.

CHAPTER 6: REVOLUTIONS NEVER GO BACKWARD

126 "Better have a *little*": Frederick Douglass, *My Bondage and My Freedom*, in *Autobiographies*, ed. Henry Louis Gates, Jr. (New York: Library of America, 1994), 367.

126 "refuses to oppose": Quoted in the superb Eric Foner, *Free Soil, Free Labor, Free Men: The Ideology of the Republican Party before the Civil War* (New York: Oxford University Press, 1995), 302.

126 Adams had said: See John Stauffer, *Giants: The Parallel Lives of Frederick Douglass and Abraham Lincoln* (New York: Twelve, 2009), 144–51. Note that many of the Liberty Party's members moved over to the Free Soil party. For a cogent analysis of Douglass's and Lincoln's different political points of view, see also the excellent volume by James Oakes, *The Radical and the Republican: Frederick Douglas, Abraham Lincoln, and the Triumph of Antislavery Politics* (New York: W. W. Norton, 2007).

127 "To him, your celebration": Frederick Douglass, " 'What to the Slave Is the Fourth of July?': An Address Delivered in Rochester, New York, on 5 July 1852," in *The Frederick Douglass Papers*, ed. John W. Blassingame, vol. 2 (New Haven, Conn.: Yale University Press, 1982), 371.

127 "We need the storm": Douglass, *My Bondage and My Freedom*, 434.

128 "that religious elevation": Thomas Wentworth Higginson, *Cheerful Yesterdays* (Boston: Houghton Mifflin, 1898), 219.

128 "a strange, resolute, repulsive": William Phillips, *The Conquest of Kansas by Missouri and Her Allies* (Boston: Philips, Sampson & Company, 1856), 333.

128 "a transcendentalist above all": Henry David Thoreau, *The Writings of Henry David Thoreau: Reform Papers*, ed. Wendell Glick (Princeton, N.J.: Princeton University Press, 1973), 115.

128 "Talk is a national institution": Quoted in John Edwin Cooke, *The Life, Trial, and Execution of Captain John Brown, Known as "Old Brown of Ossawatomie," With a Full Account of the Attempted Insurrection at Harper's Ferry* (New York: Robert M. De Witt, 1859), 21–22.

128 "swallows a Missourian": Thomas Higginson, "Antislavery Festival," *The Liberator*, Jan. 16, 1857, 1.

128 "Weird John Brown": Herman Melville, "The Portent," in *Poets of the Civil War*, ed. J. D. McClatchy (New York: Library of America, 2005), 50.

129 "Lynch-law is terrible always": Phillips, *The Conquest of Kansas*, 317.

129 "lean, strong, and sinewy": Frederick Douglass, *The Life and Times of Frederick Douglass*, in *Autobiographies*, 716.

129 "Slavery was a state of war": Ibid., 718.

130 "like some dark ghost": W. E. B. DuBois, *John Brown*, ed. David Roediger (New York: Modern Library, 2001), 148.

130 "Napoleon himself had": Quoted in Cooke, *The Life, Trial, and Execution of Captain John Brown*, 13–14.

130 "I think him equal": Odell Shephard, ed., *The Journals of Bronson Alcott* (Boston: Little, Brown, 1938), 316.

131 The Reverend Henry Ward Beecher: James Redpath, ed., *Echoes of Harper's Ferry* (Boston: Thayer and Eldridge, 1860), 6.

131 "The Beechers of our age": Ibid., 6.

132 "You, Old Hero": James Redpath, *The Roving Editor: or, Talks with Slaves in the Southern States* (New York: A. B. Burdick, 1859), iv.

133 An antislavery man: Samuel Tyler, *Memoir of Roger Brooke Taney, LL.D., Chief Justice of the Supreme Court of the United States* (Baltimore: John Murphy & Company, 1872), 391.

135 "plantations of our Southern states": Quoted in "W. H. Seward for 1860," *New York Herald*, Nov. 8, 1858, 8.

135 "Roguery Overreaches Itself": Ibid.

136 "We are two peoples": See Foner, *Free Soil, Free Labor, Free Men*, 310.

139 "I told him": Douglass, *The Life and Times of Frederick Douglass*, 278.

140 "My name is John Brown": Thomas Drew, ed., *The John Brown Invasion* (Boston: James Campbell, 1860), 13.

140 "Some sort of insurrection": George Templeton Strong, *The Diary of George Templeton Strong: 1835–1875*, vol. 2, ed. Allan Nevins and Milton Halsey Thomas (New York: Macmillan, 1952), 464.

141 "The supporters of any institution": Ibid., 474.

142 "Gerrit Smith's insanity": Thomas Higginson to Samuel Gridley Howe, Nov. 15, 1859, Higginson Papers, BPL.

143 "If the monster had one head": Lydia Maria Child, *Letters of Lydia Maria Child* (Boston, Houghton Mifflin, 1882), 143. An interesting appraisal of Child's moral certainty can be found in John Stauffer, "Embattled Manhood and New England Writers, 1860–1870," in *Battle Scars: Gender and Sexuality in the American Civil War*, ed. Catherine Clinton and Nina Silber (New York: Oxford University Press, 2006), 120–39.

145 "In this enlightened age": Lydia Child, Henry Wise, and Mrs. M. J. C. Mason, *Correspondence between Lydia Maria Child and Gov. Wise and Mrs. Mason of Virginia* (Boston: American Anti-Slavery Society, 1860), 26.

145 "I John Brown": Oswald Garrison Villard, *John Brown, 1800–1859: A Biography Fifty Years After* (New York: Houghton Mifflin, 1910), 554–55.

145 "This *is* a beautiful country": Cooke, *The Life, Trial and Execution of Captain John Brown*, 100.

145 "John Brown may be": "The Mission of John Brown," *The Liberator*, Feb. 3, 1860.

146 "I believe John Brown": Quoted in Edward Renehan, *The Secret Six: The True Tale of the Men Who Conspired with John Brown* (Columbia: University of South Carolina Press, 1997), 244.

146 "will make the gallows": Quoted in Robert D. Richardson, Jr., *Emerson: The Mind on Fire* (Berkeley: University of California Press, 1995), 545.

146 "because the acts of Brown": Quoted in George S. Merriam, *The Life and Times of Samuel Bowles*, vol. 1 (New York: Century Co., 1885), 252.

146 "condemned his past course": Sophia Hawthorne to Mary Mann, April 27, 1860, Berg Collection, NYPL.

146 "Nobody was ever": Nathaniel Hawthorne, "Chiefly about War Matters by a Peaceable Man," in *Centenary Editions of the Works of Nathaniel Hawthorne: Miscellaneous Prose and Verse*, vol. 23, ed. Thomas Woodson (Columbus: Ohio State University Press, 1994), 427.

147 "sparked the Civil War": This is in the subtitle of two recent, very good studies: David S. Reynolds, *John Brown: The Man Who Killed Slavery, Sparked the Civil War, and Seeded Civil Rights* (New York: Alfred A. Knopf, 2005); and Tony Horwitz, *Midnight Rising: John Brown and the Raid That Sparked the Civil War* (New York: Henry Holt, 2011).

147 "People of Virginia": Strong, *The Diary of George Templeton Strong*, vol. 2, 471.

147 "This must open the eyes": Edmund Ruffin, *The Diary of Edmund Ruffin: Toward Independence, October, 1856–April, 1861*, vol. 1, ed. William Kaufmann Scarborough (Baton Rouge: Louisiana State University Press, 1972), 304–5.

147 "Before me stood": Quoted in Mary Anna Jackson, *The Life and Letters of Thomas J. Jackson* (New York: Harper & Brothers, 1892), 131.

147 "abiding and impressive evidence": Quoted in Avery O. Craven, *Edmund Ruffin, Southerner: A Study in Secession* (Baton Rouge: Louisiana State University Press, 1966), 179–80.

148 "John Brown has only": *Rise and Progress of the Bloody Outbreak at Harper's Ferry*, vol. 63 (New York: New York Democratic Vigilant Association, 1859), 17.

148 "You announce your determination": *CG*, 36th Congress, 1st Session, Dec. 8, 1859, 68.

CHAPTER 7: THE IMPENDING CRISIS

149 One of those young women: Certain of the details of the disaster have been taken from the invaluable compilation by Alvin F. Oickle, *Disaster in Lawrence: The Fall of the Pemberton Mill* (Charleston, S.C.: History Press, 2008). Oickle says that the mill was six stories high, though contemporary accounts say five. However, I defer to his statistics since his research is the most comprehensive.

151 "before God and man": Quoted in ibid., 93.

151 "Of course, nobody": George Templeton Strong, *The Diary of George Templeton Strong: The Civil War, 1860–1865*, vol. 3, ed. Allan Nevins and Milton Halsey Thomas (New York: Macmillan, 1952), 4.

152 "to become a resident": Benjamin F. Butler, *Autobiography and Personal Reminiscences of Major-General Benj. F. Butler: Butler's Book* (Boston: A. M. Thayer, 1892), 91.

152 "The girls there": Lucy Larcom, *A New England Girlhood, Outlined from Memory* (Boston: Houghton Mifflin, 1889), 222–23.

152 "They are bell'd": "The Lawrence Slaughter," *The* [Cleveland] *Plain Dealer*, Jan. 19, 1860, 3.

153 "like so many": Quoted in Oickle, *Disaster in Lawrence*, 100.

154 "no one to blame": "No One to Blame," *Vanity Fair* 1 (Feb. 4, 1860), 85.

154 "Mankind has not yet learned": "The Lawrence Calamity," *Scientific American*, 2 (Jan. 28, 1860), 73.

154 "white slaves": "Verdict in the Pemberton Mills Case," *New York Herald*, Feb. 4, 1860, 4.

154 "That several hundred": "The Lawrence (Mass.) Calamity," *The Daily Federation*, Jan. 19, 1860, 2.

154 "traitors taken red-handed": *Milledgeville Federal Union*, Feb. 7, 1860, 3.

155 "His mission was one": Hinton Rowan Helper, *The Impending Crisis of the South: How to Meet It* (New York: A. B. Burdick, 1857), 106.

156 "That negro-worshipping sheet": Ibid., 108.

156 "the cities of Lowell and Lawrence": Ibid.

156 "Testimony of a Southern man": William Anthon, circular, March 9, 1859, William Henry Anthon Papers, NYPL.

156 "John Brown text-book": "The Republican Party Abolitionized," *New York Herald*, Nov. 26, 1859, 28.

157 "sectionalism, with hostility": CG, 36th Congress, 1st Session, Jan. 19, 1860, 523.

157 "as exciting as Euclid": Allan Nevins, *The Emergence of Lincoln* (New York: Charles Scribner's Sons, 1950), vol. 2, 118.

157 "Judge between the slaveholders": CG, 36th Congress, 1st Session, Jan. 19, 1860, 524.

157 "What a glorious thing": George Fitzhugh, *Sociology of the South* (Richmond, Va.: A. Morris, 1854), 68.

157 Ralph Waldo Emerson said: Ralph Waldo Emerson, *Emerson in His Journals*, ed. Joel Porte (Cambridge, Mass.: Belknap Press of Harvard University Press, 1982), 356.

158 "reputation and life": Quoted in Diane Neal and Thomas W. Kremm, *The Lion of the South: General Thomas C. Hindman* (Macon, Ga.: Mercer University Press, 1993), 26.

158 "a fugitive from justice": Ibid., 27.

159 "irrepressible conflict": Harold T. Smith, "The Know-Nothings in Arkansas," *The Arkansas Historical Quarterly* 34 (Winter 1975), 295–96.

159 "Sewardism, Helperism, and Shermanism": CG, 36th Congress, 1st Session, Jan. 19, 1860, 525.

159 After two months of wrangling: See J. J. Cardoso, "Lincoln, Abolitionism, and Patronage: The Case of Hinton Rowan Helper," *Journal of Negro History* 53 (April 1968), 147–48; see also Ollinger Crenshaw, "The Speakership Contest of 1859–1860: John Sherman's Election a Cause of Disruption?," *Mississippi Valley Historical Review* 29 (December 1942), 333–35.

160 "'gur-reat pur-rinciple'": Harold Holzer, *Lincoln at Cooper Union: The Speech That Made Abraham Lincoln President* (New York: Simon & Schuster, 2004), 269. I have taken all quotes from Lincoln's Cooper Union speech from Holzer's reproduction of it.

162 "If this country": Mary Chesnut, *Mary Chesnut's Civil War*, ed. C. Vann Woodward (New Haven, Conn.: Yale University Press, 1981), 26.

163 Lincoln doubtless knew: See Gillian Silverman, "'The Best Circus in Town': Embodied Theatrics in the Lincoln-Douglas Debates," *American Literary History* 21 (Winter 2009), 779.

163 "neither white man nor monkey": Quoted in Holzer, *Lincoln at Cooper Union*, 69.

163 "The sun is a faithful biographer": Gail Hamilton, "Brady's Gallery," *National Era* 13 (March 24, 1859), 46.

164 That photograph guaranteed: Quoted in Holzer, *Lincoln at Cooper Union*, 100. The detailing of the photograph's reproduction also depends on *Lincoln at Cooper Union*, 94–100.

CHAPTER 8: A CLANK OF METAL

165 A clairvoyant told: See Hans L. Trefousse, *Andrew Johnson: A Biography* (New York: W. W. Norton, 1997), 123–24.

166 "*Ours* is the property": Quoted in Eric Walther, *The Fire-Eaters* (Baton Rouge: Louisiana State University Press, 1992), 74.

166 "smiling like a bridegroom": Quoted in Frank L. Klement, *The Limits of Dissent: Clement Vallandigham and the Civil War* (New York: Fordham University Press, 1998), 35.

166 Georgia left too: See Murat Halstead, *Three Against Lincoln: Murat Halstead Reports the Caucuses of 1860* (Baton Rouge: Louisiana State University Press, 1960), 3–10.

166 "I will not sit": Quoted in Benson J. Lossing, *Harpers' Popular Cyclopedia of the United States from the Aboriginal Period, Containing Brief Sketches of Important Events and Conspicuous Actors* (New York: Harper and Brothers, 1881), vol. 1, 92.

167 "full measure . . . safe on slavery": Quoted in Thomas E. Schott, *Alexander H. Stephens of Georgia* (Baton Rouge: Louisiana State University Press, 1988), 292–94.

167 "selfishness and personal ambition": Ibid., 294.

167 Retrospective analyses: See again the fine discussion of the conventions in David M. Potter, *The Impending Crisis: America before the Civil War, 1848–1861*, completed and edited by Don E. Fehrenbacher (New York: Harper & Row, 1976).

167 "Submission to the rule": Quoted in Steven A. Channing, *Crisis of Fear: Secession in South Carolina* (New York: Simon & Schuster, 1970), 263.

168 there was something clubbish: See the excellent analysis and phrasing in Sean Wilentz, *The Rise of American Democracy: Jefferson to Lincoln* (New York: W. W. Norton, 2005), 758.

168 "I think the chances": Abraham Lincoln, *Lincoln: Speeches and Writings, 1859–1865*, ed. Don E. Fehrenbacher (New York: Library of America, 1989), 171–172.

169 finest hour: Allan Nevins, *The Emergence of Lincoln: Douglas, Buchanan, and Party Chaos* (New York: Scribner, 1950), 390.

169 "Whether there be secession": Quoted in Donald E. Reynolds, *Editors Make War: Southern Newspapers in the Secession Crisis* (Nashville: Vanderbilt University Press, 1970), 124, 126.

169 "an abolition party": Quoted in ibid., 127.

170 "the only conservative party": James Russell Lowell, "The Election in November," *The Atlantic Monthly*, October 1860, 501. For an incisive discussion of the response to secession from intellectual conservatives as well as abolitionists, see the indispensable George Frederickson, *The Inner Civil War: Northern Intellectuals and the Crisis of the Union* (New York: Harper & Row, 1968), 53–64.

171 "Passion is rash": Sam Houston, *The Writings of Sam Houston*, vol. 8, ed. Amelia Williams and Eugene Barker (Austin: University of Texas Press, 1943), 194.

171 "strike, strike": Quoted in Ulrich B. Phillips, *The Life of Robert Toombs* (New York: Macmillan, 1913), 201.

171 "So we go": Quoted in Schott, *Alexander H. Stephens of Georgia*, 305.

171 "Unionism is dead": Quoted in William Gilmore Simms, *The Letters of William Gilmore Simms*, vol. 4, ed. Mary C. Simms Oliphant, Alfred Taylor Odell, and T. C. Duncan Eaves (Columbia: University of South Carolina Press, 1955), 267.

171 "gallant Northern Union men": Quoted in Avery O. Craven, *The Coming of the Civil War* (Chicago: University of Chicago Press, 1966), 418.

171 "Believe me there will": Thomas Andrew Stevens, November 20, 1860, Civil War Collection, Virginia Military Institute Archives.

172 "the merchants & their clerks": Quoted in Channing, *Crisis of Fear*, 260.

172 "The Union is unnatural": Nathaniel Hawthorne to Henry Bright, Dec. 17, 1860, in *Centenary Editions of the Works of Nathaniel Hawthorne,* vol. 18, ed. Thomas Woodson et al. (Columbus: Ohio State University Press, 1987), 355.

172 "If the Cotton States": "Going to Go," *New-York Tribune*, Nov. 9, 1860, 4.

172 "If the Union can": Frederick Douglass, "Dissolution of the American Union," *Douglass' Monthly*, January 1861, 387.

173 "where is the ill in that": Quoted in James Redpath, ed., *Echoes of Harpers Ferry* (Boston: Thayer and Eldridge, 1860), 296.

173 "The only men who": "The National Crisis," *Baltimore Sun*, December 17, 1860.

173 "Abolition Is Disunion": Quoted in Howard C. Perkins, ed., *Northern Editorials on Secession* (New York: D. Appleton-Century Co., 1942), vol. 1, 94–97.

173 "I have never believed": Franklin Pierce, "Ex-President Pierce's Letter to Jeff. Davis," *New York Evening Post*, Sept. 19, 1863, 2.

173 "this wicked & crazy Republicanism": John O'Sullivan to Franklin Pierce, Feb. 7, 1861, LC.

174 "and that New England": Quoted in Allan S. Nevins, *The Ordeal of the Union: The Emergence of Lincoln*, vol. 2 (New York: Charles Scribner's Sons, 1950), 387.

174 "He is today": Quoted in Reynolds, *Editors Make War*, 146.

174 "Hasty action": Quoted in William W. Freehling and Craig M. Simpson, *Secession Debated: Georgia's Showdown in 1860* (New York: Oxford University Press, 1992), 107, 108.

174 "exulting over the destruction": Quoted in Craven, *The Coming of the Civil War*, 434.

174 "Whatever may be thought": Quoted in William J. Grayson, *James Louis Petigru: A Biographical Sketch* (New York: Harper & Brothers, 1866), xii.

174 "South Carolina is too small": Quoted in Lacy K. Ford, Jr., *Origins of Southern Radicalism: The South Carolina Upcountry, 1800–1860* (New York: Oxford University Press, 1988), 371.

174 "South Carolina has gone": Quoted in Reynolds, *Editors Make War*, 166.

175 "If these traitors": George Templeton Strong, *The Diary of George Templeton Strong: 1835–1875*, vol. 3, ed. Allan Nevins and Milton Halsey Thomas (New York: Macmillan, 1952), 64.

175 "Their suicidal frenzy": Ibid., 91.

175 "Peaceable Secession an Absurdity": Quoted in Allan Nevins, *The Evening Post: A Century of Journalism* (New York: Boni and Liveright, 1922), 270.

175 "We are worse off": *CG*, 36th Congress, 2nd Session, Jan. 7, 1861, 271.

175 "Events": Herman Melville, "The Conflict of Convictions," in *Selected Poems of Herman Melville*, ed. Robert Penn Warren (Jaffrey, N.H.: David Godine, 2004), 93.

176 "YEA AND NAY": Ibid., 95.

176 "None can foresee": Quoted in Daniel Aaron, *The Unwritten War: American Writers and the Civil War* (Madison: University of Wisconsin Press, 1987), 15.

176 "the southerners were beyond": Henry Adams, *The Great Secession Winter, 1860–61, and Other Essays* (New York: Sagamore Press, 1958), 4.

177 "The Constitution provided against": John Sherman, *John Sherman's Recollections of Forty Years in the House, Senate, and Cabinet: An Autobiography*, vol. 1 (Chicago: Werner Company, 1895), 204.

177 "If the States are": Quoted in Nevins, *Ordeal of the Union*, vol. 2, 410.

177 "The eyes of all good men": Quoted in Adam Goodheart, *1861: The Civil War Awakening* (New York: Alfred A. Knopf, 2011), 69.

178 "Mr. Crittenden's compromise": Anthony Trollope, *North America*, vol. 2 (Philadelphia: J. B. Lippincott & Co., 1863), 314.

178 "a year will not pass": Lincoln, *Lincoln: Speeches and Writings, 1859–1865*, 196.

179 "Here is a constitutional party": Houston, *The Writings of Sam Houston*, vol. 8, 153.

179 Of all the seceding states: The reasons clearly differed: see, e.g., James M. McPherson, *Battle Cry of Freedom: The Civil War Era* (New York: Oxford University Press, 1988), 235–39, for a cogent summary of different viewpoints. For a state-by-state analysis, see, e.g., Channing, *Crisis of Fear*, and Michael P. Johnson, *Toward a Patriarchal Republic: The Secession of Georgia* (Baton Rouge: Louisiana State University Press, 1977).

179 "in man's capability": *CG*, 36th Congress, 2nd Session, December 19, 1860, 134.

179 "No: I intend": Ibid., 243.

179 "In the language": Ibid.

179 "Action, action is": Carl Schurz, *Speeches, Correspondence and Political Papers of Carl Schurz*, vol. 1, ed. Frederic Bancroft (New York: G. P. Putnam's Sons, 1913), 175.

180 "ultimate extinction": Lincoln, *Lincoln: Speeches and Writings, 1859–1865*, 38.

180 "It is this perpetual putting": "The Diary of a Public Man," *North American Review* 129 (August 1879), 132.

181 "the right of revolution": Quoted in Sean Wilentz, *The Rise of American Democracy: Jefferson to Lincoln* (New York: W. W. Norton, 2005), 773. See also James Oakes, *The Ruling Race: A History of American Slaveholders* (New York: Alfred A. Knopf, 1982), 239–42.

181 "I can't stand the idea": Quoted in Channing, *Crisis of Fear*, 289.

181 "We are upholding": Jefferson Davis, *Jefferson Davis, Constitutionalist: His Letters, Papers, and Speeches*, vol. 6, ed. Dunbar Rowland (Jackson: Mississippi Department of Archives and History, 1923), 357.

182 Fear motivated them: See also the interesting argument in Kenneth Stampp, *The Imperiled Union: Essays on the Background of the Civil War* (New York: Oxford University Press, 1980), 191–270, and his contention that these Southerners may also have been plagued by the nagging, unspoken knowledge that their peculiar institution was out of step with the nineteenth-century rhetoric of freedom.

182 "On the 4th of March": Quoted in Michael P. Johnson, *Toward a Patriarchal Republic: The Secession of Georgia* (Baton Rouge: Louisiana State University Press, 1977), 36.

182 "It's a revolution": Quoted in James M. McPherson, *Battle Cry of Freedom: The Civil War Era* (New York: Oxford University Press, 1988), 237.

182 "Revolutions are much easier": Quoted in Robert Toombs, Alexander H. Stephens, and Howell Cobb, *The Correspondence of Robert Toombs, Alexander H. Stephens, and Howell Cobb: Annual Report of the American Historical Association for the Year 1911*, vol. 2, ed. Ulrich B. Phillips (Washington, D.C.: U.S. Government Printing Office, 1913), 504.

183 "to yield to necessity": *OR*, ser. I, vol. 1, December 21, 1860, 103.

184 When the unarmed: "The Diary of a Public Man," 134.

184 "crafty and sensible": Ibid., 140.

185 "no shake": Henry Adams, *The Letters of Henry Adams*, ed. Ernest Samuels (Cambridge, Mass.: Harvard University Press, 1982), 204.

186 "Soon, it will be": *CG*, 36th Congress, 2nd Session, Jan. 12, 1861, 344.

186 "God damn you, Seward": Quoted in Glyndon G. Van Deusen, *William Henry Seward* (New York: Oxford University Press, 1967), 249.

187 "If he yields the ground": John Greenleaf Whittier, *The Letters of John Greenleaf Whittier*, ed. John B. Pickard, vol. 3 (Cambridge, Mass.: Harvard University Press, 1975), 10.

187 Maybe so: One of Seward's early biographers called the speech enigmatic, conciliatory, and self-contradictory. The historian Eric Foner noted that Seward's reputation for radicalism was in large measure undeserved. See Eric Foner, *Free Soil, Free Labor, Free Men: The Ideology of the Republican Party before the Civil War* (New York: Oxford University Press, 1970), 222.

187 "Compromises based on the idea": Quoted in Doris Kearns Goodwin, *Team of Rivals: The Political Genius of Abraham Lincoln* (New York: Simon & Schuster, 2005), 303.

187 "With the human soul": Henry Wadsworth Longfellow, *Michael Angelo: A Dramatic Poem* (Boston: Houghton, Mifflin and Company, 1884), 50.

187 "The Government": "Questions in American Politics," *Sacramento Daily Union*, January 14, 1861, 4.

187 "Republicans are as much afraid": Toombs, Stephens, and Cobb, *The Correspondence of Robert Toombs, Alexander H. Stephens, and Howell Cobb*, vol. 2, 541.

188 "The hour and the man": Quoted in Allan Nevins, *The Emergence of Lincoln: Prologue to Civil War, 1859–1861*, vol. 2 (New York: Charles Scribner's Sons, 1950), 435.

188 "No compromise, no reconstruction": Quoted in William J. Cooper, Jr., *Jefferson Davis: American* (New York: Vintage, 2000), 353.

188 "illustrates the American idea": Quoted in ibid., 354.

189 "corner-stone": Quoted in Henry Cleveland, *Alexander H. Stephens in Public and Private: With Letters and Speeches, before, during, and since the War* (Philadelphia, 1866), 721–22. For a fine analysis of the relation between this speech and the thinking of Lincoln and Davis on this subject, see Harry V. Jaffa, *New Birth of Freedom: Abraham Lincoln and the Coming of the Civil War* (Lanham, Md.: Rowman and Littlefield, 2000), 215–18.

189 "the first . . . it fell": Cleveland, *Alexander H. Stephens*, 721.

189 "There is a hierarchy": Ibid., 408.

190 "You think slavery is *right*": Lincoln, *Lincoln: Speeches and Writings, 1859–1865*, 194.

190 "We have just carried": Abraham Lincoln, *The Collected Works of Abraham Lincoln*, vol. 4, ed. Roy P. Basler (New Brunswick, N.J.: Rutgers University Press, 1953), 172.

191 "motley mixture": Quoted in Van Deusen, *William Henry Seward*, 274.

191 Lincoln had also been composing: For excellent analyses of Lincoln's changes to the address, particularly after he showed it to Seward, see Ronald C. White, Jr., *The Eloquent President: A Portrait of Lincoln through His Words* (New York: Random House, 2005), and Harold Holzer, *Lincoln President-Elect: Abraham Lincoln and the Great Secession Winter, 1860–1* (New York: Simon & Schuster, 2008); see also Don E. Fehrenbacher, "The Words of Lincoln," *Lincoln in Text and Context: Collected Essays* (Stanford, Calif.: Stanford University Press, 1987), and Fred Kaplan, *Lincoln: The Biography of a Writer* (New York: HarperCollins, 2008); for knives and pistols, see Walt Whitman, *The Complete Writings of Walt Whitman*, vol. 15, ed. Richard Maurice Bucke, Thomas Biggs Harned, Horace Traubel, and Oscar Lovell Triggs (New York: G. P. Putnam's Sons, 1902), 243–44.

191 "no purpose": Lincoln, *Lincoln: Speeches and Writings, 1859–1865*, 215–24.

193 "It seemed more like escorting": Quoted in Holzer, *Lincoln President-Elect*, 448.

193 "I never expected": "Diary of a Public Man, Part III," *North American Review* 129 (October 1879), 283.

194 "grasp the circumstances": "The Inaugural Address of President Lincoln," *Charleston Mercury*, March 5, 1861.

194 "double-tongued document": Frederick Douglass, "The Inaugural Address," *Douglass' Monthly* (April 1861), in *Frederick Douglass: Selected Speeches and Writings*, ed. Philip S. Foner and Yuval Taylor (Chicago: Chicago Review Press, 2000), 433.

194 "I claim not to have": Lincoln, *Lincoln: Speeches and Writings, 1859–1865*, 586.

194 "I think there's a clank": Strong, *The Diary of George Templeton Strong: 1835–1875*, vol. 3, 106.

CHAPTER 9: ON TO RICHMOND

197 "We learned once for all": James Russell Lowell, "Democracy: Inaugural Address on Assuming the Presidency of the Birmingham and Midland Institute, Birmingham, England, 6 October, 1884," in *The Complete Writings of James Russell Lowell*, vol. 6, ed. Charles Eliot Norton (Boston: Houghton Mifflin, 1904), 24.

198 "Events are crowding": *CG*, 36th Congress, 2nd session, December 18, 1860, 116.

198 "moral anachronism": Kenneth Stampp, *The Imperiled Union: Essays on the Background of the Civil War* (New York: Oxford University Press, 1980), 230.

198 "War begins where reason ends": Frederick Douglass, "Reconstruction," *The Atlantic Monthly* 18 (December 1866), 763.

199 "They mean to compel": Quoted in William J. Cooper, Jr., *Jefferson Davis: American* (New York: Vintage, 2000), 365.

200 "I shall have no winter": Emily Dickinson, *The Letters of Emily Dickinson*, vol. 2, ed. Thomas H. Johnson and Theodora Ward (Cambridge, Mass.: Belknap Press of Harvard University Press, 1958), 377.

200 "Squads gather everywhere": Walt Whitman, "Drum Taps," in *Walt Whitman: Complete Poetry and Collected Prose*, ed. Justin Kaplan (New York: Library of America, 1982), 417.

200 "fossil court of arbitration": "Situation of Affairs," *New York Herald*, April 29, 1861.

200 The next month, Lincoln called: See James M. McPherson, *Battle Cry of Freedom: The Civil War Era* (New York: Oxford University Press, 1988), 322.

201 "Our cause is just and holy": Quoted in James D. Richardson, ed., *A Compila-tion of the Messages and Papers of the Confederacy*, vol. 1 (Washington, D.C.: U.S. Government Printing Office, 1896), 22.

201 "On to Washington": See Allan Nevins, ed., *American Press Opinion: Washington to Coolidge, a Documentary Record of Editorial Leadership and Criticism, 1785–1927*, vol. 1 (New York: Kennikat Press, 1969), 253–54.

201 "The regular cavalry": Quoted in "The Flight from the Field," in Frank Moore, ed., *The Rebellion Record: A Diary of American Events with Documents, Narratives, Illustrative Incidents, Poetry, Etc.*, vol. 2 (New York: G. P. Putnam, 1862), 87.

202 "Ayer's battery dashed": Charles Carleton Coffin, *Four Years of Fighting: A Volume of Personal Observation with the Army and the Navy, from the First Battle of Bull Run to the Fall of Richmond* (Boston: Ticknor & Fields, 1866), 23.

202 "the dust, the grime": Walt Whitman, *Specimen Days*, in *Walt Whitman: Complete Poetry and Collected Prose*, 708.

202 "rang like a reveille": John Hay, *Addresses of John Hay* (New York: Century Company, 1906), 231.

203 "a grand army, retreating": Edmund Clarence Stedman, *The Battle of Bull Run* (New York: Rudd & Carleton, 1861), 10.

203 "the scenes on the battlefield": [Henry Villard] "The Bull Run Battle. The Ad-vance into Virginia," *New York Herald*, July 24, 1861.

204 "Turn back! Turn back!": William Howard Russell, *My Diary North and South* (Boston: T. O. H. P. Burnam, 1863), 451.

204 "something extraordinary": Ibid., 454.

204 "in the hope of seeing": Ibid., 435.

204 "Their hearts were all willing": Quoted in Frank Moore, ed., *The Rebellion Record: A Diary of American Events, with Documents, Narratives, Illustrative Incidents, Poetry, Etc.*, vol. 2 (New York: G. P. Putnam, 1862), 4.

205 McDowell had no reserves: See Gary W. Gallagher, ed., *Fighting for the Confed-eracy: The Personal Recollections of General Edward Porter Alexander* (Chapel Hill: University of North Carolina Press, 1989), 48.

205 "There is Jackson": Benjamin Perley Poore, *Perley's Reminiscences of Sixty Years in the National Metropolis*, vol. 2 (Philadelphia: Hubbard Brothers, 1886), 85.

205 "For our people": Quoted in Charles Royster, *The Destructive War: William Te-cumseh Sherman, Stonewall Jackson, and the Americans* (New York: Vintage, 1993), 41. Royster's superb account of the war focuses on Jackson and Sherman.

205 "The vaunted Union": Whitman, *Walt Whitman: Complete Poetry and Collected Prose*, 710.

205 "the tone of the Northern papers": Robert Toombs, Alexander H. Stephens, and Howell Cobb, *The Correspondence of Robert Toombs, Alexander H. Stephens, and Howell Cobb*, vol. 2, ed. Ulrich B. Phillips (Washington, D.C.: U.S. Government Printing Office, 1913), 573.

206 "the best lesson": Quoted in Royster, *The Destructive War*, 93.

206 "Youth must its ignorant impulse": Herman Melville, "The March into Virginia Ending in the First Manassas," in *Selected Poems of Herman Melville*, ed. Robert Penn Warren (Jaffrey, N.H.: David Godine, 2006), 96.

207 "no preparations whatever": William C. Prime, ed., *McClellan's Own Story: The War for the Union, the Soldiers Who Fought It, the Civilians Who Directed It and His Relations to It and to Them* (New York: Charles L. Webster, 1887), 66–67.

207 "professional rivalry, jealousy": William Henry Hurlbert, *General McClellan and the Conduct of the War* (New York: Sheldon and Company, 1864), 103.

208 "the officers themselves": Ibid., 104.

208 "The men have lost": George Templeton Strong, *The Diary of George Templeton Strong*, vol. 3, ed. Allan Nevins and Milton Halsey Thomas (New York: Macmillan, 1952), 173.

208 "Repulse may do us good": R. H. Stoddard, "Resurgamus," *The Rebellion Record: A Diary of American Events, with Documents, Narratives, Illustrative Incidents, Poetry, Etc.*, vol. 2, ed. Frank Moore (New York: G. P. Putnam, 1862), 10.

208 "is one of the greatest powers": See Joseph L. Gardner, " 'Bull Run Russell,' " *American Heritage* 13 (June 1962), 59–64.

209 "I have seen a telegraph-operator": Quoted in David Homer Bates, *Lincoln in the Telegraph Office: Recollections of the United States Military* (New York: Century Company, 1907), 12.

210 "we might as well": On Uriah Painter, see J. Cutler Andrews, *The North Reports the Civil War* (Pittsburgh: University of Pittsburgh Press, 1955), 90.

210 "hybrid": Junius Henri Browne, *Four Years in Secessia: Adventures within and beyond the Union Lines* (Hartford, Conn.: O. D. Case and Company, 1865), 13.

211 "Unthinkable": Royal Cortissoz, *The Life of Whitelaw Reid*, vol. 1 (New York: Charles Scribner's Sons, 1921), 70.

211 "crushed by a shell": Samuel Wilkeson, "Details from Our Special Correspondent," *The New York Times*, July 6, 1863, 1.

211 "Many, particularly among our officers": "Agate," *Cincinnati Times*, April 14, 1862.

211 "the most contemptible race": Quoted in William T. Sherman, *Sherman's Civil War: Selected Correspondence of William T. Sherman*, ed. Brooks D. Simpson and Jean Vance Berlin (Chapel Hill: University of North Carolina Press, 1999), 212.

213 "You can send that": Quoted in Noah Brooks, *Lincoln Observed: Civil War Dispatches of Noah Brooks*, ed. Michael Burlingame (Baltimore: Johns Hopkins University Press, 2002), 9.

213 "That's good!": Browne, *Four Years in Secessia*, 238.

213 In the Midwest: See Carl R. Osthaus, *Partisans of the Southern Press: Editorial Spokesmen of the Nineteenth Century* (Louisville: University of Kentucky Press, 1994), 103.

213 At the same time: See Menahem Blondheim, *News over the Wires: The Telegraph and the Flow of Public Information in America, 1844–1897* (Cambridge, Mass.: Harvard University Press, 1994).

213 So did Lincoln: Richard Carwardine, *Lincoln and the Fourth Estate: The White House and the Press during the American Civil War* (Reading, England: University of Reading, 2004), 8.

214 "This is the Peoples war": Virginia Jeans Laas, ed., *Wartime Washington: The Civil War Letters of Elizabeth Blair Lee* (Urbana: University of Illinois Press, 1999), 450.

214 "News of the War!" *Harper's Weekly*, June 14, 1862, 378.

214 "personal courage": Henry Kyd Douglas, *I Rode with Stonewall: The War Experiences of the Youngest Member of Jackson's Staff* (Chapel Hill: University of North Carolina Press, 1940), 76.

214 There were pictures, too: See, e.g., Michael L. Carlebach, *The Origins of Photojournalism in America* (Washington, D.C.: Smithsonian Institution Press, 1992), esp. 61–72; see also Gisèle Freund, *Photography and Society* (Boston: David R. Godine, 1980).

215 "If all the terrific": Quoted in Joshua Brown, *Beyond the Lines: Pictorial Reporting, Everyday Life, and the Crisis of Gilded Age America* (Berkeley: University of California Press, 2002), 55.

215 "You fellows make the best spies": Quoted in William F. Thompson, *The Image of War* (Baton Rouge: Louisiana State University Press, 1994), 79.

215 "The above impression": Quoted in Elizabeth Johns, *Winslow Homer: The Nature of Observation* (Berkeley: University of California Press), 35.

216 "How much better": Horace Traubel, *With Walt Whitman in Camden,* vol. 3 (Boston: Small, Maynard & Company, 1906), 553.

217 Along with the copy: See "Brady's Photographs of the War," *New York Daily Tribune,* July 19, 1862, 3.

217 "I felt that I had to go": George Alfred Townsend, "Still Taking Pictures," *The World,* April 12, 1891, 26.

217 "whatisit wagons": For more information on Brady, see James Horan, *Mathew Brady: Historian with a Camera* (New York: Crown, 1955); Roy Meredith, *Mathew B. Brady: Mr. Lincoln's Camera Man* (New York: Dover, 1974); the very fine Mary Panzer, *Mathew Brady and the Image of History* (Washington, D.C.: Smithsonian Books, 1997); and the excellent work of Alan Trachtenberg in *Reading American Photographs: Images as History, Mathew Brady to Walker Evans* (New York: Hill and Wang, 1989).

218 "In every glade": Quoted in Panzer, *Mathew Brady and the Image of History,* 102.

218 The photographs taken by: See, e.g., Trachtenberg, *Reading American Photographs.*

218 "The hills were black": Edwin Forbes, *Thirty Years After: An Artist's Memoir of the Civil War* (Baton Rouge: Louisiana State University Press, 1993), 258.

218 "There were men in every state": Josiah Marshall Favill, *The Diary of a Young Officer Serving with the Armies of the United States during the War of the Rebellion* (Chicago: R. R. Donnelley & Sons, 1909), 189.

218 "dead horses, swollen": Strong, *The Diary of George Templeton Strong,* vol. 3, 260.

219 "pale faces of the dead": "Brady's Photographs," *The New York Times,* October 20, 1862, 5.

219 The photographs then appeared: See *Harper's Weekly,* October 18, 1862, 662–63.

219 "the same sun": "Brady's Photographs," *The New York Times,* October 20, 1862, 5.

220 "Don't ask awkward questions": Mary Chesnut, *Mary Chesnut's Civil War,* ed. C. Vann Woodward (New Haven, Conn.: Yale University Press, 1981), 109.

220 "Why did we not follow": Ibid., 121.

220 "On this day of the week": Quoted in Moore, *The Rebellion Record,* vol. 2, 71.

220 "There is no legitimate excuse": See Edward Porter Alexander, *Fighting for the Confederacy: The Personal Recollections of General Edward Porter Alexander,* ed. Gary Gallagher (Chapel Hill: University of North Carolina Press, 1998), 58–59.

221 "Thousands of Yankees and Rebs": James McPherson, *Battle Cry of Freedom,* 580. Thanks to Eric Wilson for reminding me of the passage.

221 And though higher: For preparations for counting and burying the dead and for tending the wounded, as inaugurated by Bull Run, see Drew Gilpin Faust's excellent *This Republic of Suffering: Death and the American Civil War* (New York: Alfred A. Knopf, 2008).

222 "The South was proud": Douglas, *I Rode with Stonewall,* 11–12.

CHAPTER 10: BATTLE CRY OF FREEDOM

223 "Either slavery is essential": Thomas Wentworth Higginson, "Ordeal by Battle," *The Atlantic Monthly* 8 (July 1861), 94.

223 "not waged upon": Quoted in Allen C. Guelzo, *Lincoln's Emancipation Proclamation: The End of Slavery in America* (New York: Simon & Schuster, 2004), 36.

224 "From the instant": John Quincy Adams, *Speech of the Honorable John Quincy Adams in the House of Representatives, May 25, 1836* (New York: H. R. Piercy, 1836), 15.

225 "Shall they [Confederates] be allowed": Benjamin F. Butler, *Private and Personal Correspondence of Gen. Benjamin F. Butler During the Period of the Civil War*, vol. 1 (Norwood, Mass.: Plimpton Press, 1917), 106.

225 "did not affect": Benjamin F. Butler, *Autobiography and Personal Reminiscences of Major-General Benjamin F. Butler: Butler's Book* (Boston: A. M. Thayer, 1892), 258. See also *OR*, vol. 2 (May 25, 1861), 649.

225 "Our troops could not act": Ibid., 650.

225 "contraband of war": Ibid.

225 "bad one": Butler, *Autobiography and Personal Reminiscences of Major-General Benjamin F. Butler*, 259.

225 "increased the dilemma": "Negroes Taking Refuge at Fortress Monroe," *Frank Leslie's Illustrated Newspaper*, June 8, 1861, 55; see also Edward L. Pierce, "The Contrabands at Fortress Monroe," *The Atlantic Monthly* 8 (November 1861), 627.

226 "$60,000 worth of them": Butler, *Autobiography and Personal Reminiscences of Major-General Benjamin F. Butler*, 258.

226 "the slave question . . . stumbling-block": Ibid., 259.

226 "The venerable gentleman": Pierce, "The Contrabands at Fortress Monroe," 627.

226 "one might reverently": Butler, *Autobiography and Personal Reminiscences of Major-General Benjamin F. Butler*, 293.

227 "Our troops have not": Allan Nevins, *The War for the Union: The Improvised War, 1861–1862*, vol. 1 (New York: Scribner's, 1959), 312.

228 "You had as well attack": Joshua F. Speed to Abraham Lincoln, Sept. 3, 1861, Abraham Lincoln Papers, LC.

228 "awkward tact": Quoted in John Hay, *Inside Lincoln's White House: The Complete Civil War Diary of John Hay*, ed. Michael Burlingame and John R. Turner Ettlinger (Carbondale: Southern Illinois University Press, 1997), 123.

228 "quite a female politician": Pamela Herr and Mary Lee Spence, eds., *The Letters of Jessie Benton Frémont* (Urbana: University of Illinois Press, 1993), 246; see also Frederick J. Blue, *No Taint of Compromise: Crusaders in Anti-Slavery Politics* (Baton Rouge: Louisiana State University Press, 2005), 258.

229 "the abolition horde in the north": Virginia Jeans Laas, ed., *Wartime Washington: The Civil War Letters of Elizabeth Blair Lee* (Urbana: University of Illinois Press, 1999), 86.

229 "without the statesman's tact": John Greenleaf Whittier, *The Poetical Works of John Greenleaf Whittier*, vol. 3 (Boston: Houghton Mifflin, 1892), 222.

229 "How many times": James Russell Lowell, *The Complete Writings of James Russell Lowell*, vol. 15, ed. Charles Eliot Norton (Boston: Houghton Mifflin, 1904), 63.

229 "was accomplishing much good": Orville H. Browning to Abraham Lincoln, Sept. 17, 1861, Abraham Lincoln Papers, LC.

229 Regardless, abolition was still unthinkable: See G. S. Boritt, "The Voyage to the Colony of Lincolnia: The Sixteenth President, Black Colonization, and the Defense Mechanism of Avoidance," *The Historian* 37 (August 1975), 619.

229 "Why, oh why": Quoted in Frederick Douglass, *Frederick Douglass, The Life and Writings of Frederick Douglass*, vol. 3, ed. Philip S. Foner (New York: International Publishers, 1950), 286; see also David W. Blight, "The Bugbear of Civilization," *Frederick Douglass' Civil War: Keeping Faith in Jubilee* (Baton Rouge: Louisiana State University Press, 1989), 122; and Guelzo, *Lincoln's Emancipation Proclamation*, 139.

230 Though Lincoln's plan: The historian Eric Foner calls it "a bold initiative"; see Foner, *The Fiery Trial: Abraham Lincoln and American Slavery* (New York: W. W. Norton, 2010), 183.

230 In early 1862: For two fine discussions of the Delaware legislative proposal and Lincoln's subsequent, almost naive, appeal to Congress, see Foner, *The Fiery Trial*, and Guelzo, *Lincoln's Emancipation Proclamation*.

230 "These terms are milestones": Edward L. Pierce, "The Freedmen at Port Royal," *The Atlantic Monthly* 12 (September 1863), 291.

230 But when they set to music: See Robert Penn Warren, *John Greenleaf Whittier's Poetry: An Appraisal and a Selection* (St. Paul: University of Minnesota Press, 1971), and Samuel T. Pickard, *Life and Letters of John Greenleaf Whittier* (Boston: Houghton Mifflin, 1894), 467–68.

230 "*I* am fighting to preserve": George B. McClellan, *The Civil War Papers of General George McClellan, 1861–1865*, ed. Stephen W. Sears (New York: Ticknor & Fields, 1989), 128.

231 "no terms except": See, e.g., William S. McFeely, *Grant: A Biography* (New York: W. W. Norton, 2002), 101.

231 "It was as if General McClellan": Nathaniel Hawthorne, "Chiefly about War Matters," *The Atlantic Monthly* 10 (July 1862), 45.

232 "the brain of Lee": John Hay, *Lincoln and the Civil War in the Diaries and Letters of John Hay*, ed. Tyler Dennett (Cambridge, Mass.: Da Capo Press, 1939), 89.

233 "The watchword": Thomas Wentworth Higginson, "The Ordeal by Battle," *The Atlantic Monthly* 8 (July 1861), 95.

234 "Colored men were good enough": "A Black Man on the War," *New-York Tribune*, Feb. 13, 1862, 7.

234 "It is as clearly a right" : Edward McPherson, *The Political History of the United States of America, during the Great Rebellion* (Washington, D.C.: Philip & Solomons, 1871), 294.

234 "Every negro ought to": Henry James, Sr., to Elizabeth Palmer Peabody, July 30 [1862], Mann Papers, Courtesy Antioch College.

234 "deep as a well": James R. Gilmore, *Personal Recollections of Abraham Lincoln and the Civil War* (Boston: L. C. Page, 1898), 44.

235 "John Brown *IS* a-marching": George Templeton Strong, *The Diary of George Templeton Strong*, vol. 3, ed. Allan Nevins and Milton Halsey Thomas (New York: Macmillan, 1952), 216.

236 Inspired by Hunter's proclamation: For information on Robert Smalls, see Willie Lee Rose, *Rehearsal for Reconstruction: The Port Royal Experiment* (New York: Oxford University Press, 1964), and more recently, the well-narrated Philip Dray, *Capitol Men* (New York: Houghton Mifflin, 2008). See also "Letter from the Negro Robert Smalls," *The Liberator*, Sept. 12, 1862, 148.

236 "for the 'old fetters'": Quoted in Edward A. Miller, Jr., *Lincoln's Abolitionist General: The Biography of David Hunter* (Columbia: University of South Carolina Press, 1997), 101.

236 "Gen. Hunter is an honest man": Abraham Lincoln, *Lincoln: Speeches and Writings, 1859–1865*, ed. Don E. Fehrenbacher (New York: Library of America, 1989), 341.

237 "Broken eggs cannot be mended": Ibid., 347.

237 "Neither confiscation of property": George B. McClellan, "The Army of the Potomac: General McClellan's Report," *The Rebellion Record: A Diary of American Events, with Documents, Narratives, Illustrative Incidents, Poetry, Etc.—Supplement*, vol. 1, ed. Frank Moore (New York: G. P. Putnam, 1864), 596.

238 "Do you know Pope is a humbug": Charles Frances Adams, *A Cycle of Adams Letters, 1861–1865*, ed. Worthington Chauncey Ford (Boston: Houghton Mifflin, 1920), 177.

238 "in danger of utter demoralization": Ibid., 178.

238 "I rather think many": Rachel Sherman Thorndike, ed., *The Sherman Letters: The Correspondence between William Tecumseh Sherman and John Sherman from 1837 to 1891* (New York: Charles Scribner's Sons, 1894), 164–66.

238 "We must free the slaves": Gideon Welles, "The History of Emancipation," *The Galaxy* 14 (December 1872), 842.

239 "I think that the best": Bell Irvin Wiley, *Life of Billy Yank: The Common Soldier of the Union* (Baton Rouge: Louisiana State University Press, 1978), 109.

239 "the perversion of the war": Quoted in Horace Greeley, *The American Conflict: A History of the Great Rebellion in the United States of America 1860–'64*, vol. 2 (Hartford: O. D. Case, 1867), 254.

239 "military necessity": Quoted in James M. McPherson, *The Struggle for Equality* (Princeton, N.J.: Princeton University Press, 1964), 91.

239 "All of that old abolition": James Robert Gilmore, "Our War and Our Want," *Continental Monthly* 1 (February 1862), 114.

239 "the Rebellion, if crushed out": Horace Greeley, "Prayer of Twenty Millions," *New-York Tribune*, August 20, 1862.

240 "My paramount object": Lincoln, *Lincoln: Speeches and Writings, 1859–1865*, 358.

240 "Was ever a more heartless": *The Liberator*, Sept. 5, 1862, quoted in McPherson, *The Struggle for Equality*, 117.

241 "arm, uniform, equip": OR, ser. 1, vol. 14, Aug. 25, 1862, 377–78.

241 This was an anomalous position: See Charlotte Forten Grimké, *The Journals of Charlotte Forten Grimké*, ed. Brenda Stevenson (New York: Oxford University Press, 1988), 405.

242 "from the dull and tedious": James Branch Cabell and A. J. Hanna, *The St. Johns: A Parade of Diversities* (New York: Farrar & Rinehart, 1943), 208.

242 "intensely human": See Brenda Wineapple, *White Heat: The Friendship of Emily Dickinson and Thomas Wentworth Higginson* (New York: Alfred A. Knopf, 2008), 125.

242 "sucks everything": Oliver Wendell Holmes, "My Hunt after 'The Captain,'" *The Atlantic Monthly* 10 (December 1862), 743.

243 "The carnage was frightful": John G. Nicolay and John Hay, *Abraham Lincoln: A History*, vol. 6 (New York: Century Co., 1890), 140.

244 To conceive of his proclamation: Benjamin H. Hill, *Senator Benjamin H. Hill of Georgia: His Life, Speeches and Writings*, ed. Benjamin H. Hill, Jr. (Atlanta: T. H. P. Bloodworth, 1893), 573.

244 "The President can do nothing": William Lloyd Garrison, *The Letters of William Lloyd Garrison: Let the Oppressed Go Free*, ed. Walter M. Merrill (Cambridge, Mass.: Belknap Press of Harvard University Press, 1979), 114–115.

244 General McClellan insisted: James Alexander Scrymser, *Personal Reminiscences of James A. Scrymser in Times of Peace and War* (New York: James A. Scrymser, 1915), 36–38.

244 In Europe, the response: See Martin Duberman, *Charles Francis Adams, 1807– 1886* (Boston: Houghton Mifflin, 1961), 299.

244 "the Emancipation Proclamation": Quoted in James McPherson, "The Saratoga That Wasn't: Confederate Recognition and the Effect of Antietam Abroad," *Inside the Confederate Nation: Essays in Honor of Emory Thomas*, ed. Lesley J. Gordon and John C. Inscoe (Baton Rouge: Louisiana State University Press, 2005), 105.

244 "of being taken back": Ralph Waldo Emerson, *The Complete Works of Ralph Waldo Emerson: Miscellanies*, vol. 11, ed. Edward W. Emerson (Boston: Houghton Mifflin, 1884), 319.

244 "We have recovered ourselves": Ibid., 320.

245 "There is now no possible hope": *OR*, ser. 1, vol. 24, pt. 3, March 31, 1863, 157.

245 "My Country, 'Tis of Thee": Elizabeth Pearson Ware, ed., *Letters from Port Royal, 1862–1868* (Boston: W. B. Clarke and Co., 1906), 130; see also "Higginson's Black Brigade," *Springfield Republican*, Jan. 1, 1863, 1.

246 "Our negro troops": Quoted in Wineapple, *White Heat*, 135.

246 "At last the North": Samuel Longfellow, ed., *The Life of Henry Wadsworth Longfellow, with Extracts from His Journals and Correspondence*, vol. 3 (Boston: Houghton Mifflin, 1891), 22.

247 A tall, thin man: See Robert Gould Shaw, *Blue-Eyed Child of Fortune: The Civil War Letters of Robert Gould Shaw*, ed. Russell Duncan (Athens: University of Georgia Press, 1999), 356.

247 "It was as abominable": Quoted in Lydia Minturn Post, ed., *Soldiers' Letters, from Camp, Battle-field and Prison* (New York: Bunce & Huntington, 1865), 252. I have also told the story of the Massachusetts 54th in *White Heat*, chapter 7, and the following section is taken from that book.

247 "This indiscriminate burning": Quoted in Wineapple, *White Heat*, 136.

247 "Then you die": George Crockett Strong to Benjamin Franklin Butler, June 29, 1863, in *Private and Official Correspondence of Gen. Benjamin F. Butler, during the Period of the Civil War*, vol. 3 (Springfield, Mass.: Plimpton Press, 1917), 94.

247 "had done it to white soldiers": Quoted in Wineapple, *White Heat*, 136.

247 "Do not think this rapid organization": Ibid.

248 "We presume too much": Thomas Wentworth Higginson, letter to the editor, *The New York Times*, February 21, 1864, 5; see also Higginson, "Appendix D," *Army Life in a Black Regiment, and Other Writings* (New York: Penguin, 1997), 222. See also Higginson, *Massachusetts in the Army and Navy during the War of 1861–1865*, vol. 1 (Boston: Wright Potter, 1895), 83, and Higginson, "The Shaw Memorial and the Sculptor St. Gaudens III. Colored Troops under Fire," *Century* 54 (June 1897), 194.

248 The physician serving: "Letters of Dr. Seth Rogers," *Proceedings of the Massachusetts Historical Society* 43 (February 1910), 346.

248 Higginson's and Montgomery's regiments: See, e.g., Thomas Wentworth Higginson, "The First Black Regiment," *Outlook* 59 (July 2, 1898), 521.

248 "Well I guess we will": Shaw, *Blue-Eyed Child of Fortune*, 51.

CHAPTER 11: THIS THING NOW NEVER SEEMS TO STOP

250 "When you meet people": Mary Chesnut, *Mary Chesnut's Civil War*, ed. C. Vann Woodward (New Haven, Conn.: Yale University Press, 1981), 370.

251 unity of Southern interests: Douglas Southall Freeman and Richard Barksdale Howell, *Lee: An Abridgment in One Volume of the Four-Volume "R. E. Lee" by Douglas Southall Freeman* (New York: Touchstone, 1997), 105.

251 "I could take no part": Rev. J. William Jones, *Personal Reminiscences, Anecdotes, and Letters of Gen. Robert E. Lee* (New York: D. Appleton and Co., 1875), 141.

251 "He moves his agencies": Quoted in Charles Royster, *The Destructive War: William Tecumseh Sherman, Stonewall Jackson, and the Americans* (New York: Vintage, 1993), 235.

251 "Confederate hero par excellence": Chesnut, *Mary Chesnut's Civil War*, 428.

251 "I always thought we ought": Thomas J. Jackson, *The Life and Letters of General Thomas J. Jackson*, ed. Mary Anna Jackson (New York: Harper & Brothers, 1892), 310.

252 "otherwise rational men proposed": E. M. Thomas, *The Confederate Nation, 1861–1865* (New York: Harper & Row, 1979), 134.

253 "These people seem, indeed": Edward L. Pierce, "The Freedmen at Port Royal," *The Atlantic Monthly* 12 (September 1863), 295.

253 "we forget there": Chesnut, *Mary Chesnut's Civil War*, 428.

253 "lamentable incapacity": William J. Cooper, Jr., *Jefferson Davis, American* (New York: Vintage, 2001), 411.

253 "the mob": Chesnut, *Mary Chesnut's Civil War*, 288.

254 There were some exceptions: See Albert Burton Moore, *Conscription and Conflict in the Confederacy* (New York: Hillary House, 1963).

254 Twenty Negro Act: Thomas, *The Confederate Nation, 1861–1865*, 134.

254 "bloodless spade": "A Cry to Arms," *Charleston Mercury and Daily Courier*, March 4, 1862.

254 "endless field": Henry Timrod, "The Cotton-Boll," in *War Poetry of the South*, ed. William Gilmore Simms (New York: Richardson and Co., 1866), 315.

255 "vaunt over our heads": Edward A. Pollard, "Hints on Southern Civilization," *Southern Literary Messenger* 32 (April 1861), 310.

255 "Are we to bend": John L. O'Sullivan, "Close the Ranks," in *War Poetry of the South*, 188–89.

255 "sacred sands": Henry Timrod, "Carolina," in *War Poetry of the South*, 113.

255 "ten times ten": Ibid., 115.

255 "Avenge the patriot gore": James Ryder Randall, "Maryland, My Maryland," in *Poets of the Civil War*, 179.

255 "codfish poltroons": Quoted in Daniel Aaron, *The Unwritten War: American Writers and the Civil War* (Madison: University of Wisconsin Press, 1987), 239.

256 "species of demon": Royster, *The Destructive War*, 44.

256 "We should be": Wendell Phillips, *Speeches, Lectures, and Letters* (Boston: James Redpath, 1863), 540.

257 "Nothing here nowadays": Laura Stedman and George M. Gould, eds., *The Life and Letters of Edmund Clarence Stedman*, vol. 1 (New York: Moffatt, Yard, 1910), 260.

257 Fat generals: See Louisa May Alcott, *Hospital Sketches* (Boston: James Redpath, 1863), 78.

257 "I must say I cannot": Karl Marx and Friedrich Engels, *The Civil War in the United States* (New York: International Publishers, 1971), 259.

257 Burnside was dubious: See James McPherson, *Battle Cry of Freedom: The Civil War Era* (New York: Oxford University Press, 1988), 570.

258 "It seemed foolhardy": George F. Williams, *Bullet and Shell: War as the Soldier Saw It* (New York: Fords, Howard, and Hulbert, 1884), 114–15.

258 "They want us to get in": Frank Moore, ed., *The Rebellion Record: A Diary of American Events*, vol. 6 (New York: G. P. Putnam, 1863), 98.

259 "A chicken could not live": James Longstreet, "The Battle of Fredericksburg," in *Battles and Leaders of the Civil War*, vol. 3, ed. Robert Underwood Johnson and Clarence Clough Buel (New York: Century Company, 1884), 79.

259 "We might as well": G. H. Washburn, *A Complete Military History and Record of the 108th Regiment N.Y. Vols., from 1862 to 1894* (Rochester: E. R. Andrews, 1894), 27.

259 "coming up in succession": Darius N. Couch, "Sumner's 'Right Grand Division,'" in Johnson and Buel, *Battles and Leaders*, vol. 3, 113.

259 "The spectacle we saw": Longstreet, "The Battle of Fredericksburg," 79.

259 "It can hardly be": Moore, *The Rebellion Record*, vol. 6, 100.

259 This was no battle: See Hannah Ropes, *Civil War Nurse: The Diaries and Letters of Hannah Ropes*, ed. John R. Brumgardt (Knoxville: University of Tennessee Press, 1980), 114.

259 "If there is a worse place": Quoted in McPherson, *Battle Cry of Freedom*, 574.

260 "Horrid war": Bronson Alcott, *The Journals of Bronson Alcott*, ed. Odell Shepherd (Boston: Little, Brown, 1938), 353.

260 "I think through all this": Ropes, *Civil War Nurse*, 93.

261 "when the great muster roll": Alcott, *Hospital Sketches*, 42.

261 "the barren honors": Ibid., 36.

261 "carelessness of the value of life": Ibid.

261 Surprisingly, Dix managed: See Helen E. Marshall, *Dorothea Dix: Forgotten Samaritan* (Chapel Hill: University of North Carolina Press, 1937), 206–10.

262 "The field is no place": Quoted in Blanche Colton Williams, *Clara Barton: Daughter of Destiny* (Philadelphia: J. B. Lippincott Co., 1941), 73.

262 Soon she was sorting: See, e.g., Charles F. Ritter and Jon L. Wakelyn, eds., "Clara Barton," in *Leaders of the American Civil War* (Westport, Conn.: Greenwood Press, 1998), 11.

262 In her plain brown frock: Williams, *Clara Barton*, 73.

262 A few weeks later: See Agatha Young and Agnes Brooks Young, *Women and the Crisis: Women of the North in the Civil War* (New York: McDowell, Obolensky, 1959), 45.

263 "I wrung the blood": Quoted in Elizabeth Brown Pryor, *Clara Barton: Professional Angel* (Philadelphia: University of Pennsylvania Press, 1987), 107.

263 "All that was elegant": Ibid.

263 "My position is one": Clara Barton to Elvira Stone, August 30, 1862, Clara Barton Papers, LC.

263 "I am singularly free": Clara Barton to Elvira Stone, [October or November,] 1863, LC.

264 "the ordinary deliberations": Quoted in Ann Douglas Wood, "The War within a War: Women Nurses in the Union Army," *Civil War History* 18 (September 1972), 211.

264 "I do not believe in missions": Pryor, *Clara Barton*, 102.

264 "This war of ours": "Our Women and the War," *Harper's Weekly*, Sept. 6, 1862, 570.

264 "Dr. Buck informed me": Quoted in Jane E. Schultz, "The Inhospitable Hospital: Gender and Professionalism in Civil War Medicine," *Signs: Journal of Women in Culture and History* 17 (Winter 1992), 375.

265 "lucky": Walt Whitman, "Our Wounded and Sick Soldiers," *The New York Times*, Dec. 11, 1864, 1.

265 "I don't want to see": William Dean Howells, *The Rise of Silas Lapham*, in *Novels, 1875–1886*, ed. Edwin Cady (New York: Library of America, 1982), 1048.

266 "a great deal of opposition": Kate Cumming, *Kate: The Journal of a Confederate Nurse*, ed. Richard Barksdale Harwell (Baton Rouge: Louisiana State University Press, 1959), 38.

266 "The women of the South": Phoebe Yates Pember, *A Southern Woman's Story* (New York: G. W. Carleton and Company, 1879), 13.

266 "The results of war": Ibid., 44.

266 "in what I consider": Ibid., 60.

267 "with a narrower scope": Henry Timrod, "The Two Armies," in *War Poetry of the South*, 159.

267 "the women of the south": William Gilmore Simms, "To the Women of the South," in *War Poetry of the South*, i.

268 A volume of Confederate verse: See Samuel Albert Link, *War Poets of the South* (Nashville, 1898).

268 "Had I Stonewall Jackson": Quoted in Mary Anna Jackson, *Memoirs of Stonewall Jackson by His Widow Mary Anna Jackson* (Louisville: Prentice Press, 1895), 611.

268 "crowded to suffocation": Chesnut, *Mary Chesnut's Civil War*, 430.

268 "Bread! Bread": See Paul D. Escott, " 'The Cry of the Sufferers': The Problem of Welfare in the Confederacy," *Civil War History* 23 (September 1977), 228–40; see also George C. Rable, *Civil Wars: Women and the Crisis of Southern Nationalism* (Urbana: University of Illinois Press, 1989).

268 "women and children": Mrs. Burton Harrison, *Recollections Grave and Gay* (New York: Charles Scribner's Sons, 1911), 137; see also Michael B. Chesson, "Harlots or Heroines? A New Look at the Richmond Bread Riot," *The Virginia Magazine of History and Biography* 92 (April 1984), 139–43.

268 When the mayor couldn't: See Varina Davis, *Jefferson Davis: A Memoir by His Wife*, vol. 2 (Baltimore: Nautical Aviation Publishing Company of America, 1990), 375; for an account of the riot, see "Richmond's Bread Riot," *The New York Times*, April 30, 1889.

269 James Seddon: See Moore, *Rebellion Record,* vol. 6, 523–24.

269 The various conflicting accounts: See "Reported Bread Riot at Richmond," *Harper's Weekly*, April 18, 1863, 243.

269 "We had forgotten Yankees": Chesnut, *Mary Chesnut's Civil War*, 436.

270 "I write from the border": Rebecca Harding Davis, *Margret Howth* (Boston: Ticknor & Fields, 1862), 3.

270 "My family lived": Rebecca Harding Davis, *Bits of Gossip* (Boston: Houghton Mifflin, 1904), 165–66.

270 "While they thought": Ibid., 32–33.

270 "the actual war": Ibid., 34.

270 "A man cannot drink": Ibid., 125.

271 "right and wrong mixing": Rebecca Harding, "David Gaunt," *The Atlantic Monthly* 10 (October 1862), 409.

271 "Does anybody wonder": Chesnut, *Mary Chesnut's Civil War*, 371.

271 "What an extraordinary paper": George W. Curtis to Charles Eliot Norton, June 26, 1862, Houghton Library, Harvard University.

CHAPTER 12: THE LAST FULL MEASURE OF DEVOTION

272 They died from cannonades: See Gary Laderman, *The Sacred Remains: American Attitudes toward Death, 1799–1883* (New Haven, Conn.: Yale University Press, 1996), 97.

272 Assuming their chances of survival: Drew Gilpin Faust, "'The Dread Void of Uncertainty': Naming the Dead in the American Civil War," *Southern Cultures* 11 (Summer 2005), 15.

273 By the time her bureau closed: Ibid., 25.

273 "The corpses seemed to be everywhere": George F. Williams, *Bullet and Shell: War as the Soldier Saw It* (New York: Ford, Howard, and Hulbert, 1882), 257.

276 "on July 1 was without order": Henry Heth, "Letter from Major-General Henry Heth, of AP Hill's Corps, ANV," *Southern Historical Society Papers* 4 (1877), 159.

276 "Can you tell me": Ibid., 156.

276 "one boot off": John Bell Hood, *Advance and Retreat: Personal Experiences in the United States and Confederate States Armies* (New Orleans: G. T. Beauregard, 1879), 57.

277 Critics later alleged: I am indebted for this summary to Kurt Silverman.

277 "desperate-looking character": Lieutenant-Colonel Arthur James Fremantle, *Three Months in the Southern States, April–June 1863* (London: William Black-wood and Sons, 1863), 253.

277 "The execution of the fire": *OR*, vol. 27, pt. 1, 1863, 884.

277 "The Rebels—three lines deep": Quoted in Horace Greeley, *The American Conflict*, vol. 2 (Hartford: O. D. Case, 1867), 386.

278 "Death! death everywhere": George F. Williams, *Bullet and Shell: A Soldier's Romance* (New York: Ford, Howard, and Hulbert, 1882), 257.

278 "That day at Gettysburg": James Longstreet, "Lee's Right Wing at Gettysburg," in *Battles and Leaders of the Civil War*, vol. 3, ed. Robert Underwood Johnson and Clarence Clough Buel (New York: Century Co., 1884), 345.

278 "I thought it would not do": James Longstreet, *From Manassas to Appomattox: Memoirs of the Civil War in America* (Philadelphia: J. B. Lippincott, 1896), 386.

278 "The rebels behaved": Henry Livermore Abbott, *Fallen Leaves: The Civil War Letters of Major Henry Livermore Abbott*, ed. Robert Garth Scott (Kent, Ohio: Kent State University Press, 1991), 188.

278 "Never mind, General": Fremantle, *Three Months in the Southern States*, 289.

279 "proceed in search of the enemy": *OR*, vol. 27, pt. 1, July 6, 1863, 80.

279 "They will be ready": Quoted in David Homer Bates, *Lincoln in the Telegraph Office* (New York: Century Co., 1907), 157.

279 "act upon your own judgment": *OR*, vol. 27, pt. 1, July 13, 1863, 92.

280 "to an attempt to lock": Shelby Foote, *The Civil War: Fredericksburg to Meridian*, vol. 2 (New York: Random House, 1963), 591.

280 "We have certain information": *OR*, vol. 27, pt. 1, July 7, 1863, 83.

280 "Your golden opportunity is gone": Ibid., 479.

280 "It's all my fault": See Edward A. Pollard, *Lee and His Lieutenants* (New York: E. B. Treat, 1867), 114.

280 "fate of the Confederacy": Ulysses S. Grant, *Memoirs and Selected Letters*, ed. Mary Drake McFeely and William S. McFeely (New York: Library of America, 1990), 381.

281 "wan, hollow-eyed, ragged": Dora Miller Richards, "A Woman's Diary of the Siege of Vicksburg," *Century Magazine* 30 (1885), 771.

281 "We are whipped": Mary Ann Webster Loughborough, *My Cave Life in Vicksburg: With Letters of Trial and Travel* (New York: D. Appleton, 1864), 42.

282 "Caves were the fashion": Ibid., 72.

282 "the burning matter": Ibid., 64.

282 "We are utterly cut off": Dora Miller Richards, "A Woman's Diary of the Siege of Vicksburg," *Century Magazine* 30 (1885), 771.

282 "sleek horses, polished arms": Ibid., 775.

283 "In boldness of plan": *OR*, vol. 24, pt. 1, August 1, 1863, 63.

283 "I can't spare this man": Quoted in *Recollected Words of Abraham Lincoln*, compiled and ed. Don E. Fehrenbacher and Virginia Fehrenbacher (Palo Alto, Calif.: Stanford University Press, 1996), 315.

283 "I posted the First and Third": *OR*, vol. 26, pt. 1, May 30, 1863, 45.

284 "completely revolutionized the sentiment": Charles A. Dana, *Recollections of the Civil War: With the Leaders at Washington and in the Field in the Sixties* (New York: D. Appleton, 1899), 86.

284 "The war is not waged": Edmund Clarence Stedman, *The Life and Letters of Edmund Clarence Stedman*, vol. 1, ed. Laura Stedman and George M. Gould (New York: Moffatt, Yard, 1910), 242.

284 "was too good a fellow": Abbott, *Fallen Leaves*, 198–99.

284 "We are for the Union": Told to the author, January 13, 2011.

284 "Shall we sink down": Quoted in Wood Gray, *The Hidden Civil War: The Story of the Copperheads* (New York: Viking, 1942), 125.

285 "[Horatio] Seymour, the New York *World*": Ibid., 303.

285 "I think, to be sure": Ibid., 310.

285 "PATRIOTISM ABOVE MOCK PHILANTHROPY": Clement Vallandigham, *The Record of Hon. C. L. Vallandigham on Abolition, the Union, and the Civil War* (Columbus, Ohio: J. Walter, 1863), 39.

286 "the Secession Rebellion South": Ibid., 146.

286 "enslavement of the white race": Ibid., 189.

286 "Ought this war": Ibid., 183.

287 "The real genuine Democracy": Quoted in Gray, *The Hidden Civil War*, 121.

287 "his sympathies for those in arms": Quoted in Vallandigham, *The Record of Hon. C. L. Vallandigham*, 253.

288 "I am a Democrat": Ibid., 254.

288 "ours is a case of rebellion": Abraham Lincoln, *Lincoln: Speeches and Writings, 1859–1865*, vol. 2, ed. Don E. Fehrenbacher (New York: Library of America, 1989), 457.

288 "shoot a simple-minded": Ibid., 460.

289 in the summer or fall of 1863: See *OR*, ser. 2, vol. 7, 233–36, 629–46.

289 "worth regarding": John Hay, *Lincoln and the Civil War in the Diaries and Letters of John Hay*, ed. Tyler Dennett (Cambridge, Mass.: Da Capo Press, 1939), 192.

290 "the Father of Waters again": Lincoln, *Lincoln: Speeches and Writings, 1850–1865*, 498.

290 "The conscription is necessary": "The Conscription and the War," *The New York Times*, July 10, 1863, 4.

290 That Saturday, July 11: For the best single volume on the draft riots, see Iver Bernstein, *The New York City Draft Riots: Their Significance for American Society and Politics in the Age of the Civil War* (New York: Oxford University Press, 1990).

290 "a proposal for the butchery": Allan Nevins, *The War for the Union*, vol. 2 (New York: Scribner's, 1959), 302.

291 The draft had taken recruitment: For a discussion of the relation between state and federal authority in this matter, see Rachel Shelden, "'Speedy Conclusion': A Reexamination of Conscription and Civil War Federalism," *Civil War History* 55 (December 2009), 469–98.

291 "Men and ladies attacked": George Templeton Strong, *The Diary of George Templeton Strong*, vol. 3, ed. Allan Nevins and Milton Halsey Thomas (New York: Macmillan, 1952), 342.

291 "They are the most peaceable": Ibid., 343.

292 "the Democratic party": Ibid., vol. 3, 340.

292 "I at once felt myself": Frederick Douglass, *Life and Times of Frederick Douglass, from 1817 to 1882* (London: Christian Age Office, 1882), 422.

292 "I have given the subject": Ulysses S. Grant, *The Papers of Ulysses S. Grant*, vol. 9, ed. John Y. Simon (Carbondale: Southern Illinois University Press, 1982), 196.

293 "To be plain": This and subsequent quotations from the famous "Conkling letter" are in Lincoln, *Lincoln: Speeches and Writings, 1859–1865*, 495–99.

CHAPTER 13: FAIRLY WON

296 "True Democracy makes no": Quoted in John Niven, *Salmon P. Chase* (New York: Oxford University Press, 1995), 85.

296 "How his example shames": Salmon P. Chase, *The Salmon P. Chase Papers*, vol. 1, ed. John Niven et al. (Kent, Ohio: Kent State University Press, 1993), 212.

296 His abolitionism too: See Albert Bushnell Hart, *American Statesmen: Salmon Porter Chase* (Boston: Houghton Mifflin, 1899); Herman Belz, "Salmon P. Chase and the Politics of Racial Reform," *Journal of the Abraham Lincoln Association* 17 (Summer 1996), 27; Stephen Maizlish, "Salmon P. Chase: The Roots of Ambition and the Origins of Reform," *Journal of the Early Republic* 18 (Spring 1998), 47–70.

297 "man of mark": Gideon Welles, *The Diary of Gideon Welles: Secretary of the Navy under Lincoln and Johnson*, vol. 2 (Boston: Houghton Mifflin, 1911), 59.

297 "inordinate ambition": Ibid., 121.

297 "He constantly indulged": Carl Schurz, *The Reminiscences of Carl Schurz*, vol. 2 (New York: McClure Company, 1907), 172.

297 "Chase is a good man": John Hay, *Lincoln and the Civil War in the Diaries and Letters of John Hay*, ed. Tyler Dennett (Cambridge, Mass.: Da Capo Press, 1939), 53.

297 "fond dreams": Noah Brooks, *Lincoln Observed: Civil War Dispatches of Noah Brooks* (Baltimore: Johns Hopkins University Press, 2002), 69.

297 "Chase keeps ahead": Ibid.

299 "like a duck hit": Hay, *Lincoln and the Civil War in the Diaries and Letters of John Hay*, 106.

299 "make capital": Ibid., 110.

299 "I suppose he will": Ibid.

300 "the country will never": Ibid.

300 "it can not be known": Abraham Lincoln, *Lincoln: Speeches and Writings, 1859–1865*, vol. 2, ed. Don E. Fehrenbacher (New York: Library of America, 1989), 504.

300 "attempt to retract": Ibid., 552.

301 "a retail policy": James McPherson, "No Peace without Victory, 1861–1865," *The American Historical Review* 109 (February 2004), 5.

301 "the best the Executive": Lincoln, *Lincoln: Speeches and Writings, 1859–1865*, 558.

301 "President's message and proclamation": George Templeton Strong, *The Diary of George Templeton Strong*, vol. 3, ed. Allan Nevins and Milton Halsey Thomas (New York: Macmillan, 1952), 379.

301 "the negro's freedom": James McPherson, *The Struggle for Equality: Abolitionists and the Negro in the Civil War and Reconstruction* (Princeton, N.J.: Princeton University Press, 1992), 242.

301 Jefferson Davis and his ilk: Elizabeth Blair Lee, *Wartime Washington: The Civil War Letters of Elizabeth Blair Lee*, ed. Virginia Jeans Laas (Urbana: University of Illinois Press, 1999), 325.

302 "The Goliath": James Harvey Young, "Anna Elizabeth Dickinson and the Civil War: For and against Lincoln," *The Mississippi Valley Historical Review* 31 (June 1944), 66.

303 "Ask no man": Quoted in Thomas Higginson, *Contemporaries* (Boston: Houghton Mifflin, 1900), 258.

303 "counterweight": Richard Hofstadter, *The American Political Tradition* (New York: Vintage, 1967), 137–38.

303 "Peace if possible": Quoted in Richard Mardock, *Reformers and the Indian* (Columbia: University of Missouri Press, 1971), 17.

303 "carved her way": Elizabeth Cady Stanton, "Anna Elizabeth Dickinson," in James Parton, *Eminent Women of the Age* (Hartford: S. M. Betts & Co., 1868), 479.

303 "the young elephant": Quoted in Eleanor Flexner, *Century of Struggle: The Women's Rights Struggle in the United States* (Cambridge, Mass.: Belknap Press of Harvard University Press, 1996), 102.

303 The Pennsylvania State Republican Party: See Giraud Chester, *Embattled Maiden: The Life of Anna Dickinson* (New York: G. P. Putnam's Sons, 1951), 71–73.

304 "what you brought away": Shelby Foote, *The Civil War: Fredericksburg to Meridian*, vol. 2 (New York: Vintage, 1986), 961; see also Stanton, "Anna Elizabeth Dickinson."

304 "crazy Jane in a red jacket": Quoted in Young, "Anna Elizabeth Dickinson and the Civil War," 70.

304 "Let no man prate": Quoted in ibid., 69.

305 A constitutional amendment: "Miss Dickinson's Lecture," *Washington Chronicle* (January 28, 1864).

305 "slavery or involuntary servitude": *CG*, 38th Congress, 1st Session, March 29, 1864, 1313 (the proposal had been made about two months earlier).

306 Raymond didn't believe: "Congress," *The New York Times*, Feb. 2, 1864, 4.

306 "Let them be free": Jean-Charles Houzeau, *My Passage at the New Orleans Tribune: A Memoir of the Civil War Era*, ed. David C. Rankin, trans. Gerald F. Denault (Baton Rouge: Louisiana State University Press, 1984), 92.

306 "Negro equality": This paragraph is derived from the report "Thirty-eighth Congress, First Session," *New-York Tribune*, Feb. 11, 1864, 8.

306 "the word *slavery*": Quoted in C. Peter Ripley, *Black Abolitionist Papers: The United States, 1859–1865*, vol. 5 (Chapel Hill: University of North Carolina Press, 1992), 300–301.

306 "By rejecting Sumner's language": Michael Vorenberg, *Final Freedom: The Civil War, the Abolition of Slavery, and the Thirteenth Amendment* (New York: Cambridge University Press, 2001), 59.

307 "*vacated*": Charles Sumner, "Our Domestic Relations," *The Atlantic Monthly* 12 (September 1863), 527.

307 "manifest tendency toward compromises": "Pomeroy Circular," quoted in John George Nicolay and John Hay, *Abraham Lincoln: A History*, vol. 8 (New York: Century Co., 1909), 318.

308 "your rose-water war": *CG*, 37th Congress, 2nd Session, Jan. 21, 1862, 511.

308 "Pomeroyism": See Edward Winslow Martin, *Behind the Scenes in Washington* (Washington, D.C.: J. D. McCabe, 1873), 176.

308 Davis, Wade, and Pomeroy: See "Pomeroy Circular," 4.

309 "This is a very pretty game": "A Game That Won't Work," *Chicago Tribune*, Feb. 24, 1864.

309 "The Salmon is": Quoted in Frederick J. Blue, *Salmon P. Chase: A Life in Politics* (Kent, Ohio: Kent State University Press, 1987), 226.

310 "What McClellan was": "M'Clellan, Buckner," *The Liberator*, May 20, 1864, 1.

310 "fanatics must make history": Rebecca Harding Davis, *Margret Howth: A Story of To-day* (Boston: Ticknor & Fields, 1862), 180.

311 "I don't believe": Quoted in Andrew Rolle, *John Charles Frémont: Character as Destiny* (Norman: University of Oklahoma Press, 1991), 230.

312 " 'You'll never fight' ": George Bodnia, "Fort Pillow 'Massacre': Observations of a Minnesotan," *Minnesota History* 43 (Spring 1973), 188.

313 twenty-nine horses: See Shelby Foote, *The Civil War: Fort Sumter to Perryville*, vol. 1 (New York: Vintage, 1986), 349.

313 "the river was dyed red": See Jack Hurst, *Nathan Bedford Forrest: A Biography* (New York: Alfred A. Knopf, 1993); for fine and comprehensive examinations of the Fort Pillow debacles, see John Cimprich, *Fort Pillow, A Civil War Massacre and Public Memory* (Baton Rouge: Louisiana State University Press, 2005), and Andrew Ward, *River Run Red: The Fort Pillow Massacre in the American Civil War* (New York: Viking, 2005).

313 "Your colors were never lowered": *OR*, ser. 1, vol. 32, pt. 1, June 28, 1864, 600.

314 "The case under consideration": Quoted in Robert Underwood Johnson and Clarence Clough Buel, eds., *Battles and Leaders of the Civil War*, vol. 4 (New York: Century Co., 1884), 418.

314 "Our Northern brethren": "Fort Pillow," *Richmond Examiner* (April 23, 1864), 2.

314 "You, Abraham Lincoln": "The Murder of Colored Troops at Fort Pillow," *The Independent*, April 21, 1864, 4.

314 The resilient abolitionist: Gerrit Smith, "The Murder of Colored Troops at Fort Pillow," *The Liberator*, April 21, 1864, 4.

315 "Once begun": Quoted in Ward, *River Run Red*, 323.

316 "protect the loyal men": Bernard Christian Steiner, *The Life of Henry Winter Davis* (Baltimore: John Murphy Co., 1916), 292.

316 "The radical Republicans": See Edmund Kirke, "Our Visit to Richmond," *The Atlantic Monthly* 14 (September 1864), 380.

316 "Everybody is looking": James G. Randall and David Herbert Donald, *The Divided Union* (Boston: Little, Brown, 1961), 473.

316 And he had strengthened: See Hans L. Trefousse, *Andrew Johnson: A Biography* (New York: W. W. Norton, 1989), 177–78.

317 "Can't you find": Quoted in ibid., 180.

317 "the most hysterical man": Nathaniel Wright Stephenson, *Lincoln: An Account of His Personal Life* (Indianapolis: Bobbs-Merrill, 1922), 327.

317 "a self-made man": Quoted in W. L. Alden, "Some Phases of Literary New York in the Sixties," *Putnam's Monthly* 3 (February 1908), 557.

318 "Meek as he looks": Harriet Beecher Stowe, *The Lives and Deeds of Our Self-Made Men* (Hartford: Worthington, Dustin, & Co., 1872), 294.

318 "He is ambitious, talented": Gideon Welles, *The Diary of Gideon Welles, Secretary of the Navy under Lincoln and Johnson*, vol. 2 (Boston: Houghton Mifflin, 1911), 104.

319 "I propose to fight": *OR*, ser. 1, vol. 37, pt. 1, 427.

319 In the tangled, dark: See William S. McFeely, *Grant: A Biography* (New York: W. W. Norton, 2002), 168.

319 "atavistic territorial battle": James McPherson, *Battle Cry of Freedom: The Civil War Era* (New York: Oxford University Press, 1988), 730.

319 "heavens are hung in black": Lincoln, *Lincoln: Speeches and Writings, 1859–1865*, 600.

319 "Many a man has gone": Oliver Wendell Holmes, Jr., *Touched with Fire: Civil War Letters and Diary of Oliver Wendell Holmes, Jr., 1861–1864*, ed. Mark DeWolfe Howe (Cambridge, Mass.: Harvard University Press, 1947), 149–50.

319 "Our bleeding, bankrupt": Quoted in Abraham Lincoln, *The Collected Works of Abraham Lincoln*, vol. 7, ed. Roy P. Basler (New Brunswick, N.J.: Rutgers University Press, 1953), 435.

320 "tall spare false looking": Quoted in John Hay, *Inside Lincoln's White House: The Complete Civil War Diary of John Hay*, ed. Michael Burlingame and John R. Turner Ettlinger (Carbondale: Southern Illinois University Press, 1997), 226.

320 "Greeley is an old shoe": Quoted in Welles, *The Diary of Gideon Welles*, vol. 2, 112.

321 "the terms and conditions of peace": "Peace Negotiations," *The New York Times*, July 22, 1864, 1.

322 "Withdraw your armies": Quoted in Kirke, "Our Visit to Richmond," 382.

322 "Mr. Lincoln is already beaten": Quoted in David Donald, *Lincoln Reconsidered* (New York: Alfred A. Knopf, 1861), 114.

323 "Lincoln's re-election will end": Lydia Minturn Post, ed., *Soldiers' Letters, from Camp, Battle-field, and Prison* (New York: Bunce & Huntington, 1865), 189–90.

323 "Why will the people": Quoted in Chester, *Embattled Maiden*, 82.

323 "The great mass": Quoted in Steiner, *The Life of Henry Winter Davis*, 302.

CHAPTER 14: ARMED LIBERTY

325 Violence: On the moral erosion of war and its connection to mass murder, see Allan Nevins, *The War for the Union: The Organized War to Victory, 1864–1865*, vol. 8 (New York: Scribner's, 1971), 61, and, on the mass destruction detailed in this chapter, see Charles Royster, *The Destructive War: William Tecumseh Sherman, Stonewall Jackson, and the Americans* (New York: Vintage, 1993).

326 "It seems to me": Oliver Wendell Holmes, Jr., *The Essential Holmes: Selections from the Letters, Speeches, Judicial Opinions and Other Writings of Oliver Wendell Holmes, Jr.*, ed. Richard Posner (Chicago: University of Chicago Press, 1997), 103.

326 "past the thoughtless": Henry David Thoreau, *Walden; or, Life in the Woods*, in *A Week, Walden, The Maine Woods, Cape Cod*, ed. Robert F. Sayre (New York: Library of America, 1985), 492.

326 "I have no objection": David Goldfield, *America Aflame: How the Civil War Created a Nation* (New York: Bloomsbury Press, 2011), 120.

327 "The essential American soul": D. H. Lawrence, *Studies in Classic American Literature* (New York: Penguin, 1961), 68.

328 "I John Brown am": Quoted in John Brown, *The Life and Letters of John Brown*, ed. Franklin B. Sanborn (Boston: Roberts Bros., 1891), 620.

329 "pestilent factional quarrel": Abraham Lincoln, *The Collected Works of Abraham Lincoln*, vol. 6, ed. Roy P. Basler et al. (New Brunswick, N.J.: Rutgers University Press, 1953), 234.

329 "It is heart sickening": Quoted in Richard S. Brownlee, *Gray Ghosts of the Confederacy: Guerrilla Warfare in the West, 1861–1865* (Baton Rouge: Louisiana State University Press, 2009), 126–127.

330 "With the view to revive": *OR*, ser. 1, vol. 13, 33.

331 "since the whole": Charles Marshall, *An Aide-de-Camp of General Robert E. Lee*, ed. Frederick Maurice (New York: Little, Brown, 1927), 32.

331 "if this detestable system": *OR*, ser. 1, vol. 34, pt. 4, 690.

331 "Arrest all bands": *OR*, ser. 1, vol. 34, pt. 4, May 27, 1864, 633.

331 "Now, whether the guerrillas": *OR*, ser. 1, vol. 13, Sept. 28, 1862, 682–83.

332 "To secure the safety": *OR*, ser. 1, vol. 31, pt. 3, Dec. 21, 1863, 459.

332 "we lived off the country": *OR*, ser. 1, vol. 32, pt. 2, Feb. 29, 1864, 498.

332 "worse than vandal hordes": Jefferson Davis, *The Essential Writings*, ed. William J. Cooper, Jr. (New York: Modern Library, 2003), 282.

333 "Should we treat": William T. Sherman and John Sherman, *The Sherman Letters: Correspondence between General and Senator Sherman from 1837 to 1891*, ed. Rachel Sherman Thorndike (New York: Charles Scribner's Sons, 1894), 230.

334 "gentleness and forbearance": *OR*, ser. 1, vol. 32, pt. 2, Jan. 31, 1864, 280–81.

335 "To make war": Quoted in Royster, *The Destructive War*, 269.

335 "I do not know": Quoted in J. Cutler Andrews, *The North Reports the Civil War* (Pittsburgh: University of Pittsburgh Press, 1955), 538.

335 "we mowed them down": Phillip Thomas Tucker, *The Forgotten "Stonewall of the West": Major General John Stevens Bowen* (Macon, Ga.: Mercer University Press, 1997), 321.

336 "A garden was": J. T. Headley, *Grant and Sherman: Their Campaigns and Generals* (New York: E. B. Treat & Co., 1865), 221.

336 According to one soldier: Charles Harding Cox, "Gone for a Soldier," ed. Lorna Lutes Sylvester, *Indiana Magazine of History* 68 (September 1972): 181–239, at 229.

337 "War, after all": David Conyngham, *Sherman's March through the South* (New York: Sheldon & Co., 1865), 334.

337 "This unprecedented measure": *OR*, ser. 1, vol. 39, pt. 1, Sept. 9, 1864, 804.

338 "wandering brood": Herman Melville, "The Scout toward Aldie," in *Selected Poems of Herman Melville*, ed. Robert Penn Warren (Jaffrey, N.H.: David Godine, 2004), 161.

338 "would run a knife": Horace Traubel, *With Walt Whitman in Camden*, vol. 4, ed. Sculley Bradley (Philadelphia: University of Pennsylvania Press, 1953), 331.

338 "I regard the whole system" *OR*, ser. 1, vol. 33, Jan. 25, 1864, 1121.

339 "crows flying over": *OR*, ser. 1, vol. 40, pt. 3, July 14, 1864, 223.

339 "I do not mean": Ibid., 253.

340 "I was sorry enough": Edward W. Emerson, *The Life and Letters of Charles Russell Lowell, Captain Sixth United States Cavalry, Colonel Second Massachusetts Cavalry, Brigadier-General United States Volunteers* (Boston: Houghton Mifflin, 1907), 353.

340 "to the death": *OR*, ser. 1, vol. 37, pt. 2, Aug. 1, 1864, 558.

341 The former West Pointer: See Emerson, *The Life and Letters of Charles Russell Lowell*, 414.

341 "With forehead of no promise": George Templeton Strong, *The Diary of George Templeton Strong*, vol. 4, ed. Allan Nevins and Milton Halsey Thomas (New York: Macmillan, 1952), 165.

341 "Face the other way": J. W. De Forest, "Sheridan's Victory of Middletown," *Harper's New Monthly Magazine* 30 (February 1865), 358.

341 "The first that the general": Thomas Buchanan Read, "Sheridan's Ride," in *Poets of the Civil War*, ed. J. D. McClatchy (New York: Library of America, 2005), 120.

342 "Relentless, merciless": W. J. Tenney, *The Military and Naval History of the Rebellion in the United States* (New York: D. Appleton, 1865), 627.

342 "The time had fully come": Frederic Denison, *Sables and Spurs: The First Rhode Island Regiment Cavalry in the Civil War, 1861–1865* (Central Falls: First Rhode Island Cavalry Veteran Association, 1876), 381.

342 Up to the door: For a penetrating discussion of the tactics of Sherman, Grant, and Sheridan on these issues, see Mark E. Neely, "Was the Civil War a Total War?," *Civil War History* 50 (December 2004), 434–58.

342 "the people must be left": Quoted in Moritz Busch, *Bismarck: Some Secret Pages of His History*, vol. 1 (London: Macmillan, 1898), 171.

342 "Death is popularly considered": Philip H. Sheridan, *Personal Memoirs of P. H. Sheridan*, vol. 1 (New York: Charles L. Webster and Co., 1888), 488.

343 Twenty-five cannon: See George Ward Nichols, *The Story of the Great March: From the Diary of a Staff Officer* (New York: Harper & Brothers, 1866), 199.

343 "There is a hope": Elizabeth Blair Lee, *Wartime Washington: The Civil War Letters of Elizabeth Blair Lee*, ed. Virginia Jeans Laas (Urbana: University of Illinois Press, 1999), 453.

343 "we should destroy slavery": For these and the other quotes, see "The Constitutional Amendment," *New York Daily Tribune*, Jan. 13, 1865, 8.

343 "I think such action": *CG*, 38th Congress, 2nd Session, Jan. 31, 1865, 524.

344 "defending [of] the State sovereignty": *CG*, 38th Congress, 2nd Session, Jan. 6, 1865, 139.

345 Stunned silence filled the room: Noah Brooks, *Washington in Lincoln's Time* (New York: Century Co., 1895), 207.

345 "It is worth while": Quoted in Allan Nevins, *The War for the Union*, vol. 8, 214.

345 "has laid nearest": Lee, *Wartime Washington*, 471.

346 "half the multitude": *The Times* [London], March 20, 1865.

347 "Johnson is either drunk": Gideon Welles, *The Diary of Gideon Welles*, vol. 2 (Boston: Houghton Mifflin, 1911), 252.

347 A man in the crowd: Ervin S. Chapman, *Latest Light on Abraham Lincoln, and War-Time Memories*, vol. 2 (New York: Fleming H. Revell, 1917), 280–92.

347 Lincoln's brief address: For an overview and analysis of the speech, see Ronald C. White, *Lincoln's Greatest Speech: The Second Inaugural* (New York: Simon & Schuster, 2002); see also Garry Wills, "Lincoln's Greatest Speech?," *The Atlantic Monthly* (September 1999), 60–70.

348 "I claim not to have": Abraham Lincoln, *Lincoln: Speeches and Writings, 1859–1865*, ed. Don E. Fehrenbacher (New York: Library of America, 1989), 586.

348 Grant, Sherman, Sheridan: See Royster, *The Destructive War*, 337; for a fine
discussion of Lincoln's Second Inaugural in the context of the theologians of
the age, see Mark A. Noll, "'Both . . . Pray to the Same God': The Singularity
of Lincoln's Faith in the Era of the Civil War Author(s)," *Journal of the Abraham
Lincoln Association* 18 (Winter 1997), 1–26.

349 "a few words": "The Inaugural Address," *The Liberator*, March 17, 1865, 4.

350 "that the newly-emancipated": Lydia Maria Child, Letter to the editor, *The
Independent*, March 7, 1865; *The Liberator*, March 24, 1865.

350 "wear as well as": Lincoln: *Lincoln: Speeches and Writings, 1869–1865*, 689.

350 "sacred effort": Frederick Douglass, *Life and Times of Frederick Douglass*, in *Autobiographies*, ed. Henry Louis Gates (New York: Library of America, 1994), 804.

350 "It is filled with texts": John Beauchamp Jones, *A Rebel War Clerk's Diary at the
Confederate States Capital*, vol. 2 (Philadelphia: J. B. Lippincott, 1866), 443.

CHAPTER 15: AND THIS IS RICHMOND

351 In Baton Rouge: See Sarah Morgan Dawson, *A Confederate Girl's Diary*, ed. Warrington Dawson (Boston: Houghton Mifflin, 1913), 213.

351 "Our rations have been": J. R. McMichael, *Autograph and Diary* (privately published), Southern Historical Collection, University of North Carolina, Chapel
Hill.

351 "The wolf is at the door": Quoted in Mary Chesnut, *Mary Chesnut's Civil War*,
ed. C. Vann Woodward (New Haven, Conn.: Yale University Press, 1981), 747.

351 "The Confederacy seemed suddenly": Quoted in Mrs. A. T. Smythe, M. B. Poppenheim, and Mrs. Thomas Taylor, eds., *South Carolina Women in the Confederacy*
(Columbia: State Co., 1903), 225.

352 "He has not the broad": J. B. Jones, *A Rebel War Clerk's Diary at the Confederate
States Capital*, vol. 2 (Philadelphia: J. B. Lippincott, 1866), 372.

352 "Disaffection is intense": Quoted in Josiah Gorgas, *The Civil War Diary of Josiah
Gorgas*, ed. Frank Vandiver (Tuscaloosa: University of Alabama Press, 1947),
154.

353 "I do not profess": Alexander H. Stephens, *A Constitutional View of the Late War
between the States: Its Causes, Character, Conduct, and Results*, vol. 2 (Philadelphia:
National Publishing Co., 1870), 613.

353 "to give to our people": Quoted in William J. Cooper, *Jefferson Davis, American*
(New York: Vintage, 2001), 551.

353 "War is a game": Quoted in Eli N. Evans, *Judah P. Benjamin: The Jewish Confederate* (New York: Free Press, 1988), 284–85.

354 "If we impress them": Ibid., 285.

354 "There is much excitement": Jones, *A Rebel War Clerk's Diary*, vol. 2, 416.

354 "Intervention on the part": Ibid., 368.

354 Kenner argued that: See John Bigelow, *Retrospections of an Active Life*, vol. 3 (New
York: Baker and Taylor Co., 1909), 80.

355 "Abolish slavery to propitiate": Chesnut, *Mary Chesnut's Civil War*, 710.

355 "Send us protection": Quoted in Stephanie McCurry, *Confederate Reckoning:
Power and Politics in the Civil War South* (Cambridge, Mass.: Harvard University
Press, 2010), 330.

355 "I think, therefore": *OR*, ser. 4, vol. 3, 1012–13.

356 "By the conscription": Robert F. Durden, *The Gray and the Black: The Confederate Debate on Emancipation* (Baton Rouge: Louisiana State University Press, 1972),
170.

356 "forth the negroes": Warren Akin, *The Letters of Warren Akin: Confederate Congressman*, ed. Bell Irvin Wiley (Athens: University of Georgia Press, 1959), 32.

356 "The proposition to make soldiers": *OR*, ser. 4, vol. 3, 1009.

356 "It is the desperate remedy": Jones, *A Rebel War Clerk's Diary*, vol. 2, 451.

357 "Slavery, from being": *OR*, ser. 1, vol. 52, pt. 2, January 8, 1865, 587.

357 "revolting to Southern sentiment": *OR*, ser. 1, vol. 52, pt. 2, 598.

357 "in advance of many": John Bell Hood, *Advance and Retreat: Personal Experiences in the United States and Confederate States Armies* (New Orleans: Hood Orphan Memorial Fund, 1880), 296.

357 Cleburne was killed: See James M. McPherson, *Battle Cry of Freedom: The Civil War* (New York: Oxford University Press, 1988), 811–13, and, for a complete study, James Lee McDonough and Thomas L. Connelly, *Five Tragic Hours: The Battle of Franklin* (Knoxville: University of Tennessee Press, 1983).

357 "And how could man": Chesnut, *Mary Chesnut's Civil War*, 692.

358 "The deep waters": Ibid., 694.

358 "Have you ever noticed": Akin, *The Letters of Warren Akin*, 33.

358 "to seek legislation": *OR*, ser. 1, vol. 46, pt. 3, 1366.

358 "What is this but abolition?": Thomas Gholson, *Speech of Honorable Thomas S. Gholson of Virginia on the Policy of Employing Negro Troops* (Richmond: George P. Evans, 1865), 6.

358 "You may make a soldier": Thomas Wentworth Higginson, "Safety Matches," *The Independent*, Sept. 21, 1865, 4.

359 "No slave will be accepted": *OR*, ser. 4, vol. 3, March 23, 1865, 1161.

359 "Assert the right": *Charleston Mercury*, Nov. 12, 1864.

359 "call on each State": *OR*, ser. 4, vol. 3, 1161.

360 the South's "peculiar institution": The question of why the Confederacy lost and what contributed to its military defeat has received much attention; see, e.g., McCurry, *Confederate Reckoning*, 293, 420n.

361 One Southern cavalry officer: See Allan Nevins, *The War for the Union: The Organized War to Victory: 1864–5*, vol. 3 (New York: Charles Scribner's Sons, 1972), 284.

361 "Secession was burned out": Thomas Morris Chester, *Thomas Morris Chester, Black Civil War Correspondent: His Dispatches from the Virginia Front*, ed. R. J. M. Blackett (Baton Rouge: Louisiana State University Press, 1989), 297.

362 Union troops riding: The descriptions are based on Brevet Brigadier General Edward H. Ripley, "The Occupation of Richmond," in *Personal Recollections of the War of the Rebellion*, ed. A. Noel Blakeman, vol. 3 (New York: G. P. Putnam's Sons, 1907), 475–80, and Chester, *Thomas Morris Chester, Black Civil War Correspondent*, 289–94.

362 "was filled with furniture": Charles Carleton Coffin, *The Boys of '61: or, Four Years of Fighting* (Boston: Estes and Lauriat, 1881), 508.

362 "There is no sound": George Alfred Townsend, *Campaigns of a Non-Combatant, and His Romaunt Abroad during the War* (New York: Blelock & Co., 1866), 336–37.

362 "Glory to God": Coffin, *The Boys of '61*, 508.

362 Still, one Federal officer: Jones, *A Rebel War Clerk's Diary*, vol. 2, 471.

363 "I know I am free": Quoted in Chester, *Thomas Morris Chester, Black Civil War Correspondent*, 297.

363 Later, the new military governor: George F. Shepley, "Incidents of the Capture of Richmond," *The Atlantic Monthly* 46 (July 1880), 28.

363 "The Confederate rear": James Longstreet, *From Manassas to Appomattox: Memoirs of the Civil War in America* (Philadelphia: J. B. Lippincott, 1895), 614. The description of Longstreet comes from Frederick C. Newhall, *With Sheridan in the Final Campaign against Lee,* ed. Eric J. Wittenberg (Baton Rouge: Louisiana State University Press, 2002), 117.

363 "My God": Longstreet, *From Manassas to Appomattox*, 615.

363 "to shift from myself": *OR*, ser. 1, vol. 46, pt. 1, April 7, 1865, 56.

364 "Not yet": Longstreet, *From Manassas to Appomattox*, 619.

364 "There is nothing left": John B. Gordon, *Reminiscences of the Civil War* (New York: Charles Scribner's Sons, 1904), 438.

365 "A stranger, unacquainted": Ibid., 457.

365 "This will have the best": This quote and the account of the meeting are taken from Horace Porter, "Grant's Last Campaign," *Century Magazine* 35 (November 1887), 148–50.

365 "The war is over": Quoted in Bruce Catton, *Grant Takes Command* (Boston: Little, Brown, 1969), 468.

365 "When our idolized leader": Randolph H. McKim, *A Soldier's Recollections: Leaves from the Diary of a Young Confederate* (New York: Longmans, Green and Co., 1910), 288.

366 The news of his surrender: See Stephen R. Mallory, "Last Days of the Confederate Government": *McClure's* 26 (December 1900), 107; see also Chester, *Thomas Morris Chester, Black Civil War Correspondent*, 299.

366 "walked empty-handed": Longstreet, *From Manassas to Appomattox*, 631.

CHAPTER 16: THE SIMPLE, FIERCE DEED

368 A few miles: For the episode, see *OR*, ser. 1, vol. 49, pt. 1, 657–58.

369 Quantrill and his boys: For this account, I've drawn extensively on William Elsey Connelley, *Quantrill and the Border Wars* (Cedar Rapids, Iowa: Torch Press, 1910), 465–82.

369 "The heaviest blow": Quoted in Thomas Reed Turner, *Beware the People Weeping: Public Opinion and the Assassination of Abraham Lincoln* (Baton Rouge: Louisiana State University Press, 1982), 90.

369 "appalling crime": *OR*, ser. 1, vol. 46, pt. 3, April 16, 1865, 787.

369 "the more violently 'Secesh' ": Sarah Morgan Dawson, *A Confederate Girl's Diary*, ed. Warrington Dawson (Boston: Houghton Mifflin, 1913), 437–38.

371 "He would have flashes, passages": Horace Traubel, ed., *With Walt Whitman in Camden*, vol. 4 (Philadelphia: University of Pennsylvania Press, 1959), 485.

372 "I was led on": Quoted in Louis J. Weichmann, *A True History of the Assassination of Abraham Lincoln and of the Conspiracy of 1865,* ed. Floyd E. Risvold (New York: Alfred A. Knopf, 1975), 431.

372 "My hopes are gone": Quoted in Benjamin Perley Poore, ed., *The Conspiracy Trial for the Murder of the President*, vol. 1 (Boston: J. E. Tilton & Co., 1865), 376.

372 "That means nigger citizenship": Quoted in William Hanchett, *Lincoln Murder Conspiracies* (Urbana: University of Illinois Press, 1983), 37.

373 "those shooting-irons ready": Quoted in Poore, *The Conspiracy Trial for the Murder of the President*, 123.

374 "Tell my mother": Quoted in Edward Steers, *Blood on the Moon: The Assassination of Abraham Lincoln* (Lexington: University of Kentucky Press, 2005), 204.

374 "Ours is a government": Howard K. Beale, ed., *The Diary of Edward Bates, 1859–66* (Washington, D.C.: U.S. Government Printing Office, 1933), 483.

375 "It is not simply": Quoted in Giraud Chester, *Embattled Maiden: The Life of Anna Dickinson* (New York: G. P. Putnam's Sons, 1951), 84.

376 George Templeton Strong heard: George Templeton Strong, *The Diary of George Templeton Strong*, vol. 3, ed. Allan Nevins and Milton Halsey Thomas (New York: Macmilllan, 1952), 596.

376 "The news of the capture": "The Capture of Jeff. Davis," *The New York Times*, May 16, 1865, 1.

377 Nearly forty: "Arrest of the Surratt Family," *The New York Times*, April 18, 1865, 1.

379 "as a point of evidence": Nathaniel Hawthorne, *The House of the Seven Gables*, in *Collected Novels*, ed. Millicent Bell (New York: Library of America, 1983), 612.

380 "gnat-brained, cowardly": John McElroy, *Andersonville: A Story of Rebel Military Prisons* (Toledo, Ohio: D. R. Locke, 1879), 143.

380 Wirz presented himself: For a discussion of Wirz and the conditions at Andersonville, I have drawn on Robert Scott Davis, ed., *Ghosts and Shadows of Andersonville: Essays on the Secret Social Histories of America's Deadliest Prison* (Macon, Ga.: Mercer University Press, 2006); Ovid Futch, *History of Andersonville Prison* (Gainesville: University of Florida Press, 1968); William B. Hesseltine, *Civil War Prisons* (Kent, Ohio: Kent State University Press, 1962); William Marvel, *Andersonville: The Last Depot* (Chapel Hill: University of North Carolina Press, 1994); U.S. Congress, "Trial of Henry Wirz. Letter," 40th Congress, 2nd Session, 1867–1868, Executive Document no. 23.

380 "It is hard on our men": *OR*, ser. II, vol. 7, August 18, 1864, 607.

380 "We ought not": *OR*, ser. II, vol. 7, August 19, 1864, 614–15.

381 "a man of iron will": "The Rebel Assassins," *The New York Times*, Aug. 22, 1865.

381 "accomplished by the rebel authorities": Quoted in Elizabeth D. Leonard, *Lincoln's Avengers: Justice, Revenge, and Reunion After the Civil War* (New York: W. W. Norton, 2004), 180.

381 Wirz was then: See Jefferson Davis, *The Rise and Fall of the Confederate Government*, vol. 2 (New York: D. Appleton and Co., 1881), 497–500.

382 "Talk about liberty": Quoted in Morgan Peoples, "'The Scapegoat of Andersonville': Union Execution of Confederate Captain Henry Wirz," *North Louisiana Historical Association Journal* 11 (Fall 1980), 13.

382 The buildings were lit: See Noah Brooks, *Washington in Lincoln's Time* (New York: Century Co., 1895), 253.

383 "The whole subject": Gideon Welles, *The Diary of Gideon Welles, Secretary of the Navy under Lincoln and Johnson*, vol. 2 (Boston: Houghton Mifflin, 1911), 98.

383 "Liberty has been won": Quoted in Eric Foner, *The Fiery Trial: Abraham Lincoln and American Slavery* (New York: W. W. Norton, 2010), 335.

383 "we should have slavery": Quoted in ibid., 320.

383 "the most liberal views": "Admiral Porter's Account of the Interview with Mr. Lincoln," in William T. Sherman, *Memoirs of General William T. Sherman*, ed. Charles Royster (New York: Library of America, 1990), 814.

383 "they would be at once": Ibid., 813.

383 It was an astonishing event: This point is emphasized in Foner, *The Fiery Trial*, 331.

384 "dignified, urbane": Strong, *The Diary of George Templeton Strong*, vol. 3, 509.

384 "It was a remarkable illustration": Brooks, *Washington in Lincoln's Time*, 274.

384 "clearly": "The President and the Rebel Chiefs," *Harper's Weekly* (May 6, 1865), 274.

384 "We have faith": George W. Julian, *Political Recollections, 1840–1872* (Chicago: Janson, McClurg and Co., 1884), 257.

384 "would prove a godsend": Ibid., 255.

386 "The glittering muskets": Sherman, *Memoirs of William T. Sherman*, 865.

386 When a young girl: See William S. McFeely, *Yankee Stepfather: General O. O. Howard and the Freedmen* (New York: W. W. Norton, 1994), 11.

386 Clover Hooper: See Marian Hooper Adams, *The Letters of Mrs. Henry Adams*, ed. Ward Thoron (Boston: Little, Brown, and Co., 1936), 5–8.

387 All the noise spooked: Ivory G. Kimball, *Recollections from a Busy Life, 1843–1911* (Washington, D.C.: Carnahan Press, 1912), 87.

387 "crowded with colored people": Ulysses S. Grant, *Personal Memoirs of U. S. Grant*, ed. Mary Drake McFeely and William S. McFeely (New York: Library of America, 1990), 769.

387 Instead, there were black laborers: See Adams, *The Letters of Mrs. Henry Adams*, 8.

387 "All felt this": Welles, *The Diary of Gideon Welles*, vol. 2, 310.

387 "It was a strange feeling": Adams, *The Letters of Mrs. Henry Adams*, 7.

388 "The martyred heroes": Bret Harte, "A Second Review of the Grand Army," in *Poets of the Civil War*, ed. J. D. McClatchy (New York: Library of America, 2005), 175.

388 "Did I ever think": Quoted in Allan Nevins, *The War for the Union*, vol. 4 (New York: Charles Scribner's Sons, 1971), 359.

CHAPTER 17: BUT HALF ACCOMPLISHED

391 "not very profound": Whitelaw Reid, *After the War: A Southern Tour* (Cincinnati: Moore, Wilstach & Baldwin, 1866), 80.

392 "what ladies would call": Ibid.

392 "rank secesh women": Diary of S. Willard Saxton, Jan. 28, 1865, MS 431, box 6, folder 32, Yale.

393 "former promises which I": *Impeachment Investigation: Testimony Taken before the Judiciary Committee of the House of Representatives in the Investigation of Charges against Andrew Johnson*, 39th Congress, 2nd Session, and 40th Congress, 1st Session (Washington, D.C.: U.S. Government Printing Office, 1867), 116. For a persuasive account of the circumstances that attest to the truth of Saxton's account, see the superb Willie Lee Rose, *Rehearsal for Reconstruction: The Port Royal Experiment* (Athens: University of Georgia Press, 1999), 328–330.

394 "every colored man": Quoted in William S. McFeely, *Yankee Stepfather: General O. O. Howard and the Freedmen* (New York: W. W. Norton, 1994), 50.

394 "possessory": Diary of S. Willard Saxton, Jan. 15, 1865, Yale.

394 Not so General Howard: See Howard C. Westwood, "Sherman Marched—and Proclaimed 'Land for the Landless,'" *South Carolina Historical Magazine* 85 (January 1984), 43.

395 "born in petticoats": John Carpenter, *Sword and Olive Branch: Oliver Otis Howard* (Pittsburgh: University of Pittsburgh Press, 1964), 24–25.

395 "a man of pure purposes": "The Bureau Afloat," *The Independent*, December 7, 1865, 5.

395 "*too much* Northern management": McFeely, *Yankee Stepfather*, 60.

396 "This is a country": Quoted in Eric McKitrick, *Andrew Johnson and Reconstruction* (New York: Oxford University Press, 1988), 184.

397 "They are doing all": Quoted in William A. Dobak, *Freedom by the Sword: The U.S. Colored Troops, 1862–1867* (Washington, D.C.: U.S. Army, Center of Military History, 2011), 464.

398 "The whites seem wholly": Sidney Andrews, "Three Months among the Reconstructionists," *The Atlantic Monthly* 17 (February 1866), 244.

398 "We heard that a negro": Emmala Reed, *A Faithful Heart: The Journals of Emmala Reed, 1865 and 1866*, ed. Robert T. Oliver (Columbia: University of South Carolina Press, 2004), 114.

398 "have the whole black population": Testimony of General Rufus Saxton, in *Report of the Joint Committee on Reconstruction, at the First Session, of the 39th Congress* (Washington, D.C.: U.S. Government Printing Office, 1866), 219.

398 "The Government is now": "Has the South Any Statesmen Still Living?," *New-York Tribune*, November 24, 1865, 4.

399 "There are large numbers": Testimony of General Rufus Saxton, in *Report of the Joint Committee on Reconstruction*, 220.

399 "It was Plymouth colony": Quoted in Rose, *Rehearsal for Reconstruction*, 331.

400 "I should break faith": *Impeachment Investigation*, 116.

400 had raised more than $300,000: See Rufus Saxton to O. O. Howard, Aug. 15, 1865, Bureau of Refugees, Freedmen, and Abandoned Lands, South Carolina, vol. 9, National Archives.

400 "have conspired together": Quoted in Martin L. Abbott, "The Freedmen's Bureau in South Carolina," PhD diss., Emory University, 1954, 17–18.

400 "only care to make": Laura M. Towne, *The Letters and Diary of Laura M. Towne: Written from the Sea-Islands of South Carolina, 1862–1884*, ed. Rufus Sargent (Cambridge, Mass.: Riverside Press, 1912), 171.

401 "Yankees and negroes": Quoted in Rose, *Rehearsal for Reconstruction*, 347.

401 "We are in no sense": Reid, *After the War*, 357.

401 "break the sad news": Diary of S. Willard Saxton, October 18–19 and 24, 1865.

401 "the negroes in public speeches": Quoted in McFeely, *Yankee Stepfather*, 124.

402 "The negro believes": Testimony of General Rufus Saxton, in *Report of the Joint Committee on Reconstruction*, 219.

403 "this unnecessary and unnatural": "The Freedmen's Bureau and the Freedmen," *DeBow's Review* (May 1866), 551.

403 In December 1865: General Rufus Saxton, "Annual Report," December 6, 1865, Bureau of Freedmen, Refugees, and Abandoned Lands, box 732, National Archives.

403 "sink to perdition": Diary of S. Willard Saxton, November 20, 1865, Yale.

403 "Here is the proof": *CG*, 39th Congress, 1st Session, Dec. 1, 1865, 257.

403 "would not touch": Diary of S. Willard Saxton, Jan. 15, 1866, Yale.

403 "O that we had": Ibid., Dec. 9, 1865.

403 "loss of rank": Rufus Saxton, "Autobiography," typescript, MS 43, Yale.

403 "It is a triumph": Diary of S. Willard Saxton, Jan. 9, 1866, Yale.

404 Ultimately, freedmen holding titles: See the indispensable Eric Foner, *Reconstruction: America's Unfinished Revolution, 1863–1867* (New York: Harper & Row, 1988), 163.

404 "All subsequent attempts": "The Educational Work of General Rufus Saxton among the Freedmen of the South," *Report of the Commissioner of Education*, vol. 1 (Washington, D.C.: U.S. Government Printing Office, 1902), 423.

404 "because he delivered": "Gen. Saxton's Removal," *Chicago Tribune*, Feb. 4, 1866, 2.

404 "a rough character": O. O. Howard, *The Autobiography of Oliver Otis Howard*, vol. 2 (New York: Baker and Taylor Co., 1907), 296.

404 "If the Freedman Bureau": Quoted in Foner, *Reconstruction*, 169.

405 "The result of Gen. Saxton's": "South Carolina," *The New York Times*, May 25, 1866, 5.

405 "that, in their own words": Testimony of General Rufus Saxton, in *Report of the Joint Committee on Reconstruction*, 217.

406 "After earning a dollar": "The South Victorious," *New York Daily Tribune*, Oct. 26, 1865, 8.

406 The French correspondent: See Georges Clemenceau, *American Reconstruction*, ed. Fernand Baldensberger, trans. Margaret MacVeigh (New York: Dial Press, 1928), 61.

409 "If, as long as": *Message of the President of the United States: Communicating in compliance with, a resolution, of the Senate. Of the 12th instant, information in relation to the States of the Union lately in rebellion, accompanied by a report of Carl Schurz on the States of South Carolina, Georgia, Alabama, Mississippi, and Louisiana; also a report of Lieutenant General Grant, on the same subject*, 39th Congress, 1st Session, no. 2 (Washington, D.C.: U.S. Government Printing Office, 1865), 39.

409 "Centuries of slavery": Ibid., 32.

409 "A voter is a man": Ibid., 43.

410 "*I* did think": Douglas L. Wilson and Rodney O. Davis, eds., *Herndon's Informants: Letters, Interview, and Statements about Abraham Lincoln* (Champaign: University of Illinois, 1998), 315.

410 "A disastrous eclipse": Diary of S. Willard Saxton, Jan. 15, 1866, Yale.

CHAPTER 18: AMPHITHEATRUM JOHNSONIANUM

412 "political agitators": Quoted in Philip H. Sheridan, *Personal Memoirs of Philip H. Sheridan*, vol. 2 (New York: D. Appleton & Co., 1888), 235.

413 "several negroes lying dead": Quoted in *Report of the Select Committee in the New Orleans Riots* (Washington, D.C.: U.S. Government Printing Office, 1867), 16.

413 "I'll shoot down": Quoted in ibid., 196–97.

413 "It seemed ridiculous": Quoted in ibid., 7.

414 "God damn you": Quoted in ibid.

414 "I have seen death": Quoted in the important volume George Rable, *But There Was No Peace: The Role of Violence in the Politics of Reconstruction* (Athens: University of Georgia Press, 1984), 58.

414 "It is 'Memphis'": See, e.g., "Great Riot . . . the Fearful Scenes of Memphis Re-Enacted," *The New York Times*, July 31, 1866, 1.

415 "some of the colored people": Quoted in Abraham Lincoln, *Lincoln: Speeches and Writings, 1859–1865*, ed. Don E. Fehrenbacher (New York: Library of America, 1989), 579.

415 After the war: See Wallace P. Reed, "Last Forlorn Hope of the Confederacy," *Southern Historical Society Papers* 30 (1902), 117–21.

415 President Johnson had issued: For a fine summary of the political conditions in postbellum New Orleans, see Scott P. Marler, " 'A Monument of Commercial Isolation': Merchants and the Economic Decline of Post–Civil War New Orleans," *Journal of Urban History* 36 (March 2010), 507–27.

417 "It is our general belief": Quoted in Joe Gray Taylor, "New Orleans and Reconstruction," *Louisiana History: The Journal of the Louisiana Historical Association* 9 (Summer 1968), 195.

417 "Reconstruction in Louisiana": W. E. B. DuBois, *Black Reconstruction in America, 1860–1880* (New York: Free Press, 1990), 482.

417 "no riot": Quoted in *Report of the Select Committee on the New Orleans Riots*, 351.

419 "just like any nigger": Quoted in Hans Trefousse, *Andrew Johnson: A Biography* (New York: W. W. Norton, 1989), 242.

419 Duplicating the civil rights bill: The second section of the amendment reduced Southern representation in the House—unless the state granted the black man suffrage. This was a compromise measure intended to placate both moderate and radical ends of the Republican party, for not everyone could yet agree that granting suffrage fell under the jurisdiction of the federal government. The third section disenfranchised former Confederate military personnel and political officeholders, though there too there was compromise, for the franchise could be reinstated by a two-thirds vote of Congress. The fourth section of the amendment declared Confederate debts null and void and did not authorize compensation for the loss of slavery or slaves.

420 "We have at last agreed": William Salter, *The Life of James W. Grimes* (New York: D. Appleton and Co., 1876), 292.

420 "there is no possibility": John B. Pickard, ed., *The Letters of John Greenleaf Whittier*, vol. 3 (Cambridge: Harvard University Press, 1975), 89.

421 "I have been opposed": Ibid., 132.

421 "If he left Washington": Ibid., 133.

421 "didn't like attending": Quoted in George Templeton Strong, *The Diary of George Templeton Strong*, vol. 4, ed. Allan Nevins and Milton Halsey Thomas (New York: Macmillan, 1952), 103.

421 "a National disgrace": Ulysses S. Grant, *The Papers of Ulysses S. Grant*, vol. 16, ed. John Y. Simon (Carbondale: Southern Illinois University Press, 1988), 308.

422 "Hang Jeff Davis": Edward McPherson, *The Political History of the United States of America during the Period of Reconstruction* (Washington, D.C.: Philip and Solomons, 1871), 135.

422 "If there is any man": Donald E. Reynolds, "The New Orleans Riot of 1866, Reconsidered," *Louisiana History* 5 (Winter 1964), 15.

422 "sunk the Presidential office": William T. Sherman and John Sherman, *The Sherman Letters: The Correspondence of General and Senator Sherman from 1837 to 1891*, ed. Rachel Sherman Thorndike (New York: Charles Scribner's Sons, 1894), 278.

422 "Does Seward mean": Quoted in Trefousse, *Andrew Johnson: A Biography*, 264.

422 "coppery": "The Seward-Johnson Reaction," *North American Review* 103 (October 1866), 524.

423 "Thomas Nast has been": Quoted in Albert Bigelow Paine, *Thomas Nast: His Period and His Pictures* (New York: Macmillan, 1904), 69.

423 Petroleum Vesuvius Nasby: Locke's Nasby was an unrepentant racist "who allus tuk his likker straight." Satirizing slavery, white supremacy, defeatism, and Copperheads, Locke once explained that "I can kill more error by exaggerating vice than by abusing it." Likened by some to Cervantes, he'd been publishing his Nasby letters since 1860 in the *Toledo Blade*, and soon they were reprinted throughout the North and collected in book form in 1864. Union soldiers loved the Nasby letters, for Nasby was the dissipated Kentucky Democrat so devoted to bigotry that he made it ludicrous. Lincoln too loved the Nasby letters, which he purportedly read before each cabinet meeting. Charles Sumner, a bit too stiff for that, nonetheless remembered Lincoln saying that "for the genius to write such things, I'd give up my office." At the war's end, George S. Boutwell, who had been in charge of the Internal Revenue Service, said that three things had been responsible for the North's victory: the army, the navy, and the Nasby letters.

423 "I have great confidence": Petroleum V. Nasby [David Ross Locke], *Andy's Trip to the West, Together with a Life of Its Hero* (New York: J. C. Haney and Co., 1867), 38.

424 "These poor men": Quoted in Drew Gilpin Faust, *This Republic of Suffering: Death and the American Civil War* (New York: Alfred A. Knopf, 2008), 230.

424 "If we had looked": "The Seward-Johnson Reaction," *North American Review* 103 (October 1866), 539–40.

425 "To fight out a war": Oliver Wendell Holmes, Jr., *The Essential Holmes: Selections from the Letters, Speeches, Judicial Opinions, and Other Writings of Oliver Wendell Holmes, Jr.*, ed. Richard A. Posner (Chicago: University of Chicago Press, 1992), 81.

426 "set Zionsward": Quoted in John Hay, *Inside Lincoln's White House: The Complete Civil War Diary of John Hay*, ed. Michael Burlingame and John R. T. Ettlinger (Carbondale: Southern Illinois University Press, 1999), 101.

426 "May I ask my friend": Quoted in Eric Foner, "Thaddeus Stevens, Confiscation, and Reconstruction," in *The Hoftstadter Aegis: A Memorial*, ed. Stanley Elkins and Eric McKitrick (New York: Alfred A. Knopf, 1974), 167.

426 "strip the Southern": "Confiscation at the South," *The New York Times*, May 2, 1867.

426 "A deep-seated prejudice": Quoted in James Albert Woodburn, *The Life of Thaddeus Stevens: A Study in American Political History, Especially in the Period of the Civil War and Reconstruction* (Indianapolis: Bobbs-Merrill Co., 1913), 429–30.

426 "This doctrine": Ibid., 430.

426 As one historian later noted: See Foner, "Thaddeus Stevens, Confiscation, and Reconstruction," 174.

426 "whole countenance": "Interview of a Southern Editor with Hon. Thaddeus Stevens," *The New York Times*, June 22, 1867.

426 And in spite of: See "The Fallen Oak," *The Independent*, Aug. 20, 1868, 4.

427 "I repose in this quiet": Thomas F. Woodley, *Great Leveler: The Life of Thaddeus Stevens* (New York: Stackpole Sons, 1937), 414.

428 "*beggary, starvation, death*": Henry Timrod, *The Poems of Henry Timrod, with a Sketch of the Poet's Life*, ed. Paul H. Hayne (New York: E. J. Hale & Son, 1873), 45.

428 "we have eaten": Ibid., 46.

428 a pretext for war: Edward A. Pollard, *The Lost Cause: A New Southern History of the War of the Confederates* (New York: E. B. Treat & Co, 1866), 47.

428 "The extreme Black Republican party": Ibid., 746.

429 "No history is a matter": James Branch Cabell, *Let Me Lie: Being in the Main an Ethnological Account of the Remarkable Commonwealth of Virginia and the Making of Its History* (Charlottesville: University of Virginia Press, 2001), 74.

429 "Civil wars, like private quarrels": Pollard, *The Lost Cause*, 729.

CHAPTER 19: POWER

430 "Society in America": Henry Adams, *The Education of Henry Adams*, in *Novels*, ed. Ernest Samuels and Jayne N. Samuels (New York: Library of America, 1983), 937.

431 "The truth is": William T. Sherman and John Sherman, *The Sherman Letters: Correspondence between General and Senator Sherman from 1837 to 1891*, ed. Rachel Sherman Thorndike (New York: Charles Scribner's Sons, 1894), 258.

433 "By means of railroads": Quoted in Robert Milder, *Reimagining Thoreau* (New York: Cambridge University Press, 1995), 100.

433 "But if we stay at home": Henry David Thoreau, *A Week, Walden, The Maine Woods, Cape Cod*, ed. Robert F. Sayre (New York: Library of America, 1985), 396.

433 "We have bound": Walt Whitman, "Passage to India," in *Leaves of Grass: A Textual Variorum of the Printed Poems*, ed. Sculley Bradley, Harold W. Blodgett, Arthur Golden, and William White, vol. 3 (New York: New York University Press, 1980), 565–68.

434 Though railroads were destroyed: See Richard White's superb *Railroaded: The Transcontinentals and the Making of Modern America* (New York: W. W. Norton, 2011), 43. See also James McPherson, *Ordeal by Fire: The Civil War and Reconstruction* (New York: McGraw-Hill, 2001), 621–30.

434 "trade dominates the world": Charles F. Adams, "A Chapter of Erie," *The North American Review* 109 (July 1869), 36–37.

434 "Great Barbecue": Vernon L. Parrington, *Main Currents in American Thought*, vol. 3 (New York: Harcourt Brace, 1930), 7–47.

434 "I am duly thanking": Quoted in Morton Keller, *Affairs of State: Public Life in Late Nineteenth Century America* (Cambridge, Mass.: Belknap Press of Harvard University Press, 1977), 45–46.

435 "the emigration of the Yankees": Lawrence N. Powell, *New Masters: Northern Planters during the Civil War and Reconstruction* (New Haven, Conn.: Yale University Press, 1980), 6.

435 Then there was Garth Wilkinson "Wilkie" James: Named for a disciple of the philosopher Emanuel Swedenborg, Wilkie James was trying to tap the power within, which is what his enlightened father, Henry, Sr., had taught him to cherish. But Henry, Sr., seemed to favor his older sons, William and Henry, Jr., over the two younger ones, Wilkie and Robertson. Unlike Wilkie and Bob, neither William nor Henry had fought in the war, but, as their father said, Wilkie and Bob were not "cut out for intellectual labors." See, for instance, Paul Jerome Croce, "Calming the Screaming Eagle: William James and His Circle Fight Their Civil War Battles," *New England Quarterly* 76 (March 2003), 13.

436 "We came down": Quoted in Jane Maher, *Biography of Broken Fortunes: Wilkie and Bob, Brothers of William, Henry, and Alice James* (New York: Archon Books, 1986), 84.

436 "We are at the mercy": Ibid.

436 "freed negro under decent": Quoted in Powell, *New Masters*, 29.

437 "the freedmen who labor": Thomas W. Conway, "On the Introduction of Capital and Men from the Northern States and from Europe, into the Southern States of the Union," in *Annual Report of the Chamber of Commerce of the State of New York*, vol. 8 (New York: John W. Amerman, 1866), 64.

437 "Cotton is gold": Ibid., 64; see also Powell, *New Masters*, which focuses on this issue.

437 "politically and privately": Quoted in Maher, *Biography of Broken Fortunes*, 106.

437 "The persons mainly responsible": Thomas Wentworth Higginson, "The Case of the Carpet Baggers," *The Nation*, March 2, 1899, 162.

437 "The men of the better class": Ibid., 163.

437 "What most men mean": Thomas Wentworth Higginson, "Too Many Compliments," *The Independent*, Oct. 26, 1865, 4.

438 "What a bitter dose": George Templeton Strong, *The Diary of George Templeton Strong*, vol. 4, ed. Allan Nevins and Milton Halsey Thomas (New York: Macmillan, 1952), 147.

438 "The President": Quoted in Michael Les Benedict, *The Impeachment and Trial of Andrew Johnson* (New York: W. W. Norton, 1999), 90.

438 "I fear he is among": Strong, *The Diary of George Templeton Strong*, vol. 4, 150.

439 "I can but regard": Quoted in Jean Edward Smith, *Grant* (New York: Simon & Schuster), 451.

439 "Stick": See Hans L. Trefousse, *Andrew Johnson: A Biography* (New York: W. W. Norton, 1989), 313.

440 "bundle of generalities": Quoted in Benedict, *The Impeachment and Trial of Andrew Johnson*, 80. This is the single best account of the impeachment and, more specifically, of the complex political divisions within the Republican Party both before and during impeachment.

440 "A moral principle": *CG*, 39th Congress, 1st Session, Feb. 7, 1866, 705.

440 "If the great culprit": Quoted in Michael Les Benedict, "From Our Archives: A New Look at the Impeachment of Andrew Johnson," *Political Science Quarterly* 113 (Autumn 1998), 504.

441 "construed by him": *CG*, 40th Congress, 2nd session, Feb. 24, 1868, 1386.

441 Johnson's defense: Eric L. McKitrick, *Andrew Johnson and Reconstruction* (New York: Oxford University Press, 1988), 506. See also Annette Gordon-Reed, *Andrew Johnson* (New York: Times Books, 2011), 120–39. Also: if Johnson had sent the act to the Supreme Court, he would have been sending Reconstruction there too, for if the Court had found the act unconstitutional, Johnson could continue to fire army officers who opposed his plans, such as Sheridan and perhaps even Grant.

441 "The dignity of the nation": "The Impeachment and the People," *The New York Times*, April 5, 1868, 4.

442 Representative James Garfield speculated: For a fine analysis of the fiscal issues and their relation to impeachment, see Benedict, *The Impeachment and Trial of Andrew Johnson*, in particular chaps. 4 and 5.

442 "I see little hope": Quoted in Hans L. Trefousse, *Thaddeus Stevens: Nineteenth-Century Egalitarian* (Chapel Hill: University of North Carolina Press, 1997), 244.

442 "May God save": Quoted in ibid., 333.

442 "Safe deliverance": Andrew Johnson, *The Papers of Andrew Johnson*, vol. 14, ed. Paul Bergeron (Knoxville: University of Tennessee Press, 1997), 113.

442 "Radicalism has gone to h—": "Impeachment," *Memphis Daily Avalanche*, May 19, 1869.

442 "will only be to inflict": Quoted in "The President's Acquittal," *The Sun* [Baltimore], May 19, 1868, 1.

442 Yet Johnson had become: See Homer Adolph Stebbins, *A Political History of the State of New York, 1865–1869* (New York: Columbia University Press, 1913), 331–35.

443 "What can we do with him": Quoted in Trefousse, *Andrew Johnson*, 327.

443 "Nobody feels more deeply": John Murray Forbes, *Letters and Recollections of John Murray Forbes*, vol. 2, ed. Sarah Forbes Hughes (Boston: Houghton Mifflin, 1899), 164–65.

443 "on every man's tongue": "How the Victim Was Chosen," *The Independent*, July 13, 1868, 4.

444 "People don't like": Quoted in Ellis Paxson Oberholtzer, *Jay Cooke: Financier of the Civil War*, vol. 2 (Philadelphia: George W. Jacobs & Co., 1907), 68.

444 "C. is as radical as ever": Quoted in ibid., 69.

444 "Chase is out of the question": Samuel J. Tilden, *Letters and Literary Memorials of Samuel J. Tilden*, vol. 1, ed. John Bigelow (New York: Harper & Brothers, 1908), 229.

445 "Everybody is heartily tired": "The Week," *The Nation* 1 (July 6, 1865), 1.

445 Or, as Henry Adams: Adams's depiction of Grant as "uniquely stupid" has been expertly analyzed in Brooks D. Simpson, "Henry Adams and the Age of Grant," *Hayes Historical Journal* 8 (Spring 1989), 5–23. See also *The Political Thought of Henry Adams* (Columbia: University of South Carolina Press, 1996), and *The Reconstruction Presidents* (Lawrence: University Press of Kansas, 1998). In addition, the derogation of Grant is well analyzed in Joan Waugh's fine *U. S. Grant: American Hero, American Myth* (Chapel Hill: University of North Carolina, 2009).

446 "put eight holes": Quoted in Maher, *Biography of Broken Fortunes*, 103.

446 "There is going on": Frederick Douglass, "Horatio Seymour's Letter of Acceptance," *The Independent*, Aug. 20, 1868, 1.

446 "To tell the plain truth": Quoted in Maher, *Biography of Broken Fortunes*, 104.

446 According to the Radical Republican: See Albion W. Tourgée, *Undaunted Radical: The Selected Writings and Speeches of Albion W. Tourgée*, ed. Mark Elliott and John David Smith (Baton Rouge: Louisiana State University Press, 2010), 47–51.

447 "Do not understand me": Quoted in Maher, *Biography of Broken Fortunes*, 104.

447 "No Northern man": Charles Stearns, *The Black Man of the South and the Rebels* (New York: American News Co., 1872), 457.

447 "This is about as bad": Ibid., 162.

448 "forced into it": Quoted in Josiah Bunting III, *Ulysses S. Grant: The American Presidents Series: The 18th President, 1869–1877* (New York: Times Books, 2004), 81; this is an excellent, short, and well-written biography.

448 "It is difficult to comprehend": George S. Boutwell, *The Lawyer, The Statesman, and the Soldier* (New York: D. Appleton, 1887), 170.

448 "Does anybody want": Frederick Douglass, "Horatio Seymour's Letter of Acceptance," 1.

449 "He could depend": Mark Twain, *Autobiography of Mark Twain*, vol. 1, ed. Harriet Elinor Smith (Berkeley: University of California Press, 2011), 83.

CHAPTER 20: DEEP WATER

450 "I have argued": Elizabeth Cady Stanton, *Elizabeth Cady Stanton as Revealed in Her Letters, Diary, and Reminiscences*, vol. 2, ed. Theodore Stanton and Harriet Stanton Blatch (New York: Harper & Brothers, 1922), 105.

450 "Our fossil is first amazed": Eleanor Kirk, "Two Women of the Present: Elizabeth Cady Stanton, Susan B. Anthony," *The Phrenological Journal and Packard's Monthly* 50 (July 1870), 58.

451 "Men came to Oberlin": Quoted in Nancy A. Hardesty, *Women Called to Witness: Evangelical Feminism in the Nineteenth Century* (Knoxville: University of Tennessee Press, 1999), 31.

452 "I forged the thunderbolts": Elizabeth Cady Stanton, *Eighty Years and More (1815–1897): Reminiscences of Elizabeth Cady Stanton* (New York: European Publishing, 1897), 165.

452 "No matter what is done": Quoted in Anna Howard Shaw, *The Story of a Pioneer* (New York: Harper & Brothers, 1915), 232.

452 "Failure is impossible": "Susan B. Anthony: An Appreciation and an Appeal," *The Westminster Review* 165 (May 1906), 547.

453 "The right of woman": Quoted in William S. McFeely, *Frederick Douglass* (New York: W. W. Norton, 1995), 268.

453 "If that word 'male'": See the important Ellen Carol DuBois, *Feminism and Suffrage: The Emergence of an Independent Women's Movement in America, 1848– 1869* (Ithaca, N.Y.: Cornell University Press, 1999), 61.

453 "The disfranchised all make": Stanton, *Elizabeth Cady Stanton as Revealed in Her Letters, Diary, and Reminiscences*, vol. 2, 110.

454 This was the *nation's* hour: See Elizabeth Cady Stanton and Susan B. Anthony, *The Selected Papers of Elizabeth Cady Stanton and Susan B. Anthony*, vol. 2, ed. Ann D. Gordon (New Brunswick, N.J.: Rutgers University Press, 2000), 28. See also Lori D. Ginzberg, *Elizabeth Cady Stanton: An American Life* (New York: Hill & Wang, 2009).

454 Everyone walks through the door: See Vivian Gornick, *The Solitude of Self: Thinking about Elizabeth Cady Stanton* (New York: Farrar, Straus and Giroux, 2005), for a particularly illuminating analysis of the radical and liberal feminism created at this juncture.

454 "If the two millions": Stanton, *Eighty Years and More (1815–1897)*, 110.

454 "The ballot and the bullet": Elizabeth Cady Stanton, *Elizabeth Cady Stanton as Revealed in Her Letters, Diary, and Reminiscences*, vol. 2, 116.

454 "Public sentiment": "The State Constitutional Convention," *National Anti- Slavery Standard*, July 6, 1867.

454 "most inopportune": Quoted in David Herbert Donald, *Charles Sumner and the Rights of Man* (New York: Alfred A. Knopf, 1970), 577.

454 "clogged, burdened": Quoted in ibid., 282.

455 "Degraded, oppressed himself": Quoted in Stanton and Anthony, *The Selected Papers of Elizabeth Cady Stanton and Susan B. Anthony*, vol. 2, 63.

455 "The wisest order": Ibid., 65.

455 "Shame! Shame! Shame": Quoted in ibid., 66.

456 "Success in Kansas": Quoted in DuBois, *Feminism and Suffrage*, 80.

456 "We climb hills": Quoted in Andrea Moore Kerr, *Lucy Stone: Speaking Out for Equality* (New Brunswick, N.J.: Rutgers University Press, 1995), 124.

456 "Kansas rules the world": Stanton and Anthony, *The Selected Papers of Elizabeth Cady Stanton and Susan B. Anthony*, vol. 2, 67.

456 "A persistent effort": Quoted in Faye E. Dudden, *Fighting Chance: The Struggle over Woman Suffrage and Black Suffrage in Reconstruction America* (New York: Oxford University Press, 2011), 125.

456 "I do not believe": Quoted in Stanton, *Elizabeth Cady Stanton as Revealed in Her Letters, Diary, and Reminiscences*, vol. 2, 112.

457 "As to woman's rights": Elizabeth Hawthorne to Una Hawthorne, May 11, 1866, Bancroft Library, University of California at Berkeley.

457 "I have often found": Olympia Brown Willis, *Acquaintances Old and New, among Reformers* (Milwaukee: S. E. Tate, 1911), 30.

457 "If only Anna E. Dickinson": Matthew Gallman, *America's Joan of Arc: The Life of Anna Elizabeth Dickinson* (New York: Oxford University Press, 2006), 86.

457 "We had no party": Willis, *Acquaintances Old and New among Reformers*, 73.

458 "an American in excess": Junius Henri Browne, *The Great Metropolis: A Mirror of New York* (Hartford: American Publishing Co., 1869), 630.

458 "The same God that made": Quoted in an important overview provided in Christine Stansell, *The Feminist Promise: 1792 to the Present* (New York: Modern Library, 2011), 88.

459 "He is a highly exaggerated": Browne, *The Great Metropolis*, 630.

459 "could speak of nothing": Quoted in Donald, *Charles Sumner and the Rights of Man*, 84.

459 "If the Devil steps forward": Quoted in Stanton and Anthony, *The Selected Papers of Elizabeth Cady Stanton and Susan B. Anthony*, vol. 2, 117.

459 "The Garrisons, Phillipses": Quoted in Willis, *Acquaintances Old and New*, 70.

459 "we shall see some": Quoted in Jean H. Baker, *Sisters: The Lives of America's Suffragists* (New York: Hill & Wang, 2005), 34.

459 "Suppose George Francis Train": Stanton and Anthony, *The Selected Papers of Elizabeth Cady Stanton and Susan B. Anthony*, vol. 2, 127.

460 "It was not": Quoted in ibid., 108.

460 As far as Anthony was concerned: Ibid., 114.

460 "When you propose": Quoted in ibid., 111.

460 "Think of Patrick": Ibid., 196.

461 "When women, because": Elizabeth Cady Stanton, Susan Brownell Anthony, and Matilda Joslyn Gage, eds., *The History of Woman Suffrage*, vol. 2 (Rochester, N.Y.: Charles Mann, 1871), 382.

462 "thousands of hungry Negroes": Quoted in Ginzberg, *Elizabeth Cady Stanton: An American Life*, 126.

462 Nor did its language: Regarding the bubbles in a bar of soap and other terrorist techniques, see Robert A. Caro, *The Years of Lyndon Johnson: Master of the Senate* (New York: Alfred A. Knopf, 2002), x.

463 "an aristocracy of sex": Quoted, e.g., in Stansell, *The Feminist Promise*, 105.

463 "We think our national life": Quoted in DuBois, *Feminism and Suffrage*, 118.

464 "without depreciating": Quoted in Stanton and Anthony, *The Selected Papers of Elizabeth Cady Stanton and Susan B. Anthony*, vol. 2, 256.

464 "The attempt to reform": Quoted in "The Enfranchisement of Women," *The Independent*, March 30, 1870.

465 "*The Revolution*": Quoted in Stacey Robertson, " 'Aunt Nancy Men': Parker Pillsbury, Masculinity, and Women's Rights Activism in the Nineteenth-Century United States," *American Studies* 37 (Fall 1996), 33.

466 "A woman is just as capable": "The Queens of Finance," *New York Herald*, Jan. 22, 1870. My discussion of Woodhull draws on, among other sources, Stanton, Anthony, and Gage, *The History of Woman Suffrage*, vol. 2, as well as the fine work of Helen Lefkowitz Horowitz, "Victoria Woodhull, Anthony Comstock, and the Conflict over Sex in the 1870s," *The Journal of American History* 87 (September 2000), 403–34, and that of Lois Beachy Underhill, *The Woman Who Ran for President: The Many Lives of Victoria Woodhull* (Bridgehampton, N.Y.: Bridge Works Publishing Co., 1995). In addition, I have consulted the excellent T. J. Stiles, *The First Tycoon: The Epic Life of Cornelius Vanderbilt* (New York: Alfred A. Knopf, 2010), which scrupulously debunks theories, often taken as fact, regarding the relationship between Woodhull and Vanderbilt. Also, Barbara Goldsmith's sympathetic study of Woodhull, *Other Powers: The Age of Suffrage, Spiritualism, and the Scandalous Victoria Woodhull* (New York: Alfred A. Knopf, 1998), though less reliable, is useful, and she draws on the excellent study of women's rights and spiritualism, Ann Braude, *Radical Spirits: Spiritualism and Women's Rights in Nineteenth-Century America* (Boston: Beacon Press, 1989).

466 "In this age": Quoted in Mary Gabriel, *Notorious Victoria: The Life of Victoria Woodhull, Uncensored* (Chapel Hill, N.C.: Algonquin Books, 1998), 80.

466 "heaven sent for the rescue": Quoted in Debby Applegate, *The Most Famous Man in America: The Biography of Henry Ward Beecher* (New York: Doubleday, 2007), 412.

467 "We have had enough": Quoted in Stanton and Anthony, *The Selected Papers of Elizabeth Cady Stanton and Susan B. Anthony*, vol. 2, 428.

467 "brigandish dash to it": Quoted in Gabriel, *Notorious Victoria*, 72.

468 "the fraudulent": Quoted in Madeleine Stern, *We the Women: Career Firsts of Nineteenth-Century Women* (Lincoln: University of Nebraska Press, 1994), 261.

468 "She who marries": Quoted in Amanda Frisken, *Victoria Woodhull's Sexual Revolution: Political Theater and the Popular Press in Nineteenth-Century America* (Philadelphia: University of Pennsylvania Press, 2004), 27.

468 "To love is a right": See Victoria Woodhull, "Speech on the Principles of Social Freedom," in *Victoria Woodhull Reader*, ed. Madeleine B. Stern (Weston, Mass.: M & S Press, 1974), 23.

468 "Sexual freedom means": Quoted in Goldsmith, *Other Powers*, 274.

469 "Beecherism—or the higher law": Quoted in Applegate, *The Most Famous Man in America*, 389.

469 "Be not deceived": Quoted in Stanton and Anthony, *The Selected Papers of Elizabeth Cady Stanton and Susan B. Anthony*, vol. 2, 347; see also "The Feud in the Woman's Rights Camp," *The Nation* 11 (Nov. 24, 1870), 346.

469 "I have asked for equality": Quoted in Goldsmith, *Other Powers*, 274.

469 "All laws shall be": Quoted in ibid., 275.

470 "Sooner or later": "The Woodhull Revolution," *Chicago Tribune*, Feb. 20, 1872, 4.

470 "those respectable women": "The Free-Love Ticket," *San Francisco Chronicle*, May 14, 1872, 2.

471 "cuts the very ground": Harriet Beecher Stowe, *The Writings of Harriet Beecher Stowe*, vol. 12: *My Wife and I* (Cambridge, Mass.: Riverside Press, 1895), 281.

471 "Two of your sisters": Victoria Woodhull, Letter to Henry Ward Beecher, reprinted in *Theodore Tilton v. Henry Ward Beecher, Verbatim Report* (New York: George W. Smith and Co., 1875), 829.

471 "One man": "Mrs. Woodhull and Her Critics," *The New York Times*, May 22, 1871, 5.

471 "Such a book is a tomb": Quoted in Goldsmith, *Other Powers*, 289.

473 "all the agitation": Kerr, *Lucy Stone*, 172.

473 "My one wish": Ibid., 168.

473 "Died of Free Love": Quoted in Goldsmith, *Other Powers*, 303–4.

CHAPTER 21: RUNNING FROM THE PAST

475 Anthony's subsequent arrest: The best summary of this movement, including the fact that two hundred black women, dressed as men, also went to the polls in Johnson County, North Carolina, can be found in Christine Stansell, *The Feminist Promise: 1792 to the Present* (New York: Modern Library, 2010), 101–3.

476 "one of the most stupendous": Quoted in Adam Tuchinsky, *Horace Greeley's New-York Tribune: Civil War–Era Socialism and the Crisis of Free Labor* (Ithaca, N.Y.: Cornell University Press, 2009), 213.

476 "best men": "Speech of Carl Schurz," in *Proceedings of the Liberal Republican Convention, in Cincinnati, May 1st, 2d and 3d, 1872* (New York: Baker & Godwin, 1872), 12.

476 "What is the chief end": Quoted in Justin Kaplan, *Mr. Clemens and Mark Twain: A Biography* (New York: Simon & Schuster, 1966), 96.

476 "saturated in corruption": Walt Whitman, "Democratic Vistas," in *Complete Poetry and Collected Prose*, ed. Justin Kaplan (New York: Library of America, 1982), 937.

477 "The power of 'Rings' ": James Russell Lowell, *Letters of James Russell Lowell*, vol. 2, ed. Charles Eliot Norton (New York: Harper & Brothers, 1894), 27.

477 "suggested survival from": Henry Adams, "The Great Gold Conspiracy," in Adams, *Historical Essays* (New York: Charles Scribner's Sons, 1891), 32, 324.

478 "noisy, boastful": Ibid., 324.

478 "Grant rarely met": Jean Edward Smith, *Grant* (New York: Simon & Schuster, 2001), 483; this biography of Grant is far more sympathetic to Grant than that of William McFeely, whose prizewinning *Grant: A Biography* first appeared in 1981 and is quoted below.

479 "Letter delivered all right": Most of the summary of this fiasco is from "Gold Panic Investigation," *CG*, 41st Congress, 2nd Session, House Report 31 (serial set 1436), 168–69, 444, 174, 230–33.

479 "Tell your husband": Ibid., 157. See also William S. McFeely, *Grant: A Biography* (New York: W. W. Norton, 2002), 325–26.

480 "Wall Street still panting": George Templeton Strong, *The Diary of George Templeton Strong*, vol. 4, ed. Allan Nevins and Milton Halsey Thomas (New York: Macmilllan, 1952), 255.

480 "Railroad Kings": Ibid., 256.

480 "law, custom, decency": Adams, "The New York Gold Conspiracy," *Historical Essays*, 365.

481 "a Fanatic": Quoted in David Herbert Donald, *Charles Sumner and the Rights of Man* (New York: Alfred A. Knopf, 1970), 382.

481 "most extravagant hostility": Ibid., 384.

481 "nothing but money making": Ibid., 385.

481 "man of huge": Ibid.

482 "What I desired above all": Quoted in Josiah Bunting III, *Ulysses S. Grant: The American Presidents Series: The 18th President, 1869–1877* (New York: Times Books, 2004), 104.

483 "the steamy pursuit of empire": McFeely, *Grant*, 339. For the theory about black labor, see Smith, *Grant*, 499–508.

483 "had no faith": Quoted in Charles Eliot Norton, *Letters of Charles Eliot Norton*, vol. 2, ed. Sara Norton and M. A. DeWolfe Howe (Boston: Houghton Mifflin, 1913), 43.

484 "an Administration man": Quoted in Donald, *Charles Sumner and the Rights of Man*, 436.

485 "entirely honest": Quoted in ibid., 445.

485 "yearn for the protection": Ulysses S. Grant, "Second Annual Message to Congress," Dec. 5, 1870, in *A Compilation of Messages and Papers of the Presidents*, ed. James D. Richardson, vol. 7 (1898), 99.

485 "settle the unhappy condition": Ibid., 100.

485 "seek the blessings": Ibid., 100.

485 "Porto Rico and Cuba": Ibid., 100.

485 "a free exercise": Ibid., 96.

485 He too repeated: *CG*, 41st Congress, 3rd Session, pt. 1, Dec. 21, 1870, 227–30.

486 "I lit my youthful candle": *CG*, 41st Congress, 3rd Session, pt. 1, Dec. 21, 1870, 239.

487 "that empire is": "Prophetic Voices about America: A Monograph," *The Atlantic Monthly* 20 (September 1867), 279.

487 "Canada and Nova Scotia": Ibid., 283.

487 "the day will come": Ibid., 298.

487 "the name of the Republic": Ibid., 306.

487 "quite compatible with": Quoted in Carl Schurz, *Speeches, Correspondence and Political Papers of Carl Schurz*, vol. 2, ed. Frederic Bancroft (New York: G. P. Putnam's Sons, 1913), 78.

488 "mixed Latin": Ibid., 94.

488 "assimilation downward": Ibid., 95.

488 "Here are the believers": W. C. Church, "Nebulae, Nebulae," *The Galaxy* 14 (September 1872), 434.

489 However, though Greeley publicized: "Amnesty—Personal Security," *New-York Tribune*, March 16, 1871, 4.

490 "Those loyal men": "Mr. Elliott on the Ku-Klux Outrages," *New-York Tribune*, March 21, 1871, 1.

491 "insane": Quoted in Eric Foner, *Reconstruction, 1863–1877: America's Unfinished Revolution* (New York: Harper & Row, 1988), 456.

491 "Though rejoiced at": Quoted in ibid., 458.

492 "The Northern mind": Quoted in Richard Zuczek, "The Federal Government's Attack on the Ku Klux Klan: A Reassessment," *South Carolina Historical Magazine* 97 (January 1996), 59.

493 "mass of ignorance and barbarism": "Notes from Washington," *New-York Tribune*, March 5, 1872, 2.

493 "Of all the mistakes": Quoted in Richard A. Gerber, "Liberal Republicanism, Reconstruction, and Social Order: Samuel Bowles as a Test Case," *New England Quarterly* 45 (September 1972), 404.

494 "Before the law": Quoted in Alice Fahs and Joan Waugh, eds., *The Memory of the Civil War in American Culture* (Chapel Hill: University of North Carolina Press, 2004), 171.

494 "Liberal Republicanism": Quoted in James M. McPherson, "Grant or Greeley? The Abolitionist Dilemma in the Election of 1872," *American Historical Review* 71 (October 1865), 59.

494 "What the South wants": "Civilization at the South," *New-York Tribune*, March 23, 1872, 4.

494 "The increase in": "State of the South," *Chicago Tribune*, April 10, 1872, 4.

495 "I don't pretend": Quoted in *CG*, 42nd Congress, 2nd Session, 973.

497 it was also said: See Richard N. Current, "Carpetbaggers Reconsidered," in *Reconstruction: An Anthology of Revisionist Writings*, eds. Kenneth M. Stampp and Leon F. Litwack (Baton Rouge: Louisiana State University Press, 1969), 238.

498 "he would not hesitate": Ulysses S. Grant, *The Papers of Ulysses S. Grant*, vol. 23, ed. John Simon (Carbondale: Southern Illinois University Press, 2000), 272.

498 "New Departure": The term was coined without reference, it seems, to the women's movement.

499 "I cannot become President": Quoted in Matthew T. Downey, "Horace Greeley and the Politicians: The Liberal Republican Convention in 1872," *Journal of American History* 53 (March 1967), 733.

500 "I don't know": Quoted in Schurz, *Speeches, Correspondence and Political Papers of Carl Schurz*, vol. 2, 376.

500 "a successful piece": Quoted in Glyndon G. Van Deusen, *Horace Greeley: Nineteenth-Century Crusader* (Philadelphia: University of Pennsylvania Press, 1953), 406.

500 "a few wry faces": Strong, *The Diary of George Templeton Strong*, vol. 4, 431.

500 "Mere coldness and hardness": Ibid., 420.

501 "Sir, I sound the cry": Sumner, *The Works of Charles Sumner*, vol. 14 (Boston: Lee & Shepard, 1883), 471.

501 "What could lead you": Quoted in James M. McPherson, "Grant or Greeley?," 57.

501 "first in nepotism": Charles Sumner, *The Works of Charles Sumner*, vol. 15 (Boston: Lee & Shepard, 1883), 168.

501 "I regret his late speech": John B. Pickard, ed., *The Letters of John Greenleaf Whittier*, vol. 3 (Cambridge, Mass.: Harvard University Press, 1975), 271.

501 "The colored man": Ibid., 276.

501 "Nearly all that legislation": Ibid., 276.

502 "The Republican party": Quoted in Smith, *Grant*, 550.

502 "You tell us that": Quoted in Foner, *Reconstruction*, 506.

502 "We hold our rights": Quoted in Philip Dray, *Capitol Men: The Epic Story of Reconstruction through the Lives of the First Black Congressmen* (Boston: Houghton Mifflin, 2008), 125.

503 Southerners did not resent: See George F. Hoar, *Autobiography of Seventy Years*, vol. 1 (Charles Scribner's Sons, 1905), 284.

503 "They receive money": Charles Francis Adams, Jr., "Railroad Inflation," *North American Review* 108 (January 1869), 148.

504 "I did not ask": Franklin Pierce, inaugural address, in *A Compilation of the Messages and Papers of the Presidents*, vol. 7, ed. James D. Richardson (Washington, D.C.: U.S. Government Printing Office, 1898), 223.

504 "I have done more": Quoted in Van Deusen, *Horace Greeley*, 423.

CHAPTER 22: WESTWARD THE COURSE OF EMPIRE

506 "The Western spirit": Herman Melville, *Israel Potter: His Fifty Years of Exile*, ed. Harrison Hayford, Hershel Parker, and G. Thomas Tanselle (Evanston, Ill.: Northwestern University Press, 1982), 149.

506 "hewn out of rock": Francis Parkman, *The Oregon Trail and the Conspiracy of Pontiac*, ed. William Taylor (New York: Library of America, 1991), 389.

506 "will sweep from the face": Ibid., 90.

506 "learn the arts": Ibid., 389.

507 "solid personality": Walt Whitman, "Democratic Vistas," in *Complete Poetry and Collected Prose*, ed. Justin Kaplan (New York: Library of America, 1982), 952.

507 "This is what the scamps": Quoted in *The Writings of Henry David Thoreau*, vol. 16, *Journal* 10, ed. Bradford Torrey (Boston: Houghton Mifflin, 1906), 89. See also the very fine Kevin Starr, *Americans and the California Dream, 1850–1915* (New York: Oxford University Press, 1973), 174.

508 He also hired: An important comparison between the work of Carleton Watkins and Timothy O'Sullivan, and the implication for the commercial development of postwar America, can be found in Joel Snyder, "Territorial Expansion," in *Landscape and Power*, ed. W. J. T. Mitchell (Chicago: University of Chicago Press, 2002), 175–201.

508 "These trees": Quoted in James Bradley Thayer, *A Western Journey with Mr. Emerson* (Boston: Little, Brown, 1884), 67.

508 "terrible mementoes": Oliver Wendell Holmes, "Doings of the Sunbeam," *The Atlantic Monthly* 12 (July 1863), 11.

509 "a gigantic institution": J. D. Whitney, *The Yosemite Guide-Book: A Description of the Yosemite Valley and the Adjacent Region of the Sierra Nevada, and of the Big Trees of California* (Cambridge, Mass.: Welch, Bigelow, and Co., 1869), 21.

509 "inalienable for all time!": Ibid., 22.

509 "give satisfaction": Ibid., chap. 1. In addition, see the superb essay by Douglas R. Nickel, "The Art of Perception," in *Carleton Watkins: The Art of Perception*, ed. Douglas R. Nickel (San Francisco: San Francisco Museum of Modern Art, 1999), for a fine discussion of the relation between Watkins and the railroad.

511 "The earth is the Lord's": Samuel Bowles, *The Switzerland of America: A Summer Vacation in the Parks and Mountains of Colorado* (Boston: Lee & Shepard, 1869), 124.

511 "He received us": Phineas T. Barnum, *Struggles and Triumphs: Or, Forty Years' Recollections of P. T. Barnum* (New York: American News Co., 1871), 856.

512 "It must have been": Quoted in Thurman Wilkins, *Clarence King: A Biography* (Albuquerque: University of New Mexico Press, 1988), 43.

513 "best and brightest": Quoted in Henry Adams, *The Education of Henry Adams*, in Henry Adams, *Novels*, ed. Ernest Samuels and Jayne N. Samuels (New York: Library of America, 1983), 1100.

513 King told a friend: See Wilkins, *Clarence King*, 34–36. Much of the biographical material on King in this chapter is drawn from this fine volume.

513 "facts are stupid things": Quoted in David McCullough, *Brave Companions: Portraits in History* (New York: Simon & Schuster, 1992), 26.

514 "the brain of the Negro": Quoted in Louis Menand, *The Metaphysical Club: A Story of Ideas in America* (New York: Farrar, Straus and Giroux, 2001), 109. Menand's is a superb overview of Agassiz and, more generally, postbellum skepticism.

514 "They will Mexicanize": Quoted in ibid., 101–2. For a full, excellent account of Agassiz's racial theories and their impact (as well as Darwin's comment on them), see Christoph Irmscher, *Louis Agassiz: Creator of American Science* (New York: Houghton Mifflin, 2013).

514 "effeminate progeny": Quoted in Menand, *The Metaphysical Club*, 114–15.

515 "I would rather be": Quoted in Carl Sagan, *Shadows of Forgotten Ancestors* (New York: Ballantine Books, 1993), 72.

515 "Better far": Clarence King, "Atrium Magister," *North American Review* 147 (October 1885), 377–78.

515 "that settled it": Rossiter W. Raymond, "Biographical Notice," *Clarence King Memoirs: The Helmet of Malbrino*, ed. James D. Hague (New York: G. P. Putnam's Sons, 1904), 315.

517 "Now, Mr. King": James D. Hague, "Memorabilia," in *Clarence King Memoirs*, 385.

517 "What would Ruskin": Raymond, "Biographical Notice," in *Clarence King Memoirs,* 319; John Hay, "Clarence King," in *Clarence King Memoirs*, 130.

517 "Am I really fallen": Clarence King, *Mountaineering in the Sierra Nevada* (New York: Charles Scribner's Sons, 1903), 220.

518 "as it really is": Ibid., 365.

518 "However complex": Clarence King, "Bancroft's Native Races of the Pacific States," *The Atlantic Monthly* 35 (February 1875), 163–64.

518 "Didn't I tell you": Clarence King, "Mountaineering in the Sierra Nevada, II," *The Atlantic Monthly* 27 (June 1871), 707–9.

519 "I take a little ride": Quoted in William Goetzmann, *Exploration and Empire: The Explorer and the Scientist in the Winning of the American West* (New York: Alfred A. Knopf, 1966), 438. Goetzmann's book is crucial.

520 "It would have been": Quoted in Robert Wilson's fine *The Explorer King: Adventure, Science, and the Great Diamond Hoax—Clarence King in the Old West* (New York: Scribner, 2006), 249.

520 "I have lain and listened": King, *Mountaineering in the Sierra Nevada*, 99.

521 "Tis wonderful how": Ralph Waldo Emerson, *The Collected Works of Ralph Waldo Emerson*, vol. 7, ed. Ronald A. Bosco and Douglass Emory Wilson (Cambridge, Mass.: Belknap Press of Harvard University Press, 2007), 10.

521 "Romance like this": Bret Harte, "Current Literature," *The Overland Monthly* 5 (October 1870), 386.

522 For King, O'Sullivan produced: O'Sullivan worked for King during the 1867–69 seasons. In 1871, he joined Lieutenant George Montague Wheeler in his survey of the American Southwest. This was a military expedition that included not only the preparation of maps and the documenting of topographical features but also the assessment of native Indian peoples. Though O'Sullivan returned to work with King in 1872, by 1873 he was again working with Wheeler, creating pared-down, almost abstract pictures, contrasting light and shadow and geometric forms.

522 "One would think": Quoted in Wilkins, *Clarence King*, 104.

522 King had commissioned: For a good discussion of these photographs as geological specimens, see Keith H. Davis, "Timothy H. O'Sullivan, Photographer," in *Timothy H. O'Sullivan: The King Survey Photographs*, ed. Keith F. Davis et al. (New Haven, Conn.: Yale University Press, 2012).

523 "It is only lesser men": Clarence King, "Catastrophism and Evolution," *The American Naturalist* 11 (August 1877), 463. Subsequent quotations in this section are from this essay unless otherwise noted. See also Robert Wilson's *The Explorer King* for an excellent account of King's expeditions and their meaning, as well as Goetzmann, *Exploration and Empire*, chap. 12.

526 "Size, brute mass": Clarence King, "Style and the Monument," *North American Review* 141 (November 1885), 450.

526 "optimism": Alexander Agassiz, *Letters and Recollections of Alexander Agassiz*, ed. George Russell Agassiz (Boston: Houghton Mifflin, 1913), 192.

526 Ada Copeland: See Martha A. Sandweiss, *Passing Strange: A Gilded Age Tale of Love and Deception across the Color Line* (New York: Penguin, 2010), for a detailed analysis of the relationship between King and Ada Copeland.

527 "I have been trying": Tyler Dennett, *John Hay: From Poetry to Politics* (New York: Dodd, Mead and Co., 1934), 161

CHAPTER 23: WITH THE TEN COMMANDMENTS IN ONE HAND

529 a "subject": William T. Sherman and John Sherman, *The Sherman Letters: Correspondence between William Tecumseh and John Sherman from 1837 to 1891*, ed. Rachel Sherman Thorndike (New York: Charles Scribner's Sons, 1894), 29.

530 "Possession is half the law": Herman Melville, *Moby-Dick* (New York: Library of America College Editions, 2000), 448.

530 "painful to behold": Quoted in Robert G. Athearn, *William Tecumseh Sherman and the Settlement of the West* (Norman: University of Oklahoma Press, 1956), 82.

530 "If the whole Army": *CG*, 40th Congress, 1st Session, July 17, 1867, 681.

530 The way west: See F. A. Walker, "The Indian Question," *North American Review* 116 (April 1873), 339.

531 "On the 27th day": *OR*, ser. I, vol. 41, pt. 1, January 15, 1865, 959–62.

532 "Bucks, women, and children": Quoted in Steve Grinstead and Ben Fogelberg, eds., *Western Voices: 125 Years of Western Writing* (Golden, Colo.: Fulcrum Publishing, 2004), 329.

532 "Any man who would": Quoted in ibid., 325.

532 "the worst passions": "Massacre of the Cheyenne Indians," in *Report of the Joint Committee on the Conduct of the War, at the Second Session of the Thirty-eighth Congress* (Washington, D.C.: U.S. Government Printing Office, 1865), v. For a good account of the Sand Creek massacre, see also Robert M. Utley, *The Indian Frontier of the American West, 1846–1890* (Albuquerque: University of New Mexico Press, 1984), chap. 3.

533 "pure beggars and poor devils": Quoted in Athearn, *William Tecumseh Sherman and the Settlement of the West*, 26. See also the most complete treatment of government policy and Native Americans: Francis Paul Prucha, *The Great Father: The United States Government and the American Indians* (Lincoln: University of Nebraska Press, 1984).

533 "Our soldiers are not": Quoted in Athearn, *William Tecumseh Sherman and the Settlement of the West*, 83.

533 "We have come to": *CG*, 40th Congress, 1st Session, July 16, 1867, 672.

533 "Whether right or wrong": Quoted in Sherman and Sherman, *The Sherman Letters*, 296.

533 The railroad, he calculated: See Athearn, *William Tecumseh Sherman and the Settlement of the West*, 252.

534 "Now and then": Quoted in R. W. Mardock, *The Reformers and the American Indian* (Columbia: University of Missouri Press, 1971), 86.

535 "If the lands": Quoted in Prucha, *The Great Father*, 491.

536 "a sort of predatory war": Sherman and Sherman, *The Sherman Letters*, 321.

536 "The red man": Walker, "The Indian Question," 338.

537 "The Indian is unfortunately": Ibid., 365.

537 "The great poison": Quoted in Mardock, *The Reformers and the American Indian*, 39.

537 "Most Indians have a personal": Quoted in Richard G. Hardorff, *The Death of Crazy Horse: A Tragic Episode in Lakota History* (Lincoln: University of Nebraska Press, 2001), 98.

537 "Wendell Phillips' new nigger": "Wendell Phillips," *New York Herald*, June 11, 1869, 6.

537 "To talk of the rights": Quoted in Mardock, *The Reformers and the American Indian*, 47.

538 "All the great points": Quoted in ibid., 39.

538 "Heaven forbid": "Wendell Phillips on the Pacific Railroad," *The New York Times*, June 10, 1868, 1.

539 "I propose to give them": Athearn, *William Tecumseh Sherman and the Settlement of the West*, 224.

539 "I hope to do": Philip H. Sheridan to Samuel J. Crawford, Sept. 26, 1868, Kansas State Historical Society.

539 "The only good Indians": Quoted in Ralph K. Andrist, *The Long Death: The Last Days of the Plains Indians* (Norman: University of Oklahoma Press, 2001), 316.

542 "The proper treatment": Ulysses S. Grant, "Inaugural Address," March 4, 1869, in *A Compilation of the Messages and Papers of the Presidents*, vol. 7, ed. James D. Richardson (Washington, D.C.: U.S. Government Printing Office, 1898), 8.

542 "a once powerful tribe": Ulysses S. Grant, *Personal Memoirs of U. S. Grant, Selected Letters 1839–1865*, ed. Mary Drake McFeely and William S. McFeely (New York: Library of America, 1990), 949.

542 "It really is my opinion": Quoted in Jean Edward Smith, *Grant* (New York: Simon & Schuster, 2001), 520.

545 "You are fools": Quoted in Charles Larpenteur, *Forty Years a Fur Trader on the Upper Missouri: The Personal Narrative of Charles Larpenteur, 1833–1872* (Lincoln: University of Nebraska Press, 1989), 360.

545 The story subsequently reported: See *CG*, 41st Congress, 2nd Session, pt. 2, Feb. 25, 1870, 1576–81.

546 "the whip was more efficient": Quoted in Richard Slotkin, *The Fatal Environment: The Myth of the Frontier in the Age of Industrialization, 1800–1890* (New York: Athenaeum, 1985), 402.

546 "accomplish little or no good": "The Poor Indian," *New York Times*, May 19, 1870, 8.

547 "the Great Spirit did not": "The Indians: Final Interview between Red Cloud and the Secretary of the Interior," *The New York Times*, June 11, 1870, 1.

547 "The Great Father may be": "The Indians," *The New York Times*, June 8, 1870, 1.

547 "I came from where": Ibid.

548 "I don't want any": "The Indians: Reception at Cooper Institute," *New-York Tribune*, June 17, 1870, 1.

548 "Indian lovers": Quoted in Mardock, *The Reformers and the American Indian*, 69.

549 "red savage" . . . "animal": Ibid., 86.

549 "I am on the Reservation": Quoted in Athearn, *William Tecumseh Sherman and the Settlement of the West*, 248–49.

549 "Extinction": *CG*, 41st Congress, 3rd Session, pt. 1, Jan. 25, 1871, 733.

549 "He who resists": *CG*, 41st Congress, 3rd Session, pt. 1, Jan. 21, 1871, 656.

549 "savage fiends": *CG*, 41st Congress, 3rd Session, pt. 1, Jan. 25, 1871, 738.

549 "Indian worshipper": Mark Twain, *Innocents Abroad; Roughing It*, ed. Guy Cardwell (New York: Library of America, 1984), 634.

549 "spare, bronze face": Clarence King, *Mountaineering in the Sierra Nevada* (New York: Charles Scribner's Sons, 1902), 364.

549 "liberating power": Ibid., 365.

551 "the rosewater Quaker": George Templeton Strong, *The Diary of George Templeton Strong*, vol. 4, ed. Allan Nevins and Milton Halsey Thomas (New York: Macmillan, 1952), 476–77.

551 "Let sniveling quakers": Quoted in Robert M. Utley, *The Indian Frontier of the American West, 1846–1890* (Albuquerque: University of New Mexico Press, 1984), 165.

551 "Treachery is inherent": Quoted in Athearn, *William Tecumseh Sherman and the Settlement of the West*, 301.

551 "It is evident": Quoted in David Goldfield, *America Aflame: How the Civil War Created a Nation* (New York: Bloomsbury Press, 2011), 454.

552 in the West, swarming grasshoppers: See Heather Cox Richardson, *West from Appomattox: The Reconstruction of America after the Civil War* (New Haven, Conn.: Yale University Press, 2007), 159.

552 "labor, the creator of wealth": Quoted in *The Prophet of Liberty: The Life and Times of Wendell Phillips* (New York: Bookman Associates, 1958), 597.

552 "From the grass roots down": William Eleroy Curtis, *Inter-Ocean*, Aug. 27, 1874, quoted in Donald Jackson, *Custer's Gold* (Lincoln: University of Nebraska Press, 1972), 90.

553 the back-and-forth demonstrates: For an excellent analysis of Grant's peace policy, see David Sim, "The Peace Policy of Ulysses S. Grant": *American Nineteenth Century History* 9 (September 2008), 241–68.

553 "I want you to go": Quoted in Thomas Powers, *The Killing of Crazy Horse* (New York: Alfred A. Knopf, 2010), 93.

554 "destroyed like ashes": Quoted in ibid., 103.

555 "the Indians were always scientific": Charles King, "Custer's Last Battle," *Harper's New Monthly Magazine* 81 (August 1890), 379.

556 "Rich men and poor men": "Immense Crowds Everywhere," *The New York Times*, May 11, 1976, 2.

556 Crazy Horse was not hit: Nick Rouleau, interview with Eli Ricker, November 20, 1906, conveying information from Austin Red Hawk, in *Lakota Recollections of the Custer Fight: New Sources of Indian Military History*, ed. Richard Hardorff (Lincoln: University of Nebraska Press, 1991), 37ff., and "The Thunder Bear Narrative," in *Indian Views of the Custer Fight: A Source Book*, ed. Richard Hardorff (Tulsa: University of Oklahoma Press, 2005), 87–92.

556 nothing remained: See John Gregory Burke, *The Diaries of John Gregory Burke*, vol. 1, ed. Charles M. Robinson (Denton: University of North Texas Press, 2003), 361.

556 "Our young men rained": Robert M. Utley, *Cavalier in Buckskins: George Armstrong Custer and the Western Military Frontier* (Norman: University of Oklahoma Press, 2001), 149.

557 "As this is the centennial": William H. Rowan to Thomas L. Jones, quoted in "The War with the Indians," *The New York Times*, July 16, 1876, 1.

CHAPTER 24: CONCILIATION; OR, THE LIVING

559 He wore civilian clothes: For most of the description of Forrest, see John A. Wyeth, *Life of General Nathan Bedford Forrest* (New York: Harper & Brothers, 1899), 628–29.

560 "a typical pioneer": Lafcadio Hearn, *Occidental Gleanings*, vol. 1 (New York: Dodd, Mead and Co., 1925), 146.

560 "If they send": Quoted in Charles Royster, "Slaver, General, Klansman," *The Atlantic Monthly* 271 (May 1993), 126.

561 "Nothing interferes more": "In Light of Conciliation," *The New York Times*, Oct. 31, 1877, 4.

562 "a deep-seated disease": Quoted in Samuel Flagg Bemis, *John Quincy Adams and the Union*, vol. 2 (New York: Alfred A. Knopf, 1956), 326.

563 "for no d—d niggers": "Slaughter of American Citizens at Hamburgh, S.C.," 44th Congress, 1st Session, Senate Executive Document 85, serial set 1664, Aug. 1, 1876, 36.

563 "insolent": See, e.g., "Negros Defy the Civil Power and Are Whipped into Obedience," *Daily Columbus Enquirer*, July 11, 1876, 1.

564 "We are going": "Slaughter of American Citizens at Hamburgh, S.C.," 47.

564 Henry Purvis: Quoted in Ulysses S. Grant, *The Papers of Ulysses S. Grant*, vol. 27,

ed. John Y. Simon, (Carbondale: Southern Illinois University Press, 1991), 233.

564 "as ever you seen it shine": "Slaughter of American Citizens at Hamburgh, S.C.," 44.

564 "There had to be": Ibid., 45.

564 "The white men": Ibid., 47.

565 helped organize a rally: See "The Meaning of Hamburg," *The New York Times*, July 24, 1876, 6.

565 "Who is Mr. Chamberlain": Quoted in Ted Tunnell, "Creating 'The Propaganda of History': Southern Editors and the Origins of Carpetbagger and Scalawag," *The Journal of Southern History* 72 (November 2006), 814.

566 "The civilization of the Puritan": Quoted in Hyman Rubin III, *South Carolina Scalawags* (Columbia: South Carolina University Press, 2006), 102.

567 "the possible return": "The Ku-Klux," *Harper's Weekly* 20 (Aug. 5, 1876), 630.

567 "Sambo takes naturally": James S. Pike, *Prostrate State: South Carolina under Negro Government* (New York: D. Appleton and Co., 1874), 29.

567 "Seven years ago": Ibid., 21.

567 "one who is really": Quoted in Walter Allen, *Governor Chamberlain's Administration in South Carolina: A Chapter of Reconstruction in the Southern States* (New York: G. P. Putnam's Sons, 1888), 112.

567 "like a wall": Quoted in Robert K. Ackerman, *Wade Hampton III* (Columbia: University of South Carolina Press, 2007), 142.

568 "Let the last": Quoted in Richard Zuczek, *State of Rebellion: Reconstruction in South Carolina* (Columbia: University of South Carolina Press, 1996), 160.

568 "the slaughter": Quoted in Grant, *The Papers of Ulysses S. Grant*, vol. 27, 234.

568 "widespread terror": Daniel H. Chamberlain to U. S. Grant, July 22, 1876, quoted in "Slaughter of American Citizens at Hamburgh, S.C.," 44th Congress, 1st Session, Senate Executive Document 85, Aug. 1, 1876 (serial set 1664), 4.

568 "a barbarous massacre": Ulysses Grant, *The Papers of Ulysses S. Grant*, vol. 27, 199–200.

569 "To say that the murder": Quoted in "President's Message on Louisiana Affairs," *Rochester* [Ind.] *Union Spy*, Jan. 22, 1875, 2.

569 "the terrorism now existing": Quoted in Grant, *The Papers of Ulysses S. Grant*, vol. 26, 19.

570 "Lawless and defiant": Quoted in William Lloyd Garrison, *The Letters of William Lloyd Garrison*, vol. 6, ed. Walter M. Merrill and Louis Ruchames (Cambridge, Mass.: Belknap Press of Harvard University Press, 1981), 361.

570 "Wendell Phillips and William Lloyd Garrison": Quoted in James M. McPherson, *The Abolitionist Legacy: From Reconstruction to the NAACP* (Princeton, N.J.: Princeton University Press, 1975), 49.

570 "If this can be done": Carl Schurz, *Speeches, Correspondence and Political Papers of Carl Schurz*, vol. 3, ed. Frederic Bancroft (New York: G. P. Putnam's Sons, 1913), 125.

571 "are not a people": Ibid., 142.

571 "Only the most morbid": Ibid., 142.

571 "To the extent": Quoted in James D. Richardson, ed., *A Compilation of Messages and Papers of the Presidents*, vol. 7 (Washington, D.C.: U.S. Government Printing Office, 1898), 313.

572 "support or oppose men": "Mississippi Democrats: Some Plain Words about Them," *The New York Times*, May 2, 1876, 1.

572 "Mississippi plan": James Redpath, "The Lesson of Mississippi," *The Independent*, Aug. 3, 1876, 4. But Redpath, the former Radical, was also turning his back on Reconstruction, which he dubbed a failure, declaring, "Fellow Republicans, it is idle to denounce the South. We are to blame. We are to blame. We knew the Negro to be timid, unarmed, illiterate; and yet we left him in the midst of the fiercest fights on this planet, and expected him to rule them. In Mississippi his power went down in violence and blood." To him, the problem did not admit of an easy solution: "If we give complete military protection to the Negro," he said, "we shall establish a system of government which no white race on the face of this earth either ought to endure or will endure." Yet, he added, "if we fail to protect the Negro in the right of suffrage we thereby surrender the states of South Carolina, Mississippi, and Louisiana to the same brutal banditti who drove those communities into civil war." The solution: he had none, though he did conclude by saying that "the rebel has rights too."

572 "collision": Quoted in George W. Curtis, "The Ku-Klux," *Harper's Weekly* (Aug. 5, 1876), 631.

572 "Negroes defy the civil": "The Races," *Columbus* [Georgia] *Daily Enquirer*, July 11, 1876, 1.

572 "expect my race": *Congressional Record*, 44th Congress, 1st Session, 4645.

573 "Then the contest was": Thomas Wentworth Higginson, "Border Ruffianism in South Carolina," *The Independent*, Aug. 10, 1876, 1.

573 "We black men in": Quoted in Grant, *The Papers of Ulysses S. Grant*, vol. 27, 204–5.

573 Cox sneeringly asked: See Okon E. Uya, *From Slavery to Public Service: Robert Smalls, 1839–1915* (New York: Oxford University Press, 1975), 106.

574 "The Yankees had saved": Quoted in Walter Allen, *Governor Chamberlain's Administration in South Carolina: A Chapter of Reconstruction in the Southern States* (New York: G. P. Putnam's Sons, 1888), 414.

575 "if ever a statesman": Quoted in Walter Brian Cisco, *Wade Hampton: Confederate Warrior, Conservative Statesman* (Washington, D.C.: Potomac Books, 2004), 280.

575 "as the Negro becomes": Quoted in Robert K. Ackerman, *Wade Hampton III* (Columbia: University of South Carolina Press, 2007), 175.

575 "prop up the waning": Francis Butler Simkins and Robert H. Woody, *South Carolina during Reconstruction* (Chapel Hill: University of North Carolina Press, 1932), 488, provides an excellent overview.

576 "When my race": And the quotations from Hampton's speech in Martin R. Delany, *Martin R. Delany: A Documentary Reader*, ed. Robert S. Levine (Chapel Hill: University of North Carolina Press, 2003), 453–54.

576 "Such delirium": "The Political Condition of South Carolina," *The Atlantic Monthly* 39 (February 1877), 183.

577 "We kept away fifty": Ibid., 187.

579 "shot to pieces": Louisiana in 1876: *Report of the Sub-Committee of the Committee on Privileges and Elections of the United States Senate* (Washington, D.C.: U.S. Government Printing Office, 1877), 18. See also *Florida Election, 1876: Report of the Senate Committee on Privileges and Elections, with the Testimony and Documentary Evidence, on the Election in the State of Florida, 1876* (Washington, D.C.: U.S. Government Printing Office, 1877).

579 "And this is equal rights": Quoted in William Gillette's fine, *Retreat from*

Reconstruction, 1869–1879 (Baton Rouge: Louisiana State University Press, 1979), 320. As for stealing the election, as the historian Ronald F. King points out, based on his study of the Louisiana elections, "It is probable that the Republican Party rightfully was allowed to assert victory in all three of the contested 1876 elections in the south. If so, the electoral commission's selection of Hayes over Tilden was justifiable; the federal concession of several state governments to the Redeemers was not." See Ronald F. King, "A Most Corrupt Election: Louisiana in 1876," *Studies in American Political Development* 15 (Fall 2001), 136.

579 "Who is Wheeler?": Quoted in Hans L. Trefousse, *Rutherford B. Hayes* (New York: Times Books, 2002), 68.

580 "no vote of his": William Dean Howells, *Sketch of the Life and Character of Rutherford B. Hayes* (New York: Hurd and Houghton, 1876), 103–4.

580 "blessings of honest": Ibid., 126.

580 "The result: what is it": Quoted in Trefousse, *Rutherford B. Hayes*, 76.

582 Rumors of a deal notwithstanding: See Michael Les Benedict, "Southern Democrats in the Crisis of 1876–1877," *The Journal of Southern History* 46 (November 1980), 489–524, and George C. Rable, "Southern Interests and the Election of 1876: A Reappraisal," *Civil War History* 26 (December 1980), 347–61.

582 "the constitutional safeguards": Quoted in Simkins and Woody, *South Carolina during Reconstruction*, 537.

583 "To permit Hampton": Allen, *Governor Chamberlain's Administration in South Carolina*, 470.

583 "It is not the duty": Rutherford B. Hayes, *The Diary and Letters of Rutherford B. Hayes*, vol. 3, ed. Charles R. Williams (Columbus: Ohio State Archaeological and Historical Society, 1924), 429.

583 "I am confident": Ibid., 430.

584 "violent exclusion": D. H. Chamberlain, "Reconstruction and the Negro," *North American Review* 128 (February 1879), 173.

585 "It was my fortune": Grant, *The Papers of Ulysses S. Grant*, vol. 28, 62–63.

586 "the gift Northern blundering": Wendell Phillips, "The Outlook," *North American Review* 127 (July–August 1878), 98.

586 "Half of what Grant": "Blast from Wendell: The Great Orator Dissects Mr. Hayes and His Advisers," *The Boston Globe*, March 27, 1877, 1.

586 "meaning thereby": William Lloyd Garrison, *The Letters of William Lloyd Garrison*, vol. 6, ed. Walter M. Merrill and Louis Ruchames (Cambridge, Mass.: Belknap Press of Harvard University Press, 1981), 459.

587 "I see no better course": John Greenleaf Whittier, *The Letters of John Greenleaf Whittier*, vol. 3, ed. John B. Pickard (Cambridge, Mass.: Harvard University Press, 1975), 374.

587 "The negro will disappear": "The Political South Hereafter," *The Nation* 24 (April 5, 1877), 202.

587 "well meaning": Quoted in the moving Nicholas Lemann, *Redemption: The Last Battle of the Civil War* (New York: Farrar, Straus and Giroux, 2006), 182.

588 "Drops of rose-water": Wendell Phillips, "The Outlook," *North American Review* 127 (July-August 1878), 100.

588 "Lamar of Mississippi": W. E. B. DuBois, *Black Reconstruction in America, 1860–1880* (New York: Free Press, 1990), 624.

590 "The country is again": Hayes, *The Diary and Letters of Rutherford B. Hayes*, vol. 3, 443.

590 For to him and other Liberal Republicans: For a cogent analysis of Hayes's
    policy, see Brooks D. Simpson, *The Reconstruction Presidents* (Lawrence: Univer-
    sity Press of Kansas, 1998), chap. 7.

590 "Whatever may have been": "Ought the Negro to Be Disenfranchised? Ought
    He to Have Been Enfranchised?," *North American Review* 128 (March 1879), 240.

590 "By a system": Ibid., 233.

590 "whenever political issues arise": Ibid., 235.

591 "The negro wielded his vote": Ibid., 257.

591 "scattered the fogs": Ibid., 258.

591 "We have believed": Ibid., 258.

592 "I stand here": Quoted in George Brown Tindall, *South Carolina Negroes,
    1877–1900* (Columbia: University of South Carolina Press, 1952), 86.

592 "viewed from the genuine": Frederick Douglass, *Frederick Douglass: Selected
    Speeches and Writings*, ed. Philip Foner (Chicago: Lawrence Hill Books, 1999),
    621.

592 "Though justice moves slowly": Quoted in Donald Yacavone, ed., *Freedom's
    Journey: African American Voices of the Civil War* (Chicago: Lawrence Hill Books,
    2004), 201.

593 "You think us dead": Wendell Phillips, "Appendix," in Lydia Maria Child,
    The Letters of Lydia Maria Child, ed. Harriet Winslow Sewall (Boston: Hough-
    ton Mifflin, 1882), 268. The actual gravestone's inscription reads "You call us
    dead. / We are not dead, / but truly living now."

SELECTED BIBLIOGRAPHY

A note to the bibliophile: Annotations and commentary about many of the fine books, articles, and memoirs listed here may be found in the notes. And while this bibliography is long, it is by no means complete; the literature about the period from 1848 to 1877 is vast—and growing vaster by the minute.

Aaron, Daniel. *The Unwritten War: American Writers and the Civil War*. Madison: University of Wisconsin Press, 1987.

Abbott, Henry Livermore. *Fallen Leaves: The Civil War Letters of Major Henry Livermore Abbott*. Ed. Robert Garth Scott. Kent, Ohio: Kent State University Press, 1991.

Abbott, Martin L. "The Freedmen's Bureau in South Carolina," PhD diss., Emory University, 1954. Microsoft Word file.

Ackerman, Robert K. *Wade Hampton III*. Columbia: University of South Carolina Press, 2007.

Adams, Bluford. *E Pluribus Barnum: The Great Showman and the Making of U.S. Popular Culture*. Minneapolis: University of Minnesota Press, 1997.

Adams, Charles Francis, Jr. *A Cycle of Adams Letters, 1861–1865*. Ed. Worthington Chauncey Ford. 2 vols. Boston: Houghton Mifflin, 1920.

———. "A Chapter of Erie." *North American Review* 109 (July 1869): 30–106.

———. "Railroad Inflation." *North American Review* 108 (January 1869): 130–64.

Adams, Henry. *Democracy, Esther, Mont Saint Michel and Chartres, The Education of Henry Adams*. New York: Library of America, 1983.

———. *Historical Essays*. New York: Charles Scribner's Sons, 1891.

———. *The Great Secession Winter of 1860–61 and Other Essays*. Ed. George Hochfield. New York: Sagamore Press, 1958.

———. *The Letters of Henry Adams*. Ed. J. C. Levenson, Ernest Samuels, Charles Vandersee, and Viola H. Winner. 3 vols. Cambridge, Mass.: Harvard University Press, 1982.

Adams, Marian Hooper. *The Letters of Mrs. Henry Adams*. Ed. Ward Thoron. Boston: Little, Brown, 1936.

Agassiz, Alexander. *Letters and Recollections of Alexander Agassiz*. Ed. George Russell Agassiz. Boston: Houghton Mifflin, 1913.

Akin, Warren. *The Letters of Warren Akin: Confederate Congressman*. Ed. Bell Irvin Wiley. Athens: University of Georgia Press, 1959.

Alcott, Bronson. *The Journals of Bronson Alcott*. Ed. Odell Shephard. Boston: Little, Brown, 1938.

———. *The Letters of Bronson Alcott*. Ed. Richard L. Hernstadt. Iowa City: University of Iowa Press, 1969.

Alcott, Louisa May. *Hospital Sketches*. Boston: James Redpath, 1863.

Alden, W. L. "Some Phases of Literary New York in the Sixties." *Putnam's Monthly* 3 (February 1908): 554–58.

Alexander, Edward Porter. *Fighting for the Confederacy: The Personal Recollections of General Edward Porter Alexander*. Ed. Gary W. Gallagher. Chapel Hill: University of North Carolina Press, 1989.

Allen, Walter. *Governor Chamberlain's Administration in South Carolina: A Chapter of Reconstruction in the Southern States*. New York: G. P. Putnam's Sons, 1888.

Andrews, J. Cutler. *The North Reports the Civil War*. Pittsburgh: University of Pittsburgh Press, 1955.

Andrews, Sidney. "Three Months among the Reconstructionists." *The Atlantic Monthly* 17 (February 1866): 2237–46.

Angle, Paul M., ed. *The Complete Lincoln-Douglas Debates of 1858*. Chicago: University of Chicago Press, 1958.

Annual Report of the Chamber of Commerce of the State of New York. Vol. 8, *For the Year 1865–1866*. New York: John W. Amerman, 1866.

Applegate, Debby. *The Most Famous Man in America: The Biography of Henry Ward Beecher*. New York: Doubleday, 2007.

Athearn, Robert G. *William Tecumseh Sherman and the Settlement of the West*. Norman: University of Oklahoma Press, 1956.

Auchampaugh, Philip G. *Robert Tyler, Southern Rights Champion, 1847–1866: A Documentary Study Chiefly of Antebellum Politics*. Duluth, Minn.: H. Stein, 1934.

Baker, Jean H. *Sisters: The Lives of America's Suffragists*. New York: Hill & Wang, 2005.

Bancroft, Frederic. *The Life of William H. Seward*. 2 vols. New York: Harper, 1900.

Bancroft, George. *The Life and Letters of George Bancroft*. Ed. M. A. DeWolfe Howe. 2 vols. New York: Scribner's, 1908.

Barnum, Phineas T. *Struggles and Triumphs; Or, Forty Years' Recollections of P. T. Barnum*. New York: American News, 1871.

Bates, David Homer. *Lincoln in the Telegraph Office: Recollections of the United States Military Telegraph Corps during the Civil War*. New York: Century Co., 1907.

Bates, Edward. *The Diary of Edward Bates, 1859–66*. Ed. Howard K. Beale. Washington, D.C.: U.S. Government Printing Office, 1933.

Belz, Herman. "Salmon P. Chase and the Politics of Racial Reform." *Journal of the Abraham Lincoln Association* 17 (Summer 1996): 22–40.

Bemis, Samuel Flagg. *John Quincy Adams and the Foundations of American Foreign Policy*. New York: Alfred A. Knopf, 1949.

———. *John Quincy Adams and the Union*. New York: Alfred A. Knopf, 1956.

Benedict, Michael Les. "From Our Archives: A New Look at the Impeachment of Andrew Johnson." *Political Science Quarterly* 113 (Autumn 1998): 493–511.

———. *The Impeachment and Trial of Andrew Johnson*. New York: W. W. Norton, 1999.

———. "Southern Democrats in the Crisis of 1876–1877." *Journal of Southern History* 46 (November 1980): 489–524.

Berlin, Ira, Joseph P. Reidy, and Leslie S. Rowlands, eds. *Freedom's Soldiers: The Black Military Experience*. Cambridge: Cambridge University Press, 1982.

Bernstein, Iver. *The New York City Draft Riots: Their Significance for American Society and Politics in the Age of the Civil War*. New York: Oxford University Press, 1990.

Bigelow, John. *Retrospections of an Active Life*. 5 vols. New York: Baker and Taylor, 1909–1913.

Bigler, David L. "A Lion in the Path: Genesis of the Utah War, 1857–1858." *Utah Historical Quarterly* 76 (Winter 2008): 4–21.

Blakeman, A. Noel, ed. *Personal Recollections of the War of the Rebellion*. Vol. 3, *The Third Series*. New York: G. P. Putnam's Sons, 1907.

Blight, David W. *Frederick Douglass' Civil War: Keeping Faith in Jubilee*. Baton Rouge: Louisiana State University Press, 1989.

———. *Race and Reunion: The Civil War in American History*. Cambridge, Mass.: Harvard University Press, 2002.

Blondheim, Menahem. *News over the Wires: The Telegraph and the Flow of Public Information in America, 1844–1897*. Cambridge, Mass.: Harvard University Press, 1994.

Blue, Frederick J. *No Taint of Compromise: Crusaders in Antislavery Politics*. Baton Rouge: Louisiana State University Press, 2005.

———. *Salmon P. Chase: A Life in Politics*. Kent, Ohio: Kent State University Press, 1987.

Bodnia, George. "Fort Pillow 'Massacre': Observations of a Minnesotan." *Minnesota History* 43 (Spring 1973): 186–90.

Bordewich, Fergus M. *America's Great Debate: Henry Clay, Stephen A. Douglas, and the Compromise That Preserved the Union*. New York: Simon & Schuster, 2012.

Boritt, Gabor S. "The Voyage to the Colony of Lincolnia: The Sixteenth President, Black Colonization, and the Defense Mechanism of Avoidance." *The Historian* 37 (August 1975): 619–32.

———., ed. *Why the Civil War Came*. New York: Oxford University Press, 1996.

Bourke, John Gregory. *The Diaries of John Gregory Bourke*. Ed. Charles M. Robinson. 4 vols. Denton: University of North Texas Press, 2003–2009.

Boutwell, George S. *The Lawyer, the Statesman and the Soldier*. New York: D. Appleton, 1887.

Bowles, Samuel. *The Switzerland of America: A Summer Vacation in the Parks and Mountains of Colorado*. Boston: Lee & Shepard, 1869.

Braude, Ann. *Radical Spirits: Spiritualism and Women's Rights in Nineteenth-Century America*. Boston: Beacon Press, 1989.

Brodie, Fawn. *Thaddeus Stevens: Scourge of the South*. New York: W. W. Norton, 1966.

Brooks, Noah. *Lincoln Observed: Civil War Dispatches of Noah Brooks*. Ed. Michael Burlingame. Baltimore: Johns Hopkins University Press, 2002.

———. *Washington in Lincoln's Time*. New York: Century Co., 1895.

Brooks, U. R., ed. *Stories of the Confederacy*. Columbia, S.C.: State Company, 1912.

Brown, Joshua. *Beyond the Lines: Pictorial Reporting, Everyday Life, and the Crisis of Gilded Age America*. Berkeley: University of California Press, 2002.

Browne, Junius Henri. *Four Years in Secessia: Adventures within and beyond the Union Lines*. Hartford: O. D. Case, 1865.

———. *The Great Metropolis: A Mirror of New York*. Hartford: American Publishing, 1869.

Brownlee, Richard S. *Gray Ghosts of the Confederacy: Guerrilla Warfare in the West, 1861–1865.* Baton Rouge: Louisiana State University Press, 2009.

Bunting, Josiah, III. *Ulysses S. Grant.* New York: Henry Holt, 2004.

Burton, Georgeanne B., and Orville Vernon Burton. "Lucy Holcombe Pickens, Southern Writer." *South Carolina Historical Magazine* 103 (October 2002): 296–324.

Busch, Moritz. *Bismarck: Some Secret Pages of His History.* 2 vols. London: Macmillan, 1898.

Butler, Benjamin F. *Autobiography and Personal Reminiscences of Major-General Benj. F. Butler: Butler's Book.* Boston: A. M. Thayer, 1892.

———. *Private and Official Correspondence of Gen. Benjamin F. Butler during the Period of the Civil War.* 5 vols. Norwood, Mass.: Plimpton Press, 1917.

Cabell, James Branch. *Let Me Lie: Being in the Main an Ethnological Account of the Remarkable Commonwealth of Virginia and the Making of Its History.* Charlottesville: University of Virginia Press, 2001.

Cabell, James Branch, A. J. Hanna, and Doris Lee. *The St. Johns: A Parade of Diversities.* New York: Farrar & Rinehart, 1943.

Caldwell, Robert Granville. *The Lopez Expeditions to Cuba.* Princeton, N.J.: Princeton University Press, 1915.

Cardoso, J. J. "Lincoln, Abolitionism, and Patronage: The Case of Hinton Rowan Helper." *Journal of Negro History* 53 (April 1968): 144–60.

Carlebach, Michael L. *The Origins of Photojournalism in America.* Washington, D.C.: Smithsonian Institution Press, 1992.

Caro, Robert A. *The Years of Lyndon Johnson: Master of the Senate.* New York: Alfred A. Knopf, 2002.

Carpenter, John. *Sword and Olive Branch: Oliver Otis Howard.* Pittsburgh: University of Pittsburgh, 1964.

Carwardine, Richard. *Lincoln and the Fourth Estate: The White House and the Press during the American Civil War.* Reading, England: University of Reading Press, 2004.

Cash, W. J. *The Mind of the South.* New York: Vintage, 1991.

Catton, Bruce. *Grant Takes Command.* Boston: Little, Brown, 1969.

Chaffin, Tom. *Fatal Glory: Narciso López and the First Clandestine American War.* Charlottesville: University of Virginia Press, 1996

———. *Pathfinder: John Charles Frémont and the Course of American Empire.* New York: Hill & Wang, 2002.

———. "'Sons of Washington': Narciso López, Filibustering, and U.S. Nationalism, 1848–1851." *Journal of the Early Republic* 15 (Spring 1995): 79–108.

Chamberlain, D. H. "Reconstruction and the Negro." *North American Review* 128 (February 1879): 161–73.

Chambrun, Marquis de. "Personal Recollections of Mr. Lincoln." *Scribner's Magazine* 13 (January 1893): 26–39.

Channing, Steven A. *Crisis of Fear: Secession in South Carolina.* New York: Simon & Schuster, 1970.

Chapman, Ervin S. *Latest Light on Abraham Lincoln, and War-time Memories.* 2 vols. New York: Fleming H. Revell, 1917.

Chase, Salmon P. *The Salmon P. Chase Papers.* Ed. John Niven. 5 vols. Kent, Ohio: Kent State University Press, 1993–1998.

Chesnut, Mary. *Mary Chesnut's Civil War.* Ed. C. Vann Woodward. New Haven, Conn.: Yale University Press, 1981.

Chesson, Michael B. "Harlots or Heroines? A New Look at the Richmond Bread Riot." *Virginia Magazine of History and Biography* 92 (April 1984): 131–75.

Chester, Giraud. *Embattled Maiden: The Life of Anna Dickinson*. New York: G. P. Putnam's Sons, 1951.

Chester, Thomas Morris. *Thomas Morris Chester, Black Civil War Correspondent: His Dispatches from the Virginia Front*. Ed. R. J. M. Blackett. Baton Rouge: Louisiana State University Press, 1989.

Child, Lydia Maria. *The Letters of Lydia Maria Child*. Ed. Harriet Winslow Sewall. Boston: Houghton Mifflin, 1882.

Child, Lydia Maria, Henry Wise, and Mrs. M. J. C. Mason. *Correspondence between Lydia Maria Child and Gov. Wise and Mrs. Mason of Virginia*. Boston: American Anti-Slavery Society, 1860.

Church, W. C. "Nebulae, Nebulae." *Galaxy* 14 (September 1872): 431–36.

Cimprich, John. *Fort Pillow, a Civil War Massacre, and Public Memory*. Baton Rouge: Louisiana State University Press, 2005.

Claiborne, J. F. H. *The Life and Correspondence of John A. Quitman*. 2 vols. New York: Harper & Brothers, 1860.

Cleveland, Henry. *Alexander H. Stephens in Public and Private: With Letters and Speeches*. Philadelphia: National Publishing Co., 1866.

Clifford, Deborah Pickman. *Crusader of Freedom: A Life of Lydia Maria Child*. Boston: Beacon Press, 1992.

Clinton, Catherine, and Nina Silver, eds. *Battle Scars: Gender and Sexuality in the American Civil War*. New York: Oxford University Press, 2006.

Coffin, Charles Carleton. *The Boys of '61: or, Four Years of Fighting*. Boston: Estes and Lauriat, 1881.

———. *Four Years of Fighting: A Volume of Personal Observation with the Army and the Navy, from the First Battle of Bull Run to the Fall of Richmond*. Boston: Ticknor & Fields, 1866.

Connelley, William Elsey. *Quantrill and the Border Wars*. Cedar Rapids, Iowa: The Torch Press, 1910.

Conyngham, David. *Sherman's March through the South*. New York: Sheldon, 1865.

Cooke, John Edwin. *The Life, Trial, and Execution of Captain John Brown*. New York: Robert M. De Witt, 1859.

Cooper, William J., Jr. *Jefferson Davis: American*. New York: Vintage, 2001.

Cortissoz, Royal. *The Life of Whitelaw Reid*. 2 vols. New York: Charles Scribner's Sons, 1921.

Cox, Charles Harding. "Gone for a Soldier: The Civil War Letters of Charles Harding Cox." Ed. Lorna Lutes Sylvester. *Indiana Magazine of History* 68 (September 1972): 181–239.

Craven, Avery. *The Coming of the Civil War*. Chicago: University of Chicago Press, 1957.

———. *Edmund Ruffin, Southerner: A Study in Secession*. Baton Rouge: Louisiana State University Press, 1972.

Crenshaw, Ollinger. "The Speakership Contest of 1859–1860: John Sherman's Election a Cause of Disruption?" *Mississippi Valley Historical Review* 29 (December 1942): 323–38.

Croce, Paul Jerome. "Calming the Screaming Eagle: William James and His Circle Fight Their Civil War Battles." *New England Quarterly* 76 (March 2003): 5–37.

Cumming, Kate. *Kate: The Journal of a Confederate Nurse*. Ed. Richard Barksdale Harwell. Baton Rouge: Louisiana State University Press, 1959.

Dana, Charles A. *Recollections of the Civil War: With the Leaders at Washington and in the Field in the Sixties*. New York: D. Appleton, 1899.

Davis, David Brion. *Inhuman Bondage: The Rise and Fall of Slavery in the New World*. New York: Oxford University Press, 2008.

———. *The Slave Power Conspiracy and the Paranoid Style*. Baton Rouge: Louisiana State University Press, 1967.

Davis, Jefferson. *Jefferson Davis, Constitutionalist: His Letters, Papers, and Speeches*. Ed. Dunbar Rowland. 10 vols. Jackson: Mississippi Department of Archives and History, 1923.

———. *The Rise and Fall of the Confederate Government*. 2 vols. New York: D. Appleton, 1881.

Davis, Keith F., and Jane L. Aspinwall, eds. *Timothy H. O'Sullivan: The King Survey Photographs*. New Haven, Conn.: Yale University Press, 2012.

Davis, Rebecca Harding. *Bits of Gossip*. Boston: Houghton Mifflin, 1904.

———. "David Gaunt." *The Atlantic Monthly* 10 (October 1862): 403–22.

———. *Margret Howth: A Story of To-day*. Boston: Ticknor & Fields, 1862.

Davis, Robert Scott, ed. *Ghosts and Shadows of Andersonville: Essays on the Secret Social Histories of America's Deadliest Prison*. Macon, Ga.: Mercer University Press, 2006.

Davis, Varina. *Jefferson Davis: A Memoir by His Wife*. 2 vols. Baltimore: Nautical & Aviation Publishing Company of America, 1990.

Dawson, Sarah Morgan. *A Confederate Girl's Diary*. Ed. Warrington Dawson. Boston: Houghton Mifflin, 1913.

DeForest, J. W. "Sheridan's Victory of Middletown." *Harper's New Monthly Magazine* 30 (February 1865): 353–360.

Delany, Martin R. *Blake: or; The Huts of America*. Boston: Beacon Press, 1970.

———. *Martin R. Delany: A Documentary Reader*. Ed. Robert S. Levine. Chapel Hill: University of North Carolina Press, 2003.

Delbanco, Andrew. *The Abolitionist Imagination*. Cambridge, Mass.: Harvard University Press, 2012.

———. *Melville: His World and Work*. New York: Alfred A. Knopf, 2005.

Denison, Frederic. *Sables and Spurs: The First Rhode Island Regiment Cavalry in the Civil War, 1861–1865*. Central Falls: First Rhode Island Cavalry Veteran Association, 1876.

Dennett, Tyler. *John Hay: From Poetry to Politics*. New York: Dodd, Mead, 1934.

Dickens, Charles. *American Notes: For General Circulation*. New York: Penguin, 2000.

Dickinson, Emily. *The Letters of Emily Dickinson*. Ed. Thomas H. Johnson and Theodora Ward. 3 vols. Cambridge, Mass.: Belknap Press of Harvard University Press, 1958.

Dobak, William A. *Freedom by the Sword: The U.S. Colored Troops, 1862–1867*. Washington, D.C.: U.S. Army, Center of Military History, 2011.

Donald, David Herbert. *Charles Sumner and the Coming of the Civil War*. New York: Alfred A. Knopf, 1960.

———. *Charles Sumner and the Rights of Man*. New York: Alfred A. Knopf, 1970.

———. *Lincoln*. New York: Simon & Schuster, 1995.

———. *Lincoln Reconsidered*. New York: Alfred A. Knopf, 1961.

Douglas, Henry Kyd. *I Rode with Stonewall*. Chapel Hill: University of North Carolina Press, 1940.

Douglass, Frederick. "Dissolution of the American Union." *Douglass' Monthly*, January 1861.

———. *Frederick Douglass: Selected Speeches and Writings*. Ed. Philip S. Foner and Yuval Taylor. Chicago: Chicago Review Press, 2000.

———. "Horatio Seymour's Letter of Acceptance." *The Independent*, Aug. 20, 1868.

——. *The Life and Times of Frederick Douglass, from 1817 to 1882*. London: Christian Age Office, 1882.

——. *The Life and Writings of Frederick Douglass*. 5 vols. Ed. Philip S. Foner. New York: International Publishers, 1950–1955.

Downey, Matthew T. "Horace Greeley and the Politicians: The Liberal Republican Convention in 1872." *Journal of American History* 53 (March 1967): 727–50.

Dray, Philip. *Capitol Men: The Epic Story of Reconstruction through the Lives of the First Black Congressmen*. Boston: Houghton Mifflin, 2008.

Duberman, Martin. *Charles Francis Adams, 1807–1886*. Boston: Houghton Mifflin, 1961.

DuBois, Ellen Carol. *Feminism and Suffrage: The Emergence of an Independent Women's Movement in America, 1848–1869*. Ithaca, N.Y.: Cornell University Press, 1999.

DuBois, W. E. B. *Black Reconstruction*. New York: Harcourt Brace, 1935.

——. *John Brown*. Ed. David Roediger. New York: Modern Library, 2001.

Dudden, Faye E. *Fighting Chance: The Struggle over Woman Suffrage and Black Suffrage in Reconstruction America*. New York: Oxford University Press, 2011.

Durden, Robert F. *The Gray and the Black: The Confederate Debate on Emancipation*. Baton Rouge: Louisiana State University Press, 1972.

Elkins, Stanley, and Eric McKitrick, eds. *The Hofstadter Aegis: A Memorial*. New York: Alfred A. Knopf, 1974.

Emerson, Edward W. *The Life and Letters of Charles Russell Lowell, Captain Sixth United States Cavalry, Colonel Second Massachusetts Cavalry, Brigadier-General United States Volunteers*. Boston: Houghton Mifflin, 1907.

Emerson, Ralph Waldo. *The Collected Works of Ralph Waldo Emerson*. Ed. Alfred R. Ferguson et al. 12 vols. Cambridge, Mass.: Belknap Press of Harvard University Press, 1971–2011.

——. *Emerson in His Journals*. Ed. Joel Porte. Cambridge, Mass.: Belknap Press of Harvard University Press, 1982.

——. *The Later Lectures of Ralph Waldo Emerson, 1843–1871*. Ed. Ronald A. Bosco and Joel Myerson. 2 vols. Athens: University of Georgia Press, 2001.

——. *Ralph Waldo Emerson: Essays and Lectures*. Ed. Joel Porte. New York: Library of America, 1983.

Escott, Paul D. "'The Cry of the Sufferers': The Problem of Welfare in the Confederacy." *Civil War History* 23 (September 1977): 228–40.

Ettinger, Amos Aschbach. *The Mission to Spain of Pierre Soulé, 1853–1855: A Study in the Cuban Diplomacy of the United States*. New Haven, Conn.: Yale University Press, 1932.

Evans, Eli N. *Judah P. Benjamin: The Jewish Confederate*. New York: Free Press, 1988.

Fahs, Alice, and Joan Waugh, eds. *The Memory of the Civil War in American Culture*. Chapel Hill: University of North Carolina Press, 2004.

Faust, Drew Gilpin. "'The Dread Void of Uncertainty': Naming the Dead in the American Civil War." *Southern Cultures* 11 (Summer 2005): 7–32.

——. *Mothers of Invention: Women of the Slaveholding South in the American Civil War*. Chapel Hill: University of North Carolina Press, 2004.

——. *This Republic of Suffering: Death and the American Civil War*. New York: Alfred A. Knopf, 2008.

Favill, Josiah Marshall. *The Diary of a Young Officer Serving with the Armies of the United States during the War of the Rebellion*. Chicago: R. R. Donnelley & Sons, 1909.

Fehrenbacher, Don E. *The Dred Scott Case: Its Significance in American Law and Politics*. New York: Oxford University Press, 1979.

————. *Lincoln in Text and Context: Collected Essays*. Palo Alto, Calif.: Stanford University Press, 1987.

————. *Prelude to Greatness: Lincoln in the 1850s*. Palo Alto, Calif.: Stanford University Press, 1962.

Fiske, John, John Wright, and John B. McMaster, eds. *Modern Development of the New World*. Vol. 23 of *A History of All Nations*. Philadelphia: Lea Brothers, 1905.

Fitzhugh, George. *Cannibals All! or Slaves without Masters*. Richmond: A. Morris, 1857.

Flexner, Eleanor. *Century of Struggle: The Women's Rights Struggle in the United States*. Cambridge, Mass.: Belknap Press of Harvard University Press, 1996.

Florida Election, 1876: Report of the Senate Committee on Privileges and Elections, with the Testimony and Documentary Evidence, on the Election in the State of Florida, 1876. Washington, D.C.: U.S. Government Printing Office, 1877.

Foner, Eric. *The Fiery Trial: Abraham Lincoln and American Slavery*. New York: W. W. Norton, 2010.

————. *Free Soil, Free Labor, Free Men: The Ideology of the Republican Party before the Civil War*. New York: Oxford University Press, 1970.

————. *Reconstruction: America's Unfinished Revolution, 1863–1867*. New York: Harper & Row, 1988.

Foner, Philip S. *History of Black Americans*. 3 vols. Westport, Conn.: Greenwood Press, 1975.

————. *A History of Cuba and Its Relations with the United States*. 2 vols. New York: International Publishers, 1962–1963.

Foote, Shelby. *The Civil War: A Narrative*. 3 vols. New York: Random House, 1958–1974.

Forbes, Edwin. *Thirty Years After: An Artist's Memoir of the Civil War*. Baton Rouge: Louisiana State University Press, 1993.

Forbes, John Murray. *Letters and Recollections of John Murray Forbes*. Ed. Sarah Forbes Hughes. 2 vols. Boston: Houghton Mifflin, 1899.

Ford, Lacy K., Jr. *Origins of Southern Radicalism: The South Carolina Upcountry, 1800–1860*. New York: Oxford University Press, 1988.

Foreman, Amanda. *A World on Fire: Britain's Crucial Role in the American Civil War*. New York: Random House, 2011.

Frederickson, George. *The Black Image in the White Imagination*. New York: Harper Torchbook, 1972.

————. *The Inner Civil War: Northern Intellectuals and the Crisis of the Union*. New York: Harper & Row, 1968.

Freehling, William W. *The Road to Disunion: Secessionists Triumphant, 1854–1861*. 2 vols. New York: Oxford University Press, 1991–2007.

Freeman, Douglas Southall, and Richard Barksdale Harwell. *Lee: An Abridgment in One Volume of the Four-Volume* R. E. Lee *by Douglas Southall Freeman*. New York: Scribner's, 1997.

Fremantle, Arthur James. *Three Months in the Southern States, April–June 1863*. London: William Blackwood and Sons, 1863.

Frémont, Jessie Benton. *The Letters of Jessie Benton Frémont*. Ed. Pamela Herr and Mary Lee Spence. Urbana: University of Illinois Press, 1993.

Frémont, John C. *Memoirs of My Life: Including in the Narrative Five Journeys of Western Explorations during the Years 1842, 1843–4, 1845–6–7, 1848–9, 1853–4*. New York: Cooper Square Press, 2001.

Freund, Gisèle. *Photography and Society*. Boston: David R. Godine, 1980.

Frisken, Amanda. *Victoria Woodhull's Sexual Revolution: Political Theater and the Popular Press in Nineteenth-Century America.* Philadelphia: University of Pennsylvania Press, 2004.

Futch, Ovid. *History of Andersonville Prison.* Gainesville: University of Florida Press, 1968.

Gabriel, Mary. *Notorious Victoria: The Life of Victoria Woodhull, Uncensored.* Chapel Hill, N.C.: Algonquin Books, 1998.

Gallagher, Gary. *The Confederate War.* Cambridge, Mass.: Harvard University Press, 1997.

———. *The Union War.* Cambridge, Mass.: Harvard University Press, 2011.

Gallman, Matthew. *America's Joan of Arc: The Life of Anna Elizabeth Dickinson.* New York: Oxford University Press, 2006.

Gardner, Joseph L. " 'Bull Run' Russell." *American Heritage* 13 (June 1962): 59–64.

Garrison, William Lloyd. *The Letters of William Lloyd Garrison.* Ed. Walter M. Merrill and Louis Ruchames. 6 vols. Cambridge, Mass.: Belknap Press of Harvard University Press, 1971–1981.

Genovese, Eugene. *Roll, Jordan, Roll: The World the Slaves Made.* New York: Pantheon, 1972.

Gerber, Richard A. "Liberal Republicanism, Reconstruction, and Social Order: Samuel Bowles as a Test Case." *New England Quarterly* 45 (September 1972): 393–407.

Gholson, Thomas. *Speech of Honorable Thomas S. Gholson of Virginia on the Policy of Employing Negro Troops.* Richmond: George P. Evans, 1865.

Gienapp, William E. *The Origins of the Republican Party.* New York: Oxford University Press, 1987.

Gillette, William. *Retreat from Reconstruction, 1869–1879.* Baton Rouge: Louisiana State University Press, 1979.

Gilmore, James R. "Our War and Our Want." *Continental Monthly* 1 (February 1862): 113–18.

———. *Personal Recollections of Abraham Lincoln and the Civil War.* Boston: L. C. Page, 1898.

Ginzberg, Lori D. *Elizabeth Cady Stanton: An American Life.* New York: Hill & Wang, 2009.

Goetzmann, William. *Exploration and Empire: The Explorer and the Scientist in the Winning of the American West.* New York: Alfred A. Knopf, 1966.

Going, Charles. *David Wilmot, Free Soiler: A Biography of the Great Advocate of the Wilmot Proviso.* New York: D. Appleton, 1924.

Goldfield, David. *America Aflame: How the Civil War Created a Nation.* New York: Bloomsbury Press, 2011.

Goldsmith, Barbara. *Other Powers: The Age of Suffrage, Spiritualism, and the Scandalous Victoria Woodhull.* New York: Alfred A. Knopf, 1998.

Goodheart, Adam. *1861: The Civil War Awakening.* New York: Alfred A. Knopf, 2011.

Goodwin, Doris Kearns. *Team of Rivals: The Political Genius of Abraham Lincoln.* New York: Simon & Schuster, 2005.

Gordon, John B. *Reminiscences of the Civil War.* New York: Charles Scribner's Sons, 1904.

Gordon, Lesley J., and John C. Inscoe, eds. *Inside the Confederate Nation: Essays in Honor of Emory M. Thomas.* Baton Rouge: Louisiana State University Press, 2005.

Gordon-Reed, Annette. *Andrew Johnson.* New York: Henry Holt, 2011.

Gorgas, Josiah. *The Civil War Diary of Josiah Gorgas.* Ed. Frank E. Vandiver. Tuscaloosa: University of Alabama Press, 1947.

Gornick, Vivian. *The Solitude of Self: Thinking about Elizabeth Cady Stanton.* New York: Farrar, Straus and Giroux, 2005.

Grant, Ulysses, S. *Memoirs and Selected Letters: Personal Memoirs of U. S. Grant, Selected Letters 1839–1865.* Ed. Mary Drake McFeely and William S. McFeely. 2 vols. New York: Library of America, 1990.

———. *The Papers of Ulysses S. Grant.* Ed. John Y. Simon. 31 vols. Carbondale: Southern Illinois University Press, 1967–2000.

———. *Personal Memoirs of U. S. Grant.* 2 vols. New York: Charles L. Webster, 1885–86.

Gray, Wood. *The Hidden Civil War: The Story of the Copperheads.* New York: Viking, 1942.

Grayson, William J. *James Louis Petigru: A Biographical Sketch.* New York: Harper & Brothers, 1866.

Greeley, Horace. *The American Conflict: A History of the Great Rebellion in the United States of America 1860–64.* 2 vols. Hartford, Conn.: O. D. Case, 1867.

———. "Prayer of Twenty Millions." *New-York Tribune,* Aug. 20, 1862.

Grimké, Charlotte Forten. *The Journals of Charlotte Forten Grimké.* Ed. Brenda Stevenson. New York: Oxford University Press, 1988.

Grinstead, Steve, and Ben Fogelberg, eds. *Western Voices: 125 Years of Western Writing.* Golden, Colo.: Fulcrum Publishing, 2004.

Guelzo, Allen C. *Lincoln's Emancipation Proclamation: The End of Slavery in America.* New York: Simon & Schuster, 2004.

Hague, James D. *Clarence King Memoirs: The Helmet of Mambrino.* New York: G. P. Putnam's Sons, 1904.

Hahn, Steven. *The Political Worlds of Slavery and Freedom.* Cambridge, Mass.: Harvard University Press, 2009.

Hallowell, Norwood P. *The Negro as a Soldier in the War of the Rebellion.* Boston: Little, Brown, 1897.

Halstead, Murat. *Three against Lincoln: Murat Halstead Reports the Caucuses of 1860.* Baton Rouge: Louisiana State University Press, 1960.

Hamilton, Holman. *Prologue to Conflict: The Crisis and Compromise of 1850.* Lexington: University of Kentucky Press, 1964.

Hanchett, William. *Lincoln Murder Conspiracies.* Urbana: University of Illinois Press, 1983.

Hardesty, Nancy A. *Women Called to Witness: Evangelical Feminism in the Nineteenth Century.* Knoxville: University of Tennessee Press, 1999.

Hardorff, Richard G. *The Death of Crazy Horse: A Tragic Episode in Lakota History.* Lincoln: University of Nebraska Press, 2001.

———, ed. *Indian Views of the Custer Fight: A Source Book.* Tulsa: University of Oklahoma Press, 2005.

———, ed. *Lakota Recollections of the Custer Fight: New Sources of Indian Military History.* Lincoln: University of Nebraska Press, 1997.

Harris, Neil. *Humbug: The Art of P. T. Barnum.* Chicago: University of Chicago Press, 1981.

Harrison, Constance Cary (Mrs. Burton Harrison). *Recollections Grave and Gay.* New York: Charles Scribner's Sons, 1911.

Hart, Albert Bushnell. *Salmon Porter Chase.* Boston: Houghton Mifflin, 1899.

Harte, Bret. "Current Literature." *Overland Monthly* 5 (October 1870): 386.

Hawthorne, Nathaniel. "Chiefly about War Matters." *The Atlantic Monthly* 10 (July 1862): 43–62.

———. *Collected Novels.* Ed. Millicent Bell. New York: Library of America, 1983.

———. *The Letters, 1843–1853.* Vol. 16 of *The Centenary Edition of the Works of Nathaniel Hawthorne.* Ed. William Charvat et al. Columbus: Ohio State University Press, 1985.

———. *The Letters, 1853–1856.* Vol. 17 of *The Centenary Edition of the Works of Nathaniel Hawthorne.* Ed. William Charvat et al. Columbus: Ohio State University Press, 1987.

———. *Miscellaneous Prose and Verse.* Vol. 23 of *The Centenary Edition of the Works of Nathaniel Hawthorne.* Ed. William Charvat et al. Columbus: Ohio State University Press, 1994.

Hay, John. *Lincoln and the Civil War in the Diaries and Letters of John Hay.* Ed. Tyler Dennett. New York: Da Capo Press, 1988.

———. *Inside Lincoln's White House: The Complete Civil War Diary of John Hay.* Ed. Michael Burlingame and John R. T. Ettlinger. Carbondale: Southern Illinois University Press, 1999.

Hayes, Rutherford B. *The Diary and Letters of Rutherford B. Hayes.* Ed. Charles R. Williams. 5 vols. Columbus: Ohio State Archaeological and Historical Society, 1922–1926.

Headley, J. T. *Grant and Sherman: Their Campaigns and Generals.* New York: E. B. Treat, 1865.

Hearn, Lafcadio. *Occidental Gleanings.* Ed. Albert Mordell. 2 vols. New York: Dodd, Mead, 1925.

Hedrick, Joan. *Harriet Beecher Stowe: A Life.* New York: Oxford University Press, 1994.

Helper, Hinton Rowan. *The Impending Crisis of the South: How to Meet It.* New York: A. B. Burdick, 1857.

Herndon, William H. *Herndon's Informants: Letters, Interviews, and Statements about Abraham Lincoln.* Ed. Douglas L. Wilson and Rodney O. Davis. Champaign: University of Illinois, 1998.

Hesseltine, William B. *Civil War Prisons.* Kent, Ohio: Kent State University Press, 1962.

Heth, Henry. "Letter from Major-General Henry Heth, of AP Hill's Corps, ANV." *Southern Historical Society Papers* 4 (1877): 159.

Higginson, Thomas Wentworth. *Army Life in a Black Regiment, and Other Writings.* New York: Penguin Classics, 1997.

———. "Border Ruffianism in South Carolina." *The Independent,* Aug. 10, 1876.

———. "The Case of the Carpet Baggers." *The Nation,* March 2, 1899, 162–63.

———. *Cheerful Yesterdays.* Boston: Houghton Mifflin, 1898.

———. *Contemporaries.* Boston: Houghton Mifflin, 1900.

———. "The First Black Regiment." *Outlook* 59 (July 2, 1898): 521–31.

———. Letter to the editor. *The New York Times,* Feb. 21, 1864.

———. *Massachusetts in the Army and Navy during the War of 1861–1865.* 2 vols. Boston: Wright & Potter, 1895–1896.

———. "The Ordeal by Battle." *The Atlantic Monthly* 8 (July 1861): 88–95.

———. *The Rationale of Spiritualism: Being Two Extemporaneous Lectures Delivered at Dodworth's Hall, December 5, 1858.* New York: T. J. Ellinwood, 1859.

————. "Safety Matches." *The Independent*, Sept. 21, 1865.

————. "The Shaw Memorial and the Sculptor St. Gaudens," pt. 3, "Colored Troops Under Fire." *Century* 54 (June 1897): 194–200.

————. "Too Many Compliments." *The Independent*, Oct. 26, 1865.

————. *Woman and Her Wishes: An Essay Inscribed to the Massachusetts Constitutional Convention*. Boston: Robert F. Walcutt, 1853.

Hill, Benjamin H. *Senator Benjamin H. Hill of Georgia: His Life, Speeches and Writings*. Ed. Benjamin H. Hill, Jr. Atlanta: T. H. P. Bloodworth, 1893.

Hindus, Milton, ed. *Walt Whitman: The Critical Heritage*. New York: Barnes & Noble, 1971.

Hoar, George F. *Autobiography of Seventy Years*. 2 vols. New York: Charles Scribner's Sons, 1905.

Hofstadter, Richard. *The American Political Tradition and the Men Who Made It*. New York: Vintage, 1951.

Hogue, James K. *Uncivil War: Five New Orleans Street Battles and the Rise and Fall of Radical Reconstruction*. Baton Rouge: Louisiana State University Press, 2006.

Holmes, Oliver Wendell. "Doings of the Sunbeam." *The Atlantic Monthly* 12 (July 1863): 1–16.

————. "My Hunt after 'The Captain.'" *The Atlantic Monthly* 10 (December 1862): 738–64.

Holmes, Oliver Wendell, Jr. *The Essential Holmes: Selections from the Letters, Speeches, Judicial Opinions and Other Writings of Oliver Wendell Holmes, Jr*. Ed. Richard Posner. Chicago: University of Chicago Press, 1996.

————. *Touched with Fire: Civil War Letters and Diary of Oliver Wendell Holmes, Jr., 1861–1864*. Ed. Mark DeWolfe Howe. Cambridge, Mass.: Harvard University Press, 1947.

Holt, Michael. *The Political Crises of the 1850s*. New York: W. W. Norton, 1983.

Holzer, Harold. *Lincoln at Cooper Union: The Speech That Made Abraham Lincoln President*. New York: Simon & Schuster, 2004.

————. *Lincoln President-Elect: Abraham Lincoln and the Great Secession Winter 1860–1861*. New York: Simon & Schuster, 2008.

Hone, Philip. *The Diary of Philip Hone*. Ed. Allan Nevins. 2 vols. New York: Dodd, Mead, 1927.

Hood, John Bell. *Advance and Retreat: Personal Experiences in the United States and Confederate States Armies*. New Orleans: G. T. Beauregard, 1879.

Horowitz, Helen Lefkowitz. "Victoria Woodhull, Anthony Comstock, and the Conflict over Sex in the 1870s." *Journal of American History* 87 (September 2000): 403–34.

Horwitz, Tony. *Midnight Rising: John Brown and the Raid That Sparked the Civil War*. New York: Henry Holt, 2011.

Houston, Sam. *The Writings of Sam Houston*. Ed. Amelia Williams and Eugene Barker. 8 vols. Austin: University of Texas Press, 1938–1943.

Houzeau, Jean-Charles. *My Passage at the New Orleans Tribune: A Memoir of the Civil War Era*. Ed. David C. Rankin. Translated by Gerald F. Denault. Baton Rouge: Louisiana State University Press, 1984.

Howard, Oliver Otis. *The Autobiography of Oliver Otis Howard*. 2 vols. New York: Baker and Taylor, 1907.

Howe, Daniel Walker. *The Political Culture of the American Whigs*. Chicago: University of Chicago Press, 1979.

————. *What God Hath Wrought: The Transformation of America, 1815–1848*. New York: Oxford University Press, 2007.

Howells, William Dean. *Sketch of the Life and Character of Rutherford B. Hayes*. New York: Hurd and Houghton, 1876.

Hurlbert, William Henry. *General McClellan and the Conduct of the War*. New York: Sheldon & Company, 1864.

Hurst, Jack. *Nathan Bedford Forrest: A Biography*. New York: Alfred A. Knopf, 1993.

Impeachment Investigation: Testimony Taken before the Judiciary Committee of the House of Representatives in the Investigation of Charges against Andrew Johnson, 39th Cong., 2nd Session, and 40th Congress, 1st Session. Washington, D.C.: U.S. Government Printing Office, 1867.

Irmscher, Christoph. *Louis Agassiz: Creator of American Science*. New York: Houghton Mifflin, 2013.

Hutton, Paul Andrew. *Phil Sheridan and His Army*. Norman: University of Oklahoma Press, 1999.

Jackson, Mary Anna. *Memoirs of Stonewall Jackson by His Widow Mary Anna Jackson*. Louisville: Prentice Press, 1895.

Jackson, Thomas J. *The Life and Letters of General Thomas J. Jackson*. Ed. Mary Anna Jackson. New York: Harper & Brothers, 1892.

Jaffa, Harry V. *Crisis of the House Divided: An Interpretation of the Issues in the Lincoln-Douglas Debates*. Chicago: University of Chicago Press, 1959.

————. *New Birth of Freedom: Abraham Lincoln and the Coming of the Civil War*. Lanham, Md.: Rowman and Littlefield, 2000.

James, Henry. *A Small Boy and Others*. New York: Charles Scribner's Sons, 1913.

Johannsen, Robert Walter. *Stephen A. Douglas*. Urbana: University of Illinois Press, 1997.

Johnson, Andrew. *The Papers of Andrew Johnson*. Ed. Leroy P. Graf, Ralph W. Haskins, and Paul H. Bergeron. 16 vols. Knoxville: University of Tennessee Press, 1967–2000.

Johnson, Michael P. *Toward a Patriarchal Republic: The Secession of Georgia*. Baton Rouge: Louisiana State University Press, 1977.

Johnson, Robert Underwood, and Clarence Clough Buel, eds. *Battles and Leaders of the Civil War*. 4 vols. New York: Century Co., 1884.

Jones, John Beauchamp. *A Rebel War Clerk's Diary at the Confederate States Capital*. 2 vols. Philadelphia: J. B. Lippincott, 1866.

Jones, J. William. *Personal Reminiscences, Anecdotes, and Letters of Gen. Robert E. Lee*. New York: D. Appleton, 1875.

Julian, George W. *Political Recollections, 1840–1872*. Chicago: Janson, McClurg, 1884.

Kahn, Edward. "Creator of Compromise: William Henry Sedley Smith and the Boston Museum's *Uncle Tom's Cabin*." *Theatre Survey* 48 (2000): 71–82.

Kaplan, Fred. *Lincoln: The Biography of a Writer*. New York: HarperCollins, 2008.

Kaplan, Justin. *Walt Whitman: A Life*. New York: Simon & Schuster, 1980.

————. *Mr. Clemens and Mark Twain: A Biography*. New York: Simon & Schuster, 1966.

Karcher, Carolyn L. *The First Woman in the Republic: A Cultural Biography of Lydia Maria Child*. Durham, N.C.: Duke University Press, 1994.

Katz, Jonathan. *Resistance at Christiana: The Fugitive Slave Rebellion, Christiana, Pennsylvania, September 11, 1851: A Documentary Account*. New York: Thomas Y. Crowell, 1974.

Keller, Morton. *Affairs of State: Public Life in Late Nineteenth Century America*. Cambridge, Mass.: Belknap Press of Harvard University Press, 1977.

Kerr, Andrea Moore. *Lucy Stone: Speaking Out for Equality*. New Brunswick, N.J.: Rutgers University Press, 1995.

Kimball, Ivory G. *Recollections from a Busy Life, 1843–1911*. Washington, D.C.: Carnahan Press, 1912.

King, Charles. "Custer's Last Battle." *Harper's New Monthly Magazine* 81 (August 1890): 378–387.

King, Clarence. "Atrium Magister." *North American Review* 147 (October 1885): 377–78.

———. "Bancroft's Native Races of the Pacific States." *The Atlantic Monthly* 35 (February 1875): 163–73.

———. "Catastrophism and Evolution." *The American Naturalist* 11 (August 1877): 449–70.

———. *Mountaineering in the Sierra Nevada*. New York: Charles Scribner's Sons, 1903.

———. "Mountaineering in the Sierra Nevada," pt. 2. *The Atlantic Monthly* 27 (June 1871): 704–15.

———. "Style and the Monument." *North American Review* 141 (November 1885): 443–53.

King, Ronald F. "A Most Corrupt Election: Louisiana in 1876." *Studies in American Political Development* 15 (Fall 2001): 123–37.

Kirk, Eleanor. "Two Women of the Present: Elizabeth Cady Stanton, Susan B. Anthony." *Phrenological Journal and Packard's Monthly* 50 (July 1870): 57–61.

Kirke, Edmund. "Our Visit to Richmond." *The Atlantic Monthly* 14 (September 1864): 372–83.

Klement, Frank L. *The Limits of Dissent: Clement Vallandigham and the Civil War*. New York: Fordham University Press, 1998.

Laderman, Gary. *The Sacred Remains: American Attitudes toward Death, 1799–1883*. New Haven, Conn.: Yale University Press, 1996.

Larcom, Lucy. *A New England Girlhood, Outlined from Memory*. Boston: Houghton Mifflin, 1889.

Larpenteur, Charles. *Forty Years a Fur Trader on the Upper Missouri: The Personal Narrative of Charles Larpenteur, 1833–1872*. Lincoln: University of Nebraska Press, 1989.

Lawrence, D. H. *Studies in Classic American Literature*. New York: Penguin, 1961.

Lee, Elizabeth Blair. *Wartime Washington: The Civil War Letters of Elizabeth Blair Lee*. Ed. Virginia Jeans Laas. Urbana: University of Illinois Press, 1999.

Lemann, Nicholas. *Redemption: The Last Battle of the Civil War*. New York: Farrar, Straus and Giroux, 2006.

Leonard, Elizabeth D. *Lincoln's Avengers: Justice, Revenge, and Reunion after the Civil War*. New York: W. W. Norton, 2004.

Lincoln, Abraham. *Abraham Lincoln: Complete Works, Comprising His Speeches, Letters, State Papers, and Miscellaneous Writings*. Ed. John G. Nicolay and John Hay. 2 vols. New York: Century, 1894.

———. *Abraham Lincoln: Speeches and Writings*. 2 vols. Ed. Don E. Fehrenbacher. New York: Library of America, 1989.

———. *The Collected Works of Abraham Lincoln*. Ed. Roy P. Basler. 8 vols. New Brunswick, N.J.: Rutgers University Press, 1953.

Lincoln, Abraham, and Stephen A. Douglas. *The Lincoln-Douglas Debates: The First Complete, Unexpurgated Text*. Ed. Harold Holzer. New York: Fordham University Press, 2004.

Link, Samuel Albert. *War Poets of the South.* Nashville, 1898.

Litwack, Leon. *Been in the Storm So Long.* New York: Vintage, 1980.

Loguen, Jermain W. *The Rev. J. W. Loguen, as a Slave and as a Freeman: A Narrative of Real Life.* Syracuse, N.Y.: J. G. K. Truair, 1859.

Longfellow, Henry Wadsworth. *Michael Angelo: A Dramatic Poem.* Boston: Houghton Mifflin, 1884.

Longfellow, Samuel. *The Life of Henry Wadsworth Longfellow, with Extracts from His Journals and Correspondence.* Boston: Houghton Mifflin, 1886–1891.

Longstreet, James. *From Manassas to Appomattox: Memoirs of the Civil War in America.* Philadelphia: J. B. Lippincott, 1896.

Lossing, Benson J. *Harper's Popular Cyclopedia of the United States from the Aboriginal Period.* 2 vols. New York: Harper & Brothers, 1881.

Loughborough, Mary Ann Webster. *My Cave Life in Vicksburg.* New York: D. Appleton, 1864.

Louisiana in 1876: Report of the Sub-committee of the Committee on Privileges and Elections of the United States Senate. Washington, D.C.: U.S. Government Printing Office, 1877.

Lowell, Charles Russell. *The Life and Letters of Charles Russell Lowell.* Ed. Edward W. Emerson. Boston: Houghton Mifflin, 1907.

Lowell, James Russell. *The Complete Writings of James Russell Lowell.* Ed. Charles Eliot Norton. 16 vols. Boston: Houghton Mifflin, 1904.

———. "The Election in November." *The Atlantic Monthly* 36 (October 1860), 492–503.

Maddox, George T. *Hard Trials and Tribulations of an Old Confederate Soldier.* Van Buren, Ark.: Argus, 1897.

Maher, Jane. *Biography of Broken Fortunes: Wilkie and Bob, Brothers of William, Henry, and Alice James.* New York: Archon Books, 1986.

Maizlish, Stephen. "Salmon P. Chase: The Roots of Ambition and the Origins of Reform." *Journal of the Early Republic* 18 (Spring 1998): 47–70.

Mallory, Stephen R. "Last Days of the Confederate Government." *McClure's Magazine* 26 (December 1900): 99–107, 239–48.

Mann, Mary Tyler Peabody. *Life of Horace Mann.* Boston: Walker, Fuller, 1865.

Mardock, R. W. *The Reformers and the American Indian.* Columbia: University of Missouri Press, 1971.

Marler, Scott P. "'A Monument to Commercial Isolation': Merchants and the Economic Decline of Post–Civil War New Orleans." *Journal of Urban History* 36 (March 2010): 507–27.

Marshall, Charles. *An Aide-de-Camp of Lee: Being the Papers of Colonel Charles Marshall, Sometime Aide-de-Camp, Military Secretary, and Assistant Adjutant General on the Staff of Robert E. Lee, 1862–1865.* Ed. Frederick Maurice. New York: Little, Brown, 1927.

Marshall, Helen E. *Dorothea Dix: Forgotten Samaritan.* Chapel Hill: University of North Carolina Press, 1937.

Martin, Edward Winslow. *Behind the Scenes in Washington.* Washington, D.C.: J. D. McCabe, 1873.

Marvel, William. *Andersonville: The Last Depot.* Chapel Hill: University of North Carolina Press, 1994.

Marx, Karl, and Friedrich Engels. *The Civil War in the United States.* New York: International Publishers, 1971.

McClatchy, J. D., ed. *Poets of the Civil War.* New York: Library of America, 2005.

McClellan, George B. *The Civil War Papers of General George McClellan, 1861–1865.* Ed. Stephen W. Sears. New York: Ticknor & Fields, 1989.

———. *McClellan's Own Story.* Ed. W. C. Prime. New York: Charles L. Webster, 1887.

McCullough, David. *Brave Companions: Portraits in History.* New York: Simon & Schuster, 1992.

McCurry, Stephanie. *Confederate Reckoning: Power and Politics in the Civil War South.* Cambridge, Mass.: Harvard University Press, 2010.

McDonough, James Lee, and Thomas L. Connelly. *Five Tragic Hours: The Battle of Franklin.* Knoxville: University of Tennessee Press, 1983.

McElroy, John. *Andersonville: A Story of Rebel Military Prisons.* Toledo, Ohio: D. R. Locke, 1879.

McFeely, William S. *Frederick Douglass.* New York: W. W. Norton, 1995.

———. *Grant: A Biography.* New York: W. W. Norton, 2002.

———. *Yankee Stepfather: General O. O. Howard and the Freedmen.* New York: W. W. Norton, 1994.

McKim, Randolph H. *A Soldier's Recollections: Leaves from the Diary of a Young Confederate.* New York: Longmans, Green, 1910.

McKitrick, Eric L. *Andrew Johnson and Reconstruction.* New York: Oxford University Press, 1988.

McMichael, J. R. *Autograph and Diary* (privately published). Southern Historical Collection, University of North Carolina, Chapel Hill.

McPherson, Edward. *The Political History of the United States of America during the Period of Reconstruction.* Washington, D.C.: Philp & Solomons, 1871.

McPherson, James M. *The Abolitionist Legacy: From Reconstruction to the NAACP.* Princeton, N.J.: Princeton University Press, 1975.

———. *Battle Cry of Freedom: The Civil War Era.* New York: Oxford University Press, 1988.

———. "Grant or Greeley? The Abolitionist Dilemma in the Election of 1872." *American Historical Review* 71 (October 1865): 43–61.

———. "No Peace without Victory, 1861–1865." *American Historical Review* 109 (February 2004): 1–18.

———. *Ordeal by Fire: The Civil War and Reconstruction.* New York: Alfred A. Knopf, 1982.

———. *The Struggle for Equality: Abolitionists and the Negro in the Civil War and Reconstruction.* Princeton, N.J.: Princeton University Press, 1964.

Melville, Herman. *Moby-Dick.* New York: Library of America College Editions, 2000.

———. *The Piazza Tales and Other Prose Pieces, 1839–1860.* Ed. Harrison Hayford, Alma MacDougall, and G. Thomas Tanselle. Evanston, Ill.: Northwestern University Press and the Newberry Library, 1987.

———. *Selected Poems of Herman Melville.* Ed. Robert Penn Warren. Jaffrey, N.H.: David Godine, 2006.

Menand, Louis. *The Metaphysical Club: A Story of Ideas in America.* New York: Farrar, Straus and Giroux, 2001.

Message of the President of the United States: Communicating in Compliance with, a Resolution, of the Senate. Of the 12th Instant, Information in Relation to the States of the Union Lately in Rebellion, Accompanied by a Report of Carl Schurz on the States of South Carolina, Georgia, Alabama, Mississippi, and Louisiana; also a Report of Lieutenant General Grant, on the Same Subject, 39th Congress, 1st Session, no. 2. Washington, D.C.: U.S. Government Printing Office, 1865.

Milder, Robert. *Reimagining Thoreau.* New York: Cambridge University Press, 1995.

Miller, Edward A., Jr. *Lincoln's Abolitionist General: The Biography of David Hunter.* Columbia: University of South Carolina Press, 1997.

Mitchell, W. J. T. *Landscape and Power.* Chicago: University of Chicago Press, 2002.

Moore, Albert Burton. *Conscription and Conflict in the Confederacy.* New York: Hillary House, 1963.

Moore, Frank, ed. *The Rebellion Record: A Diary of American Events, with Documents, Narratives, Illustrative Incidents, Poetry, Etc.* 11 vols. New York: G. P. Putnam, 1862–1868.

Nasby, Petroleum V. [David Ross Locke]. *Andy's Trip to the West, Together with a Life of Its Hero.* New York: J. C. Haney, 1867.

Neal, Diane, and Thomas W. Kremm. *The Lion of the South: General Thomas C. Hindman.* Macon, Ga.: Mercer University Press, 1993.

The Nebraska Question: Comprising Speeches in the United States Senate. New York: Redfield, 1854.

Neely, Mark E. *The Union Divided: Party Conflict in the Civil War North.* Cambridge, Mass.: Harvard University Press, 2002.

———. "Was the Civil War a Total War?" *Civil War History* 50 (December 2004): 434–58.

Nevins, Allan. *The Emergence of Lincoln.* 2 vols. New York: Charles Scribner's Sons, 1950.

———. *The Evening Post: A Century of Journalism.* New York: Boni and Liveright, 1922.

———. *Ordeal of the Union.* 8 vols. New York: Charles Scribner's Sons, 1947–1971.

———, ed. *American Press Opinion: Washington to Coolidge, A Documentary Record of Editorial Leadership and Criticism, 1785–1927.* 2 vols. New York: Kennikat Press, 1969.

Newhall, Frederick C. *With Sheridan in the Final Campaign against Lee.* Ed. Eric J. Wittenberg. Baton Rouge: Louisiana State University Press, 2002.

Nichols, George Ward. *The Story of the Great March: From the Diary of a Staff Officer.* New York: Harper & Brothers, 1866.

Nickel, Douglas R., ed. *Carleton Watkins: The Art of Perception.* San Francisco: San Francisco Museum of Modern Art, 1999.

Nicolay, John G., and John M. Hay. *Abraham Lincoln: A History.* 10 vols. New York: Century, 1890.

Noll, Mark A. "'Both . . . Pray to the Same God': The Singularity of Lincoln's Faith in the Era of the Civil War Author(s)." *Journal of the Abraham Lincoln Association* 18 (Winter 1997): 1–26.

Norton, Charles Eliot. *Letters of Charles Eliot Norton.* Ed. Sara Norton and M. A. DeWolfe Howe. 2 vols. Boston: Houghton Mifflin, 1913.

Oakes, James. *The Radical and the Republican: Frederick Douglass, Abraham Lincoln, and the Triumph of Antislavery Politics.* New York: W. W. Norton, 2007.

———. *The Ruling Race: A History of American Slaveholders.* New York: Alfred A. Knopf, 1982.

Oberholtzer, Ellis Paxson. *Jay Cooke: Financier of the Civil War.* 2 vols. Philadelphia: George W. Jacobs, 1907.

Oickle, Alvin F. *Disaster in Lawrence: The Fall of the Pemberton Mill.* Charleston, S.C.: History Press, 2008.

Orwell, George. *All Art Is Propaganda: Critical Essays.* Compiled by George Packer. Boston: Houghton Mifflin Harcourt, 2008.

Osthaus, Carl R. *Partisans of the Southern Press: Editorial Spokesmen of the Nineteenth Century.* Louisville: University of Kentucky Press, 1994.

Paine, Albert Bigelow. *Th. Nast: His Period and His Pictures.* New York: Macmillan, 1904.

Painter, John H. "The Fugitives of the Pearl." *Journal of Negro History* 1 (June 1916): 243–64.

Painter, Nell Irvin. *Sojourner Truth: A Life, a Symbol.* New York: W. W. Norton, 1996.

Panzer, Mary. *Mathew Brady and the Image of History.* Washington, D.C.: Smithsonian Books, 1997.

Parker, William. "The Freedman's Story," pt. 1. *The Atlantic Monthly* 17 (February 1866): 152–67.

Parkman, Francis. *The Oregon Trail; The Conspiracy of Pontiac.* Ed. William Taylor. New York: Library of America, 1991.

Parsons, Lynn Hudson. "The 'Splendid Pageant': Observations on the Death of John Quincy Adams." *New England Quarterly* 53 (December 1980): 464–82.

Pember, Phoebe Yates. *A Southern Woman's Story.* New York: G. W. Carleton, 1879.

Peoples, Morgan. "'The Scapegoat of Andersonville': Union Execution of Confederate Captain Henry Wirz." *North Louisiana Historical Association Journal* 11 (Fall 1980): 3–18.

Perkins, Howard C., ed. *Northern Editorials on Secession.* 2 vols. New York: Century Co., 1942.

Peterson, Merrill. *The Great Triumvirate: Webster, Clay, and Calhoun.* New York: Oxford University Press, 1987.

Phillips, William. *The Conquest of Kansas by Missouri and Her Allies.* Boston: Philips, Sampson, 1856.

———. "The Outlook." *North American Review* 127 (July–August 1878): 97–116.

———. *Speeches, Lectures, and Letters.* Boston: James Redpath, 1863.

Pickens, Lucy Holcombe. *The Free Flag of Cuba; or, The Martyrdom of Lopez.* New York: DeWitt and Davenport, 1854. Reprinted with an introduction by Orville Vernon Burton and Georgeanne B. Burton. Baton Rouge: Louisiana State University Press, 2002.

Pierce, Edward L. "The Contrabands at Fortress Monroe." *The Atlantic Monthly* 8 (November 1861): 626–40.

———. "The Freedmen at Port Royal." *The Atlantic Monthly* 12 (September 1863): 291–315.

Pierce, Franklin. "Ex-President Pierce's Letter to Jeff. Davis." *New-York Evening Post,* Sept. 19, 1863, 2.

Pike, James S. *Prostrate State: South Carolina under Negro Government.* New York: D. Appleton, 1874.

Poll, Richard D., and Ralph W. Hansen. "'Buchanan's Blunder': The Utah War, 1857–1858." *Military Affairs* 25 (Fall 1961): 121–31.

Pollard, Edward A. "Hints on Southern Civilization." *Southern Literary Messenger* 32 (April 1861): 308–11.

———. *Lee and His Lieutenants.* New York: E. B. Treat & Co., 1867.

———. *The Lost Cause: A New Southern History of the War of the Confederates.* New York: E. B. Treat & Co, 1866.

Poore, Benjamin Perley. *Perley's Reminiscences of Sixty Years in the National Metropolis.* 2 vols. Philadelphia: Hubbard Brothers, 1886.

Porter, Horace. "Grant's Last Campaign." *Century Magazine* 35 (November 1887): 126–52.

Post, Lydia Minturn, ed. *Soldiers' Letters, from Camp, Battle-field and Prison*. New York: Bunce & Huntington, 1865.

Potter, David M. *The Impending Crisis, 1848–1861*. Completed and ed. by Don E. Fehrenbacher. New York: Harper & Row, 1976.

Powell, Lawrence N. *New Masters: Northern Planters during the Civil War and Reconstruction*. New Haven, Conn.: Yale University Press, 1980.

Powers, Thomas. *The Killing of Crazy Horse*. New York: Alfred A. Knopf, 2010.

Proceedings of the First Three Republican National Conventions of 1850, 1860 and 1864. Minneapolis: C. W. Johnson, 1893.

Proceedings of the Liberal Republican Convention, in Cincinnati, May 1st, 2d and 3d, 1872. New York: Baker & Godwin, 1872.

Prucha, Francis Paul. *The Great Father: The United States Government and the American Indians*. Lincoln: University of Nebraska Press, 1984.

Pryor, Elizabeth Brown. *Clara Barton: Professional Angel*. Philadelphia: University of Pennsylvania Press, 1987.

Quarles, Benjamin. *Black Abolitionists*. New York: Da Capo, 1969.

———. *Frederick Douglass*. Washington, D.C.: Associated Publishers, 1948.

———. *The Negro in the Civil War*. New York: Da Capo, 1991.

Rable, George C. *But There Was No Peace: The Role of Violence in the Politics of Reconstruction*. Athens: University of Georgia Press, 1984.

———. *Civil Wars: Women and the Crisis of Southern Nationalism*. Bloomington: University of Illinois Press, 1989.

———. "Southern Interests and the Election of 1876: A Reappraisal." *Civil War History* 26 (December 1980): 347–61.

Randall, James G., and David Herbert Donald. *The Divided Union*. Boston: Little, Brown, 1961.

Redpath, James, ed. *Echoes of Harper's Ferry*. Boston: Thayer and Eldridge, 1860.

———. "The Lesson of Mississippi." *The Independent*, Aug. 3, 1876, 4.

———. *The Roving Editor: or, Talks with Slaves in the Southern States*. New York: A. B. Burdick, 1859.

Reed, Emmala. *A Faithful Heart: The Journals of Emmala Reed, 1865 and 1866*. Ed. Robert T. Oliver. Columbia: University of South Carolina Press, 2004.

Reed, Wallace P. "Last Forlorn Hope of the Confederacy." *Southern Historical Society Papers* 30 (January–December 1902): 117–21.

Reid, Whitelaw. *After the War: A Southern Tour*. Cincinnati: Moore, Wilstach & Baldwin, 1866.

Renehan, Edward. *The Secret Six: The True Tale of the Men Who Conspired with John Brown*. New York: Crown, 1995.

Report of the Joint Committee on the Conduct of the War, at the Second Session Thirty-eighth Congress. Washington, D.C.: U.S. Government Printing Office, 1865.

Report of the Joint Committee on Reconstruction, at the First Session Thirty-ninth Congress. Washington, D.C.: U.S. Government Printing Office, 1866.

Report of the Select Committee on the New Orleans Riots. Washington, D.C.: U.S. Government Printing Office, 1867.

Reynolds, David S. *John Brown, Abolitionist: The Man Who Killed Slavery, Sparked the Civil War, and Seeded Civil Rights*. New York: Alfred A. Knopf, 2005.

———. *Mightier Than the Sword: Uncle Tom's Cabin and the Battle for America*. New York: W. W. Norton, 2012.

———. *Walt Whitman's America: A Cultural Biography*. New York: Alfred A. Knopf, 1995.

Reynolds, Donald E. *Editors Make War: Southern Newspapers in the Secession Crisis.* Nashville: Vanderbilt University Press, 1970.

————. "The New Orleans Riot of 1866, Reconsidered." *Journal of the Louisiana Historical Association* 5 (Winter 1964): 5–27.

Richards, Dora Miller. "A Woman's Diary of the Siege of Vicksburg." *Century Magazine* 30 (September 1885): 767–76.

Richards, Leonard L. *The California Gold Rush and the Coming of the Civil War.* New York: Vintage, 2008.

Richardson, Heather Cox. *West from Appomattox: The Reconstruction of America after the Civil War.* New Haven, Conn.: Yale University Press, 2007.

Richardson, James D., ed. *A Compilation of the Messages and Papers of the Confederacy.* 2 vols. Nashville: United States Publishing, 1905.

————, ed. *A Compilation of the Messages and Papers of the Presidents, 1789–1897.* 10 vols. Washington, D.C.: U.S. Government Printing Office, 1896–1899.

Richardson, Robert D., Jr. *Emerson: The Mind on Fire.* Berkeley: University of California Press, 1995.

Ripley, C. Peter, et al., eds. *The Black Abolitionist Papers.* 5 vols. Chapel Hill: University of North Carolina Press, 1985–1992.

Rise and Progress of the Bloody Outbreak at Harper's Ferry. New York: New York Democratic Vigilant Association, 1859.

Ritter, Charles F., and Jon L. Wakelyn, eds. *Leaders of the American Civil War.* Westport, Conn.: Greenwood Press, 1998.

Robertson, Stacey. "'Aunt Nancy Men': Parker Pillsbury, Masculinity, and Women's Rights Activism in the Nineteenth-Century United States." *American Studies* 37 (Fall 1996): 33–60.

Robertson-Lorant, Laurie. *Melville: A Biography.* Amherst: University of Massachusetts Press, 1996.

Rogers, Seth. "Letters of Dr. Seth Rogers, 1862–1863; A Surgeon's War Letters." *Proceedings of the Massachusetts Historical Society* 43 (February 1910): 337–98.

Rohrs, Richard C. "Antislavery Politics and the *Pearl* Incident of 1848." *The Historian* 56 (Summer 1994): 711–24.

Ropes, Hannah. *Civil War Nurse: The Diaries and Letters of Hannah Ropes.* Ed. John R. Brumgardt. Knoxville: University of Tennessee Press, 1980.

Rose, Willie Lee. *Rehearsal for Reconstruction: The Port Royal Experiment.* Athens: University of Georgia Press, 1999.

Royster, Charles. *The Destructive War: William Tecumseh Sherman, Stonewall Jackson, and the Americans.* New York: Vintage, 1993.

————. "Slaver, General, Klansman." *The Atlantic Monthly* 271 (May 1993): 125–28.

Ruffin, Edmund. *The Diary of Edmund Ruffin.* Ed. William Kaufmann Scarborough. 3 vols. Baton Rouge: Louisiana State University Press, 1972–1989.

Russell, William Howard. *My Diary North and South.* Boston: T. O. H. P. Burnam, 1863.

Salter, William. *The Life of James W. Grimes.* New York: D. Appleton, 1876.

Samson, Robert D. *John L. O'Sullivan and His Times.* Kent, Ohio: Kent State University Press, 2003.

Sandweiss, Martha A. *Passing Strange: A Gilded Age Tale of Love and Deception across the Color Line.* New York: Penguin, 2010.

————, ed. *Photography in Nineteenth Century America.* New York: Harry A. Abrams, 1991.

Saxon, A. H. *P. T. Barnum: The Legend and the Man.* New York: Columbia University Press, 1989.

Schlesinger, Louis. "Personal Narrative of Louis Schlesinger, of Adventures in Cuba and Ceuta." *United States Magazine and Democratic Review* 31 (September 1852): 210–24.

Schott, Thomas E. *Alexander H. Stephens of Georgia.* Baton Rouge: Louisiana State University Press, 1988.

Schoultz, Lars. *Beneath the United States: A History of U.S. Policy toward Latin America.* Cambridge, Mass.: Harvard University Press, 1998.

Schultz, Duane. *Quantrill's War: The Life and Times of William Clarke Quantrill.* New York: St. Martin's Press, 1996.

Schultz, Jane E. "The Inhospitable Hospital: Gender and Professionalism in Civil War Medicine." *Signs: Journal of Women in Culture and History* 17 (Winter 1992): 363–92.

Schurz, Carl. *The Reminiscences of Carl Schurz.* 3 vols. New York: McClure, 1907.

———. *Speeches, Correspondence and Political Papers of Carl Schurz.* Ed. George Bancroft. 6 vols. New York: G. P. Putnam's Sons, 1913.

Schwekart, Larry. "The Mormon Connection: Lincoln, the Saints, and the Crisis of Equality." *Western Humanities Review* 34 (Winter 1980): 1–22.

Scrymser, James Alexander. *Personal Reminiscences of James A. Scrymser in Times of Peace and War.* New York: James A. Scrymser, 1915.

Shaw, Anna Howard. *The Story of a Pioneer.* New York: Harper & Brothers, 1915.

Shaw, Robert Gould. *Blue-Eyed Child of Fortune: The Civil War Letters of Robert Gould Shaw.* Ed. Russell Duncan. Athens: University of Georgia Press, 1999.

Shelden, Rachel. "'Speedy Conclusion': A Reexamination of Conscription and Civil War Federalism." *Civil War History* 55 (December 2009): 469–98.

Shepley, George F. "Incidents of the Capture of Richmond." *The Atlantic Monthly* 46 (July 1880): 18–28.

Sheridan, Philip H. *Personal Memoirs of P. H. Sheridan.* 2 vols. New York: Charles L. Webster, 1888.

Sherman, John. *John Sherman's Recollections of Forty Years in the House, Senate, and Cabinet: An Autobiography.* 2 vols. Chicago: Werner Company, 1895.

Sherman, William T. *Memoirs of General William T. Sherman.* Ed. Charles Royster. New York: Library of America, 1990.

———. *Sherman's Civil War: Selected Correspondence of William T. Sherman.* Ed. Brooks D. Simpson and Jean Vance Berlin. Chapel Hill: University of North Carolina Press, 1999.

Sherman, William T., and John Sherman. *The Sherman Letters: The Correspondence between General and Senator Sherman from 1837 to 1891.* Ed. Rachel Sherman Thorndike. New York: Charles Scribner's Sons, 1894.

Sherwin, Oscar. *The Prophet of Liberty: The Life and Times of Wendell Phillips.* New York: Bookman Associates, 1958.

Silverman, Gillian. "'The Best Circus in Town': Embodied Theatrics in the Lincoln-Douglas Debates." *American Literary History* 21 (Winter 2009): 757–87.

Sim, David. "The Peace Policy of Ulysses S. Grant." *American Nineteenth Century History* 9 (September 2008): 241–68.

Simkins, Butler, and Robert H. Woody. *South Carolina during Reconstruction.* Chapel Hill: University of North Carolina Press, 1932.

Simms, William Gilmore. *The Letters of William Gilmore Simms.* Ed. Mary C. Simms Oliphant, Alfred Taylor Odell, and T. C. Duncan Eaves. 6 vols. Columbia: University of South Carolina Press, 1955–1982.

Simms, William Gilmore, ed. *War Poetry of the South*. New York: Richardson, 1866.

Simpson, Brooks D. "Henry Adams and the Age of Grant." *Hayes Historical Journal* 8 (Spring 1989): 5–23.

———. *The Political Thought of Henry Adams*. Columbia: University of South Carolina Press, 1996.

———. *The Reconstruction Presidents*. Lawrence: University Press of Kansas, 1998.

Slaughter, Thomas P. *Bloody Dawn: The Christiana Riot and Racial Violence in the Antebellum North*. New York: Oxford University Press, 1992.

Slotkin, Richard. *The Fatal Environment: The Myth of the Frontier in the Age of Industrialization, 1800–1890*. New York: Atheneum, 1985.

Smith, Gerrit. "The Murder of Colored Troops at Fort Pillow." *The Liberator*, April 21, 1864, 4.

Smith, Harold T. "The Know-Nothings in Arkansas." *Arkansas Historical Quarterly* 34 (Winter 1975): 291–304.

Smith, Jean Edward. *Grant*. New York: Simon & Schuster, 2001.

Smythe, Mrs. A. T., M. B. Poppenheim, and Mrs. Thomas Taylor, eds. *South Carolina Women in the Confederacy*. Columbia, S.C.: State Company, 1903.

Solnit, Rebecca. "The Annihilation of Time and Space." *New England Review* 24 (Winter 2003): 5–19.

Stahr, Walter. *William Seward: Lincoln's Indispensable Man*. New York: Simon & Schuster, 2012.

Stampp, Kenneth. *America in 1857: A Nation on the Brink*. New York: Oxford University Press, 1990.

———. *The Era of Reconstruction, 1865–1877*. New York: Vintage, 1967.

———. *The Imperiled Union: Essays on the Background of the Civil War*. New York: Oxford University Press, 1980.

Stampp, Kenneth M., and Leon F. Litwack, eds. *Reconstruction: An Anthology of Revisionist Writings*. Baton Rouge: Louisiana State University Press, 1969.

Stansell, Christine. *The Feminist Promise: 1792 to the Present*. New York: Modern Library, 2011.

Stanton, Elizabeth Cady. "Anna Elizabeth Dickinson," in *Eminent Women of the Age*. Ed. James Parton. Hartford, Conn.: S. M. Betts, 1868, 479–512.

———. *Eighty Years and More (1815–1897): Reminiscences of Elizabeth Cady Stanton*. New York: European Publishing, 1897.

———. *Elizabeth Cady Stanton as Revealed in Her Letters, Diary, and Reminiscences*. Ed. Theodore Stanton and Harriet Stanton Blatch. 2 vols. New York: Harper & Brothers, 1922.

Stanton, Elizabeth Cady, and Susan B. Anthony. *The Selected Papers of Elizabeth Cady Stanton and Susan B. Anthony*. Ed. Ann D. Gordon. 4 vols. New Brunswick, N.J.: Rutgers University Press, 1997–2000.

Stanton, Elizabeth Cady, Susan B. Anthony, Matilda Joslyn Gage, and Ida Husted Harper, eds. *The History of Woman Suffrage*. 6 vols. Rochester, N.Y.: Charles Mann, 1881–1922.

Starr, Kevin. *Americans and the California Dream, 1850–1915*. New York: Oxford University Press, 1973.

Stauffer, John. *Giants: The Parallel Lives of Frederick Douglass and Abraham Lincoln*. New York: Twelve, 2009.

Stearns, Charles. *The Black Man of the South and the Rebels*. New York: American News Co., 1872.

Stebbins, Homer Adolph. *A Political History of the State of New York, 1865–1869*. New York: Columbia University, 1913.

Stedman, Edmund Clarence. *The Battle of Bull Run*. New York: Rudd & Carleton, 1861.

Stedman, Laura, and George M. Gould, eds. *The Life and Letters of Edmund Clarence Stedman*. 2 vols. New York: Moffatt, Yard, 1910.

Stegner, Wallace. *The Gathering of Zion: The Story of the Mormon Trail*. New York: McGraw Hill, 1964.

Steiner, Bernard Christian. *The Life of Henry Winter Davis*. Baltimore: John Murphy, 1916.

Stephens, Alexander H. *A Constitutional View of the Late War between the States: Its Causes, Character, Conduct, and Results*. 2 vols. Philadelphia: National Publishing, 1870.

———. *Recollections of Alexander H. Stephens*. Ed. Myrta Lockett Avary. New York: Doubleday, Page, 1910.

Stephenson, Nathaniel Wright. *Lincoln: An Account of His Personal Life*. Indianapolis: Bobbs-Merrill, 1922.

Stern, Madeleine. *We the Women: Career Firsts of Nineteenth-Century Women*. Lincoln: University of Nebraska Press, 1994.

Stiles, T. J. *The First Tycoon: The Epic Life of Cornelius Vanderbilt*. New York: Alfred A. Knopf, 2009.

———. *Jesse James: Last Rebel of the Civil War*. New York: Vintage, 2003.

Stovall, Pleasant H. *Robert Toombs: Statesman, Speaker, Soldier, Sage*. New York: Cassell Publishing, 1892.

Stowe, Harriet Beecher. *The Lives and Deeds of Our Self-Made Men*. Hartford, Conn.: Worthington, Dustin, 1872.

———. *The Writings of Harriet Beecher Stowe*. 16 vols. Boston: Houghton Mifflin, 1896.

Strong, George Templeton. *The Diary of George Templeton Strong*. Ed. Allan Nevins and Milton Halsey Thomas. 4 vols. New York: Macmillan, 1952.

Stout, Harry S. *Upon the Altar of the Nation: A Moral History of the Civil War*. New York: Penguin, 2007.

Sumner, Charles. "Our Domestic Relations." *The Atlantic Monthly* 12 (September 1863): 507–29.

———. *The Works of Charles Sumner*. 15 vols. Boston: Lee & Shepard, 1870–1883.

Sundquist, Eric J. *Empire and Slavery in American Literature, 1820–1865*. New York: Cambridge University Press, 1995.

———. *To Wake the Nations: Race in the Making of American Literature*. Cambridge, Mass.: Harvard University Press, 1998.

Taylor, Joe Gray. "New Orleans and Reconstruction." *Journal of the Louisiana Historical Association* 9 (Summer 1968): 189–208.

Tenney, W. J. *The Military and Naval History of the Rebellion in the United States*. New York: D. Appleton, 1865.

Thayer, James Bradley. *A Western Journey with Mr. Emerson*. Boston: Little, Brown, 1884.

Theodore Tilton v. Henry Ward Beecher. New York: McDivitt, Campbell, 1875.

Thomas, E. M. *The Confederate Nation, 1861–1865*. New York: Harper & Row, 1979.

Thomas, Hugh. *Cuba: The Pursuit of Freedom*. New York: Da Capo, 1968.

Thompson, William F. *The Image of War*. Baton Rouge: Louisiana State University Press, 1994.

Thomson, William Y. *Robert Toombs of Georgia*. Baton Rouge: Louisiana State University Press, 1966.

Thoreau, Henry David. *The Correspondence of Henry David Thoreau*. Ed. Walter Harding and Carl Bode. New York: New York University Press, 1958.

———. *Journal 10*. Vol. 16 of *The Writings of Henry David Thoreau*. Ed. Bradford Torrey. Boston: Houghton Mifflin, 1906.

———. *A Week, Walden, The Maine Woods, Cape Cod*. Ed. Robert F. Sayre. New York: Library of America, 1985.

———. *The Writings of Henry David Thoreau: Reform Papers*. Ed. Wendell Glick. Princeton, N.J.: Princeton University Press, 1973.

Tilden, Samuel J. *Letters and Literary Memorials of Samuel J. Tilden*. Ed. John Bigelow. 2 vols. New York: Harper & Brothers, 1908.

Timrod, Henry. *The Poems of Henry Timrod, with a Sketch of the Poet's Life*. Ed. and with introduction by Paul H. Hayne. New York: E. J. Hale & Son, 1873.

Tindall, George Brown. *South Carolina Negroes, 1877–1900*. Columbia: University of South Carolina Press, 1952.

Tise, Larry E. *Proslavery: A History of the Defense of Slavery in America, 1701–1840*. Athens: University of Georgia Press, 1987.

Token of a Nation's Sorrow: Addresses in the Congress of the United States, and Funeral Solemnities on the Death of John Quincy Adams. Washington, D.C.: J. and G. S. Gideon, 1848.

Toombs, Robert, Alexander H. Stephens, and Howell Cobb. *The Correspondence of Robert Toombs, Alexander H. Stephens, and Howell Cobb*. Ed. Ulrich B. Phillips. 2 vols. Washington, D.C.: U.S. Government Printing Office, 1913.

Tourgée, Albion W. *Undaunted Radical: The Selected Writings and Speeches of Albion W. Tourgée*. Ed. Mark Elliott and John David Smith. Baton Rouge: Louisiana State University Press, 2010.

Towne, Laura M. *The Letters and Diary of Laura M. Towne: Written from the Sea-Islands of South Carolina, 1862–1884*. Ed. Rufus Sargent. Cambridge, Mass.: Riverside Press, 1912.

Townsend, George Alfred. *Campaigns of a Non-Combatant, and His Romaunt Abroad during the War*. New York: Blelock, 1866.

Trachtenberg, Alan. *Reading American Photographs: Images as History, Mathew Brady to Walker Evans*. New York: Hill & Wang, 1989.

Traubel, Horace. *With Walt Whitman in Camden*. 9 vols. Boston: Small, Maynard, 1906.

Trefousse, Hans L. *Andrew Johnson: A Biography*. New York: W. W. Norton, 1997.

———. *Rutherford B. Hayes*. New York: Times Books, 2002.

———. *Thaddeus Stevens: Nineteenth-Century Egalitarian*. Chapel Hill: University of North Carolina Press, 1997.

Trollope, Anthony. *North America*. 2 vols. Philadelphia: J. B. Lippincott, 1863.

Tuchinsky, Adam. *Horace Greeley's New-York Tribune: Civil War–Era Socialism and the Crisis of Free Labor*. Ithaca, N.Y.: Cornell University Press, 2009.

Tucker, Phillip Thomas. *The Forgotten "Stonewall of the West": Major General John Stevens Bowen*. Macon, Ga.: Mercer University Press, 1997.

Tunnell, Ted. "Creating 'The Propaganda of History': Southern Editors and the Origins of Carpetbagger and Scalawag." *Journal of Southern History* 72 (November 2006): 789–822.

Turner, Thomas Reed. *Beware the People Weeping: Public Opinion and the Assassination of Abraham Lincoln*. Baton Rouge: Louisiana State University Press, 1982.

Twain, Mark. *The Autobiography of Mark Twain*. Ed. Harriet Elinor Smith. 1 vol. Berkeley: University of California Press, 2011.

———. *Innocents Abroad; Roughing It*. Ed. Guy Cardwell. New York: Library of America, 1984.

Tyler, Samuel. *Memoir of Roger Brooke Taney, LL.D., Chief Justice of the Supreme Court of the United States*. Baltimore: John Murphy, 1872.

Underhill, Lois Beachy. *The Woman Who Ran for President: The Many Lives of Victoria Woodhull*. Bridgehampton, N.Y.: Bridge Works Publishing, 1995.

Utley, Robert M. *Cavalier in Buckskins: George Armstrong Custer and the Western Military Frontier*. Norman: University of Oklahoma Press, 2001.

———. *The Indian Frontier of the American West, 1846–1890*. Albuquerque: University of New Mexico Press, 1984.

Uya, Okon E. *From Slavery to Public Service, Robert Smalls, 1839–1915*. New York: Oxford University Press, 1975.

Vallandigham, Clement. *The Record of Hon. C. L. Vallandigham on Abolition, the Union, and the Civil War*. Columbus, Ohio: J. Walter, 1863.

Van Deusen, Glyndon G. *Horace Greeley: Nineteenth-Century Crusader*. Philadelphia: University of Pennsylvania Press, 1953.

———. *William Henry Seward*. New York: Oxford University Press, 1967.

Villard, Oswald Garrison. *John Brown, 1800–1859: A Biography Fifty Years After*. New York: Houghton Mifflin, 1910.

Von Frank, Albert J. *The Trials of Anthony Burns*. Cambridge, Mass.: Harvard University Press, 1998.

Vorenberg, Michael. *Final Freedom: The Civil War, the Abolition of Slavery, and the Thirteenth Amendment*. New York: Cambridge University Press, 2001.

Walker, F. A. "The Indian Question." *North American Review* 116 (April 1873): 329–89.

Walther, Eric H. *The Fire-Eaters*. Baton Rouge: Louisiana State University Press, 1992.

War of the Rebellion: A Compilation of the Official Records of the Union and Confederate Armies. Washington, D.C.: U.S. Government Printing Office, 1880–1901.

Ward, Andrew. *River Run Red: The Fort Pillow Massacre in the American Civil War*. New York: Viking, 2005.

———. *The Slaves' War: The Civil War in the Words of Former Slaves*. Boston: Houghton Mifflin, 2008.

Ware, Elizabeth Pearson, ed. *Letters from Port Royal, 1862–1868*. Boston: W. B. Clarke, 1906.

Warren, Robert Penn, ed. *John Greenleaf Whittier's Poetry: An Appraisal and a Selection*. St. Paul: University of Minnesota Press, 1971.

Washburn, G. H. *A Complete Military History and Record of the 108th Regiment N.Y. Vols., from 1862 to 1894*. Rochester, N.Y.: E. R. Andrews, 1894.

Waugh, Joan. *U. S. Grant: American Hero, American Myth*. Chapel Hill: University of North Carolina Press, 2009.

Welles, Gideon. *The Diary of Gideon Welles, Secretary of the Navy under Lincoln and Johnson*. 3 vols. Boston: Houghton Mifflin, 1911.

———. "The History of Emancipation." *Galaxy* 14 (December 1872): 838–51.

Westwood, Howard C. "Sherman Marched—and Proclaimed 'Land for the Landless.'" *South Carolina Historical Magazine* 85 (January 1984): 33–50.

White, Richard. *Railroaded: The Transcontinentals and the Making of Modern America*. New York: W. W. Norton, 2011.

White, Ronald C., Jr. *A. Lincoln: A Biography*. New York: Random House, 2009.
———. *The Eloquent President: A Portrait of Lincoln through His Words*. New York: Random House, 2005.
———. *Lincoln's Greatest Speech: The Second Inaugural*. New York: Simon & Schuster, 2002.
Whitman, Walt. *The Complete Writings of Walt Whitman*, vol. 15. Ed. Richard Maurice Bucke, Thomas Biggs Harned, Horace Traubel, and Oscar Lovell Triggs. New York: G. P. Putnam's Sons, 1902.
———. *Leaves of Grass: A Textual Variorum of the Printed Poems*. Ed. Sculley Bradley, Harold W. Blodgett, Arthur Golden, and William White. 3 vols. New York: New York University Press, 1980.
———. *Walt Whitman: Poetry and Prose*. Ed. Justin Kaplan. New York: Library of America, 1982.
Whitney, J. D. *The Yosemite Guide-Book: A Description of the Yosemite Valley and the Adjacent Region of the Sierra Nevada, and of the Big Trees of California*, 2nd ed. Cambridge, Mass.: Welch, Bigelow, 1869.
Whittier, John Greenleaf. *The Letters of John Greenleaf Whittier*. Ed. John B. Pickard. 3 vols. Cambridge, Mass.: Harvard University Press, 1975.
———. *Life and Letters of John Greenleaf Whittier*. Ed. Samuel T. Pickard. 2 vols. Boston: Houghton Mifflin, 1894.
———. *The Writings of John Greenleaf Whittier*. 7 vols. Boston: Houghton Mifflin, 1888–1889.
Wilentz, Sean. *The Rise of American Democracy: Jefferson to Lincoln*. New York: W. W. Norton, 2005.
Wiley, Bell Irvin. *Life of Billy Yank: The Common Soldier of the Union*. Baton Rouge: Louisiana State University Press, 1978.
Wilkins, Thurman. *Clarence King: A Biography*. Albuquerque: University of New Mexico Press, 1988.
Williams, George F. *Bullet and Shell: War as the Soldier Saw It*. New York: Fords, Howard, and Hulbert, 1884.
Willis, Olympia Brown. *Acquaintances Old and New, among Reformers*. Milwaukee: S. E. Tate, 1911.
Wills, Garry. *Lincoln at Gettysburg: The Words That Remade America*. New York: Simon & Schuster, 1992.
———. "Lincoln's Greatest Speech?" *The Atlantic Monthly* 284 (September 1999): 60–70.
Wilson, Edmund. *Patriotic Gore: Studies in the Literature of the American Civil War*. New York: Oxford University Press, 1962.
Wilson, James Grant, Titus Munson Coan, and A. Noel Blakeman, eds. *Personal Recollections of the War of the Rebellion*. 4 vols. New York: G. P. Putnam's Sons, 1897–1912.
Wilson, Robert. *The Explorer King: Adventure, Science, and the Great Diamond Hoax— Clarence King in the Old West*. New York: Scribner, 2006.
Wilson, Thomas William. *An Authentic Narrative of the Piratical Descents upon Cuba Made by Hordes from the United States*. Havana, 1851.
Wineapple, Brenda. *Hawthorne: A Biography of Nathaniel Hawthorne*. New York: Alfred A. Knopf, 2003.
———. *White Heat: The Friendship of Emily Dickinson and Thomas Wentworth Higginson*. New York: Alfred A. Knopf, 2008.
Winthrop, Robert C. *A Memoir of Robert C. Winthrop*. Boston: Little, Brown, 1897.

Wood, Ann Douglas. "The War within a War: Women Nurses in the Union Army." *Civil War History* 18 (September 1972): 197–212.

Woodburn, James Albert. *The Life of Thaddeus Stevens: A Study in American Political History, Especially in the Period of the Civil War and Reconstruction.* Indianapolis: Bobbs-Merrill, 1913.

Woodhull, Victoria. *The Victoria Woodhull Reader.* Ed. Madeleine B. Stern. Weston, Mass.: M & S Press, 1974.

Woodley, Thomas F. *Great Leveler: The Life of Thaddeus Stevens.* New York: Stackpole Sons, 1937.

Yacavone, Donald, ed. *Freedom's Journey: African American Voices of the Civil War.* Chicago: Lawrence Hill Books, 2004.

Young, Agatha. *Women and the Crisis: Women of the North in the Civil War.* New York: McDowell, Obolensky, 1959.

Young, James Harvey. "Anna Elizabeth Dickinson and the Civil War: For and Against Lincoln." *Mississippi Valley Historical Review* 31 (June 1944): 59–80.

Zuczek, Richard. "The Federal Government's Attack on the Ku Klux Klan: A Reassessment." *South Carolina Historical Magazine* 97 (January 1996): 47–64.

———. *State of Rebellion: Reconstruction in South Carolina.* Columbia: University of South Carolina Press, 1996.

Zunder, Theodore A. "Whitman Interviews Barnum." *Modern Language Notes* 48 (January 1933): 40.

INDEX

ABOUT THE AUTHOR

BRENDA WINEAPPLE is the prizewinning author of several books, including *White Heat: The Friendship of Emily Dickinson and Thomas Wentworth Higginson*, a finalist for the National Book Critics Circle Award and a *New York Times* Notable Book. She teaches in the MFA programs at the New School University and Columbia University, and is the Doris Zemurray Stone Professor of Modern Literary and Historical Studies at Union College. She lives in New York City.